CPA Review Manual

fourth edition

CPA Review Manual

edited by

Herbert E. Miller
Arthur Andersen & Co.

George C. Mead
Michigan State University

PRENTICE-HALL, INC.,
Englewood Cliffs, New Jersey

Library of Congress Cataloging in Publication Data

MILLER, HERBERT E. ED.
CPA review manual.

Includes bibliographical references.
1. Accounting. I. Mead, George C., 1935- joint ed. II. Title.
HF5635.M63 1972 657.61 78-170980
ISBN 0-13-188219-8

Printed in the United States of America

10 9 8 7 6 5 4 3 2

PRENTICE-HALL INTERNATIONAL, INC., *London*
PRENTICE-HALL OF AUSTRALIA, PTY. LTD., *Sydney*
PRENTICE-HALL OF CANADA, LTD., *Toronto*
PRENTICE-HALL OF INDIA PRIVATE LIMITED, *New Delhi*
PRENTICE-HALL OF JAPAN, INC., *Tokyo*

contents

preface

It is not an uncommon experience for an accounting professor to receive requests from CPA candidates for suggested reference material on the topics commonly covered by the CPA examination. Although much material has been written on the topics that are important to the CPA candidate, the professor may justifiably surmise that the candidate is somewhat inconvenienced in his study and review by the fact that this material is widely scattered in a number of sources and frequently written not specifically with the CPA candidate in mind. This book is a collection of selected writings, covering topics that a candidate cannot safely ignore in his preparation for the CPA examination.

Parts of the book represent adaptations and condensations of material in other published writings of the authors. But whether the contributing author was breaking new ground or modifying his subject matter, each worked with the same objective—to assist the CPA candidate. With this goal much of the writing was undertaken with a belief that the candidate, in most cases, would be currently engaged in accounting work and would have completed or nearly completed his formal education. Accordingly, the chapters generally provide complete yet rapid development of their respective subject matter. For the former accounting major, this should serve to "point up" his accounting background. For the person working in accounting who has limited formal accounting training, this approach should afford an efficient and satisfactory introduction to topics he has not yet encountered.

While the authors have tried to give full consideration to the nature and scope of past examinations, they can, of course, give no assurance or guarantee that a reading or study of this book will insure a successful encounter with the CPA examination. And the candidate should be cautioned that reading is not a substitute for problem solving. However, if a candidate has cause to believe that he needs to strengthen his background in the areas covered here, it can be said in fairness that the authors have tried to develop material for such purpose.

In addition the work has other uses. Because the advanced accounting student and the CPA candidate have much in common, both in educational background and in their ultimate goals, the material is suitable as a reference text or as supplemental study material for students currently enrolled in CPA Problems courses.

The term "collectors of manuscripts," rather than "editors," more aptly describes our activities: each contributing author deserves the full credit for whatever excellence and suitability his material possesses. The authors would be the first to acknowledge that the project could not have developed without the willing and active support of the American Institute of Certified Public Accountants. The Institute material quoted herein is copyrighted by the American Institute of Certified Public Accountants and is used with its permission.

George C. Mead
Herbert E. Miller

1
introduction

George C. Mead

The CPA examination may not be taken as a casual exercise. But neither is it an impossible hurdle for the candidate who, with a reasonable background of education or experience, prepares himself conscientiously. Your preparation should be planned with regard for your own qualifications and for the purpose and form of the examination.

As a serious candidate, working with and/or educated in accounting, you are not completely unfamiliar with the meaning of "CPA" and with the examination itself. Yet the following review of the role of the Uniform CPA Examination and suggestions on preparing for and writing it may be useful. You may also wish to review the latest edition of *Information for CPA Candidates,* published by the American Institute of CPAs and available from the Institute or from your state society of CPAs.

The CPA Designation—Purpose and Requirements

Certified Public Accountant is a designation granted by each of the states to persons qualified to enter professional accounting practice. The public is served by this formal identification of professionally qualified individuals. State certification is not for the benefit of the certificate's possessor, nor is it intended to restrict arbitrarily the number of practitioners nor to prevent any qualified person from practicing. Indeed, the accountancy laws of some states and territories are of the *permissive* type. Under such legislation, anyone may practice as a public accountant—the noncertified person merely may not use the title "*certified* public accountant." A majority of states, however, do restrict public accounting practice (particularly the rendering of professional audit opinions) to certified persons, under accountancy laws commonly termed *regulatory*. In either case, an individual's CPA designation is of benefit to his present and prospective clients, to those relying on his opinions, and (obviously) to him.

In all states the conditions for certification include successful completion of the Uniform CPA Examination, some level of education (in nearly every state, a college degree), and character references. All states also require public accounting experience (in many states, prior to completion of all parts of the examination) before the individual may be fully licensed to practice as a CPA. (Most states have provisions for limited substitution of education for experience.) In combination, these requirements serve to test general and technical knowledge, practical judgment, and personal character. Other prevailing legal requirements are a twenty-one year minimum age and residence or citizenship in the state. Specific requirements vary from state to state, and occasionally a candidate's education or experience is in some way unusual, necessitating an individual interpretation.

Presumably you have information about your state's requirements. If not, this can be obtained from your state board of accountancy or state society of CPAs. You should make early application for admission to the examination, especially if your qualifications are in any way unclear.

Role of the Examination

The CPA examination serves a key function in the profession. Notwithstanding the educational requirements, the examination is the single rigorous, controlled, and nationally uniform indicator of technical and judgmental ability. As the "gateway" (or "hurdle," if you prefer) to professional status, it greatly influences the quality of the profession by controlling the quality of its entrants. Furthermore, it affects the type of person (regarding areas of qualification) who gains entry. As changes occur in typical services offered by and techniques used by CPAs, the examination evolves, sometimes following practice and sometimes preceding it.

The philosophy of initial certification is also changing. Traditionally, the new CPA has been presumed to be sufficiently competent and mature to practice immediately on his own, a "certified professional." This is a major reason for the experience requirement. However, many members of the profession believe the certificate should (and perhaps already does) designate a person qualified to "enter the profession." A comprehensive study of the "common body of knowledge" for beginning

CPAs concurred, advocating direction "toward a foundation for general practice, a foundation upon which specialization can be built by further study and experience."[1] This seems to be the trend of the examination.

The examination's basic objective is stated: "to measure basic technical competence which includes technical knowledge and the application of such knowledge, the exercise of good judgment, and the understanding of professional responsibility."[2] Indeed, many of its questions do require analytical ability and common sense. Yet it is essentially an academic examination, testing qualities learned principally in the classroom.

Structure of the Profession

The framework of the accounting profession includes a combination of state governments, voluntary professional bodies, and federal governmental agencies. Primary are the state boards of accountancy, the agencies which grant the CPA certificate.

state boards of public accountancy

State accountancy laws commonly provide for the appointment of boards of public accountancy. Typically the governor of the state appoints the board members. In most states the appointees must be CPAs, but in a few cases the state law provides for the appointment of a lawyer, an educator, or other non-CPA to the board. In some states, public accountants have minority representation on the boards in matters other than the CPA examination and the practice of CPAs.

The state boards have power to prescribe rules and regulations necessary and expedient for administration of the accountancy acts. The more important matters included are:

1. Qualifications of applicants for examination.
2. Requirements for registration to practice.
3. Conduct of examinations.
4. Grading of examinations.
5. Terms for reexamination in sections not passed.

[1] Robert H. Roy and James H. MacNeill, *Horizons for a Profession* (New York: American Institute of Certified Public Accountants, 1967), p. 28. There has been discussion of formal identification, through testing and experience, and recognition of specialists within the profession, as in the medical profession. Such "super CPA" designations, however, have not been adopted by any state or by the American Institute of CPAs.

[2] *Information for CPA Candidates* (New York: American Institute of Certified Public Accountants, 1970), p. 2.

6. Issuance of certificates.
7. Regulation of practice.
8. Reciprocity (recognition of certificates granted by other states).
9. Revocation of certificates.

Approximately two-thirds of the accountancy boards have adopted official codes of ethics. In these states, and in other states where state boards have not promulgated a compulsory code of ethics, state boards usually have power to revoke certificates for unprofessional conduct or other sufficient cause.

professional certified accounting organizations

Most CPAs choose to belong to a professional body, either the national group—the American Institute of Certified Public Accountants—or a state institute or society of CPAs, or both.

The American Institute is active in many areas. One of its functions is that of self-regulation. The Institute's Code of Professional Ethics sets standards for its members, and violation can result in suspension or expulsion from membership. (Note, however, that only the state boards can revoke a certificate.) Especially important to CPA examination candidates are the Institute's activities in formulating generally accepted auditing standards and generally accepted accounting principles. These guidelines are not "law"; however, serious violation of them is contrary to the Code of Professional Ethics and could result in loss of membership or professional embarrassment. Furthermore, since the courts and the Securities and Exchange Commission generally regard the Institute's positions as reasonable professional standards, violation can subject the CPA to reprimands, liability for faulty practice, or both.

Activities of the state societies include professional development (in general, short courses and lectures, often those written by the AICPA staff), public relations (explaining CPAs' activities to local bankers, educators, attorneys, etc.), liaison with state legislators (regarding professional accountancy practice legislation), and self-regulation. The state societies also have codes of ethics that usually parallel the AICPA Code rather closely.

The state societies and the American Institute are only loosely affiliated. Membership in both is voluntary and not coexistent.

the securities and exchange commission

The federal Securities and Exchange Commission oversees the public trading of securities of all but the smallest corporations. Of immediate influence on accountants, the SEC is concerned with the sufficiency of information given by corporations to present and prospective security holders. It has the legal authority to prescribe types of information that must be made public (if a corporation's shares are to be publicly traded), the manner in which that information is to be prepared, including accounting methods, and the type of independent review of and opinion on (audit) that information, if any. With only minor exceptions to date, the SEC has relied on the standards of accounting and auditing promulgated by the AICPA. Special technical features of SEC accounting practice are unlikely to appear on the CPA exam; however, in the law chapter there is a summary of the rather different legal situation of the auditor engaged in SEC practice.

Administration of the CPA Examination

Each state independently determines requirements for certification, administers an examination, and grants certificates to qualified candidates. There is no "national CPA certificate."

Initially, states prepared and graded their own examinations. Independently, the AICPA (then the American Institute of Accountants) administered an examination intended as a screening device for evaluating candidates for membership in the Institute. The very first of these examinations (1917) was adopted by eight states, which used it as their official CPA examination. Today every state and territory has voluntarily adopted the Uniform Examination and all use the Advisory Grading Service which the Institute offers. A few states also examine candidates in additional subjects, not part of the Uniform Examination, as required by the individual state's accountancy act or under a policy of the individual state board. The additional subjects examined most frequently are economics and finance, taxation, and professional ethics.

The preparation of the Uniform Examination is the ultimate responsibility of the Board of Examiners of the AICPA. The Board sets examination policies and gives final approval to each examination. Its sixteen members render important services in drafting and reviewing sections of the examinations, but the Board's chief function is supervisory rather than administrative. A large degree of responsibility is delegated to the Director of Examinations of the Institute and, through him, to the staff members who work under his direction.

The preparation process is described in detail in *Information for CPA Candidates*. Suffice it here to observe that great care is taken to assure that the examination is comprehensive, balanced, unambiguous, current, consistent with the always-evolving common body of knowledge for the new CPA—and secure from premature exposure.

Each state board has final authority as to the grades of its own candidates. However, the Institute's Advisory Grading Service, under the responsibility of the Board of Examiners, is used by all jurisdictions, thus assuring uniformity in grading.

The graders work under the supervision of the Director of Examinations. They are Institute members with experience in public accounting, and many of them have been accounting teachers. The graders have no information concerning the identity of the candidates. On the initial grading, each grader works with a single problem or question, rather than being responsible for the entire grade of any single paper. Then an experienced grader carefully reviews papers that are close to the passing grade to judge their overall merit. Papers just below passing grades receive a second, and at times a third and fourth, grading.[3]

Objective questions and many of the problems have only one correct answer. The objective question may have each part graded right or wrong, but the problems are graded on the basis of the knowledge and skill shown by a candidate, not on a right or wrong answer. Essay questions predominate in the Auditing, Theory, and Law examinations. Candidates should regard these questions as a test of their ability to organize ideas, to express themselves in clear and correct English, and to formulate judgments. In grading, consideration is given to these abilities as well as to technical knowledge of the subject matter of the questions. Model answers to essay questions usually involve several specific items. A grading scale is developed to allocate point credit for each of the fundamental and desirable items. Normally the candidate need not discuss all these concepts to earn maximum credit. Even so, it is obviously important that an answer be definite and comprehensive.[4]

There is no "normal quota" or "curve" of passing grades, formally or informally. Failure rates appear to be high. Such statistics are hard to interpret, however. Many candidates adopt the questionable policy of "sitting for the experience" with little preparation, by design or default. Rarely is such a person successful. Some candidates focus on only two or three sections in their preparation, hoping for a "conditional pass." Candidates such as these inflate the failure rate. On the other hand, several studies have indicated that 70 to 85% of all serious candidates do complete the examination within five years.[5]

[3] For a comprehensive statement concerning grading procedures see the section "How the Examination Is Graded" in *Information for CPA Candidates,* pp. 28–31.

[4] See the Appendix to this chapter for an example of the grading process.

[5] *Information for CPA Candidates,* p. 32.

conditional credit

You are probably aware that it is not necessary to pass all parts of the examination at one sitting. The following paragraph from *Information for CPA Candidates* (pp. 46–47) summarizes "conditioning the examination":

> The passing grade in each subject is 75 per cent. Conditional credit for subjects passed is usually given if not all subjects are passed on one examination. Some states require that only one subject must be passed to receive conditional credit, some states require that two subjects be passed, and many require a minimum grade in the subjects failed in order for a candidate to receive conditional credit for the subjects passed. Requirements also vary as to the number of opportunities the candidate will be given to pass the remaining subjects. Most states give the candidate two to five opportunities before the conditional credit expires. After expiration of the conditional credit, the candidate must be reexamined in all four subjects if he wishes to continue to work toward a CPA certificate.

If you believe it may be relevant to your preparation strategy, you may wish to determine your own state's approach.

summary

The CPA examination is continually the focus of much attention. Its fairness and general appropriateness have been affirmed in independent reviews—a crucial matter, since the content and administration of the examination is so important to thousands of candidates annually, and to the profession. The examination reflects trends in public accounting practice and in education for accounting and business. In fairness to candidates, the topics included cannot be too innovative; yet by the practice of introducing new topics first as optional questions and/or in very elementary forms, the examination can and definitely does prod laggard accounting curricula.[6]

No examination is perfect. The competence of many candidates will be imperfectly measured; given the wide and changing variety of professional accounting practice, the examination may test some of the

[6] "Within its designated scope the CPA examination should test those qualities being taught at the best business schools. It is expected, however, that the content of the examination may lag slightly behind the curricula of the very best schools, but that it will be ahead of the curricula of the poorer schools. The reason for the slight lag is that the examination tends to be less flexible than the curricula because it must test candidates from all levels of schools on a national basis." AICPA, Committee to Study the Content of the CPA Examination, Minutes of Meeting, September 27, 1967.

wrong things. However, the examination has always been very carefully constructed and administered, and fairly and expertly graded. You, the candidate, face a formidable but fair, very professional and relevant examination.

The Uniform Examination Described

The Uniform Examination is offered in mid-May and mid-November of each year. The dates and specific places of examination may be secured from each state board. Four subjects are covered, over a period of two and one-half days. The scheduling of the examination in recent years has been as follows:

First day:
Accounting Practice, Part I ....1:30 P.M. to 6:00 P.M.
Second day:
Auditing ....8:30 A.M. to 12:00 noon
Accounting Practice, Part II ....1:30 P.M. to 6:00 P.M.
Third day:
Business (Commercial) Law ....8:30 A.M. to 12:00 noon
Accounting Theory ....1:30 P.M. to 5:00 P.M.

Accounting Practice is graded as a single subject. The division into Parts I and II is made to permit a convenient time schedule. As previously noted, a few states examine candidates in additional subjects, typically using the morning of the first day for the examination on these topics.

To indicate the general scope of the examination, the Board of Examiners has stated that

> Candidates may expect the examination to measure the extent of their knowledge of:
>
> 1. Accounting concepts, postulates, and principles.
> 2. Generally accepted auditing standards, audit programs, and auditors' reports.
> 3. Business organization and operation, including a knowledge of the basic laws governing such organization and operation.
> 4. Use of accounting data for managerial purposes.
> 5. Quantitative methods and techniques as they apply to accounting and auditing.
> 6. Federal income taxation.
> 7. Current professional literature and accounting issues receiving special attention at the time of the examination.

Candidates are expected to demonstrate their ability to apply to specific situations their knowledge of the above areas with good judgment and logical reasoning, and to draw reasonable conclusions from such applications. In addition, the examination will determine the extent of their ability to:

1. Write precisely and concisely, and in good English.
2. Organize accounting data and present them in an acceptable form.
3. Discriminate among data in a complex situation, and evaluate and classify such data.
4. Apply appropriate accounting concepts and auditing procedures to given situations.
5. Use mathematics with reasonable facility.[7]

The examinations consist primarily of problems and essays (short answers), although there is a gradually growing proportion of objective (typically, multiple choice) questions. Law topics are generally limited to their own part of the examination, as are most auditing topics. However, topics covered in Theory and Practice, and to some extent in Auditing, are very interrelated. Thus study of accounting topics cannot be focused efficiently on any of these parts individually.

There are a few reasonably predictable features. Current issues, such as new Accounting Principles Board Opinions or Statements on Auditing Procedure, are quite likely to be included.[8] The Practice I Examination usually has an objective-type tax question, whereas a computational tax problem often appears in Practice II. Multiple-choice questions on statistical sampling, and often on internal control with stress on automated data processing (ADP) systems, have recently appeared in the auditing examination. The Practice sections include a "common-sense analysis of data" and/or a "general accounting analysis" problem not related to any specific accounting topic. There are a few optional problems. In recent years one of the options has usually involved a choice of governmental accounting versus, perhaps, cost accounting or (more recently) a question calling for basic knowledge of some quantitative or statistical analysis technique. The time suggested, and presumably the credit given, for these optional problems has generally appeared liberal, assuming that the candidate is reasonably acquainted with one of the optional areas.

There are trends in the examination. An example is the regular inclusion now of problems and questions on analysis of accounting and

[7] *Information for CPA Candidates,* p. 3.

[8] "Current" should be interpreted by noting that the process of preparing the examination requires more than a year.

economic data for business decisions, although facility with historical cost accounting concepts remains important. The candidate may count on facing quantitative problems or questions involving, for example, matrix algebra, linear programming, statistical correlation, and statistical decision making. Except for statistical sampling in auditing, the quantitative questions have often been optional. Some very basic problems have been mandatory, but even these problems have been constructed to allow the candidate who is calm but does not possess great quantitative knowledge an opportunity to earn at least partial credit. However, academic exposure to quantitative methods is becoming increasingly crucial to the candidate—these are now regarded as part of the new CPA's minimal qualifications, or "common body of knowledge."[9] This is true also of familiarity with ADP systems, with emphasis on internal control as such knowledge relates to auditing.

To generalize, the examination (the Law part excepted) demands (a) a common-sense ability to analyze and clearly present data and (b) a sound knowledge of basic accounting and auditing concepts, philosophy, and theory, plus a reasonable recognition of specific AICPA positions on accounting and auditing issues.

Preparing for the Examination

Preparation for the examination can appear overwhelming. And indeed, you should just not "plunge in." First obtain an impression of the examination from reading recent questions and solutions, from talking with associates, and from reading the preceding paragraphs here. Compare these data with your experience, the type and recentness of your academic background, and personal awareness of current events in professional accounting. Set a goal—to pass all sections simultaneously is the most efficient and generally most successful advice, although an individual with a glaring weakness (in, e.g., law or auditing), may reasonably decide to aim for only conditional credit on his first sitting. (In some states, of course, candidates lacking experience are ineligible to sit for all parts.) Whatever you do, avoid a defeatist attitude. Serious candidates with reasonable backgrounds do pass. Commit yourself and your time to preparing.

[9] Testing in quantitative techniques "will be progressively more extensive to the point where candidates are tested for their knowledge of the application of modern algebra (linear and nonlinear), calculus (differential and integral), probability and statistics, and other mathematical techniques developed for business applications." *Information for CPA Candidates,* pp. 7–8.

> Wrong attitudes have led some candidates to take the examination for "experience" or "practice." The candidate should take the examination only with the expectation of passing, and one can reasonably expect to pass only after relentless, habitual, and intensive review for a minimum of two or three months prior to the examination dates. Half-hearted preparation will result in failure; and failure, no matter how it is explained, is discouraging.[10]

The strength of candidates whose preparation is adequate with respect to education but inadequate with respect to experience will probably lie in familiarity with accounting literature and with the technique of taking examinations. Not all schools require the same amount of problem solving in their accounting courses. Thus various candidates may be strong or weak in this respect. However, good academic programs develop a knowledge of different points of view on controversial matters. In answering questions of this type, a candidate's classroom training should give him a distinct advantage.

If one's basic preparation is stronger in experience, he usually has no difficulty in laying out working papers or in preparing involved supporting schedules. He has probably acquired habits of accuracy and neatness. Usually he is faster in typical calculations and in statement preparation than are candidates without this experience.

Survey your strength or weakness with respect to the capabilities mentioned. Then plan a program of preparation calculated to remove your deficiencies.

Statistics on successful candidates are frequently presented as predictors of success. As you might suppose, there are no simple cause-and-effect relationships. Experience is of some help, assuming a good academic background; good quality and recent academic work in accounting, both in theory and in problem solving, is helpful—given also adequate general intelligence, ability to analyze and present matters clearly, and so on. Even if the success predictors were stronger, though, they would be of no more than passing interest to you, since your background is now settled. However, do not delay your sitting.

> Candidates should take the examination as soon as they are eligible to do so. . . . [Recent graduates'] academic knowledge is freshest and their ability to write examination papers is at a peak. Delays in writing the examination impose unnecessary handicaps on candidates.[11]

There are various methods of undertaking a review, and no single one is best for every case. Some candidates rely on home study, reread-

[10] *Information for CPA Candidates,* p. 13.
[11] *Information for CPA Candidates,* p. 34.

ing basic texts and working with the questions and answers from previous examinations. Such candidates usually have considerable difficulty in selecting material to be covered. The chapters of this book should be especially helpful to them. Others can benefit from working with a small, semiformal group of candidates, a method that can be especially helpful if there is some leadership. Some candidates are able to enroll in coaching courses. These may be short-term (two to four weeks) or intensive (full-time devoted to the review). Or they may extend over ten or more weeks, with one or two sessions per week. Many other candidates enroll in correspondence courses.

Most candidates are well advised to review with others, to undertake a formal program of study, or to use both measures. Self-discipline is often most difficult. Work with others can provide both guidance and interactive support.

You will be "reviewing," but of course much material will be new. Wherever you feel confident, assure this by a quick review and practice with a problem or question. In general, spend more time on the less familiar areas. You should have at least a fair knowledge of all financial and managerial accounting topics—this book is designed to assist you toward that goal. Review should not be restricted to textbooks and this *Manual,* however. Do not neglect AICPA publications, especially recent *Opinions of the Accounting Principles Board, Statements on Auditing Procedure,* Accounting Research Studies of the Accounting Research Division of the Institute, and the Code of Professional Ethics. The *Journal of Accountancy* regularly contains significant statements and editorials regarding current accounting and professional problems.

In your preparation, a significant choice is posed by any major area with which you are totally unacquainted. Take, for example, fund (governmental) accounting. This is usually an optional problem. Review its most recent optional alternatives (which at this writing have been on quantitative methods) and decide the better use of your time. (Facility with fund accounting sufficient for reasonable examination credit can be picked up rather rapidly by many candidates, it may be noted.)

Quantitative methods are another example. Statistical sampling in auditing is a requirement; the audit examination should not be attempted without knowledge of this area. Study of that topic in the following auditing chapter will be very beneficial. Other quantitative topics, such as linear programming, correlation analysis, queuing theory, and so on, cannot be acquired in this way, however. The candidate without prior quantitative exposure must "take his chances." Even so, it is advisable to review a few recent quantitative problems, with an eye toward how you might remain unflustered and earn at least partial credit. Parts of some quantitative problems have involved accounting and/or economic decision analysis.[12]

All examinations feature problems of types involving abilities that might be termed "general accounting sense" and "general reasoning ability." These typically do not involve major accounting topical areas and as such might be overlooked by the candidate. However, two or more of each type should be solved. (Candidates without an academic accounting major should be especially sure to work on the former type.) Review recent examinations for examples. At this writing, good recent examples were: For "general accounting," November 1969, Practice I, No. 3; November 1968, Practice I, No. 2 and Practice II, No. 4; and May 1966, Practice I, No. 2. For "general reasoning," May 1969, Practice I, No. 4; and November 1966, Practice II, No. 5.

use previous examinations

Solving the past CPA questions and problems is strongly recommended. Solving problems and writing clear and concise answers require arts that quickly fade as one leaves an academic environment. The Uniform Examination questions and answers have been published in book form by the AICPA in separate volumes, each covering the examinations of a three-year period. The questions, unofficial answers, and study references of the most recent examinations are contained in individual supplements, published each February and August. These may be obtained individually or, by subscribers to the *Journal of Accountancy,* on a regular basis.

During most of your review period it is desirable to work on single problems and questions that are selected to coordinate with the topics then being studied. Answer some of them completely, writing answers and solutions in a form you would be willing to present to the graders. Do not be concerned if early in your review you cannot comply with the recommended times. On the other hand, as you become more adept, work some others as "speed sprints," attempting to form a maximum credit answer within one-half or two-thirds of the minimum suggested time. This will allow you both to cover more material and to build confidence that may be valuable if you should encounter a difficulty with time when writing the examination. Just prior to the examination date it is advisable to set aside several three- or four-hour periods and work complete sections at single sittings under simulated examination conditions.

[12] At this writing, the four most recent examinations (through May 1970) have included a quantitative problem in the Practice I part, all optional with a fund accounting question.

You may be tempted to glance at the solution before seriously attempting to solve the problem. Be wary of this. Early in your review, while you are still "rusty" in examination writing or in the subject matter, there may be some efficiency in this procedure. As the examination date approaches, however, avoid this "preparation"—practice under actual examination conditions. Do not complacently feel able to write the examination merely because you can read and understand a prepared solution.

Obviously, working with past examinations will aid in reviewing subject matter. Equally important, however, is constant awareness of your *approach to solutions* as you compare yours with the published ones. The "unofficial answers" are so termed because they are models, perhaps more than sufficient for full credit. Also, alternative solutions and different terminology are very often acceptable. Thus, in comparing your solution with the "unofficial" one, try to emphasize the basic approach and any glaring deficiencies or errors. Do not dwell on the specific solution. There will never be another problem identical to that one, the published answer is only a model of many acceptable variations, and 75 is a passing grade. The grader will be looking for a reasonable familiarity with the subject and ability to use that knowledge. Passing, not perfection, should be your goal.[13]

other suggestions for review

Some other simple but useful suggestions may be listed:

1. Follow a definite schedule.
2. Devote the major time to the subject matter not covered in previous preparation.
3. Do not work too long at a single sitting.
4. Get normal sleep and exercise.
5. Plan rest days.
6. Do not memorize or cram.
7. Allow a two- or three-day period of relaxation before the examination.

Taking the Examination

In most states the examiners distribute printed rules and suggestions to the candidates immediately preceding the examination. It is

[13] The candidate may wish to refer also to *Information for CPA Candidates,* pp. 13–18.

helpful to study this material in advance. In addition, specific instructions are given on the front of each section of the examination along with the warning, "Disregard of these instructions may be considered as indicating inefficiency in accounting work."

The examination is carefully prepared to avoid unclear questions; it contains no trick questions. Nevertheless, candidates regularly lose points by apparent failure to read carefully the instructions and requirements—by misinterpreting, by omitting, or by doing more than necessary.

A copy of the rules may be obtained from your state board. The current rules and suggestions are reproduced on pages 16 and 17.

Be sure to have all materials necessary for taking the examination—a supply of pencils and erasers, a ruler, and perhaps some candy to break the tension and provide energy. Paper is provided. It is advisable to report early for the examination and to secure an advantageous seat from the point of view of light and physical comfort.

The examination can be completed in the available time if the candidate is qualified to pass and knows how to plan his work. The time will not be adequate if he makes "false starts" or does more than is required of him. Many have found it helpful to scan all the questions initially and to begin with those involving subjects they know well. Having one or two satisfactory answers completed aids one's confidence. It should also be possible to build a reserve of allowable time. Almost never should more than the estimated maximum time be spent on a question (until you have completed the examination and have time remaining). You may not have written all you wish, but very probably the extra time will be used more profitably on a new question.

answering essay questions

Read each essay question two or more times: once hurriedly to obtain a comprehensive view of its content and requirements; the second time carefully, underscoring important dates and amounts. Then plan your answer well before doing any writing on the answer sheet. Frequently it is helpful to make notes on the margin of the question sheet or working paper. Haste in undertaking a formal answer generally involves a waste of effort and time.

In answering essay questions, make certain that you have correctly interpreted the requirements. Emphasize the basic points involved, avoiding minor points and lengthy arguments. Short paragraphs and short sentences are generally preferable. Well-stated reasons to support an answer generally result in a better grade than would be achieved by mere citation of references as authority. The objectives should be to develop a clear, concise, and comprehensive answer with no irrelevant

UNIFORM CERTIFIED PUBLIC ACCOUNTANT EXAMINATION

General Rules Governing Examination

1. Read carefully the identification card assigned to you; sign it; make a note of your number for future reference; and return the card to the examiner when he so indicates. Only the examination number on your card shall be used on your papers for the purpose of identification. The importance of remembering this number and recording it on your examination paper correctly cannot be overemphasized. If a question calls for an answer involving a signature, do not sign your own name or initials.

2. Answers must be submitted on paper furnished by the Board and must be completed in the total time allotted for each subject stated on the printed examinations. Identify your answers by using the proper question number. Begin your answer to each question on a separate page and number pages in accordance with the instructions on the printed examinations. Arrange your answers in the order of the questions.

3. Answers may be written in pencil or in ink. If pencil is used it should be soft enough to leave an easily visible impression. Use only one side of the paper. Use the plain sheets, Form F, for calculations, working notes, etc. Neatness and orderly presentation of work are important. Credit cannot be given for answers that are illegible.

4. Use a soft pencil, preferably #2 lead, to blacken the spaces on the separate I.B.M. answer sheets for the objective-type questions.

5. Attach all computations to the papers containing your solutions. Identify them as to the problem to which they relate. The rough calculations and notes may assist the examiners in understanding your solutions.

6. Stationery and supplies furnished by the Board shall remain its property and must be returned whether used or not. You may retain the printed examinations providing you do not leave the examination room before one-half hour prior to completion time.

7. Any reference during the examination to books or other matters or the exchange of information with other persons shall be considered misconduct sufficient to bar you from further participation in the examination.

UNIFORM CERTIFIED PUBLIC ACCOUNTANT EXAMINATION

Suggestions to the Candidate

1. The estimated minimum time and the estimated maximum time that the candidate may need for giving adequate answers to each question or group of questions is given in the printed examinations. These estimates should be used as a guide to allotment of time. It is recommended that the candidate not spend more than the estimated maximum time on any one question until the others have been completed except to the extent that the maximum time has not been used on prior questions. No point values are shown for the individual questions. Points will be approximately proportionate to the time required. The following is an example of time estimates as they appear on the printed examination booklets:

	Estimated Minutes	
	Minimum	Maximum
Group I (All required):		
No. 1	25	30
No. 2	25	30
No. 3	20	25
No. 4	25	30
No. 5	25	30
No. 6	25	30
Total for Group I	145	175
Group II (One required)	30	35
Total for examination	175	210

2. If the candidate is unable to complete all the answers called for in the examination, a partial answer is better than none and will receive appropriate credit. When more questions are answered out of a group of optional questions than are required, <u>the excess answers will not be graded.</u>

3. The candidate should avoid explaining how to solve the problem instead of actually solving it in the best way he can. If time grows short, a brief statement to the point is permissible, but full credit cannot be obtained by this expedient.

4. Formal journal entries should not be prepared unless specifically required by the problem. Time may be saved by entering adjustments, reclassifications, etc., directly on the working papers. Elaborate working papers should not be prepared unless they are of assistance in solving the problem. If both working papers and formal statements are required and time is not adequate to complete both, the working papers should be completed.

5. In problems or questions which permit alternative treatment the credit given for the solution will depend on the knowledge and intelligence indicated by the candidate's presentation.

6. Due weight will be given to the arguments presented to support the candidate's answer even though the examiners may not agree with his conclusions.

7. All amounts given in a question or problem are to be considered material unless otherwise stated.

8. The CPA is continually confronted with the necessity of expressing his opinions and conclusions in written reports in clear, unequivocal language. Although the primary purpose of the examination is to test the candidate's knowledge and application of the subject matter, the ability to organize and present such knowledge in acceptable written language will be considered by the examiners.

material. As previously noted, alternative answers may often be satisfactory. In such cases, give special attention to making specific points and to supporting them with appropriate reasons rather than to emphasizing a right or wrong answer. State a personal position if one seems called for; obviously, any official AICPA position on the subject matter should be recognized. Take care to avoid conflicting statements unless a clear explanation is made that you are presenting an alternative based on different facts or assumptions.

solving problems

Careful reading of the problem and its requirements is important. Have your approach thought out before undertaking computations and the preparation of schedules or statements. Determine the chief points involved and decide on the procedure you will follow in dealing with them. If an assumption needs to be made, it should be made promptly without waste of time. Care should be taken not to overlook a discussion requirement in a problem.

Journal entries and work sheets are seldom required, and frequently it is possible to save time by eliminating them by posting entries directly to accounts on the question sheet or to T-accounts on a work sheet. In contrast, for involved problems, preparation of journal entries or a working trial balance may save time. This difficult decision must be based on your own limitations and abilities in the use of shortcuts, and this information can be acquired only by careful analysis of your capabilities and practice with past examinations.

After completing the solution to a problem, make certain that each statement and schedule is properly headed and that the solution is properly cross-referenced.

To summarize:

1. Read the question carefully. Follow the instructions.
2. Keep the examiner in mind when answering questions. Think of him as a reasonable person who will be satisfied with a reasonable answer.
3. Do not offer more than the answer requires. Note carefully whether the answer should be submitted as a definition, outline, discussion, statement, or schedule.
4. Do not waste time criticizing a question. If an assumption is necessary, state it plainly and proceed without delay.
5. Do not give conflicting statements. Avoid an indefinite position on issues.
6. Review the requirements and your answer to make certain that all the requirements are met.

7. Check the reasonableness of mathematical computations. Mathematical perfection is not expected, but glaring errors may be interpreted as indicating accounting immaturity.

8. Writing need only be legible. Do not copy questions.

9. Time may be lost in attempting a perfect answer. The answer need only be reasonably satisfactory.

10. Keep calm. Expect and utilize the normal tension that accompanies examination conditions.

Appendix

The following example illustrates how the grading process is designed to assess the candidate's knowledge and judgment, in a rigorous yet reasonable manner. Although the maximum number of points allocated to the question was 16, there were 39½ gradable points on the question. In this respect it should be noted that maximum credit can be obtained even though the solution is not letter perfect.

number 4

(Estimated time—25 to 35 minutes)

a. Goodwill that is permitted on a statement (other than a consolidated statement) is that which has been purchased. Describe briefly two explanations that have been used to justify the recording of goodwill in the balance sheet of a corporation or partnership.

b. Present two methods for estimating the value of goodwill in determining the amount that should properly be paid for it.

c. Discuss the propriety of the item "Goodwill" on the balance sheet in each of the following cases, using the "cost" concept as a guide.

(1) The excess of cost over book value of the net assets of firm A acquired by firm B.

(2) Goodwill placed on the books of an existing partnership immediately preceding the admission of a new partner.

(3) Goodwill arising from consolidation.

grading guide—question number 4

	(Maximum Points Allowed)
a. Goodwill that has been paid for is properly recorded on the balance sheet because it is an asset (i.e., it has future benefit)	2½

Discussion of—			
Excess profits			
Discontinued value	1½		
of future earnings	1½		
in excess of normal	3	5	
OR			
Allow 1 point each for stating sources of this future benefit (i.e., satisfactory customer relationship; favorable location; product marketability)		2	5
Master valuation account			
The excess of current values over book or assigned values			2
Going concern			
The excess of the value of a group of assets working together (i.e., in a going concern) over the value of the individual assets			3
Maximum for a			8
b. *Capitalized profits*			
Divides the average excess profits by an assumed interest rate . . . . (Allow 2 points for incomplete discussion—i.e., omits "excess" or "average" or "capitalize")			3½
Annuity			
The present value of an annuity equal to the estimated excess profit, for a limited number of years			2
No. of years			
Average profits multiplied by a given number of years			1½
Variation			
Where candidate's second method is an acceptable variation of an acceptable method			1½
Maximum for b			5

c. (1) *Excess only*

The proper amount for goodwill in this case is the excess of cost over current value, not book value 3

Is cost

Such goodwill has been purchased, so that this is in accordance with the cost basis .. 1½

OR

Not goodwill

Total purchase price is assigned to assets acquired on the basis of then current or market values 1½

Maximum for (1) 3

(2) *Not full amount*

If the full amount of goodwill is recorded, it is not in accordance with the cost concept 1½

Excess only

Only the excess of the amount paid in by the new partner over his share of the net assets is cost 1½

Objective evidence

However, the payment is objective evidence of the existence of a full amount of goodwill 1

Alternate answer

Allow 2 points for recognition that this transaction gives rise to goodwill in accordance with the cost concept ....

Maximum for (2) 3

(3) *Is cost to unit*

The excess of cost over book value of the subsidiary does represent cost to the consolidated group 2½

Allocate

It is possible that some part of this would have been allocated to specific assets if they had been purchased directly	1
Maximum for (3)	$3\frac{1}{2}$
Maximum for c	7

2
accounting theory

Charles T. Zlatkovich

accounting theory

Accounting is a practical service activity. Its primary function is to provide quantitative information, essentially financial in character, designed to be useful in making economic decisions about entities. It is somewhat more an art than a science and its rules are man made—those which prove useful and win general acceptance survive; those which prove less useful often are ultimately discarded.

For our purposes, accounting theory is an explanation or rationalization of the rules of accounting. Put another way, it is an explanation of accounting principles. The purpose of theory is to express the basic concepts or ideas that underlie the principles of accounting. Since there is no single accepted, complete set of accounting principles and since some of the generally accepted principles in widespread use in the United States are not in harmony with all the other generally accepted principles, it follows that there is no single accepted, complete, and unified body of theory. Terminology in the realm of accounting theory is not very uniform. More or less equal or parallel levels of ideas or thoughts are variously referred to by different writers or groups as postulates, concepts, standards, principles, and still other terms.

Some of accounting's rules are essentially mechanical or procedural and these are well settled. Increases in asset and expense accounts are recorded by means of debits, and credits cause decreases in these accounts. Mechanical accuracy of ledgers is proven by means of trial balances; the accuracy of subsidiary ledgers is checked by comparison of balances of controlling accounts with the totals of underlying subsidiary accounts, and so on. Mechanical details of some of these procedural matters have undergone methodological changes in recent years because of widespread introduction of new devices such as computers; but the fundamental recording principles have remained essentially unchanged for several centuries.

Even at the initial recording state, however, a higher order of theory can enter the picture and can determine the ultimate reporting and analysis of results. For example, determination of whether an invoice for repairs should be charged to an expense account or to some other account forces a consideration of a variety of factors, including the materiality of the charge, the nature of the repair, the period or periods to be benefited from it, and whether the entity has previously established an account to which such charges should be made.

After recording has taken place, theory considerations dictate the nature and amount of certain adjusting entries, placement, grouping and terminology used for statement presentation and analysis, and the kinds of disclosures made in supplementary fashion in connection with financial statements.

relation of accounting theory to courses and to accounting practice

For the most part CPA candidates are likely to relate their preparatory efforts to courses taken while in a college or university and to the specific segments of the Uniform CPA Examination. Although there is a segment of the examination called Accounting Theory, much of the material in this chapter relates also to the Accounting Practice parts of the examination. The following quotations from the 1970 edition of *Information for CPA Candidates* seem pertinent on this point.

> The topics covered by Accounting Theory and Accounting Practice are similar despite the difference in the emphases of the sections.[1]
>
> The candidate should not think that it is more efficient to prepare for only one or two sections at a time. On the contrary, the best performance is achieved by the candidate who prepares for all sections of the examination simultaneously. This is because Auditing, Theory, and Accounting Practice are so interrelated and interdependent that review of one is beneficial to the others. After all, good practice is nothing more than the application of good theory. Good theory, similarly, is nothing more than the explanation of good practice. And since good practice and theory have been influenced heavily by the attest function of accounting, it follows that knowledge in these two areas is essential, though insufficient of course to pass Auditing.[2]

[1] *Information for CPA Candidates* (New York: AICPA, 1970), p. 8.
[2] *Ibid,* p. 15.

The subject areas dealt with on the Accounting Theory part of the Uniform CPA Examination can be broadly categorized as "financial accounting." In collegiate courses the subject matter was often covered in Introductory, Intermediate, and Advanced Principles of Accounting courses. To some extent, however, materials covered in Cost Accounting, Managerial Accounting, and similarly titled courses are also encompassed in Accounting Theory.

This chapter is intended to provide a review of what is usually called financial accounting theory—the concepts and ideas used in the preparation of financial statements of profit-oriented business entities when such statements, designed for general public use, provide the basis for examinations to be made by independent public accountants. Those concepts and ideas relate to basic accounting principles having almost universal application. Because of their importance, these principles have been the subject of authoritative study and pronouncement.

sources of accounting theory

A single overall authoritative statement of accounting principles does not (and may never) exist. In the absence of such a statement, accounting theory (as previously explained) rests piecemeal on a variety of sources. A listing of these sources, not necessarily in the order of their importance for our purposes, is furnished here.

From the American Institute of CPAs (AICPA), 666 Fifth Avenue, New York, New York, 10019:

Opinions of the Accounting Principles Board [3]

Statements of the Accounting Principles Board [4]

Accounting Research Studies published by the AICPA Director of Accounting Research [5]

Accounting Research Bulletins of the Committee on Accounting Procedure, predecessor of the Accounting Principles Board [6]

[3] Nineteen Opinions had been issued when this book went to press. Candidates should keep in mind the importance of stressing the recent APB Opinions in their review efforts. When an Opinion has been published more than twelve months prior to a particular examination and is not more than three years old, it is especially likely to be the basis of a Theory question, a Practice problem, or both.

[4] Four Statements had been issued when this book went to press. To a fair degree, what is said about the age of Opinions and their forming the basis of questions or problems is also true of Statements.

[5] Eleven Studies had been published when this book went to press. Studies sometimes serve as the source of Theory questions or Practice problems.

[6] Accounting Research Bulletins were discontinued in 1959 with the issuance of No. 51; nonetheless, the Accounting Principles Board has adopted the bulletins of its predecessor and has made relatively few changes in them.

Accounting Terminology Bulletins of the Terminology Committe, a subgroup of the Committee on Accounting Procedure [7]

From the American Accounting Association (AAA), 653 South Orange Avenue, Sarasota, Florida, 33577:

Accounting and Reporting Standards for Corporate Financial Statements and Preceding Statements and Supplements

A Statement of Basic Accounting Theory

An Introduction to Corporate Accounting Standards

From other sources:

Various up-to-date textbooks, reference books, accounting articles, and committee reports are likely to contain authoritative expressions of accounting theory. It is obviously not feasible to attempt a listing of individual sources here.[8]

[7] The last Terminology Bulletin was published in July, 1957. Of all the AICPA-originated materials listed, the terminology materials are probably least important from the standpoint of modern theory.

[8] One of the more interesting articles germane to this chapter to appear in recent years was "Some Thoughts on Substantial Authoritative Support," *The Journal of Accountancy* (April, 1969), pp. 44–50, by Marshall S. Armstrong, an APB member who later became President of the AICPA. The article was principally concerned with informing practicing CPAs how they might locate substantial authoritative support for an accounting principle. A CPA might be launched on such a search because the governing Council of the AICPA adopted recommendations as follows:

1. "Generally accepted accounting principles" are those principles which have substantial authoritative support.
2. Opinions of the Accounting Principles Board constitute "substantial authoritative support."
3. "Substantial authoritative support" can exist for accounting principles that differ from Opinions of the Accounting Principles Board.

Thus, if a client of a CPA proposed to use a reporting practice at variance with APB recommendations, it would become necessary for the CPA to determine whether that practice had authoritative support. Armstrong suggested a search of some of the literature listed specifically and also suggested reference to rules and regulations of the SEC, written views of individuals, accounting textbooks, reference books, accounting articles, laws, pronouncements of industry regulatory authorities, and publications of industry associations.

The relation between accounting theory and generally accepted accounting principles (GAAP) is debatable. At one extreme are those who would say the two are virtually indistinguishable and that the framework of GAAP constitutes the whole of accounting theory. Those at the other extreme contend that there exists a fairly well-developed body of accounting theory and that, at best, GAAP represent rather spotty manifestations of it.

a broad structure of theory

The remainder of this chapter is structured around the following outline:

I. Fundamental Assumptions
   A. identified accounting entity
   B. continuity (going concern)
   C. quantifiability (unit of measure)
   D. time period
II. Permeative Principles—Accounting Procedures
   A. measured consideration
   B. revenue recognition
   C. objectivity of accounting data
   D. exceptions
      1. materiality
      2. conservatism
      3. industry peculiarities
III. Permeative Principles—Reporting
   A. relevance—user orientation
   B. adequacy of disclosure
   C. consistency
   D. appropriateness to expected use
IV. Miscellaneous specific topics

Fundamental Assumptions

identified accounting entity

The separate identification of the accounting unit or entity from those having interests in it is fundamental and has been verbalized by most authors or groups dealing with accounting theory. It has been well expressed by Paton and Littleton in these words:

> The business undertaking is generally conceived of as an entity or institution in its own right, separate and distinct from the parties who furnish the funds, and it has become almost axiomatic that the business accounts and statements are those of the entity rather than those of the proprietor, partners, investors, or other parties or groups concerned.[9]

[9] William A. Paton and A.C. Littleton, *An Introduction to Corporate Accounting Standards* (Columbus, O.: American Accounting Association, 1956), p. 8.

Legal form has nothing to do with it, and whether the entity is a separate legal person from its owners (as in the case with a corporation) is immaterial to the distinction. The essential point is that in carrying out the accounting function, the assets, equities, and operations are segregated for each separate entity. All records and reports are developed from the viewpoint of the entity. The personal transactions of persons closely associated with the entity are isolated from those of the entity itself, and transactions between the entity and those persons are often accounted for just as though the parties were complete strangers.[10]

Sometimes two or more entities are treated as a single entity for accounting purposes; there are also occasions when an entity is broken into smaller units which in turn are treated as reporting entities. The first situation is typified by the preparation of consolidated statements. The latter is exemplified by accounting for a branch or department as though it were an independent entity; sometimes transfer prices between divisions of a company are set in a way that allows divisions to "earn a profit" or for other reasons of managerial control.

To return for a moment to the matter of combining legally separate entities into a single superentity for accounting ends, the reason for consolidated statements has been well stated in the first paragraph of Accounting Research Bulletin No. 51:

> The purpose of consolidated statements is to present, primarily for the benefit of the shareholders and creditors of the parent company, the results of operations and the financial position of a parent company and its subsidiaries essentially as if the group were a single company with one or more branches or divisions. There is a presumption that consolidated statements are more meaningful than separate statements and that they are usually necessary for a fair presentation when one of the companies in the group directly or indirectly has a controlling financial interest in the other companies.[11]

Before leaving the subject of the accounting entity it should be pointed out that there are a number of equity theories of the enterprise, one of which is known as "the entity theory." This discussion has not related specifically to it and no attempt is made to cover the entity theory or some competitive theories known as the proprietary theory, the fund theory, the residual equity theory, the enterprise theory, or the commander theory because these theories do not seem particularly important from the standpoint of the Uniform CPA Examination. The last major

[10] There are, of course, exceptions to this statement. For example, if the owner of a proprietorship takes home merchandise for personal consumption, the transaction is recorded as a drawing rather than as a sale. Payments of salaries to partners are ultimately handled as distributions of profits rather than as expenses (employment costs).

[11] ARB No. 51.

question concerning them to appear on the examination was in May, 1959, although small portions of objective questions have since dealt with the topic.[12]

continuity

The continuity assumption is often alternatively referred to in terms of "going concern." Whatever terminology is used, there is an implication of indefinite continuance of the entity. In other words, the enterprise is not expected to liquidate or terminate in the foreseeable future. At the same time, there is no implication of permanent continuance. Indefinite continuance means that the entity will not be liquidated within a time span necessary to carry out present contractual commitments or to use up assets according to plans and expectations presently held. The assumption has been useful in widening the scope of accounting with respect to valuations and in freeing it from a strict construction of legal rights and obligations. Some specific items of evidence on this point, cited by Moonitz, are:

> 1. *Receivables.* Receivables (and the related revenues) are ordinarily recognized whenever future cash receipts from customers are definitely expected and can be measured. The amount of the receivables is geared to the amount of the anticipated future cash receipts, not to the present realizable (liquidation) value of the receivable in the market. While there may be some legal defect in the transaction such as an incomplete transfer of title to goods sold, it will ordinarily be ignored in accounting for the transaction. These considerations of liquidity and legality are of some relevance, but only in those cases in which the expected cash receipts from the customer are in doubt or in jeopardy.
>
> 2. *Inventories.* The customary valuation basis of work in process is raw materials cost plus labor and overhead costs incurred to date. At the same time, it is recognized the immediate market (liquidation) value of work in process is usually low compared with the market value of materials before processing. In pricing such inventories at cost we assume a going concern will finish the work in process and sell the finished output.[13]

[12] Readers interested in detailed treatment of these theories can find them in the following sources, among others:

Hendriksen, Eldon S., *Accounting Theory* (1970 rev. ed.), (Homewood, Ill.: Richard D. Irwin, Inc.), Chapter 17.

Vatter, William J., in "Corporate Stock Equities," *Modern Accounting Theory,* Ed., Morton Backer (1966 rev. ed.), (Englewood Cliffs, N.J.: Prentice-Hall, Inc.), pp. 250–57.

Goldberg, Louis, *An Inquiry into the Nature of Accounting,* Monograph No. 7 (Evanston, Ill.: American Accounting Association, 1965), pp. 162–74.

[13] Material in this section is paraphrased and abstracted from Maurice Moonitz, Accounting Research Study No. 1, *The Basic Postulates of Accounting* (New York: AICPA, 1961), pp. 39–40.

quantifiability (unit of measure)

Accountants assign numbers to virtually all items of information which they report. Money is the most common, but it is not the only quantitative measure used by accountants. Basic accounting assumptions with respect to money have undergone interesting changes over the past several decades. Had this chapter been written less than thirty years ago, the basic monetary assumption would probably have been satisfactory to a preponderance of the practicing accounting profession if it had been phrased somewhat in these terms: "a basic assumption for accounting purposes is that the monetary unit (dollar) is of constant dimensions; that is, the purchasing power of money remains unchanged." Clearly, world-wide monetary experience since 1940 has been such that this assumption, which was once tenable as a working basis for accounting theory and practice in the United States and many other economies, no longer has much validity. No completely acceptable alternative statement in succinct terms seems to exist today. There seem to be two leading alternatives to the earlier stability of money assumption. In 1953, for example, Carman G. Blough, then Director of Research for the AICPA, wrote:

> Changes in the Purchasing Power of the Monetary Unit are not Important—It is on the basis of this assumption that dollars of cost are intermingled in the accounts as though they were of equal purchasing power at the time incurred, although, as a matter of fact, it is well recognized that they are not. Dollars of revenue are treated as the equivalent of dollars of cost allocated to the same period regardless of any material changes in the purchasing power of the dollar between the time the costs were incurred and the time they are matched against revenues.[14]

The other leading alternative is to prepare financial statements as though the originally stated assumption or the one just quoted were acceptable (i.e., prepare "conventional" statements on the basis of historical costs), then to supplement these statements by means of price-level adjusted statements prepared according to one of a variety of techniques that have been proposed.

Because the Accounting Principles Board has such widespread influence over accounting practices in the United States, the specific techniques it has recommended to yield supplementary price-level adjusted statements to accompany regularly prepared financial statements are briefly described. At the outset it should be pointed out that some other

[14] Robert L. Kane, Jr., Chap. XVII, *CPA Handbook* (New York: AICPA, 1953) Vol. II, 13.

proposals have at least equal theoretical merit and that several of them would ordinarily yield somewhat comparable results if applied in the same circumstances. It should also be observed that the Board was somewhat restrained in its urging that its recommended techniques actually be applied in the United States. Its language on this point was as follows:

> The Board believes that general price-level financial statements or pertinent information extracted from them present useful information not available from basic historical-dollar financial statements. General price-level information may be presented in addition to the basic historical-dollar financial statements, but general price-level financial statements should not be presented as the basic statements. The Board believes that general price-level information is not required at this time for fair presentation of financial position and results of operations in conformity with generally accepted accounting principles in the United States.
>
> The Board recognizes that the degree of inflation or deflation in an economy may become so great that conventional statements lose much of their significance and general price-level statements clearly become more meaningful, and that some countries have experienced this degree of inflation in recent years.[15]

Summary of Technique of Restating Financial Statements for Price-Level Changes. In Statement No. 3 the Accounting Principles Board made the following recommendations concerning the restatement of conventionally prepared financial statements to reflect price-level changes.

1. Use an index number reflecting changes in general purchasing power. (Specifically, the GNP Deflator was recommended for use in the United States.)
2. The index value should be as of the latest balance sheet date. (This would mean that, given the "creeping inflation" experienced in the last decade, even current revenue such as Sales for the most recent period would be adjusted upward slightly.)
3. Monetary and nonmonetary items should be distinguished for the purpose of preparing general price-level statements. Monetary items include cash, receivables, most liabilities—in general all items to be realized or settled at a definite monetary sum. Nonmonetary items include most other assets (inventories, plant, etc.) and the common stockholders' equity.
4. Nonmonetary items on both the balance sheet and income statement should be restated into terms of their current general purchasing power. (Example: Land was acquired for $9,000 when the index stood at 110; the index is at 132 on the balance sheet date. The land would be reported at $10,800; $9,000 × 132/110.)

[15] *APB Statement No. 3,* p. 12.

5. General price-level gains and losses on monetary items are calculated, and the net result should be reported on the adjusted income statement as a nonoperating gain or loss.

6. Income tax amounts in general price-level statements are based on income taxes reflected in historical-dollar statements and are not computed in direct relation to income before taxes on the general price-level statements.

7. Some nonmonetary items such as inventories are stated at the lower of cost or market in historical-dollar statements; they should also be stated at the lower of cost or market in general price-level statements.

8. General price-level financial statements of earlier periods should be updated to reflect current general purchasing power at the end of each subsequent period for which they are presented as comparative information. Descriptive material accompanying such statements should make it clear that previously reported information has been updated to dollars of current general purchasing power to provide comparability with current general price-level statements.

9. All general price level information presented should be based on complete general price-level calculations; partially restated financial statements, in the view of the APB, are likely to be misleading and should not be presented.

10. General price-level financial statements should preferably be presented in separate schedules rather than in columns parallel to the historical-dollar statements. (This is in contrast to a recommendation of the American Accounting Association's Committee to Prepare a Statement of Basic Accounting Theory, which preferred the parallel column approach.)

11. The basis of preparation of general price-level information and what it purports to show should be clearly explained in the notes to the general price-level statements. The explanation should note that (a) the statements are supplementary; (b) all amounts shown are in terms of the same general purchasing power as measured by an index number; (c) the general price-level gain or loss indicates the effects of price change on the company's net holdings of monetary assets and liabilities; (d) in all other respects, the same generally accepted accounting principles are used (as used for historical-cost statements); (e) amounts do not purport to reflect appraised, replacement, or other current value measures; and (f) any general price-level statements of prior years presented for comparative purposes have been updated to current dollars.

Arguments For and Against Price-Level Adjusted Statements. On a number of occasions candidates have been asked to give arguments for and against preparation of price-level adjusted statements or the taking of other measures designed to reveal or alleviate the impact of inflation on financial statements. As long as price changes continue, there is reason to expect recurrence of this type of question on examinations and from clients, as well as continued discussion of the subject in the public press. Question No. 7 which appeared on the November, 1964, Theory examination is fairly typical, and the unofficial answer to it represented an excellent checklist of the leading arguments pro and con. Both the question and the unofficial answer are quoted.

Question: A common objective of accountants is to prepare meaningful financial statements. To attain this objective many accountants maintain that the financial statements must be adjusted for changes in price level. Other accountants believe that financial statements should continue to be prepared on the basis of unadjusted historical cost.

Required:

a. List arguments for adjusting financial statements for changes in price level.
b. List the arguments for preparing financial statements on only the basis of unadjusted historical cost.
c. In their discussions about accounting for changes in the price levels and the methods of measuring them, uninformed individuals have frequently failed to distinguish between adjustments for changes in the price levels of specific goods and services and adjustments for changes in the general purchasing power of the dollar. What is the distinction? Which are "price level adjustments"? Discuss.

Answer:

a. The following arguments are made for adjusting financial statements for changes in price level:

1. Failure to allow for the effects of changes in price level is unrealistic and causes significant errors in the determination of income and the presentation of balance sheet amounts. These errors arise from reliance on the premise that the monetary unit, the dollar, is stable. The dollar is not stable, however, and changes in its value result in the assembly of basically nonadditive amounts for balance sheet purposes and nonuniform costs for income computations.

2. Readers of the financial statements can make a better appraisal of management's effectiveness in the preservation of the current dollar equivalent of the capital invested in the business. The readers can also make a more useful analysis of the company's earning power in terms of current economic conditions. In addi-

tion, such analyses as return on stockholders' equity and return on total capital employed would be made more meaningful.

3. Computation of the gain or loss on monetary items provides information that is useful in judging how effective monetary management has been.

4. If the computation of depreciation based on costs adjusted for the effect of price level changes were permitted for tax purposes, depreciation charges would permit recovery of purchasing power that would more nearly equal the cost of new assets to replace the old.

5. The values of nearly all items, as reported on the balance sheet, would more closely approximate current values.

6. The public would be better informed regarding the effect of inflation or deflation upon the national economy in general and, more specifically, upon corporate profits, prices, etc.

7. More accurate information would be made available for governmental use in developing economic policies regarding such matters as business pricing policies, income taxation, business profits, and antitrust actions. In the cases of public utilities, transportation companies and other companies whose rates are set by government action, a more equitable method of determining the amount of capital investment and, hence, the amount of return, would be afforded by financial statements adjusted for price level changes.

8. The soundness of management's decisions concerning the business depends on the accuracy of the information upon which they are based. In those cases in which information in published financial statements is relied upon wholly or in part as a basis for management's decisions, it is argued that better decisions will be made if the financial statements have been adjusted for price level changes. To rely on "information" in unadjusted financial statements is frequently to rely on misinformation, not information.

b. The following arguments are advanced for preparing financial statements only on the basis of unadjusted historical costs:

1. Financial statements prepared on this basis provide a measure of management's accomplishments based on verifiable evidence. Such statements have been the principal communication between management and stockholders, and their limitations are so well-recognized that readers make allowances therefor.

2. The use of unadjusted historical cost is deeply imbedded in matters of law and, to a considerable extent, in income tax matters.

3. No method of adjusting for price level changes has been generally accepted; for example, there is no general agreement, among those who advocate price level adjustments, as to which

price index should be used. The application of price indexes on a subjective basis might result in varying results that would be confusing to readers of the statements. Of comparable importance, also, is the possibility of statement manipulations and other malpractices if price indexes could be applied on a subjective basis.

4. The importance of the price level problem may well be exaggerated because, in view of technological improvements, a substantial part of a typical manufacturing company's fixed assets have been recently acquired and are, therefore, valued virtually at current price levels. The turnover of inventories results in their being stated at values that approximate current costs (except for inventories valued on the LIFO basis).

5. Price level adjustments might upset the market price of corporate capital stock if investors should come to the conclusion that a less favorable financial picture is presented.

6. The use of historical costs (unadjusted for price level changes) and the placement of all information concerning values other than such costs only in footnotes permits readers of the financial statements to make whatever use of the book values they deem appropriate in making financial analyses of the statements.

7. Placing financial statements on a current price level might contribute to the inflation of prices with unforeseeable consequences for the national economy as a whole.

8. No need exists for the placing of similar assets on a common price level as is maintained by advocates of price level adjustments. Average costs have traditionally been employed by accountants with satisfactory results.

c. Changes in the prices of specific goods and services occur with fluctuations in the markets for them and may occur when the purchasing power of the dollar is stationary or when it is moving up or down. Measures of the general price level indicate the average purchasing power of the dollar and hence the amount of general inflation or deflation.

Changes in the prices of specific goods and services may be measured by appraisal procedures or by the application of price indexes especially prepared for them. For example, a price index based on the movements of the prices of the factors that enter into construction costs would be suitable for estimation of changes in the reproduction cost of a new building. On the other hand, an index based on the movement of the prices of all goods and services (or of goods and services selected to be representative of all) would be suitable for estimating changes in the purchasing power of the dollar.

The book value of the building cited above could be adjusted by means of either the construction index or the general price level index. Only the latter adjustment would properly be called a "price level adjustment" because the former index may not bear any relationship to the general price level.

time period

If an entity were concerned with a venture-type activity such as the drilling of a single oil well, development of a single real estate tract, or the like, it might be feasible to wait until the project was terminated and liquidation had occurred to determine whether a gain or loss had been realized. Such projects are comparatively rare or are undertaken by continuing entities, so determination of profit or loss at more or less regular intervals is normally required. Moonitz has pointed out that this emphasis on profits calculated in periods of equal length such as a quarter or a year is relatively recent.[16] The recency of the current emphasis on periods of equal length is closely tied to the necessity for determining the coverage of bond interest and of profits available for dividends or subject to taxation as well as to budgetary planning requirements. Regular periods are also consistent and promote comparability.

The environment—the business community and the government—has forced accountants to attempt to measure changes in the wealth of entities over comparatively short time intervals. Such measurements could be accomplished by either of two basic means:

1. By inventorying assets and liabilities at the start and end of the period chosen and calculating net changes as the income or loss after allowing for any added investment or disinvestment (withdrawal or dividends).
2. By the transactions approach, whereby revenue, expense, and other transactions for the period chosen are recorded and then an appropriate matching of earned or realized revenue against expired costs and losses at the end (after a proper recognition of accruals and adjustments) determines net income. In terms of historical dollars, the results of this matching can be verified by an inventorying of assets (and other unexpired costs) and of liabilities and a comparison of this inventorying with a similar operation as of the start of the period.

An obvious difficulty with either approach (but especially the first one) is that unless all prices have remained stationary throughout the period, the resultant income or loss is going to reflect not only the result of transactions engaged in during the period but the results of changes in the values of nonmonetary items held. Traditional accounting practice has largely refrained from inclusion of unrealized appreciation in net income. Under conditions of inflation there is a strong likelihood

[16] Moonitz, *op. cit.,* pp. 16–17.

that some appreciation would be reflected as part of income, since what is being measured is increases in the dollar values of net assets.

For a variety of reasons the most commonly used accounting period is twelve months in duration. Longer periods would furnish needed information too infrequently and would exceed the maximum term an entity can operate without filing an income tax return. Shorter periods are often heavily influenced by seasonal variations and force so many estimates that the information obtained is often less reliable than is desirable. At the same time, quarterly and even monthly reports are quite common, although they are almost always unaudited. If seasonal factors do not bulk too heavily in the operations of an entity and if factors affecting its estimates are such that about the same degree and direction of error can normally be expected in the estimates, then the statements issued at short intervals can be quite useful.

Chopping what is essentially a continuous lifestream of operating activity into arbitrary intervals such as a year, a quarter, or a month forces a large number of allocations, and many of these must be made on somewhat arbitrary bases. Some costs are identifiable with inventories or products, others identify directly with certain revenues, still others with time intervals; but some do not associate particularly with any of the aforementioned things (or with assets other than inventories) and they simply become recognized as expenses or losses more or less by default or because no future benefit can be ascribed to them. It is perhaps easier (but not always necessarily easy) to determine when revenue has been earned or what portion of a larger block of revenue has been earned. Cutting the total life of an entity into short periods forces decisions on these matters, and the shorter the periods the larger the number of decisions and the less certainty that can attend some of them.

Natural Business Year. *A Dictionary for Accountants* has defined a natural business year as "a fiscal year ending with the annual low point of business activity or at the conclusion of a season." [17] For years the accounting profession, the Securities and Exchange Commission (SEC), and others have been advocating more widespread adoption of the natural business year.[18] The end of the natural business year for any particular entity would be marked by lows or near-lows for the year of inventories, sales, production, and probably also receivables and current

[17] Eric L. Kohler, *A Dictionary for Accountants* (Englewood Cliffs, N.J.: Prentice-Hall, Inc., 1970).

[18] The 1969 edition of *Accounting Trends and Techniques,* an annual survey published by the AICPA of 600 corporate annual reports, indicates slow but steady progress in the adoption of the natural business year among the companies included in the survey. In 1968, there were 215 companies that did *not* have fiscal years in December, whereas in 1960 the number was 194 and in 1955 was only 179.

liabilities, and by annual highs of cash. In *Accounting Series Release No. 17* the SEC's Chief Accountant said:

> . . . the advantages to be obtained from the adoption of a fiscal-year-end date which coincides with the lowest point in the annual cycle of operations are clear and to my mind have never been shown to be outweighed by related disadvantages. Among the more important advantages there may be mentioned the probability of obtaining more complete and reliable financial statements, since at the close of the natural business year incomplete transactions, and such items as inventories, would ordinarily be at a minimum. Mention may also be made of the fact that the general adoption of the natural business year would facilitate the work of public accountants by permitting them to spread much of their work throughout the calendar year, and thus aid them in rendering the most effective service to their clients.

In addition to the stated and implied advantages cited in the SEC release, some other advantages of adoption of the natural business year include:

1. Future planning is simplified. There is a natural break for changes in cost standards, establishment of sales and other budget quotas, and planning of future operations.
2. The cost of inventory taking and valuation is reduced because all inventories are at a low point. Furthermore, the taking of a physical inventory would probably cause least interference with sales and production activities, and personnel to assist with the inventory would be available.
3. The workload of the accounting department is smoothed because there would be less conflict with preparation of annual government payroll, tax, and other information returns filed on a calendar-year basis (unless, of course, the natural business year and the calendar year coincided).
4. Assessment of annual operating results and of financial position can probably be done somewhat more efficiently when statements are prepared at the close of a natural cycle of operations rather than somewhere in the middle of the cycle.

Permeative Principles—Accounting Procedures

measured consideration

The term "measured consideration" was apparently first used by Paton and Littleton as generic phraseology to designate the basic subject matter of accounting. It identifies either side of a transaction or a transaction in either direction. The word "cost" covers the motion of exchange in only one direction. If a business acquires services, it thereby incurs cost, but if it renders services and we say "rendered at a cost," the reference is likely to be understood to mean the cost of production, not the price of the exchange. The word "cost" does not satisfactorily say the same thing about a purchase and a sale.[19]

When we say that transactions are expressed quantitatively as price-aggregates for the purpose of accounting, we have a statement of broad usefulness. The price-aggregate of a labor service can be called "cost"; the price-aggregate of an equipment transaction can be called "asset"; the price-aggregate of service rendered can be called "revenue"; the price-aggregate of a loan contract can be called "liability"; and the price-aggregate of a residual equity contract can be called "capital stock." The generic term "measured consideration" encompasses all these concepts. Observe that usage of the word "value" has been avoided. Accounting may record the mutual valuation accorded a transaction by seller and buyer at the moment of exchange, and as of that moment a record of such consideration or price-aggregate may be viewed as a record of value. However, after the moment of exchange the value may change but the recorded measured consideration does not.

The starting point of nearly all asset valuation or measurement is cost. In the case of assets acquired for cash or on short-term credit where no cash discount is involved, the amount of cash paid or to be paid represents the cost of the asset and its initial carrying value. If a cash discount is offered in connection with the purchase of an asset on short-term credit, the discount should theoretically be treated as a reduction of the cost of the asset, regardless of whether it is taken.

Suppose an asset costing $1,000 is offered on terms of 2/10, net/30; journalization of its purchase and payment might be recorded under either of the following alternatives:

Liability recorded gross			*Liability recorded net*		
Asset	$1,000		Asset	$ 980	
Payable		$1,000	Payable		$ 980
			Payment in 10 days		
Payable	$1,000		Payable	$ 980	
Asset		$ 20	Cash		$ 980
Cash		980			
			Payment instead after 30 days		
Payable	$1,000		Payable	$ 980	
Discount lost	20		Discount lost	20	
Cash		$1,000	Cash		$1,000
Asset		20			

[19] Paton and Littleton, *op. cit.*, pp. 11–13.

A good many accountants who would say that the cost was $980 if payment took place within the discount period would say that it was $1,000 if the discount was lost. Others would contend the financial inability of the business to take advantage of a 36% discount (2% for 20 days' payment lag annualizes to approximately 36%) does not create a future benefit which should be carried forward as an asset value.

Determining the measured consideration or cost in a noncash, non-short-term-credit, transaction is less easy. Assets are frequently exchanged for securities such as stocks or bonds. Since assets tend to be unique (this is especially true of realty) and since there is often a broader market for the securities than for the assets, it would seem that ordinarily the fair market value of the securities would provide the better measure of the transaction. This, of course, is not always true. The securities may not be very widely traded. The transaction may involve a block of securities so large that the use of market values prevailing when small blocks trade becomes questionable. It is also quite possible that recent bona fide offers for the assets in question may have served to establish their approximate value. Asset values can also be established by competent appraisers. In some cases the amounts for which they are insured or their values on tax rolls may be guides to their current values. Use of the par value of securities as a basis of valuation should always be viewed with some suspicion, especially in the case of stocks, since the latter may have been issued at par arbitrarily in order to avoid a discount.

Tangible fixed assets are often acquired by means of trade-in of used similar assets plus payment of cash (often called "boot"). Several times over the years, CPA Theory questions have dealt with this matter; one most recent occasion was the May, 1970, examination. On an earlier examination the question was stated as below:

The following information relates to the purchase of an asset which was paid for by a trade-in of an old asset and the balance in cash:

List price of new asset	$10,000
Cash payment	5,800
Cost of old asset	8,000
Depreciation reserve—old asset	5,000
Second-hand market value—old asset	3,600

Required:

a. You are to prepare journal entries to show three different methods of recording the transaction.

b. Following each entry give an explanation of the reasoning behind that method of recording and indicate the circumstances in which it might be appropriate.

Solution:

a. Journal entries were as follows:

	#1		*#2*		*#3*	
New asset	$9,400		$10,000		$8,800	
Depreciation allowance—old asset	5,000		5,000		5,000	
Old asset		$8,000		$8,000		$8,000
Cash		5,800		5,800		5,800
Gain on disposal of old asset		600		1,200		—

b. The explanations in the unofficial answer of entries in columns #1, #2, and #3 (somewhat paraphrased) were as follows:

Entry #1 reflects the view that the best measure of the cost of the new asset is the market value of the old asset plus the cash paid. Such a view is reasonable when there is a customary discount on the new asset and there is an established market price for the old asset and when a gain or loss on disposal of the old asset is indicated.

Entry #2 reflects the view that the cost of acquiring the new asset is its list price. Such a view is reasonable when there is seldom a discount on the new asset and no standard market price for the old asset. Such a view is strengthened when a gain on disposal of the old asset is indicated by a rising price level or other evidence.

Entry #3 reflects the view that the unamortized balance of the old asset plus cash constitutes the cost of the new asset. Such a view may be reasonable when there is no customary market price for either the new or old asset and when there has been no marked change in the price level. It would be inappropriate in a situation like the one set forth in the question. It might be used when the difference is immaterial and it is desirable to keep records for tax and book purposes parallel.

Beyond these three alternatives, the unofficial solution showed still a fourth answer with unknown amounts charged to the new asset and credited to gain on disposal. This was said to be appropriate where there was regularly a discount available on the cash purchase of the new asset and it differed from the total of the cash and market value of the old asset. It accepted the theory that the cost of an asset should be measured by its net cash price.

There are a few exceptional cases in which measured consideration is not the generally accepted starting point of asset valuation. One relates to self-constructed plant assets which turn out to have a cost more than they would have if acquired from outsiders. Such cost overruns should not ordinarily occur, but if they do (as might happen when plant assets are self-built to prevent idleness of facilities), the excess cost should be expensed immediately and only the costs that would have been incurred by normal purchase should be capitalized. Another exception arises in the case of an asset acquired where the consideration is wholly or partly an obligation with an extended maturity date. Suppose, for example, that a machine is bought and the consideration given is a $3,000 note due in two years. Manifestly, it would be incorrect to charge Machinery for the full $3,000. If the going rate of interest is 6%, a more correct handling would be to record the purchase as follows:

Machinery	2,670	
Deferred interest	330	
Note payable		3,000

This entry reflects applying a discount rate of 6% to the obligation and a slight bit of rounding. No doubt, had the purchase been for cash, the measured consideration would have been approximately $2,670 if the vendor was aware of the going rate of interest, as must be presumed.

revenue recognition

Statement No. 4 of the Accounting Principles Board, entitled *Basic Concepts and Accounting Principles Underlying Financial Statements of Business Enterprises,* commences its discussion of revenue and realization as follows:

> *Revenue and Realization.* Revenue is a gross increase in assets or a gross decrease in liabilities recognized and measured in conformity with generally accepted accounting principles that results from those types of profit-directed activities of an enterprise that can change owners' equity. Revenue under present generally accepted accounting principles is derived from three general activities: (a) selling products; (b) rendering services and permitting others to use enterprise resources, which result in interest, rent, royalties, fees and the like; and (c) disposing of resources other than products—for example, plant and equipment or investments in other entities. Revenue does not include receipt of assets purchased, proceeds of borrowing, investments by owners, or adjustments of revenue of prior periods.
>
> Most types of revenue are the joint result of many profit-directed activities of an enterprise and revenue is often described as being "earned" gradually and continuously by the whole of enterprise activities. *Earning* in this sense is a technical term that refers to the activities that give rise to the revenue—purchasing, manufacturing, selling, rendering service, delivering goods, allowing other entities

> to use enterprise assets, the occurrence of an event specified in a contract, and so forth. All of the profit-directed activities of an enterprise that comprise the process by which revenue is earned may be called the *earning process.*
>
> Revenue is conventionally recognized at a specific point in the earning process of a business enterprise, usually when assets are sold or services are rendered. This conventional recognition is the basis of the pervasive measurement principle known as realization.
>
> *Realization.* Revenue is generally recognized when both of the following conditions are met: (1) the earning process is complete or virtually complete, and (2) an exchange has taken place.

Although many accountants recognize that revenue may be earned in an economic sense by production, it is ordinarily held that revenue is not realized until a sale has occurred or until there has been a billing for services. There are two principal objections to recognizing revenue prior to sale: (a) lack of objective evidence about the amount that should be recognized and (b) no conversion of the asset (inventory) into a different type of asset has occurred. When a sale has been made there is evidence about the amount of revenue that has been realized, and inventory has been exchanged for a more liquid asset such as cash or a receivable. It is true that some provision for uncollectible accounts will have to be made for a block of receivables; but at the time each sale is made, the vendor believes that a collectible receivable is being created (otherwise no sale would take place).

At the same time, there are some objections to the sale basis. The sale is but one of the many steps in a sequence of business operations. The entire sequence must be carried on efficiently for the business to make a profit and to survive as a continuing entity. It can be argued that efficiency in hiring, in purchasing, or in production contribute as much to the earning of a profit as does selling. Thus adherence to the sale criterion results in a lag in profit recognition, and undoubtedly in some instances the actual making of sales is so routine that it consists more of taking orders and of making deliveries than of real selling.

Partly as a consequence of these realities and partly because of practicality or expediency, there have been some widespread (hence "generally accepted") departures from the sales basis of revenue recognition. Examples include the pricing of inventories at market in the case of certain agricultural and mineral products and precious metals, and the use of percentage of completion as a basis of revenue recognition by some contractors engaged in long-term projects. The justification in the case of certain agricultural and mineral products seems to rest on a combination of circumstances; namely, that often these products are in the nature of commodities for which well-established markets exist, and hence salability and determination of selling prices are certain and easy. Furthermore, it is often well-nigh impossible to determine the costs of inventories of such products because dozens, sometimes hundreds, of finished articles may be processed from a single raw material such as an animal or a barrel of crude oil. It is simply not worth the effort to undertake the detailed accounting that would be necessary to arrive at individual product costs if it could be done; indeed, the number of arbitrary apportionments in the process of doing so would render the end results somewhat suspect. In the case of long-term construction contracts, use of the percentage-of-completion basis is justified when estimates of cost to complete and extent of progress toward completion are reasonably dependable. Certainly partial or piecemeal recognition of some of the prospective profit in each period as progress is attained under these conditions is preferable to recognition of the entire profit in the terminal period when very little of the actual construction work may have been accomplished.

A somewhat opposite type of revenue recognition is to be found in the case of the installment sales basis. Here, when an installment sale is made, no profit is recognized unless a down payment is received. As the installment receivables are collected, a part of each collection is viewed as return of cost, whereas the other part is considered a realization of gross profit. The installment sales method is a modification of the cash basis, and its use is now regarded as justifiable only when collection of the sale price is not reasonably assured.

An even more conservative method of revenue recognition (and one that is seldom justifiably used) is the "sunk cost" basis. Under this method, all initial receipts are regarded as a recovery of investment in a project; only after the initial outlay has been fully recovered are subsequent receipts treated as revenue. Such a basis is appropriate in highly speculative ventures featuring an unusual degree of risk (e.g., purchase of a bond on which the interest payments are in default). Such a security will ordinarily sell at a very substantial discount. When or if the buyer of such a bond receives anything from it, he should credit the investment account for the entire receipts. Only if the receipts should exceed his investment will revenue be recognized.

objectivity of accounting data

Historically, the accounting data reported in statements addressed to external users (as distinguished from insiders such as management) have been as objectively determined as possible. That is to say, these data have tended to emphasize completed transactions and to minimize projections, estimates, and what might happen. Obviously, it is not possible to prepare realistic statements that are devoid of estimates and future predictions; such matters as valuation of receivables and depreciable assets, for example, necessarily involve estimates and future assumptions. Statements that did not take these factors into account could not possibly be as useful or as accurate as those that do so. At the same time, the temptation to inject a host of estimated data which proponents contend and firmly believe would improve financial statements has been consistently resisted by those elements of the profession responsible for determination of generally accepted accounting principles.[21]

Closely related to the concept of objectivity are "verifiability" and "freedom from bias," but both differ. The American Accounting Association's Committee to Prepare a Statement of Basic Accounting Theory considered both ideas and determined that they were each fundamental standards of accounting information. The committee said that verifiability, "is that attribute of information which allows qualified individuals working independently of one another to develop essentially similar measures or conclusions from an examination of the same evidence, data, or records." [22] At the same time, the committee noted, identical results are not required. Verifiability is a necessary attribute of accounting information which makes it possible for persons who have neither access to the underlying records nor competence to audit them to rely on financial statements, nevertheless. It also underlies the presentation of an independent auditor's opinion. It is important because users of accounting information sometimes have opposing interests. Freedom from bias means that facts have been determined and reported impartially. It also means that techniques used in developing data should be devoid of bias. Biased information may be useful internally, but it is generally to be avoided for external reporting.[23]

Objectivity is not guaranteed by verifiability. As was noted in *A Statement of Basic Accounting Theory:*

[21] A good example has been the recurrent efforts by various groups to substitute appraised values for historical costs of depreciable and other assets throughout the inflationary period experienced in the United States over the past three decades. Clearly, in many cases, adherence to historical costs as a basis of reporting older properties by some companies has resulted in both undervaluation of their balance sheets and understatement of their depreciation. However, the alternative of substituting appraised values would have meant the almost complete loss of objectivity and of comparability of financial statements—not only between companies whose appraisals would doubtless have differed, but also between successive statements of the same company to some degree.

[22] *A Statement of Basic Accounting Theory* (Evanston, Ill.: American Accounting Association, 1966), p. 10.

[23] As an example, merchandise may be billed to a branch at some value above cost or at selling price as a matter of internal control or as a means of keeping the manager of the branch uninformed as to the amount of profit his branch contributes. Such internal markups must be eliminated to the extent not realized when external statements are prepared.

> It is possible for accounting information to possess high degrees of relevance and verifiability and yet be biased in favor of some parties and detrimental to others. This bias may result from use of inappropriate techniques or it may be of a personal nature. The use of plant-wide overhead rates may produce a statistical bias in product cost information. Information prepared by the accountant of a corporation selling its assets to another entity may be biased in the direction of high asset valuation for possible personal gain.[24]

The newest related term germane to this discussion of *objectivity* has been injected by the Accounting Principles Board. In October 1970, the Board published Statement No. 4, *Basic Concepts and Accounting Principles Underlying Financial Statements of Business Enterprises,* and the term *neutrality* was introduced. The Statement said "Neutral financial information is directed toward common needs of users and is independent of presumptions about particular needs and desires of specific users of the information." [25] The discussion went on to point out that measurements not based on presumptions about the particular needs of specific users enhance the relevance of the information to common needs of all users. Preparers of financial accounting information were admonished not to try to increase the helpfulness of the information to a few users to the detriment of others who might have opposing interests.

materiality

Materiality is an important concept in accounting because it is synonymous with *significance.* There are few official definitions in accounting and there is no definition of materiality that could be called official. Possibly because of the difficulties involved, it appears that there have been few attempts by persons or groups to define materiality. Perhaps one of the most successful efforts was that of Grady, who suggested:

> A statement, fact, or item is material if giving full consideration to the surrounding circumstances, as they exist at the time, it is of such a nature that its disclosure, or the method of treating it, would be likely to influence or to "make a difference" in the judgment and conduct of a reasonable person. The same tests apply to such words as significant, consequential, or important.[26]

Some indication of the importance of materiality can be gleaned from the fact that the research of Donald Rappaport concentrating on

[24] *A Statement of Basic Accounting Theory,* p. 11.

[25] *Basic Concepts and Accounting Principles Underlying Financial Statements of Business Enterprises* (New York: American Institute of CPAs, 1970), p. 37.

[26] Paul Grady, *Inventory of Generally Accepted Accounting Principles for Business Enterprises* (New York: American Institute of CPAs, 1965), p. 40. Grady acknowledged that he was heavily indebted to James L. Dohr, who had somewhat similarly defined materiality in a 1950 *Journal of Accountancy* article.

three fundamental documents regulating the actions of independent auditors in respect to third party financial statements found more than 100 references to items: material and significant, immaterial, of little or no consequence, so inconsequential as to be immaterial, not so significant, substantial, materially distorting, and so on.[27]

Somewhat surprisingly, *materiality* is dealt with in two short, somewhat similar sentences in *Basic Concepts and Accounting Principles Underlying Financial Statements of Business Enterprises* (APB Statement No. 4); the thrust of the longest is to this effect: financial reporting is concerned only with information that is significant enough to affect evaluations or decisions. Although that is certainly true, there is an aspect to immateriality that warrants brief discussion. Immaterial items (because they are not big enough to be significant or make a difference) are not necessarily handled in accordance with strict theory. For example, a waste basket costing $6 may last four years; theoretically the cost should be allocated over the four years through depreciation. Since the asset obviously is immaterial when related to overall operations, it would be expensed when acquired. Observe, however, the following quotation from Accounting Principles Board Opinion No. 9 relating to the disposition of an aggregate of *material* extraordinary items in the income statement.

> The segregation in the income statement of the effects of events and transactions which have occurred during the current period, which are of an extraordinary nature and whose effects are *material* requires the exercise of judgment. (In determining *materiality,* items of a similar nature should be considered *in the aggregate*. Dissimilar nature should be considered individually; however, if they are few in number, they should be considered in the aggregate.)[28] [Italics supplied.]

There have been a few attempts to establish by mathematical means criteria or guidelines for materiality. These would necessarily have to be

[27] Donald Rappaport, "Materiality," *The Journal of Accountancy,* CXVII (April, 1964), 42–48. His research covered the AICPA's Accounting Research Bulletins and Statement on Auditing Procedure No. 33 and the SEC's Regulation S-X.

[28] *APB Opinion* No. 9, p. 114. To put this quotation in context for readers who may not be familiar with the concept of income reporting advocated in Opinion No. 9, it should be noted that a two-part income statement would be used by those companies which had *material* extraordinary items affecting net income. Such items would be reported in a lower segment beneath an intermediate income figure captioned "income before extraordinary items." The final figure after reflecting extraordinary items would be captioned "net income" (or net loss). Typical of the things to be reported in extraordinary items would be material gains or losses from sale of plant assets or of investments not acquired for resale, net of income tax effects. If such items were immaterial, unless there were an aggregate of them which amounted to a material sum, they would be reported along with normal operating items and there would be no separate section for extraordinary items.

based on averages of what qualified persons had judged to be material or not material in cases postulated to them. Thus far no accepted percentage or quantitative guidelines have been forthcoming. Most persons would tend to relate items in question to such amounts as net income for the period, total revenue for the period, or to total assets or assets of a given category.

conservatism

Conservatism, as generally applied in accounting, holds that where alternatives for an accounting determination are available, each having some reasonable support or consequences, the choice should favor the procedure having the least favorable immediate impact on owners' equity. There is a line to be drawn between sensible conservatism (which is regarded as "generally accepted") and extreme conservatism (which is unacceptable). Conservatism has a not-too-savory reputation among some accounting theorists because, as it has sometimes been practiced, it was overdone and, furthermore, because it can lead to somewhat capricious results. It is certainly a one-way street—a "heads we lose, tails we don't win" affair, hence, not very defensible on logical grounds. At the same time, experienced accountants in general, and independent CPAs in particular, have seen overoptimistic managers prepare statements and forecasts which later were simply unsupported by performance and facts, and part of their protective armor is conservatism.

Accountants' thinking on conservatism has been influenced by the shifting emphasis which accountants and others have placed on the balance sheet and the income statement. Years ago when the primary emphasis was on the balance sheet, accountants sometimes felt justified in following procedures that tended to reduce the total of assets and the corresponding capital balance soon after various assets were acquired. As the income statement grew in importance it became apparent that conservatism with respect to balance sheet accounts often resulted in a lack of conservatism in later periods' income statements. If a building is fully depreciated but is still in use, the only possible interpretation must be that depreciation expense was overstated during its early years of use and understated during the later years. Of course, the asset value and capital were understated throughout the time the asset was used. In recognition of these misleading results, accountants have now turned to what is generally referred to as sensible or reasonable conservatism. Thus we find phraseology such as the following in unofficial answers to CPA Examination questions. "The acceptable limit of conservatism permits only the choice of the lower of *reasonable* estimates in cases of uncertainty. It does not justify the use of amounts which are below a *reasonable* estimate of value for inventory. . . . The term 'conservative' means that of two alternatives, each having some *reasonable* support, one should choose the least favorable alternative from the standpoint of net equity." [29]

Just as consideration of materiality excuses some departures from strict theory (e.g., expensing some long-lived assets), so also does consideration of conservatism cause some departures from strict theory. It has already been indicated that the starting point of asset valuation is cost or measured consideration. Departures from a strictly cost basis are to be found in the case of inventories valued at the lower of cost or market, marketable securities similarly valued, or any assets written down pursuant to a quasi-reorganization. The latter can be construed as an interruption of the continuity or going-concern assumption.[30]

industry peculiarities

"Generally accepted accounting principles" are intended to apply to all profit-making entities. At the same time, the range of economic activities carried on by corporations and other entities organized for profit is so broad that it is unrealistic to expect a single set of principles to cover all industries and situations with no exceptions.

Differences arise in the application of generally accepted accounting principles as between regulated and nonregulated businesses because of the effects of the rate-making processes on the former. These differences often concern the time at which various items enter into the determination of net income in the matching process. For example, if a cost incurred by a public utility during a given period is treated for rate-making purposes by its regulatory commission as applicable to future revenues, it may be deferred in the balance sheet at the end of the current period and written off in the future period or periods in which the related revenue accrues, even though similar costs are being expensed currently by nonregulated businesses. However, this treatment is appropriate only when it is evident that the cost will be recoverable out of future revenues.

Accounting requirements not directly related to the rate-making

[29] From the answers to Theory questions on the May, 1954, and May, 1955, examinations; italics supplied.

[30] The admonition of the Committee on Accounting Procedure regarding the application of conservatism in the case of a quasi-reorganization is interesting. "A write-down of assets below amounts which are likely to be realized thereafter, though it may result in conservatism in the balance sheet at the readjustment date, may also result in overstatement of earnings or of earned surplus when the assets are subsequently realized. Therefore, in general, assets should be carried forward as of the date of readjustment at fair and not unduly conservative amounts, determined with due regard to the accounting to be employed by the company thereafter."

process are frequently imposed on regulated businesses by their regulatory authorities and other bodies having legal jurisdiction. Although such requirements are legally required, they may not conform with generally accepted accounting principles. When reporting on financial statements of a regulated business, the independent auditor should (as usual) state whether the financial statements are presented in accordance with generally accepted principles of accounting. Material variances from these principles in recognition of rate-making considerations may require a qualified or adverse opinion. *Statement on Auditing Procedures No. 33* is quite explicit on this point:

> The basic postulates and broad principles of accounting comprehended in the term "generally accepted accounting principles" which pertain to business enterprises in general also apply to companies whose accounting practices are prescribed by governmental regulatory authorities or commissions. (Such companies include public utilities, common carriers, insurance companies, financial institutions, and the like.) Accordingly, the first reporting standard is equally applicable to opinions on financial statements of such regulated companies presented for purposes other than filings with their respective supervisory agencies, and material variances from generally accepted accounting principles, and their effects, should be dealt with in the independent auditor's report in the same manner followed for companies which are not regulated. Ordinarily, this will require either a qualified or adverse opinion on such statements.[31]

The range of accepted practices within the framework of generally accepted accounting principles is quite broad. This has been a matter of some concern for some segments of the accounting profession for nearly half a century. This is not the place to argue that the existing amount of diversity is good or that there should be less diversity or even a single set of procedures. What makes mention of this topic appropriate here is the fact that in some industries the range of accepted accounting practices is especially broad, whereas there is a tendency for large segments of certain other industries to opt for a single procedure from among several acceptable alternatives.

Perhaps the extractive industries furnish the leading example of an industry group which, because of its complexity and the intricacies of its contracts and tax provisions, has developed an extremely broad set of widely used accounting procedures and principles. They alone hold the distinction of having caused publication of an AICPA Accounting Research Study.[32] No other single industry has, to date, done this. On the basis of the findings of the study, it is essentially accurate to say that

[31] *Statement on Auditing Procedure* No. 33, p. 70.

[32] Robert E. Field, Accounting Research Study No. 11, *Financial Reporting in the Extractive Industries* (New York: AICPA, 1969).

financial statements of larger oil companies and many other supposedly similar extractive companies are likely not to be comparable in many important particulars; yet all seemingly comply with generally accepted accounting principles. At the same time, the study's author developed a set of recommendations which, if adopted, would put all extractive industries on a more nearly uniform and comparable footing.

Large numbers of units in some industries or leading companies in the industry tend to adopt similar procedures from among a variety of acceptable choices. From the standpoint of enhancing statement comparability, this is a good practice, and one that is to be encouraged. The widespread adoption of LIFO retail among department stores, the trend to select October as the fiscal year end by meat packers, and the use of parallel policies for expensing of research and development costs by chemical companies afford examples of the similarities.

Permeative Principles—Reporting

relevance—user orientation

In both of the latest American Accounting Association's and the American Institute of CPAs' publications dealing with accounting theory or principles in broad terms, *relevance* has been accorded a great deal of attention. In the AAA study, *A Statement of Basic Accounting Theory,* of four basic standards for accounting information, relevance was named the primary standard. In Statement No. 4, the Accounting Principles Board said that financial accounting has seven qualitative objectives and that the primary one is relevance.

Relevance is a user-oriented concept. It is also related to materiality. Relevance implies that all information should be reported that would aid statement users in making decisions. Since immaterial information would not influence the decision of an informed user, immaterial information *per se* is irrelevant information. The distinction between relevance and materiality is not easily drawn. Obviously data can possess both properties or, as just noted, lack them. But the more crucial question is, can data possess one property and not the other? The answer would seem to be a qualified *yes* in that information that cannot be expressed in quantitative terms is very difficult to evaluate with respect to materiality; but it is more frequently possible to say with certainty that it has relevance than that it is material. Edicts such as banning cigarette ads, prohibiting use of certain chemicals in products after a set deadline, for example, or conditions such as a new unfriendly government taking power, discovery of laxity in internal control with few apparent losses to date, and the like, seem somewhat easier to assess from the standpoint of relevance than of materiality. Since much work remains to be done in the establishment of criteria for relevance and for materiality, and since both are somewhat subjective concepts whose interpretation can vary from one statement reader to the next, in the present state of the art any discussion of either term has to be somewhat general.

Both the AAA's *A Statement of Basic Accounting Theory* and the AICPA's *Statement No. 4* have considered the trade-off of relevance with other standards or objectives of information. On this point the AAA committee said:

> The standard of relevance is primary among the four recommended standards.[33] Although not sufficient as a sole criterion, it represents a necessary characteristic for all accounting information. None of the other standards has this position of primacy. Nevertheless, the committee believes that the process of judging accounting information should involve a combined and simultaneous consideration of all four standards. The required degree of adherence to each standard is conditioned by the degree to which the other standards are met. The relative significance of each standard depends upon the nature of the information and its intended use. Both the minimum conformity required with any one of the standards and rates of substitution (trade-off) among the four standards are conditioned by the circumstances.

In its discussion of the trade-off of relevance with other objectives, the APB said:

> The pursuit of one objective or one set of objectives may conflict with the pursuit of others. It is not always possible, for example, to have financial statements that are highly relevant on the one hand and also timely on the other. Nor is it always possible to have financial accounting information that is both as verifiable and as relevant as desired. Only if all other objectives are not affected will a change in information that increases compliance with one objective be certain to be beneficial. Conflicts between qualitative objectives might be resolved by arranging the objectives in order of relative importance and determining desirable trade-offs, but, except for the primacy of relevance, neither accountants nor users now agree as to

[33] Their other three standards are Verifiability, Freedom from Bias, and Quantifiability. The quotation is from pages 9–10 of *A Statement of Basic Accounting Theory*. In addition, the committee proposed five guidelines for communication of accounting information which were secondary to its four basic standards. The five guidelines were: (1) appropriateness to expected use, (2) disclosure of significant relationships, (3) inclusion of environmental information, (4) uniformity of practice within and among entities, and (5) consistency of practice through time.

their relative importance. Determining the trade-offs that are desirable requires judgment.[34]

adequacy of disclosure

Disclosure involves the whole process of financial reporting. Determination of the adequacy of disclosure involves judgment of the professional accountant on several counts. First, there is the matter of balance between giving too little information and too much. Second, there is often a choice regarding means of disclosure. The two factors complement each other because a choice of the least concise or an unattractive means of presenting information will tend either to surfeit the report reader with information or to drive him away before he has attained his goal of getting the information that is available in the report. Presentation of too much information or of irrelevant data will tend to bury the relevant information and repel the statement reader by making his task of winnowing significant material too difficult. In *The Elusive Art of Accounting,* Ross warned of the dangers of overdisclosure:

> A proliferation of irrelevant detail may serve only to obscure the picture. Moreover, a certain sense of proportion must be maintained. To refine the presentation in certain areas is useless if it must remain rough in more important areas. The added refinement of figures may be worse than useless; it may actually be distracting.[35]

The author of Accounting Research Study No. 1 examined the topic of disclosure and succinctly arrived at a conclusion, stated somewhat negatively, which was one of his five "imperative" postulates. "Postulate C-5 Disclosure. Accounting reports should disclose that which is necessary to make them not misleading."[36] The discussion preceding this conclusion was in more positive terms and included a four-way classification suggested as a means of achieving adequate disclosure. This contemplated disclosure of:

1. Items not in the normal or regular activities of the business.
2. Items reflecting changing expectations (e.g., losses on purchase commitments).

[34] The other six objectives are understandability, verifiability, neutrality, timeliness, comparability, and completeness. The quotation is from page 42 of Statement No. 4 of the Accounting Principles Board, *Basic Concepts and Accounting Principles Underlying Financial Statements of Business Enterprises.*

[35] Howard Ross, *The Elusive Art of Accounting* (New York: The Ronald Press Company, 1966), p. 69.

[36] Maurice Moonitz, Accounting Research Study No. 1, *The Basic Postulates of Accounting* (New York: AICPA, 1961), p. 50.

3. That which a law or contract requires to be disclosed (e.g., sinking fund provisions).
4. New activities or major changes in old ones.[37]

Quite a range of methods of achieving disclosure are available. Some possess the advantage of being concise or of emphasizing the particular matter at issue; others inherently lend themselves to a unique treatment. In many instances more than one alternative from among those mentioned can be selected to achieve the end of adequate disclosure. Methods of disclosure include:

1. Formal financial statements (which can be arranged and classified in a variety of ways).[38]
2. Terminology and detailed descriptions.
3. Parenthetical information.
4. Footnotes to financial statements.
5. Supplementary statements and schedules.
6. Comments in the auditor's report.[39]
7. Charts, graphs, and similar visual materials.
8. Letter of the president or board chairman or other textual material in the annual report.

Detailed discussion of any one of the eight items just enumerated could range from a single paragraph or page to several paragraphs or pages. To keep the overall discussion balanced and to shed some insight on the subject of adequacy of disclosure from the standpoint of the independent auditor, this discussion is concluded with the following quotation from the Statement on Auditing Procedure No. 33, *Auditing Standards and Procedures:*

> The third standard of reporting reads:
>
> Informative disclosures in the financial statements are to be regarded as reasonably adequate unless otherwise stated in the report.
>
> The fairness of presentation of financial statements, apart from the relationship to generally accepted accounting principles, is de-

[37] *Loc. cit.*

[38] Examples include balance sheets prepared in account form versus statement of financial position form and income statements in the single-step versus multiple-step arrangements or with costs and expenses grouped according to function or according to nature or object.

[39] Past practice was for the auditor's report or opinion to cover the balance sheet, income statement, statement of retained earnings, and funds statement (even though the latter did not have to be included prior to the appearance of APB Opinion No. 19 in March, 1971). The Opinion does not cover such supplementary data as tons mined, passenger miles flown, or the like. It does not necessarily cover the type of material that would be presented graphically or in the president's letter.

> pendent upon the adequacy of disclosures involving material matters. These matters relate to the form, arrangement, and content of the financial statements with their appended notes; the terminology used; the amount of detail given, the classification of items in the statements; the bases of amounts set forth, for example, with respect to such assets as inventories and plants; liens on assets; dividend arrearages, restrictions on dividends, contingent liabilities; and the existence of affiliated or controlling interests and the nature and volume of transactions with such interests. This enumeration is not intended to be all-inclusive, but simply indicative of the nature and type of disclosures necessary to make financial statements sufficiently informative.[40]

consistency

Consistency refers to the use of the same accounting procedures and reporting bases by an entity from period to period. It is an important factor in achieving *comparability* of the entity's financial statements over time. It does not relate to uniformity of accounting procedures between two or more entities or in an entire industry. Although comparability of financial statements of different entities is a desirable goal, it is more complex and difficult to attain than is comparability of this year's statements with those of earlier years for a single entity and is only partly related to consistency of practices.

Comparability of this year's financial statements with those of earlier years for a single entity can be affected by three kinds of changes:

1. Accounting principles or practices employed.
2. Conditions that necessitate accounting changes but do not involve changes in the accounting principles employed.
3. Business conditions and actions unrelated to accounting *per se*.

Only the first of these three classes of changes involves the necessity to observe the consistency standard of reporting on the part of the independent auditor. This standard, one of four which he must observe in the formulation of his opinion, reads: "The report shall state whether such principles have been consistently observed in the current period in relation to the preceding period."[41] Changes of the second and third class having a material effect on the financial statements will not ordinarily be commented upon in the auditor's opinion. At the same time, fair presentation or adequate disclosure may require that notes to the financial statements reflect the changes. Examples of each type of change will now be given. If a business changes its method of arriving at cost

[40] Committee on Auditing Procedure, *Auditing Standards and Procedures* (New York: AICPA, 1963), p. 54.

[41] *Ibid.,* p. 16.

of inventory from FIFO to LIFO or its depreciation method from straight-line to an accelerated method, this is a change of accounting principle of the first type and would require disclosure in the auditor's opinion.

In contrast, if a business discovers that it has been depreciating plant assets too rapidly or too slowly as a result of obsolescence or operating experience, or if it finds pension plan expenses changed materially because of a revision in actuarial assumptions based on experience under the plan, the necessary adjustments involve no changes in accounting principles. This exemplifies the second type of change. Some comment in notes to the financial statements or elsewhere in the annual report would be necessary in the interests of adequate disclosure but, because the accounting principles were applied "on a basis consistent with that of the preceding year," no qualification of the auditor's opinion would be required or even appropriate under the consistency standard of reporting.

An example of the third type of change would be the expropriation of a company's overseas assets by an unfriendly foreign government, or purchase or sale of a new plant. Again, such an event would have some effects on subsequent financial statements, but the question of the consistency standard of reporting does not arise.

When an auditor's client changes from the use of one generally accepted accounting principle to another which is also generally accepted, the independent auditor need not indicate whether he approves the change, even though reference to it is required in his opinion. However, if he wishes, he may express his approval of the change by including words in the opinion such as "in which we concur" or "to which we do not object."

Comparability of statements between entities is harder to attain than comparability of statements over a span of time for a single entity (as was noted earlier). A goal of comparability of statements as between entities is only partially attainable or, if attainable, too costly to be worthwhile. Statements of two different entities in the same unregulated industry could be made somewhat comparable if the range of generally accepted accounting principles or practices were narrowod so that, for example, there was but a single depreciation method or a single inventory flow method, and uniform rates of amortization for various kinds of assets were used. Such a lack of freedom or flexibility is probably a higher price than most managements, accountants, and many investors are willing to pay. An impliedly less drastic approach was visualized by the APB in Statement No. 4. It would admittedly be difficult to implement and could yield a greater (but still limited) degree of comparability than now exists.

> Achieving comparability between enterprises depends on accomplishing two difficult tasks: (1) identifying and describing the circumstances that justify or require the use of a particular accounting practice or method, (2) eliminating the use of alternative practices under these circumstances. If these tasks can be accomplished, basic differences under which enterprises operate can be reflected by appropriate, and possibly different, practices.
>
> Pending accomplishment of these tasks, users of financial statements should recognize that financial statements of different enterprises may not be fully comparable; that is, they may to an unknown extent reflect differences unrelated to basic differences in the enterprises and in their transactions. Evaluation of differences is not completely effective in the absence of criteria governing the applicability of various practices and methods.[42]

appropriateness to expected use

Recent accounting literature has placed increased emphasis on the preparation of accounting statements and reports with the user in mind. Perhaps the first major breakthrough along these lines was the appearance in 1966 of the American Accounting Association's *A Statement of Basic Accounting Theory*. Since its primary standard was *relevance* and the first of its five guidelines for communicating accounting information was *appropriateness to expected use,* a heavy user orientation is indicated. The Accounting Principles Board's Statement No. 4 published in 1970 also reflects a large measure of concern with uses and users of financial information. Both documents recognize a distinction between statements or reports prepared for external use and those designed for special purposes or internal use.

Generally accepted accounting principles apply primarily to financial statements prepared for general use (i.e., external users such as investors, financial analysts, and the interested public). That is not to say that these principles may not also be relevant to statements and reports prepared for managers, taxing and regulatory authorities, or other special interests; but it often happens that the latter groups have their own particular needs or requirements which supersede or transcend the more generally applicable principles.

Our knowledge of users' wants or needs for accounting and related information is less complete than it should be. Some research is being done to overcome this deficiency, but it seems safe to say that accountants are largely supplying what they presume to be the needs for information of various users. On this point the AAA's Committee to Prepare a Statement of Basic Accounting Theory said:

[42] *Basic Concepts and Accounting Principles Underlying Financial Statements of Business Enterprises,* p. 40.

> Accounting information is the chief means of reducing the uncertainty under which external users act as well as a primary means of reporting on stewardship. Ideally, more should be known about what does and should affect their decisions. The decision models used are both diverse and complex.
>
> Most decisions based on accounting information involve some kind of prediction. Common examples include forecasts of future earnings, of probable payment of debt, and of likely managerial effectiveness.
>
> It is not necessary to know in detail the needs of all the diverse users of accounting information to prepare relevant reports for them for certain classes of information are relevant to many decisions. As more is learned about external users, however, and as their decision models are refined and become better known, accounting theory and practice will change.[43]

Miscellaneous Specific Topics

The remainder of this chapter is devoted to a consideration of a number of important topics from a theory standpoint. Some have to do with statement classification, others with disclosure, still others with income determination (e.g., rate of amortization or cost accrual). The sequence in which they are presented is, generally speaking, the order in which they would appear on a balance sheet, then on an income statement.

working capital

Working capital is defined as the excess of current assets over current liabilities.

Current assets include cash and other assets or resources reasonably expected to be realized in cash or sold or consumed within one year, or during the *normal operating cycle* of the business, whichever is longer. They are listed on the balance sheet in order of their liquidity. Current assets frequently command more attention than do any others. Solvency and the financial strength to carry out expansion, dividends, and investment policies are largely dependent on the working capital position.

In addition to cash, current assets include the following major categories of items: receivables, inventories, marketable securities, prepaid expenses, and supplies.

The *operating cycle* is the period of time between the acquisition of inventory for sale and the final cash realization from its sale. Briefly stated, the cycle is cash to inventory, to sale, to receivables, to cash. For

[43] *A Statement of Basic Accounting Theory,* p. 19.

most businesses this cycle is considerably shorter than one year. For example, if a business enjoys an inventory turnover of six times per year and sells on 30-day credit terms (so that its accounts receivable turnover should be about twelve times per year), its operating cycle would be approximately three months. There are, however, certain businesses whose operating cycle extends beyond twelve months. Industry examples whose production cycles are extended include sugar plantations, distilleries, logging, and shipbuilding. Similarly, owing to the extended collection period, dealers who sell on installment terms and who carry their receivables often have an operating cycle exceeding one year. The length of the operating cycle is important because it determines whether assets and liabilities should be classed as current or noncurrent.

The AICPA's Committee on Accounting Procedure stated:

> For accounting purposes, the term *current assets* is used to designate cash and other assets or resources commonly identified as those which are reasonably expected to be realized in cash or sold or consumed during the normal operating cycle of the business. Thus the term comprehends in general such resources as (a) cash available for current operations and items which are the equivalent of cash; (b) inventories of merchandise, raw materials, goods in process, finished goods, operating supplies, and ordinary maintenance material and parts; (c) trade accounts, notes, and acceptances receivable; (d) receivables from officers, employees, affiliates, and others, if collectible in the ordinary course of business within a year; (e) installment or deferred accounts and notes receivable if they conform generally to normal trade practices and terms within the business; (f) marketable securities representing the investment of cash available for current operations; and (g) prepaid expenses such as insurance, interest, rents, taxes, unused royalties, current paid advertising service not yet received, and operating supplies. Prepaid expenses are not current assets in the sense that they will be converted into cash but in the sense that, if not paid in advance, they would require the use of current assets during the operating cycle.
>
> This concept of the nature of current assets contemplates the exclusion from that classification of such resources as: (a) cash and claims to cash which are restricted as to withdrawal or use for other than current operations, are designated for expenditure in the acquisition or construction of noncurrent assets, or are segregated for the liquidation of long-term debts; (b) investments in securities (whether marketable or not) or advances which have been made for the purposes of control, affiliation, or other continuing business advantage; (c) receivables arising from unusual transactions (such as the sale of capital assets, or loans or advances to affiliates, officers, or employees) which are not expected to be collected within twelve months; (d) cash surrender value of life insurance policies; (e) land and other natural resources; (f) depreciable assets; and (g) long-term prepayments which are fairly chargeable to the operations of several years, or deferred charges such as unamortized debt discount and

> expense, bonus payments under a long-term lease, costs of rearrangement of factory layout or removal to a new location, and certain types of research and development costs.[44]

Current liabilities were described by the AICPA's Committee on Accounting Procedure as those obligations

> . . . whose liquidation is reasonably expected to require the use of existing resources properly classifiable as current assets, or the creation of other current liabilities. As a balance-sheet category, the classification is intended to include obligations for items which have entered into the operating cycle, such as payables incurred in the acquisition of materials and supplies to be used in the production of goods or in providing services to be offered for sale; collections received in advance of the delivery of goods or performance of services; and debts which arise from operations directly related to the operating cycle, such as accruals for wages, salaries, commissions, rentals, royalties, and income and other taxes. Other liabilities whose regular and ordinary liquidation is expected to occur within a relatively short period of time, usually twelve months, are also intended for inclusion, such as short-term debts arising from the acquisition of capital assets, serial maturities of long-term obligations, amounts required to be expended within one year under sinking fund provisions, and agency obligations arising from the collection or acceptance of cash or other assets for the account of third persons.[45]

Current liabilities should not include long-term bonds or notes whose maturity dates have become imminent where such debts are expected to be refunded, but there should be disclosure that they have been omitted from current liabilities and the reason therefor given. Similarly, debts to be liquidated by use of noncurrent assets should be excluded from current liabilities. Obviously, reclassification after fourteen years of a fifteen-year bond issue and its related sinking fund would seriously distort the current ratio for the fifteenth year and render comparisons with that ratio for several preceding periods somewhat meaningless.

It is a general principle of accounting that the offsetting of assets and liabilities in the balance sheet is improper unless a legal right of setoff exists. The reason for this rule is that a business with a positive current ratio can improve its apparent liquidity by resorting to offsetting. Suppose a business has \$30,000 of current assets including cash of \$12,000 and owes current liabilities of \$15,000. If management states it intends to pay a \$7,500 debt with part of the cash which happens to be in a separate account, what had been a 2:1 current ratio (\$30,000 ÷ \$15,000) becomes 3:1 (\$22,500 ÷ \$7,500) by a mere expression of intent. An exception (aside from the legal right of setoff) occurs when a purchase

[44] *Accounting Research and Terminology Bulletins* (final ed.), pp. 20–21.
[45] *Loc. cit.*

of securities (acceptable for the payment of taxes) is in substance an advance payment of taxes payable in the near future.

Inventories are the least homogeneous of assets to be found under the current assets caption or under any other statement classification. Just about anything tangible that is owned was (or is) part of some entity's inventory at some time; other categories of assets such as receivables, buildings, equipment, and patents tend to be more homogeneous. Despite the lack of homogeneity, certain general guidelines for accounting for inventories have been laid down long ago by the AICPA's Committee on Accounting Procedure and have stood the test of time very well. Their guidelines are as follows:

Statement 1

> The term *inventory* is used herein to designate the aggregate of those items of tangible personal property which (1) are held for sale in the ordinary course of business, (2) are in process of production for such sale, or (3) are to be currently consumed in the production of goods or services to be available for sale.

Statement 2

> A major objective of accounting for inventories is the proper determination of income through the process of matching appropriate costs against revenues.

Statement 3

> The primary basis of accounting for inventories is cost, which has been defined generally as the price paid or consideration given to acquire an asset. As applied to inventories, cost means in principle the sum of the applicable expenditures and charges directly or indirectly incurred in bringing an article to its existing condition and location.

Statement 4

> Cost for inventory purposes may be determined under any one of several assumptions as to the flow of cost factors (such as first-in first-out, average, and last-in first-out); the major objective in selecting a method should be to choose the one which, under the circumstances, most clearly reflects periodic income.

Statement 5

> A departure from the cost basis of pricing the inventory is required when the utility of the goods is no longer as great as its cost. Where there is evidence that the utility of goods in their disposal in the ordinary course of business will be less than cost, whether due to physical deterioration, obsolescence, changes in price levels, or

other causes, the difference should be recognized as a loss of the current period. This is generally accomplished by stating such goods at a lower level commonly designated as *market.*

STATEMENT 6

As used in the phrase *lower of cost or market,* the term *market* means current replacement cost (by purchase or by reproduction, as the case may be) except that:
(1) Market should not exceed the net realizable value (i.e., estimated selling price in the ordinary course of business less reasonably predictable costs of completion and disposal); and
(2) Market should not be less than net realizable value reduced by an allowance for an approximately normal profit margin.

STATEMENT 7

Depending on the character and composition of the inventory, the rule of *cost or market, whichever is lower* may properly be applied either directly to each item or to the total of the inventory (or, in some cases, to the total of the components of each major category). The method should be that which most clearly reflects periodic income.

STATEMENT 8

The basis of stating inventories must be consistently applied and should be disclosed in the financial statements; whenever a significant change is made therein, there should be disclosure of the nature of the change and, if material, the effect on income.

STATEMENT 9

Only in exceptional cases may inventories properly be stated above cost. For example, precious metals having a fixed monetary value with no substantial cost of marketing may be stated at such monetary value; any other exceptions must be justifiable by inability to determine appropriate approximate costs, immediate marketability at quoted market price, and the characteristic of unit interchangeability. Where goods are stated above cost this fact should be fully disclosed.

STATEMENT 10

Accrued net losses on firm purchase commitments for goods for inventory, measured in the same way as are inventory losses, should, if material, be recognized in the accounts and the amounts thereof separately disclosed in the income statement.[46]

[46] *Accounting Research and Terminology Bulletins* (final ed.), pp. 27–34

depreciable assets and depreciation

Depreciable assets are commonly reported under balance-sheet captions such as Property, Plant, and Equipment or Fixed Assets. Such a classification would also include Land, which is not subject to depreciation, and Land Improvements, which frequently are depreciable. The caption should include only those properties which are being used in the operations of the business. Assets being held for future use (e.g., land bought as a future plant site) should be reported as Investments or as Other Assets. Assets once used as plant assets but not retired or held for disposal should similarly be reported under some classification other than Property, Plant, and Equipment, such as Other Assets. The normal carrying basis of assets properly reported under Property, Plant, and Equipment is their original cost less the accumulated depreciation recorded in connection with them; the latter is normally accumulated and reported in a separate account. At one time there was a tendency to reflect appraised values in connection with property subject to depreciation but this had waned somewhat prior to its outright ban in 1965 by the Accounting Principles Board. In that year, in reviewing some of the Accounting Research Bulletins issued by the Committee on Accounting Procedure which had preceded it, the Board stated:

> . . . property, plant and equipment should not be written up by an entity to reflect appraisal, market or current values which are above cost to the entity. This statement is not intended to change accounting practices followed in connection with quasi-reorganizations or reorganizations. . . . Whenever appreciation has been recorded on the books, income should be charged with depreciation computed on the written-up amounts.[47]

The last sentence in the quotation was obviously added to take care of situations in which appraisals had been recorded on the books prior to the effective date of the Board's edict.

Typically, property, plant, and equipment have comprised the largest portion of assets for many types of businesses and will likely continue to do so, even though an increasing number of entities now lease substantial portions of this type of property whereas they formerly had little option but to own it. Because of the significant effects on the balance sheet, income statement, and statement of changes in financial position, the Accounting Principles Board has determined that the following disclosures should be made in the financial statements or in notes thereto:

[47] *Opinion of the Accounting Principles Board No. 6,* p. 42.

a. Depreciation expense for the period.

b. Balances of major classes of depreciable assets by nature or function, at the balance-sheet date.

c. Accumulated depreciation, either by major classes of depreciable assets or in total, at the balance-sheet date, and

d. A general description of the method or methods used in computing depreciation with respect to major classes of depreciable assets.[48]

Depreciation is necessarily one of the most controversial of all expenses. Today there is virtually no argument with the proposition that a profit-oriented entity owning depreciable property should recognize some depreciation expense during each period it holds such property, regardless of whether the property was used. This viewpoint has not always prevailed. Controversy and room for arguments arise because depreciation usually involves a long look into the future with the attendant necessity to predict both the useful lives and the salvage values of properties and because there are several accepted formulas for calculating depreciation and a lack of universal agreement about circumstances under which a particular formula ought to be employed. Another controversial issue related to depreciation involves its function: most accountants believe that depreciation ought to record the expiration of cost of tangible properties over their useful lives; but a vocal minority advocates recording sufficient depreciation to provide for the expected replacement cost of facilities being depreciated. In view of the long lives of many depreciable assets (during which their replacement costs can change materially and during which technological changes can result in their being replaced with radically different properties, often before original properties are worn out), strong arguments are mustered by these persons for use of accelerated depreciation methods and for recording amounts that exceed the investment in the properties being depreciated. Accelerated methods such as "sum of the digits" and "double declining balance" are in wide use under generally accepted accounting principles (GAAP) in the United States; but the use of methods that would record depreciation amounts exceeding cost of the assets being depreciated does not conform to GAAP, and it seems unlikely that it will in the foreseeable future.

There is something less than total agreement on the kind of depreciation method or formula that ought to be selected in any given situation, as noted previously. Various methods have advantages and disadvantages.

The *straight-line method* has the advantage of being easy to calculate. Wear and tear and obsolescence—leading causes of depreciation—

[48] *Opinion of the Accounting Principles Board No. 12,* p. 188.

are factors of time and would be recognized under this method (whereas they would not under a method based on usage). Fixed assets can be likened to prepaid expenses, and the latter are often allocated on a straight-line basis. Disadvantages of the method include the fact that it causes a varying per-unit depreciation charge if usage or production varies. Moreover, it fails to relate service or usage to the expense charge. Income produced from many assets is likely to be highest during early life and cost of operations is likely to be lowest then so the method may not match costs with revenue as closely as would be desirable.

Methods based on *production* or asset usage have certain advantages. A prime cause of depreciation is use, hence a method that relates the expense charge to this factor is sound and logical. Production methods will yield a uniform cost-per-unit charge against units produced, miles driven, or the like. Disadvantages of such methods include the difficulty of estimating soundly the number of units a particular asset can produce (or, if this were possible, what the economic demand for its product might be). Assets do depreciate even when not in use, and the method would not recognize this fact. As changes occur during the life of property, new estimates of total remaining production "stored up" in it would be required.

Accelerated methods such as "sum of the digits" similarly have advantages and disadvantages. Perhaps the principal advantage claimed for them relates to the fact that during the early years of asset life when repair cost and "down time" costs are low, depreciation charges will be correspondingly high; when assets grow old opposite conditions tend to prevail. The result is a relatively uniform cost of owning and using the asset throughout its life, except that costs based on value such as insurance and taxes tend to behave as depreciation under an accelerated method. Assets tend to be more productive when new; hence, it is reasoned, more depreciation occurs in early years. Arguments against the accelerated methods or disadvantages cited concerning them include the contention that depreciation is a means of spreading cost, not of smoothing periodic income. Thus, a subsequent rise in maintenance charges should not be buried or offset by an averaging technique such as accelerated depreciation. Data exist to support the position that fixed assets do require more maintenance in later years, but there are not much data to support the notion that an accelerated formula such as sum of the digits or double declining balance is a measure of the increase in maintenance charges.

intangible assets

In 1970, the Accounting Principles Board restudied intangible assets and issued an Opinion that may have rather far-reaching effects. Prior to the new Opinion, it had been customary to classify intangibles as either type (a)—those having limited lives—or as type (b)—those with unlimited lives. Examples of the former included patents, leaseholds, and franchises, and goodwill where there was evidence of limited duration in connection with the latter. Examples of type (b) intangibles included trademarks, secret processes, perpetual franchises, and goodwill (generally). The new Opinion, in effect, declares that there is no such thing as a type (b) intangible. The cost of each intangible should be amortized over its estimated life which is presumed never to exceed 40 years. The cost should not be written off in the period of the asset's acquisition.

According to the new Opinion, a company should record as assets the costs of intangible assets acquired from other enterprises or individuals. Costs of developing, maintaining, or restoring intangible assets that are not specifically identifiable, have indeterminate lives, or are inherent in a continuing business and related to an enterprise as a whole—such as goodwill—should be deducted from income when incurred.

In determining the period of amortization (which, it is repeated, should not exceed 40 years) the following factors, among others, should be considered:

1. Legal or contractual provisions.
2. Provisions for renewal or extension.
3. Effects of obsolescence, competition, or other economic factors.
4. The useful life may parallel that of certain employees.
5. Expected actions of competitors.

Generally speaking, the Board preferred straight-line amortization in the absence of a showing that some other systematic method would be more appropriate.[49]

deferred credits and miscellaneous liabilities

Most of the important theoretical points related to current liabilities requiring coverage were included in the discussion of working capital. We now consider a number of other liability topics.

Deferred Credits. One troublesome subject, which nearly always arises in discussions of liabilities, concerns deferred credits. As a classification or balance-sheet caption, deferred credits are something of an anomaly. They do not fit the basic accounting equation: Assets − Liabilities = Owners' Equity. At the same time, after the books are closed, there often remain open one or more accounts with credit balances which do not represent debt and which are not part of capital or owners' equity.

[49] *Opinion of the Accounting Principles Board No. 17,* p. 340.

Furthermore, these accounts usually contain balances which, in time, will be transferred through the income account to owners' equity. They are the opposites or credit counterparts of deferred charges. In recently defining liabilities, the Accounting Principles Board stated that certain deferred credits were subsumed under liabilities. Their definition of liabilities reads:

> Liabilities—economic obligations of an enterprise that are recognized and measured in conformity with generally accepted accounting principles. Liabilities also include certain deferred credits that are not obligations [a] but that are recognized and measured in conformity with generally accepted accounting principles.[b] [50]

The footnotes to the APB definition are as follows:

> [a] Deferred credits from income tax allocation are an example of deferred credits that are not obligations. The term *deferred credits* is also sometimes used to refer to certain obligations, for example, subscriptions collected in advance.
>
> [b] This definition differs from that in Accounting Terminology Bulletin No. 1, paragraph 27, in that (1) it defines liabilities primarily in terms of obligations rather than as credit balances carried forward upon closing the books, and (2) it excludes capital stock and other elements of owners' equity.

It is probably true that a preponderance of the balances reported under a separate balance-sheet caption Deferred Credits could, after careful analysis, be reported more accurately as liabilities. There is usually a large element of such balances which will require the expenditure of current assets or the incurrence of other liabilities before the deferred credit can be "earned." A good case in point is subscriptions collected in advance, cited in the footnote to the APB definition of liabilities. Even if it were not true that many subscriptions are sold at breakeven or at a loss in order to boost circulation and thereby raise advertising revenue, it would still be true that to earn the balance reported in such an account would require the use of a substantial inventory of paper, ink, and supplies, the incurrence of substantial printing and editorial costs, and the payment of postage. The amount of profit (if any) left after these costs have been incurred is often quite small; in these circumstances the credit balance is more in the nature of a liability than of deferred or unearned revenue.

Because real and personal property taxes could logically be charged against income on any of several bases the Committee on Accounting Procedure (predecessor to the APB) considered the problem and in the

[50] Statement No. 4 of the Accounting Principles Board, *op. cit.*, p. 50.

interest of achieving greater uniformity and comparability recommended as follows:

> Generally, the most acceptable basis of providing for property taxes is monthly accrual on the taxpayer's books during the fiscal period of the taxing authority for which the taxes are levied. The books will then show, at any closing date, the appropriate accrual or prepayment.[51]

Convertible Debt. During the latter part of the 1960s, issuance of hybrid securities and securities with options and conversion features took place on a scale that had not been seen before. The popularity of convertible debt securities and of debt securities with detachable stock purchase warrants prompted the Accounting Principles Board to issue Opinions No. 9 (1966) and 14 (1969) dealing with how to account for them. The main provisions of these Opinions are as follows. In the case of debt securities which are convertible into common stock of the issuer or an affiliated company at the holder's option,[52] the Board determined that no portion of the proceeds from their original issuance should be accounted for as attributable to the conversion feature. In arriving at its conclusion, the Board stated it placed greater weight on the inseparability of the debt from the conversion feature than on the practical difficulty of assigning some portion of the initial lump-sum consideration to the debt and some part to the conversion feature, especially in view of the anticipatory nature of the conversion. In the case of debt sold with detachable warrants to purchase stock the Board determined that the portion of the proceeds allocable to the warrants should be accounted for as paid-in capital. The allocation should be made on the basis of relative fair values of the two securities at the time of issuance. Any resulting discount or premium on the debt securities should be accounted for as such.

Accounting theorists do not agree on how to record the conversion of debt into stock. There are basically two approaches: (a) to substitute for the book value of the debt an equivalent amount of owners' equity and (b) to consider the market values of the bonds redeemed and the stock issued at the time and to use one of these as the basis of recording the aggregate credits to owners' equity. The latter approach was favored by the American Accounting Association's Committee on Concepts and

[51] *Accounting Research and Terminology Bulletin* (final ed.), p. 83.

[52] Typically, such securities were issued at a lower interest rate than the same issuer could establish for nonconvertible debt; they provided for conversion initially at a price that was greater than market value of common stock at the time the debt was issued (i.e., the conversion feature had value only if the common stock appreciated); and their conversion price did not decrease except pursuant to antidilution provisions. Usually such securities were also callable at the option of the issuer and subordinated to nonconvertible debt.

Standards.[53] Both approaches and the use of alternate market values (i.e., both bond value and stock value) are illustrated in the following part of a question taken from the November, 1969, Theory of Accounts portion of the Uniform CPA Examination and the unofficial answer:

Zakin Co. recently issued $1,000,000 face value, 5%, 30-year subordinated debentures at 97. The debentures are redeemable at 103 upon demand by the issuer at any date upon 30 days' notice ten years after the issue. The debentures are convertible into $10 par value common stock of the Company at the conversion price of $12.50 per share for each $500 or multiple thereof of the principal amount of the debentures.

Required: Assume that no value is assigned to the conversion feature upon issuance of the debentures. Assume further that five years after issue, debentures with a face value of $100,000 and book value of $97,500 are tendered for conversion on an interest payment date when the market price of the debentures is 104 and the common stock is selling at $14 per share and that the Company records the conversion as follows:

Bonds payable	100,000	
Bond discount		2,500
Common stock		80,000
Premium on common stock		17,500

Discuss the propriety of the above accounting treatment.

Solution: The method used by the company to record the exchange of convertible debentures for common stock can be supported on the grounds that, when the company issued the convertible debentures the proceeds could, to a larger extent, represent consideration received for the stock. Therefore, when conversion occurs, the book value of the obligation is simply transferred to the stock exchanged for it.

On the other hand, recording the issue of the common at the book value of the debentures is open to question. It may be argued that the exchange of the stock for the debentures completes the transaction cycle for the debentures and begins a new cycle for the stock. The consideration or value used for this new transaction cycle should then be the amount which would be received if the debentures were sold rather than exchanged or the amount which would be received if the related stock were sold, whichever is more clearly determinable at the time of the exchange. This method recognizes changes in property values which have occurred and subordinates a consideration determined at the time the

[53] AAA, *Accounting and Reporting Standards for Corporate Financial Statements and Supplements,* 1957, p. 7.

debentures were issued. The entries which would be used to record the exchange using the market values of the debentures and the stock for valuation purposes would be:

	Debenture Value		*Stock Value*	
Bonds payable	100,000		100,000	
Bond conversion cost	6,500		14,500	
Bond discount		2,500		2,500
Common stock		80,000		80,000
Premium on common stock ..		24,000		32,000

In this instance the market value of the debentures ($104,000) is the consideration received for the stock issued, and inasmuch as the firm is bound by the bondholders' option to convert, the $8,000 excess of the market value of the stock ($112,000) over the market value of the bonds may be viewed as an opportunity cost of the funds borrowed.

owners' equity

Most of the accounting requirements with respect to owners' equity or capital are legalistic rather than theoretical. There is usually an effort to report capital by source [i.e., paid in (at par or stated value), paid in (exceeding par), earned, from donation or appraisal, etc.]. Unfortunately, these distinctions often tend to get blurred in the later life of a corporation, owing to such commonplace events as stock dividends (which result in the capitalization of earned capital), trading in treasury stock (which can have a similar result), and various kinds of recapitalization transactions.

The Accounting Principles Board and its predessor committees have issued various pronouncements pertaining to reporting capital and accounting for certain types of capital transactions. A few of these rules were adopted by the entire membership of the Institute in the 1930s; and although in the light of modern practice some of the earlier rules seem quite unnecessary and archaic, they remain in effect. Only some of the more modern pronouncements pertaining to capital are cited in this section.

Aside from the Opinions dealing with convertible debt already discussed, the APB has had relatively little to say about owners' equity. It did discuss liquidation preference of preferred shares in 1966.[54] The Board stated that when companies issue preferred or other senior stock

[54] *Opinion No. 10.* The Board also considered capital structure at length and in some detail in conjunction with earnings per share. This subject is discussed later in this chapter.

that has a preference in involuntary liquidation considerably in excess of par, this fact may be of major significance to statement readers. It accordingly recommended that the liquidation preference of the stock be disclosed in the equity section of the balance sheet in the aggregate. In addition, the balance sheet or its notes should disclose the aggregate or per-share amounts at which preferred shares may be called or are subject to redemption through sinking fund operations or otherwise and the aggregate and per-share amounts of arrearages in cumulative preferred dividends.

The Board has also dealt briefly with accounting for treasury stock in two phases. First, when the stock is retired or bought for constructive retirement, it stated an excess of purchase price over par or stated value *may* be allocated between capital surplus and retained earnings. The portion of the excess allocated to capital surplus should be limited to the sum of (a) all capital surplus arising from previous retirements and net "gains" on sales of treasury stock of the same issue and (b) the prorata portion of capital surplus paid in, voluntary tranfers of retained earnings, and capitalization of stock dividends on the same issue. For this purpose, any remaining capital surplus applicable to issues fully retired is considered to be applicable prorata to shares of common stock. Alternatively, the excess *may* be charged entirely to retained earnings, since a corporation can always capitalize or allocate retained earnings for such purposes. In case par or stated value exceeds the purchase price, capital surplus should be credited for the difference.

Second, when stock is not to be retired (or no such final decision has been reached), the cost of acquired stock may be shown separately from the aggregate of capital, or it may be accorded the accounting treatment appropriate for retired stock, or in some instances may be reported as an asset. "Gains" on sales of treasury stock not accounted for as retired should be credited to capital surplus; "losses" *may* be charged to capital surplus to the extent previous net "gains" from sales or retirements of the same class of stock are included there, otherwise the losses should affect retained earnings. Although these practices are cited by the Board as "more in accord with current developments in practice," they are not the only practices the Board regards as acceptable.[55]

Appropriations of Retained Earnings. Retained earnings are often referred to as the cushion that absorbs losses. It is the account which is diminished when actual losses occur; it is also used to reflect the effects of potential losses and to report certain managerial intentions. Reflection of the effects of potential losses and managerial intentions is generally accomplished through the medium of appropriation of portions of retained earnings. In terms of mechanics, appropriation of retained earn-

[55] *APB Opinion No. 6,* p. 40.

ings involves a charge to that account and a credit to some appropriately titled account. The credits are often made to accounts called "Reserve for . . ." (and this terminology is permissible), but use of some term such as "Retained Earnings Appropriated for . . ." is considered preferable.

Decisions to appropriate retained earnings are made by corporate directors. Four common reasons underlying such decisions are:

1. Fulfillment of legal requirements (e.g., a restriction on retained earnings equal to the cost of treasury stock held). The laws of some states require this type of restriction.
2. Fulfillment of a contractual requirement (e.g., a bond issue whose indenture requires a sinking fund and stipulates a restriction on retained earnings as well).
3. To record formally a discretionary action by the directors as a matter of financial planning (e.g., retained earnings appropriated for plant expansion).
4. To record formally a discretionary action by the directors in anticipation of possible future losses (e.g., appropriation of retained earnings for self-insurance reserves, for general undetermined contingencies, or for any other indefinite possible future losses, such as losses on inventories not on hand or contracted for).

the income statement

For many years two different concepts of income statement preparation have been prominent in accounting practice and literature. They are commonly referred to as the *current operating performance* concept and the *all-inclusive* concept.[56] They differed principally in that certain items that would appear on the retained earnings statement (rather than on the income statement) under the current operating performance concept would be reported on the income statement under the all-inclusive concept. For the most part, these items were extraordinary or nonrecurring gains and losses and corrections of the net income of prior periods. It is generally correct to say that the recommendations of AICPA committees have historically favored the use of the current operating performance concept, whereas those of the AAA committees have leaned toward the all-inclusive concept.

With the issuance of Opinion No. 9 in December, 1966, the Accounting Principles Board reversed the AICPA's long-held stand against the all-inclusive concept. The Opinion made an exception in the case of *prior period adjustments* (which were carefully defined); aside from these, all

[56] Synonyms for *current operating performance* include "earning power" and for *all-inclusive* include "clean surplus" and "historical."

items of gain or loss recognized during a period should be reported on the income statement. The Opinion states that *extraordinary items* should be segregated within the income statement unless their effects are immaterial.

Some significant excerpts from the Board's Opinion follow:

> 1. The fundamental viewpoint:
> . . . net income should reflect all items of profit and loss recognized during the period with the sole exception of the prior period adjustments described below. *Extraordinary items* should, however, be segregated from the results of ordinary operations and shown separately in the income statement, with disclosure of the nature and amounts thereof. The criteria for determination of extraordinary items are described . . . below.[57]
>
> 2. Financial statement form:
> Under this approach, the income statement should disclose the following elements:
>
> Income before extraordinary items
> Extraordinary items (less applicable income tax)
> Net income
>
> 3. Extraordinary items related to current period explained:
> Such events and transactions are identified primarily by the nature of the underlying occurrence. They will be of a character significantly different from the typical or customary business activities of the entity. Accordingly, they will be events and transactions of material effect which would not be expected to recur frequently and which would not be considered as recurring factors in any evaluation of the ordinary operating processes of the business.
>
> 4. Criteria for prior period adjustments:
> Adjustments related to prior periods—and thus excluded in the determination of net income for the current period—are limited to those material adjustments which (a) can be specifically identified with and directly related to the business activities of particular prior periods, and (b) are not attributed to economic events occurring subsequent to the date of the financial statements for the prior period, and (c) depend primarily on determinations by persons other than management, and (d) were not susceptible of reasonable estimation prior to such determination. Such adjustments are rare in modern financial accounting.
>
> Examples of items to be reported on the income statement as extraordinary items include material gains or losses from (a) sale or abandonment of a plant or major segment of the business, (b) sale of an investment not acquired for resale, (c) property condemnation or expropriation, (d) major devaluation of a foreign currency, and (e) corrections of the earnings of prior periods. Examples of gains or losses (or provisions therefor) which, regardless of size, constitute

[57] This quotation and those immediately following are rearranged to facilitate presentation, but are taken from *Opinion of the Accounting Principles Board No. 9*.

neither extraordinary items nor prior period adjustments (therefore are operating items in the income statement) include (a) write-downs of receivables, inventories, and research and development costs; (b) adjustments of accrued contract prices; and (c) gains or losses from ordinary foreign exchange fluctuations.

Examples of prior period adjustments (to be reported on the statement of retained earnings), which it is emphasized are rare, include material, nonrecurring adjustments or settlements of income taxes, of renegotiation proceedings, or of public-utility revenue under rate regulation. Settlements of significant amounts resulting from litigation or similar claims may also constitute prior period adjustments. On the other hand, treatment as prior period adjustments should *not* be applied to normal, recurring corrections and adjustments which are the natural result of the use of commonplace accounting estimates. Thus, changes in the estimated remaining lives of fixed assets affect the computed amounts of depreciation, but such changes should be viewed as prospective in nature rather than as prior period adjustments—hence, reported on the income statement as extraordinary items. Similarly, immaterial adjustments of provisions for liabilities (such as for taxes) made in prior periods should be considered recurring items to be reflected in current period operations. Other uncertainties which would *not* qualify for prior period adjustment treatment include those relating to collectibility of receivables, ultimate recovery of deferred costs, or realizability of inventories or other assets. Such items fail to qualify as prior period adjustments because *current* economic events (i.e., subsequent to the period in which they were initially recognized) enter into a determination of their most recent status or values.

reporting earnings per share

No single statistical measure in the realm of financial reporting is accorded as much attention as earnings per share (EPS). The practice of reporting EPS data on outstanding common shares has long been widespread, not only in connection with financial statements, but in many other types of releases prepared for the financial community. However, prior to issuance of APB Opinion No. 9 in 1966, reporting EPS on financial statements was completely optional. In Opinion No. 9 the APB stated:

> . . . earnings per share data are most useful when furnished in conjunction with a statement of income. Accordingly, the Board *strongly recommends* that earnings per share be disclosed in the statement of income. It is the Board's opinion that the reporting of per share data should disclose amounts for (a) income before extraordinary items, (b) extraordinary items, if any, (less applicable income tax) and (c) net income—the total of (a) and (b).[58]

[58] *APB Opinion No. 9,* p. 119 (italics supplied).

APB Opinion No. 15, issued in 1969, has changed the recommendation to a *requirement*. The new Opinion calls for two presentations of earnings per share on the income statement—(a) primary earnings per share and (b) fully diluted earnings per share. These terms are explained later in this section.

APB Opinion No. 15 is a lengthy, complex document. Only its highlights are presented here; it is not feasible to attempt a discussion of all the details covered in its approximately sixty pages of text and exhibits. Furthermore, a little over a year after its publication, Opinion No. 15 was supplemented by an interpretive booklet of well over 100 pages of explanatory material.

The simplest possible calculation of earnings per share in compliance with Opinion No. 15 would involve a company with but a single class of shares authorized, when all had remained outstanding throughout its fiscal year. If such a company had only ordinary income (i.e., no extraordinary items), calculation of its EPS for the year would merely involve dividing the net income by the number of shares.

A modest advance in complexity would have the company experience a gain or loss due to extraordinary items in arriving at its net income. In this event, EPS figures would be reported for "income before extraordinary items" and for "net income" (or net loss). A further advance in complexity would involve a company with but a single class of authorized securities which experienced an increase in the number of outstanding shares during the period. Here it would be necessary to ascertain the reason for the increase. If the shares increased because of a stock dividend or split, the year-end number of shares would be used in calculating EPS figures as though that number of shares had been outstanding for the entire year. On the other hand, if the increase were due to a sale of additional shares, a weighted average of shares outstanding would be the proper basis of determining EPS figures for the year.

Another step upward in complexity would be for a corporation to have nonconvertible senior securities outstanding. Senior securities are those for which interest or dividend requirements take precedence over common stock dividends. Generally speaking, senior securities include bonds and preferred stocks, especially cumulative preferred shares; interest or dividends on such securities ordinarily take precedence over common stock dividends. Claims of senior securities against earnings of a period should be deducted from net income (and from income before extraordinary items) before computing EPS. Dividends for cumulative preferred stock should be deducted regardless of whether they were earned. In the event of a net loss, the amount of the loss should be increased by the amount of the preferred dividend requirements for the period to arrive at loss-per-share figures on the common stock.

Companies which have complex capital structures, including convertible debt and other convertible securities, options, or warrants that upon exercise or conversion will dilute EPS, must present two per-share amounts on the face of the income statement. The first is "primary earnings per share," and the second, "fully diluted earnings per share." Furthermore, in case there is more than one income figure (as would be the case when extraordinary items are reported), both primary and fully diluted per-share figures must be presented for income before extraordinary items as well as for net income.

Some securities are to be regarded as common stock equivalents. As defined by the APB, a common stock equivalent is a security that is not a common stock in form, although it usually contains provisions to enable its holder to become a common stockholder and, because of its terms and the circumstances under which it was issued, is in substance equivalent to a common stock. The holders of these securities can expect to participate in the appreciation of the value of the common stock resulting principally from the earnings and earnings potential of the issuing corporation.[59]

Primary earnings per share should be based on the number of common shares outstanding plus common stock equivalents. A convertible security is a common stock equivalent if at the time of its issuance, its cash yield, based on its market price, is less than two-thirds of the then-current bank prime rate of interest. This determination is made when convertible securities are issued and is not altered by later events. Stock options and warrants are always regarded as common stock equivalents, but the Board's rules for determination of their dilutive effects, if any, are much too complex and lengthy for consideration here.

Fully diluted EPS are computed on the assumption that all convertible securities, options, or warrants, if dilutive, have been converted or exercised. Since the purpose is to show maximum potential dilution of current EPS on a prospective basis, the computation should exclude those securities whose conversion or issuance would have the effect of increasing earnings per share or of decreasing loss per share. However, in case any EPS amount calculated in accordance with provisions of the Opinion is diluted by less than 3%, such diluted amount need not be presented. In applying this provision, only security issues that individually reduce EPS should be considered. The 3% test is then applied in the aggregate.

A final word should be inserted in respect to presentation of "fully diluted EPS" data. In calculating the effects of potential dilution through the exercise of various conversion options, it sometimes happens that the

[59] *APB Opinion No. 15,* p. 225.

EPS figures for common shareholders derived after giving effect to the potential dilution would be more favorable (i.e., higher EPS per share) than on the actual primary basis as things really stand as of the date of the financial statements. When this is the case, no "fully diluted EPS" figures should be presented; in other words, fully diluted EPS data should be reported only when they are less favorable than the primary EPS figures.

accounting for pension costs

Before one can understand the fundamentals of accounting for pension costs, it is necessary to know something about the typical pension plan and to know the meaning of certain terms common in pension plan accounting. Most companies which have adopted pension plans have done so after the firm has existed for a number of years; at the same time, they usually provide that many of their employees who have been on their payroll for some time prior to adoption of a plan are entitled to receive benefits if they continue to work as though the plan had been in effect from the time these persons first became employees of the company. This means that from the outset the company is somewhat behind in the accrual of its pension costs. This initial cost not previously provided for is known as *past service cost.* In the rare case of a newly formed company which adopts a pension plan from the outset and accounts for its annual pension cost expense (regardless of whether funded by cash payments) annually in accordance with an accepted actuarial cost method, its *normal cost* is being met as time passes. The APB has determined that pension costs are to be recognized on an *accrual basis,* which is to say that, by and large, except for the interest effects of having prepaid or having fallen behind in one's pension payments, the funding of pension costs has little to do with annual pension plan expenses.

The APB has ruled that recognition of past service cost should affect income of the years subsequent to the adoption of a pension plan and that a lump-sum charge to retained earnings for a previously unrecognized expense is improper. Only a qualified actuary can determine the amount of unfunded past service cost a company is assuming in adopting a given pension plan with its particular set of employees. By making certain assumptions about earnings accumulations, the actuary or an investment advisor can determine what period of time would be required to fund the past service costs, provided they do not change materially and provided the assumptions with respect to employee earnings, turnover, retirements, and so on, are borne out. If at some stage it becomes necessary to revalue the plan because past actuarial assumptions have proved incorrect or because the original plan has been modified, the additional pension cost assigned under the actuarial cost method in use to years prior to the date of the valuation is known as *prior service cost.* Both *prior service cost* and *past service cost* are spread prospectively over future periods rather than being treated as retroactive corrections of prior periods.

Management of the business can make a determination of the period over which it wants to amortize the accumulated past service (and prior service) cost(s) as an expense and the period over which it feels it can fund the past service cost. The two time periods may coincide; for example, it may be decided to amortize the past service cost and to fund it over a ten-year term. On the other hand, ten years may be chosen as the amortization period and fifteen years as the funding period. If this happens, pension costs will be increased in the long run because of a lag in the accumulation of compound interest on pension fund assets, and the balance sheet through the fifteenth year will reflect a liability that might be called "provision for pension cost in excess of payments." Conversely, if amortization is effected over ten years and funding takes place in a shorter time, there will be a corresponding reduction in the net cost of the pension plan, and the balance sheet will reflect a deferred charge through the tenth year.

The Accounting Principles Board has set forth the following criteria for the basic calculation of pension costs:

> 1. The entire cost of benefit payments ultimately to be made should be charged against income subsequent to adoption (or amendment) of a plan; no portion of such cost should be levied against retained earnings directly.
> 2. The annual provision for pension cost should be based on an accounting method using an acceptable actuarial cost method resulting in a provision between the minimum and maximum prescribed below.
> 3. Both the accounting and actuarial cost methods should be applied consistently from year to year.
>
> The *maximum* annual provision for pension cost should not exceed the total of (1) *normal cost,* (2) 10% of *past service cost* until fully amortized, (3) 10% of the amounts of any increases or decreases in *prior service cost* arising from amendments of the plan until fully amortized, and (4) interest equivalents of the difference between provisions and amounts funded. The *minimum* annual provision should be not less than the total of (1) normal cost, (2) an amount equal to interest on any unfunded prior service cost, and (3) a provision for vested benefits.[60]

The Board believes pension plans are of sufficient importance that the following disclosures should be made in financial statements or their notes:

[60] *APB Opinion No. 8,* pp. 73–74.

1. A statement that such plans exist, identifying or describing the employee groups covered.
2. A statement of the company's accounting and funding policies.
3. The provision for pension cost for the period.
4. The excess, if any, of the actuarially computed value of vested benefits over the total of the pension fund and any balance-sheet pension accruals less any pension prepayments or deferred charges.
5. Nature and effect of significant matters affecting comparability for all periods presented, such as changes in accounting methods, changes in circumstances, or adoption or amendment of a plan.[61]

leasing activities [62]

Although the relation of lessor to lessee in the case of a long-term lease can, in many respects, be likened to that of bond investor to bond issuer, their respective accounting treatment of that lease is by no means reciprocal, as in the lending relationship. For this reason, discussion of accounting for leases in financial statements of lessors is undertaken separately from that for lessees.

Accounting for Leases in Financial Statements of Lessors. Lessors may engage in leasing activities for a variety of reasons including the investment of funds, facilitating sale or use of the lessor's own manufactured product, retaining control of locations when it is desirable that the property be operated by others, and making available to others property operated by the lessor for profit. Some lessors use leasing principally as a means of investing funds. Other lessors engage in the practice as incidental to entirely different and relatively more significant business operations. There are two main methods in general use for allocating lease rental revenue and expenses over the accounting periods covered by a lease; they are known as the *financing* and *operating* or *rental* methods.

Since all leases cover some period of time and since many of them extend over several years, it is apparent that most accounting problems of lessors relate to *matching* of leasehold cost with revenue. Allocation of lease revenue to the proper accounting periods and the related allocation of acquisition and operating costs of leased property and of the costs of negotiating the lease need to be governed by the consistent application of accounting principles that are both systematic and rational.

The *financing* method is applicable only to long-term leases and can be likened to the purchase of an annuity for a lump sum. The cost of

[61] *Ibid.,* p. 84.

[62] Some of the material in this section is adapted from Welsch, Zlatkovich, and White, *Intermediate Accounting* (rev. ed.), (Homewood, Ill.: Richard D. Irwin, Inc., 1968), pp. 852–54 and 858–63.

the property (net of its value, if any, upon expiration of the lease) represents the lessor's outlay, and the periodic lease rentals represent his return. The rents are comprised of two elements: (a) return of capital and (b) return on investment (interest). In the earlier years, rents consist of relatively large amounts of income (interest) and relatively small recovery of capital. Later, the proportions of the equal rents represent smaller amounts of income (since the investment has been largely recovered) and proportionately greater amounts of capital recovery.

The *operating* method may be applied to either long-term or short-term leases. Under it, rentals are reported as revenue as they are collected or accrued except when the schedule of receipts departs radically from a straight-line pattern without relation to the usefulness of the leased property. Expense allocation under the operating method is straightforward and based on usual common-sense principles applicable to expense allocation generally; more is said about this topic later.

In choosing between the two methods, consideration should be given to the general nature of the lessor's business activities and the objectives of engaging in leasing. If the lessor primarily lends money at interest—as would be the case with banks, insurance companies, pension trusts, and the like—the financing method is ordinarily more appropriate. Lease contracts made by such entities often pass along to lessees the usual risks and rewards of property ownership; lessees also commonly assume responsibility for meeting many recurring expenses incident to property ownership and use, including taxes, insurance, utility costs, and maintenance. To be sure, there are still some risks, but they are more akin to those associated with secured loans. The principal expense borne by lessors of the financial institution type is the equivalent of depreciation since, except for land, property is either not returned at all or is worn out at the end of the lease term. Even where the lessor is not essentially a financial institution, the financing method may be appropriate, provided the lease contracts have the characteristics described previously. On the other hand, where lessors retain the ordinary risks and rewards of property ownership—as would be the case with a corporation engaged principally in renting space in apartment or office buildings or in renting automobiles—the operating method is more appropriate. Rents commonly cover not only depreciation but also insurance, taxes, utilities, maintenance, and repairs of the properties and provide an adequate profit for assuming the risks involved. Here, also, the owner-operator is essentially a property manager. Rarely is the property made available to the lessee for purchase, and most of the services such as janitorial, elevator, fuel, and utilities are furnished by the lessor.

Ordinarily it is expected that the initial costs of negotiating and closing leases will be recovered from revenues; hence such costs should be deferred and allocated to future periods in which the related periodic revenues are reported. The method of allocation should be consistent with that used to recognize revenue under the financing or operating methods. When initial direct costs of lessors are reasonably constant in relation to revenues, consistent expensing of these costs will have about the same income statement effect as deferring and then amortizing them. Of course, from a balance sheet standpoint, the expensing treatment will result in lower asset and capital totals.

Where leasing activities are significant in relation to other operations, amounts related to leasing should be reported separately in the balance sheet and in the manner that best describes the nature of the resources. Under the financing method, the aggregate unpaid rentals called for in the lease should be classified with or near receivables; a description such as "due from lessees" or "contracts receivable for equipment rentals" would be appropriate. Unearned revenue (which is closely equivalent to finance charges or interest) should be shown as deductions from the receivables. The estimated residual value of property expected to be returned upon expiration of leases should be shown separately under tangible fixed assets unless the property is expected to be sold to the lessee, in which case it should be classed with or near receivables and appropriately described. This means that the principal assets to be reported are net receivables and residual values of leased properties. Classification of the receivables as current or noncurrent is determined by the same criteria as discussed in the section on working capital. On the other hand, when the operating method is used, investment in leased property (less related accumulated depreciation) is reported adjacent to the tangible fixed assets used by the lessor and appropriately described.

Accounting for Leases in Financial Statements of Lessees. Two central questions arise in connection with accounting for leases on the part of lessees:

1. Should property rights and obligations relating to future rents under true leases be capitalized and reported at some discounted values on the balance sheet?
2. How should certain contracts called leases which are, in substance, contracts for the purchase of property be accounted for and reported?

These questions, which have been accorded considerable attention by persons and committees associated with the research division of the AICPA and by others as well, are discussed here in the order stated.

True leases, mentioned in the preceding paragraph, are contracts calling for the rental rather than the purchase of property. Two basic methods of accounting for them have been proposed. For some time accountants have debated whether such contracts should be accorded recognition in the accounts and statements beyond the current and next fiscal periods (unless, of course, a prepayment extending further into the future has been made). Some contend that an asset and corresponding obligation relating to the entire span of the lease are created as soon as a lease is signed and that both items should be reflected in the accounts and reported on the financial statements. Others contend that a lease is an executory contract requiring no recognition beyond the current (or at the most the next) fiscal period, except, of course, for cost outlays already made which clearly extend further into the future.

What are the pros and cons of capitalization of leases? The principal arguments favoring capitalization are:

1. Liabilities exist under the lease and should be disclosed to statement readers and kept before management.
2. Disclosure of the liability by footnote rather than in the body of statements might not be properly related to the overall financial structure of the enterprise.
3. An investor attempting to compare a company which leased a large proportion of its facilities with one which owned them could make a better comparison if lease rights and obligations are reported among the assets and liabilities. Better comparisons could be made of return on capital, managerial efficiency, and the like.
4. Leasing is an alternative to purchasing and perhaps to borrowing; capitalization recognizes this fact.
5. Better comparisons can be made of operating results of divisions using different proportions of leased facilities.
6. Vulnerability to volume changes would be disclosed. A large fixed rental obligation would be of considerable significance.
7. Capitalization is more in accordance with the principles of revealing all assets and liabilities.
8. Capitalization accords to the "continuity assumption." Failure to capitalize merely because a lease contract is executory accentuates the liquidation viewpoint.

The principal arguments against capitalization are:

1. The tenant does not own the facilities leased and recording a substantial asset balance could be deceptive. (Use of a longer descriptive title such as "capitalization of leased facilities" could overcome this objection.)
2. Capitalization tends to violate a principle that liabilities should be recorded only when assets or services are received.
3. Computation of the amount of the asset and liability can be somewhat arbitrary; use of a higher imputed interest rate would yield lower dollar amounts.

4. There is no universal agreement on correct classification and presentation of the offsetting rights and obligations balances.
5. Capitalization reduces the overall rate of return on total assets; this might lead investors to place an unduly low value on the entity's earnings.
6. If the entity is in a regulated industry, computation of rate of return might be distorted.
7. Inclusion of the liability increases the total indebtedness; this could lead to an impairment of ability to borrow.
8. If local taxes are levied on total assets, capitalization could lead to excessive property taxation.

The accounting issue has not been finally resolved. AICPA *Accounting Research Study No. 4,* published in 1962, advocated capitalization on a broad scale. To the extent that leases give rise to property rights, those rights and related liabilities should be measured and incorporated in the balance sheet. Longer, noncancelable leases whereunder lessees pay fixed amounts sufficient to return to the lessor his investment plus a fair return are likely to reflect property rights. On the other hand, short leases that contain no options to buy at termination and provide, moreover, that the lessor will pay for taxes, insurance, and maintenance, are likely not to involve property rights. In 1964 when the Accounting Principles Board, after considering the recommendations of that study and adopting many of them, issued its first Opinion dealing with accounting for leases, it rejected the principle of capitalization (except where a lease was actually a contract to buy assets). However, when the Board issued a later Opinion dealing principally with accounting for leases by lessors, it included the following excerpt:

> There continues to be a question as to whether assets and the related obligations should be reflected in the balance sheet for leases other than those that are in substance installment purchases. The Board will continue to give consideration to this question.[63]

Accounting for "Leases" That Are Purchases. Property contracts are sometimes drawn in such a way that what is called a lease turns out, in substance, to be a purchase contract. In discussing such contracts and in setting out some criteria to identify them, the APB said:

[63] "Accounting for Leases in Financial Statements of Lessors," *Opinion of the Accounting Principles Board No. 7* (New York: AICPA, 1966), p. 60. Other relevant AICPA publications on the subject are "Reporting of Leases in Financial Statements of Lessee," *Opinion of the Accounting Principles Board No. 5* (New York: AICPA, 1964); and John H. Myers, "Reporting of Leases in Financial Statements," *Accounting Research Study No. 4* (New York: AICPA, 1962).

> The property and the related obligation should be included as an asset and a liability in the balance sheet if the terms of the lease result in the creation of a material equity in the property. It is unlikely that such an equity can be created under a lease which either party may cancel unilaterally for reasons other than the occurrence of some remote contingency. The presence, in a noncancelable lease or in a lease cancelable only upon the occurrence of some remote contingency, of either of the two following conditions will usually establish that a lease should be considered to be in substance a purchase:
>
> a. The initial term is materially less than the useful life of the property, and the lessee has the option to renew the lease for the remaining useful life of the property at substantially less than the fair rental value; or
>
> b. The lessee has the right, during or at the expiration of the lease, to acquire the property at a price which at the inception of the lease appears to be substantially less than the probable fair value of the property at the time or times of permitted acquisition by the lessee.[64]

Elsewhere in the same Opinion, the Board provided additional criteria by which determination of whether a lease is a rental or purchase contract when it noted that the existence in a noncancelable lease (or one cancelable only upon the occurrence of some remote contingency) of one or more of the following circumstances would tend to indicate that it is a purchase:

> a. The property was acquired by the lessor to meet the special needs of the lessee and will probably be usable only for that purpose and only by the lessee.
>
> b. The term of the lease corresponds substantially to the estimated useful life of the property, and the lessee is obligated to pay costs such as taxes, insurance, and maintenance, which are usually considered incidental to ownership.
>
> c. The lessee has guaranteed the obligations of the lessor with respect to the property leased.
>
> d. The lessee has treated the lease as a purchase for tax purposes.[65]

A close relation between a lessor and lessee as evidenced by common ownership, common officers or directors, or the fact the lessor is a subsidiary of the lessee or of the same parent corporation, may also indicate the propriety of treating a lease as a purchase contract.

When it has been determined that a lease is in fact an installment purchase contract, the property and the obligation should be recorded on the books of the lessee at an appropriate discounted amount of future payments under the lease agreement. The method of amortizing the amount of the asset against income should be appropriate to the nature

[64] *Opinion of the Accounting Principles Board No. 5,* p. 30.
[65] *Ibid.,* p. 31.

of the use of the asset and does not necessarily bear any relation to the period over which the related obligation is discharged. Obviously part of each payment (rent) required is interest and the remainder is a reduction of principal. As with any debt retirement calling for uniform payments, the proportion of interest to principal in early payments is relatively high; when the debt is nearly fully paid, only a small part of each payment is interest. To the extent that rental payments are for services such as property taxes, utilities, maintenance, and the like, they should be charged to current operations.

In connection with true leases (i.e., those not involving purchase of the leased assets), it should be pointed out that since the APB, at least temporarily, rejected capitalization of lease rights and recognition of a corresponding obligation on the statements, it laid down some disclosure requirements as a substitute. Succinctly, these are that "the financial statements or the accompanying notes should disclose the minimum annual rentals under such leases and the period over which the outlays will be made." [66]

The final matter to be discussed in connection with leases is "sale-and-leaseback" transactions. Principal details of any such arrangement should be disclosed in the year in which the transaction originates. A sale-and-leaseback transaction is one in which one company acquires or constructs property for another, sells it to the other company, and then proceeds to lease it from the new owner. Obviously, such transactions are planned in advance and are a means of financing fixed asset utilization in that the lessee has use of the property throughout the term of the lease in exchange for periodic rents under the lease. There also may be important tax advantages for both the lessor and lessee. Sale-and-leaseback transactions sometimes result in gains or losses; hence a question of how to deal with any difference between the cost and sales price arises. In this connection, the APB said:

> . . . material gains or losses resulting from the sale of properties which are the subject of sale-and-leaseback transactions, together with the related tax effect, should be amortized over the life of the lease as an adjustment of the rental cost (or, if the leased property is capitalized, as an adjustment of depreciation).[67]

income tax allocation

The purpose of income tax allocation is to relate the amount of tax expense reported as closely as possible to the income reported. There are two major types of income tax allocation—*interperiod allocation,*

[66] *Ibid.,* p. 32.
[67] *Ibid.,* p. 33.

which is necessitated because of differences in the *timing* of recognition of revenues or deductions for tax and accounting purposes, and *intra-statement* (or interstatement) *allocation,* which is required because the effects of various transactions can be properly reported in either of two major segments of the income statement or on the retained earnings statement.

Interperiod tax allocation is necessary when there are timing differences between pretax accounting income and taxable income. For example, rent or royalty income collected in advance is usually taxed when received but may not be earned until considerably later; depreciation may be recognized on an accelerated basis for tax return purposes but on a straight-line basis for book purposes. Such differences ultimately counterbalance themselves (i.e., the excess of tax revenue or deduction in the earlier periods in the two examples cited is exactly equal to the later excess of book revenue or deduction in some later periods). In the case of the rent income collected in advance, if the rent represents a material part of the current year's income, the amount of income tax payable will exceed considerably the income tax expense proportionate to the income reported for book purposes. It would be necessary to journalize the tax expense liability and expense at the end of the period as set out below:

Debit: Income tax expense	*Pretax income times current tax rate*
Debit: Deferred income taxes	*Squeeze amount*
Credit: Income taxes payable	*Amount actually estimated to be payable*

In subsequent periods an opposite set of conditions would prevail and the income tax expense would exceed the tax liability; accordingly, the Deferred Income Taxes balance would be amortized.

Debit: Income tax expense	*Sum of credits*
Credit: Deferred income taxes	*Amount determined by amortization schedule*
Credit: Income taxes payable	*Amount actually estimated to be payable*

In the case of the accelerated depreciation versus straight-line depreciation example, journal entries to record tax expense in the early years when the tax depreciation exceeded book depreciaton would be as follows:

Income tax expense	$XXXX	
Deferred income tax		$XXXX
Income taxes payable		XXXX

As the asset grows older and book depreciation expense exceeds the tax deduction, the annual tax entry would be:

Income tax expense	$XXXX	
Deferred income tax	XXXX	
Income taxes payable		$XXXX

Intrastatement tax allocation is necessary when some of the transactions of the period having an effect on the income tax expense of the period are reported in different segments of the income statement. For example, if a company reports that its regular operations were profitable but that it sustained a material casualty loss (an extraordinary item which would have the effect of reducing the company's income tax liability), intrastatement tax allocation is necessary. Or if another company reports that its regular operations were profitable and that it sold some fixed assets at a gain which resulted in a long-term capital gain, intrastatement tax allocation again would be necessary, and for somewhat similar reasons. In the rather rare event that a company can report part of its operating results on the income statement and some transaction having tax consequences on the retained earnings statement, interstatement tax allocation would be necessary; in other words, the tax consequences relating to that part reported on the retained earnings statement would be shown there and the tax related to what was reported on the income statement would be shown on the income statement.

It should be noted that for the company with the casualty loss the amount of tax consequences to be assigned to the casualty loss should probably be the *difference* in tax calculated with and without the casualty loss. An alternative would be to use an *average* rate calculated by dividing total income tax by net income. Since different tax rates are applied to the two forms of income, in the case of the company with income from regular operations plus a long-term capital gain, tax allocation should apportion tax expense at ordinary tax rates to income from regular income reported in the "income before extraordinary items" segment of the income statement and at capital gain rates to the gain in the "extraordinary items" segment.

Federal tax laws allow corporations which sustain losses to carry back and then carry forward such losses. The effect can be that a corporation may secure refunds of income taxes paid in three prior years, and if the loss is so large that it is not absorbed fully when offset against the profitable years to which it is carried back, it can be carried forward for as many as five years, during which it may serve to reduce taxes that would otherwise be owed on income of those years.

Where the years preceding a loss year have been profitable, there can be little doubt that a carryback equal to or less than the profits of the years to which it can be applied will be fully realized. On the other hand, uncertainty must necessarily attend the realizability of a carryforward. The following quotation from *APB Opinion No. 11* is relevant:

> The tax effects of loss carry*forwards* also relate to the determination of net income (loss) of the loss periods. However, a significant question generally exists as to realization of the tax effects of the carry*forwards,* since realization is dependent upon future taxable income. Accordingly, the Board has concluded that the tax benefits of loss carry*forwards* should not be recognized until they are actually realized, except in unusual circumstances when realization is *assured beyond any reasonable doubt* at the time the loss carry*forwards* arise. When the tax benefits of loss carry*forwards* are not recognized until realized in full or in part in subsequent periods, the tax benefits should be reported in the results of those periods as extraordinary items.
>
> In those rare cases in which realization of the tax benefits of loss carry*forwards* is assured beyond any reasonable doubt, the potential benefits should be associated with the periods of loss and should be recognized in the determination of results of operations for those periods. Realization is considered to be assured beyond any reasonable doubt when conditions such as those set forth [in the next two paragraphs] are present. The amount of the asset (and the tax effect on results of operations) recognized in the loss period should be computed at the rates expected to be in effect at the time of realization. If the applicable tax rates change from those used to measure the tax effect at the time of recognition, the effect of the rate change should be accounted for in the period of the change as an adjustment of the asset account and of income tax expense.
>
> Realization of the tax benefit of a loss carry*forward* would appear to be assured beyond any reasonable doubt when both of the following conditions exist: (a) the loss results from an identifiable, isolated and nonrecurring cause and the company either has been continuously profitable over a long period or has suffered occasional losses which were more than offset by taxable income in subsequent years, and (b) future taxable income is virtually certain to be large enough to offset the loss carry*forward* and will occur soon enough to provide realization during the carry*forward* period.
>
> Net deferred tax credits arising from timing differences may exist at the time loss carry*forwards* arise. In the usual case when the tax effect of a loss carry*forward* is not recognized in the loss period, adjustments of the existing net deferred tax credits may be necessary in that period or in subsequent periods. In this situation net deferred tax credits should be eliminated to the extent of the lower of (a) the tax effect of the loss carry*forward,* or (b) the amortization of the net deferred tax credits that would otherwise have occurred

> during the carry*forward* period. If the loss carryforward is realized in whole or in part in periods subsequent to the loss period, the amounts eliminated from the deferred tax credit accounts should be reinstated (at the then current tax rates) on a cumulative basis as, and to the extent that, the tax benefit of the loss carry*forward* is realized. In the unusual situation in which the tax effect of a loss carry*forward* is recognized as an asset in the loss year, the deferred tax credit accounts would be amortized in future periods. . . .[68]

Income tax allocation procedures are inappropriate where differences between the income tax return and income statement are more or less permanent. This is to be distinguished from situations in which there is simply a difference in the *timing* of deductions or income and the divergences will cancel out over time. A few examples of items giving rise to continuing differences between the income tax return and income statement include (a) interest income on state and municipal bonds that is exempt from federal income tax, (b) dividends received by one corporation from another that usually are effectively taxed at very low rates because of special tax law credits, and (c) depletion computed on a percentage basis for tax purposes, whereas book depletion is calculated on a cost basis. In these and other similar cases, tax allocation procedures are inappropriate because the differences between book and taxable income do not later cancel out.

concluding commentary

The early portion of this chapter was designed to provide the CPA candidate with a broad review of the foundations of accounting theory. The final segment stressed a number of more specific points of financial reporting. Throughout there has been an emphasis on the pronouncements of those segments of the American Institute of CPAs concerned with the determination of generally accepted accounting principles and the setting of standards of reporting. This stress has been deliberate. Candidates for the CPA examination should bear in mind that the examination is one for issuance of the professional designation and license to practice as a Certified Public Accountant. It is only natural that in preparing and grading the Uniform CPA Examination, the Examination Division of the American Institute would accord a high degree of recognition to positions taken by other segments of the organization.

No single chapter such as this can possibly summarize or outline all the theory which a practicing CPA needs to know or is reflected in the various reference sources cited. The purpose has been to bring out

[68] *APB Opinion No. 11,* pp. 173–74. Some footnotes are omitted from the quotation.

in a concise fashion the more basic material and to advise candidates who are in need of additional study where they might turn for more information. In addition to having adequate and current knowledge, it is important to employ sound examination techniques in taking the Theory portion of the Uniform CPA Examination. In this connection, the booklet *Information for CPA Candidates* published by the American Institute of CPAs contains many valuable suggestions as well as useful background data concerning the examination.

Some specific suggestions concerning answering Theory questions follow; to some extent they have validity for other portions of the examination as well.

1. Take with you to the examination a means of keeping track of time and maintain a "time log" of when you begin and finish each question. Do not exceed the maximum time allotment on a question until after you have gained sufficient time on questions already completed to permit such an overrun.

2. Do not answer the first question first unless it strikes you as being reasonably easy to answer. If it is not a question you are well prepared to answer, go on and find a question on a topic you are better equipped to handle. There are several reasons for this approach:

   a. It builds confidence to answer one or more questions successfully before tackling the most difficult ones.

   b. You will probably answer the easier questions in less than the maximum time and this will allow you more time for the harder questions and avoid undue time pressure as the end of the examination period approaches.

   c. If you begin with a question you cannot answer or can only partially answer, it is not only demoralizing but it is time consuming, and you are spending time you could use earning points elsewhere.

3. Read the questions very carefully. This is such obvious advice one hesitates to offer it, but it is important. From having graded hundreds of Theory papers for the AICPA, the author is quite aware that many candidates obviously misread or fail to read questions fully. Furthermore, it is not uncommon for the *"a"* part of a Theory question to be somewhat unrelated to the prefatory part of the question; indeed, it may be rather general and even deal with something that is not directly accounting-related.[69]

[69] Some examples of Theory questions in which the "*a*" part (and in some cases part "*b*" as well) was somewhat unrelated to the prefatory statement include the following: May, 1966 #2; November, 1966 #3 and #5; November, 1967 #6; May, 1968 #2; November, 1969 #2; May, 1970 #2.

4. Outline your answers briefly before beginning to answer questions. This is important because it will enable you to correct bad organization before it can be damaging. Once part of an answer is committed to paper that one intends to turn in, the time constraint often deters a candidate from scrapping what he has said, so he "writes around it" and tries to salvage his first written response in the remainder of the answer.

5. Answer fully. Supporting reasons are often more important than the actual recommendation of the answer. Furthermore, if an answer calls for a specified number of arguments for a particular treatment and you can think of a larger number, go ahead and give as many arguments as possible. If you are going to have parts of an answer that contradict other parts, this is all right, but you should indicate an awareness of the contradiction. You can cover yourself by saying in one place "Some authorities contend . . ." and elsewhere "An alternative treatment would be to . . . ." Often a question will call for the pros and cons of a given controversy; be sure you state explicitly which are the arguments for and which are those against.

6. Leave some space between the "*a*" and "*b*" parts of your answers. If you have "afterthoughts" or an opportunity to review your answer near the end of the examination, you can write in your added thoughts in these spaces. If you do not fill in these spaces, no harm is done.

3
auditing

Alvin A. Arens

The overall objective of the auditing section of the CPA examination has remained relatively unchanged in recent decades. The primary objective continues to be the testing of the candidate's knowledge and competence in the subject matter relevant to the services performed by certified public accountants. The predominant emphasis is on matters directly involving auditing, but occasionally there are also questions pertaining to such related subjects as management services, income taxes, and unaudited statements.

Although the objective of the examination has remained much the same, there have been significant changes in its substance. The most obvious change has been the recent inclusion of statistical sampling and electronic data processing (EDP) questions. Prior to 1965 it was unusual to find a required question in either of these subjects, but recently at least one required question in each examination has involved one or both of them. In addition, there is a noticeable trend toward examining at a higher level of technical competence in each of these subjects. A more subtle change is the current emphasis on the development of audit programs in a specific set of circumstances, rather than on requiring a detailed listing of a standard audit program. This change requires the candidates to have a thorough knowledge of the factors that influence audit program development as well as an understanding of the effect of these factors on evidence accumulation.

The Board of Examiners of the American Institute of Certified Public Accountants has recently revised its statement on the purpose and scope of the CPA examination. The areas of knowledge that they state will be regularly tested on the auditing examination are as follows:

Generally accepted auditing standards. Candidates should know, understand, and be able to explain the generally accepted auditing standards of the profession. Questions may require an explanation of the standards or an interpretation of their meaning. Understanding of the standards is tested by requiring their application to specific situations.

Internal control. Questions on this topic may require knowledge of controls over various assets, liabilities, expenses, and costs as well as the objectives of these controls. In given situations, candidates should be prepared to identify deficiencies in systems of internal control, make recommendations to correct the deficiencies, and suggest changes in the duties of employees to strengthen the systems. Understanding of the degree and manner by which internal controls affect audit procedures may also be tested. Questions on internal control systems may require a knowledge of flowcharting.

Automatic data processing and computers. Automatic data processing systems and computers are chiefly treated in the Auditing section as types of systems which the CPA should understand for audit purposes. Testing in this area shall be progressively more extensive until the level is reached at which candidates are required to demonstrate (1) a basic knowledge of at least one computer system —the function of the component parts, the general capabilities of the system, and the more universal terms associated with the computer, (2) the ability to design, analyze, and flowchart a system of modest complexity, (3) a working knowledge of at least one computer language sufficient to program, debug, and test a simple problem, and (4) an understanding of the control procedures and needed modification of auditing methods to conform to computerized systems.

Audit programs and procedures. As a general rule Auditing includes at least one question on audit programs and procedures. Questions may provide a situation and ask for the audit program or procedures which the CPA would apply, or may give an audit procedure and ask for a discussion of it. The emphasis of the questions is on the understanding of the objectives and purposes of the audit procedures, and not on the procedures themselves. Usually the knowledge tested is *why* the procedures are applied, and not necessarily *what* they are.

Auditing evidence. Candidates may expect to be tested on their understanding of the significance of the various kinds of evidence examined or accumulated during an audit. Such evidence is obtained by observation, inquiry, examination of documents, confirmations, client representations, comparisons, analyses, and the like. Candidates should also know the kinds and importance of information which the CPA may look for and expect to find in his examination of contracts, minutes, articles of incorporation, leases, insurance policies, partnership agreements, and other documents usually encountered in the course of an audit.

Auditing theory. This topic includes knowledge of the systematic array of ideas and basic doctrines which logically explain the nature of, the reasons for, and the societal significance of auditing. Areas to be tested include the attest function, the nature and purpose of audit evidence, the doctrine of due care, and concepts of independence, integrity, and personal responsibility.

Auditor's report. Questions dealing with the auditor's report may be expected in each examination's Auditing section. The candidate may be presented with a situation and required to write an appropriate auditor's report in which his opinion might be unqualified, qualified, or adverse, or he might disclaim an opinion. Knowledge of the implications and significance of the auditor's report may also be tested by multiple-choice questions, or by the presentation of an auditor's report on which candidates may be asked to comment.

Candidates may also expect questions pertaining to the CPA's responsibilities when he is associated with unaudited financial statements. Knowledge of the adequacy of disclosures in the auditor's report will also be tested frequently.

Inasmuch as the culmination of an audit engagement is the auditor's report, heavy emphasis is placed on this topic in the Auditing section. Therefore candidates may expect questions in the Auditing section of each examination dealing with aspects of the auditor's report. These questions may bear upon matters such as statement presentation, footnotes, disclosures, and forms of opinions.

Professional responsibility. Questions relating to professional responsibility may appear in Auditing from time to time. These questions will be based on the profession's rules of professional conduct and interpretive opinions. The subject of these questions might be such matters as professional relations with clients and other CPAs (including the confidential nature of these relations), professional independence, and professional conduct. Usually the topic of the accountant's legal responsibility appears in the Business (Commercial) Law section.

Constructive service suggestions. There may be interwoven into Auditing the testing of the candidates' ability to recognize the need for constructive service suggestions that arise from auditing engagements. Such suggestions may pertain to modifications of the accounting or costing system, realignment of personnel duties, strengthening of security measures, and the like.

Statistical sampling. Candidates should understand the theory of statistical sampling and be able to apply the techniques in auditing situations. Such questions will appear in Auditing regularly at levels of difficulty justified by current professional development in this area of knowledge.[1]

At the completion of a typical audit engagement, the auditor issues a standard short-form audit report to accompany the financial statements. Since this report summarizes the most important concepts in an ordinary audit, it is useful to state the present form of the unquali-

[1] American Institute of Certified Public Accountants, *Information for CPA Candidates* (New York: American Institute of Certified Public Accountants, 1970), pp. 5–7.

fied report that is recommended by the American Institute of Certified Public Accountants (AICPA).

> We have examined the balance sheet of X Company as of June 30, 19__ and the related statement(s) of income and retained earnings for the year then ended. Our examination was made in accordance with generally accepted auditing standards, and accordingly included such tests of the accounting records and such other auditing procedures as we considered necessary in the circumstances.
>
> In our opinion, the accompanying balance sheet and statement(s) of income and retained earnings present fairly the financial position of X Company at June 30, 19__, and the results of its operations for the year then ended, in conformity with generally accepted accounting principles applied on a basis consistent with that of the preceding year.[2]

The first part of the report (the scope paragraph) states in essence that, in the auditor's professional judgment, the evidence accumulated in the course of the audit was adequate considering the facts of the engagement. The generally accepted auditing standards referred to in the scope paragraph will be discussed shortly. The second paragraph (the opinion) states that the auditor believes, on the basis of a limited examination, that the financial statements are fairly stated in accordance with generally accepted accounting principles that have been consistently applied. Detailed attention will be given to the auditor's report in a later section of the chapter.

Responsibilities of the Auditor and Management

The objective of the ordinary examination of financial statements is to issue an audit report on the statements, based upon the extent of the auditor's examination and the results found in the audit.

The question often arises about the degree of responsibility the auditor should take for the reliability of the information included on the financial statements. The professional literature has made it clear in the following statement that the responsibility for the fairness of the representation made in the financial statements rests with management rather than with the auditor:

> Management has the responsibility for adopting sound accounting policies, for maintaining an adequate and effective system of accounts, for the safeguarding of assets, and for devising a system

[2] American Institute of Certified Public Accountants, *Statements on Auditing Procedure No. 33,* p. 57.

> of internal control that will, among other things, help assure the production of proper financial statements. The transactions which should be reflected in the accounts and in the financial statements are matters within the direct knowledge and control of management. The auditor's knowledge of such transactions is limited to that acquired through his examination. Accordingly, the fairness of the representations made through financial statements is an implicit and integral part of management's responsibility.[3]

If the auditor were responsible for making certain that all the representations in the statements were correct, it would be necessary to accumulate far more evidence than is generally obtained. The cost of the audit function would thereby be increased to such an extent that audits would not be economically feasible.

The auditor's responsibility is limited to performing the audit investigation and reporting the results in accordance with generally accepted auditing standards. In most cases, any material errors and omissions will be discovered if the audit has been so performed. Yet the possibility always exists that the auditor's selected sample will fail to uncover a material error. In this event, his best defense is that he performed the audit and prepared his report with due care in accordance with generally accepted auditing standards. That the auditor is not responsible for all undisclosed errors in the financial statements indicates that he is not a guarantor or insurer of the reliability of the financial statements.

The management's responsibility for the fairness of the representations in the financial statements carries with it the privilege of determining which disclosures it considers necessary. Although management has the responsibility for the preparation of the financial statements and the accompanying footnotes, it is acceptable for an auditor to prepare a draft for the client or to offer suggestions for clarification. In the event that management insists on financial statement disclosure that the auditor finds unacceptable, the auditor can either issue an adverse or qualified opinion or withdraw from the engagement.

The profession has been especially emphatic that the auditor is not responsible for the discovery of fraud if the examination has been performed in accordance with generally accepted auditing standards. If auditors were responsible for the discovery of all material fraud, auditing tests would have to be greatly expanded, for many types of fraud are extremely difficult if not impossible to detect. The extension of the procedures that would be necessary to uncover all cases of fraud would probably be more expensive than the benefits would justify.

[3] American Institute of Certified Public Accountants, *Statements on Auditing Procedure No. 33,* pp. 9–10.

The profession has concluded that the prevention and detection of fraud can be more economically accomplished by an adequate accounting system with appropriate internal controls. However, if the auditor has sound reasons to suspect the existence of fraud which may materially affect the reliability of financial statements, he has a responsibility to determine whether the fraud actually exists. The investigation can be made by the client, under the auditor's supervision, or by the auditor himself.

Generally Accepted Auditing Standards

Generally accepted auditing standards are regarded as the broadest guidelines that are available to auditors in the performance of the audit function. As an indication of their importance, the standard short-form audit report includes a statement that the audit was performed in accordance with generally accepted auditing standards. The purpose of most of the professional literature pertaining to auditing that is published by the AICPA is to aid in interpreting and adhering to these standards. It is essential that the candidate have a thorough knowledge and understanding of the standards. They are set forth as follows:

General Standards

1. The examination is to be performed by a person or persons having adequate technical training and proficiency as an auditor.
2. In all matters relating to the assignment, an independence in mental attitude is to be maintained by the auditor or auditors.
3. Due professional care is to be exercised in the performance of the examination and the preparation of the report.

Standards of Field Work

1. The work is to be adequately planned and assistants, if any, are to be properly supervised.
2. There is to be a proper study and evaluation of the existing internal control as a basis for reliance thereon and for the determination of the resultant extent of the tests to which auditing procedures are to be restricted.
3. Sufficient competent evidential matter is to be obtained through inspection, observation, inquiries, and confirmations to afford a reasonable basis for an opinion regarding the financial statements under examination.

Standards of Reporting

1. The report shall state whether the financial statements are presented in accordance with generally accepted principles of accounting.

2. The report shall state whether such principles have been consistently observed in the current period in relation to the preceding period.

3. Informative disclosures in the financial statements are to be regarded as reasonably adequate unless otherwise stated in the report.

4. The report shall either contain an expression of opinion regarding the financial statements, taken as a whole, or an assertion to the effect that an opinion cannot be expressed. When an over-all opinion cannot be expressed, the reasons therefor should be stated. In all cases where an auditor's name is associated with financial statements the report should contain a clear-cut indication of the character of the auditor's examination, if any, and the degree of responsibility he is taking.[4]

The general standards stress the important personal qualities that the auditor should possess. The first standard is normally interpreted as requiring the auditor to have some formal education in auditing and accounting, adequate practical experience for the work he is performing, and continuing professional education. In recent court cases it has been clearly demonstrated that the auditor must be technically qualified and experienced in those industries in which his audit clients are engaged. The second standard, concerning an independence of mental attitude, requires the auditor to use great care in maintaining an unbiased attitude. This is essential for the continued acceptance of auditing as a social benefit by users of financial information. Although independence is a state of mind that cannot be quantified, the *Code of Professional Ethics* includes several specific guidelines to aid auditors in remaining independent in both fact and appearance. The Code is quoted in full at the end of this chapter. The third standard is concerned with due care in the performance of all aspects of auditing. Simply stated, this means that the auditor is a professional who is responsible for adequately fulfilling his duties with diligence and reasonable care. As an illustration, due care includes consideration of the completeness of the working papers, the sufficiency and competence of the audit evidence, and the adequacy of the audit report. It should be kept in mind that the auditor, as a professional, must avoid negligence and bad faith, but he is not expected to make perfect judgments in every instance.

The standards of field work and reporting concern the performance of the audit and the reporting of the results. The remainder of this chapter is concerned primarily with meeting the requirements of these standards.

[4] American Institute of Certified Public Accountants, *Statements on Auditing Procedure No. 33* (New York: American Institute of Certified Public Accountants, 1963), pp. 15–16.

The Audit Examination in General

The following highly simplified summary of the four primary steps in a normal audit serves as a frame of reference for the subsequent detailed discussion in following sections.

(1) Internal Control Review. The system of internal control is thoroughly studied and evaluated as a means of understanding the client's accounting system and identifying weaknesses in the controls. Since the client's methods of record keeping and controlling assets directly affect the reliability of the information on the financial statements, it should be apparent that a thorough evaluation of internal control is an important part of every audit.

(2) Tests of Transactions. Tests of transactions are performed to determine whether the accounting information is properly recorded in the accounting journals and correctly transferred to the subsidiary ledgers and the general ledger. These tests are closely related to the internal control review because the auditor is testing the actual system for compliance with the purported system.

(3) Direct Tests of Balances. The audit procedures used to directly test the balances on the client's trial balance (also known as tests of bona fides) are determined by the adequacy of the system of internal control, the results of the tests of transactions, the evidence that is available for the auditor's use, and other circumstances of the audit. The circumstances that affect evidence accumulations are discussed in detail in a separate section of this chapter.

Tests of transactions and direct tests of balances are closely related approaches to determining whether the financial statements are fairly stated. Transactions testing is used to ascertain whether the individual transactions that make up the ending balances in the financial statements are properly recorded. Direct year-end testing is used to directly verify that the balances at the end of the year are satisfactorily stated. Of course, if the direct tests demonstrate that the account balance is incorrect, it is also an indication that the system of internal control is not functioning adequately. Similarly, when the tests of transactions indicate that the system is not adequate, the auditor has valuable evidence that the balances in certain accounts are likely to be misstated. Hence we can see that when the results of these two approaches are subjectively combined by the auditor, the evidence is more persuasive than when the results of each test are considered separately.

(4) Preparation of the Audit Report. At the completion of the audit tests, an audit report is issued. This brief statement informs financial statement users in general terms of the audit tests performed and the results found.

Internal Control

definition of internal control

Internal control has been defined by the Committee on Auditing Procedure of the AICPA as follows:

> Internal control comprises the plan of organization and all of the coordinate methods and measures adopted within a business to safeguard its assets, check the accuracy and reliability of its accounting data, promote operational efficiency, and encourage adherence to prescribed managerial policies.[5]

This definition is so broad in scope that it is generally not feasible for the auditor to adequately review and evaluate the client's system for all the aspects of internal control encompassed in the definition. As a result, the auditor generally limits himself to the parts of the definition concerned with the safeguarding of assets and the complete and accurate recording of accounting data.

purpose of the review of internal control

The primary reason for reviewing the client's system of internal control is to aid in determining the audit evidence that should be accumulated. The adequacy of the internal control system affects the auditor's expectation of errors, and the expectation of errors in turn affects the audit evidence that should be accumulated. The need for carefully reviewing the client's system of internal control in determining the appropriate evidence to accumulate is considered so important that there is a specific generally accepted auditing standard dealing with the subject:

> There is to be a proper study and evaluation of the existing internal control as a basis for reliance thereon and for the determination of the resultant extent of the tests to which auditing procedures are to be restricted.[6]

[5] American Institute of Certified Public Accountants, *Statements on Auditing Procedure No. 33,* p. 27.

[6] *Ibid.,* p. 16.

The evidence accumulated by the auditor is influenced by internal control inadequacies that affect the expectation of both fraudulent and unintentional errors. The effect of internal control evaluation in fraud detection is important because auditors have not accepted responsibility for the discovery of fraud in normal circumstances. If, however, the review of internal control indicates that there is a weakness in the system that increases the probability of fraud, the auditor then has a responsibility to perform tests to determine whether the fraud in fact exists, especially if he believes the fraud could be material. For example, when the separation of duties in a client's accounting system is such that there is a clear opportunity for the lapping of accounts receivable, it is necessary to employ procedures specifically designed to test for that type of fraud. In a similar manner, internal control evaluation affects the auditor's evidence accumulation in searching for unintentional errors. When an auditor is accumulating evidence in a situation where the system of internal control is believed to be inadequate (e.g., when the physical controls over assets are insufficient), it is reasonable to expect more extensive testing than when he believes the controls are effective.

There are two purposes, other than determining the appropriate evidence to accumulate, for reviewing the client's system of internal control. The first is to aid the auditor in understanding the client's methods of recording financial information. The internal control review helps to familiarize the auditor with the company's policies and it assists him in understanding the client's accounting system. The second purpose is to enable the auditor to inform management of any inadequacies in the system and to suggest methods to eliminate the weaknesses and improve the system.

characteristics of satisfactory internal control

A knowledge of the most important properties of good internal control is necessary before an auditor can intelligently determine when a system has weaknesses. Once the auditor understands the important properties, he can determine whether any of them are lacking in the system being evaluated. The following are the most important basic characteristics.

Clearly Defined Responsibilities for Each Function. It is important to place specific responsibility for the performance of duties with specific individuals to provide reasonable assurance that the work will be adequately performed. When jobs are carefully assigned, it is likely that the work will be done efficiently and correctly. When the function is not adequately performed, it is then possible to place responsibility with the person who had done the work. The assigned person is also motivated to work carefully, and corrective action by management is facilitated.

As a part of placing specific responsibility with specific individuals, it is necessary to provide a method of transferring the responsibility to successive functions whenever the person performing the work loses control over the reliability of the results. Thus, if the control over inventory calls for the signature of the receiving clerk when raw material is received and counted by the receiving department, it is also important to require the transfer of the responsibility to the storage department when the material is sent to stores. When stores releases the material to manufacturing, responsibility should again be transferred. If an inventory shortage develops, it is then feasible to pinpoint the department that is responsible for the shortage.

An Adequate System of Authorizations. Every transaction in an organization is either implicitly or explicitly authorized by someone. It is important that the transactions be authorized at a level in the organization that facilitates adequate control over the company's assets. As an illustration, the approval of credit should be performed by the credit manager rather than the sales manager because the latter may be tempted to approve poor credit risks as a means of increasing sales. This could result in a large number of uncollectible accounts included in accounts receivable. Similarly, the acquisition and disposal of major capital assets should be authorized by top management as a means of adequate control of assets. Another important aspect of authorizations is that they take place at the level designated by management. For example, if the board of directors designates a fixed selling price for the company's products, it is inappropriate for sales personnel to charge a different price.

Adequate Division of Duties. The appropriate segregation of duties is especially important as a means of preventing both fraudulent and unintentional errors. The following three general categories of segregation are usually considered the most important:

1. Separation of the Custody of Assets from Accounting. The primary reason for not requiring the person who has temporary or permanent custody of an asset to account for that asset is to protect the firm against fraud. When one person performs both functions, there is an excessive risk that he could dispose of the asset for personal gain and adjust the records to relieve himself of responsibility for the asset. As an illustration, if the cashier receives cash and maintains both the cash and accounts receivable records, it is feasible for him to take the cash received from a customer and adjust the customer's account by failing to record a sale or, as an alternative, record a fictitious credit to the account. As a general rule, it is desirable that any person who performs an accounting function should be prevented from having access to any asset that can be converted to personal gain.

2. *Separation of the Authorization of Transactions from the Handling of Related Assets.* It is desirable, to the extent that it is feasible, to prevent the person who authorizes transactions from having control over the related asset. For example, the same person should not authorize the payment of a vendor's invoice and also sign the check in payment of the bill. Similarly, the authority for adding newly hired employees to the payroll or eliminating those who have terminated employment should be performed by someone other than the person who is responsible for distributing the checks to the employees. As a final illustration, it is undesirable for anyone who handles incoming cash receipts to have the authority to determine which accounts should be charged off as uncollectible. In each of the foregoing examples the authorization of a transaction and the handling of the related asset by the same person reduces the control in the organization.

3. *Separation of Duties within the Accounting Function.* The least desirable accounting system is one in which one employee is responsible for recording a transaction from its origin to its ultimate posting in the general ledger. There are many opportunities for automatic cross-checking of different employees' work by simply segregating the recording in the journals from the related subsidiary ledgers. It is also possible to segregate the recording of such related journals as sales on account and cash receipts. In most cases the adequate segregation of accounting duties affords an opportunity to substantially increase the controls over errors without any duplication of effort.

Adequate Documents. Documents perform the function of transmitting information throughout the client's organization and between different organizations. The documents must be adequate, for only then does the auditor have reasonable assurance that all assets are properly controlled and all transactions correctly recorded. For example, if the receiving department is required to fill out receiving reports when material is received, the accounts payable department can verify whether the invoice from the vendor is correct by comparing the description and quantity of the vendor's invoice with the information on the receiving report.

The use of prenumbered documents is a useful means of cross-referencing interrelated documents and assuring that all transactions are recorded. When properly prenumbered, each document has a unique identification number. This is helpful both for precisely locating the desired document and for determining whether all the documents in a sequence have been included in the records.

Adequate documentation also includes a provision for acknowledging the performance of duties. When duties are assigned to different individuals in an organization, it is desirable that the completion of the work be formally documented. The documentation is useful as a means of fixing the responsibility with the person doing the work and as a way of informing management that the work has been done. For example, if vendors' invoices are checked for appropriate prices and correct extensions and footings, the person doing the work should initial the invoices to indicate that the work has been performed.

Protective Measures. The most important type of protective measure is the safeguarding of assets and records by using physical precautions. An example of this is the use of storerooms for inventory as a means of providing some protection against pilferage. When the storeroom is under the control of a competent employee, there is also further assurance that obsolescence is minimized. Fireproof safes and safety deposit vaults for the protection of such assets and records as currency, securities, and insurance policies are other important physical safeguards.

Mechanical protective devices are another desirable means of furnishing additional assurance that accounting information is correctly recorded and assets adequately protected. Cash registers, adding machines, and automatic data processing equipment are all potentially useful additions to the system of internal control.

Internal Verification. It is necessary to provide for a means of internally verifying the credibility of the records. The need for a system of "internal checks" arises because fraudulent and unintentional errors are always possible, regardless of the quality of the controls that have been established. It is essential that the persons performing the verification procedures be independent of those who were originally responsible for preparing the data.

The least expensive means of internal verification is the separation of duties in the manner previously discussed. For example, when the accounts receivable subsidiary records, the sales journal, and the general ledger are maintained by different people, each of these three employees automatically verifies, at least in part, the work of the others. Similarly, when the bank reconciliation is performed by a person independent of the accounting records and handling of cash, there is an opportunity for verification without incurring significant additional costs.

Some types of verification that should be performed can only be accomplished by a duplication of effort: for instance, the counting of physical inventory by two different teams to make certain that the count is correct. Another example is the practice of having an independent clerk verify the accuracy of the details on sales invoices before they are mailed to customers, as a means of preventing billing errors. Even though the cost of performing the same work more than once may seem excessive, it is sometimes the only feasible way of assuring that the results are accurate and trustworthy.

The existence of an internal audit staff is usually considered a highly effective method of verifying that financial information is correctly recorded. If the internal audit staff is independent of both the operating and the accounting departments, and if it reports directly to management, there is an excellent opportunity for extensive verification within the client's organization. Although the independent outside auditor is not permitted to use the internal audit staff to perform procedures during the independent audit, the existence of an adequate internal audit staff can greatly reduce the scope of the external audit. Furthermore, the internal auditors can prepare schedules and account analysis for the external auditor as a means of reducing the audit cost.

methods of internal control review

The initial step in determining the adequacy of the system of internal control is to develop a formal description of the client's system which is then studied by the auditor in determining the apparent strengths and weaknesses of the system. It should be kept in mind that in the early stages of the investigation of the client's procedures, the information is often obtained directly from the client. After the system as described by the client has been evaluated, tests of transactions are performed to ascertain whether the information obtained from the client is reliable. Both parts of the review are vital to the evaluation of the client's system. Its basic design must be satisfactory, but still there may be significant differences between the system as it is perceived by the client's supervisory personnel and the actual procedures in effect.

The two most common methods of obtaining information for the formal description of the internal control system are questionnaires and flowcharting.

(1) Internal Control Questionnaires. Most questionnaires are designed to make numerous inquiries in each audit area such that a "no" response indicates that a potential internal control weakness exists. Every "no" response should be considered in order to establish the seriousness of the weakness and to determine the effect that the weakness should have on the audit program.

The primary advantage of the questionnaire approach is the relative completeness of coverage of each audit area that a good instrument affords. Furthermore, a questionnaire can usually be prepared reasonably quickly at the beginning of the audit engagement. The primary disadvantage is that individual parts of the system are examined without providing an overall view of the client's system. In addition, a standard questionnaire is often inapplicable to some audit clients, especially smaller ones.

The following is a sample of the types of inquiries that are included in a questionnaire.

PROPERTY, PLANT, AND EQUIPMENT

1. Do the proper officials:
   _______ a. Authorize the purchase of all property, plant, and equipment?
   _______ b. Approve such purchases after purchase if not authorized prior to purchase?

_______ 2. Are actual costs checked against authorized costs?

_______ 3. Does a definite policy exist to aid the accounting department in distinguishing between capital items and repairs and maintenance, etc.?

4. Are plant ledgers, including records of accumulated depreciation:
   _______ a. Maintained?
   _______ b. Reviewed periodically?
   _______ c. Occasionally checked by actual physical inventories of the assets?
   _______ d. Balanced regularly to the control accounts?
   _______ e. Maintained for fully depreciated assets?

_______ 5. Are all pieces of equipment marked or tagged with an identifying number of the company corresponding with the identifying number shown in the plant ledger?

_______ 6. Do sales of excess and scrapped equipment require specific authorization by proper officials?

7. Do routine procedures provide for prompt and accurate reporting to the accounting department of:
   _______ a. Sales of equipment?
   _______ b. All disposals and retirements of property, plant, and equipment?

8. Are tools and small equipment:
   _______ a. Kept in special locations?
   _______ b. Accountable for by a few specific employees? [7]

[7] American Institute of Certified Public Accountants, *Case Studies in Internal Control No. 2,* "The Machine Manufacturing Company" (New York: American Institute of Certified Public Accountants, 1950), p. 33.

(2) Flowcharting. Flowcharting a client's internal control system is a symbolic diagrammatic representation of the client's documents and their sequential flow in the organization. An adequate flowchart shows the origin of each document and record in the system, the subsequent processing, and the final disposition of any document or record included in the chart. In addition, it is possible to show the separation of duties (by keeping each major function separated in the diagram) as well as the authorizations, approvals, and verifications that take place within the organization.

Flowcharting is advantageous primarily because it provides an opportunity for a concise overview of the client's system, which is useful for the auditor in his evaluation. Not only does the flowchart aid in identifying inadequacies by facilitating a clear understanding of how the system operates, similarly, it affords audit supervisors a frame of reference for evaluating the results.

The primary shortcoming of flowcharting in such evaluation is that it does not deal with all aspects of internal control. Since flowcharting is limited to furnishing information about documents and their flow, the responsibility for attention to protective controls, such as storerooms, must be placed elsewhere. Furthermore, flowcharts generally fail to show whether the documents themselves are adequate. For example, a flowchart generally does not state whether the documents in use provide space for acknowledging performance or are prenumbered.

Standard flowcharting symbols have been developed by the American National Standards Institute (formerly the United States of America Standards Institute) as a means of encouraging more uniformity in their use. The most important symbols and their meanings are as follows:

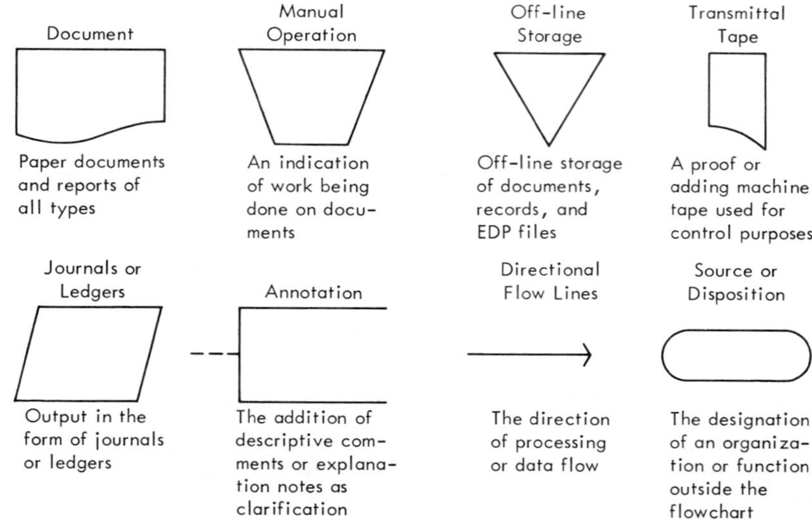

In addition, special symbols are used in flowcharting EDP systems. The most important of these are:

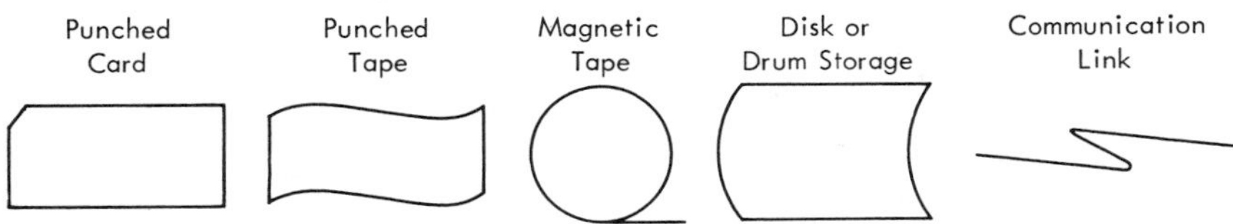

There are several rules that should be followed in developing flowcharts for reviewing internal control:

1. The flowchart should show the source and ultimate disposition of every document, tape, or record that is included in the flowchart.

2. Since flowcharts are generally read downward or to the right, directional flow lines are necessary only when the chart should be read upward or to the left.

3. The information included on the flowchart should be sufficiently self-explanatory to preclude the need to refer to supplementary data.

A brief flowcharting illustration will be useful at this point. Figure 1 furnishes a narrative description and a flowchart of the sales, billing, and shipping departments of a small wholesale company. (Accounting is excluded for purposes of simplification.)

The sales department prepares a six-part sales invoice form from the customer's order. The sales orders are filed alphabetically by customer. Part 2 of the invoice is sent to the credit department as a credit slip for approval. The remaining parts are held until credit is approved. After the credit is approved, the credit slip is returned to sales and filed with the customer's order. Parts 1 (sales invoice) and 3 (ledger) are then sent to billing; part 4 (packing slip) and part 5 (shipping order) are sent to shipping; and part 6 is sent to the customer as acknowledgment of the order.

Shipping selects the items for shipment and notes them on the shipping order. The packing slip is sent to the customer with the goods and the shipping order is sent to billing.

Billing enters the shipped items marked on the shipping order on the sales invoice and ledger copy, makes extensions and checks them, compares the prices with the price list, and runs a tape of the amounts on the ledger copy. The shipping order is then filed numerically. The sales invoice is sent to the customer and the ledger copy and the tape are sent to accounting.

FIGURE I

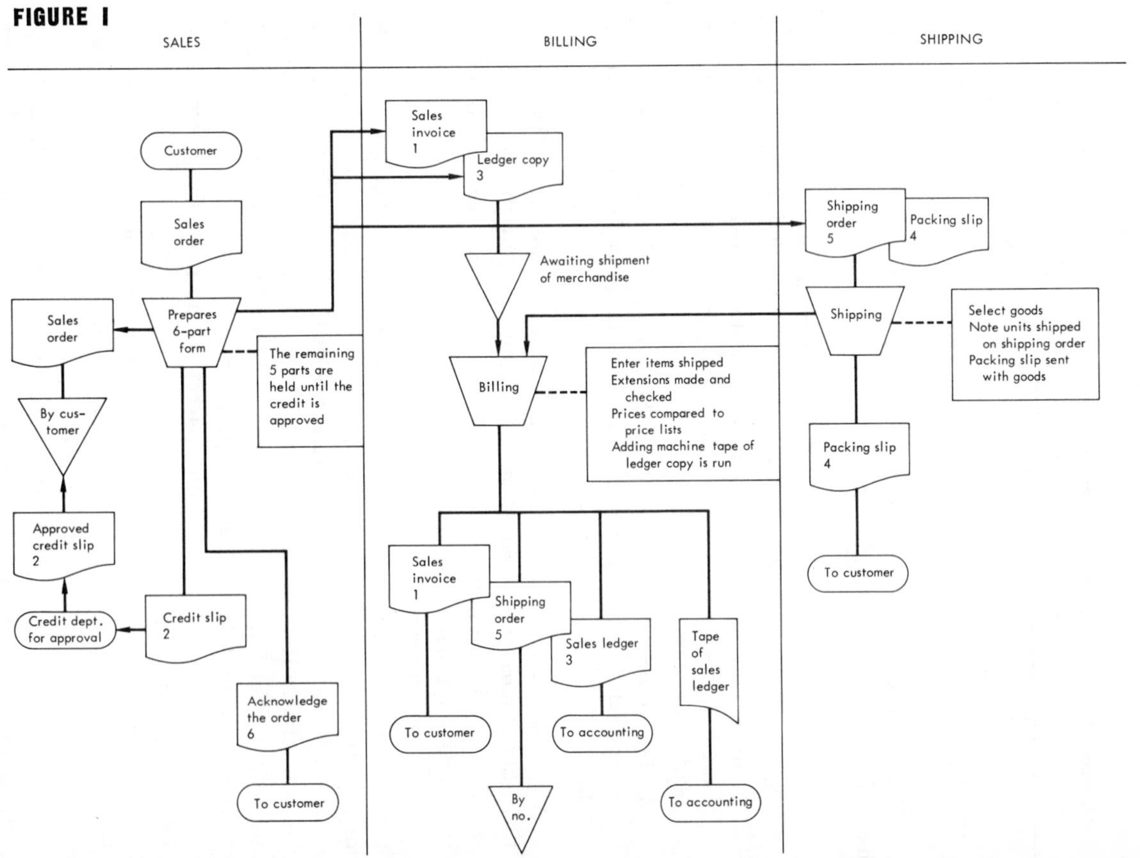
SALES
BILLING
SHIPPING
Customer
Sales order
Prepares 6-part form
Sales order
By cus-tomer
Approved credit slip 2
Credit dept. for approval
Credit slip 2
The remaining 5 parts are held until the credit is approved
Acknowledge the order 6
To customer
Sales invoice 1
Ledger copy 3
Awaiting shipment of merchandise
Billing
Enter items shipped
Extensions made and checked
Prices compared to price lists
Adding machine tape of ledger copy is run
Sales invoice 1
Shipping order 5
Sales ledger 3
Tape of sales ledger
To customer
By no.
To accounting
To accounting
Shipping order 5
Packing slip 4
Shipping
Select goods
Note units shipped on shipping order
Packing slip sent with goods
Packing slip 4
To customer

Basic Objectives of Evidence Accumulation

Having evaluated internal control as it is described by management, the auditor must then satisfy himself (a) that the system actually functions that way and (b) that the balances and other disclosures in the financial statements are fairly stated. This is accomplished by performing tests of transactions and direct tests of balances. As a means of determining the appropriate audit tests for a given set of circumstances, it is necessary for the candidate to understand (a) the basic objectives of each audit area with which the auditor is dealing, (b) the types of audit evidence that are available to satisfy the objectives, and (c) the factors or circumstances of the audit that determine which evidence should be accumulated. Questions dealing with these three related subjects arise indirectly whenever a candidate is required to prepare an audit program, but it is also common to find direct questions in the examination about each of these subjects. The basic objectives are discussed in detail in this section, and the other two topics are covered in the following two sections.

A thorough understanding of the objectives of each audit area is essential to the development of adequate audit programs. If the candidate clearly understands the audit objectives, it is relatively easy to develop a tailor-made audit program that takes into account the available evidence and the special circumstances existing in the audit. The basic objectives set forth in this section are specifically designed to be used by the candidate in developing audit programs. If the relevant procedures for any given audit area are carefully associated with each of the basic objectives, the auditor will have a satisfactory program when the procedures are combined. The basic objectives are summarized here and discussed in detail immediately following the summary:

1. Existence.

    a. The transactions and amounts that are included in the records are valid.

    b. The transactions and amounts that should be included in the records are actually recorded.

2. Ownership of assets.

    a. The recorded assets are owned.

    b. The owned assets are recorded.

3. Valuation. The recorded transactions and subsidiary account balances are stated at the correct dollar amount.

4. Classification. The recorded transactions and subsidiary account balances are properly classified.

5. Cut-off. The transactions are recorded in the proper period.

6. Mechanical accuracy. The footings, extensions, and transfers of information are correct.

7. Overall reasonableness. The balance in the account being considered appears to be reasonably correct.

8. Disclosure. The account being verified is properly disclosed on the financial statements.

(1) Existence. This objective is concerned first with assuring that the journals and subsidiary ledgers reflect only transactions and balances that actually resulted from the client's operations and second with making certain that all transactions that actually occurred and all balances that actually exist were included in the records. The first part of the objective deals with the overstatement of accounts, the second with their understatement. Both parts of the objective are important to the auditor, but their relative importance depends on the type of account being verified. When the auditor is verifying assets or revenue accounts, he is generally more concerned with overstatement, whereas he usually cares more about understatement of liabilities, expenses, and owners' equity. This attitude prevails because of the existence of the doctrine of conservatism: the notion that it is more important to avoid the overstatement of income and owners' equity than to avoid their understatement.

The application of specific procedures to the existence objective depends on the part of the objective under consideration. As an illustration, if the auditor wishes to determine whether all recorded sales were actually shipped to customers, he could trace a sample of entries recorded in the sales journal to their related shipping documents to assure himself that a valid shipping document exists for each recorded sale. On the other hand, if he wonders whether all actual shipments have been recorded as sales, the auditor could trace selected shipping documents directly to the sales journal to make certain that each shipment was included as a sale. In most cases the auditor is interested in both parts of the objective.

(2) Ownership of Assets. It is important for the auditor to distinguish between the physical presence of assets and their ownership. Some assets that are physically present may not be owned by the client in the sense that ownership is defined by generally accepted accounting principles. Similarly, it is possible that the client owns assets that are not physically located on his premises. Examples of existence without ownership are rented equipment and consignment inventory; examples of ownership outside the premises include inventory stored at a separate location or out on consignment.

In most cases, the ownership of assets is consistent with the passage of the title. For example, the appropriate timing for recording purchased inventory is when title passes. As a result, some purchases are properly recorded on the date of the shipment by the vendor and others on the date of the receipt of the merchandise, depending upon whether the merchandise was shipped F.O.B. origin or F.O.B. destination. On the other hand, there are exceptions to the general rule of recording assets as of the date title passes. As an example, to determine whether leased equipment should be recorded as an asset, the auditor must consult the conditions specified in Accounting Principles Board Opinion No. 5 rather than title passage alone. Ascertaining whether an asset is owned at a given date in a particular set of circumstances requires a knowledge of the facts in the case and a thorough understanding of generally accepted accounting principles.

(3) Valuation. Valuation provides reasonable assurance that each transaction and each subsidiary account balance are recorded at the proper dollar value. For example, in analyzing fixed asset transactions, the auditor would accomplish this objective in part by comparing the recorded amounts with supporting documents to ascertain whether the client correctly recorded such things as trade-ins, freight, installation, and cash discounts. Similarly, in testing the pricing of inventory the auditor must determine whether the individual items have been recorded at the lower of cost or market using LIFO (last-in, first-out), FIFO (first-in, first-out) or another acceptable cost method. The auditor's assurance that generally accepted accounting principles were applied on a basis consistent with that of the preceding year is an especially important facet of this objective.

In fulfilling the valuation objective for asset accounts, realizable value is an important factor in determining whether the account balance is fairly stated. This requires, for example, consideration of the collectibility of accounts receivable, the current market value of marketable securities, and the replacement cost and possible obsolescence of inventories.

(4) Classification. It is important to verify that recorded information is properly classified into the general categories of assets, liabilities, owners' equity, revenue, and expense; but the classification objective also concerns the specific classification within each of these general categories. For example, in the audit of fixed assets, the auditor tests to make certain that the recorded additions were actually capital improvements rather than repairs, rentals, or similar expenses. Similarly, he verifies that expenses for such classifications as repairs and supplies do not include transactions properly classified as capital improvements. In addition, it is necessary to verify that the fixed assets have been

correctly described with respect to the type of permanent asset, such as machinery, office equipment, or building. The last step is important because the classification can affect the depreciation expense as well as the disclosure of information on the financial statements.

(5) Cut-off. In fulfilling this objective, the auditor is ascertaining that the transactions of the current period were also recorded in the current period and the transactions of the previous or subsequent periods were not included in the current period's records. An example of this in the audit of the cut-off of accounts payable is the review of the recorded transactions in the accounts payable journal for the last few days of the current year, to determine whether any transactions that are appropriately associated with the subsequent period are erroneously recorded in the current period. Similarly, the auditor should review the transactions recorded in the first few days of the subsequent period, as well as invoices unpaid at the time of the audit, to make certain that there are no transactions that should be included in the records of the current period.

In applying procedures to fulfill this objective, it is essential that the auditor understand the proper period to which a particular transaction belongs. Generally accepted accounting principles and consistency with the preceding period both play an important role in cut-off.

(6) Mechanical Accuracy. This objective actually encompasses two subobjectives. First, the auditor must be reasonably confident of the client's arithmetical accuracy, including a wide variety of procedures such as correct extension of sales invoices and inventory, accurate footing of journals and trial balances, and proper calculation of depreciation expense and prepaid expenses. Second, the auditor wants to be certain that, when the same information is included in more than one place—such as in journals, ledgers, and subsidiary ledgers—it is recorded at the same amount each time. For example, the auditor should make limited tests to ascertain that the information included in the sales journal has been correctly included in the subsidiary accounts receivable ledger and correctly summarized in the general ledger. Similarly, the detail of the names and balances on the accounts receivable trial balance should be the same as that included on the subsidiary ledger, and the total should tie out to the general ledger. Even though both the recalculation of footings and extensions and the retracing of the detail or totals from one place to another are mechanical tasks, the auditor must verify their reliability on a test basis because there is always the possibility of fraud or unintentional errors.

(7) Overall Reasonableness. It is essential for auditors to avoid becoming so engrossed in testing the details of an account balance that

they fail to evaluate whether the total in the account is reasonable, considering the circumstances of the audit. In auditing, it is necessary to limit the testing to a sample because of the prohibitive cost of auditing the entire population. As a result, the auditor takes a risk that the sample is not representative of the population. In addition, some errors, such as the intentional or unintentional duplication or omission of amounts in the original recording processes are often difficult to discover even when extensive tests are performed. Testing the overall reasonableness of the balance is a useful supplement to the detailed procedures as a means of obtaining an indication of a possible material misstatement of a balance. There are a large number of tests the auditor can use to test for overall reasonableness; for example, the calculation of ratios and their comparison to the ratios from previous years and industry standards. The comparison of the absolute account balances with previous years' balances may also indicate the possibility of a material misstatement or misclassification in an account. The scanning of ledgers and journals for unusual amounts is also a desirable overall test.

(8) Disclosure. After an account balance has been verified, it is necessary to learn whether the necessary information is properly included in the financial statements. Disclosure involves consideration of the appropriate combination of the account being verified with other accounts, the proper title, the correct description, and the inclusion of the necessary parenthetical statements or footnotes. As an illustration, after the auditor has satisfied himself that the trial balance amount and classification of accounts receivable from officers and directors are correct, he must decide whether the amount is sufficiently material to require separate disclosure on the financial statements. If separate disclosure is deemed necessary, the auditor must decide whether the description is adequate, and he has to consider the possible need for a footnote explaining the composition of the account or the nature of any collateral that has been pledged.

Since an understanding of the basic objectives is critical in the development of adequate audit programs, the remainder of this section is devoted to the application of the foregoing objectives to specific audit areas. A complete understanding of the examples should assist the candidate in developing programs in other audit areas.

basic objectives of tests of transactions

Tests of transaction procedures for any audit area are performed in order to determine the adequacy of the system of internal control. As a means of fulfilling this overall objective, the detailed objectives are useful both as a guide to understanding what the auditor is trying to accomplish and as an aid in developing audit programs. In order to better concentrate on the detailed objectives in transactions testing, we shall use the tests of sales transactions for a client that sells merchandise as an illustration. Similar objectives apply to cash disbursements, purchases, and cash receipts.

(1) Existence. First, do the recorded sales reflect actual merchandise shipments? This objective is satisfied by selecting transactions recorded in the sales journal and ascertaining whether there are valid shipping documents and similar documents to support each transaction in the sample. Second, are all current-period merchandise shipments recorded as sales? In fulfilling this objective, the auditor usually traces a sample of shipping documents to the sales journal to find out if they have all been recorded.

(2) Ownership of Assets. The auditor reviews sales transactions for ownership to satisfy himself that the recorded sales actually represent valid title transfers rather than consignment shipments, temporary storage, or similar shipments that do not represent a change of ownership.

(3) Valuation. By sampling, the auditor can ascertain how reliable the system is with respect to the correct valuation of individual sales transactions. For example, he must see that the quantity shipped is the same as the quantity billed, that the price charged is correct, that the freight and insurance charges are correct, and that the extensions and footing are accurate. The auditor can verify valuation by tracing from duplicate sales invoices to various documents, such as shipping documents for the quantity shipped, and price lists for the proper selling price. It is also necessary to test the extensions and footings of the documents for mechanical accuracy.

(4) Classification. The purpose of the classification objective is to determine that recorded sales do not include such transactions as the disposal of permanent assets. The auditor is also concerned with the proper classification between such categories as cash and account sales, wholesale and retail sales, and sales to customers and officers.

(5) Cut-off. The audit of the cut-off for sales is usually performed only at the end of the period. The purpose of sales cut-off tests is to determine whether all shipments made before the end of the period were included in sales and all those made after the end of the period were

excluded from the current period's sales. A closely related objective is to establish that no merchandise that is included in the current year's inventory has also been included in sales, because this would mean that assets had been double counted. Similarly, the auditor wants to be sure that any merchandise not included in year-end inventory has been recorded as a current-period sale. If the auditor clearly understands the objectives to be accomplished, it is fairly easy to reason out the proper procedure to use in a specific set of circumstances.

(6) Mechanical Accuracy. This objective is designed to ensure the adequate testing of any mechanical aspect of sales that has not been verified as part of one of the foregoing objectives. Fulfilling this objective includes footing and crossfooting the sales journal and testing the consistency between the information in the sales journal, the accounts receivable ledgers, and the general ledger accounts, as well as testing the mechanical accuracy of any documents connected with sales not verified as a part of the other objectives.

(7) Overall Reasonableness. The auditor performs tests of overall reasonableness for sales transactions to look for any unusual transactions that may indicate a misstatement of sales. For example, the auditor should review the sales journal for unusually large sales transactions, unusual customers, or misclassifications. Any unusual transactions should be investigated in detail. The primary overall testing is done as a part of the direct tests of assets, liabilities, and income statement accounts. In the case of sales, this would include direct tests of accounts receivable and sales.

If the candidate carefully associates the appropriate specific audit procedures with each of the above-stated objectives in a specific set of circumstances involving sales transactions, the combined procedures should result in a satisfactory audit program for testing the internal controls over sales. Although some procedures will be used to satisfy more than one objective, these duplications can be eliminated when the procedures are combined into an overall audit program.

It should be noted in the preceding application that the tests were restricted to testing the internal control in sales. If the auditor wants to test the system for sales returns and allowances, he must consider each of the objectives separately for that account. Similarly, when the auditor is concerned about the ending balance in sales, it is necessary to perform direct tests of the sales balance as well as the tests of transactions. We shall deal with direct tests of income statement accounts shortly. The conclusion reached about the tests of sales are also applicable to other audit areas.

basic objectives of direct tests of assets and liabilities

The overall objective of performing direct tests of year-end balances for any audit area is to establish whether the balance is fairly stated. As in transactions testing, the detailed objectives are useful both as a guide to understanding what the auditor is trying to accomplish and as an aid in developing audit programs. Accounts receivable serve to illustrate the use of these objectives in the verification of asset and liability accounts. It also demonstrates the interrelations between transactions tests and direct tests of balances. (We assume that the auditor has a listing of the client's accounts receivable as a starting point for his examination.)

(1) Existence. The first part of the existence objective is to verify that all recorded accounts receivable are valid assets; then it is necessary to determine that all the accounts receivable have been recorded. It should be clear to the candidate that there is usually more concern about the first objective in the audit of assets because of the danger that they will be overstated. The first part of the objective can generally be satisfied by the confirmation of account balances. The tests of transactions for sales also aid in furnishing reasonable assurance that accounts receivable are not overstated. Since it is difficult to uncover omitted transactions by any direct tests of accounts, the auditor must rely to some degree on the client's system of internal control, which is reviewed during the tests of transactions, to fulfill the second part of the objective.

(2) Valuation. The correct valuation of the individual balances on the accounts receivable trial balance is accomplished by the confirmation of accounts receivable, with special emphasis on the accounts that are most likely to contain material errors, such as those with large balances, disputed amounts, and noncurrent balances. The tests of transactions in sales also assists in establishing the proper valuation of the account balances.

A second aspect of the valuation of accounts receivable is determining whether the overall balance is stated at realizable value. This requires the auditor to satisfy himself that the allowance for uncollectible accounts is reasonably stated.

(3) Classification. That the individual accounts receivable are actually short-term rather than notes, loans, or noncurrent assets may be verified via classification. The classification of receivables generally causes few problems if an adequate test of transactions has been performed.

(4) Cut-off. The cut-offs for sales and accounts receivable are identical and are accomplished at the same time. Since the objectives were discussed as a part of the test of sales, they are not repeated here.

(5) Mechanical Accuracy. Testing accuracy of balance sheet accounts includes footing the client's schedules and lists and tracing the balances to the subsidiary ledger and general ledger for correspondence. For accounts receivable, this entails footing the trial balance, tracing the total to the general ledger, and tracing the detail to the subsidiary ledgers.

(6) Overall Reasonableness. A great deal of skill is needed to apply overall reasonableness tests because the interpretation of the results is a highly subjective matter. For accounts receivable, the auditor should compare the individual balances of the current year with those of previous years, compute accounts receivable as a percentage of total current assets, and perform other similar tests.

(7) Disclosure. The objective of disclosure for accounts receivable and all other balance sheet accounts is to make certain that the balance is correctly set forth on the financial statements and properly described in the body and footnotes of the statements.

basic objectives of direct tests of owners' equity accounts

Although the basic objectives used for assets and liabilities is partially applicable to owners' equity accounts, the principal responsibility in verifying those accounts concerns their conformity with legal requirements. The requirements include those imposed by the corporation charter, the articles of incorporation, and the by-laws, and they disclose such information as the authorized number of shares and the par value of the stock. Verification also requires consideration of legal restrictions on capital transactions from legal contracts such as bond indenture agreements and stock option plans. Closely related to legal requirements are the actions by the board of directors that require proper accounting treatment of owners' equity, such as the declaration of cash and stock dividends and the appropriation of retained earnings. Since the fair presentation of financial statements requires adequate disclosure of any legal restrictions on owners' equity (e.g., on the payment of dividends), it is essential that the auditor have knowledge of any existing restrictions and that he assure himself of their adequate disclosure.

basic objectives of direct tests of income statement accounts

If the auditor has performed adequate tests of transactions and has sufficiently tested the asset and liability accounts, most of the income statement account balances will have been satisfactorily verified as a part of these tests. For example, if the auditor tests sales and sales returns and allowances transactions and verifies the accounts receivable balance, relatively little additional direct testing is necessary. The only additional verification that should be performed in most cases is testing the overall reasonableness of the balance by the use of comparison and ratios and by making certain that there is adequate disclosure of the balance on the financial statements.

There are a few income statement accounts that the auditor should test in detail even though adequate tests of transactions and balance sheet accounts have been completed. The first type of account requiring additional detailed testing is any one that is not verified as a part of transactions testing. Examples of this are amortization and depreciation accounts. Audit procedures for testing accounts of this type can be developed by using the basic objectives previously enumerated. A second type of income statement account that may require additional testing is any one which the auditor believes has such a high expectation of error that the general transactions testing would not be sufficient. The most likely examples are accounts such as repair and maintenance, miscellaneous income and expense, and rental expense. The auditor is primarily concerned about errors in classification for these accounts, so he generally restricts the additional verification to classification tests and tests of the overall reasonableness of the balance.

Types of Audit Evidence

In developing audit programs it is necessary to understand the basic objectives of the audit area under consideration, but it is equally important to have a thorough knowledge of the different types of evidence that are available to satisfy the objectives. The CPA examination commonly includes direct questions about certain aspects of one or more of the types of audit evidence, and every examination requires a knowledge of evidence when questions are asked requiring audit programs.

In general terms, evidence in auditing can be defined as information that is used to determine whether the overall financial statements or individual parts of the statements are fairly presented in accordance with generally accepted accounting principles. To decide what evidence should be accumulated in a given set of circumstances, we need to understand the alternative types of evidence.

physical examination

Physical examination is the inspection or count by the auditor of any tangible asset. This type of evidence is most often associated with inventory and cash, but it is also applicable to the verification of securities, notes receivable, and tangible fixed assets. The distinction between the physical examination of assets, such as marketable securities and cash, and the examination of documents, such as canceled checks and sales documents, is well defined for auditing purposes. If the object being examined has no inherent value, such as a sales invoice, it is called documentation or vouching. For example, before a check is signed it is a document; but after it is signed, it becomes an asset. When the check is canceled it becomes a document again. In the technical sense, physical examination of the check can only occur while the check is an asset.

Physical examination, which is a direct means of verifying that an asset actually exists, is regarded as one of the most reliable and useful types of audit evidence whenever it is applicable. In most cases, physical examination is an objective means of determining both the count and description of the asset. If the auditor is qualified to judge qualitative factors, it is also a useful method for determining the asset's condition or quality. On the other hand, physical examination is not sufficient evidence to verify that existing assets are owned by the client and, in many cases, the auditor is not qualified to judge such qualitative factors as obsolescence or authenticity.

When physical examination is applicable and feasible, it is highly reliable and therefore should normally be used as evidence. In the verification of inventory, the AICPA requires that the auditor physically examine inventory when inventory is material if an unqualified auditor's opinion is to be given. This is clearly stated in *Statement on Auditing Procedure No. 43:*

> When inventory quantities are determined solely by means of a physical count, and all counts are made as of the balance sheet date or as of a single date within a reasonable time before or after the balance sheet date, it is ordinarily necessary for the independent auditor to be present at the time of count and, by suitable observation, tests and inquiries, satisfy himself respecting the effectiveness of the methods of inventory-taking and the measure of reliance which may be placed upon the client's representations about the quantities and physical condition of the inventories.[8]

[8] American Institute of Certified Public Accountants, *Statements on Auditing Procedure No. 43* (New York: American Institute of Certified Public Accountants, 1970), pp. 81–82.

When the auditor is not on hand during the client's taking of the physical inventory, it is acceptable for the auditor to perform test counts at a different date if the client has adequate perpetual records. It is essential, however, that the auditor perform test counts at some time during the audit period.

The requirement of physical examination of inventory is not applicable in the case of inventory in a public warehouse. The AICPA position on inventory stored in a public warehouse is summarized in *Statements on Auditing Procedure No. 37* as follows:

> In the case of inventories, which in the ordinary course of business are in the hands of public warehouses or other outside custodians, direct confirmation in writing from the custodians is acceptable provided that where the amount involved represents a significant proportion of the current assets or the total assets, supplemental inquiries are made to satisfy the independent auditor as to the bona fides of the situation.[9]

The Committee on Auditing Procedure recommends that the supplemental inquiries include the following steps, to the extent that the auditor considers them necessary in the circumstances:

> 1. Discussion with the owner as to the owner's control procedures in investigating the warehouseman, and tests of related evidential matter.
> 2. Review of the owner's control procedures concerning performance of the warehouseman, and tests of related evidential matter.
> 3. Observation of physical counts of the goods, wherever practicable and reasonable.
> 4. Where warehouse receipts have been pledged as collateral, confirmation on a test basis, where appropriate, from lenders as to pertinent details of the pledged receipts.[10]

When dealing with assets that are susceptible to examination or count, the auditor is not responsible for the initial determination of the quantity or amount. It has been well established that the responsibility for taking the physical counts and providing adequate records of the results rests solely with management. The auditor's objective and responsibility in physical examination is to determine whether the client's methods of taking the physical count, and the records that result from the count, will lead to fairly presented statements. In fulfilling this duty, the auditor reviews and observes the client's procedures for taking counts, observes the counting, and takes limited test counts himself. Regardless

[9] American Institute of Certified Public Accountants, *Statements on Auditing Procedure No. 37* (New York: American Institute of Certified Public Accountants, 1966), p. 38.

[10] *Ibid.*, pp. 50–51.

of whether the auditor is verifying inventories, securities, cash on hand, or similar tangible assets, his objective is limited to establishing the reliability of the client's representations about those assets.

As a part of establishing the reasonableness of the client's representations about the existence of tangible assets, it is essential, especially in inventory, that the auditor determine the adequacy of the client's planning and preparation for making the counts. If the client adequately plans and controls the taking of the inventory, it is likely that the results will be accurate. The auditor's review of the advance planning and controls should include consideration of the adequacy of the initial and second-count procedures, the familiarity of the personnel performing the counts with the merchandise they are counting, the orderliness of the material being counted, the segregation of obsolete and non-owned inventory, the use of adequate prenumbered tags or similar count forms, and to cut-off procedures employed.

Whenever feasible, the auditor should be on hand to observe the personnel while they are taking the physical inventory. This enables him to learn whether the client is adhering to the prescribed plan, but more important, it facilitates corrective action early in the physical count if the procedures appear to be inadequate. For example, if the procedures call for recounts of the inventory by a separate count team to assure the accuracy of the counts, the auditor can observe whether the second team actually recounts the inventory. If the second counts are not being performed, the client should be requested to take corrective action. As a part of observing the client's counting procedures, the auditor should observe that (a) all inventory items that exist are included on tags or count sheets, (b) the inventory that is included on the tags or count sheets actually exists, and (c) the information stated on the tags or sheets is correct with respect to description and count.

Although it is management's responsibility rather than the auditor's to determine that inventory is correctly counted and valued, the auditor should be alert to the possibility of obsolete inventory and inaccurate information about its quality. Obsolescence can normally be discovered by examining the inventory for rust or damage, asking employees about its age and condition, and reviewing the perpetual records for turnover; but it is often difficult to determine the quality of some assets, such as diamonds or chemicals. If assets whose evaluation requires a high degree of technical competence represent a material dollar amount, the auditor should obtain independent technical assistance.

While the auditor is performing the physical examination procedures, it is essential that control be maintained over the flow of assets that occurs during the counting. In inventory, it is desirable that no assets be added or removed until all counts have been completed; this precaution will serve to establish an accurate cut-off and to prevent a possible transfer of inventory to a different location for intentional or unintentional duplicate counting. If an inventory movement must take place, the auditor should make a record for subsequent follow-up of all receipts and disposals of merchandise, indicating whether they have been included or excluded from inventory. In the audit of cash or securities, it is similarly important that all the assets be counted at the same time in order to prevent the intentional shift of an asset from one location to another to conceal a shortage. When simultaneous counting is not possible, the auditor should use such measures as sealed-count boxes or vaults to prevent a shifting of the assets.

Since physical examination procedures are normally performed prior to the rest of the year-end audit procedures, it is important that the auditor control the results of the client's counts to ensure that they are properly used in the preparation of the financial statements. It does little good for the auditor to review the client's counting procedures and test the reliability of the counts if he cannot be confident that the results of the physical count are used in the final preparation of the financial statements. For assets such as notes receivable, securities, and cash, this causes few problems, for the client normally provides the auditor with a complete listing of the quantity and description of the asset. After the auditor verifies that the list is a reliable representation of the actual assets on hand, he maintains control of the list in his working papers for the subsequent comparison with the work sheets or compilation that the client uses for the final asset valuation. It is seldom feasible for the auditor to keep a copy of the tags used for counting inventory because of the large volume of items involved. To maintain control of the inventory counts, the auditor uses two procedures. He documents in his working papers the tag numbers that the client used in the physical count, and he records a sample of the counts and descriptions from selected tags. The record of the tag numbers is used to verify that the final inventory compilation includes all the tags contained in the physical count but no additional ones. The records of the counts and descriptions are used to test whether the client has intentionally or unintentionally changed the information on the tags after the auditor has left the premises. If count sheets are used rather than tags, similar procedures must be carried out unless the client prepares a duplicate copy of the count sheets for the auditor.

An essential part of the physical examination of inventory is ascertaining that the inventory cut-off is adequate at the end of the year for both sales and purchases. An adequate cut-off of inventory relative to sales requires that any shipment of merchandise that has been recorded as a current-period sale must be excluded from inventory, whereas merchandise that has not been sold and therefore is excluded from sales must be included in the count. Similarly, if the inventory for purchases is included in the physical count, it must also be recorded as a current-period purchase. The auditor should review and test the client's procedures in both receiving and shipping in order to judge the adequacy of the cut-off procedures. The working papers should include a record of the receiving report numbers of the most recent receipts of inventory included in the physical inventory. This permits subsequent determination of the adequacy of purchase cut-off procedures. Similar methods should be followed for sales.

confirmation

Confirmation is a term in auditing that describes the receipt of a written response from an independent third party verifying the accuracy of information that was requested by the auditor. Confirmations are a highly regarded and often-used type of evidence because they come from a source independent of the client. On the other hand, confirmations are a relatively costly type of evidence to the auditor, and they cause some inconvenience to the persons receiving the information request. Therefore, they are not used in every instance in which they are applicable. The determination of when they should be used depends on the reliability needs of the situation as well as the alternative evidence available for the auditor's use. Traditionally, confirmations are not used for tests of transactions because the auditor can use documents to determine the adequacy of the client's system of recording information. Similarly, confirmations are seldom used in the audit of fixed asset additions because these can be adequately verified via documentation and physical observation.

The confirmation of a representative sample of accounts receivable, either during or after the period under audit, is required by generally accepted auditing procedures whenever it is practical and reasonable to do so. This requirement is included because accounts receivable usually represent a material balance on the financial statements, and confirmations are the most reliable means of verifying the fairness of the balance. The effect on the audit report when accounts receivable are not confirmed is discussed in the section on audit reports.

Although the confirmation of balances is not required for any account other than accounts receivable, the procedure is useful to verify many types of information. Some of the frequently confirmed assets in addition to accounts receivable are cash in the bank, notes receivable, inventory held in public warehouses, consigned inventory, and the cash surrender value of life insurance. Similarly, liabilities such as accounts and notes payable, advances from customers, and mortgages and bonds payable, are susceptible to confirmation. The auditor can also use confirmations to verify information that does not appear directly in the body of the financial statements. Examples of this type of confirmation include insurance coverage, contingent liabilities, bond indenture agreements, and collateral held by creditors.

For many types of information, the confirmation automatically aids in testing detailed transactions even though the primary objective may be to directly verify a balance sheet amount. For example, in confirming accounts receivable, a discrepancy in a confirmed balance may indicate that the system of internal control is not functioning properly.

It is essential that the auditor's objectives be completely understood before confirmations are prepared. In most cases the objectives vary in accordance with the type of information being confirmed. For example, when confirmations are sent to banks, the auditor is concerned with more than just verifying the balance in an account that is included on the trial balance. He also wants to know whether there are any restrictions on the account or if the client has an unrecorded account in the bank. Since banks provide multiple services, the auditor also wants to verify the existence of and the balance in notes or similar liabilities, collateral on loans, and possible contingent liabilities for discounted notes. As a result of these multiple objectives, most auditors use a standard bank confirmation request that covers the information just listed. Similarly, when confirmation requests are sent to the client's attorneys, the primary concern is the determination and valuation of possible lawsuits that may exist against the client. Since any one lawsuit may be highly material in amount, a confirmation requesting information about any litigation or other dispute should be sent to each attorney with whom the client does business. When confirming accounts receivable, the objectives of the auditor are different from those that apply when he is confirming accounts payable; and therefore different types of accounts are selected for confirmation. In verifying accounts receivable, the auditor's primary concern is whether the accounts receivable balance is overstated. As a result, when individual accounts are selected for verification, the auditor should put greater emphasis on large and noncurrent balances than on small, current balances. On the other hand, when accounts payable are confirmed, the auditor usually includes in the sample some zero balances and small active accounts because the emphasis is on avoiding possible understatement of the balance.

In order to be considered reliable evidence, confirmations must be controlled by the auditor from the time of their preparation until they are returned to the auditor. If the client prepares the confirmation, performs the mailing, or receives the responses, the confirmation comes under his own control; hence independence is lost, and the reliability of the evidence is reduced. The auditor should either prepare the confirmation request himself or check it after it has been prepared by the client. The auditor must also control the mailing to prevent the elimination or alteration of selected confirmation requests. Control over the receipt of the confirmation returns is accomplished by having the response directed to the auditor's office rather than to the client's. This is necessary as a means of preventing the destruction or alteration of a returned confirmation. Also, having the return address, the auditor's office will assure that all undelivered mail is returned directly to the auditor.

When responses to the sample of confirmation requests mailed are not received on the first request, the auditor must carry out follow-up procedures. He should send second and eventually third requests if a confirmation of important information is not received in a reasonable time period. If the auditor believes a response is critically important, a telephone call or a registered letter is appropriate. For some accounts, such as accounts receivable or payable, a 100% response is neither common nor necessary. When positive confirmations of the client's accounts receivable are not received from those customers who choose not to be cooperative or who are unable to confirm the account balances because of the set-up of their accounting systems, the auditor must resort to different methods of verifying the balance. He may, for example, examine shipping documents, customer orders, and cash remittance advices. The use of these other methods of verifying an accounts receivable balance is commonly referred to as "alternative procedures."

When there is a discrepancy between the results of the confirmation and the information stated on the client's records, the auditor must determine the cause and the implication of the difference. This requires comparing each confirmation received from the respondent with the information that is being confirmed and a reconciliation of any differences. The auditor must consider the effect of each client error on the financial statements. If there is a substantial number of errors, it may be necessary to confirm additional accounts to determine if the errors are widespread.

In confirming accounts receivable, the auditor can use positive confirmations, negative confirmations, or both. A positive confirmation requests that the debtor reply to the inquiry regardless of whether the balance is correct or incorrect, whereas a negative confirmation asks the debtor to reply only if his records disagree with the balance being confirmed. A positive confirmation is more reliable evidence because the auditor can perform follow-up or alternative procedures if a response is not received from the debtor. With the negative confirmation, on the other hand, failure to reply must be regarded as a correct response, even though the client may have ignored the confirmation.

Offsetting the reliability disadvantage, negative confirmations are less expensive to send than positives, and thus more of them can be distributed for the same total cost. The determination of which type of confirmation to be sent is an auditor's decision, and it should be based on the facts in the audit. Positive confirmations are generally used for large accounts or those in which there is a high probability of error, such as old or disputed ones. Similarly, positive confirmations are normally used when the internal control system is considered inadequate or when the auditor feels that the customer would not otherwise respond to the request. Negatives are considered acceptable when there is a large number of accounts, none of which is by itself material, and when the system of internal control is considered adequate. It is also common to combine the two methods by using positives for large and noncurrent balances and negatives for some or all of the other accounts.

As with the physical examination of inventory, it is acceptable to confirm accounts receivable at a time other than year end if the system of internal control is considered adequate. When confirmations are performed during the period or after the end of the period, it is necessary to review the sales and cash receipts transactions for reasonableness for the period between the date of the confirmation and the end of the accounting period under examination.

documentation

Documentation, which is also commonly referred to as "vouching," is the auditor's examination of the client's documents and records to substantiate the information that is or should be included in the financial statements. The documents examined by the auditor are the records that are used to provide information to the client as a means of conducting his business in an organized manner. Since each transaction that takes place in the client's organization is normally supported by at least one document, and usually more, there is a large volume of this type of evidence available for the auditor's use. For example, for each sales transaction the client normally retains a customer order, a shipping document, and a duplicate sales invoice for his information purposes. The same documents are useful evidence for the verification of the credibility of the client's records. Documentation is a widely used form of evidence in every audit because it is normally readily available for the auditor's use at a relatively low cost. Sometimes it is the only reasonable evidence available to the auditor.

Documents can be conveniently classified as internal and external. An *internal document* is one that has been prepared and used within the client's organization and is retained without its ever going to an outside party such as a customer or a vendor. Examples of internal documents include duplicate sales invoices, employee time reports, and receiving reports. An *external document* is one that is either currently in the hands of the client or is readily accessible, although it has also been in the hands of someone outside the client's organization who is a party to the transaction being documented. In some cases, external documents originate outside the client's organization and end up in the hands of the client. Examples of this type of external document are vendors' invoices, canceled notes payable, and insurance policies. In other cases, such as canceled checks, the documents originate with the client, go to an outsider, and are finally returned to the client.

The primary determinant of the auditor's willingness to accept a document as reliable evidence is whether it is an internal or external document. Since external documents have been in the hands of both the client and another party to the transaction, there is some indication that both members are in agreement with the information and the conditions stated on the document. As a result, external documents are regarded as more reliable than internal ones. For internal evidence, the adequacy of the client's internal control system that supplies the documents is a primary factor in determining its reliability. For example, if an authorized signature of a responsible official is included on a purchase order, it will normally be considered more reliable evidence than an order that contains no authorization. Similarly, if receiving reports are prepared by a separate receiving department, they are more likely to be correct than those prepared by the factory line employees.

Documentation is commonly used evidence for the support of nearly all the basic objectives stated in the previous section. In determining whether all recorded transactions are valid, a common procedure is to trace from the recorded transaction to a supporting document to determine the validity of the transaction. For example, in validating a recorded inventory purchase, it is customary to trace from the purchase journal to the related vendor's invoice and receiving report for support. Similarly, in determining whether all transactions that should be recorded are actually recorded, a common procedure is to establish whether all the documents in a sequence are recorded. For example, in cash disbursements, the auditor can prove that every check written during a period of time was actually recorded in the journal by accounting for every number of the sequence of checks being used and investigating the unrecorded numbers. In establishing the ownership of assets, the most common verification method used for permanent assets is examining documents such as titles or deeds; in the case of inventory or similar assets, the auditor examines vendors' invoices for the date of title passage. The valuation and classification of most transactions is also determined by the examination of documents. For example, in the analysis of fixed assets additions, the auditor examines external documents in the form of vendors' invoices to determine that fixed assets have been recorded at the correct cost and have been classified correctly as to the type of fixed asset. For the verification of the cut-off objective, documentation is not only applicable, it is essential. The auditor must review documents for a few days before the end of the accounting period and a few days after to establish whether transactions have been recorded in the proper period.

In addition to documents that support specific transactions, the auditor must examine more general types of documents. These include some extremely general information such as the articles of incorporation, the by-laws, and the minutes of the board of directors. Documents of this type should be carefully reviewed to determine if the client has properly made the necessary disclosures in the financial statements. The corporate charter and by-laws should be reviewed for such information as the proper corporate name, the authorized number of shares of stock, the current description for each class of stock, the frequency of required stockholders' meetings, and other data directly or indirectly related to the fairness of the presentation of financial statements. The corporate minutes book should be examined each year to determine whether all authorized transactions were correctly recorded and whether all recorded transactions pertaining to the minutes were actually authorized. Examples of important information usually found in the corporate minutes are the corporate dividends declared, officers' salaries, authorization for capital improvements, names of authorized check signers, and debt approval. A copy of these documents or an abstract of their contents should be included in the auditor's permanent file for future reference.

The careful review of somewhat more specific documents such as indenture agreements, lease agreements, and pension fund or union contracts, is also essential in determining whether the client has lived up to the requirements of the contracts and has properly recorded the transactions described in the documents. A copy of each of these documents or an abstract of the most relevant information contained therein should be included in the permanent file for any agreement that will affect subsequent years' financial statements.

inquiries of the client

Inquiry is the obtaining of written or oral information from the client in response to questions by the auditor. Although a good deal of information is obtained from the client through inquiry, it cannot usually be regarded as conclusive because it is not from an independent source and may be biased in the client's favor. Therefore, when the auditor obtains evidence through inquiry, it is normally necessary to obtain further corroborating information by other procedures. As an illustration, when the auditor acquires information about the client's system of internal control by the use of a questionnaire or flowcharting, it is common to begin by asking the client how the system operates. At a subsequent time in the audit, the auditor performs tests of transactions and other procedures to determine if the transactions are recorded and authorized in the manner stated by the client.

The *letter of representation* is one of the important statements of inquiry obtained from the client. This formal statement by the client, addressed to the CPA firm and signed by a responsible official in the client's organization, informs the auditor that the client has correctly included all information in the financial statements for the accounts mentioned in the letter. Although the letter of representation in no way relieves the auditor of responsibility for the performance of an adequate audit, it does serve to remind the client that the primary responsibility for the fair presentation of financial statements rests with him and not the auditor. Furthermore, if the letter of representation is stated in specific terms rather than in generalities, the statements made in the letter may bring to the client's mind disclosures of information that were unintentionally excluded from the financial statements. Possible examples are the obsolescence of inventory and outstanding purchase commitments or pledged assets.

The scope of the information that should appear in the letter of representation depends on the desires of the auditor. The minimum amount of subject matter normally included in the letter has to do with inventory and liabilities. Inventory is normally included because there is a higher chance of error in this area than for most other accounts. Although the representation need not take a standard form, the inventory representation often features statements referring specifically to the adequacy of physical counting procedures, ownership of the inventory, pledged inventory, the method of pricing, obsolescence, and cut-off. Representations for liability are also common, because it is often difficult for the auditor to discover unrecorded liabilities, especially contingent ones. The representation letter customarily states that all liabilities appear in the statements and all contingent liabilities, if they are material, are included in footnotes. It is also accepted practice for auditors to ask for specific reference to contingent liabilities such as notes receivable discounted, assigned accounts receivable, income tax disputes, and product warranties. Some auditors request that other accounts be specifically referred to in the letter of representation. The accounts most often referred to are property, plant and equipment, accounts receivable, and income statement classifications. It is also not unusual to ask the client to include a statement that there have been no material unreported subsequent events.

mechanical accuracy

Testing of mechanical accuracy involves rechecking a sample of the computations and the transfers of information made by the client during the period under audit. It encompasses recomputing the arithmetic work done by the client and tracing the client's recorded totals from one place to another (e.g., from the journals to the subsidiary ledgers or general ledger). Since mechanical accuracy was discussed as a part of the basic objectives in the preceding section, it need not be considered here.

comparisons and relationships

The auditor's own calculations and comparisons help him to determine the apparent reasonableness of the client's balances. This type of evidence is extremely subjective in the sense that it does not give any concrete evidence for establishing whether an account is misstated. It is useful primarily as a means of isolating accounts or transactions that should receive a more than usually detailed investigation because of an indication of a possible misstatement. As a result, much of this evidence should be obtained early in the audit to aid in determining which audit areas should be more thoroughly investigated.

There are four general classifications of comparisons and relationships.

(1) Comparison of the Current-Year Absolute Total Balance with the Balance of the Previous Year. One of the easiest ways to make this test is to include the previous year's adjusted trial balance results in a special column of the current year's unadjusted trial balance. This gives the auditor an opportunity to find out early in the audit whether

a particular account should receive more than the normal amount of attention because of a significant change in the balance. For example, if the auditor observes a substantial increase in supplies expense, this would indicate the need to determine whether the cause of the increase was the increased use of supplies, a misstatement in the account due to a misclassification, or an error in the supply inventory.

(2) Comparison of the Detail of a Total Balance with Similar Detail for the Previous Year. If there have been no significant changes in the client's operations in the current year, much of the detail making up the totals in the financial statements should also remain relatively unchanged. By briefly comparing the detail of the current period with similar detail of the preceding period, it is often possible to isolate information that needs further examination. As might be expected, there is an almost unlimited number of possibilities for this type of comparison. One common example is comparing the monthly totals for the current and previous year for sales, repairs, and other accounts. The auditor should perform a more detailed analysis and investigation of any month that shows a significantly different total. Another example is in the physical examination of inventory where the auditor can compare the current physical inventory quantities for specific items with the previous year's count. The current-year unit costs can also be compared to the costs of the previous year.

(3) Computation of the Percentage Change in Balance for Comparison with Other Percentage Changes. When there is a change in volume, it is normal to expect a similar change in accounts that vary directly with volume. As a result, a calculation of the percentage change in the account balance is often more meaningful to the auditor than the absolute value of the change. For example, if the volume of physical production has increased by 10%, it is reasonable to expect that variable maintenance costs may go up by a similar percentage. At the same time, expenses unaffected by the volume change should not have increased at all, unless some other change has occurred in the client's operation.

(4) Computation of Ratios and Percentage Relationships for Comparison with Previous Years or Industry Standards. The computation of ratios and percentage relationships for comparison with the previous year is another way to obtain an indication of whether an account is materially misstated. For example, one of the most important percentage relationships is the gross margin percentage. A significant change in this amount could be due to an error either in sales or in costs of goods sold. An error in the cost of goods sold could be caused by errors in

physical inventory or pricing, inadequate cut-off of accounts payable, or other factors. Sales could be misstated for similar reasons. A large change in the gross margin percentage would indicate to the auditor the need for a detailed investigation to determine the cause of the difference. The percentage of sales returns and allowances to sales, purchase discounts taken to total purchases, and sales commissions expense to total commission sales are a few other income statement relationships that are potentially useful for uncovering large errors. There also exists a large number of comparisons between the income statement and the balance sheet that should be computed to identify the possibility of unreasonable balances. For example, the percentage of interest expense to the average balance in notes payable outstanding or insurance expense relative to unexpired insurance might reveal unusual differences.

The foregoing types of comparisons and relationships are useful in discovering the possibility of material errors that might not be uncovered in the detail testing. The auditor who uses imagination in making comparisons and calculations can substantially increase the reliability of the audit results without a large increase in the audit cost. To adequately use these tests, it is important for the auditor to understand the client's operations and the changes that have taken place during the current year.

review of subsequent events

Examination and review of transactions and events that occurred after the end of the current accounting period but before the auditor has issued his report constitute another important type of evidence.

The review of subsequent events assists the auditor in determining whether the financial statements are correctly valued and whether they contain adequate footnote disclosure. The three types of subsequent events that are relevant to the fair presentation of financial statements are given as follows in *Statements on Auditing Procedure No. 33:*

> 1. *Subsequent events of the first type are those which affect the financial statements directly and should be recognized therein.* If subsequent information is acquired which would have been utilized had it been available at the balance-sheet date, appropriate adjustments should be made in the financial statements. Examples are collection of receivables, or settlement or determination of liabilities on a substantially different basis from that previously anticipated.
>
> 2. *Subsequent events of the second type are those which have no direct effect on the financial statements of the prior year but their effects may be such that disclosure is advisable.* These do not require adjustment. Examples of this type of transaction or event are the sale of a capital stock issue, or large bond issue with restrictive covenants, purchases of businesses, or serious damage from fire, flood or other casualty.

> 3. *Subsequent events of the third type are those not likely to require disclosure in financial statements;* for example non-accounting matters such as war, legislation, management changes, product changes, strikes, unionization, marketing agreements and loss of important customers. Disclosure of such conditions or events frequently creates doubt as to the reason therefor, and inferences drawn could be misleading as often as they are informative. However, in rare cases they may have such weighty effects as to require disclosure.[11] (Italics added.)

There are several kinds of information that should be reviewed or obtained in establishing whether any of the three types of subsequent events just specified exist. The following procedures are the most important that should be carried out:

1. Examine the minutes of the meetings of stockholders, of committees of officers, and of directors that have been prepared subsequent to year end.
2. Scrutinize the books of original entry for cut-off and other unusual entries.
3. Review the documents supporting the books of original entry that are prepared in the subsequent year as well as documents that have not been recorded.
4. Review interim statements prepared for after the year-end date.
5. Review and make excerpts of any contracts or other legal documents originating after the end of the year.
6. Read the prospectus and review other pertinent portions of the registration statements.
7. Correspond with attorneys late in the audit engagement to obtain information about the possibility of pending litigations and similar information.
8. Make inquiries of management, including a specific statement in the letter of representation, about subsequent events.

The auditor's responsibility for the review of subsequent events is generally limited to the date of the auditor's report. Since the date of the auditor's report corresponds to the completion of the important auditing procedures in the client's office, the subsequent event review should be completed near the end of the engagement. When the auditor's name is associated with a registration statement under the Securities Act of 1933, his responsibility for reviewing subsequent events extends beyond the date of the auditor's report to the date the registration statement becomes effective.

[11] American Institute of Certified Public Accountants, *Statements on Auditing Procedure No. 33,* pp. 76–77.

Factors Affecting Evidence Accumulation

It is the responsibility of the individual auditor to decide which audit evidence will be sufficient to satisfy the basic objectives in a given situation. In making this decision, there are a number of factors to be considered—the nature of the client, his organization, the scope of the engagement, the system of internal control in effect, the materiality of individual accounts and transactions, and many other matters. The auditor must evaluate the significance of each relevant factor and then obtain sufficient competent evidence, at a minimum of cost and time, to provide reasonable assurance that the financial statements are fairly stated.

Before examining the factors that should be considered in accumulating evidence, it is useful to consider the three general ways the auditor can vary the evidence he accumulates.

(1) The Auditor Can Change the Audit Procedures He Employs. Since very few procedures must be performed for each and every audit, the auditor has a considerable amount of flexibility in selecting a procedure. He can employ more procedures for a given audit area when, for instance, internal control is weak or the account being verified is material in amount. Conversely, he can eliminate some procedures if the system of internal control is considered adequate or if the account is not material.

(2) The Auditor Can Change the Extent of the Application of an Audit Procedure. The sample size that the auditor requires may be extremely small, or he may demand an examination of the entire population. It is impossible to state the precise sample size that should be used in a given set of circumstances, but it is feasible to establish in general terms the effect on the sample size of different circumstances of the audit. Although the appropriate size can best be determined by the application of statistical sampling, the effect of the circumstances of the audit on the extent of the sample should be similar in both judgmental and statistically based samples. For example, when statistical sampling is being employed, the auditor would normally demand a higher confidence level in an initial audit than for a repeat engagement. This would result in larger sample sizes in the initial engagement. The same effect would be expected if a judgmental sample had been used.

(3) The Auditor Can Change the Timing of the Procedures. There is general agreement among auditors that evidence is most reliable when

it is accumulated near the closing date of the financial statements; but as a means of spreading the auditor's work load and completing the audit work as soon after the closing date as possible, it is customary for auditors to perform audit procedures at an interim date and sometimes throughout the year. The procedures most commonly performed at an interim date are those designed to test individual transactions occurring during the year, primarily for the purpose of evaluating internal control. These procedures include the testing of sales, cash receipts, and purchases. They can also include the testing of transactions in accounts such as fixed assets and repairs and maintenance, for the early part of the year. Other common tests performed at an interim date are mechanical verifications of footings and extensions, and tracing from journals to ledgers. In some circumstances it is also acceptable to perform procedures that are typically referred to as year-end procedures at an interim date. The most common examples are the confirmation of accounts receivable and the physical examination of inventory. If the system of internal control is considered adequate, these procedures can be performed at a date close to the end of the year as a means of facilitating the timely completion of the audit. When this is done, it is necessary only to review the transactions between the confirmation or physical examination date and the year end.

In deciding on the appropriate procedures, extent, and timing for a given situation, the auditor, after a thorough study of the circumstances or factors of the audit, must exercise his professional judgment about what constitutes adequate evidence. The number of possible circumstances is so large that we cannot cover them in depth in this section. We can, however, establish the most important factors that the auditor should keep in mind throughout the engagement, explaining them in general terms.

scope of the engagement

If the auditor is to adequately perform the audit function and fulfill his responsibility to the users of financial statements, he must have complete freedom in selecting the procedures that he believes are necessary and the sample size he considers appropriate. There would be little sense in having an independent auditor perform the audit function if the evidence he accumulated were dependent on the dictates of the client. Nevertheless, occasionally some clients request the auditor to omit certain procedures. In most cases the client can be persuaded that all the procedures that the auditor considers necessary are in the client's best interest, but occasionally the client is persistent in his attitude. When he does impose restrictions on the procedures that can be performed or the extent of the application of the procedures, the auditor must either find satisfactory alternative methods of verifying the account in question or qualify his audit report. The burden of proof that satisfactory alternative means were found is on the auditor. In the case of confirmation of accounts receivable or the physical observation of inventory, the auditor must qualify the scope paragraph of his audit report even if alternative means are available to verify the account.

It is important that any restrictions imposed by the client be clearly understood by both the auditor and the client before the audit actually begins. This understanding will facilitate the acceptance of a qualified audit report by the client and it will aid the auditor in determining the possibility of using alternative procedures to verify the account. The restrictions should be included as a part of the formal letter of engagement between the client and the auditor.

Some clients request the auditor to perform procedures beyond those which are necessary for a satisfactory audit. This is an acceptable practice as long as the procedures result in additional audit evidence and are not performed to provide a service such as advertising or credit collection. The auditor can use the additional evidence to provide increased confidence that the financial statements are fairly set forth.

initial versus repeat engagement

Evidence accumulation is different when the audit is being performed for a new client and for one that has been an audit client in previous years for three primary reasons.

(1) It Is Necessary to Verify the Detail Making up Those Balance Sheet Accounts Which Are of a Permanent Nature Such As Fixed Assets, Patents, and Retained Earnings. On an initial audit it may be necessary to verify transactions that occurred several years earlier in order to establish that the current balance in the account is reasonable, whereas on repeat engagements it is necessary only to audit the transactions that took place in the current period.

(2) It Is Necessary to Verify the Beginning Balances in the Balance Sheet Accounts on an Initial Engagement. This step is essential even if comparative financial statements are not issued, because the accuracy of the current year's income statement is dependent on the accuracy of the beginning balances in the balance sheet accounts. In a repeat engagement this step is unnecessary because the prior year-end balances, which were verified in the audit of the previous year, are the current year beginning balances.

(3) The Auditor Is Less Familiar with the Client's Operations in an Initial Audit. Although the lack of knowledge about a client's operations is a highly subjective matter, it includes such considerations as unfamiliarity with the system of internal control, absence of reliable historical ratios and balances with which to compare the current year's results, and nonexistence of previous year's audit evidence and conclusions as a basis for developing a current year's audit program. As a consequence of the lack of familiarity, it may be necessary to perform more audit procedures in an initial engagement than for a repeat audit. Similarly, larger sample sizes and a more intensive evaluation of the system of internal control are appropriate in new audits.

If a new client has had audits performed in previous years by a reputable CPA firm in whom the current auditor has a high degree of confidence, it is acceptable to place some reliance on the previous auditor's results. The extent to which the current auditor should rely on a previous audit depends on his knowledge of the previous auditor, but it is always necessary at a minimum to perform sufficient procedures on beginning balances to establish that the current-period transactions are recorded on a basis consistent with that of the preceding year.

system of internal control

It is now accepted in auditing that the system of internal control is one of the most important determinants of the audit procedures performed, their extent, and the timing of the procedures. A thorough evaluation of the system must be completed before the audit can be regarded as adequate, and the results of this evaluation must then determine what evidence is to be accumulated throughout the audit. Internal control is such an important factor in evidence accumulation that it was treated in a separate section of this chapter.

materiality

The concept of materiality as it relates to auditing is simply the idea that the auditor should concentrate on the financial statement information that is most important and put less emphasis on the less significant accounts and transactions. This attitude is justified because auditors are concerned that the financial statements be reasonably stated, not that they be correct to the penny. By emphasizing the areas most likely to contain large errors, the auditor has a better chance of establishing whether the financial statements are materially misstated than he would if he spent his time verifying accounts that would not materially affect the overall financial statements even if they were misstated. For example, in most cases the auditor will have more confidence in the overall reliability of the financial statements if the verification of a small supplies account is limited to a brief review and the audit emphasis is placed on verifying accounts receivable or inventory, rather than on devoting an equal amount of time to each of these accounts.

In deciding on materiality in a given situation, the auditor must establish whether the account or transaction under consideration contains errors or omissions that, when combined with other possible errors in the statements, will make the overall financial statements misleading. Several important facets of materiality make it difficult for the auditor to decide whether any particular item is material.

(1) Materiality Is a Relative Concept Rather Than an Absolute One. An error of a given magnitude might be material for a small company, whereas the same dollar error could be immaterial for a large company. For example, a total error of $100,000 would be extremely material for a company with $200,000 total assets but it would be immaterial for a company such as General Motors. Hence it is not possible to establish any dollar-value guidelines applicable to all audit clients.

(2) A Base Is Needed for Evaluating Materiality. Since materiality is relative, it is necessary to have a basis for establishing whether an error is material. Net income is normally the most important basis for deciding what is material, because it is regarded as a critical item of information for users; but it is also important to learn whether the item in question could materially affect the reasonableness of such subtotals as current assets, total assets, current liabilities, and owners' equity. It is the responsibility of the individual auditor to decide whether the item in question contains errors that would be material when compared with any one of these bases.

(3) The Combined Errors Are More Important Than Errors in Individual Accounts. It is insufficient for the auditor to consider the materiality of the errors in a particular account in relation to the bases to which he is comparing the errors. The auditor must ultimately decide whether all the combined errors in the financial statements are sufficient to make the overall financial statements misleading. It is possible for individual errors to be immaterial when they are considered separately and for the overall financial statements to be misleading because of the combined errors. Evaluation of the reliability of the overall financial statements becomes especially difficult because the auditor, having only sampled the population, does not know the exact extent of the errors.

(4) Accounts with Small Recorded Balances Can Contain Material Errors. In judging whether an account is material enough to justify intensively verifying the balance, it is insufficient to make the decision on the basis of the recorded account balance. It is possible for an account with a small balance, or even a zero balance, to contain significant errors.

Several factors influence the auditor's decision about whether an account with a small recorded balance potentially contains material errors. First, he should consider the materiality of the transactions that affected the balance in the current period. For example, the balance in the cash account may be small, but there usually are material cash receipts and cash disbursements transactions during the year that affect the balance. Another factor is the maximum potential size of the account. As an illustration, if the income tax liability from previous years is recorded at zero, it is still necessary to examine the internal revenue agent's reports for previous years, since the unrecorded liability could be material. On the other hand, it is unlikely in most situations that the correct balance of certain accounts (e.g., unexpired insurance) would be material even if the relative error were reasonably large. Finally, the auditor should consider such other factors as the risk of error, the system of internal control, and the results of previous audits in deciding whether an account with a small balance is likely to contain a material error.

The Canadian Institute of Chartered Accountants has suggested a useful approach for reviewing accounts that appear on the surface to be immaterial; namely, to limit the tests to the following procedures:

1. Learn what the item represents.
2. Decide that it appears reasonable.
3. Check the amount to the general ledger and scrutinize the relevant accounts.
4. Decide that in comparison to similar items for the previous year it is reasonable.
5. Decide that there are no special circumstances that would render material this otherwise immaterial item.[12]

If the auditor cannot satisfy himself that the account is fairly stated by these tests alone, he must perform detailed verification procedures.

Materiality should also be a consideration in the selection of the individual items in the population for detailed verification. The auditor should emphasize the detail in the account that is most likely to contain material errors. For example, in the confirmation of accounts receivable,

[12] Canadian Institute of Chartered Accountants, Study Group on Audit Techniques, *Materiality in Auditing* (Toronto: Canadian Institute of Chartered Accountants, 1965), pp. 8–9.

the auditor should select a disproportionate percentage of large account balances and noncurrent accounts because they are more likely to contain significant errors than the small current balances. Similarly, in the review of the repair and maintenance account the auditor should concentrate on the large transactions, since the primary objective of reviewing this account is to establish whether it includes any significant transactions that should have been classified as fixed assets.

reliability of the evidence

The reliability of evidence refers to the trustworthiness, or believability, that the auditor is willing to place in the evidence he has obtained. Not all the evidence accumulated by the auditor is equally reliable. For example, external evidence such as that received from a bank or an attorney is generally regarded as more reliable than answers obtained from inquiries to the client.

Of the several considerations that determine the reliability of audit evidence, the most important are expressed in the *Statements on Auditing Procedure No. 33* as follows:

> 1. When evidential matter can be obtained from independent sources outside an enterprise it provides greater assurance of reliability for the purposes of an independent audit than that secured solely within the enterprise.
>
> 2. When accounting data and financial statements are developed under satisfactory conditions of internal control there is more assurance as to their reliability than when they are developed under unsatisfactory conditions of internal control.
>
> 3. Direct personal knowledge of the independent auditor obtained through physical examination, observation, computation, and inspection is more persuasive than information obtained indirectly.[13]

In addition to these considerations, the auditor should take into account the objectivity of the audit evidence, the timeliness of the evidence, and the qualifications of the person providing the evidence. Each of these additional considerations affects the reliability of audit evidence.

risk

In auditing, the term risk bears upon a situation or circumstance in which the auditor believes that an unusually high probability of errors exists. It is logical to expect that an auditor, when he believes that the probability of errors in a given situation is excessive, would

[13] American Institute of Certified Public Accountants, *Statements on Auditing Procedure No. 33,* p. 36.

modify his audit program to satisfy himself that the population does not contain material errors. Although it is not possible to enumerate all the circumstances of excessive risk, the following illustrations represent important situations in which the auditor can expect a high probability of errors.

(1) The Account Being Verified Is Highly Susceptible to Defalcation. The auditor should be concerned about the risk of possible defalcation in situations where it is relatively easy to convert company assets to personal use—if, for example, currency or highly marketable inventory is not closely controlled. Although it is not the auditor's primary responsibility to discover fraud, he must be aware that fraud may exist, and he must adjust his audit program accordingly if he has reason to believe that fraud may have occurred. This is especially important when the system of internal control is not considered adequate.

(2) The Account Being Verified Contains Transactions or Information That Require Considerable Accounting Judgment to Properly Record. Transactions for major repairs or partial replacement of assets are examples of this type of situation. It is common for inexperienced accountants to record these transactions as repairs when in many cases company policy dictates that they should be recorded as assets, or vice versa. When fixed assets are replaced by similar assets, it also requires an adequate knowledge of accounting theory to record the new asset at the correct amount. Similarly, legal fees are normally recorded by clients as legal expense when often part of the fee should actually be classified as patent cost, a part of a property acquisition cost, or a comparable asset. When the auditor is dealing with areas calling for considerable judgment, he must be prepared to perform more intensive auditing.

(3) The Transaction Is An Unusual One for the Client. Unusual transactions are more likely to be incorrectly recorded by the client than typical transactions because the client lacks experience in recording them. As a result, transactions that occur with relative infrequency for a particular client should be carefully scrutinized by the auditor. Possible examples include fire losses, major property acquisitions, disposals of assets, and lease agreements.

(4) The Client Is Motivated to Misstate the Financial Statements. In many situations, management may believe that it would be advantageous to misstate the financial statements. For example, if management receives a percentage of total profits as a bonus, there may be a tendency to overstate net income. Similarly, if a bond indenture requirement includes a specification that the current ratio must remain

at a certain level, the client may be tempted to overstate current assets or to understate current liabilities by an amount sufficient to meet the requirement. In other situations (e.g., when the client is in financial difficulty), management may attempt to deceive the auditor. The auditor should constantly be alert to this possibility and adjust his evidence accumulation accordingly.

results of the current and previous audits

An auditor would be considered negligent if the results of the previous year's examination were ignored during the development of the current year's audit program. If the auditor found a significant number of errors in the previous year in an audit area such as inventory pricing, extensive testing would have to be done in the current audit as a means of determining whether the deficiency in the client's system has been corrected. On the other hand, if the auditor has found no errors for the past several years in his tests of an audit area, he is justified in reducing the scope of the audit, provided always that the internal control review indicates that the system has remained unchanged.

If, during the current-year audit, the auditor finds errors in the sample that lead him to question the fairness of the total population being tested, he must ultimately establish whether the population contains material errors. Before the auditor completes his tests he must either (a) satisfy himself by additional testing that the original sample was not representative of an essentially satisfactory population or (b) take corrective action on the population. The auditor must never be put in the position of having to defend his failure to determine the actual extent of the errors in the population when the original sample indicated the possible presence of material errors.

Audit Reports

The audit report is essential to users and auditors alike because it is the vehicle available to inform financial statement users of the extent to which the auditor has performed his evidence accumulation responsibilities and the results of the findings in the audit. Earlier in the chapter it was established that management, rather than the auditor, has the basic responsibility for the fairness of the representations in the financial statements. If the auditor believes the statements are not fairly stated in accordance with generally accepted accounting principles, and the client refuses to make revisions, the auditor uses the audit report to inform users that the statements are not fairly stated. Similarly, if for any reason the auditor is unable to satisfy himself that the statements are fairly stated, the report informs users that the auditor lacks knowledge about the fairness of the financial statement presentation.

Since the only information about the audit that is normally available to statement users comes through the audit report, its wording must clearly communicate the auditor's message to users. As a result of the need for unambiguous statements about the auditor's work performed and the results found, the profession has developed standard audit reports for different circumstances and fairly precise rules for determining the appropriate type of audit report. The CPA candidate should understand completely the various types of audit reports, know when each type of report is to be used, and be able to construct a well-worded report for different circumstances.

parts of the short-form report

There are several distinct types of short-form reports: unqualified, qualified, adverse, and disclaimer. Each of them must be composed of the following five parts.

(1) The Audit Report Address. The report is usually addressed to the company, its stockholders, or the board of directors. In recent years it has become customary to address the report to the stockholders, to indicate that the auditors are independent of the company and the board of directors.

(2) The Date of the Audit Report. The appropriate date for the report is the one on which the auditor has completed the most important auditing procedures in the field. This date is important to users because it indicates the last day of the auditor's responsibility for the review of significant events that occurred after the date of the financial statements. For example, if the balance sheet is dated December 31, 1970, and the audit report is dated February 25, 1971, this indicates that the auditor has searched for material unrecorded transactions and events that occurred before February 25, 1971. The definition of the type of subsequent events that should be disclosed and the audit procedures that will facilitate their discovery were discussed earlier.

(3) The Scope of the Audit. In the scope paragraph of the audit report the auditor states which financial statements he has examined and informs users in very general terms what was done on the audit. The scope paragraph intentionally states the work performed in general terms rather than enumerating the details because no user is in a position to evaluate the adequacy of the audit unless he has professional experience and knows all the facts about the audit. The auditor is required to state

whether he has followed generally accepted auditing standards and performed all the tests that he believed were necessary.

The scope of the report is especially important as a means of revealing when the auditor has not followed generally accepted auditing standards or carried out his work with the scope that he believes was appropriate for the audit. Whenever this occurs, the auditor must specifically state the shortcoming in the scope section of the audit report and the effect that it has on his opinion in the opinion section.

(4) The Opinion of the Auditor. The opinion paragraph is an expression of the auditor's opinion about the degree to which the financial statements conform to generally accepted accounting principles, which have been applied consistently relative to the ones used in the preceding period. Since the opinion is based on a limited examination of the financial information, it does not represent a guarantee that the financial statements are accurate or correct.

The auditor must restrict his opinion to the information on the financial statements that he has verified to his own satisfaction. Furthermore, he must specify that he is not expressing an opinion on any financial information for which he has been unable to obtain adequate verification. Care must also be taken to withhold expression of an opinion on all totals on which the unverified information has a material effect. For example, the balances in accounts receivable directly affect current assets and total assets, and they indirectly affect sales, gross profit, and net income.

On the parts of the financial statements that have been verified to the auditor's satisfaction, there must be a straightforward expression of whether, in the auditor's opinion, the financial statements are reported by the client in accordance with generally accepted accounting principles that have been consistently applied. The opinion covers the quantitative information in the statements as well as all other necessary informative disclosures such as footnotes and parenthetical explanations. If the auditor believes the financial statements are not fairly expressed, he must clearly state the nature and amount of the misstatement.

(5) Signature of the Auditor. The signature identifies the CPA or the CPA firm that has performed the audit.

standard unqualified report

The AICPA has recommended a standard short-form report when the auditor has followed generally accepted auditing standards, has accumulated all the evidence considered necessary in the audit, and has found the client's financial statements fairly stated. The standard short-form report was reproduced early in the chapter (p. 96).

The first paragraph in the report is the standard scope paragraph and the second paragraph is a standard opinion. In subsequent discussion, mention of a standard scope or a standard opinion refers to this form.

Departures from the Unqualified Report. Three primary types of reports are departures from the standard unqualified report. These are the qualified report, the adverse opinion, and the disclaimer of opinion. First, a brief explanation is given of each type of report. This is followed by the circumstances requiring a deviation from the standard unqualified report and some examples of reports that are appropriate in different circumstances.

1. Qualified Report. The qualified report can result from a limitation of the scope of the audit, the lack of fairly represented information in the financial statements, or the existence of unusual circumstances that prevented the auditor from knowing whether information on the statement is fairly presented. *This report can be used to disclose any of the foregoing circumstances only when the auditor believes that the overall financial statements are fairly presented.* A disclaimer or adverse report must be used if the exceptions being reported are extremely material in amount. For this reason the qualified report is considered the least severe type of report for disclosing exceptions.

The qualified report can take the form of an opinion qualification only or a qualification of both the scope and opinion. The appropriate form of the report in different circumstances is clarified in the remainder of this section.

2. Adverse Opinion. This type of report is not used unless the auditor believes that the financial statements are so materially misstated or misleading that they do not present fairly the financial position or results of operations. The adverse report can be used only when the auditor has knowledge, after an adequate investigation, that the financial statements are not fairly stated.

The distinction between an adverse opinion and a qualified opinion resulting from financial statements that are not fairly presented is entirely a matter of materiality. An adverse opinion is required if the exception is so material that the auditor believes that the overall financial statements are not fairly presented, whereas a qualified opinion can be issued if he believes that the overall statements are fairly stated but that existing exceptions must be disclosed.

3. Disclaimer of Opinion. A disclaimer is issued whenever the auditor has been unable to satisfy himself that the overall financial statements are fairly presented. The necessity for disclaiming an opinion arises (a) from a severe limitation of the scope of the audit examination or (b) from the existence of unusual uncertainties concerning the amount of an item or the outcome of a matter materially affecting the financial position or the results of operations. Both these situations prevent the auditor from forming an opinion on the financial statements as a whole.

The disclaimer is distinguished from an adverse opinion in that it can arise only from the *lack* of knowledge by the auditor, whereas in an adverse opinion the auditor must have knowledge that the financial statements are not fairly stated.

The distinction between a qualified report resulting either from a scope limitation or from the existence of future uncertainties and a disclaimer is entirely a question of materiality. A disclaimer of opinion is required if the scope limitation or the presence of the unusual uncertainty is so material that the auditor cannot determine if the overall financial statements are fairly presented. A qualified opinion can be issued if he believes that the scope limitation or the existence of unusual uncertainty must be disclosed, but the overall statements are fairly stated.

Whenever any type of qualification is included in the audit report, it is essential that the auditor clearly state the nature of the qualification and the degree of responsibility he is taking for the fair presentation of the financial statements. If there is a significant restriction in the evidence accumulated by the auditor, the report must name the restrictions in the scope paragraph and present the effect on the opinion, if any, in the opinion paragraph. If during the course of the audit the financial statements are found to be not fairly stated in accordance with generally accepted accounting principles applied consistently with those of the previous period, the opinion must specify the nature of the qualification and the responsibility the auditor is taking. Although there is no standard form recommended for departures from the standard qualified audit report, examples taken from the professional literature are given as an aid to the candidate.

Certain categories of circumstances require a deviation from the standard unqualified opinion. The appropriate type of report depends on the circumstances in the audit and the materiality of the circumstances in question. It should be borne in mind that, if the circumstances in question do not have a significant effect on the financial statements, it is unnecessary to disclose the exception in the report at all. In dealing with materiality, the auditor must consider the combined effect of several items that are immaterial when they are considered individually.

Conditions Requiring a Qualified Report. The circumstances that may require a deviation from the standard unqualified report follow.

1. The Auditor Did Not Perform the "Extended Procedures." The only audit procedures that are formally required by the AICPA are the confirmation of accounts receivable by direct communication with the customers of the client and the observation by the auditor of the client's taking of physical inventory. These two procedures are called the extended auditing procedures.

Although it is desirable for the auditor to be present during the actual taking of inventory, he may issue an unqualified audit report even if it is not practical for him to be on hand during the count if he performs the necessary alternative procedures. The alternative procedures must include sufficient tests of the client's perpetual records and the examination of enough physical counts of the inventory at a different date to satisfy the auditor that the inventory was fairly stated at the balance sheet date.

When the auditor is unable, by the application of the specified alternative procedures, to satisfy himself that the inventory is fairly stated, he must issue a qualification in the scope paragraph and also, depending on the materiality of the amounts, either a qualified opinion or a disclaimer of opinion. For example, the following report would be appropriate if the auditor had not been on hand to observe inventory and could not satisfy himself by alternative procedures:

> (scope paragraph—qualified)
>
> We have examined the balance sheet of X Company as of December 31, 19__, and the related statements of income and retained earnings for the year then ended. Our examination was made in accordance with generally accepted auditing standards, and accordingly included such tests of the accounting records and such other auditing procedures as we considered necessary in the circumstances, except as stated in the following paragraph.
>
> (middle paragraph—part of scope)
>
> We did not observe the taking of physical inventories as of December 31, 19__, since these dates were prior to our initial engagement as auditors for the company. The company's records do not permit adequate retroactive tests of inventory quantities.
>
> (opinion paragraph—qualified)
>
> In our opinion, except for the effect of such adjustments, if any, as might have been disclosed had we been able to observe the physical inventory taken as of December 31, 19__, or to make retroactive tests, the statements present fairly. . . .

When the amounts are so material that a disclaimer of opinion is required, the scope and middle paragraph could remain the same, but the opinion might be as follows:

(opinion paragraph—disclaimer)

Because the inventories referred to in the preceding paragraphs enter materially into the determination of financial position and the results of operations, we are unable to express an opinion on the accompanying financial statements taken as a whole.

For accounts receivable, confirmation must be performed whenever the procedure is feasible, but it is acceptable to issue an unqualified report if the balance in the account can be verified by using such alternative procedures as the examination of evidence of subsequent cash receipts, sales and shipping documents, and other records.[14] A qualified scope and either a qualified opinion or a disclaimer similar to the example shown for inventory must be given if alternative procedures are not feasible.

When he does not confirm receivables or observe inventory *because of a restriction imposed by the client,* the auditor cannot issue an unqualified report even if he has satisfied himself via alternative procedures that the balance is fairly stated. He must issue a report with a qualified scope paragraph and, depending on the materiality of the balance in question, either a qualified opinion or a disclaimer of opinion. As might be expected, the auditor is more likely to issue a disclaimer of opinion when the scope restrictions are imposed by the client than when circumstances prevent the auditor from performing the procedures. The appropriate wording for either a qualified opinion or a disclaimer could be the same as the preceding illustration, except that it is desirable to state in the middle paragraph that a restriction was imposed by the client.

2. *Other Limitations in the Scope.* Although the two extended auditing procedures are the only ones specifically required for all audits, the auditor must be satisfied that every account balance and financial statement disclosure is fairly presented if the item is material in amount. When the auditor can neither perform procedures that he considers necessary nor satisfy himself by using different procedures, a scope qualification and, again depending on the materiality, either an opinion qualification or a disclaimer of opinion is necessary. For example, if the auditor is unable to examine the client's recorded minutes, it is normally necessary to issue a disclaimer of opinion, since the minutes often include vital information that cannot be found elsewhere. When

[14] Prior to the issuance of *Statement on Auditing Procedure No. 43* it was necessary to qualify the scope paragraph whenever confirmation of receivables and physical examination of inventory were not performed, even if alternative procedures were performed. The Committee on Auditing Procedures abolished this requirement because they felt that it might be misleading to qualify the scope paragraph and still issue an unqualified opinion.

the auditor cannot perform procedures that he considers desirable, but he *is* able to satisfy himself with alternative procedures that the information being verified is fairly stated, an unqualified report is acceptable.

3. Part of the Examination Is Made by Other Independent Accountants. When the examination is shared by other auditors, the auditor signing the report may assume full responsibility for the work of the others, he may assume responsibility only for the audit work that he has performed, or he may refuse any responsibility for the fairness of the financial statements. If the principal auditor is willing to take full responsibility for the work of the other auditors, no report qualification is needed. At the other extreme, it is necessary for the principal auditor to issue a scope qualification and either a disclaimer or a qualified opinion if he is unwilling to utilize another auditor's report. When the principal auditor is willing to utilize the report of another auditor but does not wish to take full responsibility for the report, the AICPA has recommended that the following report be issued:

> (scope paragraph—shared responsibility)
>
> We have examined . . . and such other auditing procedures as we considered necessary in the circumstances. We did not examine the financial statements of B Company, a consolidated subsidiary, which statements were examined by other certified public accountants whose report thereon has been furnished to us. Our opinion expressed herein, insofar as it relates to the amounts included for B Company, is based solely upon such report.[15]
>
> (opinion paragraph—unqualified)
>
> In our opinion, based upon our examination and the aforementioned report of other certified public accountants, the accompanying consolidated financial statements present fairly. . . .[16]

4. The Financial Statements Have Not Been Prepared in Conformity with Generally Accepted Accounting Principles. When the auditor knows that the financial statements may be misleading because they were not prepared in accordance with generally accepted accounting principles, the auditor must issue a qualified or an adverse opinion, depending on the materiality of the item in question. The opinion must clearly state the nature of the deviation from the accepted principles and the amount of the misstatement, if it is known. Following is an example from *Statements on Auditing Procedure No. 33* of a qualified report based on financial statements in which the client failed to set up a provision for deferred income taxes.

[15] American Institute of Certified Public Accountants, *Statements on Auditing Procedure No. 33,* p. 68.

[16] *Ibid.,* p. 68.

(scope paragraph—unqualified)

(middle paragraph—part of opinion)

Although the proceeds of sales are collectible on the installment basis over a five-year period, revenue from such sales is recorded in full by the Company at time of sale. However, for income tax purposes, income is reported only as collections are received and no provision has been made for income taxes on installments to be collected in the future, as required by generally accepted accounting principles. If such provisions had been made, net income for 1961 and retained earnings as of December 31, 1961, would have been reduced by approximately $________ and $________, respectively, and the balance sheet would have included a liability for deferred income taxes of approximately $________.

(opinion paragraph—qualified)

In our opinion, except that provision has not been made for additional income taxes as described in the foregoing paragraph, the accompanying financial statements present fairly. . . .[17]

If the auditor felt that the amounts were so materially misstated that an adverse opinion was required, the scope and middle paragraph would remain unchanged but the opinion would be adverse.

(opinion paragraph—adverse)

Because of the materiality of the amounts of omitted income taxes as described in the preceding paragraph, we are of the opinion that the financial statements do not present fairly the financial position of X Company at December 31, 1961 or the results of its operations for the year then ended in conformity with generally accepted accounting principles.[18]

5. *The Accounting Principles Used in Financial Statements Have Not Been Consistently Applied.* Whenever there is a change in accounting principles having a material effect on the current year's statements or expected to have a material effect in future years, it is necessary to report the change in the opinion even if the change has been fully disclosed in the financial statements.

If the accounting principle used in the current period's financial statements is generally accepted, it is sufficient to issue a qualified opinion. For example, if the client changed from the accelerated to the straight-line method of computing depreciation, the following wording would be appropriate:

(opinion paragraph—qualified)

. . . in conformity with generally accepted accounting principles applied on a basis consistent with that of the preceding year, except for the change, (insert expression of approval), in depreciation methods . . . as described in Note ___ to the financial statements.[19]

[17] *Ibid.*, pp. 69–70.
[18] *Ibid.*, p. 70.
[19] *Ibid.*, pp. 46–47.

If there were no footnotes in the financial statements explaining the nature of the above-mentioned change and the effect on the financial statements, this information would have to be included directly in the opinion, rather than by reference to the footnotes. The inclusion of the auditor's expression of approval in the opinion is optional.

When there is a change from a generally accepted accounting principle to a principle that lacks general acceptance, the auditor is required to issue either a qualified or an adverse opinion, depending on the materiality of the effect on the financial statements.

There are a number of specific situations in which a consistency qualification is not required. If the client altered his accounting because of a change in conditions, but used the same accounting principles, it would be unnecessary to issue a qualified report. For example, a decrease in the life of fixed assets due to unexpected obsolescence would not require a consistency exception. Similarly, a new accounting practice adopted because of a new business circumstance, such as the adoption of a pension plan, is not an accounting inconsistency. In such cases, if the amount is material and if the client has not made adequate footnote disclosures, inadequate disclosure would still make it necessary to qualify the report. The final situation where a consistency exception is not required is when there has been a reclassification in the statements that is adequately explained in the financial statements.

6. The Financial Statements Do Not Include Adequate Disclosure. When the client fails to include information that is necessary for the fair presentation of financial statements in the body of the statements or in the related footnotes, it is the responsibility of the auditor to present the information in the audit report. It is common to put this type of qualification in a middle paragraph and to refer to the middle paragraph in the opinion paragraph. An example of an audit report in which the auditor considered the financial statement disclosure inadequate is as follows:

> (scope paragraph—unqualified)
> (middle paragraph)
>
> In January 15, 19___, the company issued debentures in the amount of $____________ for the purpose of financing plant expansion. The debenture agreement restricts the payment of future cash dividends to earnings after December 31, 19___.
>
> (opinion paragraph—qualified)
>
> In our opinion, the accompanying financial statements, except for the omission of the information in the preceding paragraph, present fairly. . . .[20]

[20] *Ibid.*, p. 72.

7. Unusual Uncertainties Exist Concerning the Future Outcome of Pending Matters. If the auditor is unable to determine whether certain information is fairly stated because of unusual uncertainties, it may be necessary to issue a qualified opinion or disclaimer of opinion, depending on the materiality of the amount in question. The most likely cases have to do with contingent or actual liabilities resulting from lawsuits, income tax disputes, or renegotiation contracts, but uncertainties in the valuation and reevaluation of assets can also be causes for a qualified opinion or a disclaimer. For example, it may be necessary to qualify the opinion if the financial statements include a material amount for pending patents if the value of the product being researched is questionable.

In *Statements on Auditing Procedure No. 33* there is an example of a qualification that resulted from the client's contesting an income tax assessment by the Internal Revenue Service in which there were conflicting federal court decisions:

> (scope paragraph—unqualified)
> (opinion paragraph—qualified)
>
> In our opinion, subject to any adjustments to the balance sheet and statement of retained earnings which may result from the final determination of the company's income tax liability for prior years as indicated in Note A to the financial statements, the accompanying financial statements present fairly. . . .[21]

When the amounts are so large that the uncertainty materially affects the overall fairness of the statements, a disclaimer is required.

8. The Auditor Is Lacking in Independence. If the auditor has not fulfilled the independence requirements specified by the Code of Professional Ethics, quoted in full near the end of this chapter, he must disclaim an opinion on the financial statements even though he may have performed all the audit procedures he considered necessary in the circumstances. The following report is recommended by the Committee on Auditing Procedure of the AICPA when the auditor is not independent.

> We are not independent with respect to XYZ Company, and the accompanying balance sheet as of December 31, 19___ and the related statement(s) of income and retained earnings for the year then ended were not audited by us; accordingly, we do not express an opinion on them.[22]

[21] *Ibid.*, p. 73. There is a useful distinction between the "subject to" exception in this opinion and the "except for" used in previous qualified opinions. "Except for" is generally the most desirable qualifying phrase, but "subject to" is acceptable if the qualification arises when the outcome of a matter is uncertain.

[22] American Institute of Certified Public Accountants, *Statements on Auditing Procedure No. 42*, p. 76.

It is *not* permissible to include a statement that certain procedures were performed.

other types of reports

Several other specific kinds of auditor's reports have received sufficient special attention by the auditing profession to justify their inclusion here. These reports are for the most part a special case or an extension of the reports that have been previously discussed.

(1) Piecemeal Opinions. When an auditor uses an adverse opinion or a disclaimer of opinion, it is also possible to state, by issuing a piecemeal opinion, that specific items in the financial statements have been fairly stated. A piecemeal opinion associated with an adverse opinion has the effect of stating that, even though the overall financial statements are not fairly stated, the auditor is willing to express an opinion on the fairness of some of the individual accounts. A similar relation exists between a disclaimer and a piecemeal opinion.

If the auditor issues a piecemeal opinion, he must be careful that the adverse opinion or disclaimer of opinion is not overshadowed or contradicted by the piecemeal opinion. The best way to make certain that this does not happen is to use the disclaimer or adverse opinion to make an overall statement about the financial statements and then to list in detail the specific accounts or disclosures that, to the auditor's satisfaction, are fairly stated. No specific account listed should be one that is affected by the cause of the disclaimer or adverse opinion.

(2) Unaudited Statements. When the CPA has been associated with financial statements but no audit has been performed, or the auditing procedures are insignificant, the CPA must issue a disclaimer of opinion and clearly mark each page of the financial statements as unaudited. This situation usually occurs when the CPA is retained by the client to do routine services such as preparing the financial statements rather than performing an audit. When all footnotes or other disclosures that the auditor believes are necessary have been included in the statements, the following disclaimer has been recommended:

> The accompanying balance sheet of X Company as of December 31, 19___ and the related statement(s) of income and retained earnings for the year then ended were not audited by us and accordingly we do not express an opinion on them.[23]

If the CPA has knowledge that the financial statements are not fairly stated, the preceding disclaimer of opinion is not satisfactory. For example, when the unaudited financial statements are for internal

[23] American Institute of Certified Public Accountants, *Statements on Auditing Procedure No. 38,* p. 54.

purposes only and lack the necessary footnotes or other disclosures that would be important to external users, the auditor should include a disclaimer and a sentence to the effect that the statements are for internal purposes only and therefore do not necessarily include all the information necessary for adequate disclosure. On the other hand, if the statements *are* for external purposes and are known to include information that is not in accordance with generally accepted accounting principles, the auditor must include a statement in the disclaimer informing the reader of the auditor's reservations about the financial statements. If the client refuses to revise his statements or to permit such a statement in the disclaimer, the auditor must withdraw from the engagement.

The only exception to the requirement that an auditor must issue a disclaimer for unaudited statements occurs when the auditor merely types on plain paper or reproduces unaudited financial statements prepared by the client and submits the statements directly to the client. If the auditor has been associated with the preparation of the statements, has his name associated with the statements in any way, or submits the statements to someone other than the client, a disclaimer must be issued and each page must be marked unaudited.

(3) Long-Form Report. A long-form report generally includes the financial statements associated with a short-form report plus additional information that is considered useful for management and other statement users. The profession has intentionally refrained from defining or restricting the appropriate supplementary information included in the long-form report. This enables auditors to individualize each long-form report to meet the needs of the users. However, several standard types of information are commonly included in the supplementary information of a long-form report. For example, it is normal to find detailed comparative statements supporting the control totals on the primary financial statements for accounts, such as cost of goods sold, operating expenses, and miscellaneous assets. Other customary types of information include such statistical data for past years as ratios and trends, a schedule of insurance coverage, and specific comments on the changes in the financial statements that have taken place. The supplemental information is not restricted to the foregoing information, and in many cases some of these items may be excluded.

It is important that the auditor clearly distinguish between the responsibility that he is taking for the primary financial statements and the supplemental information. Usually, the auditor has not performed a sufficiently detailed audit to justify an opinion on the supplementary information. In some instances, however, the auditor may be confident that all the information in the long-form report is fairly presented. The profession's standards of reporting require the auditor to make a clear statement about the degree of responsibility he is taking for the additional information.

When long-form reports are issued to some users and only the basic financial statements are issued to others, the auditor should exercise special care to assure himself that the long-form report does not include information that might support a claim that there is inadequate disclosure in the short-form report. For example, if the supplementary comments contain exceptions, reservations, or material disclosures that do not appear in the short-form report, there is a basis for potential legal claims against the auditor for failure to qualify his short-form report because of inadequate disclosure.

(4) Special Reports. A large variety of special reports arise in auditing. They include, but are not limited to, reports for organizations that do not follow generally accepted accounting principles because of government or association restrictions, reports that relate only to certain aspects of the financial statements such as the determination of profit-sharing bonuses, and cash basis statements.

The auditor is required to follow generally accepted auditing standards to the extent that it is possible when he is dealing with engagements that involve special reports. In most cases the general standards and field standards are applicable in the engagement, but the reporting standards often cannot be followed because generally accepted accounting principles and consistency are not germane to these reports.

In preparing reports for special audits, the auditor must make certain the statements clearly state the nature of the information being presented, as well as the basis on which they have been prepared. The auditor has a responsibility to include in his report an expression of opinion regarding the fairness of the information being presented or an expression to the effect that no opinion can be given. If there is any possibility that users will mistakenly believe that the information was prepared in accordance with generally accepted accounting principles, it is essential that the auditor insert in his report a qualified or an adverse opinion. But if statements prepared on a cash basis are clearly labeled in such a manner that users will not interpret them as statements prepared on the accrual basis, the following audit opinion is acceptable:

> In our opinion, the accompanying statements present fairly the assets and liabilities of the XYZ Company, at __________ 19___, arising from cash transactions, and the revenues collected and expenditures made by it (and changes in proprietary interest, fund balances, etc., where reflected in cash basis statements) during the year then ended, on a basis consistent with that of the preceding year.[24]

[24] American Institute of Certified Public Accountants, *Statements on Auditing Procedure No. 33,* p. 89.

When the auditor believes that misleading inferences may be drawn from the cash basis report, he should insert a middle paragraph in the report making it clear that the statements present neither the financial position nor the results of operation. The preceding cash basis opinion can then follow the middle paragraph. On the other hand, if the statements are on a modified accrual basis, it is necessary to issue an adverse or qualified opinion.

A special provision has been made in *Statements on Auditing Procedure No. 33* for nonprofit organizations that do not follow generally accepted accounting principles but do have clearly defined principles established by a recognized agency or association. Even though the established principles differ from those of the AICPA, it is appropriate to state in the report that the financial statements have been prepared in accordance with generally accepted accounting principles. In the case of regulated companies, a qualified or an adverse opinion must be issued if the statements are not prepared in accordance with generally accepted accounting principles, but it is also permissible to express an opinion in the same report upon the fair presentation of the statements in accordance with the accounting requirements set forth by the regulating agency.

subsequent discovery of facts existing at the date of the auditor's report

If the auditor becomes aware, after the audited financial statements have been released, that some information included in the statements was materially misleading, he has an obligation to make certain that users who are relying on the financial statements are informed about the misstatements.

The most desirable approach is to request the client to issue as soon as possible a revised set of financial statements containing an explanation of the reasons for the revision and a new audit report. If a subsequent period's financial statements were completed before the revised statements could be issued, it is acceptable to disclose the misstatement in the current statements. In the event that the revised statements cannot be completed within a reasonable length of time, the client should inform users who are likely to be relying on the statements that the data are misleading and should not be relied upon. Whenever it is pertinent, the Securities and Exchange Commission and other regulatory agencies should be informed, by the client, of the misleading financial statements. The auditor has a responsibility to make certain that the client has taken the appropriate steps in informing users of the misleading statements.

When the client refuses to cooperate in disclosing the misstated information, the auditor must inform the board of directors of this fact. He must also notify the regulatory agencies having jurisdiction over the client and each person who, in his knowledge, relies on the financial statements that the statements are no longer trustworthy. If the stock is publicly held, it is permissible to request the Securities and Exchange Commission and the stock exchange to notify the stockholders. The auditor should inform the users of the nature of the subsequently acquired information and its effect on the previously issued financial statements. In the event that the auditor has not been able to satisfactorily determine the effect of the acquired information on the financial statements because the client has refused to cooperate, he should inform the users of his belief that the statements are unreliable. In addition, the users should be told of the unwillingness of the client to cooperate in allowing the auditor to investigate the facts. The auditor should not comment about the motives or the conduct of the client.

Working Papers

Working papers are the written records kept by the auditor of the evidence that has been accumulated during the course of the audit. They should include all the information that the auditor believes is necessary to adequately conduct his examination and provide support for his audit report.

purposes of working papers

The overall objective of the current-period working papers is to aid the auditor in providing reasonable assurance that an adequate audit was conducted in accordance with generally accepted auditing standards. In more specific terms, the purposes of the working papers as they pertain to the current year audit include the following:

1. *Provide the basis for planning the audit.* If the auditor is to adequately plan the current year's audit, he needs the reference information available in the working papers to aid him in his decision making. The papers include such diverse planning information as the evaluation of internal control, a time budget for individual audit areas, the audit program, and the results of the previous year's audit.
2. *Provide a record of the evidence accumulated and the results of the tests.* The working papers are the primary means of documenting that an adequate audit was conducted. It is essential that the auditor be able to demonstrate to commissions and courts, if the need arises, that the audit was well planned and adequately supervised, that the evidence accumulated was both competent and

sufficient, and that the audit report was proper, considering the results of the audit.

3. *Provide data for determining the proper type of audit report.* The working papers provide an important source of information to assist the auditor in deciding on the appropriate audit report to issue in a given set of circumstances. The data in the papers are useful for evaluating the adequacy of the scope of the examination and the fairness of the financial statement presentation.

4. *Provide the basis for review by supervisors and partners.* The working papers are the primary frame of reference used by supervisory personnel in evaluating whether sufficient competent evidence has been accumulated to justify the audit report that is issued.

In addition to the purposes directly related to the current year's audit, the working papers are useful for related activities. Adequate working papers are needed as a basis for preparing the tax returns if the CPA firm provides that service. They are also useful as a source of information for issuing a management letter to the client for improving operations. Finally, working papers are an excellent frame of reference for the training of personnel and the planning for future audits.

essential features of working papers

Working papers must possess certain characteristics if they are to fulfill their purpose.

1. Each working paper must be properly identified with such information as the client's name, the period covered, a description of the contents, the initials of the preparer, and the date of preparation.

2. Each working paper should include sufficient information to fulfill the objectives for which it was designed. For the auditor to properly prepare working papers, he must be clearly aware of his goals. For example, if a working paper is designed to list the detail and show the verification in support of a balance sheet account, such as unexpired insurance, it is essential for the detail on the working paper to reconcile to the trial balance. In addition, the verification procedures should be indicated on the working paper.

3. All unanswered questions, exceptions, and inconsistencies existing in the working papers must be resolved and clearly explained.

4. The conclusions that were reached about the segment of the audit under consideration must be plainly stated.

5. The working papers should be sufficiently clear and self-explanatory to enable supervisory personnel to make an adequate review and evaluation without resorting to additional data to determine the reliability of the information.

permanent working papers

In addition to the current-period working papers, it is also normal to find a set of permanent working papers associated with each audit engagement. The permanent file of working papers provides a convenient source of information about the audit that is of continuing interest from year to year. The most important kinds of information typically included in the permanent file are:

1. *Extracts or copies of such company documents of continuing significance as the articles of incorporation, the by-laws, bond indentures, and contracts.* The contracts are pension plans, leases, stock options, and so on. Each of these documents is of significance to the auditor for as many years as it is in effect.

2. *Information related to the evaluation of internal control.* This includes organization charts, flowcharts, and internal control questionnaires, as well as the enumeration of the strengths and weaknesses in the system that have been isolated by the auditor.

3. *Analyses from previous years of accounts that have continuing importance to the auditor.* These include such accounts as long-term debt, stockholders' equity accounts, goodwill, and fixed assets. Having this information in the permanent file enables the auditor to concentrate on analyzing only the changes in the current year's balance while retaining the results of previous year's audits in a form accessible for review.

4. *The results of overall testing from previous year's auditing.* Among these data are ratios and percentages computed by the auditor, as well as the total balance or the balance by month for selected accounts. This information is useful in helping the auditor to decide whether there are unusual changes in the current year's account balance that should be investigated more extensively than usual.

Statistical Sampling

The previous sections have dealt with the traditional approach to evidence accumulation and evaluation. One of the readily apparent difficulties in auditing is the complexity of the judgments that must be made by auditors. In recent years statistical sampling has become recognized as a useful tool to assist the auditor in making professional judgments.

Candidates who consider themselves technically weak in statistical sampling as it is applied to auditing are referred to the AICPA's programmed books on statistical sampling. These materials are specifically designed for use on a self-study basis.

Auditors use statistical sampling to assist in solving three problems: determining the appropriate sample size for a given set of circumstances, selecting the particular items in the population for testing, and evaluating the population being verified on the basis of the sample. It should be emphasized that it has been well established in the auditing literature that the role of statistics in auditing is to aid the auditor in achieving his evidence accumulation objectives rather than to eliminate or reduce his professional judgment.

Statistical sampling is applicable to auditing because the auditor is interested in evaluating a population which, for economic reasons, he is compelled to judge on the basis of a sample. In generalizing from the sample to the population, it is not valid to assume that the actual, but unknown, characteristics in the population are identical with the ones found in the sample. For example, if the auditor finds one error in testing 100 duplicate sales invoices for the appropriate sales price, it is not justifiable to conclude that 1% of the total population of sales invoices contains pricing errors. It is possible that the actual population error rate is larger or smaller than 1%, depending on how representative the sample is of the population. Statistical sampling is a tool to help determine the actual population characteristics. Once they are known, the auditor is in a position to evaluate whether the population is acceptable.

The principal advantage of statistical sampling is that it is an objective and defensible means of providing the auditor with an opportunity to use his professional judgment in a desirable manner. Once the auditor decides on the permissible population characteristics, he can compute the sample size that is needed and select the items for testing in a completely unbiased manner. After the selected sample has been examined for errors, the population characteristics can be objectively estimated. When statistical sampling is used, the auditor is in a position to objectively defend his conclusions about the population to his supervisor, the client, or to outside parties, if questions arise about the sample. In addition, this method frequently allows him to attain a satisfactory level of assurance about a population at less cost.

sampling plans

The three statistical methods or plans that have been most successfully applied to auditing are variables sampling, attributes sampling, and discovery sampling. Each of these is briefly described here and discussed at greater length throughout this section.

(1) Variables Sampling. Variables sampling, or variables estimation, is employed when the specific audit objective is to estimate the value of a total or of an average. In most cases it measures dollar amounts such

as the total value of sales during a period or the average account balance in accounts receivable. Whenever variables sampling is used, the amount being measured is stated in terms of a range of values rather than as a single precise amount. For example, if the total value of inventory is being estimated, it might be stated with a certain degree of confidence, on the basis of statistical calculation, that the true value of the inventory is between $250,000 and $275,000.

(2) Attributes Sampling. Attributes sampling measures the frequency with which a specified occurrence or attribute exists in the population. The most common type of attribute of interest in auditing is the frequency with which errors occur in the population being tested. When the auditor is concerned with errors, the population results are ultimately stated in terms of the maximum population error rate that is believed to exist. The auditor may desire to know, for example, what percentage of receiving reports are not attached to vendors' invoices in a particular situation. If one error is found in a sample of 100, the auditor can statistically conclude with a high degree of confidence that the true population error rate does not exceed a computed percentage, such as 4%.

It is important to distinguish between variables and attributes sampling. In variables sampling, each item in the population has a specific value and the auditor computes the total or the average value of the population on the basis of a sample. In attributes sampling, every item in the population either does or does not contain the attribute being measured. The auditor computes the percentage of the population that contains the attribute on the basis of a sample. As an illustration, if accounts receivable are being confirmed, either variables or attributes sampling methods can be used. If variables sampling is used, the auditor determines the correct dollar value of each account in his sample. On the basis of the results of the sample, the total value of the population is estimated. Alternatively, under an attributes sampling plan, each confirmation result is defined as correct or incorrect. The auditor then estimates, on the basis of the sample, the total percentage of accounts containing errors in the accounts receivable trial balance.

(3) Discovery Sampling. Discovery sampling is similar to attributes sampling in the sense that in both plans the rate of occurrence of errors in the population is being measured. An important difference is that a discovery sampling plan is used only when the auditor expects to find no errors in the sample. If an error is found, there must be an extension of the testing to determine the extent of the errors in the population.

As might be imagined, discovery sampling should be used only when an error has been defined as a serious deviation from acceptable practice. It is common to test for fraudulent transactions via discovery sampling, because one error uncovered in the sample would cause the auditor to greatly expand his testing. The method can also be advantageous for testing such attributes as significant unintentional classification errors or errors directly affecting the income statement. Usually, when discovery sampling is used in testing for unintentional errors, a mistake would not be defined as an error unless it exceeded a certain dollar amount, perhaps $100 or $500.

attributes sampling

If the auditor is to remain objective in evaluating a population on the basis of a sample, the technical requirements of statistical sampling must be carefully followed. The general requirements are similar for each of the sampling plans discussed, but the applications for the plans differ somewhat. In the interest of clarity, the methodology of attributes sampling is discussed first, followed by an explanation of the methodology and differences for discovery sampling and variables sampling.

The following points provide an outline of the methodology for using attributes sampling:

1. State the objective of the audit test.
2. Define the population.
3. Decide on the appropriate upper precision limit.
4. Decide on the appropriate confidence level.
5. Make an advance estimate of the population occurrence rate.
6. Determine the proper sample size.
7. Randomly select the sample.
8. Perform the audit procedures.
9. Generalize from the sample to the population.
10. Decide on the acceptability of the population.

(1) The Objective of the Audit Test. An attributes sampling plan is usually employed to assist in determining the rate of error existing in the population. In most cases attributes sampling is used in tests of transactions as a means of establishing the reliability of the system of internal control, but occasionally it is used to verify that an account balance is fairly stated.

It is essential that the auditor carefully define the characteristics of an error whenever attributes sampling is used. Unless a precise statement of what constitutes an error is made in advance of the testing, the staff man who carries out the audit procedures will not be in a position to identify an exception in the sample. For example, in performing tests of cash disbursement transactions, an error could be defined as any vendor's invoice that is recorded at the incorrect dollar amount. Alternatively, it could be defined to include such characteristics as a vendor's invoice without a receiving report or the improper approval for payment of an invoice. The auditor should think of the objective of the audit procedure when he establishes the definition of an error.

(2) Definition of the Population. The population represents the body of data about which the auditor wishes to generalize. The auditor can define the population to include whatever data he desires as long as he keeps in mind that he must randomly sample from the entire population as he has defined it. And it is both logical and important to realize that he may generalize only about that population from which he has sampled. For example, in performing tests of disbursement transactions, the auditor generally defines the population as all checks written for the year. If, however, the auditor restricts his random sample to the selection of checks from one month's transactions, he cannot statistically generalize about the disbursement transactions for the entire year. As a result, it is important that the auditor carefully define the population in advance. The total number of items or elements in the population can be determined after the population is defined.

(3) The Upper Precision Limit. One can do no more than generalize about a population on the basis of a sample. The exact population characteristics are still not known and cannot be stated. *Precision* is the statistical measure of the range of values, less than or more than the sample results, within which the true population value is expected to fall. The lower and upper extremes of this range are known as the precision limits. As an example, using attributes measurement, assume that the auditor took a random sample of 200 sales invoices and found 6 errors when he compared shipping documents to sales invoices as a test of the correctness of the quantity and description in the billing of sales. The true, but unknown, population error rate is probably not exactly 3%, but it can be statistically calculated that it is likely to be within ± 2% of the sample error rate. Stated differently, the true population error rate is probably between 1 and 5% (3% ± 2%). In this case the precision is 2%, the upper precision limit is 5%, and the lower precision limit is 1%. Usually in attributes sampling the auditor is interested only in the upper precision limit. This is because, if the true population error rate is large, the auditor will want to know about it, but if the true population error rate is small, the population is acceptable.

(4) The Confidence Level. When the auditor computes an upper precision limit there is still a chance that the true population error rate will exceed the computed value if the sample happens to be nonrepresentative (i.e., an unusually error-free sample from an error-prone popula-

tion). The possibility that the same results will not correctly reflect the true population characteristics is a risk the auditor must take regardless of whether he uses judgment sampling or statistical sampling. The advantage of statistical sampling methods is that this risk can be measured. In attributes testing the confidence level is the means of expressing the probability that the true population error rate is less than the upper precision limit. The confidence level, often referred to as *reliability,* is traditionally expressed as a percentage. Referring to the foregoing example, assume that the auditor calculates the confidence level at 90% when the upper precision limit is an error rate of 5 per hundred. The auditor can now state in statistical terms that he is 90% confident that the true population error rate is 5% or less. Another way of saying this is that there is a risk of 10% (100% − 90%) that the true population error rate exceeds 5%. The auditor must decide for himself if the computed reliability and upper precision limit are satisfactory.

Choosing the upper precision limit and the reliability that are appropriate in a particular situation is difficult, and the auditor must make this decision using his best judgment based on his professional experience. The suitable upper precision limit is a question of materiality and is therefore affected by the definition of the error and the importance of the population being estimated, as well as by the factors that auditors have traditionally considered in deciding what constitutes a material error. Since reliability is a measure of the confidence that the auditor desires, the primary considerations in deciding on reliability are the system of internal control and the upper precision limit that has been established. When internal control is considered inadequate, the auditor needs a larger confidence level than he otherwise requires. Similarly, a large upper precision limit also implies a higher confidence level.

(5) The Advance Estimate of the Population Occurrence Rate. In attributes sampling, an advance estimate of the population error rate (expected error rate) is necessary to determine the appropriate sample size. If the estimate of the population error rate is small, the auditor will be able to limit himself to a relatively small sample size to satisfy his upper precision limits. It is common to use the results of the previous year's audit as the current year's advance estimate, but if last year's results are not available or if they are considered unreliable, the auditor can take a small preliminary sample of the current year's population. It is not critical for the estimates to be absolutely correct because the current year's sample error rate is ultimately used to estimate the population characteristics.

(6) Determine the Proper Sample Size. Four factors determine the sample size the auditor should use in attributes sampling: the population

size, the advance estimate of the population error rate, the upper precision limit believed by the auditor to be appropriate, and the reliability desired by the auditor. Once these factors have been determined, the auditor can calculate the necessary sample size by using one of the available attributes sampling tables. (Some attributes tables such as the ones developed by the AICPA, do not include the population size as a factor affecting the sample size. When the population size is not included as a factor, the table assumes an infinite population.)

It should be stated at this point that it is more important for the candidate to understand the concepts underlying statistical sampling in auditing than it is to be able to use the statistical sampling tables or formulas. The determinants of any sample size or the statistical calculation of the results of any sample shown in this section are included only for purposes of illustrating the theory.

The CPA candidate should understand the effect on the sample of individually changing each of the four factors that determine its size when the other factors remain constant. The following table illustrates the effect on the sample of increasing each of the four factors. A decrease of any of the factors will have the opposite effect.

Change the Following Factor while the Three Other Factors are Held Constant	*Effect on the Required Sample Size*
1. Increase reliability	Increase
2. Increase upper precision limit	Decrease
3. Increase the advance estimate of the population error rate	Increase
4. Increase population size	Increase

A change in the population size has a relatively small effect on the sample size in attributes sampling, especially for population sizes greater than 2,000. Although this is inconsistent with the approach of most auditors when applying judgmental sampling, the relatively small effect that different population sizes should have on the sample size is a statistical fact.

(7) Random Selection of the Sample. After the auditor has computed the appropriate sample size for the circumstances, he must choose the particular elements in the population to be included in the sample (e.g., he must pull a sample of invoices from a file). This is accomplished by employing random sampling techniques to select the sample in a completely unbiased manner, thus ensuring that every item in the population has an equal chance of appearing in the sample. It is important to recall that results based on statistical calculation can be considered valid only if the sample is completely random. Two prevalent methods of random

selection are considered acceptable: random number tables and systematic sampling.

A random number table is a table of numbers in which each number, or combination of numbers, is completely independent of all other numbers in the table. The first step in using a random number table is to establish a correspondence between the digits in the table and the elements in the population. This is generally easy because most documents with which auditors are associated are consecutively prenumbered; but occasionally it is necessary to renumber a population to obtain correspondence. The second step is to select a method of consistently reading the table. The numbers from the table are then read and the elements of the population corresponding to the number in the table are included in the sample. When the auditor has arrived at the sample size he needs, he can stop. In using the table, it is desirable to choose a random starting point for picking the numbers. The auditor usually does this by simply closing his eyes and dropping a pencil onto a starting point on the table.

A facsimile of a small random number table appears below. To illustrate its use, assume that an auditor desires to select five canceled checks for detailed investigation from a check register in which the check numbers range from 47 to 875. If the auditor uses the first three digits in each column and selects row 2, column 2, as a starting point, the sample would comprise check numbers 720, 83, 185, 816, and 589. The numbers 41 and 923 would not be included because there is no population number that corresponds to these two numbers. The fourth digit in each row is not used in this illustration because the largest check number is only three digits.

	Column			
Row	*1*	*2*	*3*	*4*
1	1842	1468	8167	1859
2	0594	7202	0410	6908
3	9515	0833	9230	5955
4	7966	1856	5891	5970

In selecting a sample using a random number table, there is a distinction between replacement and nonreplacement sampling. In replacement sampling, an element in the population can be included in the sample more than once if the random number corresponding to that element is selected from the table more than once, whereas in nonreplacement sampling an element can be included only once. If the random number corresponding to an element is selected more than once in nonreplacement sampling, it is simply not included the second time. If, in the previous example, a sample size of 6 was being used, rather than 5, the next number included for replacement sampling would be check number 185, whereas for nonreplacement sampling we would skip this number, which has already been used, and take the next one—check 690. The distinction between the two types of random sampling is important because, whenever replacement sampling is used, it is necessary to assume that the population size is infinite, regardless of the actual number of elements in the population. As a result, the population size does not affect the sample size under conditions of replacement sampling.

In systematic sampling, the auditor calculates an interval and then methodically selects the items for the sample based on the size of the interval. The interval is determined by dividing the population size by the sample size. For example, if the population size is 2,500 and the sample size is 125, the interval is 20. The auditor then randomly selects a number from 1 to 20 and adds 20 to each result. If the randomly selected number is 9, the 125 items included in the sample will be 9, 29, 49, and so on to 2,489. The number in the first interval must be chosen by the use of a random table.

(8) Performing the Audit Procedures. The audit procedures are performed in the same manner in statistical sampling as in judgmental sampling. The auditor examines each randomly chosen item in the sample according to the objective of the audit test (definition of error), and he maintains a record of all the errors found. It is important that the staff man performing the steps have an adequate knowledge of the specified definition of an error. One or two improper evaluations in a small sample can have a great effect on generalizations about the population.

(9) Generalizing from the Sample to the Population. After the auditor has completed his tests of the sample, he is in a position to generalize about the population. It is critically important that he not conclude that the population error rate is the same as the sample error rate. Instead, he must compute the upper precision limit and the reliability for the population based on the actual sample results. This is easily accomplished by using an attributes sampling table which is essentially the same table by which the proper sample size was determined. To find the upper precision limit and the confidence level, it is necessary to know the error rate that was found in the sample, the actual sample size, and the population size. As an illustration, if the auditor has taken a random sample of 160 items from a population of 10,000 and determined that there were five errors (roughly 3%) in the sample, he can generalize about the population at any confidence level he desires. The following population generalizations can be made about the sample results just described, using the AICPA attributes evaluation tables.

Computed Upper Precision Limit, %	*Computed Reliability Level, %*
6	90
7	95
8	99

The results mean that, on the basis of the statistical calculations, the auditor believes there is a 10% risk (100% − 90%) that the true population error rate (upper precision limit) does not exceed 6%. With 99% confidence (reliability level) it can also be stated that true population error rate does not exceed 8%. This result is consistent with what should be expected. The auditor can be more confident that the true population error rate is less than 8% than he can be that it is less than 6%.

The preceding results are a useful means of illustrating an important concept in statistical sampling, namely, that it is inappropriate to state an upper precision limit without associating it with a reliability level. As we can see from the calculated upper precision limits, the values of upper precision limits may differ for different reliability levels. It would be misleading to state that the maximum error rate expected in the population is 6% without also noting that there is a 10% risk that the actual error rate exceeds 6%.

(10) Deciding on the Acceptability of the Population. It is important to distinguish between the upper precision limit and reliability that were set by the auditor before the tests were performed and the computed upper precision limit and reliability that resulted from the sample. The first set represents the standards that are deemed necessary by the auditor and the second set is the result that is objectively computed on the basis of the sample.

The results computed on the basis of the actual sample results must be at least as good as the standards that are demanded in advance of the actual tests. This means that the computed upper precision limit must be less than or equal to the prespecified upper precision limit, and the computed reliability must be more than or equal to the prespecified reliability level. In the example just given, if the auditor had prespecified that he would tolerate a 7% population error rate at a 95% confidence level, the requirements of the sample would have been met, and no further testing would be needed in the audit area being evaluated. Similarly, it can be seen from the above table that the population is acceptable as it currently stands if the auditor is willing to tolerate an upper precision limit of 9% at a reliability of 95% or an upper precision limit of 6% with a confidence level of 85%. On the other hand, if he demands a maximum upper precision limit of 6% at a reliability of 95% or an upper precision limit of 5% at a 90% confidence level, the auditor must take additional action.

When the reliability and upper precision limit standards have not been satisfied by the upper precision limits and reliability computed on the basis of the sample, there are two feasible courses of action: the auditor can increase his sample size to the point of certainty that the actual population error rate is acceptable or unacceptable, or he can request the client to take corrective action on the population. No matter which alternative is selected, it is important that the standards initially set be ultimately fulfilled. If it is not feasible to fulfill the reliability and upper precision limit standards, the working papers must contain a complete explanation of the implication of the excessive population error rate and a description of the auditor's corrective action.

It is an acceptable practice for the auditor to evaluate the population based upon the actual sample results at any time during the sampling as long as the sample is completely random. For example, if the auditor expected a population error rate of 2% but found only one error after selecting a random sample of 100, he could stop sampling at that point to determine if the upper precision limits and reliability standards had been fulfilled.

discovery sampling

Discovery sampling is a plan that enables the auditor to estimate the upper precision limit in the population at a specified confidence level when a random sample of the population yields no errors in the sample. Since discovery sampling is concerned with determining the rate of error in the population, rather than measuring value, it is a special case of attributes sampling.

The only differences between discovery and attributes sampling are in the definitions of the error, the expected error rate, and the upper precision limit. In discovery sampling, an error is so defined that its occurrence will be seriously regarded. For example, we might say that any misstated transaction that has the effect of misstating net income by more than $1,000 constitutes an error in the audit of cash disbursements. Another example is defining an error as any fraudulent transaction. If an anomalous occurrence in the population is called an error only when it is considered serious, the tolerable upper precision limit is usually small. Furthermore, since the auditor would normally not expect to find any of these critical errors in the sample, the expected error rate for discovery sampling is always zero.

The methodology for using discovery sampling to determine the sample size is similar to the methodology previously described for attributes. In both cases the auditor must decide in advance what constitutes an error and define the population about which he wishes to generalize. The auditor must also determine the population size and decide on both the maximum tolerable population error rate (upper precision limit) and the desired reliability level for both plans. The only difference in approach is that the expected error rate is always zero for discovery sampling. A standard table is used to determine the necessary sample size for both attributes and discovery sampling, but the tables are slightly different for each sampling plan.

After the sample size has been determined, the auditor must randomly select his sample and perform the audit procedures to determine if there are errors in the sample. Once the auditor has completed his tests, he must evaluate the results; but evaluation is carried out somewhat differently in discovery sampling and in attributes sampling. When the auditor who has used discovery sampling finds no errors in the sample, he can conclude, with the level of confidence set when the sample size was determined, that the population error rate is no greater than his originally stated level of tolerability. For example, if the auditor stated he would tolerate an upper precision limit (maximum error rate) of 1% at a confidence (reliability) level of 95% for an audit test with a population of 8,000, a discovery sampling table will show that the required sample size is 300. If no errors are found in the random sample, it is possible to automatically conclude (without referring to the tables) that the maximum expected population error rate is 1% at a reliability of 95%. It is also possible to evaluate the population at different upper precision limits and reliability levels for a sample size of 300 by using discovery sampling tables in the same manner used for attributes sampling.

When errors are discovered in the sample, the population cannot be evaluated via discovery sampling methods. Instead, it is necessary to switch to an attributes sampling table, and the results are evaluated in a manner identical to that previously described for attributes sampling. In most cases, an error found in discovery sampling leads to an extension of the audit testing, because the upper precision limit at a given confidence level will exceed the standards that were initially specified.

It is common for auditors to use attributes and discovery sampling simultaneously in the performance of an audit test. When this is done, errors are defined in such a manner that discovery sampling is used to evaluate the population for critical errors and attributes sampling is used for evaluating less important errors. If the auditor discovers some noncritical errors but no critical errors in the random sample, he can conveniently evaluate the population for both types of errors. An example of this approach is found in the testing of cash disbursements. The definition of an error for attributes sampling could include such characteristics as the lack of an invoice approval, a missing receiving report, or an error in an account classification; a discovery sampling error might be defined as any misstatement exceeding $200 that affects net income. The auditor generally would specify different confidence levels and upper precision limits for these two types of tests. A rational auditor would be willing to tolerate a larger upper precision limit for noncritical errors than he would for critical errors.

The effect of independently changing each of the factors affecting the sample size in discovery sampling is the same as for attributes sampling, except that the expected error rate cannot be changed from zero in discovery sampling. In both cases an increase in the population size or an increase in the desired confidence level increases the required sample size if the other factors are held constant; however, an increase in the upper precision limit demanded permits a decrease in the sample size. If a simultaneous increase is desired in both the upper precision limit and the confidence level, the effect on the sample size cannot be determined without the use of a statistical table, since the confidence level change increases the required sample size while the precision limit change decreases its size.

variables estimation

The objective in the use of variables estimation, which is also called variables sampling, is the measurement of the total or average value of a population, usually in terms of dollars. Since the main goal of auditing is to determine whether account balances are fairly stated on the financial statements, the use of variables sampling is often considered more directly applicable to auditing than attributes sampling. For example, variables sampling can be conveniently used to find the correct dollar balance in the inventory or accounts receivable account, whereas attributes sampling is primarily a test of the reliability of the system of internal control. Even if the auditor is satisfied that the system is adequate, he must also verify the balance in inventory and accounts receivable via variables sampling or judgmental sampling techniques.

The conclusions about the population that are reached following variables estimation are similar in concept to those resulting from attributes sampling, except that the former are stated in dollar terms rather than in terms of percentage error rates. In variables sampling, the true population value is set forth in terms of an upper and lower precision limit, in a dollar amount, at a stated reliability level. For example, in estimating inventory the auditor could calculate on the basis of his audit tests that the true population value is $90,000 ± $5,000 at a 95% reliability level. Stated in another way, he could state that he believes, with a 95% degree of confidence, that the true value of the population is between $85,000 and $95,000. The $90,000 amount is the one best estimate of the population value based on the sample; $5,000 is the precision measure and $85,000 and $95,000 are the lower and upper precision limits, respectively.

In determining the appropriate sample size to use in variables sampling, the auditor must know the population size and the standard deviation of the population, and he must specify the acceptable reliability level and precision. Although three of these terms have been explained previously, they are discussed again in connection with variables sampling to assure a complete understanding of the terms.

(1) Population Size. The population size is the total number of elements in the population being tested. It has an identical definition for variables and attributes sampling.

(2) Reliability. The reliability or confidence level is a measure of the assurance that the true dollar value of the population neither exceeds the upper precision limit nor falls below the lower precision limit. The same definition applies to variables and attributes sampling alike, except that in attributes sampling it is associated only with the upper limit. The appropriate reliability in a given set of circumstances is decided on by the auditor, using his professional judgment.

(3) Precision. Precision is a measure of the inability to extrapolate directly from the sample value to the population value. Its most important function is to enable the computation of the lower and upper percision limits. This concept is similar to attributes sampling, but it is stated in dollar amounts rather than as the percentage of errors in the population. Another relevant difference is that the auditor is concerned with both the upper and lower precision limit in variables sampling, whereas in attributes sampling he is not interested in the lower limit. The reason for this is that the auditor must determine whether the correct dollar value of an account is probably materially greater or less than the recorded value, but he need not be concerned if the true error rate in the population value is extremely small.

(4) Population Standard Deviation. The population standard deviation is a statistical measure of the variability among the values of the individual items in the population. If there is a large amount of variation in the population, the standard deviation will be larger than when the variation is small. For example, the set of values $4, $14, and $26 has far less variation than the set $2, $275, and $812. Therefore the standard deviation will be smaller in the first case.

The standard deviation is important to the auditor because its value has a significant effect on the sample size that is necessary to satisfy a specified precision. As might be expected, the ability to precisely predict the value of a population is better when there is a small amount of variation in the individual values of the population than when the variation is great. As a result, the sample size required to satisfy a specified precision is directly related to the size of the population standard deviation.

An estimated value of the population standard deviation is computed by the auditor using a standard statistical formula, on the basis of a small presample taken from the population. The size of the standard deviation estimate is determined solely by the characteristics of the population and is not affected by the professional judgment of the auditor.

Once the population size and standard deviation have been determined by estimation and the precision level and reliability that the auditor demands have been specified, the appropriate sample size can be determined either by the use of a formula or by using variables sampling tables. The calculation of the actual sample size is less important than understanding the factors that affect the result.

It is important that the CPA candidate realize the effect on the sample of individually changing each of the four factors that determine its size. The relationships are as follows:

Change the Following Factor while the Three Other Factors are Held Constant	*Effect on the Required Sample Size*
1. Decrease reliability	Decrease
2. Decrease precision level	Increase
3. Decrease the population standard deviation	Decrease
4. Decrease the population size	Decrease

These results are consistent with the conclusions that were reached earlier when the four factors that affect attribute sampling were individually changed. Like attributes sampling, the effect of changing the population size in variables sampling is usually not significant, especially for populations greater than 2,000.

The selection of the particular items for inclusion in the sample and the performance of the audit tests are accomplished in much the same manner for variables estimation as for attributes sampling. The auditor must use random selection techniques for obtaining the sample and he can only generalize to the population from which he has selected the sample. The major difference is that, in performing the audit tests for variables sampling, it is necessary to ascertain the individual values of each item in the sample. The auditor then computes the estimated total population value on the basis of the combined sample values.

The calculation of the upper and lower precision limits of the population is accomplished by separately calculating the one best population estimate and the precision at a given reliability level. These two calculations are then combined. The one best estimate of the population is computed by multiplying the population size by the average value of the individual items in the sample. For example, in calculating the value of inventory with a sample of 200 items from a population of 1,000, assume that the auditor arrived at a total sample value of $19,600. He can calculate that the one best estimate of the population is $98,000 (1,000 × $19,600/200). As a means of determining the precision, it is necessary to first estimate the standard deviation based on the sample selected. The precision at the desired confidence level can then be found from a formula or a prepared table. As an illustration, assume that the auditor has computed the population standard deviation at $45 in the example just given. The population precision can then be calculated from a different formula as $5,600 at a 95% reliability level. By combining the results of the one best estimate of the population value and the precision, it is possible to arrive at the statistical estimate of the population value in terms of precision limits at a given confidence level. As with attributes sampling, the precision limits must always be stated at a given level of reliability. The estimated value of the population in our example can be stated as being $98,000 ± $5,600 at a reliability of 95%, or stated in terms of precision limits, the estimated population value is between $92,400 and $103,600 ($98,000 ± $5,600) at a reliability of 95%.

Different precision levels and precision limits can also be computed for the same sample by changing the desired reliability level. For example, with the sample cited previously of 200 at only a 90% confidence level, the population precision would be less than $5,600 and the upper and lower precision limits would be narrower than presently stated. At a 99% reliability, the precision level would be larger than it is in the example.

The final step in variables sampling is the auditor's decision to accept or reject the recorded value of the account being tested. The rule that should be used for making this decision is as follows: if the values of the computed upper and lower precision limits are both between the upper and lower precision limits required by the auditor, the population is satisfactory as stated. Otherwise the auditor must take further action. The required upper and lower precision limits are determined by adding and subtracting the precision that was specified by the auditor in advance of the testing to the recorded book value.

As an illustration of an appropriate method for determining whether the auditor's specifications have been met, the following information is summarized:

1.	Recorded book value	$100,000
2.	Precision demanded by the auditor	6,000
3.	Reliability level demanded by the auditor	95%
4.	Auditor's single best estimate of the population based upon the sample	$98,000
5.	Computed precision at a reliability of 95% based on the sample	$5,600
6.	Computed upper and lower precision limits at a reliability of 95%	$92,400–103,600

On the basis of the recorded book value, the auditor requires each of the computed precision limits to be between $94,000 and $106,000 ($100,000 ± $6,000). The computed upper precision limit of $103,600 is satisfactory because it is between the required limits, but the lower precision limit of $92,400 falls below the required standard of $94,000. As in attributes sampling, there are two courses of action available to the auditor: the sample size can be increased until the auditor knows whether the population value is acceptable or unacceptable, or the client can be requested to take corrective action. In some cases the corrective action is simply to adjust the book value. In this example, if the recorded balance is decreased to $98,000 by an adjusting entry, the requirements are satisfied because the new required precision limits are changed to $92,000 and $104,000 ($98,000 ± $6,000). Now the computed upper and lower precision limits both fall within the required precision limits and therefore the adjusted population is satisfactory.

In some cases it is not possible to adjust the account balance to satisfy the required precision limits. This occurs whenever the computed precision is larger than the required precision. When that happens, either the auditor must increase the sample size as a means of reducing the computed precision or the client must correct the population errors.

stratified random sampling

Stratified random sampling is an extension of variables sampling in which all the elements in the total population are divided into two or more subpopulations. Each subpopulation is then independently tested and statistically measured in the manner explained for variables estimation. After the results of the individual parts have been computed, they are combined into one overall population measurement in terms of an upper and lower precision limit at a specified reliability. Subdividing or stratifying a population is not unique to statistical sampling, of course. Auditors have traditionally emphasized certain types of items when they are testing a population. For example, in confirming accounts receivable, it has been customary to place more emphasis on large accounts than on small ones. The major difference is that in statistical stratified sampling the approach is more objective and better defined than it is under most traditional stratification methods.

In a statistical sense, the purpose of stratification is to reduce the overall population standard deviation by redefining the population into several smaller populations. It will be recalled from the discussion of variables sampling that (a) the standard deviation is an important determinant of the required sample size, (b) the standard deviation is a measure of the variation of the individual items in the population, and (c) the size of the standard deviation is determined by calculation. By subdividing the population into separate populations, it is possible in many cases to reduce the overall standard deviation and thereby reduce the sample size needed to fulfill the precision and reliability requirements that have been specified. A simple example will demonstrate how the standard deviation can be reduced.

Inventory Elements in the Population	*Book Value*
1	$ 10
2	1,900
3	1,950
4	14
5	8
6	1,850

An examination of this population indicates that its standard deviation is fairly large because there is a large variation from the smallest to to the largest item. In this case, when the population is properly divided into a stratum of large items (elements 2, 3, and 6) and another stratum of small items (elements 1, 4, and 5), the variations in the individual strata are greatly reduced. In any population that contains a great deal of variation it is usually advantageous to stratify and test each stratum separately.

It is up to the auditor to decide the number of strata and the characteristics of the elements to be included in each stratum in a particular situation. Although there are no absolute rules for making the decision, the most important factor to be weighed is the cost saving arising from the reduced sample size relative to the additional costs that accrue owing to the increased calculations and the burdensome selection of samples from different strata when stratified sampling is used. If there is a considerable variation in the elements in the population, several strata may be desirable; whereas in cases of small variation it may not be worthwhile to stratify at all.

In using stratified random sampling, the following steps are necessary:

1. Establish the precision and confidence level for the overall population desired by the auditor. This requirement is fulfilled by the use of professional judgment in the same manner as for variables sampling.
2. Design the strata in the manner desired. This step entails defining the number of strata to use and setting the characteristics of each. In composing the stratification design, it is important to remember that each element in the population must be included in only one stratum and that all elements must appear.
3. Estimate the standard deviation for each stratum in the population. This is usually done by the use of a preliminary sample of each stratum.
4. Compute the sample size that must be taken from each stratum with a special statistical formula.
5. Select the items for testing. It is necessary to treat each stratum as a separate population and randomly select the corresponding required sample from that stratum. As might be imagined, this can be somewhat time consuming when the client's data are not conveniently arranged to keep the different strata separate. Often the problems of selecting the items for testing take so much time that stratified sampling is not economically feasible.
6. Compute the best single estimate of the overall population and the precision at a specified reliability from the results of the sample. This is done in a manner similar to variables sampling, but a different statistical formula is used.

A study of these six steps indicates that there is no substantial conceptual difference between stratified sampling and simple random variables sampling.

Auditing EDP Systems

The use of computers for recording, analyzing, and storing accounting information has had a significant effect on auditing during the past decade. The importance of computers has been reflected in the increasing frequency of questions concerning electronic data processing in the Auditing section of the CPA examination. For the most part, four general aspects have been emphasized (a) the effect of EDP on the traditional audit trail, (b) the types of controls available in an EDP system which are not applicable to non-EDP systems, (c) the evaluation of internal control in an EDP system, and (d) the use of the computer as an audit tool. Special emphasis has been put on the candidate's knowledge and understanding of the types of controls applicable to EDP systems. In this part of the chapter we shall discuss each of the four aspects of EDP listed, but the controls relevant to EDP systems will receive the heaviest emphasis.

A satisfactory solution to most of the questions on recent CPA examinations could have been found by a careful study of *Auditing and EDP,* by Gordon P. Davis (see note 25). As a result, that book is frequently quoted in this section. It is suggested that any candidate with an inadequate background in EDP thoroughly study *Auditing and EDP,* including Appendices A and C.

effect of EDP on the traditional audit trail

The audit trail is the accumulation of source documents and records maintained by the client which are the support for the transactions which occurred during the period. It includes such things as duplicate sales invoices, vendors' invoices, canceled checks, general and subsidiary ledgers, and all types of journals. Since the audit trail is a primary source of evidence used by auditors, it is important that an adequate trail be available for verification needs. Traditionally, for every transaction that occurs there should be support by one or more visible source documents and a record in a journal and sometimes in a subsidiary ledger.

The effect of the computer on the audit trail depends on the level of sophistication of the system. When the computer is used only as an accurate high-speed calculator, the audit trail may not be affected, especially if management desires to maintain the traditional source documents and records. In highly integrated on-line systems, on the other hand, the traditional audit trail can be substantially eliminated unless specific provision is made for some detailed records. The most common changes that can occur in the audit trail are stated in *Auditing and EDP* as follows:

> 1. Source documents, once transcribed onto a machine-readable input medium, are no longer used in the processing cycle. They may be filed in a manner which makes subsequent access difficult.
>
> 2. In some systems, traditional source documents may be eliminated by the use of direct input devices.
>
> 3. Ledger summaries may be replaced by master files which do not show the amounts leading up to the summarized values.
>
> 4. The data processing cycle does not necessarily provide a transaction listing or journal. To provide such a listing may require a specific action at a recognizable cost.
>
> 5. It is sometimes unnecessary to prepare frequent printed output of historical records. Files can be maintained on computer media and reports prepared only for exceptions.
>
> 6. Files maintained on a magnetic medium cannot be read except by use of the computer and a computer program.

7. The sequence of records and processing activities is difficult to observe because much of the data and many of the activities are contained within the computer system.[25]

When the client is designing an EDP system, it is essential for management to include adequate provisions for an audit trail that will satisfy both the operational needs of the organization and the verification needs of the auditor. In most cases it is desirable for the auditor to carefully review the system design at the planning stage to make certain that the audit trail will be adequate. This approach is useful because it enables the auditor to influence the design of the system before it becomes operational, and it reduces the likelihood that the auditor will have to disclaim an opinion or spend excessive audit time because important records were unavailable. According to *Auditing and EDP,* the general principles governing the design of proper audit trails are:

1. For all transactions affecting the financial statements there must be a means for establishing the account to which the transaction is posted.
2. For all accounts reflected in the financial statements there must be a means for tracing the summary amount back to the individual transaction elements.
3. For all transactions and accounts drawing a large number of inquiries, regular provision should be made to supply the records necessary for answering the inquiries.
4. For all transactions and accounts not typically subject to inquiries there must be a means for tracing, even though regular provisions are not made.[26]

types of controls in EDP systems

In general, the concern for adequate controls in EDP systems is the same as for noncomputerized data processing and management control systems. The controls, as they pertain to the audit function, are designed to reduce the likelihood of errors, either by prevention or early detection.

The controls that are applicable to a firm which uses EDP equipment include those previously discussed as well as some that are unique to EDP systems. Since many of the controls that are applicable to non-EDP systems are not directly concerned with the recording of transactions, they also affect an organization with an EDP system (e.g., the physical protection of assets by such means as storerooms and cash registers). Other controls are concerned with the recording of transactions, but they are applicable to any kind of a system. For example, adequate documents, such as receiving reports and shipping documents, ensure the correctness

[25] Gordon L. Davis, *Auditing and EDP* (New York: American Institute of Certified Public Accountants, 1968), pp. 119–20.

[26] *Ibid.,* p. 123.

of the information received by those responsible for recording it. Although the following discussion considers only the controls that are unique to EDP systems, auditors must also evaluate the adequacy of the controls that were previously discussed. The three major categories of controls included in this section are:

1. Organizational controls.
2. Controls over input, processing, and output.
3. Safeguarding records and files.

Organizational Controls. In a computer system it is impossible to segregate the recording function in a manner that produces the automatic cross checks that have traditionally been available in a manual system. In a manual system it is desirable to have one person record accounting information in the journals while a different person records the same data in the related subsidiary ledger; but in most EDP systems the function of recording the journals, the subsidiary ledgers, and the general ledger are performed simultaneously by the computer. Since no organizational checks are available for EDP systems, different kinds of controls are needed over input, processing, and output to compensate for the inability to segregate the recording functions. These controls are discussed shortly.

The most important data processing functions that are unique to an EDP system should be segregated as a means of reducing the likelihood of errors, both intentional and unintentional, but such segregation is especially important for the control of fraud. The three functions that should be kept apart are programming, the operation of the equipment, and the control of the output. Programming and equipment operation should be separated to prevent the operator from having sufficient knowledge of the program to modify it immediately before or during its use. In several cases of recorded fraud, the operator had covered an embezzlement by temporarily changing his original program. The control function in an EDP system is concerned with checking to determine that the output being generated is reliable. If the control function is to be adequately performed, it is essential that it be independent of both programming and equipment operation.

It is essential that an internal audit or control function be included in any organization that generates its accounting information via an EDP system, because the computer is unable to make judgments about incorrect inputs or outputs. The most important control responsibilities performed by the control group in the EDP function are shown in *Auditing and EDP* as follows:

1. Logging of input data and recording of control information.
2. Recording of progress of work through the department.
3. Reconciliation of computer controls with other control information.
4. Supervision of distribution of output.
5. Scrutiny of console logs and printed control information in accordance with control instructions.
6. Liaison with users regarding errors and logging of correction requests and recording of corrections made.
7. Scrutiny of error listings and maintenance of error log or error report.[27]

Controls Over Input, Processing, and Output. An input error is generally defined as any error that occurs in the data up to the time it is entered into the computer in machine-readable form; processing errors are those that occur during the operation performed by the computer. Errors in output thus result from either input or processing errors. Although a knowledge of the distinctions between the general type of controls is desirable, it is less important than an understanding of the types of specific controls and their purposes.

There are a substantial number of controls available in an EDP system to control input and processing errors. Although it is not feasible to consider them all, the most important controls are reviewed in this section.

(1) Keypunch Verifying. Having different operators check part or all of the original keypunching is a means of controlling errors from this source. The procedure consists of inserting the punched card into the verifier and rekeying data from the original documents. If the results do not match, the card is rejected. Since the operators are generally instructed to keypunch the information exactly as it is stated on the original documents, this means of control is useful only as a means of detecting keypunch errors. Although keypunch verification is expensive, it is normally performed on the most important data because of the importance of correct inputs.

(2) Check Digit. A check digit is a number that is a part of an identification number. It is used as a means of determining whether a recorded identification number is correct. As a highly oversimplified example of check digits, assume that salesmen identification numbers range from 1 to 9000. For the salesman with the identification number 3624, the number 15 (the summation of the 4 digits is the check digit in this example) could be added to the number for a new identification number of 362415. After this is done for each salesman, the computer

[27] Davis, *Auditing and EDP,* p. 20.

can be easily programmed to determine whether the sum of the first four digits of each salesman identification number equals the last two digits. This is a useful control for detecting keypunch, machine, or programming errors. It is unnecessary to keypunch verify identification numbers if check digits are used.

(3) Tests for Valid Data. The computer can provide some assurance that the inputs and outputs are correct by means of different types of tests. Valid data tests are performed to aid in determining whether information that should be included does in fact appear, as well as whether the information in question is correct. Davis lists the following examples of valid data tests:

> 1. *Valid code.* If there is only a limited number of valid codes (say, for coding expenses), the code being read may be checked to see that it is one of the valid codes.
>
> 2. *Valid character.* Certain characters only are allowed in a data field, so the computer can test the field to determine that no invalid characters are used.
>
> 3. *Valid field size, sign, and composition.* If a code number should be a specified number of digits in length, the computer may be programmed to test that the field size is as specified. If the sign of the field should always be positive or always negative, a test may be made to ensure that the sign is correct. If the field should contain only numerics or only alphabetics, a test may be made to determine that the field does indeed contain the proper composition of characters.
>
> 4. *Valid transaction.* There is usually a relatively small number of valid transactions processed with a particular file. For example, there is a limited number of transaction codes that can apply to accounts receivable file updating. As part of input error control, the transaction code can be tested for validity.
>
> 5. *Valid combination of fields.* Combinations, besides individual fields, may be tested for validity. For example, a salesman code that can be associated with only a few territory codes can be checked for invalid combinations.
>
> 6. *Missing data test.* The program may check the data fields to make sure that all data fields necessary to code a transaction have data.
>
> 7. *Sequence test.* In batch processing, the data to be processed must be arranged in a sequence identical to that of the file. Both the master file and the transaction file may be tested to ensure that they are in correct sequence—ascending or descending, as the case may be. The sequence check can also be used to account for all documents numbered sequentially.[28]

An examination of these examples should make it clear that valid data tests must be programmed by the user only after a careful study of

[28] Davis, *Auditing and EDP,* pp. 64–65.

the coding system, data fields, and other relevant information of the system.

(4) Control Totals. Control totals are used to determine whether all the data that were put into the system were processed. Generally, the purpose of a control total is to make certain that no data are lost in handling or processing, but in some cases it is used to verify that the dollar amount is correct. A count or summation of a batch of input must be completed before the input goes into the system. The control total is compared with the final output at a later date. An example of this might be to foot a batch of sales invoice documents before they are given to keypunching and then, after the information has been processed by the computer, to compare this total to the output. In most cases the final comparison of the control total to the output total is performed by the computer. The three general types of control totals are defined by Davis:

> *Financial totals.* Financial totals are totals such as sales, payroll amounts, inventory dollar amounts, etc., which are normally added together in order to provide financial summaries.
>
> *Hash totals.* Hash totals are totals of data fields which are usually not added. The total has meaning only as a control and is not used in any other way in data processing. To determine that all inventory items are processed, a control total may be developed of the inventory item numbers and this control total compared with the sum of the item numbers obtained during the processing run.
>
> *Document or record count.* In many cases, instead of obtaining a financial total or hash total, it may be sufficient merely to obtain a count to ensure that all documents or records have been received and processed.[29]

(5) File Label Controls. To ensure that the proper transaction or master file is being used with the program being run, file labels that identify the proper file and summarize the results of the information are customarily included in the file. An internal file label has the relevant information in machine language at both the beginning and the end of the file. The information at the beginning typically includes the file name, its identification number, and the reel number (in a multireel file). At the end of the file we usually find the record count and the applicable control totals, as well as an indication that this point is the end of the file. External file labels in a readable form aid operators, librarians, and other users to correctly identify the files. When magnetic tape is used, the external label is attached directly to the tape reel, whereas in a punched card file the information is normally written on the top of the file of cards.

[29] *Ibid.*, p. 67.

(6) Transmittal Controls and Route Slips. Both of these are forms used by organizations to help ensure that all batches of data are entirely processed. The transmittal control form is used to log the receipt of data, the date they are processed, and the release of the data. This control device is useful both for determining which data have been received but not processed and for isolating where unprocessed data are located. The route slip is attached to the file of data to inform the processing center of the proper path of processing and as a record of the actual processing performed.

(7) Crossfooting Tests. Crossfooting tests in an EDP system are similar to those normally found in a manual accounting system. Individual categories are totaled independently by the computer and are then combined to make sure that they are equal to other related totals. Examples of this include crossfooting the individual categories in the sales journal or the payroll journal. If the totals are not equal, an error message is printed out.

(8) Reasonableness Tests. Reasonableness tests constitute a general control that serves to identify a total or transaction that exceeds some predesignated reasonable limit. One example of a reasonableness check consists of testing whether the recorded payroll hours worked by an employee who is paid on a weekly basis exceeds a specified number, such as 70 hours. Similar examples are reasonableness tests of each office employee's salary for the month, the maximum number of units of merchandise sold to a retail customer, and the minimum and maximum supplies expenses for a given month. This type of test is useful for the control of all kinds of large errors including keypunch errors, loss of documents, machine failures, and program errors. Clearly, adequate reasonableness checks are important to the auditor as a means of preventing material errors.

(9) Hardware Controls. Hardware controls are built into the equipment by the manufacturer to detect equipment failure. There are a considerable number of possible specific hardware controls available in EDP systems. Davis describes the five general types of controls:

> *Redundant character check.* A redundant character is a character attached to a data item for the purpose of providing for error detection. The redundant character is developed from the characteristics of the data item to which it is attached. After an operation such as the moving of a data item in the system, the computation used to obtain the redundant character is repeated to derive a second character. The two redundant characters are compared and, if they are the same, it is assumed that there has been no malfunction affecting the data during the transfer or some other operation.

Duplicate process check. Another type of equipment control involves having the same process performed twice and the results of the two operations compared. Any difference between the first operation and the second signals an error. The duplicate process may be a complementary action such as reading after writing to check what was written.

Echo check. In an echo check the central processor sends a command to an input or output device to perform an operation. The device returns a signal that verifies that the proper mechanisms for performing the actions have been activated. This check verifies that the equipment was activated without testing the actual results obtained.

Validity check. Since, on many operations, only certain results can be considered correct, one method of checking is to compare a result obtained against all valid results. Any result not fitting into this set of valid results is considered incorrect.

Equipment check. In this control, the computer checks the equipment to see if it is functioning properly instead of checking the results from the operation. It is not a positive check, since the equipment may be working properly while defective media or other factors are causing improper results.[30]

From an internal control point of view, the independent auditor is less concerned about the adequacy of the hardware controls in the system than he is about the organization's methods of handling the errors that the computer identifies. The hardware controls are usually carefully designed by the manufacturer to adequately discover and report all machine failures. It is obvious, however, that unless the client's organization has made specific provision for handling machine errors, the output data will remain uncorrected.

(10) Console Messages. It is desirable for the computer program to include a provision for informing the operator through the use of console messages of any operational errors that have been made. The operator can be informed of errors such as the incorrect setting of console switches and the use of incorrect files.

(11) Output Control. Control over the reliability of output of an EDP system is dependent primarily on the reliability of the input and the processing. In addition, it is desirable to have a final review in the data processing department to check for obvious output errors such as incomplete output, control totals that do not reconcile, and missing information. It is also useful to secure final reasonableness tests as a means of avoiding material errors. The users of the output are another potential source of control over errors in the output when they use the data for their information needs. It is important that provisions be made for a

[30] Davis, *Auditing and EDP,* pp. 39–40.

formal feedback mechanism from the users to the data processing center as a means of making certain that the cause of the errors is corrected.

(12) Error Listing. An error listing is a common means of communicating errors that have been discovered in a data processing system. The system can be programmed to automatically report errors discovered during the processing of data (e.g., invalid data, control data differences, internal file label errors, and hardware malfunctions). Similarly, input errors and keypunch errors should result in a manually prepared error listing.

The error listing represents an essential method of controlling and evaluating the system for both the auditor and the client. The client should use the control listing as a means of making certain that all errors are corrected; but even more important, he should use it as a means of correcting the cause and thus prevent future errors. Similarly, the auditor learns from the error listing the kinds of errors that are occurring in the system, as well as the corrective measures the client has taken to eliminate the cause.

Safeguarding Records and Files. The auditor is interested in the client's means of safeguarding the EDP records and files to ensure that there is an adequate audit trail for the auditor's evidence accumulation needs and to permit advising the client about the potential loss of records that are important to the client's accounting and operating requirements.

The physical safeguards over records and files that are important in an EDP system are not significantly different from those that should exist in a manual accounting system. However, it is more crucial that the former be adhered to because of the greater potential for the destruction of the total record. The compactness of EDP records and the possibility of erasing a large amount of information on some storage media make such records highly vulnerable to accidental or intentional destruction, and thus it is essential that fire and security protection be provided by the use of adequate vaults and off-premises storage.

File protection rings are a useful safeguard against the erasure of information stored on magnetic tape. The file protection ring permits the reading of information on the tape as long as the ring is attached. Similarly, the internal and external file labels previously discussed are a means of protecting the information in files.

evaluating internal control in an EDP system

The objective of the review of the system of internal control in an EDP system is the same as for a manual system: to aid in determining, on the basis of the adequacy of existing controls, the audit evidence that should be accumulated. Similarly, the technique of internal control evaluation for both EDP and non-EDP systems is to obtain information about the client's prescribed system, to evaluate its weakness, and to ascertain that the system is actually operating in accordance with the plan.

In obtaining information about the client's prescribed system and evaluating the system for weaknesses, the auditor is concerned with determining the existence and adequacy of the EDP controls that were enumerated in the preceding pages. Of course, it is also necessary to evaluate the non-EDP controls discussed earlier in the chapter, such as the separation of the custody over assets from the recording function.

The three most important means of obtaining information about the client's EDP controls are flowcharting, EDP questionnaires, and a study of the error listing generated by the system. The first two approaches have counterparts in non-EDP systems, and error listing is unique to EDP systems. In most cases it is desirable to use all three approaches in evaluating internal control, because they offer different types of information that can be subjectively combined by the auditor. The flowchart emphasizes the organization of the company and the flow of information throughout the system, whereas the internal control questionnaire emphasizes specific controls without relating individual controls to one another. The error listing supports both these approaches by showing the actual errors that were reported by the EDP system. Ultimately, the auditor must use the information obtained about the system to determine the most important weaknesses in the internal control system. Although this is a difficult part of evaluating internal control, and one requiring considerable professional experience, generally accepted auditing standards cannot be met if it is not done.

The final step in evaluating internal control—testing whether the system operates properly—can be performed with or without the computer. These two approaches are briefly described in the remaining pages of this section.

auditing without the use of the computer

In auditing without the use of the computer, which is commonly referred to as "auditing around the computer," the auditor reviews internal control and performs tests of transactions and account balance verification procedures in the same manner as in non-EDP systems. However, there is no attempt to test the client's computer programs or to use the computer to perform audit procedures.

In order to audit without using the computer, the auditor must have access to sufficient source documents and a detailed listing of output in a readable form. This is possible only when all the following conditions are met:

1. The source documents are available in a nonmachine language.
2. The documents are filed in a manner that facilitates locating them for auditing purposes.
3. The output is listed in sufficient detail to enable the auditor to trace individual transactions from the source documents to the output, or vice versa.

If any of these conditions does not exist, the auditor will have to use the computer for carrying out his procedures. Auditing without the use of the computer is an acceptable and often desirable approach when the informational needs of the client's organization require him to maintain the necessary source documents and detailed output.

Failure of the auditor to use the computer in carrying out audit procedures does not imply that he ignores the EDP installation. He continues to have a responsibility for a thorough review of the system of internal control to determine the weaknesses in the system as an aid in deciding on the appropriate audit procedures and the sample size necessary for each procedure. Davis suggests the following general steps in reviewing the system and performing the procedures when the auditor does not use the computer.

Audit Approach	*Implementation*
Review of system	Interview with personnel in data processing Use of questionnaire Examination of general system description General review of major controls Review of controls for each application vital to the audit
Tests of systems	Examination of evidence for controls (error listings, batch control records, authorizations, etc.) Use of printouts to trace items in output to source documents to reports, report totals to controls, etc. Checking of transaction sample for correct processing Other typical tests
Evaluation of records	Tests to check correctness of summary accounts (foot, crossfoot, etc.) Tests of samples of detail items by confirmation, reasonableness tests, etc.[31]

[31] *Ibid.*, p. 133.

auditing with the use of the computer

There are two distinct ways that the auditor uses the computer to perform audit procedures: the processing of the auditors' test data on the client's computer system as a part of the review of internal control and the testing of the records maintained by the computer as a means of verifying the client's financial statements.

Test Data Approach. The objective of the use of the test data approach is to determine whether the client's computer program can correctly handle valid and invalid transactions as they arise. To fulfill this objective, the auditor develops different types of transactions that are processed under the auditor's control using the client's computer program on the client's EDP equipment. The auditor's test data must include both valid and invalid transactions in order to determine whether the client's computer program will react properly to different kinds of data. Since the auditor has complete knowledge of the errors that exist in the test data, it is possible for him to check whether the client's system has reacted properly to the auditor's input. The auditor does this by examining the error listing and the details of the output resulting from the test data.

Test data are helpful in reviewing the client's system of processing data and its control over errors, but there are several difficulties that must be overcome before this approach can be used. The most important of these are as follows:

1. *The Test Data Must Comprise All Relevant Conditions That the Auditor Desires to Test.* This should include testing the adequacy of all the controls discussed previously that are applicable to the client's program under review. Because a great deal of competence is required in developing data to test for all the relevant types of errors that could occur, this approach generally requires the assistance of an EDP specialist.

2. *The Program Tested by the Auditor's Test Data Must Be the Same Program That Is Used Throughout the Year by the Client.* One approach the auditor can take to assure that this condition is met is to run the test data on a surprise basis, possibly by randomly repeated use of the test data throughout the year. This approach is both costly and time consuming. A more realistic method is to rely on the client's system of internal control over the use of the program and changes in the program.

3. In Some Cases the Test Data Must Be Eliminated from the Client's Records. The elimination of the test data is necessary if the program being tested is for the updating of a master file such as the accounts receivable trial balance. It is not difficult to imagine that a client would not tolerate the permanent inclusion of fictitious test transactions in a master file. There are several feasible methods of eliminating the test data, but each requires the assistance of an EDP specialist.

Auditor's Computer Program Approach. The second approach to auditing with the computer is to run the auditor's computer program on a computer controlled by the auditor, in order to verify the client's data recorded in a machine language. The auditor's computer program and the test data approach are complementary rather than mutually exclusive, in the same manner that tests of transactions and year-end balance verification are complementary. When the auditor uses test data he is evaluating the ability of the client's system to handle different types of transactions, whereas in the auditor's computer program approach the output of the system is being tested for correctness.

The auditor can potentially perform a large variety of tests with a computer program if the client's data are in a machine language. The general categories of tests that can be performed are listed by Davis as follows:

> 1. *Testing extensions and footings.* The computer can be used to perform simple summations and other computations to test the correctness of extensions and footings.
>
> 2. *Selecting and printing confirmation requests.* The computer can select and print out confirmation requests on the basis of quantifiable selection criteria. The program can be written to select the accounts according to any set of criteria desired and using any sampling plan. The format of the request can be designed to facilitate mailing and audit follow-up.
>
> 3. *Examining records for quality (completeness, consistency, valid conditions, etc.).* The quality of visible records is readily apparent to the auditor when he makes use of them in his examination. Sloppy record-keeping, lack of completeness, and so on, are thus observed by the auditor in the normal course of the audit. If machine-readable records, however, are evaluated manually, a complete printout is needed to examine their quality. The auditor may choose to use the computer for examining these records for quality.
>
> 4. *Summarizing data and performing analyses useful to the auditor.* The auditor frequently needs to have the client's data analyzed and/or summarized. Such procedures age accounts receivable, prepare annual usage requirements, analyze for obsolescence of parts in an inventory, list all credit balances in accounts receivable and all debt balances in accounts payable, and so on.
>
> 5. *Selecting and printing audit samples.* The computer may be programmed to select audit samples by the use of random numbers or by

systematic selection techniques. The samples selected in this way can be used for such audit tests as confirmations, price tests or inventory items, and so on.

6. *Comparing duplicate data (maintained in separate files) for correctness and consistency.* Where there are two or more separate records having identical data fields, the computer can be used in testing for consistency. For instance, the cost prices in the master inventory file may be compared with the cost figures used by the billing program.

7. *Comparing audit data with company records.* Audit data such as inventory test counts can be compared with the company inventory records by using a computer program. For this procedure the audit data must be converted to machine-readable form.[32]

The most serious problem in the use of computer programs for testing client data is to obtain a suitable program at a reasonable cost. Three approaches are available to auditors.

(1) Use the Client's Program. This is an acceptable and economical alternative when the client already has a program that the auditor can use, such as for extensions of inventory and footing of totals. When this approach is followed, it is important to test the client's program carefully for reliability before it is used.

(2) Use a Generalized Program. A generalized program is a computer program developed by a CPA firm which can be used on different audits for most of the seven types of application listed previously. Generalized programs are recent developments in auditing that greatly increase the potential use of the computer for handling audit tasks and have two important advantages. First, generalized programs are developed in such a manner that most of the audit staff can be quickly trained to use the program even though the personnel have no formal EDP education. The second advantage is the wide range of application that can be made with a single program without having to incur the cost or inconvenience of developing an individualized program. The most important disadvantage of generalized computer programs is the high initial cost of their development and their relatively inefficient processing speed.

(3) Use a Program Written by the Auditor for the Specific Audit. This approach is applicable when the client's programs are not available and when a generalized program is not feasible because of high processing cost, inaccessibility, or similar reasons. A computer program written by the auditor does fit the audit application for which it is being developed, but it has the disadvantage of high program development cost.

The decision whether to use test data and auditor computer programs or to audit without the use of a computer must be made by the auditor on

[32] *Ibid.*, pp. 186–87.

the basis of his professional experience. Sometimes the auditor is forced to use the computer to perform procedures by the inaccessibility of source documents and detailed listing of output. Even if there are accessible records, however, it may be desirable to perform tests with the computer if sufficient competent evidence can be accumulated at a cost reduction.

Professional Conduct

Whenever services are performed for the public by members of a profession who possess a high degree of technical competence, it is essential that standards exist to guide the professional conduct of those who perform the services. The need for adequate standards of conduct arises from the importance of providing assurance to users that the service will be adequately performed regardless of the identity of the particular professional who does the work. The accounting profession has developed stringent standards of conduct, as well as means to enforce the standards, and these provide CPAs with guidelines that must be followed in their professional activities.

codes of professional ethics

The most important standards of conduct are the various codes of professional ethics of the separate states and the AICPA Code of Professional Ethics. Although there are some differences between the requirements of the various states, they are all in substantial accord with the AICPA Code. Only CPAs who are members of the AICPA are restricted by the Code, but the individual states are in a position to enforce their requirements for every CPA in their jurisdiction, even to the extent of permanently revoking the CPA certificate for serious breaches of codes.

The Code of Professional Ethics of the AICPA has changed significantly over the past few decades as a result of the profession's attitudes about the appropriate conduct of a CPA. The current Code is printed here in its entirety because an understanding of its contents is necessary for an adequate preparation for the CPA examination. It is important for the candidate to review the current professional literature for any changes that have occurred since this writing.

Article 1: Relations with Clients and Public

1.01 Neither a member or associate, nor a firm of which he is a partner, shall express an opinion on financial statements of any enterprise unless he and his firm are in fact independent with respect to such enterprise.

Independence is not susceptible of precise definition, but is an expression of the professional integrity of the individual. A member or associate, before expressing his opinion on financial statements, has the responsibility of assessing his relationships with an enterprise to determine whether, in the circumstances, he might expect his opinion to be considered independent, objective and unbiased by one who had knowledge of all the facts.

A member or associate will be considered not independent, for example, with respect to any enterprise if he, or one of his partners, (a) during the period of his professional engagement or at the time of expressing his opinion, had, or was committed to acquire, any direct financial interest or material indirect financial interest in the enterprise, or (b) during the period of his professional engagement, at the time of expressing his opinion or during the period covered by the financial statements, was connected with the enterprise as a promoter, underwriter, voting trustee, director, officer or key employee. In cases where a member or associate ceases to be the independent accountant for an enterprise and is subsequently called upon to re-express a previously expressed opinion on financial statements, the phrase "at the time of expressing his opinion" refers only to the time at which the member or associate first expressed his opinion on the financial statements in question. The word "director" is not intended to apply to a connection in such a capacity with a charitable, religious, civic or other similar type of nonprofit organization when the duties performed in such a capacity are such as to make it clear that the member or associate can express an independent opinion on the financial statements. The example cited in this paragraph, of circumstances under which a member or associate will be considered not independent, is not intended to be all-inclusive.

1.02 A member or associate shall not commit an act discreditable to the profession.

1.03 A member or associate shall not violate the confidential relationship between himself and his client.

1.04 Professional service shall not be rendered or offered for a fee which shall be contingent upon the findings or results of such service. This rule does not apply to cases involving federal, state, or other taxes, in which the findings are those of the tax authorities and not those of the accountant. Fees to be fixed by courts or other public authorities, which are therefore of an indeterminate amount at the time when an engagement is undertaken, are not regarded as contingent fees within the meaning of this rule.

Article 2: Technical Standards

2.01 A member or associate shall not express his opinion on financial statements unless they have been examined by him, or by a member or employee of his firm, on a basis consistent with the requirements of Rule 2.02.

In obtaining sufficient information to warrant expression of an opinion he may utilize, in part, to the extent appropriate in the circumstances, the reports or other evidence of auditing work performed by another certified public accountant, or firm of public accountants, at least one of whom is a certified public accountant, who is authorized to practice in a state or territory of the United States or the District of Columbia, and whose independence and professional reputation he has ascertained to his satisfaction.

A member or associate may also utilize, in part, to the extent appropriate in the circumstances, the work of public accountants in other countries, but the member or associate so doing must satisfy himself that the person or firm is qualified and independent, that such work is performed in accordance with generally accepted auditing standards, as prevailing in the United States, and that financial statements are prepared in accordance with generally accepted accounting principles, as prevailing in the United States, or are accompanied by the information necessary to bring the statements into accord with such principles.

2.02 In expressing an opinion on representations in financial statements which he has examined, a member or associate may be held guilty of an act discreditable to the profession if:

(a) he fails to disclose a material fact known to him which is not disclosed in the financial statements but disclosure of which is necessary to make the financial statements not misleading; or

(b) he fails to report any material misstatement known to him to appear in the financial statement; or

(c) he is materially negligent in the conduct of his examination or in making his report thereon; or

(d) he fails to acquire sufficient information to warrant expression of an opinion, or his exceptions are sufficiently material to negative the expression of an opinion; or

(e) he fails to direct attention to any material departure from generally accepted accounting principles or to disclose any material omission of generally accepted auditing procedure applicable in the circumstances.

2.03 A member or associate shall not permit his name to be associated with statements purporting to show financial position or results of operations in such a manner as to imply that he is acting as an independent public accountant unless he shall:

(a) express an unqualified opinion; or

(b) express a qualified opinion; or

(c) express an adverse opinion; or

(d) disclaim an opinion on the statements taken as a whole and indicate clearly his reasons therefor; or

(e) when unaudited financial statements are presented on his stationery without his comments, disclose prominently on each page of the financial statements that they were not audited.

2.04 A member or associate shall not permit his name to be used in conjunction with any forecast of the results of future transactions in a manner which may lead to the belief that the member or associate vouches for the accuracy of the forecast.

Article 3: Promotional Practices

3.01 A member or associate shall not advertise his professional attainments or services.

Publication in a newspaper, magazine or similar medium of an announcement or what is technically known as a card is prohibited.

A listing in a directory is restricted to the name, title, address and telephone number of the person or firm, and it shall not appear in a box, or other form of display or in a type or style which differentiates it from other listings in the same directory. Listing of the same name in more than one place in a classified directory is prohibited.

3.02 A member or associate shall not endeavor, directly or indirectly, to obtain clients by solicitation.

3.03 A member or associate shall not make a competitive bid for a professional engagement. Competitive bidding for public accounting services is not in the public interest, is a form of solicitation, and is unprofessional.[33]

3.04 Commissions, brokerage, or other participation in the fees or profits of professional work shall not be allowed or paid directly or indirectly by a member or associate to any individual or firm not regularly engaged or employed in the practice of public accounting as a principal occupation.

Commissions, brokerage, or other participation in the fees, charges or profits of work recommended or turned over to any individual or firm not regularly engaged or employed in the practice of public accounting as a principal occupation, as incident to services for clients, shall not be accepted directly or indirectly by a member or associate.

Article 4: Operating Practices

4.01 A firm or partnership, all the individual members of which are members of the Institute, may describe itself as "Members of the American Institute of Certified Public Accountants," but a firm or partnership, not all the individual members of which are members of the Institute, or an individual practicing under a style denoting a partnership when in fact there be no partner or partners, or a

[33] On the advice of legal counsel that Rule 3.03 subjects the Institute and its representatives to risks under the federal antitrust laws, the Institute's Board of Directors, Council and division of professional ethics have decided that the Institute will continue to refrain from taking any disciplinary action against any member or associate under Rule 3.03 until there has been a change in circumstances that would justify a different opinion on the legal status of the Rule.

corporation, or an individual or individuals practicing under a style denoting a corporate organization shall not use the designation "Members of the American Institute of Certified Public Accountants."

4.02 A member or associate shall not practice in the name of another unless he is in partnership with him or in his employ, nor shall he allow any person to practice in his name who is not in partnership with him or in his employ.

This rule shall not prevent a partnership or its successors from continuing to practice under a firm name which consists of or includes the name or names of one or more former partners, nor shall it prevent the continuation of a partnership name for a reasonable period of time by the remaining partner practicing as a sole proprietor after the withdrawal or death of one or more partners.

4.03 A member or associate in his practice of public accounting shall not permit an employee to perform for the member's or associate's clients any services which the member or associate himself or his firm is not permitted to perform.

4.04 A member or associate shall not engage in any business or occupation conjointly with that of a public accountant, which is incompatible or inconsistent therewith.

4.05 A member or associate engaged in an occupation in which he renders services of a type performed by public accountants, or renders other professional services, must observe the bylaws and Code of Professional Ethics of the Institute in the conduct of that occupation.

4.06 A member or associate may offer services of a type performed by public accountants only in the form of either a proprietorship, or a partnership, or a professional corporation or association whose characteristics conform to resolutions of Council.

Article 5: Relations with Fellow Members

5.01 A member or associate shall not encroach upon the practice of another public accountant. A member or associate may furnish service to those who request it.

5.02 A member or associate who receives an engagement for services by referral from another member or associate shall not discuss or accept an extension of his services beyond the specific engagement without first consulting with the referring member or associate.

5.03 Direct or indirect offer of employment shall not be made by a member or associate to an employee of another public accountant without first informing such accountant. This rule shall not be construed so as to inhibit negotiations with anyone who of his own initiative or in response to public advertisement shall apply to a member or associate for employment.[34]

interpretive opinions

Since the Code of Ethics is stated in somewhat general terms, members of the profession have raised a substantial number of questions concerning interpretation. As a response to the need for expanding and interpreting the Code, the Committee on Professional Ethics of the AICPA has issued a limited number of opinions setting forth in more detail the meaning of the proper conduct of a CPA. The great preponderance of these interpretive opinions have dealt with the committee's interpretation of advertising, independence, and the conditions under which engagements involving taxes, management services, and EDP are appropriate. Although space precludes the inclusion of the detailed opinions in this chapter, the candidate is advised to be familiar with them.

standards of conduct in tax practice

The applicability of the Code of Professional Ethics to the tax practice of CPAs is clearly stated by the Committee on Professional Ethics of the AICPA in Opinion No. 13 as follows:

> It is the opinion of the committee that the Code of Professional Ethics applies to the tax practice of members and associates except for Article 2, relating to technical standards, and any other sections of the code which relate only to examinations of financial statements requiring opinion or disclaimers.
>
> The committee is of the opinion that the statements, affidavit or signature of preparers required on tax returns neither constitutes an opinion on financial statements nor requires a disclaimer within the meaning of Article 2 of the Code.
>
> In tax practice, a member or associate must observe the same standards of truthfulness and integrity as he is required to observe in any other professional work. This does not mean, however, that a member or associate may not resolve doubt in favor of his client as long as there is reasonable support for his position.[35]

The preparation of tax returns by a CPA requires a reasonable understanding of the information in the tax return by inquiry or investigation of the client's records. The CPA should refuse to have his name associated in any way with a tax return that he believes materially

[34] American Institute of Certified Public Accountants, *Code of Professional Ethics* (New York: American Institute of Certified Public Accountants, 1970), pp. 2–8.

[35] *Ibid.*, p. 25.

falsifies information or omits important data. This does not preclude his being an advocate for the client when the proper handling of a transaction is not clearly established by the tax laws.

The Committee on Federal Taxation of the AICPA has issued a number of advisory opinions on the responsibility of CPAs in tax practice. Although the Committee has no official power to enforce these statements, they are considered useful as a means of establishing the extent of a CPA's responsibility to his client, the public, the government, and the profession. The most important recommendations that they have made to date are summarized as follows:

1. A CPA should sign as a preparer any federal tax return that he has prepared regardless of whether it was prepared for compensation. The CPA is deemed to have prepared the tax return when he has done a substantial amount of the assembling of the information on the tax return, but he is not considered a preparer if he has merely typed the return, assembled a minor part of it, or only advised the client on the taxability or deductibility of certain items. If the CPA's work is restricted to reviewing the tax return, he can still sign it as the preparer if his review gives him a knowledge similar to that which he would have acquired if he had prepared the return.

2. If a CPA discovers a material error in a previously filed tax return, the client should be promptly informed of the error and advised to take corrective action with the Internal Revenue Service. The confidential relationship provision of the Code of Professional Ethics prohibits the CPA from informing anyone of the erroneous tax return. In case the CPA is preparing the current year's tax return for a client who has not taken corrective action on a material error in a return of the previous year, the CPA should consider withdrawing from the tax engagement.

standards of conduct in management services

The applicability of the Code of Professional Ethics to the performance of management services by CPAs is clearly stated in Opinion No. 14:

> Inquiries have been received as to the applicability of the Code of Professional Ethics to management advisory services. It is the opinion of the committee that all the provisions of the Code of Professional Ethics apply to management advisory services, except those rules solely applicable to the expression of an opinion on financial statements.[36]

[36] American Institute of Certified Public Accountants, *Code of Professional Ethics* (New York: American Institute of Certified Public Accountants, 1970), pp. 25–26.

A serious problem in applying standards of conduct to management services lies in establishing the appropriate scope of service that should be performed by the CPA. Instead of defining the boundaries of management service that are acceptable for CPAs to perform, the profession has concluded that the scope of the services provided should be determined by the individual CPA firm, based on its competence to complete the engagement in an adequate manner. Competence in management services should be evaluated in terms of the technical qualifications of the firm's personnel as well as their ability to evaluate and supervise the results of the engagement. It is the responsibility of the individual CPA firm to carefully evaluate the technical competence of its personnel to successfully perform the services.

The role of the CPA in management services should be that of objective adviser who does not take part in the client's decision-making process. A CPA is engaged to provide technical assistance and an objective point of view about a problem faced by management. He can perform this function best by working with the client in ascertaining the relevant facts, enumerating the feasible alternatives, and establishing the advantages and disadvantages of alternative courses of action. The course of action ultimately chosen for a particular set of circumstances must be made by management, not by the CPA, because only management commands the resources necessary to implement the decision. As a means of retaining this independence, it is essential that the CPA not be involved in the final decision-making process. This point is very important when the CPA also provides auditing service. Once a course of action has been adopted by management, it is acceptable for the CPA to provide technical assistance in implementing the decision.

4 fund accounting

Edward S. Lynn
Robert J. Freeman

The Board of Examiners of the American Institute of Certified Public Accountants has listed fund accounting among the topics that are to be covered on the Theory and Practice portions of the Examination. There has been a problem on fund accounting in the Accounting Practice section of nearly all CPA Examinations of recent years and auditing questions have occasionally been posed in a fund accounting context. The fund accounting problem is ordinarily optional; but fund problems are required quite frequently, and the candidate cannot rely on their being optional. There is also a policy of mixing the subjects of optional problems so that the candidate should not expect to find specific topics presented as options on a regular or even frequent basis.

Governments are the largest kinds of organizations that use fund accounting; but hospitals, universities, religious and charitable organizations, and others use, with appropriate variations, the same principles found in governmental accounting. Fund problems most often appear in a governmental context, with hospitals a distant second in frequency.

Although governmental problems nearly always require a knowledge of General fund accounting, a knowledge of the other fund and nonfund groups of accounts is often needed, as well. Accordingly, a candidate should be familiar with the accounting for and statements of the several funds and account groups.

The most frequent single requirement of governmental CPA problems calls for the preparation of journal entries either in general journal form or as a part of a worksheet. The entries may be those required to journalize transactions; when this requirement appears in a worksheet, the worksheet headings are approximately the following:

	Opening	*Transactions*		*Closing*
Account Title	*Balance*	*Debit*	*Credit*	*Balance*

The entries may be those required to journalize corrections; when this requirement appears in a worksheet, the worksheet headings are approximately as follows:

	Unadjusted	*Corrections*		*Adjusted*
Account Title	*Balance*	*Debit*	*Credit*	*Balance*

Candidates may also be required to prepare adjusting and closing entries, either in journal or worksheet form.

In another variant, the opening or unadjusted balances of the accounts of all the funds of the organization may be commingled in a single trial balance. In such cases the candidate must determine which funds or account groups should be used and either (a) prepare a series of transaction or correction worksheets similar to the foregoing examples, or (b) journalize appropriate transaction or correcting entries on a single worksheet and sort the resulting balances into a series of separate fund and account group closing or adjusted balance columns. The latter case obviously necessitates expanding the worksheets illustrated so that several columns are provided for closing (or adjusted) balances:

Closing (or Adjusted) Balances					
General Fund	*Special Revenue Fund*	*Debt Service Fund*	*General Fixed Assets Account Group*	*General Long-Term Debt Account Group*	*Enterprise Fund*

Column headings are frequently given. Perhaps the most complicated worksheet required in recent years was one that provided the following headings:

Account Title
Opening Balances
Transactions (Debit and Credit)
Estimated Revenues
Actual Revenues
Encumbrances and Expenditures
Appropriations and Other Authorizations
Closing Balances

The stated purpose of the worksheet was "to compare estimated revenues with actual revenues and encumbrances and expenditures with appropriations and other authorizations."

The actual preparation of statements is required often enough that candidates should be acquainted with the form and content of the statements associated with the several funds and account groups. Sometimes the candidate is not required to prepare formal journal entries or worksheets, but finds it necessary to do so in order to arrive at the account balances to be used in preparing the required statements. On the other hand, worksheets may be required, as illustrated in the preceding paragraph, in terms that necessitate a knowledge of statements if the worksheets are to be prepared in conformity with the instructions.

To solve CPA problems, then, the candidate must not only be able to journalize, he must also be familiar with the form and content of typical governmental and institutional accounting statements and must know how and why these statements differ from financial statements of commercial enterprises. This part of the Manual, therefore, deals with typical governmental transactions, the related entries, and the forms of statements commonly employed, and also with the theories underlying them. Moreover, since the text discusses the entire theory of fund accounting, it should prove of help also in solving institutional accounting problems. Further assistance in solving these problems is furnished by the last part of this chapter, which describes the funds employed by such institutions as hospitals, colleges, and universities and illustrates some of the statements to be prepared for them.

General Nature of Governmental Accounting

Governmental accounting is essentially different from financial accounting, and knowledge of the environments and pressures involved facilitates one's understanding of what it is and why it is that way.

commercial versus governmental accounting

There are many similarities in the accounting for private enterprise and that for governments. A double-entry system of accounts is recommended for both. The mechanics of record keeping are the same: documents form the basic record, books of original entry are kept and posted to general ledgers and subsidiary ledgers, trial balances are drawn to prove the equality of debits and credits, a chart of accounts properly classified and properly fitted to the organization's structure is essential to good accounting, and of course uniform terminology is highly desirable in both fields. The accrual basis of accounting is recommended for private enterprises, and a modified accrual basis is recommended for governments.

Some governmental activities, such as utilities, public transportation, and parking facilities, have objectives that are similar to those of organizations of like kind in the profit-seeking section of the economy. In such cases the accounting for the governmentally operated enterprises is similar to the accounting for their private counterparts, and the accrual basis is used.

In most of their operations governments are engaged in providing services to the general public, and the profit motive is absent. Governments do not intend to make a profit from their typical activities, and in general it may be said that their accounting is not pointed toward an evaluation of profitability of their activities. Thus governmental accounting is substantially different from that of profit-oriented organizations. For example, the determination of a value for inventory is not needed for the determination of a profit, and the general operations of governments do not involve commitments in inventories intended for resale. Another example may be found in fixed assets, which in the government environment do not serve as a basis for credit. Similarly, determination of depreciation is not required for the determination of profit nor for the proper accounting for general government operations.

Other major differences arise because governments are creatures of law; in finances as in other aspects, they are governed by the law in an all-pervading sense that is not applicable to private enterprises nor even to the regulated public utility. Governments come into existence by means of constitutions or charters; their every action is governed by the provisions of constitutions, charters, statutes, ordinances, administrative regulations, legislative intents, and judicial interpretations of the foregoing laws. In this legal environment, the accounting system must assist all the operations of the government agencies in complying with the law and must provide proof of compliance with financial requirements. The two most important kinds of legal provisions affecting accounting relate to appropriations (the expenditures authorized by the legislative body) and funds.

compliance with legal provisions

Appropriations and Revenue Laws. A budget is an expression in financial terms of the planned operations of an entity for a specified period of time, or of a project, and the proposed means of financing them. The preparation of the executive budget, legislative enactment of the budget, and the execution of the budget are governed by legal provisions. When the budget has been converted by legislative action into an appropriation law that grants spending authority to the executive branch, the appropriations authorize maximum amounts of expenditures beyond which the executive branch may not go. Detailed operating and accounting requirements may be specified in the appropriation ordinance. The accounting system should assist executives to operate in such a way that expenditures will be made in accordance with legislative intent as expressed in the appropriation acts or ordinances.

The accounting system must also provide for the compilation of revenue data to serve as a guide in the preparation of future budgets. Revenues should be recorded in such a manner and under such classifications that comparison of estimated revenues with actual revenues during the current year will be possible. Such a comparison will reveal the extent to which estimates were in error; it may prevent repetition of the errors, and it will permit more accurate planning of expenditures in the future. The recording of revenue estimates on the books of account deserves special mention because it is frequently not required by law and therefore may be neglected.

The Fund Concept. Governments must raise their revenues and make their expenditures in accordance with the legally imposed regulations, restrictions, and limitations. One of the ways to ensure that money will be expended for designated purposes is to establish funds. A fund has been defined as

> . . . an independent fiscal and accounting entity with a self-balancing set of accounts recording cash and/or other resources together with all related liabilities, obligations, reserves, and equities which are segregated for the purpose of carrying on specific activities or attaining certain objectives in accordance with special regulations, restrictions, or limitations.[1]

The term "fund" as defined here should be sharply distinguished from the term as used in private enterprise operations. A fund of a commercial enterprise is simply a part of the assets of the enterprise and is not a distinct accounting entity; revenue or expense accounts related to it are a part of the enterprise's operations and appear side-by-side with other enterprise revenue or expense accounts in the general ledger. On the other hand, a fund in the governmental sense of the word is a self-contained unit with its own asset, liability, revenue, expenditure, and fund balance accounts—with its own general ledger.

Establishment and Abolition of Funds. Funds may be established in accordance with legal requirements or at the order of the executive

[1] The National Committee on Governmental Accounting [N.C.G.A.], *Governmental Accounting, Auditing, and Financial Reporting* (Chicago: The Committee, 1968), p. 161.

branch of the government. In the case of municipalities the charter may contain such requirements, the legislative body may include them in its ordinances, or the chief executive may order funds to be created. An accounting distinction must be maintained between the funds in order that moneys may be spent solely for designated purposes. For example, a government ordinarily may not make even a temporary loan from one fund to another.

Authority for abolition of funds must come from a source in the legal hierarchy as high as or higher than the creating authority. That is to say, a fund created by administrative action may be abolished by administrative action, by act of the legislative body, or by a constitutional or charter amendment, whereas a fund created by a charter provision can be abolished only by a change in the charter.

Funds and Appropriations Distinguished. The creation of a fund ordinarily does not include the authority to make expenditures from it. Expenditures must be made on the authority of appropriations, which are authorizations by the legislative body to make expenditures for specified purposes. An appropriation must indicate the fund from which the expenditure is to be made. It specifies the purposes for which expenditures may be made, the maximum amounts that may be spent, and the period of time during which the expenditures are to be made. Finally, a department or activity may be financed from several funds. If that is the case, at least one appropriation must be made from each fund; it is the appropriations that provide authority for expenditure.

Kinds of Funds to Be Established. To permit effective budgetary control and to establish uniformity in financial reports, the National Committee on Governmental Accounting has recommended the following classification of funds: [2]

1. *General fund.* The General fund is used to account for revenues not allocated to specific purposes by law or by contractual agreement. Any activities that are not properly financed from other funds are financed and accounted for through the General fund.

2. *Special Revenue funds.* Special Revenue funds are like the General fund; the only distinction is that the former are usually limited by law or administrative action to a single purpose.

3. *Capital Projects funds.* Capital Projects funds are used to account for the receipts and disbursement of the proceeds from the sale of bonds and for other moneys to be used for the acquisition of capital facilities, except when the facilities are being provided by special assessment or enterprise resources.

[2] *Ibid.*, pp. 7–8.

4. *Special Assessment funds.* Special Assessment funds are used to account for charges levied against properties or persons benefiting from special services rendered by the governmental unit.

5. *Debt Service funds.* Debt Service funds are used to account for the accumulation and disbursement of resources for the payment of interest and principal on general long-term debt—that is, debt other than that to be paid by special assessment and enterprise revenues.

6. *Trust and Agency funds.* Trust funds and Agency funds are set up to account for assets received by governmental units in the capacity of trustee or agent.

7. *Intragovernmental Service funds.* Intragovernmental Service funds are established to account for service activities performed by a department or bureau for other departments or bureaus of the same governmental unit.

8. *Enterprise funds.* Enterprise funds account for the services that a city renders primarily to the general public and for which the public pays all or most of the cost.

In order to provide for complete accounting records and fiscal information, two other self-balancing groups of accounts have been recommended by the National Committee on Governmental Accounting. They cannot be called funds because they do not meet the criteria set out in the committee's definition of the term:

The *General Fixed Asset group* of accounts is used to account for the fixed assets of a governmental unit other than those carried in an Intragovernmental Service fund, a Trust fund, or an Enterprise fund.

The *General Long-Term Debt group* of accounts is used to account for the principal of all unmatured general obligation bonds or other long-term debt except that payable from (and therefore recorded in the accounts of) a Special Assessment fund or an Enterprise fund.

Every governmental unit must have a General fund, but not all need to use all the other types of funds and account groups. The extent to which the others will be used will depend on the kinds of activities carried on by a particular governmental unit, the means of financing them, and the legal restrictions imposed. The operations of each of the foregoing types of funds and account groups are discussed in detail throughout this chapter, and a summary is presented at the end.

the government as an entity

Although there is full agreement among authorities that the fund device is essential to the financial operation of governments, its use has an unfortunate fragmenting effect on the accounting and reporting of governmental finances. The statements of a profit-seeking enterprise present in one place all the information regarding that enterprise. It is possible to tell, by looking at the balance sheet, the nature and amount of the firm's assets, liabilities, and stockholders' equity. Inspection of its operating statements reveals the amounts and the nature of the components of change.

It may not be possible to produce significant combined data for the typical governmental unit of substantial size. Even a summation of the cash that may be on hand in a number of funds is a meaningless exercise if each of the funds has specified objectives and restrictions that prevent the use of the moneys for other purposes. If the government needs more money for a specified purpose than the related fund contains, it may have to seek new resources for that fund rather than use existing cash that may be available in excess of needs in another fund. A similar analysis could be made for the other assets of funds as well as for liabilities and fund balances. The result of the fund concept is that, rather than comprising a single economic entity, a government's assets and liabilities are recorded in a number of independent fiscal and accounting entities that render an evaluation of the government's overall financial position and results of operation frustratingly difficult if not impossible.

bases of accounting

Some of the most difficult problems of accounting, whether for profit-seeking or nonprofit entities, arise from the need to measure financial position and results of operations at periodic intervals. The flows of revenue and expenditure are necessarily divided into periodic components by the measurement process. When the measurement depends solely on the amount of cash received and disbursed, the strict cash basis is being used. It should be noted that even under the cash basis not all receipts are revenues; the receipt of cash from the issuance of notes is not a revenue because it gives rise to a liability. Similarly, even under the cash basis not all disbursements are expenses; the payment of the notes is not an expense because it results in the reduction of a liability. Basing accounts on cash flows produces inaccurate and hence misleading results if an organization has an appreciable inventory, prepayments, or other assets, or if it has appreciable obligations or debt for current expenses. Therefore the cash basis is not suitable for the accounting of substantial organizations.

The full accrual basis is typified by generally accepted principles of accounting for profit-seeking enterprises. Under a strict accrual basis, revenues are taken into account when they are earned, regardless of the period in which they are collected, and expenses are matched with revenues and recorded as soon as liabilities are incurred, regardless of the period in which they are paid.

If the legal provisions of a governmental unit permit the use of the accrual method, it should as a general rule be used. It furnishes accurate data on both revenues and expenses and hence allows accurate comparisons of (a) revenues and expenses of the same period or periods and (b) the operations of several different periods. It tends, therefore, to provide better managerial control of operations and better accountability of the executive department to the legislative body and to the public than does the cash basis. The National Committee on Governmental Accounting has recommended the use of the accrual basis for Enterprise, Capital Projects, Special Assessment, Intragovernmental Service, and Trust funds.[3] These include the funds that use accounting similar to that of profit-seeking counterparts, and these types of funds seldom have legal restrictions that hinder the use of the accrual basis.

Between the cash and accrual bases of accounting lies a continuum of modifications. Although the accrual basis is generally considered ideal, the requirements of legal provisions that are traditional in local government, together with the lack of a profit motive to require matching of expenses and revenues, led the National Committee on Governmental Accounting to recommend a carefully designed modified accrual basis for the General, Special Revenue, and Debt Service funds:

> The modified accrual basis of accounting is defined as that method of accounting in which expenditures other than accrued interest on general long-term debt are recorded at the time liabilities are incurred and revenues are recorded when received in cash, except for material or available revenues which should be accrued to reflect properly the taxes levied and the revenues earned.[4]

The definition of the recommended modified accrual basis requires three comments. First, the term "revenues" as used here does not mean the same thing as "revenues" of profit-seeking enterprises. Accrual basis revenues are defined as

> . . . additions to assets which: (a) do not increase any liability; (b) do not represent the recovery of an expenditure . . . and (d) do not represent contributions of fund capital in Enterprise and Intragovernmental Service Funds. [Revenues also arise from] the cancellation of certain liabilities without a corresponding increase in other liabilities or a decrease in assets.[5]

[3] *Ibid.,* p. 11.
[4] *Loc. cit.*
[5] N.C.G.A., *op. cit.,* p. 168.

The segregation of the accounts of a governmental unit into funds and account groups, together with the prescribed operational definition of revenues, produces classifications that are not accurate for the governmental unit taken as a whole. For example, the proceeds of a bond issue qualifies as revenue of the Capital Projects fund that is to account for the spending of the proceeds. Similarly, the portion of the cost of a project that is paid to the Capital Projects fund by the General fund qualifies as revenue of the former fund. In neither example does the transaction produce revenue, under the prescribed definition, for the governmental unit taken as a whole.

Second, the portion of the definition of the modified accrual basis that pertains to revenues does not alter the generally accepted conception of the accrual basis. The latter does not require accrual of a revenue when an entity has not earned the revenue, and there are many instances in accrual basis accounting in which revenue is not recorded until cash is received.

Third, the definition of the modified accrual basis uses the term "expenditures" rather than "expenses." Accrual basis expenditures are then defined as

> . . . the cost of goods delivered or services rendered [to the fund], whether paid or unpaid, including expenses, provision for debt retirement not reported as a liability of the fund from which retired, and capital outlays.[6]

Expenses, in turn, are defined for governmental accounting purposes as they are defined for profit-seeking enterprises. The "expenditures" mentioned in the definition of the modified accrual basis, then, include such departures from the accrual basis as charging debt retirement to expenditures of a fund, charging purchases of fixed assets to expenditures of a fund, and charging purchases rather than usage of supplies to expenditures.

budgets and the accounting basis

The budget is an entity's plan of operation expressed, ultimately, in financial terms. When the proposed revenues and expenditures have been approved (or altered and approved) by legislative action, the term "budget" applies to the annual revenue and appropriation ordinances that contain the legislative body's decisions. The accounting basis of the legislatively approved budget must be used in accounting for revenues and expenditures during the budget year in order that appropriate comparisons of results and plans may be made. For example, if the

[6] *Ibid.*, p. 160.

appropriations are made on the cash basis, it would be incorrect and misleading to record as expenditures purchases made on account near the year end. If the sum of cash expenditures and purchases that were made on account just before the year end exceeded the appropriations, using the accrual basis for expenditures would improperly indicate that appropriations had been exceeded.

classification of accounts

Because municipalities and other governmental units are large and complicated organizations, their accounting systems must provide an elaborate classification of accounts. Because the appropriations and estimated revenues of governments are recorded in the accounts, there is a primary classification, namely *budgetary accounts,* which show budgetary operations and the condition of the budget. *Proprietary accounts* show the actual financial condition and the results of operation. A peculiarity of governmental accounting is that the subsidiary ledger accounts for revenues and expenditures contain both proprietary and budgetary information. They thus serve as proprietary accounts by indicating actual revenues or expenditures and as budgetary accounts by revealing the amount of the original estimates of revenues or appropriations, together with the estimated unrealized revenues and the remaining appropriations.

Another primary classification basis is the set of funds that a governmental unit uses. Revenues must be deposited in the proper funds, appropriations must be made from specific funds, and expenditures are related to the funds because they can only be made on the authorization of appropriations.

Revenues are usually classified by sources. The principal sources are taxes, licenses and permits, intergovernmental revenue, charges for services, fines and forfeits, and a miscellaneous category. Detailed accounts for each of these principal revenue sources should be maintained. Examples of some of the detailed revenues falling within each main revenue class are given in the revenue statement illustrated in Figure 8 (p. 237).

Expenditures are basically classified by funds because appropriations must be made from specified funds and expenditures are related to the appropriations that authorize them. Expenditures of the fund are classified by function, activity, organizational unit, character, and object. A *function* is a broad general purpose or aim of the government. Examples of functions are general government, public safety, public works, and health and welfare. There may be subfunctions within the broad categories; for example, there are the police protection, fire protection, correction, and protective inspection functions within the public safety function.

Each function is made effective by performing one or more activities. An *activity* is a specific line of work carried on by a governmental unit in order to perform one of its functions. For example, the police protection function requires administration, crime control and investigation, traffic control, training, and other activities.

Ideally each of the activities of a governmental unit would be assigned to a department, bureau, division, or other *organizational unit.* To have sound budgetary control, the authority and responsibility for carrying on the activities of the government must be assigned to its officials in a definite fashion. The allocation of appropriations and their related expenditures to organizational units is essential if department heads are to be held responsible for planning their activities and for controlling those activities that are authorized by the legislative body through the appropriation process. As a minimum requirement, responsibility for a single activity should be assigned to only one organization unit.

The classification by *character* is a classification by period benefited by the expenditure. The three character groupings are current expenses, capital outlays, and debt service. *Current expenses* benefit the current period; *capital outlays* are expected to benefit not only this period but also several or many periods in the future; and *debt service* includes payments of debt principal, interest on debt, and related service charges.

Finally, expenditures are classified by *object of expenditure*—articles purchased or services obtained. The following classification of objects of expenditure is a standard way of relating these items to character classification:

Character	*Object of Expenditure*
Current expenses	
	Personal services
	Supplies
	Other services and charges
Capital outlays	
	Land
	Buildings
	Improvements other than buildings
	Machinery and equipment
Debt service	
	Debt principal
	Interest
	Debt service charges

The objects of expenditure listed under current expenses are major classifications. A small municipality or a small organizational unit might find the major categories adequate, but in most cases each classification would be broken down into greater detail. For example, personal services could be subdivided into salaries, wages, employer contributions to the retirement system, insurance, sick leave, and terminal pay.

To summarize, expenditures of a fund may be classified by function, organization unit, activity, character, and object. The following ledger sheet heading illustrates the application of the expenditure classification to the sanitation division of a city:

Function:	Sanitation
Activity:	Sanitary administration
Organization unit:	Sanitation division administration
Character:	Current expenses
Object:	Other services and charges

budgeting

A budget is a plan of operation for a period of time or for a project. As a minimum, a budget contains information about the types of proposed expenditures and the proposed means of financing them.

The estimate of most types of revenues set forth in the budget is computed by applying an existing rate against an estimate of the base to which the rate will be applied. For example, assuming that a state or city has imposed a 2% sales tax, the amount of revenue that will be collected will depend, among other things, on business conditions and on the enforcement measures adopted. The 2% rate would continue in effect year after year until it was changed. On the other hand, general property taxes must be levied each year. At the time the budget is adopted, or shortly thereafter, the legislative body must levy property taxes by means of a tax levy ordinance.

The expenditure portion of the budget may consist solely of a description of the types of proposed expenditures. If this is the case, it is said to be an object-of-expenditure budget because it contains only object of expenditure information by organizational unit. But the budget *should* contain a description of the purposes for which the expenditures are to be made. The activities or programs for which the money is to be spent should be described, units of output of the programs should be developed, and, where possible, the levels of output in the past and the levels expected for the future should be described. A budget that contains information regarding programs or activities is called a program or performance budget.

The expenditure budget is adopted through the passage of an appropriation act or ordinance by the legislative body. This act or ordinance may indicate merely the total amount to be spent during the budget period by each organizational unit, or it may specify the amount to be spent by each organizational unit for each object of expenditure, such as personal services, supplies, land, and buildings. An appropriation ordinance that makes specific appropriations for each line of the budget (each object of expenditure) is called a line-item budget. When an appropriation represents the total amount to be spent during a budget period by an organization unit, it is called a lump-sum appropriation.

General and Special Revenue Funds

When revenues have been allocated by law or by contractual agreement to specific purposes, Special Revenue funds are established to account for the resources. The General fund is used to account for all revenues not allocated to specific purposes. The General fund is established at the inception of a government and may be expected to exist throughout the government's life; the Special Revenue funds, on the other hand, exist only as long as the government has resources dedicated to their specific purposes. In the typical case the resources of both kinds of funds are expended wholly or almost wholly each year and are replenished on an annual basis.

The essential character of both kinds of funds is determined by an emphasis on the recurring nature of their revenues and commitments and the necessity of meeting current commitments from the currently expendable (appropriable) resources. *There is almost complete disregard of the expense concept developed for profit-seeking organizations; the accounting principles for General and Special Revenue funds are essentially related to the funds flow concept.* For example, the purchase of fixed assets by these funds results in a decrease in the fund balances—the disbursements for such acquisitions have exactly the same status within the funds as disbursements for materials and supplies or salaries and wages, whereas the fixed assets are carried as assets of other entities within the government. Similarly, if maturing general obligation bonds of the government have to be paid from the resources of these funds, the disbursements are treated exactly like the disbursements for materials and supplies, and they have the same effect on fund balance.

In accordance with the flow of funds concept, the balance sheet for these funds is prepared so that information will be supplied to assist in solving the problem: "How shall the requirements of the succeeding period be met out of the available resources?" The balance sheet at the end of the year presents the resources on hand to meet the requirements of the following year; the fund balance is expected to be available, together with the revenues of the following year, to meet the needs of that year.

Examples of Special Revenue funds are those established for the purpose of financing institutions, such as schools, parks, or hospitals. It is assumed, however, that the institution is part of a governmental unit—for example, a municipality. If the institution is an independent governing unit, the fund constitutes the General fund of the particular "government." For example, a statute might provide that the proceeds from a certain tax levy and certain other revenues shall be used solely for school purposes. In such a case, if the schools are operated by an independent board, the fund through which these revenues are handled will constitute the General fund of the school board. On the other hand, if the schools are a part of the county or municipal government, the proceeds constitute a Special Revenue fund of the municipality or county, to be used solely for the operation of schools. Since the accounting for such a fund is similar to that for the General fund, Special Revenue funds are not considered further. The discussion of the General fund should be understood to apply also to Special Revenue funds.

operation of the general fund, 19X1

In a newly organized government, the accounting for the General fund begins as soon as the budget is adopted. At the time of such adoption, the following entry is made:

		Debit	Credit
Estimated revenues		798,000	
Appropriations			788,000
Fund balance			10,000
To record estimated revenue and appropriations.			
Entries in subsidiary ledgers:			
Debit: subsidiary estimated revenue accounts:			
General property taxes	$576,000		
Interest and penalties on taxes	4,000		
Motor vehicle licenses	66,000		
Building permits	15,000		
Municipal court fines	15,000		
Forfeited contractors' deposits	1,000		
Interest on bank deposits	4,000		
Rents	10,000		
Share of income taxes	100,000		
Charges for private police service	3,000		
Street sprinkling	4,000		
	$798,000		

Credit: subsidiary appropriation accounts:	
Police department—other services and charges	$ 10,000
Police department—personal services	85,000
Police department—supplies	5,000
Police department—equipment	22,000
Fire department—personal services	100,000
Fire department—other services and charges	10,000
Fire department—supplies	8,000
Fire department—equipment	30,000
General government	98,000
Highways and streets	75,000
Sanitation	78,000
Health	115,000
Welfare	30,000
Libraries	25,000
Interest	29,000
Debt principal	68,000
	$788,000

Several facts should be noted about this entry:

1. The entry contains both general ledger accounts and subsidiary accounts.

2. The accounts, of course, all relate to the General fund. The name of the fund was not stated in the entry because it is assumed that all entries in this subsection involve only General fund accounts. In actual practice, one journal may be used to record the entries for all funds. Consequently, in practice, it may be necessary to indicate at the head of each entry the fund to which that entry applies.

3. A separate general ledger is provided for each fund and for each group of subsidiary accounts of each fund. For example, as is apparent from the above entry, the General fund has both a general ledger and subsidiary ledgers. One subsidiary ledger contains the revenue accounts and another contains the appropriation and expenditure accounts.

4. To keep the illustration within reasonable limits, only a few of the many possible revenue sources are illustrated. Similarly, detailed appropriations are shown for the public safety function alone; for the remaining functions, only totals are given.

Property taxes, usually the most important revenues of the General fund, should be accrued at the time they are levied by the following entry:

Taxes receivable—current	600,000	
Estimated uncollectible current taxes		24,000
Revenues		576,000
To record accrual of taxes. Entries in subsidiary ledgers: *Debit:* individual taxpayers' accounts for a total of $600,000. *Credit:* General property taxes, $576,000.		

The Estimated Uncollectible Current Taxes account is an allowance for uncollectible accounts for taxes. The estimate itself is made in much the same way as for financial accounting; but the amount is a direct deduction from revenues. This treatment is used in fund accounting because to treat the estimate as an expenditure would require an appropriation for an amount that is actually not to be expended. Taxes ascertained to be uncollectible are written off against the estimate.

As other revenues accrue, the following entry is made:

Accounts receivable	4,000	
Estimated uncollectible accounts receivable		160
Revenues		3,840
To record accrual of miscellaneous revenues. Entries in subsidiary ledgers: *Debit:* individual debtors' accounts for a total of $4,000. *Credit:* Street sprinkling revenues, $3,840.		

To ensure that appropriations will not be overexpended, provision is usually made for reducing the appropriations account by the estimated amount of proposed expenditures. This is accomplished by means of *encumbrances* accounts. As orders are placed, entries are made setting up encumbrances. The amount of the encumbrance, in addition to being posted to the general ledger Encumbrances account, is posted as a debit to the particular appropriation account in the subsidiary appropriation ledger. The recording of an encumbrance results in a reduction in available appropriations. When the actual expenditure is known, the entry setting up the encumbrance is reversed, and the appropriation is reduced by the amount of the actual expenditure. Thus, if we assume that an order was placed for supplies for the police department at an estimated cost of $2,000, the entry at the time the order was placed would be as follows:

Encumbrances	2,000	
Reserve for encumbrances, 19X1		2,000
To record encumbering of appropriation. Entry in subsidiary appropriation ledger: *Debit:* Police department—supplies, $2,000.		

Assume, however, that subsequently, when the supplies and the bill are received, it is found that the supplies cost $2,100. In that case the entries would be as follows:

Reserve for encumbrances, 19X1	2,000	
Encumbrances		2,000
To reverse entry encumbering the appropriation. Entry in subsidiary appropriation ledger: *Credit:* Police department—supplies, $2,000.		
Expenditures	2,100	
Vouchers payable		2,100
To record expenditures. Entry in subsidiary appropriation ledger: *Debit:* Police department—supplies, $2,100.		

The two immediately preceding entries accomplish two things. The appropriation against which the expenditures for supplies are chargeable was first reduced by the estimated amount of the expenditure. Now, however, the exact amount of the expenditure is known; accordingly, the entry setting up the encumbrance is reversed. The actual liability incurred must also be recorded, and the appropriation must be reduced by the amount of the actual expenditure. The second entry accomplishes this.

In certain cases the appropriation is not encumbered first but is reduced only at the time the expenditure is actually made. This is often true with payrolls. Thus, if the payroll at the end of a pay period were $50,000, the entry at the time the payroll was approved would be as follows:

Expenditures		50,000	
Vouchers payable			50,000
To record approval of payroll. Entries in subsidiary appropriation ledger: *Debit:*			
Police department—personal services	$ 7,000		
Fire department—personal services	8,000		
General government	6,000		
Highways	9,000		
Sanitation	5,000		
Health	10,000		
Welfare	3,000		
Libraries	2,000		
	$50,000		

Additional Typical Transactions. The following transactions and related entries are also typical of General fund accounting.

Taxes receivable and accounts receivable were collected:

		Debit	Credit
Cash		503,000	
Taxes receivable—current			500,000
Accounts receivable			3,000
Entries in subsidiary ledgers: *Credit:* each taxpayer's account for tax collections and each debtor's account for collections on accounts receivable.			

Current taxes have become delinquent:

		Debit	Credit
Taxes receivable—delinquent		100,000	
Taxes receivable—current			100,000
No entries in subsidiary ledger.			
Estimated uncollectible current taxes		24,000	
Estimated uncollectible delinquent taxes			24,000
No entries in subsidiary ledger.			

Revenues *not* previously accrued were collected:

		Debit	Credit
Cash		213,100	
Revenues			213,100
Credit: entries in subsidiary ledger:			
Motor vehicle licenses	$ 65,000		
Building permits	15,500		
Municipal court fines	13,200		
Forfeited contractors' deposits	800		
Interest on bank deposits	3,500		
Rents	10,000		
Share of income taxes	102,000		
Charges for private police service	3,100		
	$213,100		

The outstanding voucher for supplies recorded in one of the preceding entries was paid:

		Debit	Credit
Vouchers payable		2,100	
Cash			2,100
No entries in subsidiary ledger.			

Taxes were collected in advance of their levy:

Cash	500	
Taxes collected in advance		500
Entries in subsidiary ledger: *Credit:* the individuals from whom these taxes were collected.		

Orders were placed as follows:

Order No. 3.	Police department—equipment .	$20,000
Order No. 4.	Police department—equipment .	2,000
Order No. 5.	Fire department—supplies	1,500
Order No. 6.	Fire department—services	2,000
		$25,500

Encumbrances	25,500	
Reserve for encumbrances, 19X1		25,500
Debit: entries in subsidiary appropriation ledger:		

Police department—equipment .	$22,000
Fire department—supplies	1,500
Fire department—services	2,000
	$25,500

Order No. 3 was received; the actual cost was $21,000:

Reserve for encumbrances, 19X1	20,000	
Encumbrances		20,000
To reverse entry for order No. 3. Entry in subsidiary appropriation ledger: *Credit:* Police department—equipment, $20,000.		
Expenditures	21,000	
Vouchers payable		21,000
To record expenditure on account of order No. 3. Entry in subsidiary appropriation ledger: *Debit:* Police department—equipment, $21,000.		

The city council authorized the writing off of certain delinquent taxes which had become uncollectible:

Estimated uncollectible delinquent taxes	6,000	
Taxes receivable—delinquent		6,000
Entries in subsidiary taxes receivable ledger: *Credit:* each taxpayer's account written off.		

Delinquent taxes in the amount of $10,000, together with interest and penalties thereon of $600, were collected. Since the interest and penalties were collected before the end of the year, these amounts have not been set up as receivable.

Cash	10,600	
Taxes receivable—delinquent		10,000
Revenues		600

Entries in subsidiary ledgers: *Credit:* each taxpayer from whom cash was received for a total of $10,000. *Credit:* interest and penalties on taxes, $600.

At the end of the year, interest and penalties accrued on delinquent taxes were set up on the books and an allowance was provided for uncollectible interest and penalties:

Interest and penalties receivable	3,200	
Estimated uncollectible interest and penalties		130
Revenues		3,070

Entries in subsidiary ledgers: *Debit:* each taxpayer from whom interest and penalties are receivable for a total of $3,200. *Credit:* Interest and penalties on taxes, $3,070.

Various other expenditures were incurred, and, although ordinarily they should first be vouchered, to simplify the discussion it is assumed that they were paid without having been vouchered:

Expenditures	605,950	
Cash		605,950

Debit: entries in subsidiary appropriation ledger:

Police department—personal services	$ 78,000
Police department—services	9,500
Police department—supplies	2,800
Fire department—personal services	91,400
Fire department—services	8,000
Fire department—supplies	5,500
Fire department—equipment	28,100
General government	90,000
Highways	65,000
Sanitation	72,900
Health	105,000
Welfare	26,850
Libraries	22,900
	$605,950

Supplies were furnished to the Fire Department by the Intragovernmental Service fund:

Expenditures	1,000	
Due to Intragovernmental Service fund		1,000
Entry in subsidiary appropriation ledger: *Debit:* Fire department—supplies, $1,000.		

Payment to the Debt Service fund for principal and interest became due; $82,500 was paid:

Expenditures	97,000	
Cash		82,500
Due to Debt Service fund		14,500
Entries in subsidiary appropriation ledger: *Debit:* debt principal, $68,000; interest, $29,000.		

subsidiary revenue and expenditure ledgers

Revenue and Expenditure accounts are handled differently in the general ledger and in the subsidiary ledgers. In the general ledger, separate accounts are provided for Estimated Revenues and (actual) Revenues. In the subsidiary revenue ledger (see Figure 1) the same account is

FIGURE I

A GOVERNMENTAL UNIT
Revenue Ledger

Account No.: ________
Class: Taxes
Account: Property Taxes

Date	Explanation	Ref.	Debit	Credit	Balance
19X1					
Jan. 1	Estimate		576,000		576,000
	Levy			576,000	-0-

used to show both the estimated and actual revenues. The balance of the account will normally be a debit, which will indicate the excess of estimated over actual revenues to date. When actual revenues exceed the estimate, the balance will of course be a credit. The difference between the two general ledger control accounts, Estimated Revenues and Revenues, at any point in time should be equal to the sum of the balances of the revenue accounts in the revenue subsidiary ledger.

Similarly, the accounts for appropriations, expenditures, and encumbrances in the general ledger are control accounts for the subsidiary appropriation–expenditure ledger (see Figure 2). The recording of the appropriation in a subsidiary appropriation–expenditure ledger account results in the creation of a credit balance. This balance is reduced as encumbrances and expenditures are recorded and is increased for cancellations of encumbrances. At any point in time, if the sum of the Encumbrances and Expenditures accounts is deducted from the balance of the Appropriations account in the general ledger, the difference should be equal to the sum of the balances of the accounts in the subsidiary appropriation–expenditure ledger accounts.

FIGURE 2

A GOVERNMENTAL UNIT
Appropriation-Expenditure Ledger

Code No: 2105-C
Function: Public Safety
Organization Unit: Department of Police
Activity: Investigation
Character: Current Expenses
Object: Supplies
Year: 19X1

Date	Description	Encumbrances				Expenditures			Appro-priations	Unen-cumbered Balance
		Order								
		No.	Issued Dr.	Filled or Cancelled Cr.	Balance Dr.	Voucher No.	Amount Dr.	Total Expendi-tures Dr.	Cr.	Cr.
1	2	3	4	5	6	7	8	9	10	11
Jan. 1	Appropriation								8,000	8,000
	Order		2,000		2,000					6,000
	Order filled			2,000						8,000
	Expenditure						2,100	2,100		5,900
	Expenditure						2,800	4,900		3,100

balance sheet during the fiscal year

On the basis of the transactions thus far illustrated, the balance sheet in Figure 3 can be prepared. The difference between estimated and actual revenues appearing on the debit side of the balance sheet is an estimate of the resources that are expected to become available during the remainder of the fiscal year. The difference between the sum of expenditures and encumbrances and the appropriations figure represents unexpended and unencumbered appropriations, which may require the use of resources during the remainder of the fiscal year. The Reserve for Encumbrances account is a reservation of Fund Balance in the amount of purchase orders outstanding.

FIGURE 3

A GOVERNMENTAL UNIT

GENERAL FUND
BALANCE SHEET
DURING 19X1

Assets

Cash			$ 36,650
Taxes receivable—delinquent		$ 84,000	
Less: Estimated uncollectible delinquent taxes		18,000	66,000
Interest and penalties receivable		$ 3,200	
Less: Estimated uncollectible interest and penalties		130	3,070
Accounts receivable		$ 1,000	
Less: Estimated uncollectible accounts		160	840
Estimated revenues		$798,000	
Less: Revenues		796,610	1,390
			$107,950

Liabilities, Appropriations, Reserves, and Fund Balance

Liabilities:			
Vouchers payable		$ 71,000	
Due to Intragovernmental Service fund		1,000	
Due to Debt Service fund		14,500	
Taxes collected in advance		500	$ 87,000
Appropriations:			
Appropriations		$788,000	
Less: Expenditures	$777,050		
Encumbrances	5,500	782,550	5,450
Reserve for encumbrances, 19X1			5,500
Fund balance			10,000
			$107,950

Closing Entries. Let us assume that no additional transactions have taken place between the preparation of the balance sheet and the end of the fiscal year. At the end of the year, entries would be made closing out the budgetary accounts and the actual revenue and expenditure accounts. The entry to close out the estimated and actual revenue accounts is as follows:

Revenues	796,610	
Fund balance	1,390	
Estimated revenues		798,000

Entries in subsidiary revenue ledger:

	Debit	*Credit*
Interest and penalties		$ 330
Motor vehicle licenses		1,000
Building permits	$ 500	
Municipal court fines		1,800
Forfeited contractors' deposits		200
Interest on bank deposits		500
Share of income taxes	2,000	
Charges for private police service	100	
Street sprinkling		160
To balance	1,390	
	$3,990	$3,990

The following points should be noted about the preceding entry:

1. Before the subsidiary revenue accounts were closed out, some of them had debit balances and some had credit balances. Those accounts which showed greater estimated revenues than actual revenues had debit balances, whereas those with greater actual revenues than estimated revenues had credit balances.

2. Accounts whose actual revenues were greater than their estimated revenues were debited, whereas those in which estimated revenues exceeded actual revenues were credited.

3. The total of the credits is greater than the total of the debits by $1,390. In other words, estimated revenues exceeded actual revenues by this amount. Consequently, the Fund Balance account was debited for $1,390.

4. The reader should compare the amounts shown in the explanation to the previous entry with the amounts exhibited in the last column of Figure 8, p. 237.

The entry to close out the appropriation, expenditure, and encumbrance accounts is as follows:

Appropriations	788,000	
Expenditures		777,050
Encumbrances		5,500
Fund balance		5,450

Entries in the subsidiary appropriation ledger:

	Debit	*Credit*
Police department—services	$ 500	
Police department—supplies	100	
Police department—equipment ..		$1,000
Fire department—personal services	600	
Fire department—equipment	1,900	

General government	2,000	
Highways	1,000	
Sanitation	100	
Welfare	150	
Libraries	100	
To balance		5,450
	$6,450	$6,450

Note the following points about the foregoing entry:

1. Before the subsidiary appropriation accounts were closed out, they had, with one exception, credit balances, which represented the unencumbered balance of each appropriation. The only exception is the Police Department—Equipment account, in which the actual expenditures and encumbrances exceeded the amount of the appropriation. All the accounts, except the Police Department —Equipment account, were debited in order to close out their credit balances. On the other hand, the Police Department—Equipment account was credited in order to close out its debit balance.
2. The excess of debits over credits, namely, $5,450, represents unused appropriation balances and goes to increase the balance of the Fund Balance account. This fact is also evident from the general ledger entry showing a credit of $5,450 to the Fund Balance account.
3. The information in the explanation to the entry under discussion is also reflected in the last column of the statement illustrated in Figure 9 (p. 239). Note that some of the accounts listed in Figure 9 do not appear in the explanation to the current entry: they have no preclosing balances because appropriations are equal to expenditures plus encumbrances.

balance sheet at the close of the fiscal year

Assuming that the closing entries just illustrated had been posted, the balance sheet of the General fund would appear as in Figure 4.

FIGURE 4

A GOVERNMENTAL UNIT

General Fund
Balance Sheet
December 31, 19X1

Assets

Cash		$ 36,650
Taxes receivable—delinquent	$84,000	
Less: Estimated uncollectible delinquent taxes	18,000	66,000

Interest and penalties receivable	$ 3,200	
Less: Estimated uncollectible interest and penalties	130	3,070
Accounts receivable	$ 1,000	
Less: Estimated uncollectible accounts	160	840
		$106,560

Liabilities, Reserves, and Fund Balance

Liabilities:		
Vouchers payable	$71,000	
Due to Intragovernmental Service fund	1,000	
Due to Debt Service fund	14,500	
Taxes collected in advance	500	$ 87,000
Reserve for encumbrances, 19X1		5,500
Fund balance (Fig. 5)		14,060
		$106,560

comments on balance sheet

Although the balance sheet is for the most part self-explanatory, a few additional comments will furnish a clearer picture of the characteristics of this financial statement. The comments deal with: (1) the exclusion of general fixed assets and general bonds from the General fund balance sheet; (2) the significance of the Fund Balance account; and (3) the nature of the Reserve for Encumbrances, 19X1, account.

(1) Exclusion of Fixed Assets and Bonds. Although some General fund expenditures represent outlays that should be capitalized, fixed assets are not included in the balance sheet of the General fund. For example, in one of the preceding entries, it was assumed that $21,000 was spent for equipment for the police department. In commercial accounting, this $21,000 would be shown in the general balance sheet as part of the assets. But not so in governmental accounting. Here, too, the expenditures are capitalized, but the resulting fixed assets are reported in a separate group of accounts rather than in the General fund. Again, although bonds may ultimately be payable out of the General fund, and even if they have been issued to eliminate a deficit in the General fund, they are not recorded as a liability of the fund but in a separate group of accounts.

Fixed assets are excluded from the General fund balance sheet because they do not represent expendable resources out of which the government intends to meet its liabilities or by means of which it is enabled to earn revenue. These assets are acquired for the purpose of rendering service.

Bonds are not included as part of the liabilities of the General fund because the resources of the fund in any one year are not to be used to pay all the bonds. The governmental unit's taxing power will ultimately provide resources to pay them. As these bonds mature, taxes are levied to provide revenue for their retirement. If the levy is to be paid to the General fund, the General fund will ordinarily transfer appropriate amounts to the Debt Service fund, which is responsible for the payment of principal and interest.

(2) Fund Balance. The Fund Balance amount represents the excess of the assets of the fund over its liabilities and reserves. Usually a government intends to create neither a positive balance nor a deficit in the General fund. Accordingly, if the fund shows a positive balance, the legislative body is likely to use it in financing the budget for the succeeding year. To avoid the future appropriation of resources already earmarked for some specific purpose, fund balance reserves, such as the Reserve for Encumbrances, are set up. Certain assets are segregated for a particular use and a like amount of the fund balance is tagged to indicate the segregation. For example, that portion of the fund balance represented by stocks of supplies is frequently earmarked in a Reserve for Inventories account. The entry to create the account or to increase it is a debit to Fund Balance and a credit to the Reserve for Inventories account.

The analysis of changes in fund balance (Figure 5) will help to

FIGURE 5

A GOVERNMENTAL UNIT

GENERAL FUND
ANALYSIS OF CHANGES IN FUND BALANCE
FOR THE YEAR ENDING DECEMBER 31, 19X1

Fund balance, January 1, 19X1		$ –0–
Add: Excess of revenues over expenditures:		
Revenues (Fig. 8)	$796,610	
Expenditures (Fig. 9)	777,050	19,560
Total balance and additions		$19,560
Deduct:		
Reserve for encumbrances, 19X1 (Fig. 9)		5,500
Fund balance, December 31, 19X1		$14,060

clarify the nature of this account. The amounts are identical with those used in the illustrative entries. Note that opposite the Revenues account in the statement, reference is made to Figure 8, which shows details concerning estimated and actual revenues. Also, opposite the Expenditures account and the Reserve for Encumbrances, 19X1, account reference is made to Figure 9, which shows in detail the amount appropriated to each department, the amount expended, the amount of encumbrances outstanding, and the unencumbered balance of each appropriation.

(3) Reserve for Encumbrances, 19X1. The Reserve for Encumbrances, 19X1, represents a reservation of a part of an appropriation against which future expenditures are to be charged. The reserve, as previously indicated, is established by a debit to Encumbrances and a credit to Reserve for Encumbrances, 19X1, this entry being reversed when the actual liability is determined. However, any balance remaining in the Encumbrances account at the end of the year is closed into fund balance, whereas the Reserve for Encumbrances, 19X1, is carried into the balance sheet.

During 19X2 two Reserve for Encumbrances accounts must be kept: one for encumbrances carried forward from the preceding year and one for encumbrances of the current year. The Reserve for Encumbrances, 19X1, must have a subsidiary ledger to record the details of orders outstanding at the beginning of the year. If the governmental unit uses a new expenditures subsidiary ledger for 19X2, the old expenditures ledger accounts may be carried forward as the subsidiary for the Reserve for Encumbrances, 19X1. Of course a new subsidiary ledger for Reserve for Encumbrances, 19X1, could be set up.

Let us assume that the materials, equipment, and services covered by the 19X1 encumbrances were received in 19X2 and that actual costs were $5,400. The entry to record these transactions would be as follows:

Expenditures, 19X1	5,400	
Vouchers payable		5,400
To record expenditures on account of purchase orders placed during the preceding year.		

Note the distinction between expenditures chargeable against current (19X2) appropriations and those chargeable against the Reserve for Encumbrances, 19X1. The latter group of expenditures must be kept distinct from current-year expenditures because they do not again affect appropriations. At the end of 19X2 they are closed out against the Reserve for Encumbrances, 19X1, account; the entry, assuming the accounts just illustrated, is as follows:

Reserve for encumbrances, 19X1	5,500	
Expenditures, 19X1		5,400
Fund balance		100
To close out reserve for encumbrances of prior year.		

The statements previously illustrated were based on the assumption that the governmental unit was in its first year of operation and that there were no expenditures chargeable against the prior year's encumbrances. However, the statements would not have to be materially changed to take account of these expenditures. For example, the only change necessary in the General fund balance sheet prepared *during* the fiscal year (Figure 1) is to show the reserve for encumbrances for the preceding year as well as the expenditures chargeable thereto as follows (located above Reserve for Encumbrances):

Reserve for encumbrances, 19X1	$5,500	
Less: Expenditures chargeable thereto	5,400	$100

Encumbrances are seldom carried forward more than one year. Consequently, the balance sheet prepared at the end of a year will not normally contain any Reserve for Encumbrances—Prior Year account. The statement analyzing the changes in fund balance would be the same as the one in Figure 5, except that recognition would have to be given to changes in fund balance arising from the difference between expenditures chargeable against the reserve for encumbrances of the preceding year and the amount encumbered. For example, assuming the amounts given in the immediately preceding entry, the statement illustrated in Figure 5 would be changed to resemble that in Figure 6.

FIGURE 6

A GOVERNMENTAL UNIT

General Fund
Analysis of Changes in Fund Balance
For the Year Ended December 31, 19X2

Fund balance, January 1, 19X2		$14,060
Add: Excess of revenues over expenditures:		
Revenues	$796,610	
Expenditures	777,050	19,560
Reserve for encumbrances, 19X1, canceled:		
Reserve for encumbrances, 19X1	$ 5,500	
Expenditures chargeable thereto	5,400	100
Total balances and additions		$33,720
Deduct: Reserve for encumbrances, December 31, 19X2		4,000
Fund balance, December 31, 19X2		$29,720

lapsing of appropriations

Closing entries and accounting for operations in a subsequent year are affected by the laws governing the lapsing of appropriations and related matters. The accounting for three assumptions as to such legal provisions is illustrated in Figure 7. Of the three assumptions summarized hereafter, note that Assumption A has already been described and illustrated; it is repeated for the sake of comparison.

Assumption A. Encumbered appropriations do not lapse; the closing entry should leave on the books the Reserve for Encumbrances account which becomes the authorization for the purchase of the encumbered article in the year or years following the year of appropriation.

Assumption B. Unexpended appropriations lapse; the closing entry should close everything pertaining to the appropriation. If an encumbered article is to be purchased in the year or years following the year of appropriation, the appropriation for the year in which it is purchased must contain authority for the expenditure.

Assumption C. Encumbered appropriations do not lapse; the closing entry should leave the Appropriations, Encumbrances, and Reserve for Encumbrances accounts on the books in the amount encumbered. Expenditures made in a subsequent year or years will be identified with the appropriations which authorized them.

making assumptions from year-end balances

The solution of problems in governmental accounting frequently requires that conclusions be drawn from a year-end balance sheet or trial balance regarding the type of closing entries made and hence the legal provisions governing such entries. For example, the presence in a year-end balance sheet of Reserve for Encumbrances, Encumbrances, and Appropriations accounts, all having the same amount, indicates that encumbered appropriations do not lapse and that expenditures incurred on account of the purchase orders represented in the Encumbrances account are to be charged to the carryover Appropriations account in the new year. The absence of the three accounts mentioned previously indicates that all appropriations lapse at the end of the year; the presence of a Reserve for Encumbrances account without an Encumbrances account is the signal that Assumption A has been used. In the absence of a clear indication of a change of legal provisions, the operating and closing entries should be prepared using the assumption that was used in the preparation of the previous year's closing entries. Similarly, the absence of accounts for current taxes from a year-end balance sheet or

FIGURE 7

A GOVERNMENTAL UNIT

Summary of Appropriation—Expenditure Accounting Under Three Assumptions with Respect to the Lapsing of Appropriations *

	Assumption					
	A		*B*		*C*	
	Dr.	*Cr.*	*Dr.*	*Cr.*	*Dr.*	*Cr.*
December 31, 19X1:						
Appropriations, 19X1	$788,000		$788,000		$782,500	
Reserve for encumbrances, 19X1			5,500			
Expenditures, 19X1		$777,050		$777,050		$777,050
Encumbrances, 19X1		5,500		5,500		
Fund balance		5,450		10,950		5,450
To record the closing of accounts related to appropriations.						
January 1, 19X2:						
Fund balance	800,000		805,500		800,000	
Appropriations, 19X2		800,000		805,500		800,000
To record the budget for 19X2.						
Encumbrances, 19X2			5,500			
Reserve for encumbrances, 19X2				5,500		
To record as encumbrances of 19X2 the orders placed but not filled in 19X1.						

* This summary is based upon the illustration for A Governmental Unit and the legal assumptions described therein. Assumptions have been made about 19X2 amounts as necessary—the significant information is obtainable by analyzing the differences between amounts on the same line, not by analyzing the absolute amounts. The procedure of dating the accounts has been followed to emphasize the sources of authority to spend. Note that the dating renders unnecessary the entry converting the Reserve for Encumbrances to Reserve for Encumbrances of Prior Years.

FIGURE 7 (Continued)

	Assumption					
	A		B		C	
	Dr.	Cr.	Dr.	Cr.	Dr.	Cr.
Transactions, 19X2:						
Encumbrances, 19X2	$440,000		$440,000		$440,000	
Reserve for encumbrances, 19X2		$440,000		$440,000		$440,000
To record reduction of appropriations by amount of estimated cost of purchase orders placed.						
Reserve for encumbrances, 19X2	420,000		425,500		420,000	
Encumbrances, 19X2		420,000		425,500		420,000
To reverse the entry encumbering appropriations.						
Expenditures, 19X2	775,000		780,400		775,000	
Vouchers payable		775,000		780,400		775,000
To record expenditure and the resulting liability.						
Expenditures, 19X1	5,400					
Vouchers payable		5,400				
To record expenditures and the resulting liability.						
Reserve for encumbrances, 19X1					5,500	
Encumbrances, 19X1						5,500
To reverse the entry recording all unfilled orders placed in first year.						
Expenditures, 19X1					5,400	
Vouchers payable						5,400
To record expenditures and the resulting liability.						

FIGURE 7 (Concluded)

	Assumption					
	A		B		C	
	Dr.	Cr.	Dr.	Cr.	Dr.	Cr.
December 31, 19X2:						
Appropriations, 19X2	$800,000		$805,500		$780,000	
Reserve for encumbrances, 19X2			20,000			
Expenditures, 19X2		$775,000		$780,400		$775,000
Encumbrances, 19X2		20,000		20,000		
Fund balance		5,000		25,100		5,000
To close appropriations, expenditures and encumbrances of 19X2.						
Reserve for encumbrances, 19X1	5,500					
Expenditures, 19X1		5,400				
Fund balance		100				
To close accounts relating to orders first placed in 19X1.						
Appropriations, 19X1					5,500	
Expenditures, 19X1						5,400
Fund balance						100
To close accounts relating to orders first placed in 19X1.						

trial balance means that taxes become delinquent before the end of the year and that the balances of Taxes Receivable—Current and Estimated Uncollectible Taxes—Current should be transferred to their delinquent counterparts before the balance sheet is prepared at the end of subsequent fiscal years.

revenue statement

A statement comparing estimated and actual revenues is illustrated in Figure 8. The statement is based on the subsidiary revenue accounts illustrated thus far in this section.

FIGURE 8

A GOVERNMENTAL UNIT

GENERAL FUND
STATEMENT OF REVENUES—ESTIMATED AND ACTUAL
FOR THE YEAR ENDED DECEMBER 31, 19X2 †

Revenue Source	*Estimated Revenues*	*Actual Revenues*	*Excess or Deficiency* †
Taxes:			
General property taxes	$576,000	$576,000	$ —
Interest and penalties	4,000	3,670	330 *
Total taxes	$580,000	$579,670	$ 330 *
Licenses and permits:			
Motor vehicle licenses	$ 66,000	$ 65,000	$1,000 *
Building permits	15,000	15,500	500
Total licenses and permits	$ 81,000	$ 80,500	$ 500 *
Fines and forfeits:			
Municipal court fines	$ 15,000	$ 13,200	$1,800 *
Forfeited contractors' deposits	1,000	800	200 *
Total fines and forfeits	$ 16,000	$ 14,000	$2,000 *
Intergovernmental revenue:			
Share of income taxes	$100,000	$102,000	$2,000
Charges for services:			
Charges for private police service	$ 3,000	$ 3,100	$ 100
Street sprinkling	4,000	3,840	160 *
Total charges for services	$ 7,000	$ 6,940	$ 60 *
Miscellaneous revenue:			
Interest on bank deposits	$ 4,000	$ 3,500	$ 500 *
Rents	10,000	10,000	—
Total miscellaneous revenue	$ 14,000	$ 13,500	$ 500 *
Total revenue (Fig. 5)	$798,000	$796,610	$1,390 *

† It has been assumed that the data for 19X1 and 19X2 are identical.

The significance of comparing estimated and actual revenues cannot be overemphasized. In the first place, the comparison is valuable in the preparation of future estimates because it shows to what extent forecasted revenues came up to expectations. Wide variations call for further investigation, in the process of which errors in estimating methods may be discovered and corrected. Also, the statement is likely to prevent the finance officer from purposely overestimating or underestimating revenues, because his errors become a matter of public attention.

statement of expenditures and encumbrances compared with authorizations

A statement comparing authorizations with expenditures and encumbrances appears as Figure 9. This statement is based on the entries to the subsidiary Appropriations, Expenditures, and Encumbrances accounts illustrated earlier in this section and on the Reserve for Encumbrances, 19X1, and Expenditures, 19X1, entries. This statement shows in detail the information presented in summary form in the preceding Balance Sheet (Figure 3) and Analysis of Changes in Fund Balance (Figure 5).

Capital Projects Funds

Capital Projects funds are employed to account for resources (a) received from bond or other long-term general obligation debt issues, grants or shared revenues from other governments, transfers from other funds, or other sources; and (b) used to acquire major, long-lived capital facilities. A Capital Projects fund is, in substance, a special type of Special Revenue fund, differing from the latter in two principal ways. First, resources are used to acquire capital facilities rather than to finance current operations, and second the accountability focus is on compliance with provisions of bond indentures, grant stipulations, or similar constraints and on the project, whose duration may span several operating periods.

Capital Projects funds constitute both a replacement and expansion of the "Bond Fund" formerly recommended by the N.C.G.A. (Bond funds were used to account for the proceeds of all general obligation bond issues except those of Special Assessment and Enterprise funds.) A major purpose of the change was to have capital projects accounted for uniformly in a manner that articulates with the capital program or budget. The intent of the present recommendations seems to be that proceeds of all general obligation long-term debt should be accounted

FIGURE 9

A GOVERNMENTAL UNIT

GENERAL FUND

STATEMENT OF EXPENDITURES AND ENCUMBRANCES COMPARED WITH AUTHORIZATIONS FOR THE YEAR ENDED DECEMBER 31, 19X2 †

	Reserve for Encumbrances 19X1	*Expenditures 19X1*	*Credit or Charge* to Fund Balance*	*Appropriations*	*Expenditures*	*Encumbrances*	*19X2 Unencumbered or Over-encumbered† Balance*
General government	$ —	$ —	$—	$ 98,000	$ 96,000	$ —	$2,000
Public safety							
Police:							
Personal services	$ —	$ —	$—	$ 85,000	$ 85,000	$ —	$ —
Other services	—	—	—	10,000	9,500	—	500
Supplies	—	—	—	5,000	4,900	—	100
Capital outlays	2,000	2,000	—	22,000	21,000	2,000	1,000 *
Total police	*$2,000*	*$2,000*	*$—*	*$122,000*	*$120,400*	*$2,000*	*$ 400* *
Fire:							
Personal services	$ —	$ —	$—	$100,000	$ 99,400	$ —	$ 600
Other services	2,000	1,900	100	10,000	8,000	2,000	—
Supplies	1,500	1,500	—	8,000	6,500	1,500	—
Capital outlays	—	—	—	30,000	28,100	—	1,900
Total fire	*$3,500*	*$3,400*	*$100*	*$148,000*	*$142,000*	*$3,500*	*$2,500*
Total public safety	$5,500	$5,400	$100	$270,000	$262,400	$5,500	$2,100
Highways and streets	$ —	$ —	$—	$ 75,000	$ 74,000	$ —	$1,000
Sanitation	$ —	$ —	$—	$ 78,000	$ 77,900	$ —	$ 100
Health	$ —	$ —	$—	$115,000	$115,000	$ —	$ —
Welfare	$ —	$ —	$—	$ 30,000	$ 29,850	$ —	$ 150
Libraries	$ —	$ —	$—	$ 25,000	$ 24,900	$ —	$ 100
Debt service	$ —	$ —	$—	$ 97,000	$ 97,000	$ —	$ —
Grand totals	$5,500	$5,400	$100	$788,000	$777,050	$5,500	$5,450

† It has been assumed that appropriations, expenditures, and encumbrances for 19X2 are the same as for 19X1.

for through Capital Projects funds *except* refunding issues, which are expended and accounted for through Debt Service funds, and Special Assessment and Enterprise fund issues, which are primary obligations of (and will be serviced and accounted for by) those types of funds. The recommendations are somewhat vague, however, and it would appear that proceeds of long-term general obligation debt incurred for purposes other than capital outlay or refunding (e.g., to finance operating deficits or to provide disaster relief) could be acceptably accounted for through Capital Projects, Special Revenue, or Bond funds.

Note that all fixed asset acquisitions need not be financed through Capital Projects funds. Not only may fixed assets with a comparatively limited life be acquired with the resources of almost any fund, but major fixed assets may be acquired through the General or Special Revenue funds (where no borrowing is involved), as well as through Special Assessment and Enterprise funds.

Note also that a separate Capital Projects fund is usually established for each project or debt issue and is abolished at the conclusion of the project. Where debt issues or donations are involved, a major purpose of the Capital Projects fund is to show that the proceeds were used only for authorized purposes and that unexpended balances or deficits have been handled in accordance with applicable contractual or other agreements. A single Capital Projects fund would suffice, however, where (a) a single debt issue is used to finance several projects or (b) a series of closely related projects is financed by internal transfers from the General fund, Special Revenue funds, or both. Combined statements are generally used to present financial operation or position data when a government has more than one Capital Projects fund in operation during a given year.

establishment of fund

Upon project authorization, a Capital Projects fund ledger is established and details related to the authorization are entered therein, preferably by means of a narrative memorandum entry. Alternatively, the authorization may be formally recorded by an entry such as:

Project authorized	400,000	
Fund balance		400,000
To record project authorization.		

As assets are accrued or received, the entries are as follows:

If memorandum authorization entry was made:

Due from General fund	50,000	
Due from county	50,000	
Due from federal government	200,000	
Revenues (or fund balance or appropriations)		300,000
To record accrual of project resources other than from borrowing.		

Cash	101,000	
Revenues (or fund balance or appropriations)		100,000
Premium on bonds		1,000
To record sale of bonds at a premium.		

If formal authorization entry was made:

Due from General fund	50,000	
Due from county	50,000	
Due from federal government	200,000	
Projects authorized		300,000
To record accrual of project resources other than from borrowing.		

Cash	101,000	
Projects authorized		100,000
Premium on bonds		1,000
To record sale of bonds at a premium.		

The foregoing example brings up several points. First, if a formal project authorization entry is made, it is in substance reversed when assets are received or accrued. Second, a premium on bonds does not serve to increase the magnitude of the project authorization, and finally, Appropriations and Estimated Revenue accounts need not be employed in accounting for Capital Projects funds. Estimated Revenue accounts would serve little purpose as resources for capital projects are generally few and estimation presents little problem. An Appropriations account may, if desired, be used in the same manner as in General Fund accounting.

Premiums and discounts on debt issuances are interest rate adjustments. Therefore, premiums are transferred to the appropriate Debt Service fund and, theoretically, the Debt Service fund should transfer an amount equal to any discount to the Capital Projects fund. When a series of issuances is involved, only the net premium or discount is of concern. Because of legal difficulties—and since at the origin of the project there probably will be no resources in the appropriate Debt Service fund—a discount must usually be written off and the project authorization reduced. Had these bonds sold at a $1,000 discount and had the project been scaled down accordingly, the entry would have been:

If memorandum entry was made:

Cash	99,000	
Discount on bonds	1,000	
Revenues (or fund balance or appropriations)		100,000
To record sale of bonds at a discount.		

Revenues (or fund balance or appropriations)	1,000	
Discount on bonds		1,000
To reduce the project authorization and write off bond discount.		

(Alternatively, the sale of bonds could have been recorded net—that is, only $99,000 credited to Revenues and no discount account established—if it had been known at the time of the bond sale that the discount would serve to reduce the project authorization.)

If formal authorization entry was made:

Cash	99,000	
Discount on bonds	1,000	
Projects authorized		100,000
To record sale of bonds at a discount.		

Fund balance (or appropriations)	1,000	
Discount on bonds		1,000
To reduce the project authorization and write off bond discount.		

Had resources been transferred in from another fund, the entry in either case would have been:

Cash	1,000	
Discount on bonds		1,000
To record transfer to make up for bond discount.		

operation of fund

The Capital Projects fund continues in existence until the project(s) is completed and the related resources have been expended or transferred to other funds. In extremely simple situations, such as a project that consists of purchasing existing facilities for a single payment or transferring resources to another fund (e.g., to finance a deficit or establish an Enterprise fund), the life of the Capital Projects fund may be brief and its accounting entries uncomplicated. If we assume in the example of the bonds sold at a premium, which has been transferred to the Debt Service fund, that receivables were collected and the assets expended or transferred immediately, the following entries would be made:

Cash	300,000	
Due from General fund		50,000
Due from county		50,000
Due from federal government		200,000
To record collection of receivables.		

Expenditures (or fund balance or appropriations)	400,000	
Cash		400,000
To record immediate expenditure or transfer of all assets of the fund.		

Any necessary closing entries could then be made and the fund abolished. Had Revenues and Expenditures accounts been used, the closing entry would be simply:

Revenues	400,000	
Expenditures		400,000
To close fund accounts.		

Had both the Fund Balance account or the Appropriation account been credited for asset accruals and debited on expenditure of asset accruals, no closing entries would be required.

In the usual case, however, a Capital Projects fund is used to finance construction projects; the government may use a general contractor or its own employees for all or part of the work. In this situation, accounting procedures are more complicated and closely resemble those of the General fund, although the differences warrant attention. The following examples serve to illustrate some of the transactions involved and the related entries. Only general ledger accounts are used.

In the illustration it is assumed (a) that the bonds sold at a discount, which has been written off, leaving a $399,000 project authorization; (b) that the Revenues account has been credited for assets received or accrued, and (c) that an Appropriations account is not used, since the entire fund balance is considered to be appropriated for the project and the expenditure subsidiary ledger (if used) would be controlled only by the Encumbrances and Expenditures accounts. In this project a bridge is to be constructed partly by a contractor and partly by city labor. A contract has been entered into with Jones & Company for the construction of certain parts of the bridge, the estimated cost being $300,000.

Encumbrances	300,000	
Reserve for encumbrances		300,000
To record the construction contract.		

Orders for materials, amounting to $5,000, were placed.

Encumbrances	5,000	
Reserve for encumbrances		5,000
To record purchase orders for materials.		

The payroll for the month amounted to $16,000 and was paid.

Expenditures	16,000	
Cash		16,000
To record payment of payroll.		

A bill for $120,000 was received from Jones & Company for part of the work.

Reserve for encumbrances	120,000	
Encumbrances		120,000
To reverse, in part, entry setting up the contract.		

Expenditures	120,000	
Contracts payable		120,000
To record expenditures.		

All the materials previously ordered were received, along with a bill for $4,800.

Reserve for encumbrances	5,000	
Encumbrances		5,000
To reverse entry setting up encumbrances.		

Expenditures	4,800	
Vouchers payable		4,800
To record expenditures.		

Payment of $120,000 was made to Jones & Company.

Contracts payable	120,000	
Cash		120,000
To record payment to the contractor.		

An order estimated to cost $12,000 was placed.

Encumbrances	12,000	
Reserve for encumbrances		12,000
To record a purchase order for materials.		

Had several related projects been financed through the fund, several Appropriations accounts would have been established or separate Expenditures accounts would have been employed. Again, nothing precludes use of a complete budgetary accounting approach (including Estimated Revenues and Appropriations accounts) in a manner similar to General fund accounting.

closing entry—project uncompleted

Unlike General fund appropriations, authorizations to make Capital Projects expenditures are not limited with respect to time; that is, the authorization continues until the project is completed. Although it may be argued that closing entries need not be prepared for uncompleted projects, the preferred approach is to close the Revenues, Expenditures, and Encumbrances accounts to Fund Balance in order to summarize operating results to date and fund financial status at year end. If closing entries were made, they would be as follows:

Revenues	399,000	
Fund balance		399,000
To close revenues at year end.		
Fund balance	332,800	
Expenditures		140,800
Encumbrances		192,000
To close expenditures to date and encumbrances at year end.		

Major Statements at Close of the Fiscal Year. Assuming that the journal entries illustrated thus far for the Capital Projects fund had been posted to the accounts, the statements in Figures 10 and 11 would be prepared.

Expenditures and encumbrances should be itemized either within the statement analyzing changes in fund balance or in schedules cross-referenced to that statement. A separate statement of estimated and actual revenues is recommended, although revenues could be itemized within the Analysis of Changes in Fund Balance or in supplementary schedules thereto if there were neither a large number of sources nor significant variation between estimated and actual amounts.

FIGURE 10

A GOVERNMENTAL UNIT

CAPITAL PROJECTS FUND
BALANCE SHEET
AT CLOSE OF FISCAL YEAR 19X1

Assets	
Cash	$263,000
Liabilities, Reserves, and Fund Balance	
Vouchers payable	$ 4,800
Reserve for encumbrances	192,000
Fund balance	66,200
	$263,000

FIGURE 11

A GOVERNMENTAL UNIT

CAPITAL PROJECTS FUND
ANALYSIS OF CHANGES IN FUND BALANCE
FOR THE FISCAL YEAR 19X1

Initial project authorization		$400,000
Less: Discount on bonds		1,000
Net project authorization		$399,000
Fund balance, beginning of year		$ –0–
Add: Revenues		399,000
		$399,000
Less: Expenditures	$140,800	
Encumbrances	192,000	332,800
Fund balance, end of year		$ 66,200

Note particularly that neither the long-term debt incurred to finance the project nor the fixed assets acquired thereby appear in statements of the Capital Projects fund. The long-term debt is established in the General Long-Term Debt account group when it is incurred; fixed assets are capitalized at year end in the General Fixed Assets account group.

transactions and entries—second fiscal year

To complete the illustration, let us assume that the project was concluded in the next fiscal year and that the events and the corresponding entries were as follows:

The Encumbrances account is reestablished in its usual offset relation with the Reserve for Encumbrances account by reversing the previous closing entry as it related to Encumbrances.

Encumbrances	192,000	
Fund balance		192,000
To reestablish encumbrances closed at end of previous year.		

The materials ordered were received; and an invoice for $12,400 was received.

Reserve for encumbrances	12,000	
Encumbrances		12,000
To reverse entry setting up encumbrances.		

Expenditures	12,400	
Vouchers payable		12,400
To record expenditures.		

Jones & Company completed its part of the work; its bill was for $180,000.

Reserve for encumbrances	180,000	
Encumbrances		180,000
To reverse entry setting up encumbrances.		

Expenditures	180,000	
Contracts payable		180,000
To record expenditures.		

Total additional payments for labor amounted to $60,000.

Expenditures	60,000	
Cash		60,000
To record payment of payroll.		

Jones & Company's bill was paid, except for 5% of the total contract, which was retained pending inspection and final approval of the completed project.

Contracts payable	180,000	
Contracts payable—retained percentage		15,000
Cash		165,000
To record partial payment and retained percentage.		

All other outstanding bills were paid.

Vouchers payable	17,200	
Cash		17,200
To record payment of vouchers.		

closing entry—project completed

As soon as the project is completed, even if it is completed before the close of the fiscal year, an entry is made closing Expenditures into the Fund Balance account. The entry is as follows:

Fund balance	252,400	
Expenditures		252,400
To record closing out of expenditures.		

balance sheet—project completed

After the foregoing entries have been posted, the balance sheet of Figure 12 can be prepared.

FIGURE 12

A GOVERNMENTAL UNIT

CAPITAL PROJECTS FUND
BALANCE SHEET
DURING, OR AT CLOSE OF, FISCAL YEAR 19X2

Assets

Cash	$20,800

Liabilities and Fund Balance

Contracts payable—retained percentage	$15,000
Fund balance	5,800
	$20,800

Note that the resulting fixed assets are not set up in the Capital Projects fund even when the project is completed. Instead, as already indicated, they are shown as part of the General Fixed Assets group of accounts. Again, bonds payable do not appear in the Capital Projects fund balance sheet, but are carried within the General Long-Term Debt accounts. As soon as the project is completed, the fund has accomplished its purpose and ceases to exist. For example, from Figure 12 it is evident that, were it not for the fund balance, the fund would cease to exist as soon as the completed project had been approved and the retained percentage on the contract paid.

disposing of fund balance or deficit

From the foregoing example it is apparent that any existing fund balance must be disposed of before the fund is completely dissolved. Frequently the law specifies what shall be done with such balance. In the absence of legislated restrictions, however, the balance is usually transferred to the Debt Service fund, which will pay off the bonds or other related debt, if any. The reason for such action is that the balance arose because expenditures had been overestimated, with the result that a larger amount than necessary was borrowed. Where resources were provided by intergovernmental grants or intragovernmental transfers, it may be necessary or appropriate to refund a portion of these resources in disposing of the fund balance.

If, on the other hand, the fund had a deficit, it would ordinarily be disposed of in one of two ways. A small deficit would probably be eliminated by transferring money from the General fund; a large deficit would be disposed of by additional borrowing.

analysis of changes in fund balance—project completed

The Analysis of Changes in Fund Balance is the major statement of the Capital Projects fund. A statement similar to the one in Figure 13 would be prepared at the end of the year in which the project was completed and the fund balance disposed of.

Special Assessment Funds

Special Assessment funds are established to account for the financing of improvements, such as the widening of streets, or services, such as street cleaning, from special charges levied against the properties or persons benefited. The accounting procedure for assessment funds established to finance service activities is simple. Such a procedure requires that proper records be kept of the amount assessed against and

FIGURE 13

A GOVERNMENTAL UNIT

Capital Projects Fund
Analysis of Changes in Fund Balance
For the Fiscal Year 19X2

Net project authorization		$399,000
Fund balance, beginning of year		$ 66,200
Add: Revenues	$ –0–	
Prior year encumbrances re-established	192,000	192,000
		$258,200
Less: Expenditures	$252,400	
Transfers to Debt Service fund	5,800	258,200
Fund balance, end of year		$ –0–

collected from each property or person and that the money be applied to the purposes of the fund. Since, however, special assessments are more significant in the financing of construction projects, this section deals primarily with special assessments for construction.

The financing of construction through special assessments presents various problems. First, proper construction records must be maintained in order to determine the actual cost of the project. Second, because the individual assessments in such cases are usually large, special assessment payers are frequently extended the privilege of paying assessments in installments over a number of years. In the meantime, construction expenditures must be financed from other sources, such as bonds, notes, or a combination of the two. Third, all the cash collected by a Special Assessment fund is to be used for specified purposes, and the accounts will preferably provide for a segregation by purpose. Accounts entitled Cash for Construction, Cash for Payment of Notes and Interest, Cash for Bond Payments, and Cash for Interest Payments may be used.

Similarly, since a Special Assessment fund is, in substance, a Capital Projects–Debt Service fund hybrid, it is useful to segregate the fund balance according to its origin and the use to which the net assets it represents may be put. In Figure 14 a schematic arrangement indicating possible sources of the several kinds of cash is presented. The candidate will find Figure 14 a useful reference guide to the recording of cash collections.

FIGURE 14

SPECIAL ASSESSMENT FUND

TYPICAL SOURCES OF CASH

Case A: The project is financed by contribution from the government and by assessment. The governmental unit pays its share of the costs promptly. Bonds are issued to permit deferral of assessment payments.

Case B: The project is financed by contribution from the government and by assessment. The governmental unit defers one-half of its payments to future years. Notes are issued to finance construction and to permit the issuance of bonds for the exact amount necessary to finance the deferred assessments. Assessments are levied upon completion of the project.

Cash Account Debited	*Source of Cash*	
	Case A	*Case B*
Cash for construction	Governmental unit's share of cost First assessment installment(s) Bond proceeds (excluding premiums)	One-half of governmental unit's share of cost Note proceeds
Cash for payment of notes and interest		Installment(s) of governmental unit's share of cost Bond proceeds (excluding premiums) Installment(s) of assessments receivable
Cash for payment of bonds	Assessment collections	Assessment collections
Cash for payment of interest	Bond premium Interest on assessment installments	Bond premium Interest on assessment installments

authorization of project

The first step in special assessment construction procedure is the authorization of the project. Projects are authorized by the legislative body or special district commissioners after due notice and hearings. Such authorization is recorded by the following entry:

Improvements authorized	750,000	
Fund balance—construction (or appropriations)		750,000
To record authorization of special assessment project.		

The Improvements Authorized "plug" account will be reversed when fund resources are accrued or received.

authorization and sale of bonds

If construction is to be financed from the sale of bonds, the next step is the authorization to issue bonds. In contrast with the alternate procedure illustrated for the Capital Projects fund, no entry need be made in the Special Assessment fund to show bond authorizations; a narrative memorandum entry will suffice. One of the reasons for this difference is that the entry in the Capital Projects fund indicates not only the authorization to issue bonds but also the authorization to incur expenditures. In the Special Assessment fund, the authorization to incur expenditures is covered by the opening entry.

If we assume that bonds in the amount of $525,000 are sold at a premium of $1,000, the entry is as follows:

Cash for construction	525,000	
Cash for interest payments	1,000	
Premium on bonds payable		1,000
Bonds payable		525,000
To record sale of bonds at a premium.		

Here a segregation is made between cash to be used for construction purposes and cash available for the payment of interest. In its dual Capital Projects–Debt Service fund role, the Special Assessment fund accounts not only for the expenditure of bond proceeds for construction purposes but also for the payment of bonds and interest. Since the proceeds from the sale of bonds are to be used for financing construction, the cash received from the sale is specifically earmarked for this purpose. On the other hand, premium on bonds represents an interest adjustment and should therefore be used only for making interest payments. Although such segregation is not mandatory, it is considered preferable from both managerial and accountability standpoints.

Had the bonds been sold at a discount, the entry would have been as follows:

Cash for construction	524,000	
Discount on bonds	1,000	
Bonds payable		525,000
To record sale of bonds at a discount.		

Note that the bond liability is established within the Special Assessment fund accounts rather than in the General Long-Term Debt account group. This is because these bonds are specific liabilities of the Special Assessment fund and both interest and principal payments will be paid from its resources. Since discount on bonds also represents an interest rate adjustment, cash for construction should theoretically be reimbursed for the discount through a transfer from cash for interest payments. Ordinarily, this is not done for technical and legal reasons, and only the amount received from the sale of the bonds is made available for construction.

levying and collecting assessments

The levy of assessments is the next step in special assessment financing. Assessments are generally levied when the project is completed, but sometimes the levy is made as soon as construction is authorized. The advantage of waiting until the project is completed and all costs are known is the avoidance of supplemental assessments or rebates inherent when assessments are levied at the beginning of a project. Assessments of the cost of the project are levied against the benefited property on the basis of the proportion of the benefit estimated to be derived from the project by each property. The city as a whole frequently pays a part of the cost for one or more of the following reasons: (a) it has property in the benefited area, (b) total costs exceed total benefits, or (c) the property owners in the immediate vicinity of the project are not the only beneficiaries—the city as a whole gains.

The entry to record the levy of special assessments and the governmental unit's share of the cost of the project is as follows:

Assessments receivable—current	75,000	
Assessments receivable—deferred	525,000	
Governmental unit's share of cost	150,000	
Improvements authorized		750,000
To record levy of assessments and government's share of cost.		

It should be noted that no provision has been made for uncollectible special assessments. Some special assessments, like some taxes, prove to be uncollectible. But, unlike taxes, uncollectible special assessments are subject to legal restrictions and thus cannot be provided for in advance by increasing the total amounts of assessments levied. Instead, losses from uncollectible assessments must be met through additional contributions by the municipality. However, if the assessments were to have been used to pay off special bonds which are not a charge against the city's faith and credit, the loss might have to be borne by the bondholders.

Again like taxes, special assessments are a lien against the benefited property, and the government can therefore proceed to sell the delinquent property. Theoretically, the loss would consist of the difference between the amount of the assessment and the amount received from the sale of the property, and more than minimal losses would be rare. Of far more consequence are assessments, levied against indigent property owners, which are ultimately assumed by the government.

The governmental unit may finance its share of the cost through issuing bonds, through levying special taxes, or through an appropriation from the General fund. If bonds are issued for the government's share of special assessment costs, they are treated in the same manner as other general obligation bonds; that is, bond proceeds are handled first through a Capital Projects fund and from there are transferred to the Special Assessment fund.

The entry to record the collection of current assessment installments is:

Cash for construction	70,000	
Assessments receivable—current		70,000
To record collection of current assessments.		

Similarly, the receipt of cash to cover the government's share of the cost is recorded as follows:

Cash for construction	150,000	
Governmental unit's share of cost		150,000
To record collection of government's share of cost.		

The Cash for Construction account was debited in both the preceding entries because it is assumed that the *first* installments, as well as the government's contribution, are to be used for the payment of construction costs.

When deferred assessments become due, they are transferred to the Assessments Receivable—Current account, the entry being:

Assessments receivable—current	60,000	
Assessments receivable—deferred		60,000
To record assessments becoming currently receivable.		

Delinquent assessments are set up through the following entry:

Assessments receivable—delinquent	5,000	
Assessments receivable—current		5,000
To record delinquent assessments representing first installments.		

Should it be necessary to begin foreclosure procedures on delinquent assessments receivable, all receivables and accrued interest or other charges related to that property are reclassified:

Assessment liens receivable	6,500	
Assessments receivable—delinquent		2,000
Assessments receivable—current		1,000
Assessments receivable—deferred		3,000
Interest receivable		400
Interest revenues		100
To record conversion of delinquent receivables into specific legal liens.		

Subsequent legal and sale costs would be added to the Special Assessment Liens Receivable account and, should the property be sold, any excess of proceeds over the lien would be paid to the property owner or mortgagor. Similarly, should the property owner wish to redeem his property prior to sale, he would be liable for all costs occasioned by his delinquency and he might be obliged to forfeit the right to spread his assessment payments over several years; that is, the due date of all deferred assessments receivable might be accelerated.

accounting for interest

Since bonds are issued and interest costs arise because property owners are permitted to pay by installments, the owners are expected to bear the interest cost. As interest on assessments becomes receivable, it is set up through the following entry:

Interest receivable	11,025	
Interest revenues		11,025
To record interest receivable on unpaid installments.		

When interest on bonds becomes due, an entry is made setting up interest expenses and the resulting liability. Any material premiums and discounts should be amortized in a systematic and rational manner over the period the bonds are outstanding. The entry in this case is as follows:

Premium on bonds payable	100	
Interest expenses	10,400	
Interest payable		10,500
To record interest due on bonds.		

The entries to record interest receipts and payments are:

Cash for interest payments	10,700	
Interest receivable		10,700
To record receipt of interest.		

Interest payable	10,500	
Cash for interest payments		10,500
To record payment of interest.		

accounting for construction expenditures

Special assessment projects may be constructed by contract, by the government's own labor forces, or by a combination of the two. In the present case it is assumed that most of the work is to be performed by contract but that certain parts of the project involving labor and equipment are to be performed by the government itself. If we assume that the contract was for $600,000, the following entry would be made at the time the contract was awarded:

Encumbrances	600,000	
Reserve for encumbrances		600,000
To record awarding of contract.		

The contractor submits bills from time to time as the work progresses. As bills are received, the following entries are made:

Reserve for encumbrances	200,000	
Encumbrances		200,000
To record cancellation of encumbrances by amount of actual liability.		

Expenditures	200,000	
Contracts payable		200,000
To record liability on account of contract.		

Expenditures incurred by the government are recorded as follows:

Expenditures	75,000	
Cash for construction		75,000
To record construction expenditures.		

closing entries at end of fiscal year

At the end of each year an entry is made closing out the Interest Revenues and the Interest Expenses accounts. If revenues exceed expenses, the entry is as follows:

Interest revenues	11,025	
Interest expenses		10,400
Fund balance—interest		625
To record closing out of interest accounts.		

If interest expenses had exceeded revenues, the deficiency would, of course, have been charged against the Fund Balance—Interest account. The accounting procedure involved in the disposal of fund balance surpluses and deficits is discussed later.

As noted earlier, premiums and discounts on special assessment bonds should be amortized unless they are immaterial, in which case they may be closed out at the end of the fiscal year. Premiums are closed out through the following entry:

Premiums on bonds	200	
Fund balance—interest		200
To record closing out of premium on bonds into fund balance for interest.		

Discounts, since they reduce the cash available for construction, are usually closed directly into the Fund Balance—Construction account if they are not amortized. If, however, the fund has (or anticipates) a balance arising from an excess of Interest Revenues over Interest Expenses, the discount may be charged to this account. In that case, a corresponding transfer is ultimately made from Cash for Interest Payments to Cash for Construction. Specifically, the entries would be as follows:

Fund balance—interest	200	
Discount on bonds		200
To record closing out of discount on special assessment bonds.		

Cash for construction	200	
Cash for interest payments		200
To record transfer of interest cash, equivalent to the amount of the discount, to cash for con- construction.		

Discounts are frequently made up in this fashion, that is, by charging interest on assessments receivable at the bond yield rate in order to recoup the bond discount.

It is preferable to close out the Expenditures account at the end of each fiscal year, although it may be closed out only when construction is completed. If expenditures are closed out at the end of the fiscal year, the entry is as follows:

Fund balance—construction (or appropriations) ..	675,000	
Expenditures		275,000
Encumbrances		400,000
To record closing out of construction expenditures and encumbrances at end of fiscal year.		

A corresponding entry would be made in the General Fixed Assets group of accounts setting up the expenditures of $275,000 as cost of work in progress.

special assessment fund statements

Three statements are normally prepared each period for Special Assessment funds: (a) a balance sheet, (b) a statement analyzing the changes in the fund balance account(s); and (c) a statement of cash receipts and disbursements.

As in the case of Capital Projects funds, combined statements may be prepared where a government maintains more than one Special Assessment fund. Also, a total column may be used without fear of engendering misleading inferences, so long as adequate separate fund detail is presented within Special Assessment fund statements.

balance sheet—uncompleted projects

After the previously described entries have been posted, the Special Assessment fund balance sheet would appear as in Figure 15. The Fund Balance—Construction account balance represents the amount available for commitment at the balance sheet date; the Reserve for Encumbrances also represents construction fund balance, but this balance has already been committed. The Fund Balance—Interest account presents the cumulative difference between interest revenues and expenses to date.

analysis of change in fund balances

A statement analyzing the changes in the Fund Balance account(s) should be prepared each year. Figure 16 illustrates such a statement prepared at the end of the first year of a special assessment project. Recall

FIGURE 15

A GOVERNMENTAL UNIT

SPECIAL ASSESSMENT FUND
BALANCE SHEET
AT CLOSE OF FISCAL YEAR 19X1

Assets

Cash:			
For construction		$670,000	
For interest payments		1,200	$ 671,200
Assessments receivable:			
Current		$ 60,000	
Delinquent (to be used to finance construction)		5,000	
Deferred		465,000	530,000
Interest receivable			325
Total assets			$1,201,525

Liabilities, Reserves, and Fund Balances

Liabilities:			
Contracts payable		$200,000	
Bonds payable	$525,000		
Premium on bonds payable	900	525,900	
Total liabilities			$ 725,900
Reserves and fund balances:			
Reserve for encumbrances		$400,000	
Fund balance—construction		75,000	
Fund balance—interest		625	
Total reserves and fund balance			475,625
Total liabilities, reserves, and fund balances			$1,201,525

that only the information in the total column is deemed "required," although the other information is certainly useful.

statement of cash receipts and disbursements

A statement of Special Assessment fund cash receipts and disbursements should also be prepared at the end of each year. Such a statement for the first year of a fund's activities might appear as in Figure 17. Recall again that cash segregation is optional, but it is preferred by the authors.

FIGURE 16

A GOVERNMENTAL UNIT

SPECIAL ASSESSMENT FUND
ANALYSIS OF CHANGES IN FUND BALANCE
FOR THE FISCAL YEAR 19X1

	Total	*Construction*	*Interest*
Project authorization	$750,000	$750,000	—
Fund balances, beginning of year	$ –0–	$ –0–	$ –0–
Additions:			
Project authorization	$750,000	$750,000	$ –0–
Interest revenues	11,025	–0–	11,025
Total additions	$761,025	$750,000	$11,025
Total balances and additions	$761,025	$750,000	$11,025
Deductions:			
Expenditures	$275,000	$275,000	$ –0–
Encumbrances	400,000	400,000	–0–
Interest expenses	10,400	–0–	10,400
Total deductions	$685,400	$675,000	$10,400
Fund balances, end of year	$ 75,625	$ 75,000	$ 625

FIGURE 17

A GOVERNMENTAL UNIT

SPECIAL ASSESSMENT FUND
STATEMENT OF CASH RECEIPTS AND DISBURSEMENTS
FOR THE FISCAL YEAR 19X1

	Total	*For Construction*	*For Interest*
Cash balance, beginning of year	$ –0–	$ –0–	$ –0–
Receipts:			
Sale of bonds	$526,000	$525,000	$ 1,000
Governmental unit's share of construction costs	150,000	150,000	–0–
Current assessments	70,000	70,000	–0–
Interest on assessments	10,700	–0–	10,700
Total receipts	$756,700	$745,000	$11,700
Total cash available	$756,700	$745,000	$11,700
Disbursements:			
Capital outlay	$ 75,000	$ 75,000	$ –0–
Interest on bonds	10,500	–0–	10,500
Total disbursements	$ 85,500	$ 75,000	$10,500
Cash balance, end of year	$671,200	$670,000	$ 1,200

transactions and entries during second year

Let us assume that construction of the project was completed during the second year. The following list of transactions or events and entries illustrates the operation of the fund during the year:

Encumbrances were reestablished in the usual Encumbrances—Reserve for Encumbrances offset relation by reversing the portion of the prior year closing entry applicable thereto:

Encumbrances	400,000	
Fund balance—construction		400,000
To reestablish prior year encumbrances.		

Contracts payable in the amount of $200,000 were paid:

Contracts payable	200,000	
Cash for construction		200,000

Current assessments in the amount of $58,000 were collected. (Note: these collections are segregated for bond payments.)

Cash for bond payments	58,000	
Assessments receivable—current		58,000

Bonds in the amount of $55,000 were paid.

Bonds payable	55,000	
Cash for bond payments		55,000

Delinquent assessments in the amount of $4,000 were collected.

Cash for construction	4,000	
Assessments receivable—delinquent		4,000

Deferred assessments amounting to $60,000 became due.

Assessments receivable—current	60,000	
Assessment receivable—deferred		60,000

Current assessments in the amount of $2,000 became delinquent. (Note: these were "earmarked" for construction use.)

Assessments receivable—delinquent	2,000	
Assessments receivable—current		2,000

Interest of $9,665 became receivable.

Interest receivable	9,665	
Interest revenues		9,665

Interest of $9,900 was collected.

Cash for interest payments	9,900	
Interest receivable		9,900

Interest payable was accrued and bond premium amortized:

Premium on bonds payable	75	
Interest expense	9,325	
Interest payable		9,400

Interest payable of $9,400 was paid.

Interest payable	9,400	
Cash for interest payments		9,400

Additional construction expenditures incurred by the city amounted to $71,000, and $12,000 of this amount was paid in cash, the remainder being due the Intragovernmental Service fund.

Expenditures	71,000	
Cash for construction		12,000
Due to intragovernmental service fund		59,000

The project was completed and a bill was received from the contractor for the remaining part of the contract ($400,000).

Reserve for encumbrances	400,000	
Encumbrances		400,000
To reverse remaining part of entry setting up encumbrances on account of contract.		

Expenditures	400,000	
Contracts payable		400,000
To record construction expenditures.		

The amount due on the contract was paid except for $30,000, which was retained pending final inspection and approval of the project.

Contracts payable	400,000	
Contracts payable—retained percentage		30,000
Cash for construction		370,000

An entry was made at the end of the year, closing out the Interest Revenues and Interest Expenses accounts.

Interest revenues	9,665	
Interest expenses		9,325
Fund balance—interest		340

Finally, an entry was made at the end of the year, closing out the construction expenditures for the period.

Fund balance—construction	471,000	
Expenditures		471,000

balance sheet for completed project

If the foregoing entries had been posted to the accounts, the balance sheet in Figure 18 could have been prepared. That actual expenditures were $4,000 less than authorized is reflected in the Fund Balance—Construction account. The Fund Balance—Interest account indicates that interest revenues to date have exceeded interest expenses to date by $965.

Even though most of the construction cost has been financed from special assessments, the resulting improvements are considered government property. Consequently, the entire cost of the project—in this case $746,000—would be capitalized. Note again that the resulting fixed assets are not carried in the Special Assessment fund but in the General Fixed Assets account group. There the $275,000 capitalized at the end of the first year would be reclassified from Construction in Progress to the Improvements other than Building account; the $471,000 current-year expenditures would also be capitalized to the Improvements other than Building account to bring its total from this special assessment project to $746,000.

On the other hand, recall that the special assessment bonds appear as a liability in the Special Assessment Fund balance sheet because the resources of the fund will be used to retire these bonds. Since, however, the constructed project will not provide resources for retiring such bonds, the improvement does not appear among the Special Assessment fund assets.

Notice also that there is no Fund Balance—Bond Principal Retirement or similar account in the balance sheet. Such an account would arise only if assets to be used for bond retirement exceeded the principal of the bonds payable. Again, the Fund Balance—Interest account represents the cumulative excess of interest revenues over interest expenses.

FIGURE 18

A GOVERNMENTAL UNIT

Special Assessment Fund
Balance Sheet
At Close of Fiscal Year 19X2

Assets

Cash:			
For construction		$ 92,000	
For interest payments		1,700	
For bond payments		3,000	$ 96,700
Assessments receivable:			
Current		$ 60,000	
Delinquent (of which $1,000 is for construction)		3,000	
Deferred		405,000	468,000
Interest receivable			90
Total assets			$564,790

Liabilities and Fund Balances

Liabilities:			
Due to Intragovernmental Service fund		$ 59,000	
Contracts payable—retained percentage		30,000	
Bonds payable	$470,000		
Premiums on bonds payable	825	470,825	
Total liabilities			$559,825
Fund Balances:			
Construction		$ 4,000	
Interest		965	
Total fund balances			$ 4,965
Total liabilities and fund balances			$564,790

analysis of changes in fund balance(s)

A statement analyzing the changes in Fund Balance accounts should be prepared at the end of each fiscal year. Figure 19 exhibits such a statement in which all three Fund Balance accounts are displayed. Separate statements could be prepared, of course, and combined statements may be used if several Special Assessment funds are present. Use of distinctly labeled Fund Balance accounts as illustrated here is not mandatory, but is preferred by the authors.

FIGURE 19

A GOVERNMENTAL UNIT

SPECIAL ASSESSMENT FUND
ANALYSIS OF CHANGES IN FUND BALANCES
FOR THE FISCAL YEAR 19X2

	Total	*Construction*	*Interest*
Project authorization	$750,000	$750,000	
Fund balances, beginning of year	$ 75,625	$ 75,000	$ 625
Additions:			
Encumbrances reestablished	$400,000	$400,000	
Interest revenues	9,665		$ 9,665
Total additions	$409,665	$400,000	$ 9,665
Total balances and additions	$485,290	$475,000	$10,290
Deductions:			
Expenditures	$471,000	$471,000	
Interest expenses	9,325		$ 9,325
Total deductions	$480,325	$471,000	$ 9,325
Fund balances, end of year	$ 4,965	$ 4,000	$ 965

statement of cash receipts and disbursements

As indicated earlier, a statement of cash receipts and disbursements should be prepared for each year in the life of a Special Assessment fund. Such a statement for the fund's second year of operation appears in Figure 20.

fund activities subsequent to project completion

Once project construction is finished, the Capital Projects fund aspects of the Special Assessment fund are complete and it becomes, in effect, a special assessment Debt Service fund. Significant construction fund balances or deficits are appropriately disposed of upon project completion; disposal of minor balances or deficits may be deferred until the debt service aspects are completed.

The Special Assessment fund will continue to operate in a debt service capacity until all assessments receivable and interest thereon have been collected and all special assessment bond interest and principal have been paid. At that time, any remaining fund balances or deficits are suitably disposed of and the fund is abolished.

FIGURE 20

A GOVERNMENTAL UNIT

SPECIAL ASSESSMENT FUND
STATEMENT OF CASH RECEIPTS AND DISBURSEMENTS
FOR THE FISCAL YEAR 19X2

	Total	*Construction*	*Interest*	*Bond Retirement*
Cash balance, beginning of year	$671,200	$670,000	$ 1,200	$ –0–
Receipts:				
Current assessments	$ 58,000			$58,000
Delinquent assessments	4,000	$ 4,000		
Interest on assessments	9,900		$ 9,900	
Total receipts	$ 71,900	$ 4,000	$ 9,900	$58,000
Total cash available	$743,100	$674,000	$11,100	$58,000
Disbursements:				
Capital outlay	$582,000	$582,000		
Retirement of bonds	55,000			$55,000
Interest on bonds	9,400		$ 9,400	
Total disbursements	$646,400	$582,000	$ 9,400	$55,000
Cash balance, end of year	$ 96,700	$ 92,000	$ 1,700	$ 3,000

Disposing of Balances or Deficits. The Special Assessment fund thus far considered really consists of three funds within a fund: a fund used to finance construction, a fund used to retire bonds, and a fund used to pay interest. To illustrate this distinction, the balance sheet of Figure 18 has been set up differently (see Figure 21).

Maintaining the distinction between these funds within the Special Assessment fund is essential for two reasons. First, cash belonging to one fund cannot be used to meet the liabilities of either of the other two funds without proper authorization. Second, the balance of any of these funds cannot be used to make up a deficit in the other two funds without the approval of the proper authorities.

Assuming that legislative authorization has been given, the unneeded construction fund balance may be disposed of through one of the following means: (a) by making rebates to property owners and the governmental unit, (b) by reducing unpaid assessments, (c) by retiring bonds, or (d) by making up an interest deficit. A construction deficit, on the

FIGURE 21

A GOVERNMENTAL UNIT

SPECIAL ASSESSMENT FUND
BALANCE SHEET
AT CLOSE OF FISCAL YEAR 19X2

Assets

	Total	*Construction*	*Retirement of Bonds*	*Payment of Interest*
Cash	$ 96,700	$92,000	$ 3,000	$1,700
Assessments receivable:				
Current	60,000		60,000	
Delinquent	3,000	1,000	2,000	
Deferred	405,000		405,000	
Interest receivable				90
Total assets	$564,790	$93,000	$470,000	$1,790

Liabilities and Fund Balances

	Total	*Construction*	*Retirement of Bonds*	*Payment of Interest*
Liabilities:				
Contracts payable—retained percentage	$ 30,000	$30,000		
Due to Intragovernmental Service fund	59,000	59,000		
Bonds payable	470,000		$470,000	
Premium on bonds payable	825			$ 825
Total liabilities	$559,825	$89,000	$470,000	$ 825
Fund balances	4,965	4,000		965
Total liabilities and fund balances	$564,790	$93,000	$470,000	$1,790

other hand, might be wiped out through supplemental assessments plus the receipt of a supplemental contribution from the governmental unit. An interest "surplus" might be used to make up a bond deficit.

The following typical transactions and entries are illustrative of the accounting procedure involved in disposing of surpluses and deficits.

An unneeded construction fund balance amounted to $85,000, and cash rebates were made as follows: to property owners, $10,000; to the governmental unit, $5,000. A reduction of $70,000 was made in assessments.

Fund balance—construction	85,000	
Reserve for rebates		85,000

Reserve for rebates	85,000	
Cash for construction		15,000
Assessments receivable—deferred		70,000

Cash representing construction fund balance in the amount of $50,000 was used to retire bonds.

Fund balance—construction	50,000	
Cash for construction		50,000

Cash for bond payments	50,000	
Fund balance—bonds		50,000

Bonds payable	50,000	
Cash for bond payments		50,000

A construction deficit of $75,000 was eliminated through supplemental assessments of $55,000 together with a supplemental contribution by the governmental unit of $20,000.

Assessments receivable—supplemental	55,000	
Governmental unit's share of cost—supplemental	20,000	
Fund balance—construction		75,000

Interest cash in the amount of $5,000 was used to make up a bond deficit.

Cash for bond retirement	5,000	
Cash for interest payments		5,000

Fund balance—interest	5,000	
Fund balance—bond retirement		5,000

Debt Service Funds

The purpose of Debt Service funds is "to account for the payment of interest and principal on long-term debt other than special assessment and revenue bonds." [7] The responsibility of providing for the retirement of long-term, general obligation debt is ordinarily indicated by the terms of the indenture or other contract by which the debt is created. (The

[7] N.C.G.A., *op. cit.*, p. 7.

term "general obligation" indicates that the "full faith and credit" of the governmental unit has been pledged to the repayment of the debt.) Even when the governmental unit so obligates itself, the primary responsibility for repayment may be assigned to resources—and funds—other than taxes and Debt Service funds. For example, we have observed that long-term debt issued to finance improvements that are to be paid for by owners of benefited property is to be repaid by the Special Assessment fund. Again, long-term debt issued to finance the assets of public enterprises is ordinarily to be repaid by the Enterprise fund out of the revenues of the fund. In both the foregoing cases, repayment is as stated even though the terms of the debt may specify that the full faith and credit of the governmental unit has been pledged to the repayment of the debt—neither requires a Debt Service fund.

There are three kinds of long-term debt: bonds, notes, and time warrants. Term bonds are those for which all the principal is payable at a specified maturity date. Serial bonds, which are by far the most widely used, provide for periodic maturities ranging up to the maximum period permitted by law. Regular serial bonds are repayable in equal annual installments over the life of the issue. Other arrangements may be specified by the bond indenture.

Notes that are to be repaid within one year of the date of issue are normally carried as liabilities of the General fund; notes to be repaid over a longer period of time, however, justify the creation of related Debt Service funds. Similarly, warrants that are to be paid more than one year after the date of issue also justify the Debt Service fund treatment. Since the accounting for notes and warrants is similar to that for bonds, the remainder of the discussion of Debt Service funds is in terms of bonds.

sources of financing

The money for repayment of long-term debt may come from a number of sources with varying legal restrictions. The typical source is property taxes. A special tax rate may be assessed for a single bond issue, or a total annual rate may be used with proration of the proceeds to several debt issues. There is also a growing tendency for legislative bodies to earmark a tax for a specified purpose, with a proviso that the proceeds may be used either for current operating expenses or to repay debt that has been created in order to finance a specified purpose. The total proceeds of the tax would in such a case go into a Special Revenue fund; the portion of the proceeds allocated to debt repayment would be transferred to a Debt Service fund (and the portion to be used for construction might be transferred to a Capital Projects fund).

Still another method of payment is required by a bond indenture that specifies repayment of the debt out of "the first revenues accruing to the treasury." The effect of such an agreement is to cause the General fund to contribute the necessary amounts to the Debt Service fund.

When a term issue is to be repaid by a fund accumulating to the amount of the issue at date of maturity, the assets of the fund during its lifetime will be invested in income-producing securities. Income from these securities constitutes still another form of revenue for the Debt Service fund. Here the contract with the bondholders ordinarily requires equal annual revenues for the fund from contributions or from special tax levies of the same annual amount. This requirement is the typical sinking fund arrangement.

debt service fund for a serial issue

To illustrate the operation of a Debt Service fund for a serial issue, we shall assume that A Governmental Unit issued 5% Flores Park Serial Bonds on January 1, 19X1, in the amount of $1 million to finance the purchase and development of a park. The bond indenture calls for annual payments of $100,000 per year to retire the principal. The debt service requirements (principal and interest) are to come from a property tax levied for the specific purpose. The following journal entries record the transactions for the first year of operation of the Flores Park Debt Service Fund:

	Debit	Credit
1. Estimated revenues	155,000	
Appropriations		150,000
Fund balance		5,000
To record the budget for the fund for the fiscal year.		
2. Taxes receivable—current	156,000	
Estimated uncollectible current taxes		1,000
Revenues		155,000
To record the taxes levied for the year.		
3. Cash	151,000	
Taxes receivable—current		151,000
To record collection of taxes for the year.		
4. Expenditures	100,000	
Bonds payable		100,000
To record the fund's liability for payment of the first annual serial maturity.		
5. Expenditures	50,000	
Interest payable		50,000
To record the accrual of interest payable at the end of the year.		

	Debit	Credit
6. Bonds payable	100,000	
Interest payable	50,000	
Cash		150,000
To record payment of liabilities.		
7. Taxes receivable—delinquent	5,000	
Estimated uncollectible current taxes	1,000	
Taxes receivable—current		5,000
Estimated uncollectible delinquent taxes		1,000
To record the transfer of taxes receivable and the related estimated uncollectible taxes from current to delinquent status.		

CLOSING ENTRIES

	Debit	Credit
C1. Revenues	155,000	
Estimated revenues		155,000
To close the revenue accounts.		
C2. Appropriations	150,000	
Expenditures		150,000
To close the expenditure accounts.		

It should be emphasized that the operations of the Debt Service Fund—Flores Park Serial Bonds could have been financed by any one or a combination of the revenue sources described earlier in this chapter.

sinking fund requirements

Term bonds ordinarily are repaid from a fund accumulated over the life of the bonds by means of annual additions to the fund and by earnings of the fund assets. Figure 22, "Schedule of Sinking Fund Requirements," has been prepared for the City Hall Bonds of A Governmental Unit. These are 5.5%, 20-year term bonds issued January 1, 19X0. They are to be repaid out of "the first revenues accruing to the Treasury."

The first payment to the sinking fund is scheduled for the end of year 1. A similar payment will be made at the end of each succeeding year until, at the time of the twentieth payment, the fund should equal $1 million. An assumed earnings rate of 6% has been used in the development of Figure 22. The amount of the required annual additions was determined by selecting from a table the amount of an ordinary annuity of one dollar per period at 6% for 20 periods. This amount, $36.7855912, is the amount to which an annual annuity of one dollar would accumulate in 20 years at 6%. Since the desired amount to be accumulated is $1 million, it is necessary to divide that figure by $36.7855912 to obtain the $27,185 which is the amount of the required annual additions.

The schedule of sinking fund requirements provides the amounts of the budgetary requirements for the Debt Service fund for the duration of the fund, provided the accumulation process proceeds as planned (or departs from the plan by immaterial amounts). The required fund

FIGURE 22

SCHEDULE OF SINKING FUND REQUIREMENTS

(ASSUMING AN ANNUAL EARNINGS RATE OF 6%)

Year	*Required Annual Additions*	*Required Fund Earnings*	*Required Fund Increases*	*Required Fund Balances*
1	$ 27,185		$ 27,185	$ 27,185
2	27,185	$ 1,631	28,816	56,001
3	27,185	3,360	30,545	86,546
4	27,185	5,193	32,378	118,924
18	27,185	46,018	73,203	840,168
19	27,185	50,410	77,595	917,763
20	27,171 *	55,066	82,237	1,000,000
	$543,686	$456,314	$1,000,000	$1,000,000

* The last year's addition needs to be only $27,171 because of rounding errors.

balance at the end of each year furnishes a standard against which to compare the actual accumulation. If the actual accumulation falls short of or exceeds the required fund balances by substantial amounts, a new schedule of sinking fund requirements should be computed. To accomplish this, start from the actual accumulation and calculate the annual additions and fund earnings required to produce $1 million by the end of the twentieth year. The calculation of the new schedule may be based on an altered expected annual earnings rate.

The decision to retire or not to retire treasury bonds should be made by balancing the costs of continuing the bonds alive in the fund with the cost of recalculating the accumulation schedule and changing the annual revenues required by the fund.

debt service fund for a term issue

To illustrate the operation of a Debt Service fund for a term issue we shall use the City Hall Bonds described previously and the schedule of sinking fund requirements presented in Figure 22. At the end of the first year of the fund's operation, 19X0, there would have been a balance of $27,185 in both the Fund Balance and Cash accounts of the Debt Service fund. These would have resulted from the first payment to the sinking fund of the required annual additions. The following journal entries record the transactions of the City Hall Debt Service fund for the second year of operation, 19X1:

1. Required additions	82,585	
Required earnings	1,631	
Appropriations		55,400
Fund balance		28,816
To record the budget for 19X1.		

The budget for 19X1 is as follows:

Required additions (to be provided by the General fund)	$82,585
Appropriations:	
Annual interest charges	$55,000
Fiscal agent's fee	400
	$55,400

The so-called required additions figure is computed as follows:

Required addition to sinking fund	$27,185
Annual interest charges	55,000
Fiscal agent's fee	400
	$82,585

The term "required additions" is the account title used by the National Committee on Governmental Accounting; in this set of circumstances perhaps a better term would be "required contributions." Note that the credit to Fund Balance is the amount of "Required Fund Increases" in Figure 22.

2. Investments	26,000	
Unamortized premiums on investments	270	
Interest receivable on investments	520	
Unamortized discounts on investments ..		80
Cash		26,710
To record the purchase of investments, together with the related premiums, accrued interest, and discounts.		

	Debit	Credit
3. Due from General fund	82,585	
Revenues		82,585
To record accrual of the contribution from the General fund.		
4. Cash	82,585	
Due from General fund		82,585
To record the receipt of the contribution from the General fund.		
5. Interest receivable on investments	1,650	
Interest earnings		1,650
To record accrual of interest revenue on investments.		
6. Cash	1,750	
Interest receivable on investments		1,750
To record collection of interest receivable.		
7. Unamortized discounts on investments	20	
Interest earnings	10	
Unamortized premiums on investments ..		30
To record amortization of premiums and discounts on investments and the resultant correction of interest earnings.		
8. Expenditures	55,400	
Interest payable		55,000
Vouchers payable		400
To record accrual of interest payments on the bonds and the payment of agent's fees.		
9. Cash with fiscal agent	55,000	
Cash		55,000
To record transfer of cash for payment of interest on the bonds to the fiscal agent.		
10. Interest payable	55,000	
Vouchers payable		55,000
To record the vouchering of the interest liability.		
11. Vouchers payable	55,000	
Cash with fiscal agent		55,000
To record payment of the interest by the fiscal agent.		
12. Vouchers payable	400	
Cash		400
To record payment of the fiscal agent's fee.		
C1. Revenues	82,585	
Required additions		82,585
To record the closing of the revenues and required additions accounts.		

C2. Interest earnings	1,640	
Required earnings		1,631
Fund balance		9
To close the earnings and estimated earnings accounts and to transfer the difference to fund balance.		

When the budget was recorded in journal entry 1, the credit to Fund Balance was $28,816, the amount of the required fund increase for the second year according to Figure 22. The $9 difference between estimated and actual earnings for year 2 will produce a higher figure for Fund Balance at the end of year 2 than that required by the schedule of sinking fund requirements.

C3. Appropriations	55,400	
Expenditures		55,400
To close the estimated and actual expenditures accounts.		

accrual of interest payable

The National Committee on Governmental Accounting does not recommend accrual of the year-end balances of interest payable on term or serial bonds unless the revenues to pay the interest have been accrued or received. If a fund on a calendar year basis paid the interest on its bonds as the amount fell due on, let us say, October 31, 19X1, there is no question but that the Debt Service fund would be obligated, as of December 31, 19X1, for the interest for the additional two months of 19X1. On the other hand, the 19X1 budget has provided for the payment of the interest expense falling due in the current year, and the following year's budget will provide for payment of interest falling due in 19X2. Since there is no way to show as assets, as of December 31, 19X1, the revenues that will be used to pay the interest for the months of November and December, 19X1, the accrual of the interest of those two months would result in an unwarranted deficit in a Debt Service fund servicing serial bonds and an unwarranted shortage of the required fund balance in a fund accounting for the service of term bonds.

balance sheet

Separate balance sheets for each of the Debt Service funds of A Governmental Unit could of course be prepared; but when there are a number of funds, it is customary to combine them, as in Figure 23. The balance sheet might contain such additional assets as cash with fiscal agents, taxes receivable—current, tax liens receivable, and interest and penalties receivable on taxes. In addition, the unamortized premiums and discounts on investments may be presented in the balance sheet rather than showing the investment figure at net cost. Similarly, there may be such liability accounts as Bonds Payable (for matured bonds) and Interest Payable. In the case of term bonds it is essential that the actuarial requirement for the fund be footnoted, so that readers of the statement may compare the actual achievement of the fund with the actuarial requirement.

FIGURE 23

A GOVERNMENTAL UNIT

DEBT SERVICE FUNDS
BALANCE SHEET
DECEMBER 31, 19X1

	Total	19Z0 Flores Park	19Y9 City Hall
Assets			
Cash	$30,410	$1,000	$29,410
Taxes receivable, delinquent, net of estimated uncollectible taxes	4,000	4,000 *	
Investments	26,180		26,180 †
Interest receivable on investments	420		420
Total assets	$61,010	$5,000	$56,010
Liabilities and Fund Balances			
Fund balances	$61,010	$5,000	$56,010 ‡

* A "Combined Schedule of Delinquent Taxes by Funds" will be included in the annual report to provide an overview of the success of the collection of taxes on a government-wide basis. The net delinquent tax figure for each fund should be referenced to and supported by it.

† A "Combined Schedule of Investments—All Funds" will be included in the annual report to provide complete information regarding individual investments (interest rates, maturity dates, par value and unamortized premiums and discounts) of each fund. The net investment figure should be referenced to and supported by it.

‡ The actuarial requirement is $56,001.

balance sheet at maturity

The balance sheet of A Governmental Unit's City Hall Bonds Debt Service fund at the date of maturity of the bonds, December 31, 19Y9, is presented in Figure 24. The disposition of the fund balance presents an interesting problem. If the law permits, the balance will be transferred to another Debt Service fund, especially if the latter's contributions or earnings are short of requirements. Similarly, if the fund had a deficit, it might be made up by transfers from the General fund, by an additional tax levy, or by transfers of surpluses of other Debt Service funds. Normally the fund balance or deficit of a Debt Service fund is small because adjustments have been made from time to time throughout the life of the fund.

FIGURE 24

A GOVERNMENTAL UNIT

CITY HALL BONDS DEBT SERVICE FUND
BALANCE SHEET
DECEMBER 31, 19Y9

Assets

Cash	$ 975,000
Investments	26,000
Interest receivable on investments	1,500
Total assets	$1,002,500

Liabilities and Fund Balance

Matured bonds payable	$1,000,000
Fund balance	2,500
Total liabilities and fund balance	$1,002,500

statements of operation

The management of Debt Service funds and the investing and tax-paying public will be interested in the results of the funds' operation. Two statements are available for this purpose: a statement of cash receipts and disbursements and a statement of revenues, expenditures, and fund balances. The former is not considered because the authors believe that it is in general not as useful as the latter, and because it is largely self-explanatory. Figure 25 comprises a statement of revenues, expenditures, and fund balances for the Debt Service funds of A Governmental Unit. Additional revenue accounts that might appear in the statement include Interest and Penalties on Property Taxes, Revenue from other Agencies (such as shared taxes from higher governments), and Gains or Losses on Disposition of Investments. It is important to compare the actuarial requirement for the increases in fund balances with the actual accomplishment of the funds; for this reason the actuarial requirements are footnoted.

Interim financial statements for the benefit of management may be prepared. However, the few expenditures of a Debt Service fund are more precisely budgetable than those of, for example, the General fund and hence are more easily controlled by the single finance officer who is usually in charge of them. Accordingly, the National Committee on Governmental Accounting recommends that summary interim statements of expenditures and encumbrances compared with appropriations be prepared for all funds, rather than individual statements for each fund.[8]

FIGURE 25

A GOVERNMENTAL UNIT

DEBT SERVICE FUNDS
STATEMENT OF REVENUES, EXPENDITURES, AND FUND BALANCES
FOR THE YEAR ENDED DECEMBER 31, 19X1

	Total	*19Z0 Flores Park*	*19Y9 City Hall*
Revenues:			
Property taxes	$155,000	$155,000	
Contribution from general fund	82,585		$82,585
Interest on investments	1,640		1,640
Total revenues	$239,225	$155,000	$84,225
Expenditures:			
Redemption of serial bonds	$100,000	$100,000	
Interest on bonds	105,000	50,000	$55,000
Fiscal agent's fees	400		400
Total expenditures	$205,400	$150,000	$55,400
Excess (deficit) to fund balance	$ 33,825	$ 5,000 *	$28,825 †
Fund balances, January 1, 19X1	27,185	-0-	27,185
Fund Balances, December 31, 19X1	$ 61,010	$ 5,000	$56,010

* The actuarial requirement for 19X1 was $0.
† The actuarial requirement for 19X1 was $28,816.

Trust and Agency Funds

A Trust fund is established to account for assets received and held by the government in the capacity of trustee or custodian. Trust funds are classified as expendable or nonexpendable, depending on whether their resources may be used up or must be kept intact. An Agency fund is

[8] N.C.G.A., *op. cit.*, p. 40.

established to account for assets received by a government in its capacity as agent for individuals, businesses, or other governments.

The difference between Trust funds and Agency funds is often one of degree. Trust funds, for example, may be subject to complex administrative and financial provisions set forth in trust agreements; they may be in existence for long periods of time, and may involve investment of trust assets. Agency funds, on the other hand, are primarily clearance devices for cash collected for others, held briefly, and then disbursed to authorized recipients. In all these situations, however, the government acts in a fiduciary capacity. Too, the accounting for Agency funds and for expendable Trust funds is virtually identical. Trust and Agency funds may therefore be considered together as a single class. It is important to note that enterprise trust and agency relationships (such as utility customer deposits) are accounted for in Enterprise funds; separate Trust or Agency funds need not be established in such cases.

expendable trust funds

A guarantee-deposits fund is an example of a rather simple Expendable Trust fund. Most governments require deposits for some purpose. For example, contractors may have to leave deposits with the government as a guarantee of the performance of their contracts. These deposits must be accounted for, so that they may be returned to the depositors.

The accounting procedure in this situation is simple. As deposits are received, Cash is debited and Fund Balance is credited. Subsequently, as deposits are refunded, these entries are reversed. The balance sheet of such a fund would, therefore, consist of few accounts, as indicated in Figure. 26.

FIGURE 26

A GOVERNMENTAL UNIT

DEPOSITS FUND
BALANCE SHEET
AT CLOSE OF FISCAL YEAR 19X1

Assets	
Cash	$ 7,500
Investments	25,000
	$32,500
Fund Balance	
Deposits fund balance	$32,500

retirement funds

Public employee retirement plans are examples of more complex Expendable Trust funds common to governments. Pension or retirement plans for governments, like those of businesses, should be managed and accounted for on an actuarial basis, and the provisions of Accounting Principles Board Opinion 8 are generally applicable to them.

There are many types of retirement plans in existence in governments, and the degree to which actuarial considerations are recognized varies widely. In order to illustrate the general accounting approach for a public employee retirement fund, assume that such a fund is already in operation and that its beginning trial balance appears as in Figure 27. Assume also that (a) the equity of employees resigning or dying prior to retirement is rebated to the individual or to his estate, but the employer contributions on the workers' behalf remain in the fund; (b) employer contributions and earnings thereon vest to the benefit of the employee only upon retirement, and his benefits fluctuate somewhat with performance of the fund; and (c) earnings are apportioned according to a predetermined formula among employee equity, employer equity, and retiree equity in the fund.

FIGURE 27

A GOVERNMENTAL UNIT

PENSION OR RETIREMENT FUND
TRIAL BALANCE
AT BEGINNING OF FISCAL YEAR 19X1

	Debit	*Credit*
Cash	$ 56,000	
Due from general fund	8,000	
Interest receivable	3,000	
Investments	980,000	
Unamortized premium on investments	5,000	
Due to resigned employees		$ 3,000
Annuities payable		2,800
Reserve for employee contributions		470,200
Reserve for employer contributions		260,100
Actuarial deficiency—reserve for employer contributions		300,000
Reserve for retiree annuities		315,900
Fund balance (deficit)		(300,000)
	$1,052,000	$1,052,000

Assume that the following transactions or events occurred during the year:

Employer and employee contributions were accrued in the General fund.

Due from General fund	175,000	
Contributions—employees		125,000
Contributions—employer		50,000

A check was received from the General fund.

Cash	170,000	
Due from General fund		170,000

Accrued interest and premium amortization on investments was recorded.

Interest receivable	45,000	
Unamortized premium on investments		200
Interest earnings		44,800

A portion of the interest receivable was collected.

Cash	40,000	
Interest receivable		40,000

An employee retired; employer contributions in his behalf vested, and his retirement benefit formula was determined.

Reserve for employee contributions	10,000	
Reserve for employer contributions	5,000	
Reserve for retiree annuities		15,000

One employee resigned and two died prior to retirement.

Reserve for employee contributions	25,000	
Due to deceased employees' estates		10,000
Due to resigned employees		15,000

Checks were mailed to a resigned employee and to the estates of deceased employees.

Due to deceased employees' estates	10,000	
Due to resigned employees	12,000	
Cash		22,000

Annuities payable were accrued.

Expenditures	24,000	
Annuities currently payable		24,000

Annuities payable were paid, except for that to one employee, who is out of the country.

Annuities payable	23,000	
Cash		23,000

Additional investments were made.

Investments	150,000	
Unamortized discount on investments		7,000
Cash		143,000

At year end the following adjusting and closing entries were made.

Contribution accounts were closed to the respective reserve accounts. (Note: Alternatively these contributions might have been credited to the reserve accounts originally.)

Contributions—employees	125,000	
Contributions—employer	50,000	
Reserve for employee contributions		125,000
Reserve for employer contributions		50,000

Interest earnings were apportioned.

Interest earnings	44,800	
Reserve for employee contributions		18,300
Reserve for employer contributions		15,700
Reserve for retiree annuities		10,800

The Expenditures account was closed.

Reserve for retiree annuities	24,000	
Expenditures		24,000

The actuary indicated that additional contributions would need to be made if the fund were to be actuarially sound.

Fund balance	20,000	
Actuarial deficiency—reserve for employer contributions		20,000

The following statements should be prepared annually for *all* trust and agency funds: (a) balance sheet; (b) analysis of changes in fund balance(s); and (c) cash receipts and disbursements statement. In addition, a statement analyzing reserve accounts should be prepared for pension or retirement funds (and for other funds, if changes are significant), and actuarial assumptions and actuarial position should be disclosed by footnote. The required statements are illustrated, using the retirement fund data given, in Figures 28, 29, 30, and 31.

It may be contended that most of the "reserves" shown on the pension or retirement fund balance sheet are actually liabilities. Inasmuch as this terminology persists in the pension industry, and because some are proper reserves whereas others may represent liabilities, separate liability, reserve, and fund balance subheadings are seldom employed within this statement or in combined statements including pension or retirement fund data.

FIGURE 28

A GOVERNMENTAL UNIT

PENSION OR RETIREMENT FUND
BALANCE SHEET
AT CLOSE OF FISCAL YEAR 19X1

Assets

Cash		$ 78,000
Due from General fund		13,000
Interest receivable		8,000
Investments (at par; fair market value, $xx)	$1,130,000	
Unamortized premium on investments	4,800	
Unamortized discounts on investments	(7,000)	1,127,800
Total assets		$1,226,800

Liabilities, Reserves, and Fund Balances

Due to resigned employees	$ 6,000
Annuities currently payable	3,800
Reserve for employee contributions	578,500
Reserve for employer contributions	320,800
Actuarial deficiency—reserve for employer contributions	320,000
Reserve for retiree annuities	317,700
Fund balance (deficit)	(320,000)
Total liabilities, reserves, and fund balances	$1,226,800

FIGURE 29

A GOVERNMENTAL UNIT

PENSION OR RETIREMENT FUND
ANALYSIS OF CHANGES IN FUND BALANCE
FOR THE FISCAL YEAR 19X1

Fund balance, beginning of year	$ (300,000)
Increase in actuarial deficiency—reserve for employer contributions	(20,000)
Fund balance, end of year	$ (320,000)

FIGURE 31

A GOVERNMENTAL UNIT

PENSION OR RETIREMENT FUND
STATEMENT OF CASH RECEIPTS AND DISBURSEMENTS
FOR THE FISCAL YEAR 19X1

Cash balance, beginning of year		$ 56,000
Receipts:		
Employee contributions	$125,000	
Employer contributions	45,000	
Interest	40,000	
Total receipts		210,000
Total cash available		$266,000
Disbursements:		
Investments purchased	$143,000	
Rebates—resignations	12,000	
Rebates—deaths	10,000	
Annuity payments	23,000	
Total disbursements		188,000
Cash balance, end of year		$ 78,000

nonexpendable trust funds

There are two types of Nonexpendable Trust funds: those in which neither the principal nor the earnings of the fund may be expended, and those whose earnings may be expended but whose principal must be

FIGURE 30

A GOVERNMENTAL UNIT

Pension or Retirement Fund
Analysis of Changes in Retirement Reserves
For the Fiscal Year 19X1

	Total	*Reserve for Employee Contributions*	*Reserve for Employer Contributions*	*Actuarial Deficiency—Reserve for Employer Contributions*	*Reserve for Retiree Annuities*
Balances, beginning of year	$1,346,200	$470,200	$260,100	$300,000	$315,900
Additions:					
Employee contributions	$ 125,000	$125,000	—	—	—
Employer contributions	50,000	—	$ 50,000	—	—
Interest earnings	44,800	18,300	15,700	—	$ 10,800
Total additions	$ 219,800	$143,300	$ 65,700	—	$ 10,800
Total balance and additions	$1,566,000	$613,500	$325,800	$300,000	$326,700
Transfers: Annuities awarded	—	(10,000)	(5,000)	—	15,000
Actuarial adjustments	20,000	—	—	20,000	—
Total revised balances	$1,586,000	$603,500	$320,800	$320,000	$341,700
Deductions:					
Expenditures—annuities	$ 24,000	—	—	—	$ 24,000
Rebates—deaths	10,000	$ 10,000	—	—	—
Rebates—resignations	15,000	15,000	—	—	—
Total deductions	$ 49,000	$ 25,000	—	—	$ 24,000
Balances, end of year	$1,537,000	$578,500	$320,800	$320,000	$317,700

kept intact. A loan fund is an example of the former type; some common forms of endowment funds are typical of the latter. The accounting procedure for Nonexpendable Trust funds does not differ materially from that for Expendable Trust funds, although a careful distinction between trust principal (corpus) and income must be maintained. The same principles and distinction apply as in estate accounting. These are discussed in the section on estate accounting in Chapter 7.

Loan Funds. The following transactions and corresponding entries illustrate the operation of a loan fund.

A cash donation of $150,000 was received for the purpose of establishing a loan fund.

Cash	150,000	
Loan fund balance		150,000

Loans amounting to $90,000 were made.

Loans receivable	90,000	
Cash		90,000

A loan of $1,000 was repaid with interest of $20.

Cash	1,020	
Loans receivable		1,000
Earnings		20

Earnings were closed out.

Earnings	20	
Loan fund balance		20

A loan fund balance sheet based on the foregoing entries appears in Figure 32.

Earnings are added to the capital of the fund and increase the amount of money available for loans. Although theoretically the fund is nonexpendable, in actual practice the fund balance may be reduced through bad debts.

If costs of administration are payable out of a loan fund, the fund ceases to be strictly nonexpendable, since administrative expenses reduce its balance. Sometimes however, provision is made for meeting administrative expenses out of earnings. In that case, we have the other type of trust fund, one whose *principal* must be kept intact but whose *earnings* may be expended. We shall now discuss this type of fund in detail.

FIGURE 32

A GOVERNMENTAL UNIT

LOAN FUND
BALANCE SHEET
AT CLOSE OF FISCAL YEAR 19X1

Assets

Cash	$ 61,020
Loans receivable	89,000
	$150,020

Balance

Loan fund balance	$150,020

Endowment Funds. When only the principal of a Trust fund is nonexpendable, the principal is segregated for accounting purposes from the income by establishing two funds: a Nonexpendable Trust fund to account for the principal and an Expendable Trust fund to account for earnings.

The following list of transactions and entries illustrates the operation of these related funds:

Cash in the amount of $200,000 was received for the establishment of a fund whose income is to be used in granting scholarships.

Entry in Endowment Principal Fund:

Cash	200,000	
Endowment principal fund balance		200,000

Investment of $200,000 was made. (For the sake of simplicity, assume that no premiums, discounts, or accrued interest purchases are involved. If they were, premiums and discounts would normally be amortized and only the net earnings would accrue to the Endowment Earnings fund.)

Entry in Endowment Principal Fund:

Investments	200,000	
Cash		200,000

Interest accrued on investments, $5,000.

Entry in Endowment Principal Fund:

Interest receivable	5,000	
Interest revenues		5,000

Net earnings were set up as payable to the Endowment Earnings fund.

Entry in Endowment Principal Fund:

Interest revenues	5,000	
Due to endowment earnings fund		5,000

Entry in Endowment Principal Fund:

Due from endowment principal fund	5,000	
Revenues		5,000

Interest receivable collected, $4,000.

Entry in Endowment Principal Fund:

Cash	4,000	
Interest receivable		4,000

Available cash is paid to Endowment Earnings fund.

Entry in Endowment Principal Fund:

Due to endowment earnings fund	4,000	
Cash		4,000

Entry in Endowment Earnings Fund:

Cash	4,000	
Due from endowment principal fund		4,000

Payment of $2,000 as a scholarship grant was made. (This is an outright grant, however, not a loan.)

Entry in Endowment Earnings Fund:

Scholarship expenditures	2,000	
Cash		2,000

The Endowment Earnings fund operating accounts were closed. (Note: In very simple funds with few transactions, revenues and expenditures may be debited and credited directly to the Fund Balance account. In such cases, as with the Endowment Principal fund, no closing entry would be required.)

Revenues	4,000	
Scholarship expenditures		2,000
Endowment earnings fund balance		2,000

If there are no other transactions, the endowment funds balance sheets would resemble Figures 33 and 34.

FIGURE 33

A GOVERNMENTAL UNIT

ENDOWMENT PRINCIPAL FUND
BALANCE SHEET
AT CLOSE OF FISCAL YEAR 19X1

Assets

Investments	$200,000
Interest receivable	1,000
	$201,000

Liabilities and Fund Balance

Due to endowment earnings fund	$ 1,000
Endowment principal fund balance	200,000
	$201,000

FIGURE 34

A GOVERNMENTAL UNIT

ENDOWMENT EARNINGS FUND
BALANCE SHEET
AT CLOSE OF FISCAL YEAR 19X1

Assets

Cash	$2,000
Due from endowment principal fund	1,000
	$3,000

Fund Balance

Endowment earnings fund balance	$3,000

If endowments are in the form of fixed properties, the latter constitute the nonexpendable fund principal, and the net income therefrom is transferred to an expendable fund. It is important, in such cases, to account carefully for the income and expenses of the principal fund. Whether depreciation is charged as an expense will depend on the provisions of the grant. Both the revenues and the expenses connected with administering the property (e.g., rents, repairs, decorating expenses, janitor's wages) would normally be accounted for in the principal fund, although the trustor could specify otherwise. Similarly, if the trust instrument is silent with respect to gains and losses on investments, these are usually identified with trust principal. The net earnings would, however, be transferred to the earnings fund and expended for the purpose designated—for example, granting scholarships.

agency funds

The following entries illustrate the operation of an Agency fund. It is assumed that the fund is established by a governmental unit to account for the taxes which it collects for other units.

When taxes become receivable, the entry is:

Taxes receivable for other units	98,000	
Taxes fund balance		98,000
To record taxes receivable for other governmental units.		

As taxes are collected, the entry is as follows:

Cash	58,000	
Taxes receivable for other units		58,000
To record collection of part of taxes receivable for other units.		

When the money is paid over to the governmental units, the entry is as follows:

Taxes fund balance	55,000	
Cash		55,000
To record paying over of part of collections to governmental units.		

For handling collections, the collecting unit usually charges a fee, which is ordinarily deducted from the proceeds before they are turned over to the proper unit. The entry to record this transaction in the Agency fund is a debit to Fund Balance and a credit to Cash.

Figure 35 is an illustration of an Agency fund balance sheet.

FIGURE 35

A GOVERNMENTAL UNIT

TAXES AGENCY FUND
BALANCE SHEET
AT CLOSE OF FISCAL YEAR 19X1

Assets

Cash	$ 3,000
Taxes receivable for other units	40,000
	$43,000

Fund Balance

Taxes fund balance	$43,000

combined statements for trust and agency funds

If numerous Trust and Agency funds exist, combined balance sheets, analyses of changes in fund balances, and cash receipt and disbursement statements may be prepared. These combined statements distinguish among Expendable Trust funds, Nonexpendable Trust funds, and Agency funds. The combined balance sheet in Figure 36 is illustrative of the appropriate approach to the preparation of combined statements for Trust and Agency funds. Observe also that (a) as is usual in governmental accounting, interfund receivables and payables are not eliminated, and (b) in this case the "total all funds" column is acceptable, although optional.

Intragovernmental Service Funds

Intragovernmental Service funds, sometimes referred to as "working capital" or "revolving" funds, are established to finance and account for the provision of goods and services by one department of a government to the other departments. This type of fund serves internal users only and should be distinguished from Enterprise funds, through which provision of goods or services for compensation to the general public is financed and accounted for. The operation of central garages, central storerooms, central printing plants, two-way radio facilities, cement plants, asphalt plants, and prison industries (such as license-plate factories established in penal institutions) are activities financed and accounted for through intragovernmental service funds.

FIGURE 36

A GOVERNMENTAL UNIT

TRUST AND AGENCY FUNDS
COMBINED BALANCE SHEET
AT CLOSE OF FISCAL YEAR 19X1

		Expendable Trust Funds			*Nonexpendable Trust Funds*		*Agency Funds*
Assets	*Total All Funds*	*Deposits Fund*	*Pension or Retirement Fund*	*Endowment Earnings Fund*	*Endowment Principal Fund*	*Loan Fund*	*Taxes Fund*
Cash	$ 151,520	$ 7,500	$ 78,000	$2,000		$ 61,020	$ 3,000
Interest receivable	9,000		8,000		$ 1,000		
Due from general fund	13,000		13,000				
Due from endowment principal fund	1,000			1,000			
Investments (par)	1,355,000	25,000	1,130,000		200,000		
Unamortized premium—investments	4,800		4,800				
Unamortized discount—investments	(7,000)		(7,000)				
Loans receivable	89,000					89,000	
Taxes receivable for other units	40,000						40,000
Total assets	$1,656,320	$32,500	$1,226,800	$3,000	$201,000	$150,020	$43,000
Liabilities, Reserves, and Fund Balances							
Due to resigned employees	$ 6,000		$ 6,000				
Annuities currently payable	3,800		3,800				
Due to endowment earnings fund	1,000				$ 1,000		
Reserve for employee contributions	578,500		578,500				
Reserve for employer contributions	320,800		320,800				
Actuarial deficiency—reserve for employer contributions	320,000		320,000				
Reserve for retiree annuities	317,700		317,700				
Fund balance (deficit)	108,520	$32,500	(320,000)	$3,000	200,000	$150,020	$43,000
Total liabilities, reserves, and fund balances	$1,656,320	$32,500	$1,226,800	$3,000	$201,000	$150,020	$43,000

establishment of intragovernmental service fund

An Intragovernmental Service fund is established by setting aside a certain sum of money or other assets for the fund's use. Money may be obtained by appropriation from the General fund, through the sale of bonds, or through capital advances from other funds or even other governments. The fund continues to operate as long as the activity it finances is carried on. The cash of the fund is reduced as the expenditures incurred in performing these activities are paid, but it is subsequently replenished by cash received for services rendered.

The first step in the establishment of the fund is the receipt of capital. The entry to record this transaction is a debit to Cash (or other asset accounts) and a credit to a Capital or Advance account. The next step is to secure the fixed assets with which the government is to carry on its service operations. Let us assume that these assets have already been obtained and have been set up on the records of the fund. At this point, a balance sheet of the Intragovernmental Service fund would resemble that in Figure 37 (if we assume the figures shown).

FIGURE 37

A GOVERNMENTAL UNIT

INTRAGOVERNMENTAL SERVICE FUND
BALANCE SHEET
EARLY IN FISCAL YEAR 19X1

	Assets	
Current assets:		
Cash		$150,000
Fixed assets:		
Land	$20,000	
Buildings	80,000	
Machinery	20,000	120,000
		$270,000
	Capital	
Capital		$270,000

operation of intragovernmental service fund

In studying the operations of the Intragovernmental Service fund, it is important to remember that the fund is usually intended to be self-supporting; that is, the accounting procedure must ensure that the capital of the fund remains intact. The fund must thus be accounted for on the same basis as a private enterprise. Only in that way is it possible to tell whether operations have resulted in a profit or a loss or whether the activity has broken even during a particular period. This is not to say that intragovernmental service activities are carried on for profit. Rather, the object is to recover the costs of operations, including overhead, without significant profit or loss in the long run.

In substance, an Intragovernmental Service fund is an intermediary fiscal entity through which some of the expenditures of the other departments are made. Thus the appropriations of the departments served constitute a limitation on expenditures which the fund can incur, and formal budgetary control is optional. The budget for the fund is comprised of expenditure estimates and estimates of billings to departments; an appropriation for the fund is required only if estimated expenditures exceed anticipated billings and borrowing.

Cost accounting records must be maintained for purposes of billing as well as income determination. Depreciation is recognized on those fixed assets which will be replaced from the fund's resources; depreciation is not recorded on any other general fixed assets utilized in the fund's activities, since these assets will presumably be replaced from other resources. Billings to departments may be rendered only at year end, after all costs are known; it is customary, however, to render billings monthly on a direct cost plus estimated overhead rate basis. If billings exceed *expenses* incurred, rebates may be made to the departments served; alternatively, the difference may be closed to Retained Earnings. Should expenses incurred exceed billings, supplemental charges may be made; alternatively, the loss may be closed to Retained Earnings.

For purposes of illustration, let us assume that the fund is established to finance the operations of a central equipment bureau. The hypothetical bureau owns automobiles, trucks, tractors, and similar equipment and operates them for the benefit of other departments. The procedure in accounting for the operations of such a bureau may be summarized as follows. The number of hours or miles that each piece of equipment serves each job or each department is recorded. A record is also kept of the cost of operating each piece of equipment. Subsequently, departments are billed for an amount sufficient to recover the full cost of rendering the service. The following is a list of some of the typical transactions involved in the operation of such a bureau. Since the entries are similar to those that would apply to a privately owned company, they are not reproduced here.

1. Purchased equipment on account for $80,000.
2. Materials and supplies purchased on account for $20,000.

3. Heat, light, and power paid, $4,000.

4. Office expenses paid, $400.

5. Salaries and wages paid amounted to $40,000, distributed as follows:

Direct labor	$20,000
Indirect labor	6,000
Superintendent's salary	7,000
Office salaries	7,000

6. Depreciation:

Buildings	$ 4,800
Machinery	2,400
Equipment	16,000

7. Vouchers payable in the amount of $85,000 paid.

8. Gas, oil, and other materials and supplies issued during the period, $14,000.

9. Total billings to departments for services rendered amounted to $85,600, of which $1,000 is receivable from the General fund, $25,600 is receivable from the Enterprise fund, and $59,000 from the Special Assessment fund.

balance sheet

If entries (including closing entries) had been made to reflect the previous transactions, and the entries had been posted to the accounts listed in the balance sheet illustrated in Figure 37, the resulting account balances could be used to prepare the balance sheet shown in Figure 38.

Note that the balance sheet contains fixed as well as current assets. These fixed assets are necessary in the earning of the fund's revenues, as are inventories. Their existence is essential to the continued operation of the activities. Consequently, not only must they be included in the Intragovernmental Service fund balance sheet, but provision must be made for their eventual replacement. Since departments are billed for overhead charges, including depreciation, part of the money received from departments for services represents depreciation charges. The money representing depreciation charges may be set up in a separate fund, or it may be made part of the Intragovernmental Service fund's general cash and used for various purposes pending the replacement of the assets. In the present case, it is assumed that no segregation is made.

statement of operations

As in the case of the balance sheet, if the transactions enumerated before had been journalized and posted to accounts, the resulting account balances could be used to prepare the statement of operations illustrated

FIGURE 38

A GOVERNMENTAL UNIT

INTRAGOVERNMENTAL SERVICE FUND
BALANCE SHEET
AT CLOSE OF FISCAL YEAR 19X1

Assets

Current assets:			
Cash		$20,600	
Due from general fund		1,000	
Due from enterprise fund		25,600	
Due from special assessment fund		59,000	
Inventory of materials and supplies		6,000	$112,200
Fixed assets:			
Land		$20,000	
Buildings	$80,000		
Less: Allowance for depreciation	4,800	75,200	
Machinery	$20,000		
Less: Allowance for depreciation	2,400	17,600	
Equipment	$80,000		
Less: Allowance for depreciation	16,000	64,000	176,800
			$289,000

Liabilities, Capital, and Retained Earnings

Vouchers payable	$ 15,000
Capital	270,000
Retained earnings (Fig. 40)	4,000
	$289,000

in Figure 39. The statement would be prepared and interpreted as would a similar statement for a private enterprise.

analysis of changes in retained earnings

As in commercial accounting, a statement analyzing the changes in Retained Earnings should be prepared unless changes are detailed in the capital section of the balance sheet. Similarly, analyses of other capital accounts should be prepared, or changes should be detailed in the balance sheet, if significant changes occurred during the period. The analysis of changes in Retained Earnings for the fund's initial year of operation would appear as in Figure 40.

FIGURE 39

A GOVERNMENTAL UNIT

INTRAGOVERNMENTAL SERVICE FUND
STATEMENT OF OPERATIONS
FOR THE FISCAL YEAR 19X1

Billings for services			$85,600
Less: Direct costs:			
Materials and supplies	$14,000		
Direct labor	20,000		
Depreciation—equipment	16,000	$50,000	
Less: Other costs:			
Indirect labor	$ 6,000		
Superintendent's salary	7,000		
Depreciation—buildings	4,800		
Depreciation—machinery	2,400		
Heat, light, and power	4,000		
Office salaries	7,000		
Office expenses	400	31,600	
Total costs of services rendered			81,600
Excess of billing over costs (Fig. 40)			$ 4,000

FIGURE 40

A GOVERNMENTAL UNIT

INTRAGOVERNMENTAL SERVICE FUND
ANALYSIS OF CHANGES IN RETAINED EARNINGS
FOR THE FISCAL YEAR 19X1

Balance, beginning of year	$ –0–
Add: Excess of net billings to departments over costs (Fig. 39)	4,000
Balance, end of year (Fig. 38)	$4,000

summary

The accounting procedure for an Intragovernmental Service fund is similar in most respects to that of a business enterprise carrying on like activities. As in business, it is important to determine whether the endeavor is being operated at a profit or a loss or is breaking even. Since appropriations are not normally made for the Intragovernmental Service fund, budgetary accounts need not be set up in this fund.

Enterprise Funds

Enterprise funds are established to account for the financing of services rendered to the public at large on a user charge basis. These funds must be distinguished from Intragovernmental Service funds, which finance services rendered for other departments of the government. Electric plants, water plants, natural gas distribution systems, sewer systems, public docks and wharves, hospitals, off-street parking lots and garages, public housing, airports, public transportation, swimming pools, and golf courses are among the many types of self-supporting activities carried on by governments and financed through Enterprise funds.

In all cases the Enterprise fund must be accounted for in the same manner as a similar privately owned commercial enterprise. The distinction between invested capital and retained earnings must be maintained, and the operations of the fund should be recorded in such a manner that net income or loss may be determined. Whenever possible, Enterprise fund accounting and reporting principles and procedures should follow those prescribed or generally used by privately owned businesses offering similar goods or services.

Since the same accounting principles apply to a government Enterprise fund as to similar privately owned businesses, transactions and entries for these funds are not included here. Instead, certain pertinent characteristics of Enterprise fund accounting are commented on briefly, and typical major financial statements are identified and illustrated in order to familiarize the reader with Enterprise fund accounts and statements.

comments on enterprise fund accounting

Normally a separate fund should be established for each enterprise, although related activities (e.g., water and sewer systems) may be accounted for within a single fund. Sales to government departments should be treated like those to any other customer; that is, other government departments served should be billed at standard rates. Failure to do so would result in enterprise charges to the public constituting, in part, a hidden tax used to support general government functions.

Formal budgetry control is not exercised in Enterprise fund accounting. Flexible budgeting techniques should be employed as in business, and it is preferable to present budgetary comparisons within the body of the operating statement(s).

If terms of bond indentures, council action, or administrative decisions necessitate the use of debt service, trust or agency, special revenue, or other enterprise-related funds, these are handled as in commercial accounting. That is, they are accounted for through restricted asset and reserve accounts on a "funds within a fund" basis, rather than by setting up a series of separate fund entities. Revenues and expenses of these "funds within a fund" are identified as nonoperating items within the Enterprise fund income statement.

Note again that all assets and liabilities related to the enterprise are recorded within the Enterprise fund accounts. Its fixed assets are not General Fixed Assets, nor is its debt General Long-Term Debt. Most enterprise long-term debt is in the form of revenue or mortgage serial bonds. In some cases, however, general obligation debt is issued by the government and the proceeds advanced to the Enterprise fund, through which the debt interest and principal are paid. In such cases it has been suggested that (a) the debt issue proceeds be placed first in a Capital Projects fund, then transferred to the Enterprise fund; (b) the debt be set up as a liability in the General Long-Term Debt group of accounts; and (c) an Advance From Municipality liability account be credited in the Enterprise fund. Interest expenses on the debt outstanding are paid by the Enterprise fund and constitute enterprise nonoperating expenses. When the debt principal is retired through the Enterprise fund, the Advance From Municipality account is debited; simultaneously, the liability is removed from the General Long-Term Debt group of accounts. Although this awkward approach results in a single liability being shown twice (both in the Enterprise fund and in the General Long-Term Debt group of accounts), and although no Receivable from Enterprise Fund account exists in another fund, this approach is defended on the grounds that it is necessary to report the liabilities of each fund and account group on a strict entity basis, without regard to the consolidated liability status of the government as a whole.

financial statements

The principal financial statements prepared for Enterprise funds are similar to those for private business. These are: a balance sheet; a statement of revenue and expense (income statement), preferably with budgetary comparisons; an analysis of changes in Retained Earnings; and a cash flow statement (see Figures 41–44). Other statements recommended for Enterprise funds are: a detailed statement of operating expenses, preferably with budgetary comparisons, and a schedule of fixed assets and depreciation, including current-year changes therein. Other statements or schedules might, of course, be appropriate in specific circumstances.

In reviewing the balance sheet (Figure 41), observe the use of subheadings to separate unrestricted current assets from restricted current

FIGURE 41

A GOVERNMENTAL UNIT

WATER AND SEWER FUND
BALANCE SHEET
AT CLOSE OF FISCAL YEAR 19X1

Assets

Current assets:			
Cash		$ 75,000	
Accounts receivable	$ 24,000		
Less: Allowance for uncollectible accounts	2,000	22,000	
Notes receivable		3,000	
Due from general fund		4,000	
Unbilled accounts receivable		7,000	
Inventory—materials and supplies		15,000	
Prepaid expenses		6,000	
Total current assets			$ 132,000
Restricted assets:			
Cash with fiscal agent		$ 100,000	
Revenue bond debt service fund:			
Cash		8,000	
Revenue bond retirement fund:			
Cash	$ 12,000		
Investments (net of premium amortization)	108,000	120,000	
Revenue bond construction fund:			
Cash		209,000	
Customer deposits fund:			
Investments	$ 65,000		
Interest receivable—investments	1,000	66,000	
Total restricted assets			503,000
Utility plant in service:			
Land		$ 200,000	
Buildings	$ 500,000		
Less: Allowance for depreciation	100,000	400,000	
Improvements other than buildings	$4,000,000		
Less: Allowance for depreciation	500,000	3,500,000	
Machinery and equipment	$2,000,000		
Less: Allowance for depreciation	700,000	1,300,000	
Total utility plant in service			5,400,000
Construction work in progress			25,000
Total assets			$6,060,000

Liabilities, Reserves, Contributions, and Retained Earnings

Current liabilities:		
Payable from current assets:		
Vouchers payable	$ 26,000	
Accrued wages payable	2,000	
Construction contracts payable	15,000	
Accrued general obligation bond interest payable	14,000	
Advance from municipality—general obligation bonds	50,000	$ 107,000
Payable from restricted assets:		
Construction contracts payable	$ 20,000	
Due to fiscal agent	1,000	
Accrued revenue bond interest payable	30,000	
Revenue bonds payable—current portion	100,000	
Customer deposits	65,000	216,000
Total current liabilities		$ 323,000
Other liabilities:		
Revenue bonds payable	$2,500,000	
Advance from municipality—general obligation bonds	800,000	
Total other liabilities		3,300,000
Total liabilities		$3,623,000
Reserves:		
Reserve for revenue bond debt service	$ 8,000	
Reserve for revenue bond retirement	120,000	
Reserve for new construction	209,000	
Total reserves		337,000
Contributions:		
From municipality	$ 500,000	
From customers	100,000	
From subdividers	900,000	
Total contributions		1,500,000
Retained earnings		600,000
Total liabilities, reserves, contributions, and retained earnings		$6,060,000

assets and the corresponding classifications of current liabilities. Two other features should be noted. First, certain restricted assets, along with related liability or reserve accounts, comprise the "funds within a fund" discussed earlier, and second, the distinction between contributed capital and retained earnings is clearly maintained. Balance sheets for public utilities may be presented in inverse order to that illustrated; that is, utility plant in service may be listed first, followed by restricted assets and current assets. In that case, invested capital and retained earnings will be listed first, followed by other liabilities and current liabilities.

The revenue and expense statement format (Figure 42) is also patterned after those typical of the regulated utility industry. Expenses are referred to as "operating revenue deductions"; a clear-cut operating–nonoperating distinction is maintained throughout. "Operating income

FIGURE 42

A GOVERNMENTAL UNIT

WATER AND SEWER FUND
STATEMENT OF REVENUE AND EXPENSE
FOR THE FISCAL YEAR 19X1

	Budget	*Actual*	*Actual over (under) Budget*
Operating revenues:			
Metered water sales	$590,000	$600,000	$10,000
Bulk water sales	10,000	9,000	(1,000)
Sewer service charges	145,000	150,000	5,000
Other	15,000	16,000	1,000
Total operating revenues	$760,000	$775,000	$15,000
Less: Operating revenue deductions (except depreciation):			
Operating expenses	$380,000	$400,000	$20,000
Other	32,000	25,000	(7,000)
Total operating deductions before depreciation	$412,000	$425,000	$13,000
Operating income before depreciation	$348,000	$350,000	$ 2,000
Less: Depreciation	150,000	150,000	—
Operating income	$198,000	$200,000	$ 2,000
Nonoperating income:			
Add: Rentals of nonoperating properties	$ 1,000	$ 6,000	$ 5,000
Interest earnings	3,000	4,000	1,000
Total nonoperating revenues	$ 4,000	$ 10,000	$ 6,000
Less: Interest expense—revenue bonds	$ 70,000	$ 70,000	—
Interest expense—general obligation bonds	30,000	30,000	—
Fiscal agent fees	1,000	1,000	—
Total nonoperating expenses	$101,000	$101,000	—
Net income	$101,000	$109,000	$ 8,000

before depreciation" is presented in addition to "operating income" and "net income."

FIGURE 43

A GOVERNMENTAL UNIT

WATER AND SEWER FUND
ANALYSIS OF CHANGES IN RETAINED EARNINGS
FOR THE FISCAL YEAR 19X1

Retained earnings, beginning of year		$524,000
Add:		
Net income (Figure 42)		109,000
Total balance and additions		$633,000
Deduct:		
Increase in reserve for revenue bond debt service	$ 3,000	
Increase in reserve for revenue bond retirement	30,000	
Total deductions		33,000
Retained earnings, end of year (Figure 41)		$600,000

General Fixed Assets

The General Fixed Asset group of accounts, logically enough, is used to account for the fixed assets of a governmental unit other than those carried in an Intragovernmental Service fund, a Trust fund, or an Enterprise fund. The general fixed assets may be financed from General or Special Revenue fund revenues, from special assessments, from private gifts, or from Capital Projects funds that account for the proceeds of general obligation bonds or for grants from other governments.

principles of accounting for general fixed assets

The general fixed assets acquired by gift should be valued at their fair market value at date of acquisition. All other assets should be valued at their cost to the governmental unit, no matter which fund provides the financing. Cost in the fund context is the same as cost for financial accounting purposes. It includes legal fees, title fees, surveying fees, site preparation costs, transportation costs, and the like. The same distinction should be maintained between capital and revenue expenditures as is maintained for financial accounting purposes.

FIGURE 44

A GOVERNMENTAL UNIT

WATER AND SEWER FUND
STATEMENT OF SOURCES AND USES OF CASH
FOR THE FISCAL YEAR 19X1

Cash was provided by:		
Operations:		
Income from operations	$200,000	
Adjustments to net income to arrive at cash provided:		
Depreciation	150,000	
Other	5,000	$355,000
Other sources:		
Issuance of bonds	$100,000	
Contributions from subdividers	80,000	
Contributions from customers	20,000	
Rentals	6,000	
Interest received	3,000	209,000
Total cash provided		$564,000
Cash was applied to:		
Purchase of investments	$100,000	
Additions to utility plant in service	200,000	
Retirement of revenue bonds	40,000	
Retirement of general obligation bonds	50,000	
Interest paid	101,000	
Other	5,000	
Total cash applied		496,000
Increase in cash during the year		$ 68,000
Cash balances, beginning of year		336,000
Cash balances, end of year		$404,000
Cash balances, end of year, distributed as follows:		
Unrestricted		$ 75,000
With fiscal agent		100,000
Revenue bond debt service fund		8,000
Revenue bond retirement fund		12,000
Revenue bond construction fund		209,000
		$404,000

The National Committee on Governmental Accounting has adopted the following position regarding depreciation of general fixed assets:

> Depreciation on general fixed assets should not be recorded in the general accounting records. Depreciation charges on such assets may be computed for unit cost purposes, provided such charges are recorded only in memorandum form and do not appear in the fund accounts.[9]

The Committee of course recognizes the physical and economic fact of depreciation, but in its view the recording of depreciation would serve no useful purpose. It believes that the reasons for computation of depreciation for a profit-seeking enterprise do not exist in the case of governments. The committee also believes that the recording of depreciation on general fixed assets might be misleading to those who read the financial statements. Its reasoning is that

> . . . the charging of current operations with depreciation indicates a matching of costs with directly related revenues in the generally accepted commercial accounting sense when, in fact, no causative relationship between revenues and expenditures exists for most general government operations.[10]

The committee has prescribed the following classifications of fixed assets:

1. Land.
2. Buildings.
3. Improvements other than Buildings.
4. Machinery and Equipment.[11]

Since the General Fixed Asset group of accounts is self-balancing, and since knowledge of the sources of financing is of interest, the committee has recommended the following set of equity accounts:

Investment in general fixed assets from—
- Capital Project Funds:
  - General Obligation Bonds
  - Federal Grants
  - State Grants
  - Local Grants
- General Fund Revenues
- Special Revenue Fund Revenues
- Special Assessments
- Private Gifts[12]

[9] N.C.G.A., *op. cit.*, p. 10.
[10] *Ibid.*, p. 11.
[11] *Ibid.*, p. 191.
[12] *Ibid.*, pp. 94–95.

entries in the general fixed asset group of accounts

In the General fund presentation an entry was made debiting Expenditures for $21,000 representing equipment purchased for the police department. The corresponding entry to be made in the General Fixed Asset group of accounts is

Machinery and equipment	21,000	
Investment in general fixed assets from general fund revenues		21,000

A similar entry would also be made for the equipment purchase for the fire department in the amount of $28,100 included in the General fund presentation:

Machinery and equipment	28,100	
Investment in general fixed assets from general fund revenues		28,100

As previously indicated, the Expenditures and Encumbrances accounts in both the Special Assessment fund and Capital Projects fund may be left on the books at the end of the year, although it is preferable to close them out at the end of the year to provide an indication of activity to date. Regardless of the treatment of the accounts in the originating funds, an entry should be made in the General Fixed Assets group of accounts at the end of the year to recognize the *expenditures* made to date in each of the two kinds of funds. In the Capital Projects funds section of this chapter, the expenditures of $140,800 made during the first year of the life of the project were closed to the Fund Balance account. In the General Fixed Asset group of accounts, the following corresponding entry would be made:

Construction work in progress	140,800	
Investment in general fixed assets from general fund revenues		17,600
Investment in general fixed assets from capital projects funds—general obligation bonds		35,200
Investment in general fixed assets from capital projects funds—federal grants		70,400
Investment in general fixed assets from capital projects funds—local grants		17,600

The foregoing credits were computed by applying to the expected contribution of each source the percentage that the total of expenditures to date bears to the expected cost of the project.

Upon completion of the project, an entry was made in the Capital Projects fund closing Expenditures in the amount of $252,400 into the fund balance. The corresponding entry in the General Fixed Asset group of accounts is as follows:

Buildings	393,200	
Construction work in progress		140,800
Investment in general fixed assets from general fund revenues		32,400
Investment in general fixed assets from capital projects funds—general obligation bonds		58,000
Investment in general fixed assets from capital projects funds—federal grants		129,600
Investment in general fixed assets from capital projects funds—local grants		32,400

The foregoing entry is based on the assumption that the project described in the Capital Projects fund section of this chapter was for a building. Note that the planned $100,000 contribution to the project from General Obligation Bonds has been reduced to a total of $93,200 because of the discount on the sale of the bonds and because the fund balance of $5,800 was transferred to the Debt Service fund.

In the section on Special Assessment funds, we saw that the closing entry for construction at the end of the first year of the fund's operation closed $275,000 of Expenditures to the Fund Balance—Construction account. The corresponding entry in the General Fixed Assets group of accounts is as follows:

Construction work in progress	275,000	
Investment in general fixed assets from general fund revenues		55,000
Investment in general fixed assets from special assessments		220,000

The credits in the foregoing entry were determined by applying to the construction expenditures figure fractions determined by dividing the total assessments and the governmental unit's share of the cost by the total of improvements authorized for the Special Assessment fund.

At the end of the second year of operation, the special assessment project was completed and Expenditures of the second year, $471,000, were closed into the Fund Balance—Construction account. The corresponding entry in the General Fixed Assets group of accounts is as follows:

Improvements other than buildings	746,000	
Construction work in progress		275,000
Investment in general fixed assets from general fund revenues		94,200
Investment in general fixed assets from special assessments		376,800

This entry assumes that the construction fund balance is to be rebated to the property owners and the governmental unit in proportion to the original commitments to the financing of the project.

When a general fixed asset is retired, for whatever reason, an entry is made debiting an Investment in Fixed Assets account and crediting Land, Buildings, Improvements other than Buildings, or Machinery and Equipment, as the case may be, with its book value. The specific investment in General Fixed Assets should of course be debited if the records indicate the source of the asset's cost. If such identification cannot be made, then the debit should be to Investment in General Fixed Assets from General fund revenues. If a salvage value is realized, no entry is necessary in the General Fixed Assets group of accounts for the amount of the salvage, but an entry is made in the General fund debiting Cash and crediting Revenues (with a posting to an appropriate subsidiary revenue account).

statements

If the foregoing journal entries are posted to accounts, the resulting account balances may be used to prepare the statement of general fixed assets in Figure 45. Information regarding the uses to which general fixed assets are being put can be provided by a schedule of General Fixed Assets by Functions and Activities. It has the descriptive heading "Function and Activity" and the following dollar column headings:

Total
Land
Buildings
Improvements other than Buildings
Equipment

General Long-Term Debt

General long-term debt may be defined as all the debt, having a stated life longer than one year, that is to be repaid from general revenues. The term includes time warrants and notes having a stated life longer than one year and excludes Special Assessment fund debt, as well

FIGURE 45

A GOVERNMENTAL UNIT

STATEMENT OF GENERAL FIXED ASSETS
AT CLOSE OF FISCAL YEAR 19X1

General fixed assets:	
Land	$ –0–
Buildings	393,200
Improvements other than buildings	746,000
Machinery and equipment	49,100
Total general fixed assets	$1,188,300
Investment in general fixed assets from:	
Capital Projects funds:	
General obligation bonds	$ 93,200
Federal grants	200,000
State grants	–0–
Local grants	50,000
General fund revenues	248,300
Special Revenue fund revenues	–0–
Gifts	–0–
Special assessments	596,800
Total investment in general fixed assets	$1,188,300

as Enterprise debt that is legally required to be repaid out of Enterprise revenues. If debt created to provide capital for an Enterprise fund is general obligation debt, although plans exist to pay it from the Enterprise fund, the debt should be recorded as a liability of the Enterprise fund *and* in the General Long-Term Debt group of accounts. On the other hand, special assessment debt that is secured by the full faith and credit of the governmental unit may be footnoted in the Statement of General Long-Term Debt as a contingent liability.

entries

Entries are made in the General Long-Term Debt group of accounts when bonds are sold, when amounts become available in Debt Service funds for the retirement of debt, and when debts mature and are taken over as obligations of the Debt Service fund that is to pay them off. Since Debt Service funds may receive many different kinds of revenue at different times of the year, it is customary to wait until year end, when the total increase in the Debt Service funds has been determined, before making the entry in the General Long-Term Debt group of accounts to record the increase. Since the accumulation of assets in

Debt Service funds designed to repay serial bonds is likely to be only minimally in excess of periodic payments of serial issues, recording the increase in the assets of such Debt Service funds is optional.

In the section of this chapter on Debt Service funds, the Flores Park Serial Bonds and the City Hall Bonds were described and the transactions of the related Debt Service funds were given.

At the time the Flores Park Serial Bonds were issued, the transaction would have been recorded in a Capital Projects fund, and the following entry would have been made in the General Long-Term Debt group of accounts:

Amount to be provided for payment of Flores Park serial bonds	1,000,000	
Flores Park serial bonds payable		1,000,000

Similarly, the issuance of the City Hall Bonds would have been the signal for an entry in the General Long-Term Debt group of accounts as follows:

Amount to be provided for payment of City Hall term bonds	1,000,000	
City Hall term bonds payable		1,000,000

At or near the end of the first year of the life of the Flores Park Debt Service fund, the fund paid the first serial maturity of $100,000. The corresponding entry in the General Long-Term Debt group of accounts is as follows:

Flores Park serial bonds payable	100,000	
Amount to be provided for payment of Flores Park serial bonds		100,000

Since the fund balance in the Flores Park Debt Service fund is only $5,000 at the end of the first year of operation, we shall assume that the city exercises the option not to record the increase of the fund in the General Long-Term Debt group of accounts.

At the end of the first year of operation of the City Hall Bonds Debt Service fund, there was a balance of $27,185. Since the balance represented the amount of the increase in the fund for the year, there would have been a corresponding entry in the Long-Term Debt group of accounts as follows:

Amount available in City Hall bonds debt service fund	27,185	
Amount to be provided for payment of City Hall term bonds		27,185

Similarly, at the end of the second year of the fund's operation, the fund balance of the City Hall Bonds Debt Service fund had grown to $56,100, an increase of $28,825. At the end of the second year, the amount of this increase would have been recorded in the General Long-Term Debt group of accounts as follows:

Amount available in City Hall bonds debt service fund	28,825	
Amount to be provided for payment of City Hall term bonds		28,825

When sinking fund bonds mature, the liability for them is recorded in the Debt Service fund, which presumably has accumulated enough assets by the date of maturity to pay off the bonds. In the General Long-Term Debt group of accounts the entry to record, for example, the maturity of City Hall Bonds is:

City Hall term bonds payable	1,000,000	
Amount available in City Hall bonds debt service fund		1,000,000

statement of general long-term debt

Assuming that all the previous General Long-Term Debt entries except the last have been posted to accounts, the Statement of General Long-Term Debt presented in Figure 46 could be prepared.

Interfund Relationships

The entries for the General Fixed Assets group of accounts and the General Long-Term Debt group of accounts were, in the main, based on transactions that had been initiated in other funds. Many other transactions affect more than one fund or group of accounts, and additional transactions and their related entries are presented here.

transactions originating in the general fund

Money was advanced by the General fund to the Intragovernmental Service fund for the purpose of providing capital for that fund.

Entry in General Fund:

Expenditures	50,000	
Cash		50,000

Entry in Intragovernmental Service Fund:

Cash	50,000	
Contributions from general fund		50,000

FIGURE 46

A GOVERNMENTAL UNIT

STATEMENT OF GENERAL LONG-TERM DEBT
AT CLOSE OF FISCAL YEAR 19X1

Amount Available and To Be Provided
For the Payment of General Long-Term Debt

Term bonds:		
Amount available in debt service funds	$ 56,010	
Amount to be provided	943,990	
Total, term bonds		$1,000,000
Serial bonds:		
Amount to be provided		900,000
Total available and to be provided		$1,900,000

General Long-Term Debt Payable

Term bonds:	
City Hall bonds	$1,000,000
Serial bonds:	
Flores Park bonds	900,000
Total general long-term debt payable	$1,900,000

A loan was made by the General fund to the Debt Service fund.

Entry in General Fund:

Due from debt service fund	40,000	
Cash		40,000

Entry in Debt Service Fund:

Cash	40,000	
Due to general fund		40,000

A contribution was made by the General fund to the Debt Service fund.

Entry in General Fund:

Expenditures	50,000	
Cash		50,000

Entry in Debt Service Fund:

Cash	50,000	
Revenues		50,000

The governmental unit is required to pay part of the cost of special assessment improvements.

Entry in General Fund:

Expenditures	100,000	
Due to special assessment fund		100,000

Entry in Special Assessment Fund:

Governmental unit's share of cost	100,000	
Improvements authorized		100,000

Services were performed by the General fund for the Special Assessment fund.

Entry in General Fund:

Due from special assessment fund	10,000	
Expenditures		10,000

Entry in Special Assessment Fund:

Expenditures	10,000	
Due to general fund		10,000

A contribution was made by the General fund to a Trust fund.

Entry in General Fund:

Expenditures	10,000	
Cash		10,000

Entry in Trust Fund:

Cash	10,000	
Fund balance		10,000

transactions originating in capital projects fund

Premiums on bonds were transferred to the Debt Service fund.

Entry in Capital Projects Fund:

Premiums on bonds	1,000	
Cash		1,000

Entry in Debt Service Fund:

Cash	1,000	
Revenues		1,000

Proceeds from the sale of bonds issued were transferred out of the Capital Projects fund to finance:

1. The governmental unit's share of special assessment improvement costs.
2. The governmental unit's contribution toward the establishment of an Intragovernmental Service fund.

3. A deficit in the General fund.
4. The acquisition of a utility (the bonds to be repaid from taxes).

Entry in Capital Projects Fund:

Appropriations (or expenditures)	100,000	
Cash		100,000

a. Entry in Special Assessment Fund:

Cash for construction	100,000	
Governmental unit's share of cost		100,000

b. Entry in Intragovernmental Service Fund:

Cash	100,000	
Capital		100,000

c. Entry in General Fund:

Cash	100,000	
Fund balance		100,000

d. Entry in Enterprise Fund:

Cash	100,000	
Governmental unit's contribution		100,000

Services were rendered by the Capital Projects fund for the General fund.

Entry in Capital Projects Fund:

Due from general fund	5,000	
Expenditures		5,000

Entry in General Fund:

Expenditures	5,000	
Due to capital projects fund		5,000

The Capital Projects fund balance was transferred to the Debt Service fund.

Entry in Capital Projects Fund:

Fund balance	4,000	
Cash		4,000

Entry in Debt Service Fund:

Cash	4,000	
Fund balance (or revenues)		4,000

transactions originating in intragovernmental service fund

Services were rendered by the Intragovernmental Service fund for departments whose activities are financed from the General, Special Assessment, and Enterprise funds.

Entry in Intragovernmental Service Fund:

Due from general fund	15,000	
Due from special assessment fund	10,000	
Due from enterprise fund	8,000	
Billings for services		33,000

a. Entry in General Fund:

Expenditures	15,000	
Due to intragovernmental service fund		15,000

b. Entry in Special Assessment Fund:

Expenditures	10,000	
Due to intragovernmental service fund		10,000

c. Entry in Enterprise Fund:

Expenses	8,000	
Due to intragovernmental service fund		8,000

groups of related funds

A municipality will have only one General fund, but it may have more than one of each of the other funds. For example, it may have several Special Revenue funds, Capital Projects funds, and Intragovernmental Service funds. Each group of funds is known as a *group of related funds.* A separate balance sheet must be prepared for each fund in a related fund group. These individual fund balance sheets may be arranged in columnar form and the total of each type of asset, liability, reserve, and fund balance may be shown in a "Total" column. These totals are essential in the preparation of the combined balance sheet for all funds.

The following is an example of a heading for a balance sheet covering a group of Capital Projects funds. Note the distinction made between completed and uncompleted projects.

A GOVERNMENTAL UNIT

CAPITAL PROJECTS FUNDS
BALANCE SHEET
DURING, OR AT CLOSE OF, FISCAL YEAR 19X1

		Completed Projects		*Uncompleted Projects*	
Assets	*Total, All Capital Projects Funds*	*Hospital Capital Projects Fund*	*School Capital Projects Fund*	*Bridge Capital Projects Fund*	*Street-Widening Capital Projects Fund*
Cash	$490,000	$10,000	$5,000	$175,000	$300,000

combined balance sheet—all funds

Although each fund constitutes an independent entity, it is desirable to bring together in one place, in summary form, the financial data of all funds and account groups. This can be accomplished best by preparing a combined balance sheet in columnar form. The simplest version of the combined balance sheet would have a column heading for each of the governmental unit's funds and account groups. In practice, however, a governmental unit is likely to have a number of funds of certain types, and the typical sheet of paper is not large enough to permit such a detailed listing. Instead, the balance sheets of funds of the same type are combined, as illustrated in the paragraph heading entitled "Groups of Related Funds," into totals for each type. By this device the Combined Balance Sheet—All Funds may be limited to the following ten columns:

General Fund
Special Revenue Funds
Debt Service Funds
Capital Projects Funds
Enterprise Funds
Intragovernmental Service Funds
Trust and Agency Funds
Special Assessment Funds
General Fixed Assets
General Long-Term Debt

Note that the suggested columns do not include one for "Total." The reason is that the assets and liabilities of the several different funds and account groups are so different in nature, so subject to differing legal limitations and requirements, that no total figures would be appropriate. Even a total for such an asset as Cash is meaningless because of the restrictions surrounding the uses of Cash in the several funds.

The National Committee on Governmental Accounting has taken a strong position opposing the use of *consolidated* balance sheets. Profit-seeking parent companies in the private sector of our economy have virtually unlimited control of their subsidiary corporations, and therefore the parent and its subsidiaries are a single economic entity. As we have seen, this is not at all the situation with respect to funds. Each fund is a separate legal and economic entity subject to its own rules and regulations, which prevent free access by the management of the governmental unit to the resources of the funds. Another argument against consolidation is the dissimilarity of the funds and account groups. The Committee feels strongly that the preparation of the consolidated balance sheet would provide misleading results and implications. In a consolidated balance sheet, for example, the excess of general fixed assets over general long-term debt might overshadow substantial deficits in the General fund or in one or more special revenue funds, although such excess would not be available for carrying out the general purposes of the revenue funds.

Operating Statements. The National Committee on Governmental Accounting strongly recommends that no combined statement of revenues and expenditures be prepared for all funds. This position is adopted because the revenues and expenditures of the several different kinds of funds vary so widely, and because no legitimate comparison of revenues and expenditures on a total basis may be made. For example, it is likely that all the revenues of a Special Assessment fund will be accounted for in a single year, whereas expenditures may be spread over several years as construction proceeds. Another example of variances is found in the differing concepts of expenditures in the General and other funds as compared with expenses in the Enterprise funds. Finally, revenues of some funds (e.g., Capital Projects funds) are not revenues of the municipality as a whole.

It *is* feasible and desirable to prepare "Combined Statements of Revenue—Estimated and Actual, General and Special Revenue Funds" and "Combined Statement of General Governmental Expenditures and Encumbrances Compared with Authorizations, General and Special Revenue Funds." These schedules have the same column headings as similar statements recommended in the General fund section of this chapter, but the financial data from the Special Revenue funds are added to those of the General fund. These types of combined statements are logical and desirable because the Special Revenue funds have essentially the same broad objective as the General Revenue fund—that is, to carry out the broad functional objectives of the governmental unit.

Combined Subsidiary Statements. Many of the balance sheet accounts should be supported by subsidiary schedules. Some of these subsidiary statements that are applicable to the same type of account in different funds can be presented in a single statement. In these cases it is necessary to reveal full details concerning each fund. For example, it is possible to prepare a combined statement showing details for bonds payable out of the different funds. An example of such a statement is presented in Figure 47. This statement shows details concerning general, special assessment, and enterprise bonds, a separate section being provided for each group of bonds.

FIGURE 47

A GOVERNMENTAL UNIT

COMBINED SCHEDULE OF BONDS PAYABLE
AT CLOSE OF FISCAL YEAR 19X1

Description	*Interest Rate, %*	*Date Issued*	*Last Maturity Date*	*Amount Issued*	*Retired to End of This Year*	*Outstanding at Close of Year*
		Special Assessment Bonds				
Paving	5	5/1/74	5/1/79	$100,000	$ 20,000	$ 80,000
Widening	5	6/1/74	6/1/79	200,000	40,000	160,000
Total special assessment bonds				$300,000	$ 60,000	$240,000
		Enterprise Bonds				
First mortgage	4.5	7/1/72	7/1/82	$500,000	$150,000	$350,000
Betterments	4	8/1/73	8/1/83	100,000	20,000	80,000
Total enterprise bonds				$600,000	$170,000	$430,000
		General Bonds				
Schools	4	3/1/63	3/1/83	$400,000	$ 40,000	$360,000
Fire station	4	6/1/64	6/1/84	100,000	5,000	95,000
Total general bonds				$500,000	$ 45,000	$455,000

Combined schedules may also be prepared for such accounts as Taxes Receivable and Investments.

general summary of fund accounting

The outstanding characteristic of governmental accounting is the use of funds. The details of fund accounting are apparent from the discussion of the individual funds. At this point, therefore, we shall only summarize some of the main principles that evolve from the discussion of the detailed accounting procedure for each fund.

First, it is apparent that a fund is an independent fiscal entity and must be accounted for as such. The accounting system must be so devised that the assets, liabilities, reserves, fund balances, revenues, and expenditures or expenses can be identified with the particular fund to which they apply. It follows that each fund must have a self-balancing group of accounts. A fund need not necessarily consist of cash only; it may even have fixed assets. On the other hand, the mere setting aside of cash to be used for certain purposes does not create a fund (as is true in the case of funds established under commercial accounting procedures).

In some cases, assets are shown in one fund but the liabilities incurred in their acquisition are shown in another fund. For example, special assessment improvements are shown in the General Fixed Assets group of accounts, whereas special assessment bonds payable are shown as a liability of the Special Assessment fund. Again, although the Capital Projects fund receives the proceeds from the sale of bonds, the liability is not shown in that fund.

The second important fact is that, as already indicated, a governmental unit may have many funds of the same type. That is, it may have Capital Project funds, Debt Service funds, and so forth, and each group is known as a *group of related funds*. The accounting procedure is the same for all the related funds of a group.

The third fact to note is the variation in the accounting procedure for the several funds with respect to accruing similar items, use of budgetary accounts, and excluding certain assets and liabilities. The accrual basis of accounting is followed more consistently in the Enterprise and Intragovernmental Service funds than in any other funds. Since it is essential there to arrive at the profit or loss figure for a period, all the revenues and expenses properly allocable to a period must be accounted for. Revenues are set up as soon as they become receivable, and expenses are set up as soon as they are incurred. Furthermore, depreciation expenses are recorded periodically. In the other funds the degree of accrual varies. Some transactions are recorded on an accrual basis, whereas others are not. For example, accrued interest payable on general bonds is usually not set up because the appropriation for it will not be made until the beginning of the following fiscal year. If the interest were set up, therefore, the expenditure would have to be charged against this year's appropriations, whereas actually it is chargeable to the following year's appropriations.

Both budgetary and proprietary accounts are used in all funds except the Enterprise and Intragovernmental Service funds. Since appropriations need not be made for the Intragovernmental Service fund or Enterprise fund expenditures, it is not necessary to set up budgetary accounts as a formal part of their accounting systems.

From the discussion in the earlier part of this section, it appears that identical types of assets and liabilities may be included in some funds and excluded from others. For example, fixed assets and bonds payable are included in the Enterprise fund but not in the General fund. Special assessment bonds payable are shown as a liability of the Special Assessment fund, but the special assessment improvements do not appear as assets of this fund.

Statistical Statements

Throughout this chapter heavy emphasis has been placed, and properly so, on the necessity of using accounting and accounting statements (a) to assist in enforcing and to demonstrate compliance with legal provisions and (b) to furnish financial information that will be of value to management, to the legislative body, to investors, and to the public. But accounting statements do not convey all the necessary information. For certain managerial purposes, as well as for the purpose of making intercity comparisons, it may be necessary to prepare *statistical statements,* which ignore fund restrictions. One of the characteristics of statistical statements is that in their case it is not necessary to identify the assets, liabilities, reserves, or balances with the individual funds to which they apply, because statistical statements are not used to show accountability or to indicate compliance with legal provisions. Another characteristic of such statements is that, unlike financial statements, they may not necessarily be prepared exclusively from the accounts, they may contain nonfinancial data, and they may cover a period of several years. In other words, statistical statements are a valuable supplement to accounting statements but they cannot take the place of the latter.

Statistical statements deal with such matters as assessed valuations, tax rates, tax levies, tax collections, and bonded indebtedness. Examples of statistical statements are presented in Figures 48, 49, and 50.

FIGURE 48

A GOVERNMENTAL UNIT

PROPERTY TAX LEVIES AND COLLECTIONS
LAST TEN FISCAL YEARS

Fiscal Year	*Total Tax Levy*	*Current Tax Collections*	*Percentage of Levy Collected*	*Delinquent Tax Collections*	*Total Tax Collections*	*Total Collections as Percentage of Current Levy*	*Outstanding Delinquent Taxes*	*Outstanding Delinquent Taxes as Percentage of Current Levy*
19X1								
19X2								
19X3								
19X4								
19X5								
19X6								
19X7								
19X8								
19X9								
19Y0								

Note: Only the taxes levied by the reporting governmental unit are included. Collections by the unit for other governmental units do not appear.

Source: *Governmental Accounting, Auditing, and Financial Reporting,* p. 123.

FIGURE 49

A GOVERNMENTAL UNIT

RATIO OF NET GENERAL BONDED DEBT
TO ASSESSED VALUE AND NET BONDED DEBT PER CAPITA,
LAST TEN FISCAL YEARS

Fiscal Year	*Population **	*Assessed Value*	*Gross Bonded Debt*	*Less Debt Service Funds*	*Net Bonded Debt*	*Ratio of Net Bonded Debt to Assessed Value*	*Net Bonded Debt per Capita*
19X1							
19X2							
19X3							
19X4							
19X5							
19X6							
19X7							
19X8							
19X9							
19Y0							

* Only official census figures or reliable estimates should be used. Source of population data should be indicated in all cases.
Source: *Governmental Accounting, Auditing, and Financial Reporting*, p. 122.

FIGURE 50

A GOVERNMENTAL UNIT

COMPUTATION OF LEGAL DEBT MARGIN
END OF FISCAL YEAR

Assessed value		$________
Debt limit__________percentage of assessed value *		$
Amount of debt applicable to debt limit:		
Total bonded debt	$	
Other debt	________	
Less:		
Assets in debt service funds	$	
Other deductions allowed by law: (Itemize. Include revenue and special assessment bonds where not general obligations)	________	
Total amount of debt applicable to debt limit		$________
Legal debt margin		$________

Note: The debt limit referred to in this computation is one mandated by law and does not refer to debt limits used as criteria in security analysis. If no debt limit is mandated by law, this computation should be replaced by a single comment to that effect. When the legal debt limit is expressed in terms other than a relationship to assessed value, the computation made should be in terms of the legally specified basis. When legal debt limits exist, appropriate footnotes to this computation should quote and/or explain their source and scope.

* Assessed value of property subject to taxation.

Source: *Governmental Accounting, Auditing, and Financial Reporting,* p. 123.

Accounting for Institutions

The principles discussed thus far apply also to institutions, such as hospitals, colleges, and universities. For example, if institutions are government owned, they are subject to the same restrictions as any other governmental organization. Even if they are privately owned, institutions have at least one characteristic in common with government: they must use fund accounting, since they obtain some of their income and property through gifts, which frequently include restrictions. Through the use of funds, the institutions are able to show that they have complied with these restrictions.

The funds that are used by institutions are similar to one another of the types of government funds that have been described. However, there are sufficient differences between usages of the funds and account groups to justify a brief description of the practices of the institutions.

In the discussion, hospital funds are described first and a brief description of the funds of colleges and universities follows.

hospitals

Hospital accounting contains elements of both commercial and governmental accounting. Fund accounting techniques are employed, but hospital financial statements should be prepared, for the most part at least, in accordance with generally accepted accounting principles for commercial endeavors. Although there are some differences both in accounting principles and in their application, hospitals usually adhere to the accrual basis; depreciation is recognized, and net income for the organization as a whole is determined and reported. The widely accepted principles and procedures recommended by the American Hospital Association (AHA) in *Chart of Accounts For Hospitals* (1966) form the principal basis for our discussion.

Funds. The AHA recommends that the accounts of a hospital be separated into no more than five funds:

1. The *Operating* or General fund is used to account for all resources which are not externally restricted, that is, whose use is within the discretion of the board of directors. Board-restricted assets and related liabilities are included within this fund, not specific purpose funds, and unrestricted income from other funds may be attributed to and/or transferred to the Operating fund.
2. The *Specific Purpose* fund is equivalent to a municipal Special Revenue or Expendable Trust fund and is used to account for externally restricted expendable resources to be used for specified operating purposes. Its revenues generally arise from (a) public donations for purposes such as equipment acquisition, student nurse scholarships, and provision of "free" services to indigent patients; (b) research grants; (c) endowment fund earnings which are externally restricted; and (d) investment income.
3. The *Endowment* fund is employed to account for externally restricted resources, held in trust by the hospital. They are comparable to nonexpendable trust funds of municipalities in that the fund principal must be maintained intact. Earnings of this fund may be restricted, in which case they are transferred to Specific Purpose funds; if unrestricted, earnings are transferred to the Operating fund.
4. The *Plant* fund is used to account for (a) long-lived assets such as land, buildings, and equipment, net of accumulated depreciation; (b) fixed asset related long-term debt; (c) assets earmarked for fixed asset replacement or additions; and (d) the net amount invested in, or to be invested in, fixed assets by the hospital. It has no counterpart in contemporary municipal accounting, being a com-

bination of General Fixed Assets and General Long-Term Debt account groups and Special Revenue or Capital Projects funds.

5. A *Construction* fund may be established separate from the Plant fund to account for the receipt and expenditure of resources earmarked for capital outlay purposes. Use of a Construction fund, the counterpart of municipal Capital Projects funds, is optional; a Construction fund is used mainly where major projects are financed through grants or debt issues.

To repeat, a hospital is to have no more than *one* of each of the above-mentioned funds. If several funds of a given type are required they are handled on a "funds within a fund" basis; that is, they are separate funds only in the commercial accounting usage of that term. It is also important to note (see Figure 55) that the overriding classification is by funds that are *externally* restricted, termed "restricted funds," and unrestricted *externally,* although possibly restricted by the board, referred to as "unrestricted funds."

Unique Income Determination Features. Although hospital accounting conforms to commercial accounting principles for the most part, it has several unique distinguishing features. One of the most significant of these is that the AHA recommends that income be recognized only in the period when it becomes available for unrestricted use by the board of directors or is expended for the specified purpose. Under this method, unrestricted revenues would be recognized on the accrual basis. However, unexpended restricted assets, such as the principal of living trusts, would be reported only in the period in which they become unrestricted; and assets expended for specified purposes, such as research or construction grants, would be considered realized in the period of expenditure.

Two acceptable methods of income determination and reporting—which may yield different reported operating results—are recognized by the AHA. Under the "single income statement method" preferred by the AHA, all income recognized is attributed to and/or transferred to the Operating fund. Attributing revenues or expenses of other funds to the Operating fund under the single income statement method requires simultaneous entries in all funds involved. For example, depreciation would be recognized as follows:

Entry in Operating Fund:

Depreciation expenses	xx	
Operating fund balance		xx

Entry in Plant Fund:

Fund balance invested in plant	xx	
Accumulated depreciation		xx

To record the sale of a fixed asset at a loss, the following entries would be required:

Entry in Operating Fund:

Loss on disposal of fixed assets	xx	
Operating fund balance		xx

Entries in Plant Fund:

Plant fund cash	$Proceeds	
Accumulated depreciation	xx	
Fund balance invested in plant (loss) ..	xx	
Fixed asset		xx
Fund balance invested in plant	$Proceeds	
Fund balance reserved for plant improvement or expansion		$Proceeds

Where revenues of a Specific Purpose fund are to be transferred to the General fund, the necessary entries would be:

Entry in Operating Fund:

Due from specific purpose fund	xx	
Income transfers from specific purpose fund		xx

Entries in Specific Purpose Fund:

Assets	xx	
Specific purpose fund income (or specific purpose fund balance) ...		xx
Specific purpose fund balance	xx	
Due to operating fund		xx

The format of the income statement prepared under the single income statement method is illustrated in Figure 51.

The *consolidated income statement method,* which is acceptable to the AHA so long as the income it reports is at least as great as that which would be reported under the preferred single income statement method, has two features. First, the revenues and expenses of each fund are accounted for in that fund; and second, the income of each fund and the total for the hospital are reported in a columnar consolidating income statement. The format of such an income statement is illustrated in Figure 52. The consolidated income statement method, although not the choice of the AHA, requires fewer interfund entries than does the single income statement method and more closely corresponds with usual fund accounting.

Regardless of the income determination and reporting method used, there are seven important conditions to note under AHA pronouncements.

1. Operating revenues should be recognized under the accrual basis at standard rates set for services rendered; uncollectible accounts, discounts to employees, rate reductions afforded insurors, charity write-offs, and similar items should be shown separately as "Deductions from Patient Service Revenues" in arriving at "Net Patient Service Revenues."
2. Investments are preferably valued at year end at market value, thereby reporting as income price changes that are generally considered unrealized.
3. When the endowment fund includes annuities, the difference between annuity fund assets and the actuarially computed liability may be recognized as income; subsequent changes in the excess may be reflected as gains or losses.
4. When the fair market value of donated services may be objectively measured and there is, in substance, an employer–employee relationship between the hospital and the unpaid (or underpaid) worker, the excess of the fair market value of services received over compensation paid, if any, is simultaneously recognized as both operating revenue and operating expense.
5. Assets are preferably recorded at replacement cost and depreciation charges based thereon.
6. The initial supply of minor equipment should be amortized over a period of three years or less, and replacements should be charged to operating expense.
7. A clear distinction should be maintained between operating expenses paid or accrued through any fund and expenses chargeable to Capital Outlay or Fund Balance of the fund.

Financial Statements. The principal financial statements recommended for hospitals are a balance sheet, a statement of changes in fund balance, and an income statement. Recommended income statements are shown in Figures 51 and 52. The balance sheet recommended by the AHA is illustrated in Figure 53 and the statement of changes in fund balances appears in Figure 54.

Tentative AICPA Committee Position. The AICPA Committee on Health Care Institutions considers the AHA pronouncements in *Chart of Accounts For Hospitals* generally compatible with the pertinent opinions of the Accounting Principles Board and with the committee's audit guide. It takes exception, however, to AHA recommendations: (a) that long-term security investments should preferably be valued at current

FIGURE 51

COMMUNITY HOSPITAL

INCOME STATEMENT
YEAR ENDED SEPTEMBER 30, 19X1
(000's OMITTED)

Patient Service Revenue		
Nursing Revenues	$3,636	
Other Professional Service Revenues	1,618	
Gross Patient Service Revenues		$5,254
Deduction From Patient Service Revenues		
Charity Service	$ 541	
Contractual Adjustments	182	
Policy Discounts	25	
Administrative Adjustments	2	
Provision for Bad Debts	47	
Total Deductions from Patient Service Revenues		797
Net Patient Service Revenues		$4,457
Other Revenues		
Educational Programs	$ 56	
Contributions and Grants	84	
Income From Operating Fund Investments	22	
Income Transferred From Specific Purpose Fund	236	
Income Transferred From Endowment Fund	528	
Income Transferred From Plant Fund	253	
Other Revenues	73	
Total Other Revenues		1,252
Total Revenues		$5,709
Expenses		
Nursing Expenses	$1,763	
Other Professional Service Expenses	1,409	
General Service Expenses	1,783	
Fiscal Service Expenses	235	
Administrative Service Expenses	497	
Total Expenses		5,687
Net Income for the Year		$ 22

Reprinted, with permission, from *Chart of Accounts for Hospitals,* published by the American Hospital Association, 1966, p. 117.

market value in the accounts, and (b) that assets should preferably be recorded at current replacement cost and depreciation calculated thereon. Neither of these two practices are deemed acceptable by the AICPA Committee.

FIGURE 52

COMMUNITY HOSPITAL

INCOME STATEMENT
YEAR ENDED SEPTEMBER 30, 19X1
(000's OMITTED)

	Operating Fund	*Specific Purpose Fund*	*Endowment Fund*	*Plant Fund*	*Total*
Patient Service Revenue					
Nursing Revenues	$3,636				$3,636
Other Professional Revenues	1,618				1,618
Gross Patient Service Revenues	$5,254				$5,254
Deductions From Patient Service Revenues					
Charity Service	$ 541				$ 541
Contractual Adjustments	182				182
Policy Discounts	25				25
Administrative Adjustments	2				2
Provision for Bad Debts	47				47
Total Deduction from Patient Service Revenues	$ 797				$ 797
Net Patient Service Revenues	$4,457				$4,457
Other Revenues					
Educational Programs	$ 56				$ 56
Contributions and Grants	84				84
Income From Operating Fund Investments	22				22
Income—Specific Purpose Fund		$236			236
Income—Endowment Funds			$528		528
Income—Plant Funds				$253	253
Miscellaneous	73				73
Total Other Revenues	$ 235				$1,252
Total Revenue	$4,692	$236	$528	$253	$5,709
Expenses					
Nursing Expenses	$1,763				$1,763
Other Professional Service Expenses	1,409				1,409
General Service Expenses	1,783				1,783
Fiscal Service Expenses	235				235
Administrative Service Expenses	497				497
Total Expenses	$5,687				$5,687
Net Income for the Year	($ 995)	$236	$528	$253	$ 22

Reprinted, with permission, from *Chart of Accounts for Hospitals,* published by the American Hospital Association, 1966, p. 118.

FIGURE 53

COMMUNITY HOSPITAL

BALANCE SHEET
SEPTEMBER 30, 19X1
(000's OMITTED)

Assets

Operating Fund		
Cash in Bank and Imprest Funds		$ 79
Investments		97
Accounts and Notes Receivable—Patients	$ 780	
Less Allowance for Uncollectible Receivables	82	
Net Accounts and Notes Receivable—Patients	$ 698	
Other Receivables	25	
Due from Other Funds	–0–	
Total Receivables		723
Inventories		187
Prepaid Expenses		19
Total Operating Fund Assets		$ 1,105
Specific Purpose Fund		
Cash		$ 16
Investments		3,910
Receivables		–0–
Total Specific Purpose Fund Assets		$ 3,926
Endowment Fund		
Cash		$ 4
Investments		10,384
Receivables		–0–
Total Endowment Fund Assets		$10,388
Plant Fund		
Cash	$ 4	
Investments	366	
Receivables	–0–	$ 370
Land	$ 170	
Land Improvements	81	
Buildings	10,729	
Fixed Equipment	575	
Major Movable Equipment	325	
Minor Equipment	–0–	
Total Land, Buildings, and Equipment	$11,880	
Less Accumulated Depreciation	1,363	
Net Land, Buildings, and Equipment		10,517
Total Plant Fund Assets		$10,887

FIGURE 53 (Continued)

Liabilities and Capital

Operating Fund		
Accounts payable	$ 137	
Salaries, Wages, and Fees Payable	75	
Payroll Taxes and Other Withholdings Payable	97	
Notes and Loans Payable	40	
Accrued Expenses Payable	15	
Deferred Income	10	
Due to Other Funds	–0–	
Total Operating Fund Liabilities		$ 374
Operating Fund Balance		731
Total Operating Fund Liabilities and Balance		$ 1,105
Specific Purpose Fund		
Accounts Payable		–0–
Due to Other Funds		–0–
Total Specific Purpose Fund Liabilities		–0–
Specific Purpose Fund Balance		3,926
Total Specific Purpose Fund Liabilities and Balance		$ 3,926
Endowment Fund		
Accounts Payable	$ –0–	
Accrued Interest Payable	–0–	
Due to Other Funds	–0–	
Mortgages Payable	–0–	
Total Endowment Fund Liabilities		$ –0–
Endowment Fund Balance—Income Restricted	$3,210	
Endowment Fund Balance—Income Unrestricted	7,178	
Total Endowment Fund Balance		10,388
Total Endowment Fund Liabilities and Balance		$10,388
Plant Fund		
Accounts Payable	$ 7	
Due to Other Funds	–0–	
Mortgages Payable	1,213	
Bonds Payable	30	
Total Plant Fund Liabilities		$ 1,250
Plant Fund Balance—Invested in Plant	$9,267	
Plant Fund Balance—Reserved for Plant Replacement and Expansion	370	
Total Plant Fund Balance		9,637
Total Plant Fund Liabilities and Capital		$10,887

Reprinted, with permission, from *Chart of Accounts for Hospitals,* published by the American Hospital Association, 1966, pp. 88–89.

FIGURE 54

COMMUNITY HOSPITAL

STATEMENT OF CHANGES IN FUND BALANCES
YEAR ENDED SEPTEMBER 30, 19X1
(000'S OMITTED)

	Operating Fund	*Specific Purpose Fund*	*Endowment Fund*	*Plant Fund*
Fund Balance October 1, 19X0	$709	$3,865	$10,210	$9,670
Excess Revenue over Expense	22			
Donor-Restricted Funds:				
Research Awards and Grants		225		
Contributions—Specific Purpose		30		
Endowment Fund Income for Specific Purpose		12		
Income on Investments—Specific Purpose		30		
Contributions—Endowment Fund			150	
Income on Investments—Endowment Fund			528	
Net Gain Disposal of Investments—Endowment Fund			28	
Contributions—Plant Fund				12
Income Investments—Plant Fund				15
Addition to Fund Balance—Replacement				216
Transfers to Operating Fund				
Specific Purpose—Expenditures		(206)		
Investment Income		(30)		
Endowment—Investment Income			(528)	
Plant—Investment Income				(15)
Net Loss—Disposal of Investments—Plant Fund				(45)
Accumulated Depreciation—Plant Fund				(216)
Fund Balance September 30, 19X1	$731	$3,926	$10,388	$9,637

Reprinted with permission, from *Chart of Accounts for Hospitals*, published by the American Hospital Association, 1966, p. 90.

The AICPA commmittee also emphasizes and illustrates the need for a clearer distinction between restricted and unrestricted funds (see Figure 55) than is illustrated by the AHA. It notes in particular that improper presentation of the Plant fund can result in misstatement of working capital and financial position of the unrestricted Operating fund. In addition, it recommends interperiod revenue allocation where accelerated depreciation is used in reimbursable cost calculations but the straight-line method is used in the accounts. Finally, it considers pertinent opinions of the Accounting Principles Board and pronouncements in the Accounting Research Bulletins of the AICPA applicable to hospitals, except when they are clearly inappropriate.

colleges and universities

The principles and procedures of accounting and financial reporting for colleges and universities have recently been set out by the National Committee to Revise Volumes I and II, *College and University Business Administration*.[13] There is a marked similarity to accounting for governmental units. As might be expected, there are some differences in the classifications of revenues and expenditures. Of greater significance is the general recommendation that no depreciation be computed on fixed assets used by colleges and universities to carry on operations. The only activity for which depreciation is recommended is that of Endowment funds in which depreciation may be used as a part of the calculation of net income. The committee has recommended the accrual basis of accounting.

The committee has recommended the use of the following fund groups: Current funds, Loan funds, Endowment and Similar funds, Annuity and Life Income funds, Plant funds, and Agency funds. The emphasis in financial reporting is on these fund groups rather than on individual funds, although fund identities are maintained.

Current Funds. Current funds, which are similar in many respects to the General fund and Special Revenue funds employed by governments, are of two types: unrestricted and restricted. These funds finance and account for the typical educational, research, and public service activities of the university, as well as for auxiliary enterprises such as residence halls, dining halls, student unions, and book stores.

Loan Funds. Loan funds are usually available to students, but sometimes they may also be made available to faculty and staff. If only the income of a fund may be loaned, the principal should be grouped with

[13] *College and University Business Administration* (rev. ed.), American Council on Education, Washington, D.C., 1968.

FIGURE 55

SAMPLE HOSPITAL

BALANCE SHEET
DECEMBER 31, 19X1
WITH COMPARATIVE FIGURES FOR 19X0

Unrestricted Funds

Assets	*Current Year*	*Prior Year*
Current:		
Cash	$ 133,000	$ 33,000
Receivables (note 2)	1,382,000	1,269,000
Less estimated uncollectibles and allowances	160,000	105,000
	1,222,000	1,164,000
Due from restricted funds	215,000	—
Inventories *	176,000	183,000
Prepaid expenses	68,000	73,000
Total current assets	$ 1,814,000	$ 1,453,000
Board-designated funds:		
Cash	$ 143,000	$ 40,000
Investments (note 1)	1,427,000	1,740,000
Total board-designated funds	$ 1,570,000	$ 1,780,000
Property, plant and equipment (notes 3 and 4)	$11,028,000	$10,375,000
Less accumulated depreciation	3,885,000	3,600,000
Net property, plant, and equipment	$ 7,143,000	6,775,000
Total unrestricted funds	$10,527,000	$10,008,000

Liabilities and Fund Balances	*Current Year*	*Prior Year*
Current:		
Notes payable to banks	$ 227,000	$ 300,000
Current installments of long-term debt (note 4)	90,000	90,000
Accounts payable	450,000	463,000
Accrued expenses	150,000	147,000
Advances from third-party payors	300,000	200,000
Deferred income	10,000	10,000
Total current liabilities	$ 1,227,000	$ 1,210,000
Deferred third-party reimbursement (note 3)	$ 200,000	$ 90,000
Long-term debt (note 4):		
Housing bonds	$ 500,000	$ 520,000
Mortgage note	1,200,000	1,270,000
Total long-term debt	$ 1,700,000	$ 1,790,000
Fund balances	$ 7,400,000	$ 6,918,000
Total unrestricted funds	$10,527,000	$10,008,000

FIGURE 55 (Continued)

Assets	*Current Year*	*Prior Year*	*Liabilities and Fund Balances*	*Current Year*	*Prior Year*
		Restricted Funds			
Specific purpose funds:			Specific purpose funds:		
Cash	$ 1,260	$ 1,000	Due to unrestricted funds	$ 215,000	$ —
Investments (note 1)	200,000	70,000	Fund balances:		
Grants receivable	90,000	—	Research grants	15,000	30,000
			Other	61,260	41,000
				76,260	71,000
Total specific purpose funds	$ 291,260	$ 71,000	Total specific purpose funds	$ 291,260	$ 71,000
Plant replacement and expansion funds:			Plant replacement and expansion funds:		
Cash	$ 10,000	$ 450,000	Fund balances:		
Investments (note 1)	800,000	290,000	Restricted by third-party payors	$ 380,000	$ 150,000
Pledges receivable, net of estimated uncollectible	20,000	360,000	Other	450,000	950,000
Total plant replacement and expansion funds	$ 830,000	$1,100,000	Total plant replacement and expansion funds	$ 830,000	$1,100,000
Endowment funds:			Endowment funds:		
Cash	$ 50,000	$ 33,000	Fund balances:		
Investments (note 1)	6,100,000	3,942,000	Permanent endowment	$4,850,000	$2,550,000
			Term endowment	1,300,000	1,300,000
Total endowment funds	$6,150,000	$3,975,000	Total endowment funds	$6,150,000	$3,975,000

See accompanying notes to financial statements (not included in this figure).

* When material, state basis.

Source: Committee on Health Care Institutions, American Institute of Certified Public Accountants, *Hospital Audit Guide,* (Re-exposure draft, January 22, 1971), pp. 53–54.

the Endowment funds and the income should be included with the Loan funds. The accounting procedure for these funds is similar to that described for such funds for governmental accounting.

Endowment and Similar Funds. Assets that cannot themselves be expended (although the income from them may be) are accounted for by Endowment and similar funds. Again, the accounting for these funds is like that of similar funds of municipalities, previously described in this chapter.

Annuity and Life Income Funds. Assets that belong to the institution but are subject to annuity contracts, living trust agreements, or reservations of life income to one or more beneficiaries are accounted for through Annuity and Life Income funds. For example, an individual may donate cash, securities, or other assets under an agreement that he is to receive a fixed or variable amount as an annuity for life. The transactions and entries for these funds are similar to those for Endowment funds.

Plant Funds. Plant funds are used to account for (a) cash or securities earmarked for the construction or purchase of fixed assets, (b) cash or securities for renewals and replacements of fixed assets, (c) cash or securities accumulated for the purpose of retiring bonds or other indebtedness incurred in connection with the acquisition of fixed assets, and (d) fixed assets used to carry on operations (as distinguished from fixed assets held as endowments), together with the liabilities outstanding against these assets, such as mortgages or bonds. A separate group of accounts is necessary for each of the foregoing categories (see Figure 56).

Agency Funds. Assets that do not belong to the institution having custody of them are accounted for by agency funds. Universities often serve as depositories or fiscal agents for student organizations, faculty organizations, or even for individual students or faculty members.

Financial Statements. Financial statements for colleges and universities are, in general, similar to those for municipalities. They include balance sheets, statements of revenues and expenditures (and transfers), schedules of changes in fund balances, and appropriate subsidiary schedules. Because Plant funds of colleges and universities have peculiarities of their own, the balance sheet for Plant funds has been presented. The data in that balance sheet could have been included in a balance sheet for the entire university, which would have also contained categories for Current funds, Loan funds, Endowment and similar funds, Annuity and Life Income funds, and Agency funds. A statement of revenues and expenditures for Current funds is presented in Figure 57. If there had been transfers from Current funds to other fund groups, such as Loan funds or Plant funds, they would have been added at the foot of the statement to obtain "Excess of Revenues over Expenditures and Transfers."

FIGURE 56

A COLLEGE OR UNIVERSITY

Plant Funds Balance Sheet
At Close of Fiscal Year 19X1

Assets

Unexpended plant fund:		
Cash	$ 5,000	
Investments	20,000	
Receivables	15,000	$ 40,000
Improvements and replacement fund:		
Cash	$ 10,000	
Investments	20,000	30,000
Retirement of indebtedness fund:		
Cash	$ 2,000	
Investments	18,000	20,000
Investment in plant fund:		
Land	$100,000	
Buildings	700,000	
Equipment	105,000	905,000
Total plant funds		$995,000

Liabilities and Fund Balances

Unexpended plant fund:		
Advance from current fund	$ 4,000	
Fund balance	36,000	$ 40,000
Improvements and replacement fund:		
Fund balance		30,000
Retirement of indebtedness fund:		
Fund balance		20,000
Investment in plant fund:		
Bonds payable	$300,000	
Investment in plant	605,000	905,000
Total plant funds		$995,000

FIGURE 57

A COLLEGE OR UNIVERSITY

CURRENT FUNDS
STATEMENT OF REVENUES AND EXPENDITURES
FOR FISCAL YEAR 19X1

	Total	*Unrestricted*	*Restricted*
Revenues:			
Educational and general:			
Student fees	$ xx	$ xx	$ —
Endowment income	xx	xx	xx
Gifts and grants	xx	xx	xx
Sales and services of educational departments	xx	xx	—
Organized activities relating to educational departments	xx	xx	—
Other sources	xx	xx	—
Total educational and general	$1,100,000	$1,000,000	$100,000
Student aid	xx	—	xx
Auxiliary enterprises	xx	xx	—
Total revenues	$1,400,000	$1,200,000	$200,000
Expenditures:			
Educational and general:			
General administration	$ xx	$ xx	$ xx
General expenses	xx	xx	—
Instructional and departmental research	xx	xx	xx
Organized activities relating to educational departments	xx	xx	—
Organized research	xx	xx	xx
Extension and public services	xx	xx	—
Libraries	xx	xx	—
Operation and maintenance of physical plant	xx	xx	xx
Total educational and general	$ 950,000	$ 900,000	$ 50,000
Student aid	xx		xx
Auxiliary enterprises	xx	xx	—
Total expenditures	$1,250,000	$1,100,000	$150,000
Excess of revenues over expenditures	$ 150,000	$ 100,000	$ 50,000

Selected Glossary [14]

Abatement. A complete or partial cancellation of a levy imposed by a governmental unit.

Activity Classification. A grouping of expenditures on the basis of specific lines of work performed by organization units. For example, sewage treatment and disposal, garbage collection, garbage disposal, and street cleaning are activities performed in carrying out the function of sanitation, and the segregation of the expenditures made for each of these activities constitutes an activity classification.

Allot. To divide an appropriation into amounts which may be encumbered or expended during an allotment period or for designated purposes.

Amount Available in Debt Service Funds—Term Bonds. An account in the General Long-Term Debt group of accounts which designates the amount of assets available in a Debt Service Fund for the retirement of general obligation term bonds.

Amount to be Provided for the Payment of Term Bonds. An account in the General Long-Term Debt group of accounts which represents the amount to be provided from taxes or other general revenue to retire outstanding general obligation term bonds.

Appropriation. An authorization granted by a legislative body to make expenditures and to incur obligations for specific purposes.

Assess. To value property officially for the purpose of taxation.

Assessed Valuation. A valuation set upon real estate or other property by a government as a basis for levying taxes.

Capital Budget. A plan of proposed capital outlays and the means of financing them for the current fiscal period. It is usually a part of the current budget.

Capital Outlays. Expenditures which result in the acquisition of or addition to fixed assets.

Capital Resources. Resources of a fixed or permanent character, such as land and buildings, which cannot ordinarily be used to meet current expenditures.

Character Classification. A grouping of expenditures on the basis of the time periods they are presumed to benefit. The three

[14] Adapted, with permission, from the terminology developed by the National Committee on Governmental Accounting and included in the Appendices of its publication, *Governmental Accounting, Auditing, and Financial Reporting,* 1968. The term "Debit" or "Credit" in parentheses following an account title indicates the account's typical balance.

groupings are: (1) expenses, presumed to benefit the current fiscal period; (2) provisions for retirement of debt, presumed to benefit prior fiscal periods primarily but also present and future periods; and (3) capital outlays, presumed to benefit the current and future fiscal periods.

Debt Limit. The maximum amount of gross or net debt which is legally permitted.

Debt Service Requirement. The amount of money required to pay the interest on outstanding debt, serial maturities of principal for serial bonds, and required contributions to a Debt Service fund for term bonds.

Deferred Special Assessments. Special assessments which have been levied but which are not yet due.

Encumbrances. Obligations in the form of purchase orders, contracts, or salary commitments which are chargeable to an appropriation and for which a part of the appropriation is reserved. They cease to be encumbrances when paid or when the actual liability is set up.

Estimated Uncollectible Current Taxes (Credit). A provision out of tax revenues for that portion of current taxes receivable which it is estimated will never be collected. The amount is shown on the balance sheet as a deduction from the *Taxes Receivable—Current* account in order to arrive at the net taxes receivable.

Expenditures. Where the accounts are kept on the accrual basis or the modified accrual basis, this term designates the cost of goods delivered or services rendered, whether paid or unpaid, including expenses, provision for debt retirement not reported as a liability of the fund from which retired, and capital outlays.

Expenses. Charges incurred, whether paid or unpaid, for operation, maintenance, interest, and other charges which are presumed to benefit the current fiscal period.

Force Account Method. A method employed in the construction and/or maintenance of fixed assets whereby a governmental unit's own personnel are used instead of an outside contractor.

Full Faith and Credit. A pledge of the general taxing power for the payment of debt obligations. *Note:* Bonds carrying such pledges are usually referred to as general obligation bonds or full faith and credit bonds.

Functional Classification. A grouping of expenditures on the basis of the principal purposes for which they are made. Examples are public safety, public health, public welfare, etc. See also **Activity, Character,** and **Object Classification.**

Fund. An independent fiscal and accounting entity with a self-balancing set of accounts recording cash and/or other resources together with all related liabilities, obligations, reserves, and equities which are segregated for the purpose of carrying on specific activities or attaining certain objectives in accordance with special regulations, restrictions, or limitations.

Fund Balance. The excess of the assets of a fund over its liabilities and reserves except in the case of funds subject to budgetary accounting where, prior to the end of a fiscal period, it represents the excess of the fund's assets and estimated revenues for the period over its liabilities, reserves, and appropriations for the period.

General Obligation Bonds. Bonds for whose payment the full faith and credit of the issuing body are pledged.

Lapse. (Verb) As applied to appropriations, this term denotes the automatic termination of an appropriation.

Levy. (Verb) To impose taxes, special assessments, or service charges for the support of governmental activities. (Noun) The total amount of taxes, special assessments, or service charges imposed by a governmental unit.

Lump-Sum Appropriation. An appropriation made for a stated purpose, or for a named department, without specifying further the amounts that may be spent for specific activities or for particular objects of expenditure.

Matured Bonds Payable. Bonds which have reached or passed their maturity date but which remain unpaid.

Object Classification. A grouping of expenditures on the basis of goods or services purchased; for example, personal services, materials, supplies, and equipment.

Overlapping Debt. The proportionate share of the debts of local governmental units located wholly or in part within the limits of the reporting government which must be borne by property within each governmental unit.

Performance Budget. A budget wherein expenditures are based primarily upon measurable performance of activities and work programs. A performance budget may also incorporate other bases of expenditure classification, such as character and object, but these are given a subordinate status to activity performance.

Program Budget. A budget wherein expenditures are based primarily on programs of work and secondarily on character and object. A program budget is a transitional type of budget between the traditional character and object budget, on the one hand, and the performance budget, on the other.

Reserve for Encumbrances. A reserve representing the segregation of a portion of a fund balance to provide for unliquidated encumbrances.

Resources. The actual assets of a governmental unit, such as cash, taxes receivable, land, buildings, etc. plus contingent assets such as estimated revenues applying to the current fiscal year not accrued or collected and bonds authorized and unissued.

Retained Earnings. The accumulated earnings of an Enterprise or Intragovernmental Service fund which have been retained in the fund and which are not reserved for any specific purpose.

Revenue Bonds. Bonds whose principal and interest are payable exclusively from earnings of a public enterprise.

Shared Revenue. Revenue which is levied by one governmental unit but shared, usually in proportion to the amount collected, with another unit of government or class of governments.

Special Assessment Liens Receivable. Claims which a governmental unit has upon properties until special assessments levied against them have been paid. The term normally applies to those delinquent special assessments for the collection of which legal action has been taken through the filing of claims.

Tax Anticipation Notes. Notes (sometimes called warrants) issued in anticipation of collection of taxes, usually retirable only from tax collections, and frequently only from the proceeds of the tax levy whose collection they anticipate.

Tax Liens Receivable. Legal claims against property which have been exercised because of nonpayment of delinquent taxes, interest, and penalties. The account includes delinquent taxes, interest, and penalties receivable up to the date the lien becomes effective and the cost of holding the sale.

Taxes Collected in Advance. A liability for taxes collected before the tax levy has been made or before the amount of taxpayer liability has been established.

Unencumbered Appropriation. That portion of an appropriation not yet expended or encumbered.

Unexpended Allotment. That portion of an allotment which has not been expended.

Unexpended Appropriation. That portion of an appropriation which has not been expended.

Warrant. An order drawn by the legislative body or an officer of a governmental unit upon its treasurer directing the latter to pay a specified amount to the person named or to the bearer.

5
consolidated statements

Herbert E. Miller
George C. Mead

what are consolidated statements?

Consolidated statements are the combined statements of several related corporations, made after all intercompany duplications have been eliminated. To justify this accounting treatment, the corporations whose statements are thus combined must share certain qualifications. Although each corporation is in fact a separate legal entity, ownership of its shares and the nature of its business can make it a part of a larger business entity or organization. Consolidated statements show the position and progress of a parent company and its legally separate subsidiaries as if the group were one firm with several divisions or branches.

If several corporations are to function as parts of a single business entity, sufficient control must reside with some member corporation to permit the achievement of a unity of operation from the group. One of the most common and convenient ways of gaining control of a corporation is through ownership of the voting shares. Through this device, effective operating control can be attained without disturbing the separate legal existence of the controlled subsidiary corporation.

In a legal sense, then, consolidated statements are fictions. However, this admission does not justify abandoning the notion of consolidated statements, nor does it constitute a serious weakness. Indeed, consolidated statements are usually the principal statements in the annual report to stockholders, especially if the parent company is mainly a holding company rather than an operating company.

when should statements be consolidated?

A 1956 survey indicated that the principal considerations when deciding whether to combine the financial statements of a subsidiary with those of the parent were: "(1) The degree of control by the parent company, (2) the extent to which the subsidiary is an integral part of the operating group, and (3) whether the subsidiary is a domestic or a foreign corporation."[1] Ownership of a majority of the voting stock of a subsidiary is a necessary, although not self-sufficient, reason for consolidation. In actual practice, control and even relatively coordinated operation may occur with less than 50% ownership. In spite of this possibility, a large portion of the subsidiaries are wholly owned, and some accountants believe that subsidiaries in which the parent holds interests of less than 60 to 70% of stock ownership should not be consolidated.

These matters are of some relevance to practicing accountants, but they are of slight consequence to the candidate confronting an examination problem on consolidated statements. For examination purposes, the question of when to consolidate is answered by the percentage of ownership of outstanding voting shares—51% or above being considered an acceptable criterion.

A subsidiary may be once removed (or several times removed) from the top parent company. Such subsidiaries are frequently termed "grandson" subsidiaries. In the following illustration, Company G is a grandson of Company P, and the consolidation of the statements of Companies P, S, and G is justified without question.

ILLUSTRATION

Company P owns 90% of the voting shares of Company S.
Company S owns 95% of the voting shares of Company G.

It may be pertinent in this connection to note that a company may be a subsidiary company without having the majority of its voting shares held by any one corporation. This would be the case under the following circumstances:

Company P owns 90% of Company S, 90% of Company R, and 10% of Company Q.
Company S owns 40% of Company Q.
Company R owns 40% of Company Q.

[1] *Survey of Consolidated Financial Statement Practices* (New York: American Institute of Certified Public Accountants, 1956), p. 7.

Here, also, consolidated statements are justified for Company P and subsidiaries S, R, and Q.

Reporting as a consolidated entity generally presumes continuity of control. Thus if a subsidiary is being held by the parent as a temporary investment it need not, or perhaps should not, be consolidated. A subsidiary in legal reorganization or bankruptcy should not be consolidated because control does not rest with the owners. Controlled foreign subsidiaries should not be consolidated whenever their value to the parent company is made uncertain by volatile exchange rates, severe restrictions on repatriation of funds, or instability and "nationalistic" tendencies in the foreign government. Certain financial or regulated operations, such as insurance and finance subsidiaries of manufacturing or retail firms, have often not been consolidated on the grounds that their operations or accounting methods are materially different; however, the number of exclusions for this reason appears to be diminishing.

unconsolidated subsidiaries

The investment in any unconsolidated subsidiary is reported in a parent company's balance sheet as a single asset and the earnings derived from the investment in the subsidiary as a single item in the parent's income statement. Two methods have existed for the parent's accounting for that investment and related income, "cost" and "equity," as is discussed in a later section. The equity (or "book value") method is now favored for unconsolidated subsidiaries.[2] However, neither method provides information as comprehensive as that furnished by consolidated statements, assuming the parent and subsidiary do form an economic unity of operation and control.

Thus, whenever conditions justify not combining the financial statements of one or more subsidiary companies, adequate disclosure relating to such exclusions should accompany the consolidated statements. It is generally held that the following information regarding excluded subsidiaries is pertinent:

1. Reasons for nonconsolidation (disclosure of consolidation policy).
2. Identity of excluded subsidiaries.
3. Extent of parent's ownership therein.

Unconsolidated subsidiaries are accounted for as investments. Cost is no longer favored as a method of accounting for unconsolidated sub-

[2] The theory of accounting for unconsolidated subsidiaries, and the position of the Accounting Principles Board (APB), is discussed in a later section entitled "One-Line Consolidations."

sidiaries, unless great uncertainty surrounds the investment. The favored equity method adjusts the investment account each period by recognizing as income to the controlling company its share of the subsidiary's net income, regardless of whether it is distributed. Losses incurred by a subsidiary would be similarly taken up in the accounts of the parent. Intercompany profit on transactions with unconsolidated subsidiaries should be eliminated.

other common stock investments

A stock holding of 50% or less does not entail absolute voting control; the investor–investee relation cannot be termed "parent–subsidiary." The cost method of accounting has usually been used by investors for such holdings. However, the Accounting Principles Board in Opinion 18 concluded that the equity method should be applied whenever the investor can "exercise significant influence over operating and financial policies of an investee . . . an investment of 20% or more of the voting stock of the investee should lead to a presumption . . . [of] . . . ability to exercise significant influence over the investee." [3]

business combinations and consolidated statements distinguished

The operations of two or more companies may be joined or combined in a number of ways. The manner of accounting for the newly formed operating unit depends on the answers to the questions: Was the subsidiary corporation dissolved with a single entity emerging, or did a continuing parent–subsidiary relation result? Did a firm purchase another firm, or did the firms merge their assets and equities in a "pooling of interests"?

This chapter deals almost entirely with situations in which a purchased subsidiary is continued in existence. In contrast, however, when a business combination results in a single corporation, one or more predecessor entities are terminated. The surviving legal entity may be one of the predecessor firms (e.g., Companies A and B combine, Company B being liquidated) or a new organization may be chartered (e.g., Company C is organized to take over the assets and equities of Companies A and B, which are then liquidated). Some accountants term the former a "merger" and the latter, in which a new corporation is created, a "consolidation." There is, however, no complete consensus on terminology in the business combination area.

[3] APB Opinion 18: *The Equity Method of Accounting for Investments in Common Stock,* paragraph 17.

When a single entity survives, all or a substantial portion of the assets and liabilities of the terminated firms are transferred to the successor firm. There is then no place for consolidated statement techniques, because no subsidiary company continues with its own accounts and financial statements. However, the questions of basic accounting policy are the same as those encountered in preparing consolidated statements (except for absence of minority interest), questions concerning measurement of the transferred assets and liabilities, and their later effect on entity income determination.

The position of the profession on accounting for business combinations—pooling versus purchase—is set forth in Accounting Principles Board Opinion 16; also, an overview is contained in a later section of this chapter.

fundamental consolidation concepts and techniques

The basic concepts underlying consolidated statements can be presented by the use of illustrative working papers. Indeed, CPA problems typically require preparation of working papers showing adjustments and eliminations rather than the formal financial statements.

Because there is no "official" working paper form for CPA examination purposes, any reasonable form is acceptable; however, the candidate is often provided a worksheet with trial balances printed on it. Thus facility with the form imposed by the preprinted worksheet is important in the interests of conserving examination-writing time. The form adopted for the following illustrations has often been used. A complete example toward the end of the chapter shows another form.[4]

Consolidated financial statements are basically aggregations of the separate statements of the several related companies with duplications having been eliminated. One of the main functions of working papers is to provide an organized framework within which to make the required eliminations and aggregations.

The main area of duplication is the asset on the parent company's books representing the investment in the subsidiary and the related stockholders' equity on the books of the subsidiary. This elimination is quite simple if the parent acquired all the subsidiary's capital stock for its book value. However, two circumstances commonly occur to reduce the simplicity of the elimination. First, the parent may pay more or less

[4] The candidate is urged to work through some working paper problems. The majority of examinations includes such a problem. Recommended as of this writing are No. 3 (November, 1967—Practice II) and No. 4 (May, 1970—Practice I).

than book value for the subsidiary's stock. Such difference, traditionally identified as "consolidated goodwill," is not eliminated when consolidated statements are prepared. Second, the parent may not have acquired all of the outstanding shares of the subsidiary, in which case there is a minority interest to account for. It should be noted in passing that the term "consolidated goodwill" has generally been replaced. Such terms as "excess of cost over book value acquired" or "excess of book value acquired over cost," as the case may be, are often used. However, in the interest of brevity, many accountants continue to use the older terminology, particularly in working papers.

Both consolidated goodwill and minority interest are involved in the following simplified illustration. On January 1, 1971, Company P acquired 90% of the outstanding common stock of Company S, paying the former owners $72,500. The working papers of Illustration 1 reveal the elimination that would be required if immediately thereafter a consolidated balance sheet were prepared for the newly related group. (Their

ILLUSTRATION I

COMPANY P AND SUBSIDIARY COMPANY S

CONSOLIDATED STATEMENT WORKING PAPERS
JANUARY 1, 1971

	Company P	*Company S*	*Adjustments and Eliminations*		*Consolidated Balance Sheet*
			Debit	*Credit*	
Cash	27,500	10,000			37,500
Receivables	30,000	20,000			50,000
Inventories	35,000	24,000			59,000
Investment in Company S	72,500			(1) 67,500	5,000 (G)
Fixed assets	45,000	36,000			81,000
	210,000	90,000			232,500
Liabilities	25,000	15,000			40,000
Common stock ($10 par):					
Company P	150,000				150,000
Company S		60,000	(1) 54,000		6,000 (M)
Retained earnings:					
Company P	35,000				35,000
Company S		15,000	(1) 13,500		1,500 (M)
	210,000	90,000	67,500	67,500	232,500

respective balance sheets are exactly as they were before the purchase, except that "Investment in Company S" has replaced "Cash" to the extent of $72,500 in Company P's books.)

The equity of the minority shareholders, designated by (M) in the working papers, and the excess of the amount paid over the book value acquired, designated by (G) in the working papers, can be computed as follows:

Cost of 90% interest acquired as of January 1, 1971			$72,500
Stockholders' equity—Company S as of January 1, 1971:			
	10%	*90%*	
Common stock	$6,000	$54,000	
Retained earnings	1,500	13,500	67,500
Minority interest	$7,500		
Excess of cost over book value (consolidated goodwill)			$5,000

The dollar amount for consolidated goodwill is determined by comparing the acquisition cost with the book value of the equity acquired *as of the date of acquisition.* Such difference, or excess, can be either a debit or credit amount. It appears *only* in the consolidated statements; it does not appear in the financial statements of either the parent or subsidiary companies.

This matter is discussed in greater detail later in the chapter.

consolidated statements subsequent to acquisition

The eliminations are somewhat more involved and the working papers must be expanded when consolidated statements subsequent to acquisition, including both balance sheet and income statement, are required. To illustrate, Company P's 90% investment in Company S, acquired January 1, 1971, will be carried forward for a year. That is, using Illustration 1 as the starting point, it will be assumed that during 1971 Company P earned $10,000 and Company S $8,000 from their separate operations. Rather unrealistically, there were no transactions between the two firms and the net of the revenues and expenses has been reflected in cash, all other accounts being held constant.

Although the account balances for Illustration 2 are as of December 31, 1971, one year after the parent–subsidiary relationship was established, the single working paper elimination is identical to that in Illustration 1. The investment in Company S, being carried at cost, continues to require a $67,500 credit elimination, which amount is 90%

ILLUSTRATION 2

COMPANY P AND SUBSIDIARY COMPANY S

CONSOLIDATED STATEMENT WORKING PAPERS
FOR THE YEAR ENDED DECEMBER 31, 1971

	Company P	Company S	Adjustments and Eliminations		Consolidated Income Statement *	Consolidated Retained Earnings	Consolidated Balance Sheet
			Debit	Credit			
Cash	37,500	18,000					55,500
Receivables	30,000	20,000					50,000
Inventories	35,000	24,000					59,000
Investment in Company S	72,500			67,500			5,000 (G)
Fixed assets (net)	45,000	36,000					81,000
Cost of sales	50,000	12,000			(62,000)		
Operating expenses	40,000	20,000			(60,000)		
	310,000	130,000					250,500
Liabilities	25,000	15,000					40,000
Common stock:							
Company P	150,000						150,000
Company S		60,000	54,000				6,000 (M)
Retained earnings (January 1):							
Company P	35,000					35,000	
Company S		15,000	13,500				1,500 (M)
Sales	100,000	40,000			140,000		
	310,000	130,000	67,500	67,500			
					18,000		
Minority interest in Company S earnings					(800)		800 (M)
Consolidated net income					17,200	17,200	
Consolidated retained earnings (December 31)						52,200	52,200
							250,500

* Parentheses denote deduction.

of the book value of the subsidiary's stockholders' equity at acquisition. The $5,000 remainder, or the uneliminated amount of the investment which is extended to the Consolidated Balance Sheet column, is the excess of cost over book value (i.e., the consolidated goodwill). The debits of $54,000 and $13,500 eliminate the parent's 90% interest in the stockholders' equity of the subsidiary at acquisition. The uneliminated amounts of the stockholders' equity of the subsidiary, $6,000 and $1,500, make up the minority interest as of the beginning of the year. Of course, the minority interest will be modified by the results of the operations of the subsidiary for 1971. Specifically, the minority interest at the end of 1971 will include the minority's share of the 1971 earnings of the subsidiary. This share, as shown by the working papers, amounts to $800. Thus the total minority interest as of December 31, 1971, is $8,300 ($6,000 + $1,500 + $800).

As we can see from the working papers for Illustration 2, the consolidated net income is $17,200. This amount can be determined as follows:

Net income of the parent from its own operations:			
Sales		$100,000	
Deduct:			
Cost of sales	$50,000		
Operating expenses	40,000	90,000	$10,000
Parent's share of the net income of the subsidiary:			
Sales		$40,000	
Deduct:			
Cost of sales	$12,000		
Operating expenses	20,000	32,000	
Net income		$ 8,000	
Deduct minority interest in net income of subsidiary—10%		800	7,200
Consolidated net income			$17,200

In the foregoing determination of consolidated net income, no provision was made for the amortization of consolidated goodwill. Amortization of consolidated goodwill is required by Accounting Principles Board Opinion No. 17, but discussion of this matter is postponed until later in the chapter to keep the beginning illustrations less involved.

Because there were no intercompany transactions affecting the revenue and expense accounts, the consolidated income statement will show the combined amounts, as follows:

COMPANY P AND SUBSIDIARY COMPANY S

CONSOLIDATED INCOME STATEMENT
FOR THE YEAR ENDED DECEMBER 31, 1971

Sales		$140,000
Deduct:		
Cost of sales	$62,000	
Operating expenses	60,000	122,000
Total entity earnings		$ 18,000
Deduct minority interest in subsidiary net income		800
Consolidated net income		$ 17,200

According to the working papers for Illustration 2, the December 31, 1971 consolidated retained earnings amount to $52,200. At any point in time after the parent–subsidiary relationship has been established, consolidated retained earnings can be computed by the following method:

CONSOLIDATED RETAINED EARNINGS
AS OF DECEMBER 31, 1971

Retained earnings of the parent company:		
Retained earnings, beginning of year	$35,000	
Net income of parent	10,000	
Deduct dividends declared by parent	–0–	$45,000
Add (deduct) the parent's share of the change in the subsidiary's retained earnings since the company became a subsidiary:		
Retained earnings of subsidiary, beginning of year	$15,000	
Net income of subsidiary	8,000	
Deduct dividends declared by subsidiary	–0–	
Retained earnings of subsidiary, December 31, 1971	$23,000	
Retained earnings of subsidiary, at acquisition	15,000	
Increase since acquisition	$ 8,000	
Parent's share—90%		7,200
Consolidated retained earnings		$52,200

Incidentally, at the date when the parent–subsidiary relationship is established, the consolidated retained earnings will always equal the parent's retained earnings (unless the merger is a pooling of interests, as discussed in a later section). The retained earnings of the newly acquired subsidiary are eliminated to the extent of the parent's percentage of interest in the subsidiary; any remainder is assigned to the minority interest.

In practice, of course, the consolidated retained earnings, and changes thereto, are reported in a separate statement. In the absence of unusual transactions, such statement is composed of the following items:

1. Beginning-of-period consolidated retained earnings.
2. Add (deduct) consolidated net income (loss) for the period.
3. Deduct dividends declared by the parent (there were none in Illustration 2).
4. End-of-period consolidated retained earnings.

cost and equity methods

There are two well-established methods of accounting for the investment in consolidated subsidiaries on the parent's books: (a) cost, and (b) equity or "book value." As the term implies, under the cost method, the investing corporation maintains its investment in subsidiaries at cost. Under this approach, the only entries in the investment account will reflect additional acquisitions or disposals of the particular subsidiary's stock. This generalization should be amended by noting that the investment account should be credited upon receipt by the parent of dividends declared out of retained earnings existing at the date of acquisition. (Such receipts should be properly viewed not as a share of the subsidiary's post-acquisition earnings but, instead, as a partial return of capital.) If the equity method is used, the investment account, although starting with cost, will be revised each period to reflect the parent company's share of the increase or decrease in the stockholders' equity of the subsidiary. (A later section entitled "One-line Consolidations" discusses further features of the equity method.)

The two methods are contrasted by the following illustration:

	Parent Corporation's Books					
Data	*Cost Method*			*Equity Method*		
Co. P acquires a 90% interest in the voting shares of Co. S—Cost, $150,000	Investment in Co. S	150,000		Investment in Co. S	150,000	
	Cash ...		150,000	Cash ...		150,000

Data	*Parent Corporation's Books* — *Cost Method*			*Equity Method*		
First-year earnings of Co. S—$20,000	No entry.			Investment in Co. S	18,000	
				Income from investment in subsidiaries		18,000
Dividends declared and paid by Co. S—$15,000	Cash	13,500		Cash	13,500	
	Dividend income ..		13,500	Investment in Co. S .		13,500
Second year, Co. S has a loss of $3,000	No entry.			Loss on investment in subsidiaries	2,700	
				Investment in Co. S		2,700

Consolidated statements are not affected by the method adopted by the parent for accounting for its investment in subsidiaries. The consolidated statements will be the same whether the parent maintains its investment account at cost or adjusts the account periodically for its share of the increase or decrease in the subsidiary's stockholders' equity that results from operations and related activities. However, the adjusting and elimination entries on the consolidated statement working papers will be affected by the method of accounting adopted by the parent, and it is through these working paper entries that the methods are brought to equivalence.

For example, assume in Illustration 2 that Company P adopted the equity (book value) method rather than the cost method for carrying its investment in Company S. The following tabulation shows the accounts that would be affected by this different policy, along with the working paper elimination. Note that after the elimination, the amounts extended to the Consolidated Balance Sheet column would be identical to those of Illustration 2.

	Company P	*Company S*	*Adjustments and Eliminations*		*Consolidated Balance Sheet*
Investment in Co. S	79,700			74,700	5,000 (G)
Common stock		60,000	54,000		6,000 (M)
Retained earnings		15,000	13,500		1,500 (M)
Income from investment in subsidiary	7,200		7,200		

additional events subsequent to acquisition

Let us carry the assumptions of Illustration 2 on to the next year, 1972. Assume that Companies P and S operated exactly as in 1971, with two exceptions: (a) both firms declared and paid cash dividends in the amounts shown in Illustration 3 and (b) the parent made a noninterest-bearing advance to the subsidiary. The example also illustrates the use of a column for accumulating elements of the minority interest.

The $900 dividend from Company S was properly (under the cost method) recorded by the parent as dividend income. However, since the source of that income was not external to the consolidated group, the $900 amount should be eliminated when determining consolidated net income. Elimination (1) accomplishes this. It also removes the same amount from dividends, leaving to be extended only the $2,500 of dividends paid to parent-company shareholders and $100 to minority owners of the subsidiary. Such amounts are extended as negative elements of consolidated retained earnings and of minority interest, respectively.

Elimination (2) removes all but the initial $5,000 "consolidated goodwill" from the investment in Company S account. For simplicity, subsequent amortization of goodwill has been omitted.[5] The second entry also eliminates the parent's 90% interest in the subsidiary's *beginning-of-year* stockholders' equity, leaving the minority's 10% interest. The $7,200 credit adjusts the parent company's retained earnings for its 90% share of the increase in the subsidiary's undistributed earnings, which occurred between acquisition date and the beginning of the current year. When the $7,200 is added to the *parent's* January 1, 1972 retained earnings, the total—$52,200—is the *beginning-of-year consolidated* retained earnings. The other elements of consolidated retained earnings and of minority interest are self-explanatory.

If Illustration 3 had been based on the equity (or book value) method of accounting for the parent's investment in Company S instead of the cost method, the eliminations would have been slightly different, but the resulting consolidated statement would be the same. The affected accounts and eliminations would have appeared as follows:

[5] In CPA examination problems, the goodwill amount, computed as of acquisition date, will usually be amortized. And other considerations may affect the goodwill amount. For instance, a reduction will be required if a portion of the parent's holding of subsidiary shares has been sold. Also, such goodwill may be allocated to other assets, as discussed in a later section.

ILLUSTRATION 3

COMPANY P AND SUBSIDIARY COMPANY S

CONSOLIDATED STATEMENT WORKING PAPERS
FOR THE YEAR ENDED DECEMBER 31, 1972

	Company P	Company S	Adjustments and Eliminations		Consolidated Income Statement *	Consolidated Retained Earnings	Minority Interest	Consolidated Balance Sheet
			Debit	Credit				
Cash	42,900	28,000						70,900
Receivables	30,000	20,000						50,000
Inventories	35,000	24,000						59,000
Advance to Company S	3,000			(3) 3,000				
Investment in Company S	72,500			(2) 67,500				5,000 (G)
Fixed assets (net)	45,000	36,000						81,000
Cost of sales	50,000	12,000			(62,000)			
Operating expenses	40,000	20,000			(60,000)			
Dividends:								
Company P	2,500					(2,500)		
Company S		1,000		(1) 900			(100)	
	320,900	141,000						265,900
Liabilities	25,000	15,000						40,000
Advance from Company P		3,000	(3) 3,000					
Common stock:								
Company P	150,000							150,000
Company S		60,000	(2) 54,000				6,000	
Retained earnings (1/1):								
Company P	45,000			(2) 7,200		52,200		
Company S		23,000	(2) 20,700				2,300	
Sales	100,000	40,000			140,000			
Dividend income	900		(1) 900					
	320,900	141,000	78,600	78,600				
Minority interest in Company S net income					18,000 (800)		800	
Consolidated net income					17,200	17,200		
Consolidated retained earnings						66,900		66,900
Minority interest							9,000	9,000

	Company P	Company S	*Adjustments and Eliminations*		*Minority Interest*	*Consolidated Balance Sheet*
Investment in Company S	86,000			81,000		5,000 (G)
Dividends		1,000		900	(100)	
Common stock		60,000	54,000		6,000	
Retained earnings (1/1):						
Company P	52,200					
Company S		23,000	20,700		2,300	
Income from investment in subsidiary	7,200		7,200			

The balance of the investment in Company S account reflects the original investment ($72,500), plus the parent's 90% share of the subsidiary's earnings for the two-year period ($7,200 times 2), minus the dividend received ($900). The January 1, 1972 retained earnings of the parent include its share of the 1971 subsidiary-company income, and thus the balance is $7,200 larger than the amount appearing in Illustration 3.

The eliminating entry may be analyzed as follows: "consolidated goodwill" is $5,000, as determined earlier in Illustration 1. To extend that amount to the Consolidated Balance Sheet column, an $81,000 credit is needed in the Adjustments and Eliminations columns. Minority interest in the beginning-of-year Company S stockholders' equity is extended after the parent's 90% share, $54,000 and $20,700, has been eliminated. Finally, amounts relating to intercompany income and dividends are eliminated.

intercompany transactions and profits

If consolidated statements are to reflect the position and progress of what is in fact a single business organization, then *all* intercompany duplications must be eliminated, not just the parent company's investment accounts and the related stockholders' equity accounts of subsidiary companies. Intercompany duplications may develop from a variety of business transactions and arrangements, but the results are basically the same—debit balances are created on the books of one of the related companies and these are offset by credit balances on the books of some other corporation within the related group.

This situation is particularly obvious in the case of advances or loans extended by one of the member corporations, frequently the parent, to another related corporation. Under such circumstances, as in Illustration 3, the receivable on the credit grantor's books is matched by the liability on the borrower's books. These items must be eliminated during the preparation of consolidated statements. Otherwise the asset and liability picture could be inflated or distorted by intercompany transactions having no actual significance on the financial position of the group of related corporations when viewed as a single business organization. Interest income and expense on intercompany indebtedness provide an example of an elimination, required when consolidated statements are prepared in order to avoid overstatement of the consolidated entity's total revenues and total expenses. Another example of a required elimination is intercompany sales of goods or services.

The elimination is less straightforward when the selling company shows a profit from intercompany sales. The existence of intercompany profit in the accounts of related companies is perhaps one of the most commonly recurring features of CPA problems requiring consolidated statements. From the point of view of the individual corporation, a profit can be considered as having been realized upon the transfer of goods or services to the vendee. Viewing a group of related companies as a single business entity, profit is not realized until the goods or services reach an "outsider," and "sales" should include only transactions with "outsiders." Accordingly, in the preparation of consolidated statements, all amounts of intercompany sales, cost of goods sold, and unrealized profit must be eliminated. On the consolidated balance sheet, the assets acquired from affiliated companies are presented net after eliminating the intercompany profit.

The accounts most likely to be affected by intercompany profit are inventory accounts, fixed asset accounts, and accounts representing investments in stock or bonds. These items are more commonly subject to intercompany transactions. The problems created by the existence of intercompany profit, though varied in detail, can be classified under three primary questions:

1. What is the amount of intercompany profit?
2. Does intercompany profit affect minority interest?
3. When may intercompany profit be treated as having been earned?

What is the Amount of Intercompany Profit? Concerning the dollar amount of intercompany profit, the candidate may have to determine whether the correct measure is gross profit or net profit. For example, one CPA problem disclosed that the parent corporation's purchases from the subsidiary amounted to $350,000 for the year, and that at the end of the year $80,000 of these purchases was included in the parent's inventory. The problem data included a complete trial balance of the subsidiary, but no mention was made of profit rates. In this instance, the candidate had to decide on the correct measure of intercompany profit, compute the relevant percentage, and then apply it to the $80,000 inventory secured from the subsidiary.

Most textbooks use gross profit as the measure of intercompany profit. Although this practice is well established and hence attractive to the candidate, in certain instances the accountant can fairly say that the gross profit basis may be unduly conservative. Some of the services performed by a subsidiary in supplying inventory to the parent corporation are reflected in operating expense accounts typically presented below gross profit. Freight and cartage out may be classified by a subsidiary among its operating expenses. This item of cost is an acceptable addition to inventory cost, and if the subsidiary were organized as a branch it would be so treated generally. But if gross profit of a subsidiary is used as the basis for "deflating" the inventory to "cost," it may result in an unjustified understatement of the inventory. On the other hand, the elimination of intercompany net profit would generally result in the capitalization of many costs not associated with inventory accounts. The answer appears to fall within the extremes of gross profit and net profit. In general terms, the amount of intercompany profit to be eliminated can be defined as gross profit less those operating expenses incurred by the seller that are necessary in placing the inventory in the related company's possession in the required condition. As in so many accounting matters, it is unlikely that the answer can be reduced to a definite and generally applicable formula. For this reason, accountants prefer the more conservative basis of gross profit as the measuring device.

In many instances this particular feature is settled in CPA problems by the data supplied. As the following quotations from former problems reveal, the candidate seldom has to be concerned on this point, for he is not given sufficient information to enable him to make a choice between gross profit and net profit.

> For several years a part of the output of B Company (a subsidiary of A Company) has been an intermediate product sold to A Company at a uniform markup of 20 per cent (on sales). Sales of this character recorded on B's books were $258,000 for 1970, of which $64,500 remained in A Company's inventory at the end of the year. . . .

> Inventories at December 31, 1970, include intercompany items as follows:

	Company		*Amount*	
Date of Transaction	*Purchaser*	*Seller*	*Inventory*	*Seller's Cost*
April 5, 1970	H	A	$ 3,600	$ 3,000
August 15, 1970	H	B	5,000	4,500 *
October 5, 1970	H	A	10,000	9,000
May 15, 1970	A	B	7,000	6,200
September 26, 1970	A	B	6,000	4,800
November 12, 1970	B	A	16,000	14,000

* Acquired on July 20, 1970, by B from A, A's cost then being $4,200.

In some instances, the affiliated corporations are vertically integrated, with raw material being successively processed as it is passed forward by sale and resale from corporation to corporation. Under such conditions, the calculation of intercompany profit requires an accumulation of several profit elements. In these circumstances, the intercompany profit in an inventory of finished goods may relate only to the raw material content, because the processing corporation purchased the raw material from an affiliated company at a profit to the selling company.

While discussing intercompany profit in inventories, the possibility of encountering intercompany losses in inventories should be mentioned. Intercompany sales at less than cost may be produced by "artificial" prices, in which case the seller's cost could be properly reestablished for purposes of consolidated statements. On the other hand, if the transfer price coincides with market prices, the intercompany loss, although still unrealized, is nevertheless the result of an actual decline in value and the seller's cost should not be reestablished.

Having computed the amount of intercompany profit, there may be some question about the portion of that profit to be eliminated in the preparation of the consolidated statements. For many years, there were two widely accepted schools of thought among accountants:

1. Eliminate 100% of the intercompany profit.
2. Eliminate only the parent corporation's share of the intercompany profit.

To explore these alternatives, let us continue the preceding series of illustrations by assuming that in the next year, 1973, Company S sold merchandise to Company P at an average gross profit of 40%. (This is the same as a gross markup of 66.67% on cost.) Company P's ending inventory included $2,000 of these goods. The unrealized intercompany profit is thus $800. Should the entire $800 be eliminated as the unrealized intercompany profit in the inventory, or should only the parent's share, $720, be removed?

Prior to the issuance of *Accounting Research Bulletin No. 51* in 1959, there was much support for partial elimination. From the position that consolidated statements should be prepared from the point of view of parent-company stockholders (generally referred to as the "proprietary theory" approach to consolidated statements), it follows that 10% of the above-mentioned $800 intercompany gross profit relates to goods bought, so to speak, by the parent-company shareholders from minority owners of the subsidiary. Thus $80 represents cost (over and above the original $1,200 cost to the subsidiary) of inventoriable assets acquired "from outsiders in an arm's-length transaction." This line of reasoning would lead to a conclusion that only the parent's proportionate share is unrealized and therefore should be eliminated.

However, ARB No. 51 came out squarely in favor of 100% elimination, which is now the favored position. The theory supporting full elimination takes the position that the consolidated group carries on a homogeneous operation under unified management which happens to have at least two classes of ownership interests—parent-company owners and minority holders of subsidiary stock. Under this "entity theory" approach, it is unrealistic to assume that intercompany transactions were carried out partially with "independent" minority shareholders. The entire transaction was between related parties, and full elimination of intercompany profit should follow. "The amount of intercompany profit or loss to be eliminated . . . is not affected by the existence of a minority interest." [6]

Occasionally the problem of computing the amount of intercompany profit may be complicated by the particular dates on which the intercompany transactions occurred. For instance, the transaction may have occurred before the parent-subsidiary relationship developed. An example involving inventories may be cited as follows. On May 1, when Company P and Company S are unrelated, Company S sells merchandise in the amount of $5,000 to Company P. On this transaction assume that Company S shows a gain of $800. Assume further that in the following month, June 1, Company P acquires a 100% interest in the capital stock of Company S. Suppose that one-half the merchandise involved resides in Company P's inventory on December 31. Is there an element of intercompany profit in P's inventory on December 31? On this point the authors prefer a negative answer.

Does Intercompany Profit Affect Minority Interest? Let us return to the example in which the parent's ending inventory included $2,000 of merchandise acquired from its 90%-owned subsidiary, which had cost only $1,200.

Assuming elimination from the asset account of the full $800 unrealized profit, which of the following alternatives is preferred?

1. The assignment of the entire $800 reduction to consolidated retained earnings.
2. The allocation of reduction between the consolidated retained earnings ($720) and the minority interest ($80).

There is impressive authority for the position that the minority interest should receive its share of the reduction produced by the 100% elimination of intercompany profit. Both the 1954 Committee on Accounting Concepts and Standards of the American Accounting Association [7] and the Institute's "unofficial answer" to a recent examination

[6] *ARB No. 51,* paragraph 4.
[7] See *The Accounting Review,* Vol. 3. No. 2 (April, 1955), p. 197.

question on the subject (May, 1969) have supported this alternative. This is consistent with the entity theory approach in that the unrealized profit is eliminated ratably from the two ownership classes of the subsidiary, which has recorded profit "prematurely."

Although explicit in favoring 100% elimination of intercompany gross profit, ARB No. 51 took a permissive position on the effect on minority interest: "The elimination of the intercompany profit or loss may be allocated proportionately between the minority and majority interests." There was no specific mention, much less prohibition, of the alternative approach, that is, assignment of the entire intercompany profit elimination to consolidated retained earnings. Certainly the candidate may be confident if he employs the allocation method.

When is Intercompany Profit Earned? For this question it is necessary to distinguish between assets held for sale and assets held for use. The first group is composed chiefly of inventories, and the test of realization from the point of view of the affiliated group is their sale to a nonaffiliated purchaser.

Intercompany profit on assets held for use arises most frequently when a subsidiary company constructs or manufactures plant assets for members of the affiliated group and sells such assets to a related company at a profit. In this situation also, realization would occur from the point of view of the affiliated group, should the asset be sold to an outsider. This may happen occasionally, but customarily plant assets are acquired for use. Under these circumstances, the realization of intercompany profit in plant assets is a continuous process coinciding with the utilization of the particular plant asset. Thus, given a use life of 12 years and an intercompany profit of $3,600, the passage of each year will be accompanied by a $300 reduction in the amount of unrealized intercompany profit.

Intercompany profit may also arise from transactions involving securities held as investments. Intercompany profit of this origin is similarly handled.

illustrative working papers for intercompany profit

In order to provide a complete example of working paper techniques involving intercompany profit eliminations, the series of illustrations used earlier in this chapter is extended. The candidate may wish to refer briefly to Illustration 3 for review.

You are given the following information. In the year 1973, Companies P and S again operated at the same general levels. No dividends were paid. However, there did occur some integration of operations: (1) Company S sold merchandise to Company P in the amount of $10,000 at an average gross profit of 40%, and (2) Company P manufactured (at a cost of $1,000) and sold (for $1,600) to Company S an item of equipment. The December 31, 1973, inventory of Company P included $2,000 of goods acquired from Company S. Company P owed $500 for a shipment from Company S dated December 27, 1973. Depreciation taken by Company S in 1973 on the above-mentioned equipment was $80.

Now refer to the information in Illustration 4 regarding 1973 operations of Companies P and S and assume that consolidated working papers for the full complement of financial statements are required.

Adjustments and Eliminations

(a) Liabilities	500	
Receivables		500
Amount owed by Company P on December 27, 1973, purchase from subsidiary.		
(b) Sales	10,000	
Inventories		800
Cost of sales		9,200
Intercompany sales, unrealized intercompany profit on goods purchased from Company S which remain in Company P's inventory, and cost of goods sold by P which had been acquired from S.		

The consolidated income statement should include only sales to outside parties. Similarly, consolidated cost of sales should measure the original cost to the consolidated group of goods sold during the period to outside parties.

	Total	*Subsequently Sold by P*	*In P's 12/31/73 Inventory*
Sold by Company S to Company P	$10,000	$8,000	$2,000
Original cost to Company S (40% markup)	6,000	4,800	1,200
Unrealized intercompany profit			$ 800

The $9,200 elimination may be computed in either of the two following ways:

Total recorded cost of sales by Company S	$ 6,000
Total recorded cost of sales by Company P	8,000
	$14,000
Original cost of completed sales to outside parties (see above)	4,800
To be eliminated	$ 9,200

or

Superfluous cost recorded for completed sales to "outsiders"	$ 8,000
Cost of sales recorded relative to goods not yet sold to outside parties	1,200
To be eliminated	$ 9,200

(c) Sales	1,600	
Fixed assets		600
Cost of sales		1,000

Intercompany profit on fixed assets sold by Company P to its subsidiary.

The sale having been made this period, the profit resides in the two nominal accounts which are adjusted to eliminate the effects of the intragroup transaction.

(d) Accumulated depreciation	30	
Operating expenses		30

Intercompany profit element in accumulated depreciation and in operating expenses. Intercompany profit element in accumulated depreciation is three-eighths [intercompany profit ($600) divided by selling price ($1,600)] of $80.

(e) Common stock—Company S	54,000	
Retained earnings—Company S	27,000	
Investment in Company S		67,500
Retained earnings—Company P		13,500

Parent's 90% interest in subsidiary.

The amount added to parent company (and thus consolidated) retained earnings to balance the elimination represents the parent's 90% share of the realized increase in the retained earnings of Company S from acquisition date to the beginning of the current year, January 1, 1973, that is, 90% of $30,000 – $15,000.

A key factor in Illustration 4 is the determination of the minority stockholders' share in the income of the subsidiary. The minority interest should be increased by its share of the subsidiary's net income which has been realized by the consolidated group, and the same amount should be deducted in arriving at consolidated net income. In Illustration 4, the subsidiary had a profit in 1973 of $7,920 (sales, $40,000, less cost of sales, $12,000, and operating expenses, $20,080). However, that amount includes the $800 of unrealized intercompany profit in inventory, eliminated in full by entry (b). Thus, to effect the allocation of part of the intercompany profit elimination to the minority interest, 10% of only $7,120 ($7,920 minus $800) is credited to minority interest. The unrealized profit in the

ILLUSTRATION 4

COMPANY P AND SUBSIDIARY COMPANY S

CONSOLIDATED STATEMENT WORKING PAPERS
FOR THE YEAR ENDED DECEMBER 31, 1973

	Company P	Company S	Adjustments and Eliminations		Consolidated Income Statement	Consolidated Retained Earnings	Consolidated Balance Sheet
			Debit	Credit			
Cash	55,900	31,400					87,300
Receivables	30,000	20,000		(a) 500			49,500
Inventories	35,000	24,000		(b) 800			58,200
Investment in Company S	72,500			(e) 67,500			5,000 (G)
Fixed assets (net)	45,000	37,520	(d) 30	(c) 600			81,950
Cost of sales	50,000	12,000		(b) 9,200 (c) 1,000	(51,800)		
Operating expenses	40,000	20,080		(d) 30	(60,050)		
	328,400	145,000					281,950
Liabilities	25,000	15,000	(a) 500				39,500
Common stock:							
Company P	150,000						150,000
Company S		60,000	(e) 54,000				6,000 (M)
Retained earnings (January 1):							
Company P	53,400			(e) 13,500		66,900	
Company S		30,000	(e) 27,000				3,000 (M)
Sales	100,000	40,000	(b) 10,000 (c) 1,600		128,400		
	328,400	145,000	93,130	93,130	16,550		
Minority interest in Company S net income—10% of ($40,000 – $12,000 – $20,080 – $800)					(712)		712 (M)
Consolidated net income					15,838	15,838	
Consolidated retained earnings						82,738	82,738
							281,950

depreciable asset is not involved in this computation because the parent, not the subsidiary, made the sale.

Beginning-of-Period Intercompany Profit. The preceding elimination of intercompany sales, cost of goods sold, and gross profit in ending inventory would have been more complex if there had been intercompany gross profit in the beginning inventory as well. To illustrate this added difficulty, let us carry the data in Illustration 4 forward one more year, concentrating on intercompany sales of merchandise.

Recall that on December 31, 1973, there was $800 of unrealized intercompany profit in the ending inventory. Now assume that, during 1974, Company S sold $12,000 of merchandise to Company P, and the price reflected an average gross profit of 33.3% of selling price. The year-end (December 31, 1974) inventory includes $900 of goods acquired by P from S, the entire amount having been shipped during the current year.

The December 31, 1974 elimination would be as follows (assume that the intercompany profit elimination is allocated in part to minority interests):

	Company P	*Company S*	*Adjustments and Eliminations*	
			Debit	*Credit*
Inventories	35,000	24,000		300
Cost of sales	55,000	14,000		12,500
Operating expenses	42,000	22,000		
Retained earnings (January 1):				
Company P	63,400			
Company S		37,920	800	
Sales	110,000	45,000	12,000	

The elimination may be analyzed thus. Starting with the more obvious point, the $12,000 sale by Company S to Company P was not a sale to outside parties—except as resold by the parent and included in its sales. Intercompany profit in ending inventory, $300, is eliminated. Next, recall that beginning-of-year balances of consolidated retained earnings and of minority interest were affected by eliminations for the December 31, 1973, intercompany profit in inventory, although these eliminations were made only in the working papers (see Illustration 4) and not in the accounts of the respective companies. The $800 amount was an element of the subsidiary's profit and was subtracted from it, with the result that 10% of the $800 elimination affected the minority interest and the remaining 90% affected consolidated retained earnings. To reintroduce this elimination into the 1974 working papers, the beginning-of-year intercompany profit is eliminated from the retained earnings where it resides—those of the subsidiary. The subsequent 90% elimination of the beginning-of-year stockholders' equity of Company S will then bring about the proper allocation.

The $12,500 credit to cost of goods sold may appear to be a mere remainder, and under examination conditions it probably should be just "plugged." It may be explained, however:

1. The $2,000 of goods in the beginning inventory acquired by Company P from Company S was charged to cost of goods sold during this year; the cost to Company S (and to the consolidated group), however, was only $1,200. Overstatement of consolidated cost of sales equals	$ 800
2. During the year, Company S sales to Company P were $12,000, of which Company P subsequently sold $11,100 (original cost to Company S was $7,400); the total recorded cost of goods sold (Company S's $8,000 and Company P's $11,100), overstates the $7,400 cost to the consolidated entity by	11,700
Total	$12,500

Finally, the $300 intercompany profit should be subtracted from Company S's book income in determining the amount of the minority interest's share in current earnings.

Incidentally, the minority interest in the 1974 earnings of the subsidiary would be computed as follows:

Net income of subsidiary—per books	$9,000
Add unrealized intercompany profit existing at the beginning of the year	800
Total	$9,800
Deduct unrealized intercompany profit existing at the end of the year	300
Adjusted net income (i.e., realized from consolidated entity point of view)	$9,500
Minority interest	10%
Minority interest in 1974 earnings of subsidiary	$ 950

Intercompany Profit—Change in Percentage of Control. If there has been a change in the percentage of control exercised by the parent, and if there remains some unrealized intercompany profit on assets acquired from the subsidiary during a prior period, how should the unrealized profit be allocated between the parent and the minority interest? (Assume, of course, that the accountant has been following the practice of allocation.)

The following guideline has support. Assign to the minority the percentage equal to its interest at the time of the intercompany transaction, or the new percentage, whichever is higher. Thus, if the minority interest has declined from 20% to 10%, the 20% rate would continue to apply to any unrealized intercompany profit traceable to sales made by the subsidiary in prior periods.

illustrative working papers—balance sheet alone

Illustrations 2 through 4 have dealt with postacquisition situations in which data for the full set of consolidated financial statements (i.e., income statement, statement of retained earnings, and statement of financial position) were presented. This approach to the present review of consolidated statement working papers has been used because it is complete. However, actual CPA examination problems have quite often called for only the consolidated balance sheet.[8]

To show the similarities and differences when working with balance sheet data only, Illustration 4—B/S takes the same basic facts used in Illustration 4. The only change is that the revenue and expense accounts have been closed and the balance of the two firms' retained earnings accounts represent the year-end amounts, rather than those of the beginning of the year. The working papers and adjusting entries would appear as follows.

Adjustments and Eliminations

(a) Liabilities	500	
Receivables		500
Amount owed by Company P on December 27, 1973 purchase from subsidiary.		
(b) Retained earnings—Company S	800	
Inventories		800
Unrealized intercompany profit (40% of $2,000) on goods purchased from Company S which remain in Company P's inventory.		

By removing the intercompany profit from the retained earnings which benefited from the intercompany sale (i.e., the retained earnings of Company S, the seller) the reduction for the intercompany profit is allocated between the consolidated retained earnings and the minority interest. Such allocation becomes apparent by noting that the $3,712 extended to the Minority Interest column is $80 (10% of $800) less than it

[8] As of this writing, good recent examples are No. 5 (May, 1969—Practice II) and No. 4 (May, 1970—Practice I).

ILLUSTRATION 4—B/S

COMPANY P AND SUBSIDIARY COMPANY S

CONSOLIDATED BALANCE SHEET WORKING PAPERS
DECEMBER 31, 1973

	Company P	Company S	Adjustments and Eliminations		Minority Interest	Consolidated Balance Sheet
			Debit	Credit		
Cash	55,900	31,400				87,300
Receivables	30,000	20,000		(a) 500		49,500
Inventories	35,000	24,000		(b) 800		58,200
Investment in Company S	72,500			(e) 67,500		5,000 (G)
Fixed assets (net)	45,000	37,520	(d) 30	(c) 600		81,950
	238,400	112,920				281,950
Liabilities	25,000	15,000	(a) 500			39,500
Common stock:						
Company P	150,000					150,000
Company S		60,000	(e) 54,000		6,000	
Retained earnings (December 31):						
Company P	63,400		(c) 600	(d) 30 (e) 19,908		82,738
Company S		37,920	(b) 800 (e) 33,408		3,712	
					9,712	9,712 (M)
	238,400	112,920	89,338	89,338		281,950

would have been if the $800 had been assigned to the retained earnings of the parent company.

(c) Retained earnings—Company P	600	
Fixed assets		600

Intercompany profit on fixed asset sold by Company P to its subsidiary.

Such profit resides in the retained earnings of the parent, hence it is appropriate that the $600 is debited to Company P's retained earnings.

(d) Accumulated depreciation	30	
Retained earnings—Company P		30

Intercompany profit element in accumulated depreciation is three-eighths [intercompany profit ($600) divided by selling price ($1,600)] of $80.

Eliminations (c) and (d) might well be handled as one. As shown, first the $600 gross profit is removed from the fixed asset account as well as from the retained earnings of Company P, the seller. Thus the asset is reduced to cost to the consolidated group. Next, the accumulated depreciation is reduced to the same cost basis by removing the depreciation on the intercompany profit element. Thus the net amount of unrealized intercompany profit is $570 as of December 31, 1973.

Because the parent made the sale, there was no question of allocating the elimination between the controlling and minority interests.

(e) Common stock—Company S	54,000	
Retained earnings—Company S [90% of ($37,920 – $800)]	33,408	
Investment in Company S		67,500
Retained earnings—Company P		19,908

Parent's 90% interest in subsidiary.

The amount added to parent-company retained earnings to balance the elimination represents the parent's 90% share of the increase in the retained earnings of Company S, after adjustments have been made for the unrealized intercompany profit, from acquisition date to December 31, 1973.

Retained earnings of Company S	$37,920
Elimination (b)	800
Balance	$37,120
Retained earnings of Company S at acquisition	15,000
Increase since acquisition	$22,120
Parent's share	90%
Increment to consolidated retained earnings	$19,908

intercompany bonds and interest

A very common feature of consolidated problems is the purchase of the bonds of one of the affiliated companies by another member of the affiliation. Usually the elimination of intercompany obligations is perfectly straightforward because the amounts requiring elimination have been produced by transactions between related companies *directly*. Hence the dollar amounts involved are equivalent. For example, suppose that the parent corporation purchases directly from its subsidiary an entire 6% bond issue (maturing in ten years) of the subsidiary at a five-point discount. The related entries for the example are as follows:

Parent's Books			*Subsidiary's Books*		
Investment—Bonds of S Co.	95,000		Cash	95,000	
Cash		95,000	Bond discount	5,000	
			Bonds payable		100,000

If consolidated statements were prepared as of the bond-issuance date, the following elimination entry should be made on the working papers:

Bonds payable	100,000	
Bond discount		5,000
Investment—Bonds of S Co.		95,000

One year later, provided that the companies have adopted a policy of straight-line amortization, the elimination entry to be made on the consolidated balance sheet working papers would be as follows:

Bonds payable	100,000	
Bond discount		4,500
Investment—Bonds of S Co.		95,500

If the full set of consolidated statements were called for, an entry in addition to the preceding one would be required to eliminate the intercompany interest from the consolidated income statement:

Interest income (parent's books)	6,500	
Interest expense (subsidiary's books)		6,500

The $6,500 represents the $6,000 cash interest plus the $500 discount amortization for the year.

Of course, if either company fails to amortize the bond discount, or if different amortization policies are adopted by the companies, an adjusting entry on the working papers must be made to bring the intercompany accounts into the necessary agreement to permit their elimination. Suppose, for example, that the parent corporation fails to adjust its bond investment account for periodic amortization. In this event, the related accounts would appear as listed on the following partial working papers prepared one year after the bond purchase transaction. Because the parent corporation has failed to amortize the bond discount, the working paper adjusting entry keyed as (1) is a necessary prerequisite to elimination (a).

Debits	*P Co.*	*S Co.*	*Adjustments and Eliminations*		*Con-solidated*
Investment—Bonds of S Co.	95,000		(1) 500	(a) 95,500	
Bond discount		4,500		(a) 4,500	
Interest expense		6,500		(b) 6,500	
Credits					
Bonds payable		100,000	(a) 100,000		
Interest income	6,000		(b) 6,500	(1) 500	

In order to achieve adequate disclosure, it may be desirable to present the "eliminated" bonds on the consolidated balance sheet in a contra fashion. For instance, where all or a portion of a bond issue is held internally (i.e., within the family of related corporations), the consolidated balance sheet would convey more information by showing the internally held bonds as a deduction from bonds payable in much the same fashion as treasury bonds may be presented.

Long-term liabilities:		
Bonds, 4%, due in 1995	$300,000	
Less: Bonds held by subsidiary companies	120,000	$180,000

The writers believe that this contra treatment should be favored only if the amounts involved are substantial and if the obligations held are reasonably negotiable. A contra treatment would hardly be warranted for ordinary receivables and payables.

Thus far the discussion on the elimination of intercompany bonds and interest has dealt with accounts created by direct transactions between two related companies. The problem can become more complicated when the intercompany items were acquired indirectly or circuitously. Let us assume that on January 1, 1963, a wholly owned subsidiary, Subco, issued $200,000 of ten-year, 4% bonds at face value. On January 1, 1970, three years before maturity, the parent company, Parco, purchased $150,000 (face value) of these bonds in the open market at 98. Under these conditions the intercompany accounts were not stated on a comparable basis. That is, whereas Parco's investment in bonds is shown (at acquisition date) at cost, $147,000, the same securities are carried by Subco at a book value of $150,000.

If a consolidated balance sheet were prepared just after the bond acquisition, the elimination entry would be handled as though there had been a prematurity retirement of a portion of a bonded debt; and this, from the viewpoint of the overall consolidated group, was the case. The following partial working papers illustrate the required adjustment and elimination as of the bond acquisition date.

ILLUSTRATION 5A

PARTIAL BALANCE SHEET WORKING PAPERS
AS OF JANUARY 1, 1970
(THE DATE OF THE INTERCOMPANY BOND ACQUISITION)

Debits	*Parco*	*Subco*	*Adjustments and Eliminations*		*Consolidated*
Investment—Bonds of Subco	147,000		(1) 3,000	(a) 150,000	
Credits					
Bonds payable		200,000	(a) 150,000		50,000
Retained earnings of purchasing company (Gain from acquisition of bonds)	xxxx			(1) 3,000	xxxx

The $3,000 debit adjusts the bonds held as an investment to their face amount, thus facilitating their elimination; the companion credit may be viewed as a gain from the "retirement" of the bonds, $147,000 cash having been used to "retire" a book liability of $150,000.

If a full set of statements for the year ended December 31, 1970, is called for, the $3,000 gain would appear in the consolidated income statement. Of course, the intercompany interest must be eliminated. In this connection, the partial working papers in Illustration 5B reveal that the interest amounts for 1970 relating to the intercompany-held bonds differ by $1,000; the interest expense applicable to such bonds is $6,000, but the interest income is $7,000. Such difference is caused by the amortization on Parco's books of one year's portion of the bond discount.

ILLUSTRATION 5B

PARTIAL WORKING PAPERS
FOR THE YEAR ENDED DECEMBER 31, 1970
(FIRST YEAR AFTER BOND ACQUISITION)

Debits	*Parco*	*Subco*	*Adjustments and Eliminations*		*Consolidated*
Investment—Bonds of Subco	148,000		(1) 2,000	(a) 150,000	
Interest expense		8,000		(b) 6,000	2,000
Credits					
Bonds payable		200,000	(a) 150,000		50,000
Interest income	7,000		{(1) 1,000 {(b) 6,000		
Gain from acquisition of bonds				(1) 3,000	3,000

For the sake of completeness, let us carry the illustration forward one more year.

ILLUSTRATION 5C

PARTIAL WORKING PAPERS
FOR THE YEAR ENDED DECEMBER 31, 1971
(SECOND YEAR AFTER BOND ACQUISITION)

Debits	*Parco*	*Subco*	*Adjustments and Eliminations*		*Consolidated*
Investment—Bonds of Subco	149,000		(1) 1,000	(a) 150,000	
Interest expense		8,000		(b) 6,000	2,000
Credits					
Bonds payable		200,000	(a) 150,000		50,000
Interest income	7,000		{(1) 1,000 {(b) 6,000		
Retained earnings of Parco—beginning of year	xxxx			(1) 2,000	xxxx

Perhaps only the $2,000 credit to the beginning-of-year retained earnings of Parco needs explanation.

Gain from acquisition of bonds—shown on the 1970 consolidated income statement	$3,000
The gain appeared only in the consolidated working papers and statements for 1970 and has not "reached" the retained earnings account on Parco's books.	
Deduct the discount amortization taken into income by Parco in the years prior to 1971	1,000
This amount has reached the retained earnings account on Parco's books.	
Adjustment of beginning-of-year retained earnings of purchasing company	$2,000

At the end of next year, 1972, the credit adjustment to the beginning-of-year retained earnings of Parco would amount to $1,000.

The problem becomes slightly more involved if the bonds were issued originally at either a premium or a discount. In that event, the proportionate share of issuance premium or discount must be eliminated, along with the face value of the bonds internally held. To illustrate, suppose that the ten-year bonds in the preceding example were issued at 98 and acquired, as in that example, seven years later at 98. Again, the working paper eliminations are handled as if a bond retirement situation existed. The $2,100 net credit to Retained Earnings may be viewed as a gain from the "retirement" of the bonds, $147,000 cash having been used to "retire" a book liability of $149,100 ($150,000 face value less $900, the unamortized issuance discount applicable to acquired bonds).

ILLUSTRATION 6A

PARTIAL BALANCE SHEET WORKING PAPERS
AS OF JANUARY 1, 1970
(THE DATE OF THE INTERCOMPANY BOND ACQUISITION)

Debits	*Parco*	*Subco*	*Adjustments and Eliminations*		*Consolidated*
Investment—Bonds of Subco	147,000		(1) 3,000	(a) 150,000	
Discount on bonds . . .		1,200		(2) 900	300
Credits					
Bonds payable		200,000	(a) 150,000		50,000
Retained earnings:					
Of purchasing company	xxxx			(1) 3,000	xxxx
Of issuing company .		xxxx	(2) 900		

If the full complement of statements for the year of acquisition is called for, the following partial working papers indicate the required adjustments and eliminations.

ILLUSTRATION 6B

PARTIAL WORKING PAPERS
FOR THE YEAR ENDED DECEMBER 31, 1970
(FIRST YEAR AFTER BOND ACQUISITION)

Debit	*Parco*	*Subco*	*Adjustments and Eliminations*		*Consolidated*
Investment—Bonds of Subco	148,000		(1) 2,000	(a) 150,000	
Discount on bonds		800		(1) 600	200
Interest expense		8,400		(1) 300	2,100
				(b) 6,000	
Credits					
Bonds payable		200,000	(a) 150,000		50,000
Interest income	7,000		(1) 1,000		
			(b) 6,000		
Gain from acquisition of bonds				(1) 2,100	2,100

Completing the series of illustrations, the adjustments and eliminations as of December 31, 1971 (analogous to Illustration 5C), would be:

ILLUSTRATION 6C

PARTIAL WORKING PAPERS
FOR THE YEAR ENDED DECEMBER 31, 1971
(SECOND YEAR AFTER BOND ACQUISITION)

Debits	*Parco*	*Subco*	*Adjustments and Eliminations*		*Consolidated*
Investment—Bonds of Subco	149,000		(1) 1,000	(a) 150,000	
Discount on bonds		400		(2) 300	100
Interest expense		8,400		(2) 300	2,100
				(b) 6,000	
Credits					
Bonds payable		200,000	(a) 150,000		50,000
Interest income	7,000		(1) 1,000		
			(b) 6,000		
Retained earnings, beginning of year:					
Parco	xxxx			(1) 2,000	xxxx
Subco		xxxx	(2) 600		

(1) Discount elements in accounts of Parco relating to bond purchase.
(2) Discount elements in accounts of Subco applicable to intercompany-held bonds.
(a) Elimination of intercompany-held bonds.
(b) Elimination of cash interest on intercompany-held bonds.

Thus far the question of the effect of intercompany bond holdings on minority interest has been avoided. If there is a minority interest in the purchasing company, and if the intercompany bonds are purchased for an amount other than face value, the minority interest will be affected to the extent of its share of the purchase premium or purchase discount. For example, assume that a 90%-owned subsidiary purchases from outsiders $150,000 face value of its parent's bonds for $147,000. The bonds mature in three years and carry an interest rate of 4%. Thus the income to the subsidiary from its investment in parent-company bonds will be as follows:

	Year			
	1	*2*	*3*	*Total*
Cash interest—$150,000 × 4%	$6,000	$6,000	$6,000	$18,000
Amortization of discount	1,000	1,000	1,000	3,000
Interest income	$7,000	$7,000	$7,000	$21,000

For the three-year period, the share applicable to the 10% minority interest amounts to $2,100. However, two different methods may be used in making the annual computation for the minority's interest in the net income of the subsidiary, which amount is deducted in arriving at consolidated net income.

Method 1 Apply the minority's percentage to the income of the subsidiary as reported. In effect this would credit the minority interest with $700 per year as a result of the investment in intercompany bonds.

Method 2 Apply the minority's percentage to:

a. The total purchase discount or premium on the intercompany bonds in the year of acquisition;

b. The cash income from the bond investment.

The consequences of these methods can be noted as follows:

	Year			
	1	*2*	*3*	*Total*
Minority interest in income from investment in intercompany bonds:				
Method 1:				
10% of book income	$700	$700	$700	$2,100
Method 2:				
10% of purchase discount	$300			
10% of cash income	600	$600	$600	
	$900	$600	$600	$2,100

Both methods are acceptable. However, method 2 is probably more compatible with the theory that allocates to minority interest its share of any gain or loss whenever recognized for consolidated statement purposes.

ILLUSTRATION OF DETERMINATION OF CONSOLIDATED NET INCOME UNDER BOTH METHODS

Data: $150,000 of parent's bonds purchased by 90%-owned subsidiary three years before maturity at a $3,000 discount.
Bonds issued by parent at face value.
Date of acquisition—December 31, 1973.
Annual net income per books:

Parent	$20,000
Subsidiary	10,000

		Deduction for Minority Interest	*Consolidated Net Income* — *Method* *1*	*2*
1973 net income per books:				
Parent	$20,000			
Subsidiary	10,000			
Gain from acquisition of bonds	3,000			
Total	$33,000			
Deduct minority interest:				
Method 1:				
10% of $10,000 (book income of subsidiary)		$1,000	$ 32,000	
Method 2:				
10% of $13,000 (net income of subsidiary plus the $3,000 of purchase discount)		1,300		$ 31,700
1974 net income per books:				
Parent	$20,000			
Subsidiary (which includes cash income from the bond investment plus $1,000 of discount amortization)	10,000			
Total book income	$30,000			
Effect of elimination of cash interest on intercompany-held bonds:				
On parent's net income	+6,000			
On subsidiary's net income	−6,000			
Effect of elimination of amortization element in subsidiary's interest income account	−1,000			
Total (forward)	$29,000			

Total (forwarded)	$29,000		
Deduct minority interest:			
Method 1:			
10% of $10,000		1,000	28,000	
Method 2:			
10% of $9,000 (net income of subsidiary minus the discount amortization)		900		28,100
1975—Same as 1974			28,000	28,100
1976—Same as 1974 and 1975			28,000	28,100
The bonds matured during 1976.				
Total consolidated net income for period during which intercompany bonds were held as an investment			$116,000	$116,000

Note that in 1973, the year of bond acquisition, under method 1 the entire $3,000 gain is included in consolidated net income with no effect on minority interest. Under method 2, however, the minority interest receives its 10% share. This is accomplished by including in the "deduction for minority interest" the minority's $300 share of the gain. Thus, although the full $3,000 will appear as a gain in the statement of consolidated income for 1973, $300 is allocated (immediately rather than over the years 1974–1976) to the equity of the minority owners, with only the $2,700 remainder flowing to consolidated retained earnings.

Under method 2, for 1974–1976, the $1,000 of discount amortization should be deducted from the subsidiary's earnings before the minority interest is computed. Because under method 2 the minority interest is credited for its share of the $3,000 purchase discount (the gain from the acquisition of bonds) when the bonds are acquired, duplication would result if the minority interest were to receive credit again when the discount was amortized.

Thus the difference between methods 1 and 2 is only a matter of timing. As noted earlier, both procedures are acceptable and apparently the candidate can take his choice. However, the candidate is encouraged to make a footnote reference to the method not selected. This would serve to notify the examiner that the candidate was aware of the alternative and that his choice was made for purposes of the solution of the particular problem in question.

"consolidated goodwill"

Questions of Theory. Most of the consolidated statement problems used by the AICPA Board of Examiners have featured a difference between the book value of the parent's equity in the subsidiary's net assets and cost to the parent of its investment in the securities of the subsidiary.

Such was the case in the series of illustrations earlier in this chapter. There it was assumed that Company P acquired 90% of the outstanding stock of Company S for $72,500. The difference, termed there "consolidated goodwill," was derived as follows:

Cost of investment in Company S		$72,500
Stockholders' equity of Company S at acquisition:		
Common stock	$60,000	
Retained earnings	15,000	
Total	$75,000	
Acquired by Company P	90%	
Equity (book value) acquired		67,500
Excess of cost over equity acquired		$ 5,000

If the acquisition price in the preceding illustration had been $62,500, a "negative difference," excess of equity acquired over cost of investment, would have appeared. The difference, either positive or negative, arises only in the consolidation process. It does not appear on the individual financial statements of either the parent corporation or the subsidiary corporation.

To this point, the examples and discussion have had three characteristics: (a) they have simply labeled as "goodwill" the cost–book value difference (at acquisition date), (b) they have assumed that the resulting amount would continue to appear in successive consolidated balance sheets, and (c) they have assumed that the parent pays cash for the subsidiary's shares, leaving no doubt about the measurement of the investment. This was useful for purposes of introduction, but quite simplified.

Regarding item (a), a parent company's cost may exceed the book value acquired for two primary reasons: certain assets may be understated or omitted on the subsidiary's books, or alternatively, the subsidiary may have a favorable earnings potential not reflected in the book values of the individual assets. In the first case, it is preferable to identify the excess with specific, undervalued assets and thus to adjust, for consolidated statement purposes, the subsidiary's assets. In the second case (when cost exceeds the fair value of the individual assets), the excess payment is for an anticipated stream of superior profits, expected to result from such factors as loyal customers, superior management, established trade position, and so forth, which accountants have long and reasonably labeled "goodwill." As stated by the Accounting Principles Board in Opinion 16:

> First, all identifiable assets acquired, either individually or by type, and liabilties assumed in a business combination, whether or

not shown in the financial statements of the acquired company, should be assigned a portion of the cost of the acquired company, normally equal to their fair values at date of acquisition.

Second, the excess of the cost of the acquired company over the sum of the amounts assigned to identifiable assets acquired less liabilities assumed should be recorded as goodwill.[9]

To illustrate, assume that Parco has paid $189,000 for 90% of Subco's net assets, which have a total book value of $160,000. There is, however, sufficient evidence that their fair value is $200,000, the difference being due to "undervaluation" of depreciable assets. In summary:

	100%	*90%*
Net book value	$160,000	$144,000
Net fair value of identifiable assets	200,000	180,000
Cost of investment		189,000

If a consolidated balance sheet were to be prepared as of acquisition date, the following working paper elimination is indicated:

Debits	*Parco*	*Subco*	*Adjustments and Eliminations*		*Consolidated*
Investment in Subco . .	189,000			180,000	9,000 (G)
Fixed assets (net)	120,000	160,000	36,000		316,000
Credits					
Common stock		60,000	54,000		6,000 (M)
Retained earnings		100,000	90,000		10,000 (M)

The $45,000 excess ($189,000 − $144,000) is thereby allocated, $36,000 as fixed asset adjustment and $9,000 as goodwill. Notice that the $36,000 ($180,000 − $144,000) fixed asset adjustment, and the goodwill as well, occur only in the working papers, not in the accounts of Subco.

After acquisition date, the adjustment also affects expenses, and thus the determination of consolidated net income, as illustrated by carrying the preceding example forward to the end of the first year (assume a ten-year life for the Subco assets):

Debits	*Parco*	*Subco*	*Adjustments and Eliminations*		*Consolidated*
Investment in Subco . .	189,000			180,000	9,000 (G)
Fixed assets (net)	110,000	144,000	32,400		286,400
Depreciation expense .	10,000	16,000	3,600		29,600
Credits					
Common stock		60,000	54,000		6,000 (M)
Retained earnings, beginning of year		100,000	90,000		10,000 (M)

[9] Paragraph 87.

Regarding item (b), amortization of consolidated goodwill, APB Opinion 17 states:

> The Board believes that the value of intangible assets at any one date eventually disappears and that the recorded costs of intangible assets should be amortized by systematic charges to income over the periods estimated to be benefitted. . . . The straight-line method of amortization . . . should be applied . . . [normally, over] . . . a reasonable estimate of the useful life . . . [which] . . . should not, however, exceed forty years. The cost . . . should not be written off in the period of acquisition.[10]

Consolidated goodwill, a purchased intangible asset, thus must be amortized. Indeed, goodwill amortization has appeared in CPA problems for many years. To illustrate, let us extend the example just given, assuming that the goodwill is to be amortized over a nine-year period. The annual charge of $1,000 must be deducted in arriving at consolidated net income. This could be done in the parent's books, amortizing the investment account by a charge to parent company (and thus consolidated) income. Alternatively, if the amortization policy were to be handled through the consolidated working papers, adjusting entries like the following would be made in the Adjustments and Eliminations columns (in addition to entries of the type illustrated just previously).

	Year					
	1		*2*		*3*	
Parco (consolidated) retained earnings, beginning of year			1,000		2,000	
Amortization of goodwill (shown among the expenses in the consolidated income statement)	1,000		1,000		1,000	
Investment in Subco (reducing the amount extended to the Consolidated column as unamortized goodwill)		1,000		2,000		3,000

Regarding item (c), determination of the parent's cost, most examination questions to date (other than those involving poolings of interest) have assumed cash payment. Yet the medium of payment may be shares of the parent's own stock or its bonds. Where the consideration is not cash, Opinion 16 has reaffirmed the prevailing theory that cost is measured by the fair value of the parent's stock (or other consideration) given or by the fair value of the equity (subsidiary's net assets, including any goodwill) acquired, whichever is more determinable.[11] The candidate may

[10] Paragraphs 27–30.

[11] Paragraph 67. Also, paragraphs 74 and 75.

expect that the appropriate measure will be fairly obvious in a complete working paper problem; however, a theory question could require familiarity with this matter.

Entity Theory. In relation to less-than-wholly-owned subsidiaries, it may be suggested that, theoretically, if a parent is willing to pay more than book value for its equity in net assets, it is illogical to do something that has the effect of revaluing the subsidiary's assets only partially. To illustrate, note that in our example the consolidated balance will include the subsidiary's fixed assets at $196,000, although their fair value is $200,000. Furthermore, it could be argued that if $189,000 were paid for a 90% equity, the total value of the going concern must be $210,000 ($189,000 divided by 0.90); that is, $200,000 of identifiable assets and $10,000 goodwill. Under this "entity theory" approach, the working paper elimination as of acquisition date would be as follows (note the contrast with the first example, p. 381):

Debits	*Parco*	*Subco*	*Adjustments and Eliminations*		*Consolidated*
Investment in Subco . .	189,000			(b) 189,000	
Fixed assets (net)	120,000	160,000	(a) 40,000		320,000
Goodwill			(a) 10,000		10,000 (G)
Credits					
Common stock		60,000	(b) 54,000		6,000 (M)
Retained earnings		100,000	(b) 135,000	(a) 50,000	15,000 (M)

Entry (a) in effect revalues Subco to current fair values. Entry (b) merely eliminates 90% of the equity, as revalued. Note that the additional $4,000 assigned to fixed assets and $1,000 goodwill are all reflected in minority interest. The minority's $21,000 here (10% of total fair value) contrasts with $16,000 (10% of book value) in the first example.

The candidate should recognize this argument, although he is not likely to encounter the entity theory approach in a complete working paper problem. It is obviously a more complex procedure. Yet partial (parent's share only) adjustment of book values does seem inconsistent with the fundamental assumption that the several firms are one economic entity. The concept of entity versus proprietary theory is summarized in a later section.

"Negative Goodwill." It is entirely possible that equity in a subsidiary may be acquired at a cost less than book value. "Negative goodwill" may be indicative of mediocre earnings prospects or of the overstatement of some of the subsidiary's assets. In the latter event, the approach discussed previously may be used by the accountant; the overstated assets should be reduced by an adjusting entry on the working papers.

In some cases, though, notably poor prospective earnings could produce a very low purchase cost. What if only part of the excess of book value over cost (a credit balance item) can be allocated to writing down specific assets to fair value? ARB No. 51 took the position that "the amount at which (the subsidiary's) net assets are carried in the consolidated statements should not exceed the parent's cost." [12] Thus it advocated treating the unallocated credit balance, the "true" negative goodwill, as a blanket valuation reserve and accordingly deducted from total assets.

Opinion 16, the current "official" position, has amended that treatment slightly. As before, all the subsidiary's assets should be adjusted (presumably downward) to fair value. The remaining excess should then be arbitrarily allocated as further adjustments of the subsidiary's noncurrent assets. Then if unallocated excess should still remain, even after the noncurrent assets are reduced to zero value, that amount "should be classified as a deferred credit and should be amortized systematically to income. . . . No part of the excess of acquired net assets over cost should be added directly to stockholders' equity at the date of acquisition." [13]

goodwill—specific complications

Having considered theory relating to the proper disposition of the difference between cost and book value, let us turn now to some complications that can arise in the determination of that difference.

(1) Piecemeal Acquisitions. The computation of the cost–book value difference is complicated slightly whenever the investment is acquired by piecemeal acquisitions—particularly if the first acquisition gives the parent-to-be less than 51% voting control. This matter can be illustrated by the following data, which assume that G Company acquired 25% of the outstanding stock of K Company on January 1, 1971, and another 50% one year later.

	K Company—Total Book Value	*Percentage Acquired*	*Book Value Acquired*	*Cost of Investment*
January 1, 1971	$10,000	25	$2,500	$3,000
1971 income (no dividends)	2,000			
January 1, 1972	12,000	50	6,000	8,000

[12] *ARB No. 51,* paragraph 8.

[13] Paragraphs 87, 91, and 92. Negative goodwill is not very likely to be encountered in a working paper problem. However, it is a reasonable theory question, and candidates in the November, 1970, theory examination were asked: "The term 'goodwill' often appears in connection with business combinations. 1. What is goodwill? Explain. 2. What is 'negative' goodwill? Explain."

The question confronting the candidate is whether (a) the outlays are accumulated until control is achieved, with the sum of the outlays, \$11,000, being compared to the acquired book value at the date control is achieved, \$9,000 (75% of \$12,000), or (b) a computation for the difference should be undertaken at each purchase date, regardless of whether control is present (\$500 + \$2,000).

The latter step-by-step alternative is taken in the following January 1, 1972 elimination:

Debits	*G Company*	*K Company*	*Adjustments and Eliminations*		*Consolidated*
Investment in K Company	11,000			8,500	2,500 (G)
Credits					
K Company stockholders' equity (total)		12,000	9,000		3,000 (M)
G Company retained earnings ..		xx		500 *	

* Included in consolidated retained earnings, representing G Company's 25% share of K Company's undistributed 1971 income of \$2,000.

Under alternative (a), the entire \$9,000 credit would be against the investment, leaving \$2,000 extended as goodwill.

Apparently either approach is acceptable. ARB No. 51 states: "If small purchases are made over a period of time and then a purchase is made which results in control, the date of the latest purchase, as a matter of convenience, may be considered as the date of acquisition." However, the fundamental position of ARB No. 51 is that when "two or more purchases are made over a period of time, the earned surplus of the subsidiary at acquisition should generally be determined on a step-by-step basis." Published solutions have always followed that basis when a parent has added to its already controlling interest.

It may occur to the candidate that this illustration does not involve the entity theory approach; that is, there is no attempt to adjust the subsidiary's assets or minority interest to the value(s) implied by the parent company's purchase price(s) (cost). The process of following entity theory in piecemeal acquisitions can be quite complex and it is not likely that the candidate will be required to discuss it in the examination.

(2) Adjustments Before Computation. Although it is a relatively minor point, the candidate must be alert to detect the need for any adjustments or corrections that must precede the computation of the cost–book value difference. Perhaps the most common instance of this problem characteristic involves the stockholders' equity accounts of the just-acquired subsidiary, for some of these may need to be corrected or adjusted as a preliminary step in computing "consolidated goodwill."

Unless the subsidiary's stockholders' equity is correctly stated, the consolidated goodwill, being measured by the difference between the acquisition cost and the book value of the equity acquired, will be incorrect. The candidate needs cautioning on this matter, not because the accounting involved is particularly difficult, but because the information disclosing the necessary revision is typically presented in such a casual, incidental fashion. In other words, the design or arrangement of the problem data usually will not emphasize the necessity for any preliminary adjustments or revisions. This is demonstrated by the XYZ problem from a former CPA examination.

From the following information prepare:

(a) Consolidated work sheet.
(b) Statement of consolidated retained earnings for the year 1973.

DECEMBER 31, 1973

	Company X	*Company Y*	*Company Z*
Assets			
Sundry assets	$450,000	$400,000	$350,000
Investment in Company Y—90% (cost)	150,000		
Investment in Company Z—90%		130,000	
	$600,000	$530,000	$350,000
Liabilities and Stockholders' Equity			
Sundry liabilities	$300,000	$250,000	$200,000
Capital stock	200,000	150,000	100,000
Retained earnings—January 1, 1973	72,000	91,000	40,000
Net income—January 1, 1973 to June 30, 1973	20,000	20,000 *	30,000 *
Net income—July 1, 1973 to December 31, 1973	10,000	70,000	50,000
Dividends paid (December, 1973)	20,000 *	20,000 *	10,000 *
Dividends received from subsidiaries	18,000	9,000	
	$600,000	$530,000	$350,000

* An asterisk denotes a "red" figure.

On January 1, 1967, Company X purchased 80% of the stock of Company Y for $120,000. At that date Company Y had capital stock of $150,000 and retained earnings of $20,000. On *July 1, 1973,* Company X purchased an additional 10% interest in Company Y for $30,000.

On January 1, 1968, Company Y purchased 100% of the stock of Company Z for $150,000. At that date Company Z had capital stock of

$100,000 and retained earnings of $30,000. On June 30, 1973, Company Y sold 10% of Company Z for $20,000.

The need for preliminary adjustments arises as a result of the purchase by Company X of an additional 10% interest in Company Y. On the purchase date, July 1, 1973, the stockholders' equity of Company Y is listed at $221,000. Using this figure as a basis for determining the difference between cost and book value would be incorrect for two reasons: Y's accounts do not reflect Y's share of the net increase or decrease in stockholders' equity experienced by Company Z during the period subsequent to Y's investment in Z, and the sale by Company Y of 10% of its interest in Company Z was incorrectly handled, since the entire $20,000 proceeds were credited to the investment account. The following schedule reveals the required revisions that should precede the computation of the excess of cost over book value arising from the July 1, 1973, acquisition.

Stockholders' equity of Company Y—July 1, 1973—per books		$221,000
Adjustment for sale of 10% interest in Company Z:		
Proceeds from sale of June 30, 1973	$20,000	
Cost of the 10% interest sold	15,000	5,000
Y's 90% share of the net reduction in Z's stockholders' equity since acquisition		18,000 *
Adjusted stockholders' equity of Company Y		$208,000
Cost of 10% interest in Company Y		$ 30,000
10% of Y's adjusted stockholders' equity as of July 1, 1973		20,800
Additional excess of cost over book value acquired arising from the acquisition of an additional 10% interest in Company Y		$ 9,200

It is apparent from the preceding discussion that the difference between cost and book value can be correct only if there has been (a) a correct calculation of the subsidiary's stockholders' equity at the time of affiliation and (b) a correct determination of the share of the subsidiary's stockholders' equity assignable to the stock interest acquired by the parent corporation.

(3) Complex Capital Structures. No special problems arise in those cases in which the subsidiary has a simple capital structure with only one class of stock outstanding, because the entire stockholders' equity is assignable to that class. The determination of the share of the subsidiary's stockholders' equity assignable to the stock interest acquired by the parent can become complicated if the subsidiary has two or more classes of outstanding stock. If the subsidiary should have both preferred and common

stock outstanding, it is necessary to allocate the aggregate stockholders' equity to the several stockholder classes. Essentially it is a problem of computing the book value of the stock interest acquired by the parent. The calculation of book value must give due recognition to the particular preference features attaching to the preferred shares. Those preference features most relevant to the book value problem relate to rights regarding liquidation, dividends, and participation in earnings.

Many of our accounting concepts are based on the assumption that the business will continue to function as a going concern. This assumption, although theoretically acceptable, is somewhat unattractive in the case of book value computations. For reasons of expediency, book value per share is most conveniently defined as dissolution value of the share, assuming that all corporate assets can be liquidated at carrying value.

The many shades and varieties of preferred stock make it unwise to generalize in much detail regarding the calculation of book value. The basic issues involved can be illustrated by applying the following suggestions to a specific example:

1. If any dividends are in arrears on *cumulative* preferred stock, assign to the preferred stock an amount equal to the dividend arrearage.
2. If the preferred stock has a liquidation value in excess of par or stated value, assign to the preferred stock an amount equal to the liquidation preference.

CRISTINA COMPANY

STOCKHOLDERS' EQUITY OF SUBSIDIARY
DECEMBER 31, 1973

Preferred stock, \$100 par, 5% cumulative, \$105 upon liquidation, 10,000 shares authorized and outstanding (See Note)	\$1,000,000
Common stock, \$10 stated value, 200,000 shares authorized and outstanding	2,000,000
Additional paid-in capital	800,000
Reserve for sinking fund	40,000
Retained earnings	160,000
Total stockholders' equity	\$4,000,000

NOTE: **Arrears dividends on preferred stock aggregate \$100,000.**

On December 31, 1973, Corporation P acquires 150,000 shares of Cristina Company common stock for \$2,225,000 cash.

COMPUTATION OF EXCESS OF COST OVER BOOK VALUE

	Equity Assignable to	
	Preferred	*Common*
Par or stated value	$1,000,000	$2,000,000
Liquidation premium	50,000	
Dividends in arrears	100,000	
Retained earnings ($160,000 − $150,000)		10,000
Additional paid-in capital		800,000
Reserve for sinking fund		40,000
Total	$1,150,000	$2,850,000
Cost of 150,000 shares of Cristina Company common (75% interest)		$2,225,000
75% of stockholders' equity assignable to common equity		2,137,500
Excess of cost over book value acquired		$ 87,500

(4) *Acquisition of Preferred Shares.* Occasionally a parent corporation acquires an interest in the preferred stock, as well as in the common stock, of a subsidiary. Because most preferred shares carry no voting rights, or only conditional voting rights, acquisitions of preferred shares would not increase the percentage of control held by a parent in the usual case. Nevertheless, there are instances in which parent corporations own a portion of the preferred shares issued by a subsidiary. For that reason it should be noted that consolidated goodwill, positive or negative, can arise from an investment in preferred shares.

This was the case in the American Company problem when the parent acquired 50% of the preferred stock and 90% of the common stock of Banner Corporation. At acquisition date, Banner's retained earnings were $60,000 with no preferred dividends in arrears. The cost–book value differences were to be computed.

	Common	*Preferred*	*Combined*
Book value at acquisition:			
Stock at par	$200,000	$100,000	$300,000
Retained earnings	60,000		60,000
Total book value	$260,000	$100,000	$360,000
Book value acquired	$234,000	$ 50,000	$284,000
Cost of investment	195,000	55,000	250,000
Excess of book value over cost	$ 39,000	$ (5,000)	$ 34,000

Thereupon, according to APB Opinion No. 16 (paragraph 91) the "negative goodwill" would be assigned to identifiable assets wherever necessary to reduce them to fair value; any remainder would then be arbitrarily assigned to write down further the noncurrent assets (even to zero value), and if any amount still remains, "it should be classified as a deferred credit and amortized systematically to income."

(5) Direct Issues. In the vast majority of problems, the parent company's control is achieved through the purchase of *outstanding* shares of the subsidiary. In this way, the acquisition by the parent has no effect on the stockholders' equity accounts of the subsidiary. But it is perfectly possible for the parent to acquire its control or to supplement it by subscribing to new stock issues of the subsidiary or to purchase from the treasury shareholdings of the subsidiary. These alternatives must be carefully distinguished from the more typical case involving outstanding shares, because the stockholders' equity accounts of the subsidiary are directly affected by the transaction. This feature is mentioned at this point because although the method is unchanged, the computation of the difference between cost and book value appears to be more complicated.

The arrangements leading to direct issues have many variations, but the following example based on a CPA examination problem will serve to illustrate the point under discussion. The stockholders' equity of the subsidiary on December 31, 1973, was as follows:

Common stock, \$100 par value, 4,000 issued	\$400,000	
Deduct treasury stock, 500 shares, at par	50,000	\$350,000
Additional paid-in capital		74,300
Retained earnings		85,830
Stockholders' equity		\$510,130

At this time the parent corporation owned 3,000 shares of the subsidiary's stock, thus giving the parent a six-sevenths interest in the subsidiary. As of December 31, 1973, by agreement with the minority stockholders, the parent acquired for \$90,000 the 500 shares held in the treasury of the subsidiary. Thus the parent's interest was increased from six-sevenths to seven-eighths, and the excess of cost over book value associated with this direct acquisition would be computed as shown on page 391.

(6) Contingent Consideration.[14] In most problems, the amount of the parent's payment for a given equity in the subsidiary is settled as of acquisition date. However, business combination agreements can provide

[14] This section is based on APB Opinion 16, paragraphs 77–86.

	Before Treasury Stock Disposal	*After Treasury Stock Disposal*
Capital stock	$400,000.00	$400,000.00
Treasury stock	50,000.00 *	
Additional paid-in capital	74,300.00	114,300.00
Retained earnings	85,830.00	85,830.00
Stockholders' equity of subsidiary	$510,130.00	$600,130.00
Parent's interest in stockholders' equity	6/7	7/8
After treasury stock disposal		$525,113.75
Before treasury stock disposal	$437,254.28	437,254.28
Stockholders' equity acquired by outlay of $90,000 for treasury stock		$ 87,859.47
Cost to parent		90,000.00
Additional excess of cost over book value resulting from treasury stock acquisition		$ 2,140.53

* An asterisk denotes a "red" figure.

for the transfer of additional consideration, depending on events in the future. The issuance of financial statements, of course, cannot wait until such contingencies are resolved. Accordingly, APB Opinion 16 advises that the parent's investment be measured by the consideration given unconditionally as of acquisition date. In addition, there should be footnote disclosure of the type, amount, and terms of conditionally issuable consideration. (It would not be recorded as a liability or shown as outstanding securities.)

As the contingency later becomes determinable beyond reasonable doubt, the actual (or "accrued") transfer is recognized.

Opinion 16 recognizes contingencies of two general types—those which depend on subsequent earnings and those based on later security prices. In the former case, a "bonus" payment may be due the former owners of the subsidiary if its postacquisition performance meets a certain standard. When such additional amount becomes determinable, the parent should record the current fair value of that consideration as additional cost of the acquired equity.[15]

[15] The November 1970 theory examination included a contingent consideration question. There Beach negotiated the purchase of most of Cedar's assets, including (at book value) $500,000 in tangible assets and $50,000 goodwill (on Cedar's books). No indication of any current values was given. Cedar asked $600,000 cash, but accepted $450,000 plus 1% of net sales of the next five years (which it expected to exceed $15 million). The question was asked: "How should Beach record this transaction?"

According to Opinion 16, the cost to Beach is $450,000, which amount would then be allocated first to the current assets (the $180,000 book value presumed to be reasonably indicative of current value) and the remaining $270,000

In the latter case, assuming that the original consideration was parent company shares, the agreement may require issuance of more shares (or other consideration) to make the value of the total consideration equal to a specified amount at a given future date. Opinion 16 states: "The cost of an acquired company recorded at the date of acquisition represents the entire payment, including contingent consideration. Therefore, the issuance of additional securities or distribution of other consideration does not affect the cost of the acquired company. . . ." The parent must record the fair value of the additional consideration issued, but simultaneously it would reduce the initial amount in its investment account (which was derived from the fair value of the original shares issued) by an equal amount. Said simply, nothing changes in the balance sheet but the number of shares outstanding.

entity theory and proprietary theory

At this point let us summarize the two theories about the nature of the parent–subsidiary arrangement. Whenever a minority interest exists, some of the amounts set forth in consolidated statements are affected differently, depending on the theory or point of view followed. One theory, usually labeled *proprietary* theory, emphasizes the interests of the controlling stockholders. Under such theory, consolidated statements are prepared "primarily for the benefit of the shareholders and creditors of the parent company." [16] This has been the conventional approach. The other approach, the *entity* theory, views the nature of the affiliated group as a single body under unified control which has two classes of proprietary interests—the majority, or controlling, interest and the minority interest.

Although much of the procedure of consolidated statement preparation is the same under either theory, the following list summarizes the important differences.

	Minority Interest
Under proprietary theory:	Excluded from Stockholders' Equity section of consolidated balance sheet.
Under entity theory:	Included as a subsection of the Stockholders' Equity section.

to the tangible fixed assets (presumably written down arbitrarily from their total book value of $320,000 in proportion to their relative current values). None of Cedar's goodwill would be recognized. Then as Beach made further payments, those amounts would be recorded as retroactive adjustments of the purchase price and added as cost of the acquired fixed assets. Once the cumulative total of payments equaled the total current value of tangible assets (as of acquisition date), any further payments would be classified as consolidated goodwill.

[16] ARB No. 51, paragraph 1.

Minority Interest in Periodic Income

Under proprietary theory:	A necessary deduction to arrive at consolidated net income.
Under entity theory:	Shown as a distributive share of consolidated net income.

Elimination of Unrealized Intercompany Profit or Loss

Under proprietary theory:	Eliminate only the parent company's share.
Under entity theory:	Eliminate 100% of the intercompany profit and allocate proportionately between majority and minority interests (see p. 360 and 361).

Excess of Cost Over Book Value (Or Excess of Book Value over Cost)

Under proprietary theory:	Based on the parent's percentage of interest: the cost of the parent's (less than 100%) equity in the subsidiary versus the book value of that equity interest.
Under entity theory:	Based on total (parent plus minority) interests: the value of the subsidiary's total equity (as derived from the price of the parent's share) versus the subsidiary's total book value (see p. 383).

At the time of writing, the proprietary theory continues to predominate. However, it seems clear that support for the entity theory has increased significantly in recent years. Some parts of it (e.g., the theory relating to intercompany profit) have the formal support of the accounting profession, and the part relating to goodwill has been seriously considered.

The exposure draft leading to APB Opinions 16 and 17 included specific preference for the entity theory approach in determining the cost–book value difference, thus affecting the valuation of identifiable assets, goodwill, and minority interest. However, because of certain unresolved difficulties involving piecemeal acquisitions, the published opinions omitted all reference thereto.

other applications of consolidation techniques

Consolidation techniques are used most frequently with related corporate entities. However, other types of related entities, each having its own set of accounts, may be consolidated. Reference may be made to these recent examination problem examples:

1. Parent "company" is an estate, consolidated with two controlled corporate subsidiaries (November, 1969).
2. "Parent company" is a home office, consolidated with a foreign branch office (having accounts stated in pesos) (May, 1968).
3. Home office–branch office consolidation, the working papers to show the home office income statement, branch office income statement, and combined balance sheet (November, 1966).

The candidate will find that each of these involves basic consolidation concepts and techniques, plus an ability to adapt for "nonstandard" matters: as in the foregoing problems, estate accounting principles, translation of foreign currency, and separate income statements, respectively.

As another application, the statements of firms under a third party's common ownership (neither firm owning the other) may be combined if their operations are coordinated to the extent that the resulting combined statements would reflect a meaningful economic entity.

complete example in "statement form"

The May, 1965, examination included a worksheet problem which included most of the routine consolidation matters, as well as some interesting features that are less usual. The problem and solution are reproduced here (as modified) to provide a complete example covering many of the points discussed in the chapter to this point. Liberty has been taken with the style of working papers employed, however. For longer consolidation problems, the candidate is usually provided with working papers having preprinted trial balances, and in recent years the accounts have nearly always been presented in trial balance order. Thus the trial balance arrangement has been used in the preceding series of illustrations. However, another style, sometimes termed "statement form working papers," is quite popular in practice and may warrant the candidate's attention.

The trial balances as given in the May, 1965, examination in the consolidated working papers were prepared after examination of the December 31, 1964, financial statements of Adam Corporation and its subsidiaries, Seth Corporation and Cain Corporation (the latter acquired at midyear). The subsidiary investments are accounted for by the cost method. The sales, costs, and expenses of the subsidiaries are to be included in the consolidation as though the subsidiaries had been acquired at the beginning of the year; then the current year's preacquisition earnings of Cain Corporation will be deducted at the bottom of the consolidated income statement.[17]

[17] The example illustrates concepts basic in accounting for midyear acquisitions. A later section, "Reporting Midyear Combinations," discusses specific reporting requirements under APB Opinion 16.

The working papers are presented in Figure 1. Additional information given with the examination and explanations of the adjusting and eliminating entries are as follows:

(a) Seth Corporation was formed by Adam Corporation on January 1, 1964. To secure additional capital, 25% of the capital stock was sold at par value in the securities market. Adam Corporation purchased the remaining capital stock at par value for cash.

Capital stock—Seth Corporation	200,000	
Investment in Seth Corporation		150,000
Minority interest—Seth Corporation		50,000
To eliminate the intercompany investment and to set out the minority interest in Seth Corporation.		

(b) On July 1, 1964, Adam Corporation acquired from stockholders 4,000 shares (80%) of Cain Corporation's capital stock for $175,000. Cain Corporation's net income for the first half of 1964 was $44,000.

Minority interest in Cain Corporation income	44,000	
Retained earnings—Cain Corporation		44,000
To adjust Cain Corporation retained earnings for income earned prior to acquisition and to remove the same amount as an element of consolidated net income.		

(c) Cain Corporation paid cash dividends in 1964 as follows: $6,000 on June 30 and $14,000 on December 31.

Retained earnings—Cain Corporation	6,000	
Dividends—Cain Corporation		6,000
To adjust Cain Corporation retained earnings for dividends paid prior to acquisition and to remove the same amount as an element of consolidated retained earnings.		

(d)

Dividend income	11,200	
Minority interest—Cain Corporation	2,800	
Dividends—Cain Corporation		14,000
To eliminate the intercompany dividends (80%) and to reduce minority interest (20%) for dividends paid after acquisition date.		

(e)

Capital stock—Cain Corporation	80,000	
Retained earnings—Cain Corporation	64,000	
Excess of cost over equity at acquisition date	31,000	
Investment in Cain Corporation		175,000

To eliminate 80% of the Cain Corporation's stockholders' equity at date of acquisition, July 1, 1964, as follows:

Retained earnings, January 1, 1964	$42,000	
Add: Income, January 1 to June 30	44,000	
Deduct:		
Dividends paid June 30	(6,000)	
Retained earnings, July 1		$ 80,000
Capital stock		100,000
Stockholders' equity		$180,000
80% thereof		$144,000
Cost of investment		175,000
Excess of cost over book value		$ 31,000

(f)

Retained earnings—Cain Corporation	16,000	
Capital stock—Cain Corporation	20,000	
Minority interest—Cain Corporation		36,000

To record minority interest as of acquisition date. (The same result could be obtained by extending these amounts to a minority interest column instead of using a new line as done here.)

(g) The following intercompany sales of certain products were made in 1964:

	Sales	*Gross Profit on Sales, %*	*Included in Purchaser's Inventory at December 31, 1964, at Lower of Cost or Market*
Adam Corporation to Cain Corporation	$ 40,000	20	$15,000
Seth Corporation to Cain Corporation	30,000	10	10,000
Cain Corporation to Adam Corporation	60,000	30	20,000
	$130,000		$45,000

In valuing the Adam Corporation inventory at the lower of cost or market, the portion of the inventory purchased from Cain Corporation was written down by $1,900.

Sales		130,000	
Cost of sales			121,330
Inventories			8,670

To eliminate intercompany sales, cost of sales, and unrealized profit in inventory, the latter computed as follows:

Adam Corporation sold to Cain Corporation (20% of $15,000)	$ 3,000
Seth Corporation sold to Cain Corporation (10% of $10,000)	1,000
Cain Corporation sold to Adam Corporation (see below)	4,670
	$ 8,670

In Adam Corporation's inventory at lower of cost or market	$20,000
Add write-down to market	1,900
Inventory at cost	$21,900
Gross profit percentage	30%
Unrealized intercompany gross profit included in inventory at cost	$ 6,570
Less write-down to lower of cost or market	1,900
Remaining intercompany profit to be eliminated	$ 4,670

(h) On January 2, 1964, Adam Corporation sold a punch press to Seth Corporation. The machine was purchased originally on January 1, 1962, and was being depreciated by Adam Corporation by the straight-line method over a ten-year life. Seth Corporation computed depreciation by the same method based on the remaining useful life. Details of the sale are as follows:

Cost of punch press	$25,000
Accumulated depreciation	5,000
Net book value	$20,000
Sales price	24,000
Gain on sale	$ 4,000

Gain on sales of assets	4,000	
Fixed assets	1,000	
Accumulated depreciation		5,000

To eliminate intercompany profit in fixed assets.

Accumulated depreciation	500	
Operating expenses		500

To eliminate depreciation computed on the intercompany profit, computed as follows: $3,000 (one-eighth of $24,000) less $2,500 (one-tenth of $25,000).

(i) Adam Corporation billed each subsidiary $6,000 at year end for executive services in 1964. The billing was treated as an operating expense by each subsidiary and as a reduction of operation expenses by Adam Corporation. The invoices were paid in January, 1965.

Accounts payable	12,000	
Accounts receivable		12,000

To eliminate the intercompany obligations. (Note that the parent's way of accounting for executive services "revenues" obviates the need for any expense-revenue elimination.)

(j) At year end Cain Corporation appropriated $10,000 for a contingent loss in connection with a lawsuit that had been pending since 1962.

Minority interest—Cain Corporation	2,000	
Appropriated for contingency		2,000

To allocate the contingent loss to interests that would be affected if the loss were to occur—20% as a reduction of minority interest and the remaining 80% extended as a reduction of consolidated retained earnings. Note that the full $10,000 retained earnings reserve will appear on the consolidated balance sheet.

Another acceptable method would be to reverse, in effect, the appropriation entry, that is, debit Appropriation for Contingency, $10,000; and credit Appropriated for Contingency, $10,000. Footnote disclosure of the contingency could then be made in the consolidated balance sheet.

(k)

Minority interest—Seth Corporation	15,250	
Minority interest in Seth Corporation loss		15,250

To record minority interest in Seth Corporation operating loss, computed as follows:

Net loss per books	$60,000
Unrealized profit in intercompany sale of merchandise [see entry (g)]	1,000
Realized net loss	$61,000
Minority percentage	25%
Minority share	$15,250

(l)

Minority interest in Cain Corporation income . . .		26,266	
Minority interest—Cain Corporation			26,266
To record minority interest in Cain Corporation net income, computed as follows:			
Net income per books, 1964	$180,000		
Less 1964 income prior to acquisition	44,000		
Net income per books, July–December	$136,000		
Less unrealized profit in intercompany sale of merchandise [see entry (g)]	4,670		
Realized net income	$131,330		
Minority percentage	20%		
Minority share	$ 26,266		

This completes the necessary adjustments and eliminations and leaves only extensions and footings. Note the manner by which the Adjustments and Eliminations columns are subfooted and the subtotals carried down from one statement to the next (see Figure 1).

statement of consolidated retained earnings

On occasion the candidate will encounter a type of question that focuses on consolidated retained earnings—for example, given selected data, prepare a reconciliation of parent-company retained earnings with consolidated retained earnings, or prepare a statement of consolidated retained earnings. The data available or time limits may preclude the preparation of complete working papers. Therefore the candidate should know how to compute the amounts set forth in the statement of consolidated retained earnings.

The typical statement of consolidated retained earnings covers a period of time and is composed of only four items:

1. Consolidated retained earnings at the beginning of the period, plus
2. Consolidated net income for the period, minus
3. Dividends declared by the *parent* corporation during the period, equals
4. Consolidated retained earnings at the end of the period.

If any three of these amounts are known, the statement can be completed; the fourth need not be computed except as a check on the accuracy of the other amounts. An awareness of this may be of some practical significance to a candidate pressed for time. In any event, there is at least

FIGURE I

ADAM CORPORATION AND SUBSIDIARIES

CONSOLIDATED STATEMENT WORKING PAPERS
FOR THE YEAR ENDED DECEMBER 31, 1964

	Adam Corporation	*Seth Corporation*	*Cain Corporation*	*Adjustments and Eliminations*		*Consolidated*
Income Statement:						
Sales	960,000	275,000	570,000	(g) 130,000		1,675,000
Gain on sales of assets	9,000			(h) 4,000		5,000
Dividend income	18,000			(d) 11,200		6,800
Cost of sales	(820,000)	(300,000)	(350,000)		(g) 121,330	(1,348,670)
Other expenses	(60,000)	(35,000)	(40,000)		(h) 500	(134,500)
Minority interest in Seth Corporation loss					(k) 15,250	15,250
Minority interest in Cain Corporation income				(b) 44,000 (l) 26,266		(70,266)
Totals forward	107,000	(60,000)	180,000	215,466	137,080	
Consolidated net income						148,614
Statement of Retained Earnings:						
Retained earnings, January 1, 1964:						
Adam Corporation	611,000					611,000
Cain Corporation			42,000	(c) 6,000 (e) 64,000 (f) 16,000	(b) 44,000	
Appropriated for contingency			(10,000)		(j) 2,000	(8,000)
Dividends:						
Adam Corporation	(48,000)					(48,000)
Cain Corporation			(20,000)		(c) 6,000 (d) 14,000	
Net income (loss) (forwarded)	107,000	(60,000)	180,000	215,466	137,080	148,614
Totals forward	670,000	(60,000)	192,000	301,466	203,080	
Consolidated retained earnings						703,614

FIGURE I (Continued)

	Adam Corporation	Seth Corporation	Cain Corporation	Adjustments and Eliminations		Consolidated
Balance Sheet:						
Cash	82,000	11,000	27,000			120,000
Accounts receivable	104,000	41,000	143,000		(i) 12,000	276,000
Inventories	241,000	70,000	78,000		(g) 8,670	380,330
Investment in Seth Corporation	150,000				(a) 150,000	
Investment in Cain Corporation	175,000				(e) 175,000	
Investments—other	185,000					185,000
Fixed assets	375,000	58,000	99,000	(h) 1,000		533,000
Accumulated depreciation	(96,000)	(7,000)	(21,000)	(h) 500	(h) 5,000	(128,500)
	1,216,000	173,000	326,000			
Excess of cost over equity at acquisition date				(e) 31,000		31,000
						1,396,830
Accounts payable	46,000	33,000	24,000	(i) 12,000		91,000
Capital stock:						
Adam Corporation	500,000					500,000
Seth Corporation		200,000		(a) 200,000		
Cain Corporation			100,000	(e) 80,000 (f) 20,000		
Retained earnings (forwarded)	670,000	(60,000)	192,000	301,466	203,080	703,614
Appropriation for contingency			10,000			10,000
	1,216,000	173,000	326,000			
Minority interest—Seth Corporation				(k) 15,250	(a) 50,000	34,750
Minority interest—Cain Corporation				(d) 2,800 (j) 2,000	(f) 36,000 (l) 26,266	57,466
				666,016	666,016	1,396,830

some merit in adopting a policy of computing the easiest items first, leaving until last the item that appears most difficult.

Dividends. On the statement of consolidated retained earnings, only the dividends declared by the parent corporation are shown. This amount is usually set forth in the problem.

Consolidated Retained Earnings. The following paragraphs apply for either beginning-of-period or end-of-period consolidated retained earnings.

When the parent-subsidiary relationship first arises, consolidated retained earnings equal the retained earnings of the parent company (unless a pooling of interests is involved, as discussed later). Any retained earnings on the books of the subsidiary at acquisition date are either eliminated or assignable to the minority interest. If the parent-subsidiary relationship is only one year old, often the easiest approach to the determination of beginning-of-year consolidated retained earnings is to work back to the beginning-of-year balance of the parent's retained earnings account, which equals consolidated retained earnings at that date.

The preceding paragraph pertains, of course, to a special circumstance. To generalize, consolidated retained earnings (at the beginning of the year, end of the year, or any time) equal:

1. Parent-company retained earnings; plus (minus)
2. The parent's share of the *undistributed* earnings (losses) recognized by the affiliated subsidiary company (-ies) since the date of affiliation; minus (plus)
3. The parent's share of any unrealized intercompany profit (loss) in inventory, fixed assets, or other assets; minus (plus)
4. Any working paper, in contrast to recorded, amortization or lump-sum write-offs to date of excess of cost over equity acquired (excess of equity acquired over cost).

Some further elaboration is called for.

If the percentage interest in the subsidiary has changed during the period of affiliation, generalization 2 should be refined as follows. If the shareholding has increased, the appropriate shares are the various percentages held during the several periods in which earnings were realized and reported by the subsidiary. If the shareholding has been reduced, the appropriate share is the percentage interest held at the date as of which the computation of consolidated retained earnings is being made.

Statements 1 and 2 hold when the cost method is used by the parent in accounting for its investment in the subsidiary. If, however, the parent uses the equity (or book value) method in accounting for investments in subsidiaries, the parent's retained earnings will already reflect its share of the earnings or losses of its subsidiaries, and statement 2 becomes unnecessary.

Statement 4 pertains to amortization or other write-offs of "excess" (consolidated goodwill) that have been made only in the consolidated working papers. In contrast, if the parent has been amortizing in its own books the "excess" element of its investment in subsidiary account, the write-off will already be reflected in the parent's retained earnings, making statement 4 irrelevant.

The significance of the word "undistributed" as used in the statement 2 may deserve some emphasis. Under the cost method, dividends from subsidiary companies are treated as income by the parent in the year the dividends are declared, unless such dividends are a distribution of earnings that were realized by the subsidiary prior to the parent-subsidiary relationship; in this case the dividends are merely a return of capital to the parent. Therefore, to the extent that subsidiary earnings have been distributed, they have reached the retained earnings of the parent. It is the undistributed earnings of subsidiary companies that require attention in the computation of consolidated retained earnings, unless, of course, the equity method is in use. This matter can be clarified by following the computation of consolidated retained earnings as of December 31, 1974, for the A B C problem, an adaptation from an old CPA examination.

COMPANIES A, B, AND C

BALANCE SHEETS
DECEMBER 31, 1974

	Company A	*Company B*	*Company C*
Sundry assets	$5,500,000	$3,400,000	$3,000,000
Investment in Company B (90%)	1,000,000		
Investment in Company C (90%)		1,500,000	
	$6,500,000	$4,900,000	$3,000,000
Sundry liabilities	$2,000,000	$3,000,000	$ 500,000
Capital stock:			
Company A (20,000 shares, par $100)	2,000,000		
Company B (no par value)		1,000,000	
Company C (10,000 shares, par $100)			1,000,000
Retained earnings	2,500,000	900,000	1,500,000
	$6,500,000	$4,900,000	$3,000,000

1. Company A acquired 90% of the stock of Company B on January 1, 1961, for $1 million. At that date, Company B had capital stock of $1 million and retained earnings of $200,000.

2. Company B acquired the stock of Company C on January 1, 1966, for $1.5 million. At that date, Company C had capital stock of $500,000 and retained earnings of $1.2 million.

3. On January 1, 1967, Company C declared a stock dividend of 100%.

RETAINED EARNINGS

	Company A	*Company B*	*Company C*
Balance, December 31, 1973	$2,300,000	$ 800,000	$1,200,000
Add: Net income (including dividends received from subsidiary companies)	400,000	150,000	400,000
Total	$2,700,000	$ 950,000	$1,600,000
Deduct: Dividends paid	200,000	50,000	100,000
Balance, December 31, 1974	$2,500,000	$ 900,000	$1,500,000

In the A B C problem, it is apparent that the investment accounts are maintained on a cost basis. The computation of consolidated retained earnings for the end of year 1974 follows:

Retained earnings of Company A, December 31, 1974		$2,500,000
Undistributed earnings of Company C:		
Company C retained earnings, December 31, 1974	$1,500,000	
Add back the retained earnings capitalized by Company C's stock dividend	500,000	
Total	$2,000,000	
Company C retained earnings, January 1, 1966, acquisition date	1,200,000	
Undistributed earnings	$ 800,000	
Company A's share: 90% × 90%		648,000
Undistributed earnings of Company B:		
Company B retained earnings, December 31, 1974	$ 900,000	
Company B retained earnings, January 1, 1961, acquisition date	200,000	
Undistributed earnings	$ 700,000	
Company A's share: 90%		630,000
Consolidated retained earnings, December 31, 1974		$3,778,000

The November, 1958, theory of accounts examination included a question that involved a reconciliation of parent-company retained earnings with consolidated retained earnings. The following facts were given or determinable: parent's retained earnings at December 31, $200,000;

subsidiary's retained earnings at acquisition, $100,000, and at December 31, $160,000; intercompany profit (of the parent) on goods in the subsidiary's ending inventory, $8,000; and nonrecurring loss upon the subsidiary's acquisition (for $103,000) of parent company bonds (book value equal to their face, $100,000). The subsidiary was 70% owned by the parent. Consolidated retained earnings are computed as follows:

Parent company retained earnings, December 31	$200,000
Parent's share of subsidiary's undistributed earnings since acquisition: 70% of $60,000	42,000
Parent's share (100%, since sale was by parent) of intercompany profit in ending inventory	(8,000)
Parent's share of loss on purchase of parent company bonds by subsidiary: 70% of $3,000	(2,100)
Consolidated retained earnings	$231,900

Consolidated Net Income. Several working paper illustrations of consolidated net income computations appeared earlier in this chapter. Yet when less complete data are provided, it may be helpful for the candidate to recognize that consolidated net income equals:

1. Parent company net income, after deducting any dividend income from the subsidiary; plus (minus)

2. The parent's share of the book income (loss) of the subsidiary; minus

3a. The parent's share of any end-of-period unrealized intercompany profit included in 1 or 2; plus

3b. The parent's share of any intercompany profit unrealized as of the beginning of period; plus (minus)

4. Any working paper amortization for this period of excess of cost over equity acquired (excess of equity acquired over cost).

Again, let us elaborate on these points.

Statements 1 and 2 pertain to the cost method of accounting for investments in affiliated companies. Under this method, dividends from subsidiaries will be included in the parent's net income. But dividends from subsidiaries are mere transfers of assets and do not increase the earnings of the affiliated group. For this reason, dividend income from subsidiaries should be deducted to avoid double counting when the parent's share of the subsidiary's income (statement 2) is added. However, if the book value (or equity) method is used, the parent's share of the subsidiary's income will already be included as income on the parent company's books. Under that method, too, dividends received from affiliated companies are not treated as income, and therefore no duplication is produced.

In the preceding paragraphs, the phrase "the parent's share of the earnings or losses of its subsidiaries" has been used several times. This phrase may be slightly misleading where a subsidiary has an issue of preferred stock in the hands of "outsiders." Under these conditions it should be recognized that, to arrive at the parent's share of the earnings or losses of its subsidiaries, preferred dividends must first be deducted from reported earnings. Preferred dividends are not treated in the accounts as expenses, although they reduce the amount of earnings assignable to the common stock equity held by the parent.

Statement 3a may be expanded as follows. The entire amount of any end-of-period unrealized profit included in the parent's net income should be subtracted; the parent's share of any end-of-period unrealized profit included in the subsidiary's net income should be subtracted.

Statement 3b is essentially the reverse of statement 3a. It pertains to amounts that would not be included in the book incomes of the affiliated companies of the current period, having been booked already in the preceding period. However, these amounts generally will have been realized, from the consolidated point of view, during the current period, and the parent's share of such amounts must be picked up through this addition. (Any amounts still unrealized at the end of the period would be included in the end-of-period amount.)

Statement 4 pertains to working paper amortization of "excess." If the parent has recorded in its books any such amortization for the period, statement 4 becomes irrelevant.

To summarize, given any three of the four ordinary elements of consolidated retained earnings—beginning-of-period balance, consolidated net income for the period, dividends of parent company, and end-of-period balance—or given the data to compute any three, a complete statement of consolidated retained earnings may be obtained.

Business Combinations—Purchase Versus Pooling of Interests

The process of consolidating parent and subsidiary statements allows financial reports to appear exactly as if the single economic entity were merged into a single legal entity as well. Thus the basic accounting policy question in business combinations—purchase versus pooling of interests —arises whether formal merger has occurred or whether a subsidiary still exists to be consolidated. Most consolidation problems found on the CPA examination specify that the parent has paid cash for all or most of the subsidiary's stock. Thus "purchase accounting" properly and obviously applies in these situations (indeed, in all this chapter up to this point). Yet in fact, the acquiring company often issues its own shares in payment and until recently a choice of accounting policies was usually available in this event.

This choice between "purchase" and "pooling" quite often affected subsequent financial reports very materially. APB Opinion 16 resulted from the profession's effort to achieve greater comparability among reporting practices. Accounting for business combinations has long been important and controversial; the candidate is encouraged to be familiar with the issues. The following paragraphs (a) review the mechanics and contrasting effects of the two methods and (b) summarize the positions of Opinion 16. Then, because the pooling of interest method may be required in some cases in which both combining companies continue in legal existence, (c) an example of consolidation technique under the pooling method is given.

Basic Example. The following adaptation of a problem included in the May, 1958, examination illustrates the meaning of the purchase-pooling choice. Assume that Company Z acquired all the outstanding shares of Company M by giving its own previously unissued shares (par value, $125,000; fair market value at transaction date, $325,000). Company M's condensed balance sheet included:

Current assets	$150,000	Common stock	$100,000
Fixed assets	200,000	Additional paid-in capital	100,000
Current liabilities	(50,000)	Retained earnings	100,000
Net assets	$300,000	Stockholders' equity	$300,000

The individual current assets were appraised at $150,000 and the individual fixed assets at $220,000. Company M was then liquidated and its assets and liabilities transferred to Company Z. That transfer would be recorded in Z's books as follows:

As a Purchase

Investment in Company M	325,000	
Capital stock		125,000
Additional paid-in capital		200,000
Current assets	150,000	
Fixed assets	220,000	
Goodwill	5,000	
Current liabilities		50,000
Investment in Company M		325,000

As a Pooling of Interests

Investment in Company M	125,000	
Capital stock		125,000
Current assets	150,000	
Fixed assets	200,000	
Current liabilities		50,000
Investment in Company M		125,000
Additional paid-in capital		75,000
Retained earnings		100,000

"Purchase accounting" handles the combinaiton exactly as if Company Z stock were issued for cash at the going market price, the cash being used immediately to buy the net assets of Company M. The distinctive accounting characteristics are (a) the net assets are recorded at fair market value, with only the unallocable amount remaining as goodwill, and (b) no retained earnings (or deficit) are brought over from Company M. This is, it should be noted, precisely the same result that would have occurred if Company M had continued in existence as a wholly owned subsidiary. Then consolidated statement procedures would have developed an "excess cost over book value acquired."

In contrast, "pooling accounting" interprets the arrangement as two groups of owners merely joining forces. As such, there is no obvious purchase transaction in which owners of the former firm are bought out and cease to have proprietary rights in the surviving firm. Instead, those owners, because they continue to be shareholders, retain proprietary rights, however small their portion, in the larger surviving combined business. It follows that the balance sheets of the two are merged directly with little or no adjustment of either. Thus the example shows two things: the net assets recorded at their old book values when brought over from Company M books, with no goodwill (or asset revaluation) arising, and the major categories of Company M stockholders' equity—significantly, any retained earnings *or deficit*—transplanted to the accounts of Company Z. Slight modification was necessary, of course, because equal par values were not exchanged. Nevertheless, total paid-in capital of $200,000 and retained earnings of $100,000 were brought over intact. The solution would be modified only slightly in cases in which the par value of the newly issued stock exceeds the total paid-in capital of the terminated firm. If Company Z stock had had a par value of $225,000, for example, the second entry under a pooling of interests would have been:

Current assets	150,000	
Fixed assets	200,000	
Current liabilities		50,000
Capital stock		225,000
Retained earnings		75,000

Thus the two methods interpret the merger transaction differently and produce contrasting balance sheets. The difference does not end there, however. Almost always of greater importance is the subsequent income measurement effect. As in the example, the purchase method will result in greater fixed asset depreciation charges totaling $20,000, and the $5,000 goodwill must also be amortized. Lower reported income, due to these factors, usually results from choosing the purchase method. And noting that reported total assets are a greater amount, both the lower income and the greater investment act to produce a lower reported return on investment than if the pooling method were adopted. Obviously, pooling was the more common choice.

Purchase versus Pooling—Accounting Principles Board Opinion 16.

> The Board concludes that the purchase method and the pooling of interests method are both acceptable in accounting for business combinations, although not as alternatives in accounting for the same business combination. A business combination which meets specified conditions requires accounting by the pooling of interests method. A new basis of accounting is not permitted for a combination that meets the specified conditions, and the assets and liabilities of the combining companies are combined at their recorded amounts. All other business combinations should be accounted for as an acquisition of one or more companies by a corporation. (Opinion 16, paragraph 8)

Opinion 16 removes the purchase–pooling option. There remains only the interpretation of the facts of an actual or contemplated merger to determine which method is required.

Very simply, the Board holds that mergers effected by pure common-for-common exchanges (with no contingency clauses, unusual extra agreements, convertible or otherwise complex securities, etc.) must be accounted for as poolings; all other mergers must be treated as purchases. Paragraphs 45–48 spell out the conditions under which pooling is required. All these conditions must prevail, and they are summarized as follows: (a) independent ownership interests are combined to continue previously separate operations; (b) all or nearly all the common shares of one company are exchanged for another firm's common shares, with all shareholders retaining the same relative and unrestricted rights—in a single transaction which involves no planned or contingent realignment of rights in the near future; and (c) intention to continue substantially all the operations and normal stockholder relationships of the combining companies.

This position contrasts with the prior AICPA approach. The basic philosophy of a pooling of interests had been that of a merger of relatively equal partners whose proportional ownership, management participation, and operations were to continue. This general view proved difficult to interpret and even more difficult to administer. Opinion 16 drops the relative size and management continuity tests, attempts to define criteria clearly, and (as previously stated) removes any choice of method (other than that provided by judicious planning of a merger's terms).

Advantages and disadvantages, both theoretical and practical, may be noted for both methods (see Opinion 16, paragraphs 15–41). Pooling is charged with ignoring the economic substance of a bargaining transaction —values given and received are ignored. Under pre-Opinion 16 practices, "instant earnings" are alleged to have resulted (a) by the early sale of newly pooled assets, which were carried at their pre-merger (often quite low) book value, and (b) by a reporting practice which required that the merged firm report earnings for the year of merger as if it had been merged during that entire year (even though the merger may have occurred well along in that year or even after the fiscal year-end but before publication of the financial statements). In addition, highly complex securities evolved during the 1960s, apparently greatly influenced in many cases by a desire to use the pooling method.

Pooling is defended, on the other hand, on the grounds that it is more objective than the purchase method (no appraisals of assets or stock values are necessary), that it merely and properly continues generally accepted accounting principles rather than introducing extensive appraisal-based data, and that it avoids accounting for one part of the merged company on a fair market value basis and the other part on historical cost. And, fundamentally:

> Those who endorse the pooling of interests method believe that an exchange of stock to effect a business combination is in substance a transaction between the combining stockholder groups and does not involve the corporate entities. The transaction therefore neither requires nor justifies establishing a new basis of accountability for the assets of the combined corporation. (paragraph 16)

Those who endorse the purchase method believe that one company clearly acquires another in almost every business combination, control passing to the dominant corporation in a transaction bargained on the basis of current fair values given and received, regardless of the nature of the consideration (cash, stock, etc.). However, with the purchase method there are the alleged problems with objective determination of current values and the apparent inconsistency of accounting for only part of the merged company on an updated basis. Goodwill and the related amortization charges often may materially affect financial reports although, being derived from current valuations (appraisals, etc.) of stock issued and tangible assets received, they are less than convincing measures. Indeed, some dispute the theoretical as well as the practical efficacy of periodic goodwill charges against income and urge instead that goodwill be written off entirely and immediately on the merger date.[18]

The purchase–pooling controversy can be focused on two general issues: the basic nature of a merger and the practical effects of each accounting method on the appearance and credibility of financial statements. On the "basic nature" issue, Opinion 16 embraces both merger philosophies, although pooling of interests is seemingly accepted as a special case. Regarding practical effects, Opinion 16 should improve the credibility of merger reporting by removing the option of method and by dealing with the "instant earnings" defects of past pooling accounting practices by means of changed reporting requirements (see paragraphs 56, 59, and 60). The simple common-for-common conditions required for the pooling method should reduce the incentive for artificially complex merger plans. However, the effect of mandatory goodwill amortization on financial statement credibility and, more fundamentally, on actual business merger activity itself remains to be seen.

Consolidation under the Pooling Method. If consolidated statements are prepared under the pooling-of-interests concept, the result will be analogous to statements that would have been drawn from the accounts of the combined business entity if it had become the single surviving company and had used pooling accounting to merge the sets of predecessor company accounts. That is, the subsidiary's assets and liabilities will be consolidated at their carrying values and there will be no goodwill (excess of cost over equity acquired) at all. Also, since a pooling is not an acquisition but is viewed as a mutual sharing and continuation of interests, it is proper to indulge in a practice forbidden under purchase accounting consolidation theory, namely, including the parent's share of the subsidiary's retained earnings prior to acquisition in consolidated retained earnings.

The candidate usually receives explicit directions about which method to use. That was the case on the November, 1963, examination, a good example of the pooling treatment in consolidated balance sheet working papers. The problem and solution are reproduced here to illustrate both the pooling-of-interests treatment and working papers for the consolidation of balance sheets only, rather than the full set of financial statements.

[18] George R. Catlett and Norman O. Olson, Accounting Research Study No. 10, *Accounting for Goodwill* (New York: American Institute of Certified Public Accountants, 1968).

Prior to January 1, 1962, the stockholders of Big Company and Little Company approved the merger of the two companies. On January 1, 1962, the Little Company stockholders were issued 5,000 shares of Big Company common stock in exchange for the 3,000 shares of Little Company common stock outstanding.

December 31, 1962, post-closing balance sheets of the two companies are given as they appear in the working papers.

The following additional information is available:

1. Net income for 1962 (disregard income taxes):

Big Company	$21,700
Little Company	10,200

2. On December 31, 1962, Little Company owed Big Company $16,000 on open account and $8,000 in interest-bearing notes. Big Company discounted $3,000 of the notes received from Little Company with First State Bank.

3. On December 31, 1962, Little Company accrued interest payable of $120 on the notes payable to Big Company: $40 on the notes of $3,000 discounted with the bank and $80 on the remaining notes of $5,000. Big Company did not accrue interest receivable from Little Company.

4. During 1962, Big Company sold merchandise which cost $30,000 to Little Company for $40,000. Little Company's December 31 inventory included $10,000 of this merchandise priced at Little Company's cost.

5. On July 1, Little Company sold equipment that had a book value of $15,000 to Big Company for $17,000. Big Company recorded depreciation on it in the amount of $850 for 1962. The remaining life of the equipment at the date of sale was ten years.

6. Little Company shipped merchandise to Big Company on December 31, 1962, and recorded an account receivable of $6,000 for the sale. Little Company's cost for the merchandise was $4,800. Because the merchandise was in transit, Big Company did not record the transaction. The terms of the sale were f.o.b. shipping point.

7. Little Company declared a dividend of $1.50 per share on December 30, 1962, payable on January 10, 1963. Big Company made no entry for the declaration.

Required: Prepare a consolidated balance sheet worksheet (Figure 2). The consolidation is to be accounted for as a pooling of interests. Formal journal entries are not required.

Solution:

BIG COMPANY AND LITTLE COMPANY

Adjusting and Elimination Journal Entries

(1)

Capital stock—Little Company	60,000	
Investment in Little Company		50,000
Capital in excess of par		10,000
To eliminate reciprocal elements in investment and equity accounts.		

Notice that the investment was not recorded at fair market value. The entry, in effect, substitutes $50,000 of Big Company stock plus $10,000 "consolidated premium" for the $60,000 of Little Company stock.

(2)

Notes payable—Little Company	8,000	
Accounts payable—Little Company	16,000	
Notes receivable—Big Company		8,000
Accounts receivable—Big Company		16,000
To eliminate intercompany notes and accounts.		

(3)

Notes receivable discounted—Big Company	3,000	
Notes payable—Little Company		3,000
To reclassify notes receivable discounted with bank as a primary liability of Little Company.		

(4)

Accruals receivable—Big Company	80	
Accruals payable—Little Company	80	
Retained earnings—Big Company		80
Accruals receivable—Big Company		80
To record interest receivable in Big Company's accounts and to eliminate intercompany receivables and payables.		

(5)

Retained earnings—Big Company	2,500	
Inventories—Little Company		2,500
To eliminate intercompany profit in Little Company's inventory.		

(Note that there is no elimination of intercompany sales and cost of sales here because only balance sheets are involved.)

Purchases from Big Company included in Little Company's inventory	$10,000
Big Company's cost computed on basis of gross profit rates ($30,000 is 75% of $40,000)	7,500
Intercompany profit in inventories	$ 2,500

(6)

	Dr.	Cr.
Retained earnings—Little Company	2,000	
Accumulated depreciation—Big Company	100	
Plant and equipment—Big Company		2,000
Retained earnings—Big Company		100

To eliminate intercompany profit and to adjust accumulated depreciation on equipment purchased by Big Company from Little Company.

	Equipment	*Depreciation*
Sales price	$17,000	$850
Cost	15,000	750
Excess	$ 2,000	$100

(7a)

	Dr.	Cr.
Inventories—Big Company	6,000	
Accounts payable—Big Company		6,000

To adjust the accounts of Big Company.

(7b)

	Dr.	Cr.
Accounts payable—Big Company	6,000	
Retained earnings—Little Company	1,200	
Accounts receivable—Little Company		6,000
Inventories—Big Company		1,200

To eliminate the intercompany obligation and unrealized gross profit.

(In this 100% ownership case, the quickest method would have been merely to remove the effects of the sale from Little Company's books, i.e., debit Inventory $4,800; debit Retained Earnings $1,200; credit Accounts Receivable $6,000.)

(8)

	Dr.	Cr.
Dividends receivable—Big Company	4,500	
Dividends payable—Little Company	4,500	
Retained earnings—Big Company		4,500
Dividends receivable—Big Company		4,500

To record dividend receivable in Big Company's accounts and to eliminate intercompany receivable and payable.

FIGURE 2

BIG COMPANY AND SUBSIDIARY

WORKING PAPERS FOR CONSOLIDATED BALANCE SHEET
DECEMBER 31, 1962

	Big Company	Little Company	Adjustments and Eliminations		Consolidated Balance Sheet
			Debit	Credit	
Cash	36,400	28,200			64,600
Notes receivable	22,000	9,000		(2) 8,000	23,000
Accounts receivable	20,900	21,700		(2) 16,000	20,600
				(7b) 6,000	
Accruals receivable	13,000	3,300	(4) 80	(4) 80	16,300
Inventories	81,200	49,600	(7a) 6,000	(5) 2,500	133,100
				(7b) 1,200	
Plant and equipment	83,200	43,500		(6) 2,000	124,700
Accumulated depreciation	(12,800)	(9,300)	(6) 100		(22,000)
Investment in Little Company	50,000			(1) 50,000	
Dividends receivable			(8) 4,500	(8) 4,500	
	293,900	146,000			360,300
Notes payable	4,000	12,000	(2) 8,000	(3) 3,000	11,000
Accounts payable	42,000	19,600	(2) 16,000	(7a) 6,000	45,600
			(7b) 6,000		
Dividends payable		4,500	(8) 4,500		
Accruals payable	2,600	2,100	(4) 80		4,620
Notes receivable discounted	8,100		(3) 3,000		5,100
Capital stock, $10 par value	120,000				120,000
Capital stock, $20 par value		60,000	(1) 60,000		
Capital in excess of par	28,500	20,000		(1) 10,000	58,500
Retained earnings	88,700	27,800	(5) 2,500	(6) 100	115,480
			(6) 2,000	(8) 4,500	
			(7b) 1,200	(4) 80	
	293,900	146,000	113,960	113,960	360,300

(9)

Note that there is no elimination of the subsidiary's retained earnings as of acquisition date because this solution is in accordance with the pooling-of-interests concept.

reporting midyear combinations

The majority of consolidation problems date the acquisition as of January 1 for the sake of simplicity. Similarly, theory questions, such as on the purchase and the pooling methods, are more likely to deal with fundamental concepts. Yet a philosophy of disclosure, as well as the concepts of "purchase" and "pooling," is evident in the reporting requirements of Opinion 16 for midyear mergers.

The concept of a purchase requires that the *basic* consolidated income statement for the year of acquisition include the subsidiary's income earned only after the acquisition date. The postacquisition revenues and expenses of the acquired company thus included should be based on the cost to the acquiring company (paragraph 94). The comparative statements for prior years should include only the acquiring company's (parent's) data. In addition, the following pro forma *supplemental information* is necessary for fair presentation:

> a. Results of operations for the current period as though the companies had combined at the beginning of the period . . . .
>
> b. Results of operations for (only) the (one) immediately preceding period as though the companies had combined at the beginning of that period . . . .
>
> The supplemental pro forma information should as a minimum show revenue, income before extraordinary items, net income, and earnings per share. . . . (Accounting bases and interest and dividend requirements) should be adjusted to (those) recognized in recording the combination (paragraph 96).

The concept of pooling, which assumes a commingling of assets and operations, requires that the *basic financial statements* "report the results of operations for the period in which the combination occurs as though the companies had been combined as of the beginning of the period" (paragraph 56). The comparative statements for prior years "should also be restated on a combined basis to furnish comparative information" (paragraph 57). In addition, there should be disclosed as *supplemental information* "the revenue, extraordinary items, and net income of each of the separate companies from the beginning of the period to the date the combination is consummated" (paragraph 56).

A special case arises when a pooling is consummated after the close of the acquiring company's fiscal year but before its financial statements are issued. Then the *basic financial statements* for that completed year should not include the newly pooled company. (This is directly contrary to pooling practice prior to Opinion 16.) In addition, however, required as *supplemental information* are the pro forma "effects of the combination on reported financial position and results of operations" (paragraph 61). "The details should include revenue, net income, earnings per share, and the effects of anticipated changes in accounting methods as if the combination had been consummated at the date of the financial statements" (paragraph 65).

"one-line consolidations"

In order to round out the discussion of combined business enterprises under unified management, recall that if a company continues in a subsidiary relationship to a dominant company, there are circumstances (discussed in a previous section) under which the subsidiary's statements need not, and possibly should not, be consolidated with the parent's. In such cases, the parent's balance sheet includes only the parent's own assets, one of which is its investment in the unconsolidated subsidiary, and liabilities. Similarly, the parent's income statement contains only its own revenues and expenses, plus or minus any recognized income or loss from its investment in the subsidiary.

For many years the two accepted ways of accounting for investments in unconsolidated subsidiaries have been the "cost" and the "book value" or "equity" methods. However, APB Opinion 18 (paragraph 14) requires a third method (more accurately, a complete version of the equity method) in reporting the financial effects of unconsolidated domestic subsidiaries, a method sometimes termed "one-line consolidation."

To illustrate, we shall again use the data from the Company Z–Company M example (pp. 407–9). Assume that Company Z purchased Company M, with the firms continuing in a parent-subsidiary relationship. Also assume that for good and sufficient reasons the financial statements of subsidiary Company M were not consolidated with those of the parent. Assume further that subsidiary Company M's income for the year following acquisition was $40,000 and that dividends paid to the parent, Company Z, amounted to $30,000. Let us review the cost and simple equity methods of accounting for an investment in a subsidiary.

Cost Method			*Equity Method*
		At time of acquisition	
Investment in Company M	325,000		Same as cost method
Cash (or stock plus premium).		325,000	

		When the subsidiary's earnings are reported			
No entry			Investment in Company M	40,000	
			Income from investment in subsidiary		40,000
		When dividends are received from subsidiary			
Cash	30,000		Cash	30,000	
Income from investment in subsidiary		30,000	Investment in Company M ..		30,000

Under the cost method, it is unlikely that the net income shown by an unconsolidated income statement would closely approximate that shown by a consolidated income statement for the same parent and subsidiary companies. For a close approximation to exist, the dividends declared by the subsidiary would have to come close to matching its annual earnings.

On the other hand, a statement issued under the simple equity method would include the parent's share of the earnings of the subsidiary, and therefore the net income shown by an unconsolidated income statement would closely approximate, and might agree with, the net income reported on a consolidated income statement for the same parent and subsidiary companies. Any difference between the net income on an unconsolidated income statement (following the equity method) and the net income on a consolidated income statement would be attributable to (a) the amortization of any excess of either cost or book value (or depreciation on that portion of the excess allocated to depreciable assets), and (b) the elimination of unrealized intercompany profit. (Income tax considerations are being ignored.) Thus the simple equity method does not take into account modern thought on the handling of the excess of either cost or book value. For instance, the excess of cost over book value should be allocated to adjust the carrying value of the assets (for consolidated statement purposes) to fair market value at acquisition, with any unallocated remainder (goodwill) often amortized against consolidated income. It is here that the close parallel between the simple equity method and consolidated statement technique breaks down.

To continue with the Company Z–Company M example, if subsidiary Company M's statements had been consolidated, an excess of cost over book value in the amount of $25,000 would have resulted. Of this, $20,000 would have been apportioned to specific assets with the remaining $5,000 appearing as "goodwill." In subsequent years, the fixed assets (with, e.g., ten-year lives) including the $20,000 adjustment would be depreciated. Consolidated income would be less by $2,000 each year as a result of the adjustment. (Again, income taxes are being ignored.) In addition, if the $5,000 goodwill were amortized over ten years, consolidated income would be less by another $500 per year.

The simple equity method would not accomplish this result because that procedure requires the parent to pick up its share of the subsidiary's income unadjusted for the preceding considerations. Noting this inconsistency with preferred consolidated statement practice, Opinion 10 states that, in accounting for unconsolidated subsidiaries, "The amount of . . . (the unconsolidated subsidiary's earnings included in the parent's net income) . . . should give effect to amortization . . . of any difference between the cost of the investment and the equity in net assets at the date of acquisition. . . ."[19]

The result of amortizing the $25,000 "excess" element of Company Z's investment in Company M account would be that, after ten years, the balance of that account would be equal to Company Z's (100%) share in Company M's net assets per *Company M's* books. Recall that the process of consolidating the balance sheets of parent and subsidiary companies accomplishes essentially the same effect, the difference being that consolidated balance sheets combine the subsidiary's assets and liabilities with those of the parent on a line-by-line basis, rather than disclosing the subsidiary's assets and liabilities (less any minority interest) all netted on one line.

The "one-line" distinction is true also of the income statement. A consolidated income statement includes the subsidiary's revenues and expenses commingled line by line with the parent's, including the single or combined effects of any goodwill amortization or adjustment of depreciation expense. A "one-line consolidation" income statement, under the complete equity method, would show the same final net income but would consist of the parent's own operating revenues and expenses plus, on one line, its share of the subsidiary's net income after allowance had been made for the amortization or depreciation of the "excess."

Also, unrealized intercompany gross profit should be considered in accounting for a parent company's investment in, and income from, an unconsolidated subsidiary. The preceding citation from Opinion 10 continued: ". . . and to any elimination of intercompany gain or loss that would have been made had the subsidiary been consolidated." Thus, if the subsidiary's income includes profit on items which the parent bought and still has on hand, the parent should not take up its share of the un-

[19] Paragraph 3. Opinion 18 reaffirmed the positions discussed in this section and extended them to joint ventures and, as noted earlier in this chapter, to most investments comprising 20% to 49% of the investee company's voting stock.

realized profit. The same applies in the case of a sale that went from parent to subsidiary.

The May, 1957, examination, for example, included a problem in which the parent company had made a sale of equipment to an unconsolidated subsidiary, which then leased the asset to a third party. In such a case, the gross profit from the sale should be regarded as not validated by an arm's-length transaction. The unofficial answer showed the parent company taking up the gross profit over a period of years as the subsidiary realized rental income, rather than immediately upon sale.

accounting problems of business combinations

Whenever businesses are exploring the desirability of consolidating several companies, one of the foremost problems confronting the parties to the proposed plan is forecasting the earnings contributions the several companies will make to the combination. It is reasonably certain that some of the businesses being consolidated will be worth more than others, and some equitable solution must be reached in fairness to the owners of the individual companies. Frequently, since book values of assets and past earnings may suggest approximate exchange value, the books of account provide the starting basis for price negotiations. It is at this point that the services of a professional accountant are often solicited, because the several books of account may not have been maintained on a reasonably comparable basis.

It is, however, the accountant's primary function in investigations in anticipation of a business combination to prepare accounting data for the several companies on a reasonably comparable basis in order that book values and past earnings of each company may carry approximately the same implications. For this purpose, various adjustments of recorded results may be necessary. The necessity for some adjustments arises because of different accounting policies. Other adjustments may be needed in order to avoid the possibility that misleading impressions will be produced by unusual or nonrecurring transactions.

For these reasons, certain accounts should be analyzed in considerable detail. For example, the accountant should analyze the depreciation accounts of the several companies to determine whether the depreciation policies were comparable. If differences are revealed, the influence of these differences on book values and reported earnings must be computed in order to place the accounting data on a reasonably comparable basis. Similarly, the "surplus" accounts should be analyzed for prior-period adjustments and for evidence of any entries reflecting appraisals or write-downs.

The following list suggests some of the areas in which differences are most likely to be discovered:

1. Depreciation and maintenance policies.
2. Provision for uncollectible accounts.
3. Inventory pricing policy.
4. Accounting for intangibles.
5. Valuation of investments.
6. Provisions for contingencies or losses.
7. Officers' salaries.
8. Differences in accounting policy—such as capitalizing or expensing certain expenditures.
9. Fixed asset valuations in the accounts—cost or appraisal.
10. Accrual and prepayment policies.
11. Accounting for extraordinary items.

It should be recognized that these differences may not be an indication of incorrect or improper accounting. In many areas generally accepted accounting principles permit alternative accounting procedures. That is, books of account may not be comparable because of clerical mistakes, incorrect accounting, or the application of equally acceptable alternatives. In any event, comparability of accounting data is the objective under these circumstances (i.e., when a business combination is being developed).

After reasonable comparability of accounting data has been achieved, as a general rule the interested parties endeavor to use the data in an intelligent fashion in arriving at a program for effecting the combination. Accountants generally recognize that book values, even when determined on a comparable basis, are not the only matters to be given consideration. Technological change and decline in purchasing power of money, to mention only two considerations, may substantially impair the significance of recorded amounts. Furthermore, settlement prices will be influenced not only by the separate values of the assets being transferred but by their expected earning power when combined with other assets. If the accountant is asked to review estimates of earning power, he would work with the following illustrative list of possible pertinent considerations:

1. Will any items of expense be higher or lower after the combination is effected?
2. Will key personnel continue with the consolidated company?
3. Will any products or productive capacity be discontinued? If so, what will be the effect on earnings?
4. What is the trend of earnings? Of sales? Of selling prices? Of unit costs?

The following summarizes an examination problem in which the candidate was asked to prepare an estimate of the fair market value (cash purchase price) of the stock of a going concern. Sales of the concern for the next three or four years were expected to average \$110,000; estimated annual expenses (the actual problem called for extensive adjustments here) were \$95,490. Book value of the stock, after adjustments, was \$160,-000. The problem further disclosed that, if the purchaser did acquire control, it expected to raise \$25,000 for new equipment through the issuance of capital stock; 6% was mentioned as an ordinary rate of return. The tentative purchase price of the stock, including the goodwill element, was computed as follows:

Estimated gross revenue		\$110,000
Estimated annual expenses		95,490
Estimated annual income		\$ 14,510
Return at 6% on adjusted book value:		
6% of \$160,000	\$9,600	
Return at 6% on new capital:		
6% of \$25,000	1,500	11,100
Excess annual earnings to be capitalized		\$ 3,410

The problem states that it is unsafe to assume that the profit rate will exceed an ordinary rate after four years. Therefore, if the excess annual earnings of \$3,410 are believed to be temporary and are capitalized on a 6% basis, the computation is completed:

Adjusted book value (present value of a perpetual stream of \$9,600 annual earnings)	\$160,000
Present value of the \$3,410 estimated excess annual earnings for four years only:	
$\$3,410\left[\frac{1-1/(1.06)^4}{.06}\right]=$	11,816
Total estimated value of the going concern	\$171,816

reciprocal affiliations[20]

"Reciprocal holdings" or "mutual holdings" exist when two or more companies hold stock in each other. In its simplest form, a reciprocal hold-

[20] The candidate may consider this section optional; although some familiarity with reciprocal holding situations may be advisable, no problem involving reciprocal holdings has appeared in the CPA examination between 1953 and the date of this writing (April, 1971).

ing arises when a subsidiary corporation owns a portion of the outstanding shares of its parent. An example of a more complex situation is one in which a parent owned two subsidiaries and each of them owned shares of the other. Obviously, reciprocal relationships can become quite complex.

A reciprocal affiliation between a parent and a subsidiary can be diagrammed as follows:

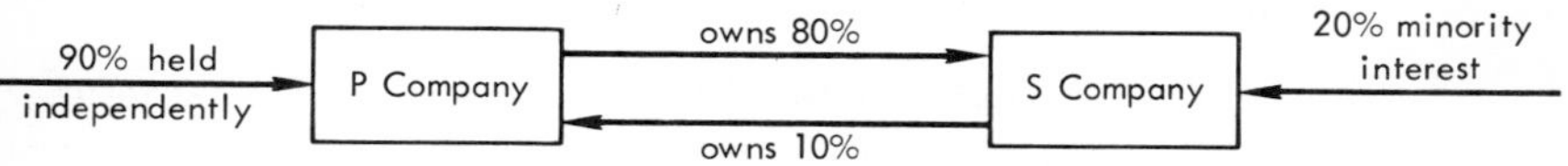

Ninety per cent of the parent's stock is held by outsiders and the rest is held by the subsidiary. The parent owns 80% of the stock of the subsidiary.

Because the cost method of accounting for investments in affiliated companies is the most widely used approach, the circular effects produced by mutual stockholdings on the income and retained earnings of the related companies are usually not reflected on the books of the individual companies. Thus preparation of consolidated statements, which are fundamentally concerned with combining data that have been adjusted to the viewpoint of the single consolidated entity, may not proceed correctly until book net income and retained earnings figures have been adjusted for any unrecognized circular effects.

To illustrate, let us assume that P Company (see diagram) reported the year's income as $30,000 and S Company reported $10,000 (after any intercompany dividend income in both cases had been eliminated). In the absence of any intercompany profit eliminations, partial consolidated working papers would show:

	P Company	*S Company*	*Consolidated Net Income*
Sales	xx	x	xxx
Costs and expenses	xx	x	xx
Total	$30,000	$10,000	$40,000
Minority interest in S Company income			?
Consolidated net income			?

If there were no reciprocal affiliation, the minority interest in the subsidiary's income would be computed by multiplying the subsidiary's net income (adjusted for any unrealized intercompany profits on sales made by the subsidiary) by the minority's percentage interest in the subsidiary. But here the subsidiary's net income, on a consolidated basis, includes not only the net income from its own operations, but also its proportionate share of the net income of the parent. A less simple procedure for determining minority interest in subsidiary net income is required.

The problem of apportioning the $40,000 between consolidated net income and minority interest is handled easily by elementary algebra.

Let P = the net income of parent on a consolidated basis
S = the net income of subsidiary on a consolidated basis (20% of S will then give the desired minority interest in S Company net income)
then $S = \$10{,}000 + .10P$
and $P = \$30{,}000 + .80S$

$$S = \$10{,}000 + .10P$$
(substitute for P) $$S = \$10{,}000 + .10(\$30{,}000 + .80S)$$
$$S = \$10{,}000 + \$3{,}000 + .08S$$
$$.92S = \$13{,}000$$
$S = \$14{,}130$ = S Company net income on a consolidated basis
= S Company net income on a consolidated basis
20% of S = $ 2,826 = minority interest in S Company net income

To continue the preceding partial working paper example:

Total	$40,000
Minority interest in S Company income	2,826
Consolidated net income	$37,174

As a proof, note that consolidated net income may be defined as the share of parent company income, on a consolidated basis, accruing to independent holders of the parent company stock. It should be (and is) possible to solve for the $37,174 amount algebraically:

$$P = \$30{,}000 + .80S$$
$$S = \$14{,}130 \text{ (as solved previously)}$$
$$P = \$30{,}000 + \$11{,}304$$
$$P = \$41{,}304$$
$$90\% \text{ of } P = \$37{,}174 = \text{consolidated net income}$$

It should be emphasized that the preliminary income figures ($30,000 and $10,000 in the example) relate to each firm's own operations; that is, exclusive of dividend income from affiliates to be consolidated. In addition, any unrealized intercompany profits must be allowed for. To illustrate, again using the facts of the preceding example, assume that S Company's inventories contained intercompany profits, made on sales by P Company, in these amounts:

In inventory at beginning of year	\$ 500
In inventory at end of year	1,500

Consolidated net income is determined as follows:

P Company net income (realized from a consolidated viewpoint) exclusive of its share of S Company income: \$30,000 + \$500 − \$1,500	\$29,000
S Company net income, exclusive of its share of P Company income	10,000
Total	\$39,000
Minority interest in S Company income (computed below)	2,804
Consolidated net income	\$36,196

$$S = \$10{,}000 + .10P$$
$$P = \$29{,}000 + .80S$$
$$S = \$10{,}000 + .10(\$29{,}000 + .80S)$$
$$S = \$12{,}900 + .08S$$
$$.92S = \$12{,}900$$
$$S = \$14{,}022$$
$$20\% \text{ of } S = \$\ 2{,}804 = \text{minority interest in S Company net income}$$
$$P = \$29{,}000 + .80(\$14{,}022)$$
$$P = \$40{,}218$$
$$90\% \text{ of } P = \$36{,196} = \text{consolidated net income}$$

Let us turn now from a consideration of the minority interest in the periodic income of a subsidiary to the determination of the minority interest to be shown in the consolidated balance sheet.

To derive the minority interest, apply the minority's percentage interest to the total of the following:

1. The common stock of the subsidiary plus any related paid-in capital.
2. The retained earnings of the subsidiary at the date the reciprocal relationship became effective.
3. The earnings of the subsidiary since such effective date, on a *consolidated basis.*

The minority interest as of any balance sheet date can be determined by another approach. In certain instances, the arrangement of the problem data makes the alternative approach the more convenient. The first step is the computation of the net, nonduplicated assets of each individual corporation. This terminology is perhaps needlessly literal, but the computation proceeds as follows:

1. Total reported assets.
2. Deduct investments in related companies.
3. Deduct liabilities.
4. Add excess of cost over book value (or deduct excess of book value over cost). This part of the "Investment" account does *not* duplicate net assets on the books of related companies.

The total of items 1–4 equals the net, nonduplicated assets.

To illustrate, the alternative method is applied to the 80%–10% case previously diagrammed.

	P Company		*S Company*	
Total assets		$395,000		$200,000
Deduct:				
Investments in related companies	$ 95,000		$25,000	
Liabilities	130,000	225,000	75,000	100,000
Balance		$170,000		$100,000
Add excess of cost over book value		26,000		–0–
Net, nonduplicated assets		$196,000		$100,000

Let P = stockholders' equity of parent on a consolidated basis
Let S = stockholders' equity of subsidiary on a consolidated basis

$$
\begin{aligned}
P &= \$196{,}000 + .80S \\
S &= \$100{,}000 + .10P \\
S &= \$100{,}000 + .10(\$196{,}000 + .80S) \\
S &= \$100{,}000 + \$19{,}600 + .08S \\
.92S &= \$119{,}600 \\
S &= \$130{,}000 \\
20\% \text{ of } \$130{,}000 &= \$\ 26{,}000 = \text{minority interest in S Company} \\
P &= \$196{,}000 + .80(\$130{,}000) \\
P &= \$300{,}000 \\
90\% \text{ of } \$300{,}000 &= \$270{,}000 = \text{consolidated stockholders' equity}
\end{aligned}
$$

6 managerial accounting

Kenneth W. Perry

In recent years, problems related to managerial accounting have constituted more than 20% of the problems given in the Practice sections of the Uniform CPA Examination. (Whereas financial accounting is concerned primarily with the preparation and presentation of accounting data for the use of groups or persons other than management, managerial accounting deals chiefly with the preparation and presentation of data for management's use.) In addition, questions related to managerial accounting frequently appear in the Theory section. With so much emphasis currently being placed on the managerial aspects of accounting, it is perhaps needless to point out that the serious CPA candidate must prepare himself thoroughly in this area before sitting for the examination. However, once he has mastered the subject, he should look forward to encountering one or more problems of this kind, because ordinarily they are relatively easy to solve.

Managerial problems appearing on the CPA examination generally fall into one of three broad categories: problems requiring the application of special-purpose analyses and techniques, cost accounting problems, and budgeting problems. Although the following coverage is not exhaustive, it is indicative of the type of managerial material with which the candidate should be thoroughly familiar.

Special-Purpose Analyses and Techniques

Management sometimes requires more specialized information than that which is readily obtainable from an analysis of the basic financial statements in order to draw sound conclusions regarding specific facets of an organization's liquidity, stability, and profitability. The following are representative of special-purpose managerial analyses and techniques frequently encountered in problems appearing on the CPA examination:

1. Gross margin analysis
2. Break-even analysis
3. Marginal analysis
4. Segmental analysis
5. Capital expenditure analysis
6. Mathematics of inventory management

gross margin analysis

Although comparative income statements reflect net changes in gross margin (gross profit) from one period to another, they do not reveal the underlying reasons for the changes. For decision-making purposes, the causes of changes may be more significant than the net amounts; therefore, it is often desirable to break net changes down into their basic components.

Because gross margin is determined by deducting the cost of goods sold from net sales, a change in the amount of gross margin may result from:

1. An increase or decrease in sales.
2. An increase or decrease in the cost of goods sold.
3. A combination of the two.

An increase or decrease in sales may be the result of:

1. A change in the per-unit selling price.
2. A change in the number of units sold.
3. A combination of the two.

An increase or decrease in the cost of goods sold may be the result of:

1. A change in the per-unit cost price.
2. A change in the number of units sold.
3. A combination of the two.

If we let *NCGM* represent the net change in gross margin, the breakdown may be depicted in tree form as in Figure 1.

FIGURE 1

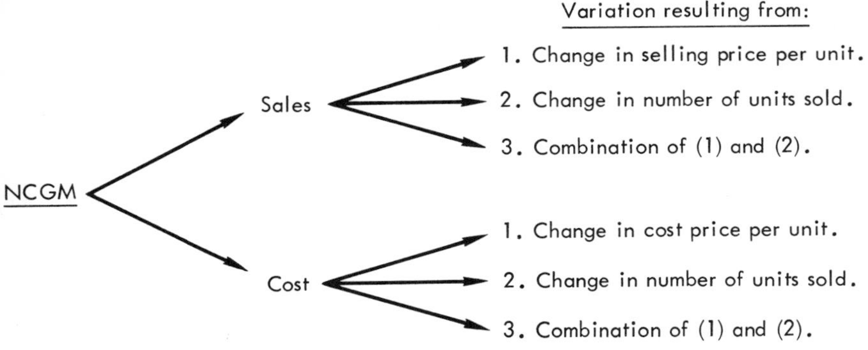

Although six possible variations appear in the tree diagram, all result from changes in either price, volume, or a combination of the two. The variances may be summarized as follows:

1. A *price variance* results from a change in either the unit selling price or the unit cost price. It is computed by multiplying the price change per unit by the number of units sold in the preceding period. It is possible to have a price variance for both sales and cost of goods sold.
2. A *volume variance* results from a change in the number of units sold. It is computed by multiplying the change in the number of units sold by the unit price for the preceding period. If there is a volume variance, there will, of course, be one for both sales and cost of goods sold.
3. A *price–volume variance* results from a change in both a unit price and the number of units sold. It is computed by multiplying the change in price per unit by the change in the number of units sold. Again, it is possible to have a price–volume variance for both sales and cost of goods sold.

The following problem is illustrative of the CPA examination requirements in this area.

Problem: Assuming that the Farmbrook Manufacturing Company manufactures and sells only one product, prepare from the following data a detailed analysis of the causes of the $7,960 change in gross margin.

	19X2		*19X1*	
	Amount	*Per Unit*	*Amount*	*Per Unit*
Sales	$112,200	$10.20	$100,000	$10.00
Cost of sales	64,240	5.84	60,000	6.00
Gross margin	$ 47,960	$ 4.36	$ 40,000	$ 4.00

Solution:

FARMBROOK MANUFACTURING COMPANY

Gross Margin Analysis

Increase in sales resulting from:		
Price variance [($10.20 − $10.00) × 10,000]		$ 2,000
Volume variance [(11,000 − 10,000) × $10.00]		10,000
Price–volume variance [($10.20 − $10.00) × (11,000 − 10,000)]		200
Increase in sales		$12,200
Increase in cost of goods sold resulting from:		
Price variance [($6.00 − $5.84) × 10,000]	$(1,600)	
Volume variance [(11,000 − 10,000) × $6.00]	6,000	
Price–volume variance [($6.00 − $5.84) × (11,000 − 10,000)]	(160)	
Increase in cost of goods sold		4,240
Increase in gross margin		$ 7,960

Instructional Note. When studying the solution, note that the net increase in gross margin of $7,960 was the result of an increase in sales of $12,200 and an increase in the cost of goods sold of $4,240. The $12,200 increase in sales was the result of a favorable price variance of $2,000, a favorable volume variance of $10,000, and a favorable price–volume variance of $200. The $4,240 increase in the cost of goods sold resulted from a favorable price variance of $1,600, an unfavorable volume variance of $6,000, and a favorable price–volume variance of $160.

break-even analysis

The *break-even* point is that point at which the total of all revenues is exactly equal to the total of all expenses. Thus at the break-even point an organization neither makes a profit nor sustains a loss. Although break-even analysis can be applied to past operations, it is particularly useful as a means of investigating projected activities. For example, management may wish to know what effect an increase or decrease in selling prices or sales volume will have on its break-even point.

Break-even analysis is based upon certain assumptions about the behavior of revenues and expenses. In the computation of the break-even point, a fixed sales price is assumed, whereas expenses are considered to be either "fixed" or "variable."

A *fixed expense* is constant in amount within a particular range of activity (often referred to as the *relevant range*). Depreciation, property taxes, and rent are examples of fixed expenses.

A *variable expense* fluctuates in total amount with changes in volume, increasing proportionately with increases in volume and decreasing with decreases in volume. The cost of goods sold, sales commissions, and supplies used are examples of variable expenses.

Break-Even Computations. The basic formula for break-even analysis is the one used to compute the break-even point. If we let S equal sales at the break-even point, FE equal fixed expenses, and VE equal variable expenses, the formula may be written as

$$S = FE + VE$$

To illustrate the computation, let us assume that fixed expenses at a projected level of activity are expected to be \$90,000 and variable expenses are expected to equal 40% of sales. To break even, the organization must generate sales of \$150,000, determined as follows:

$$\begin{aligned} S &= FE + VE \\ S &= \$\ 90{,}000 + .40S \\ .60S &= \$\ 90{,}000 \\ S &= \$150{,}000 \end{aligned}$$

In addition to determining break-even points, break-even analysis may be used to estimate the sales volume required to provide a specified net income, or rate of return, under given conditions. Using the data in the preceding illustration, let us assume that the organization wants to earn a net income of 15% on its sales. If we let RS equal the required sales and NI equal the desired net income, we can determine that the organization must generate sales of \$200,000:

$$\begin{aligned} RS &= FE + VE + NI \\ RS &= \$\ 90{,}000 + .40RS + .15RS \\ .45RS &= \$\ 90{,}000 \\ RS &= \$200{,}000 \end{aligned}$$

The following problem is indicative of CPA examination requirements in this area.

Problem: Assuming that the Atlas Sales Company has yearly fixed expenses of $1.6 million and that its variable expenses ordinarily run about 60% of sales, determine:

1. The amount of Atlas' net income or loss at a sales volume of
   a. $6,000,000.
   b. $3,000,000.
2. Atlas' break-even point.
3. The amount of sales needed by Atlas in order to generate a net income of $200,000.

Solution:

1. a. $800,000 net income [$6,000,000 – $1,600,000 – (60% × $6,000,000)].
   b. $400,000 net loss [$3,000,000 – $1,600,000 – (60% × $3,000,000)].
2. $4,000,000.

$$\begin{aligned} \text{Let } S &= \text{sales at the break-even point} \\ S &= FE + VE \\ S &= \$1{,}600{,}000 + 60\%\,(S) \\ .40S &= \$1{,}600{,}000 \\ S &= \$4{,}000{,}000 \end{aligned}$$

3. $4,500,000.

$$\begin{aligned} \text{Let } RS &= \text{required sales} \\ RS &= FE + 60\%\,(RS) + \$200{,}000 \\ RS &= \$1{,}600{,}000 + .60RS + \$200{,}000 \\ .40RS &= \$1{,}800{,}000 \\ RS &= \$4{,}500{,}000 \end{aligned}$$

Break-Even Chart. The relation of fixed and variable expenses to revenue at different volume levels is often portrayed graphically on a *break-even chart.* Revenue points are plotted on the graph at various levels and the *revenue curve* is sketched in by joining the various points with a line. Expense points are plotted on the graph at various levels and the *cost curve* is sketched in by connecting the total expense points at the various levels. The point at which the revenue curve and the cost curve intersect is the break-even point. On a recent CPA examination the candidates were required to identify the numbered components on Figure 2.

FIGURE 2

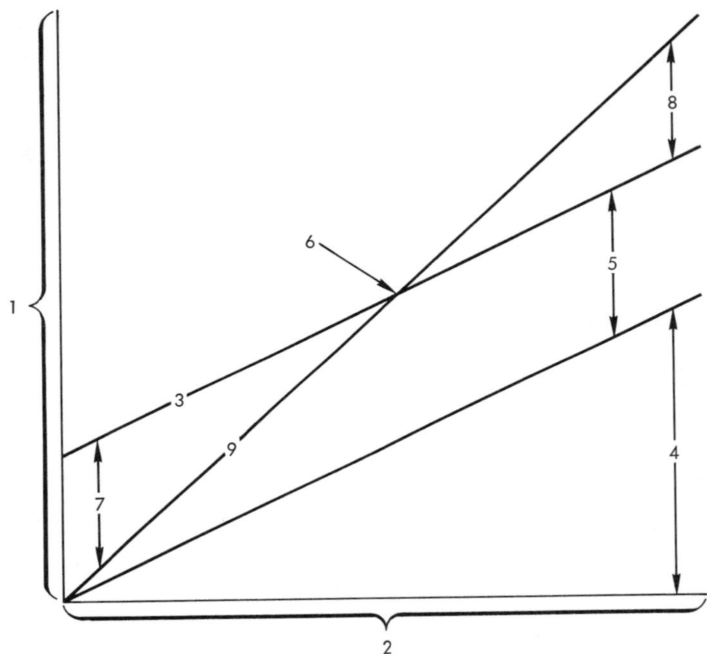

Solution:

1. Dollar values.
2. Volume or activity.
3. Total cost curve.
4. Variable expenses.
5. Fixed expenses.
6. Break-even point.
7. Loss area.
8. Profit area.
9. Revenue curve.

marginal analysis

All except the most routine managerial actions involve a choice of alternatives. For example, management may have to decide at one time or another whether to raise or lower prices, accept or reject sales orders, hire or fire employees, expand or contract operations, and so on.

When choosing among alternative courses of action, a profit-oriented management usually will give considerable weight to two factors commonly known as marginal revenue and marginal expense. *Marginal revenue* is the difference between the amount of revenue expected to be realized under one alternative and that expected to be realized under another; *marginal expense* is the difference between the total expenses expected to be incurred under one alternative and those expected to be incurred under another.

The following problem is indicative of the CPA examination requirements in the area of marginal analysis.

Problem: The Commercial Products Corporation has requested your assistance in determining the potential loss on a binding purchase contract that will be in effect at the end of the corporation's fiscal year. The corporation produces a chemical compound that deteriorates and must be discarded if it is not sold by the end of the month during which it is produced.

The total variable cost of the manufactured compound is $25 per unit and it is sold for $40 per unit. The compound can be purchased from a competitor at $40 per unit plus $5 freight per unit. It is estimated that failure to fill orders would result in the complete loss of eight out of ten customers placing orders for the compound.

The corporation has sold the compound for the past 30 months. Demand has been irregular and there is no sales trend. During this period sales per month have been:

Units Sold per Month	*Number of Months* *
4,000	6
5,000	15
6,000	9

* Occurred in random sequence.

Required:

1. Determine the probability of sales of 4000, 5000, or 6000 units in any one month.

2. Prepare a schedule showing marginal income if sales of 4000, 5000, or 6000 units are made in one month and 4000, 5000, or 6000 units are manufactured in the same month. (Assume that all sales orders are filled regardless of the circumstances.)

3. Prepare a schedule showing the average monthly marginal income the corporation might expect over the long run if 5000 units are manufactured every month and all sales orders are filled.

Solution:

1. There is a twenty percent (6/30) probability of selling 4000 units in any one month, a fifty percent (15/30) probability of selling 5000 units, and a thirty percent (9/30) probability of selling 6000 units.

2.

SCHEDULE OF MARGINAL INCOME
FOR VARIOUS COMBINATIONS OF UNIT SALES
AND UNITS MANUFACTURED

	Units Manufactured (and Purchased)		
Unit Sales	*4,000*	*5,000*	*6,000*
4,000	\$60,000 [a]	\$35,000 [b]	\$10,000 [b]
5,000	55,000 [c]	75,000 [a]	50,000 [b]
6,000	50,000 [c]	70,000 [c]	90,000 [a]

Computation of Marginal Income:

[a] When all units manufactured are sold:

4,000 × (\$40 − \$25) = \$60,000
5,000 × (\$40 − \$25) = 75,000
6,000 × (\$40 − \$25) = 90,000

[b] Reduction per 1,000 units when more units are manufactured than are sold:

1,000 × \$25 = \$25,000

[c] Reduction per 1,000 units when units must be purchased to fill sales orders:

1,000 × [\$40 − (\$40 + \$5)] = \$5,000

3.

SCHEDULE COMPUTING EXPECTED
MARGINAL INCOME IF 5,000 UNITS ARE MANUFACTURED
AND ALL SALES ORDERS ARE FILLED

Unit Sales	*Probability*	*Marginal Income*	*Expected Value*
4,000	.2	\$35,000	\$ 7,000
5,000	.5	75,000	37,500
6,000	.3	70,000	21,000
Expected average monthly marginal income			\$65,500

Two of the more useful analytical techniques based on the concept of the margin are the contribution margin ratio and the margin of safety. When studying these techniques, note their close relation to break-even analysis.

Contribution Margin Ratio. In financial analysis the excess of sales over variable expenses is known as the *contribution margin.* The *contribution margin ratio,* sometimes referred to as the *profit–volume ratio,* expresses the relation between the contribution margin and sales. The ratio is normally stated as a percentage of sales. It is the complement of the *variable expense ratio,* which expresses the relation between variable expenses and sales. If we let *CMR* stand for the contribution margin ratio, *S* for sales, and *VE* for variable expenses, the formula for determining the contribution margin ratio will appear as follows:

$$CMR = \frac{S - VE}{S}$$

Like break-even analysis, the contribution margin ratio may be used to determine the break-even point or to estimate the sales volume required to provide a specified income under given conditions. To illustrate its use, let us assume the same data used in the foregoing break-even illustrations; that is, fixed expenses are expected to be $90,000 and variable expenses are expected to equal 40% of sales for a projected level of activity. Since the contribution margin ratio is the complement of the variable expense ratio, it will be 60% of sales. It was determined in the earlier computation that to break even the organization must generate sales of $150,000. If we let *S* equal the sales at the break-even point, we can determine the $150,000 using the contribution margin ratio as follows:

$$\begin{aligned} S &= \frac{FE}{CMR} \\ S &= \frac{\$90{,}000}{.60S} \\ .60S &= \$\ 90{,}000 \\ S &= \$150{,}000 \end{aligned}$$

If the organization wishes to earn a net income of 15% on its sales, it must, as you will recall, generate sales of $200,000. If we let *RS* equal the required sales and *NI* the desired net income, using the contribution margin we can determine the $200,000 as follows:

$$\begin{aligned} RS &= \frac{FE + NI}{CMR} \\ RS &= \frac{\$90{,}000 + .15RS}{.60RS} \\ .60RS - .15RS &= \$\ 90{,}000 \\ .45RS &= \$\ 90{,}000 \\ RS &= \$200{,}000 \end{aligned}$$

Margin of Safety. The excess of projected or actual revenue over the amount of revenue required for the organization to break even is known as the *margin of safety.* It indicates the amount by which revenue may decrease without the organization's sustaining a loss. The margin of safety may be stated in dollar terms or expressed as a percentage. If we continue our previous illustration and assume that the projected sales for the next period are \$200,000, the margin of safety may be stated as either \$50,000 or 25%. The \$50,000 is determined simply by subtracting sales at the break-even point of \$150,000 from the projected sales of \$200,000. If we let *MS* equal the margin of safety, *PS* the projected sales, and *S* the sales at the break-even point, a margin of safety of 25% may be determined as follows:

$$MS = \frac{PS - S}{PS}$$

$$MS = \frac{\$200{,}000 - \$150{,}000}{\$200{,}000}$$

$$MS = \frac{\$\ 50{,}000}{\$200{,}000}$$

$$MS = 25\%$$

The following problem is illustrative of the examination requirements in this area.

Problem: Assuming that the Apex Sales Company has yearly fixed expenses of \$120,000 and a *CMR* (contribution margin ratio) equal to 20% of sales, determine:

1. Apex's break-even point.
2. The amount of sales needed by Apex in order to generate a net income of \$300,000.
3. Apex's margin of safety at a sales volume of \$660,000.

Solution:

1. \$600,000.

$$\textit{Let } S = \text{sales at the break-even point}$$

$$S = \frac{FE}{CMR}$$

$$S = \frac{\$120{,}000}{20\%\ (S)}$$

$$S = \frac{\$120{,}000}{.20S}$$

$$.20S = \$120{,}000$$

$$S = \$600{,}000$$

2. \$2,100,000.

$$\textit{Let } RS = \text{required sales}$$

$$RS = \frac{FE + NI}{CMR}$$

$$RS = \frac{\$120{,}000 + \$300{,}000}{20\%\ (RS)}$$

$$.20RS = \$\ \ 420{,}000$$

$$RS = \$2{,}100{,}000$$

3. \$60,000.

$$\$660{,}000 - \$600{,}000 \text{ (break-even)} = \$60{,}000$$

or 9.09%.

$$MS = \frac{PS - S}{PS}$$

$$MS = \frac{\$660{,}000 - \$600{,}000}{\$660{,}000}$$

$$MS = 9.09\%$$

Marginal Analysis and Break-Even Chart. The contribution margin and the margin of safety may be depicted graphically on a break-even chart as in Figure 3.

FIGURE 3

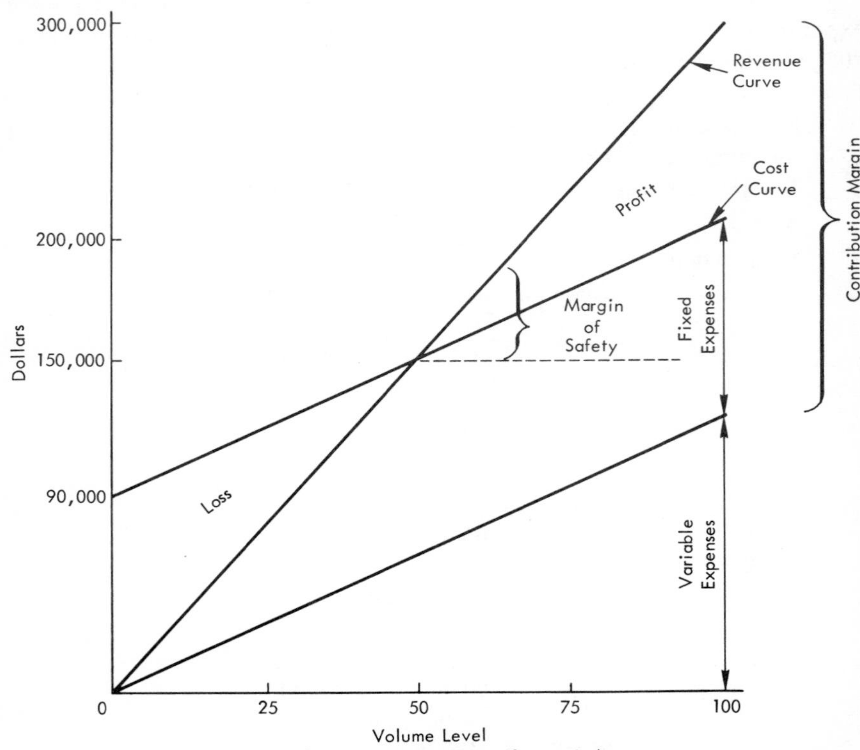

segmental analysis

In today's business environment, the successful organization must rely on sound planning and control to achieve maximum profits and realize minimum losses. This is especially important in the large, highly diversified concern that sells more than one kind of product or service. The overall operation of a business of this kind is ordinarily broken down into divisions, departments, or product lines. The analysis of the operations of such business subdivisions is commonly known as *segmental analysis.* Segmental analysis is particularly useful to management in making decisions in such areas as product planning and pricing.

Segmental Analysis and Product Planning. To illustrate the use of segmental analysis in the area of product planning, let us assume that the ABC Company has been producing and selling three products, A, B, and C. Management is given the following current year's data at a time when it is considering what products to produce and sell during the next year.

	Products			
	A	*B*	*C*	*Total*
Sales	$450,000	$400,000	$200,000	$1,050,000
Fixed expenses	$200,000	$100,000	$150,000	$ 450,000
Variable expenses	50,000	200,000	100,000	350,000
Total expenses	$250,000	$300,000	$250,000	$ 800,000
Net income (loss)	$200,000	$100,000	($ 50,000)	$ 250,000

A casual glance at the data might lead one to suggest discontinuing product C, which appears to be unprofitable. On closer analysis, however, as indicated in the following data, we can see that product C is actually contributing $100,000 (which in reality is the excess of $200,000 sales over $100,000 of variable expenses) to the overall net income, assuming that the fixed expenses are rigidly fixed and the variable expenses are strictly variable.

	Totals	
	Including Product C	*Excluding Product C*
Sales	$1,050,000	$850,000
Fixed expenses	$ 450,000	$450,000
Variable expenses	350,000	250,000
Total expenses	$ 800,000	$700,000
Net income (loss)	$ 250,000	$150,000

The following problem is illustrative of the examination requirements in the area of product planning.

Problem: The management of the Southern Cottonseed Company has engaged you to assist in the development of information to be used for managerial decisions. The company has the capacity to process 20,000 tons of cottonseed per year. The yield of a ton of cottonseed is as follows:

Product	*Average Yield per Ton of Cottonseed (in pounds)*	*Average Selling Price per Trade Unit*
Oil	300	$ 0.15 per lb
Meal	600	50.00 per ton
Hulls	800	20.00 per ton
Lint	100	3.00 per cwt
Waste	200	

A special marketing study revealed that the company can expect to sell its entire output for the coming year at the listed average selling prices.

You have determined the company's costs to be as follows:

Processing costs:

Variable: $9 per ton of cottonseed put into process

Fixed: $108,000 per year

Marketing costs:

All variable: $20 per ton sold

Administrative costs:

All fixed: $90,000 per year

Required: From the foregoing information you prepared and submitted to management a detailed report on the company's break-even point. In view of conditions in the cottonseed market, management told you that they would also like to know the average maximum amount that the company can afford to pay for a ton of cottonseed.

Management has defined the average maximum amount that the company can afford to pay for a ton of cottonseed as the amount that would result in the company's having losses no greater when operating than when closed down under the existing cost and revenue structure. Management states that you are to assume that the fixed costs shown in your break-even point report will continue unchanged even when operations are shut down. Determine the average maximum amount that the company can pay per ton.

Solution:

Computation of the Average Maximum Amount
to be Paid per Ton of Cottonseed

Sales:		
Oil—(300 × 20,000 × \$0.15)		\$ 900,000
Meal—(600/2,000 × 20,000 × \$50)		300,000
Hulls—(800/2,000 × 20,000 × \$20)		160,000
Lint—(20,000 × \$3)		60,000
Total sales		\$1,420,000
Less: Variable costs:		
Processing—(20,000 × \$9)	\$180,000	
Marketing—[\$20 (20,000 − 2,000 *)]	360,000	540,000
Maximum total amount that can be paid for 20,000 tons of cottonseed that would cause the company's losses to be no greater when operating than when closed down		\$ 880,000

Average maximum amount per ton = \$880,000/20,000 = \$44 per ton

* Waste (20,000 × 10%).

Segmental Analysis and Product Pricing. To illustrate the use of segmental analysis in the area of product pricing, let us assume in addition to the basic data used in our preceding illustration that the company produced 10,000 units of product C during the current year (full capacity being 15,000 units per year), and that the total expense at full capacity is \$300,000 per year, with the fixed and variable elements being equal. While planning for next year's production, a year in which the domestic sales of product C are expected to remain at last year's level (10,000 units), management must make a decision regarding an offer from an exporter for the excess capacity. Sales management is confident that acceptance of the exporter's offer will not affect the present domestic market. Whereas the domestic price is \$20 per unit, the exporter offers only \$15 per unit for the excess capacity of 5000 units. Since actual cost during the current year was \$25 per unit [(\$150,000 *FE* + \$100,000 *VE*) ÷ 10,000], at first glance it would appear that the \$15 per unit offer should be rejected. However, after the situation is analyzed as follows, the answer might be different:

	Product C	
	Domestic Sales Only	*Both Foreign and Domestic Sales*
Sales	$200,000	$275,000
Fixed expenses	$150,000	$150,000
Variable expenses	100,000	150,000
Total expenses	$250,000	$300,000
Net income (loss)	($ 50,000)	($ 25,000)

Although product C still appears to be unprofitable in spite of the potential foreign sales, it should be recognized that acceptance of the offer will result in a $25,000 addition to the company's overall net income. This can be seen in the following data:

	Including Only Domestic Sales of Product C	*Including Foreign and Domestic Sales of Product C*
Sales	$1,050,000	$1,125,000
Fixed expenses	$ 450,000	$ 450,000
Variable expenses	350,000	400,000
Total expenses	$ 800,000	$ 850,000
Net income (loss)	$ 250,000	$ 275,000

The next problem is illustrative of the type of problem the candidate may be required to solve on the CPA Examination in the area of product pricing.

Problem: The TBZ Company produces a single product. The company has a maximum productive capacity of 100,000 units a year. According to TBZ's marketing department, the market for its product varies with the price at which it is offered for sale, as follows:

Sales Price	*Predicted Market*
$15	70,000 units
14	80,000 units
12	90,000 units
10	100,000 units

Required: Assuming that the company's fixed expenses are $300,000 a year and that its variable expenses average 40% of gross sales, determine the selling price for the company's product which you would recommend.

Solution: $14 (see schedule of selling prices)

TBZ COMPANY

SCHEDULE OF SELLING PRICES

Sales price per unit	$15	$14	$12	$10
Number of units	70,000	80,000	90,000	100,000
Gross sales	$1,050,000	$1,120,000	$1,080,000	$1,000,000
Fixed expenses	$ 300,000	$ 300,000	$ 300,000	$ 300,000
Variable expenses	420,000	448,000	432,000	400,000
Total expenses	$ 720,000	$ 748,000	$ 732,000	$ 700,000
Gross margin	$ 330,000	$ 372,000	$ 348,000	$ 300,000

capital expenditure analysis

Making capital expenditure decisions (decisions regarding the acquisition of long-lived assets) is one of the most important of all management activities in the area of long-range planning. Typical capital expenditures range from the replacement of individual items of machinery and equipment to complex projects such as plant expansion and the development of new products.

In today's large business organization, the competition among various departments and divisions for funds and other concessions is usually intense, and for this reason management must thoroughly examine all possibilities before making capital expenditure decisions. The estimated amount of investment required for a proposed asset or project, its estimated economic life, estimated earnings, and the degree of risk involved must be given serious consideration, and all possible alternatives must likewise be studied. In many instances the very future of the organization may depend on whether the right decision is reached.

Sound capital expenditure decisions are based upon a combination of engineering, marketing, and financial analysis plus a high degree of management judgment. The profitability of a proposal is of particular importance. Three basic types of analysis, or some variation or combination thereof, are used to evaluate the profitability of capital expenditure proposals. They are:

1. Average investment method
2. Payback method
3. Discounted cash flow method

Average Investment Method. The *average investment method,* or as it is sometimes called, the *average rate of return method,* merely relates the average earnings of a project or an asset to the average investment over its lifetime. The amount of average earnings is estimated, whereas the average investment is commonly considered to be equal to one-half of the original investment. (One-half of the original investment is used as the average investment because it is equal to the average carrying value of an asset as determined by straight-line depreciation, assuming that the asset has no salvage value.) When the method is stated as a formula, we have:

$$\text{average rate of return} = \frac{\text{average earnings}}{\text{average investment}}$$

To illustrate the average investment method, let us assume that management is considering the acquisition of an asset costing \$100,000 with an estimated useful life of ten years, and that estimated earnings from the asset after all expenses including depreciation are deducted are \$50,000 for the ten-year period. If we let *ARR* equal the average rate of return, *AE* equal average earnings, and *AI* equal the average investment, a rate of return of 10% would be determined as follows:

$$ARR = \frac{AE}{AI}$$

$$ARR = \frac{(\$50{,}000/10)}{(\$100{,}000/2)}$$

$$ARR = \frac{\$\ 5{,}000}{\$50{,}000}$$

$$ARR = 10\%$$

Although the average investment method is easy to apply and can be used as a simple screening device to eliminate unprofitable proposals from consideration early in capital expenditure deliberations, it does have limitations. A serious weakness of the method is that it fails to take into consideration the timing of the earnings; that is, it makes no distinction between investments returning capital outlays at an early date and those which return them sometime in the future. Obviously, the sooner capital outlays can be recovered, the sooner they can be reinvested in something else.

Payback Method. The *payback method,* sometimes called the *payout method,* is a procedure for determining the *payback period,* which is the amount of time required for a project or an asset to earn enough to return the original outlay. Stated another way, it is the number of years needed for the accumulated cash earnings from a project or asset to equal the original cash outlay. The formula is:

$$\text{payback} = \frac{\text{investment}}{\text{annual net cash flow}}$$

Technically, *net cash flow* is the excess of cash flowing into an organization from revenue over cash flowing out for expenses. For purposes of simplicity, however, in payback computations the term is used in much the same way the term "funds provided by operations" is used on the funds statement; that is, net cash flow is considered to be equal to reported earnings plus depreciation. Letting *PBP* equal the payback period, *I* equal the investment, or original outlay, *NCF* equal the predicted annual net cash flow, and assuming the same data that were used in the preceding illustration, we can determine a payback period of $6\frac{2}{3}$ years as follows:

$$PBP = \frac{I \text{ (investment)}}{NCF \text{ (annual earnings plus depreciation)}}$$

$$PBP = \frac{\$100{,}000}{\$5{,}000 + \$10{,}000}$$

$$PBP = 6\tfrac{2}{3} \text{ years}$$

The payback method of analysis is very popular. Like the average investment method, it is easily applied and can be used to eliminate unprofitable proposals from consideration early in deliberations. For instance, a proposed project with a payback period of $6\frac{2}{3}$ years would automatically be screened out if an organization demanded a payback period of five years or less, whereas it would be retained for further consideration if the payback criterion were ten years. Also like the average investment method, the payback method has weaknesses. It does not, for example, take into account the time value of money—the notion that time is worth money, or stated another way, that a dollar today is worth more than the promise of a dollar at some time in the future. Moreover, it does not reflect the overall profitability of one project as compared to that of another. To illustrate the second disadvantage assume:

Proposed Projects	*Investment*	*Annual Net Cash Flow*
A	$100,000	$15,000
B	120,000	18,000

Both projects have payback periods of $6\frac{2}{3}$ years ($I \div NCF$). Thus, if evaluated strictly on payback periods, they would appear to be equally desirable. Further analysis, however, indicates that project A has an estimated useful life of ten years, and project B an estimated useful life of twenty years. Therefore the projects really are not equally desirable. Project B has the greater potential because it is capable of generating

$18,000 a year for 13⅓ years (20 years − 6⅔ years) after the initial investment is recovered. Project A, on the other hand, is capable of generating only $15,000 a year for 3⅓ years (10 years − 6⅔ years) after its initial investment has been recouped.

Discounted Cash Flow Method. Both the average rate of return and payback methods provide rather simple approaches to the evaluation of capital expenditure proposals. In order to include a consideration of the time value of money, many organizations use the more sophisticated *discounted cash flow method* of analysis. Under this procedure a capital expenditure is viewed as the acquisition of a series of future net cash flows composed of two elements: the return of the original outlay and net income from the project. When it employs this method, an organization will not invest more in a given project than the sum of the net cash flows discounted back to the present at the desired rate of return.

The idea of discounting future amounts is not new to us as accountants. The candidate will recall from previous studies that if we invest $1 for one year at 6% interest, the $1 will grow to be $1.06 at the end of the year. To determine the amount, we simply multiply $1 by 1.06. If we were to work backward to the present, we would merely divide $1.06 by 1.06 and determine that the present value is $1. Thus if we wanted to know the present value of a net cash flow of $1,000 for the first year, we would divide $1,000 by 1.06 (assuming the desired rate of return is 6%) and obtain a present value of approximately $943. The present value of a net cash flow of $1,000 for the second year would be determined by dividing $1,000 by 1.06, obtaining $943, and then by dividing $943 by 1.06 and obtaining roughly $890. (Of course, as the candidate will recall, the detailed computations can be eliminated if we take the correct factor from predetermined annuity tables and multiply it by the future amount in order to convert the future amount into the present value.)

To illustrate the discounted cash flow method, let us assume the same data used in the preceding illustrations: that is, a proposed capital expenditure requires a $100,000 outlay, the estimated useful life of the asset under consideration is ten years, and a net cash flow of $15,000 ($5,000 income plus $10,000 depreciation) per year is expected. In addition, let us assume that the organization requires that at least 6% be earned on all capital expenditures. As shown in Schedule A (Table 1), the amount to be invested ($100,000) is less than the present value ($110,385) of the expected cash flows. Thus, the proposal meets the discounted cash flow requirement.

If the requirement were 10% rather than 6%, the proposal would not meet it. As we can see in Schedule B (Table 2), the present value of

TABLE 1

SCHEDULE A

NET CASH FLOW DISCOUNTED AT 6%

Year	Net Cash Flow		Present Value of 1 at 6%		Present Value of Net Cash Flow
1	$15,000	×	.943	=	$ 14,145
2	15,000	×	.890	=	13,350
3	15,000	×	.840	=	12,600
4	15,000	×	.792	=	11,880
5	15,000	×	.747	=	11,205
6	15,000	×	.705	=	10,575
7	15,000	×	.665	=	9,975
8	15,000	×	.627	=	9,405
9	15,000	×	.592	=	8,880
10	15,000	×	.558	=	8,370
Present value of net cash flow					$110,385
Amount to be invested					100,000
Excess of present value of net cash flow over amount to be invested					$ 10,385

the net cash flow when discounted at 10% is $7,840 less than the amount to be invested.

TABLE 2

SCHEDULE B

NET CASH FLOW DISCOUNTED AT 10%

Year	Net Cash Flow		Present Value of 1 at 6%		Present Value of Net Cash Flow
1	$15,000	×	.909	=	$ 13,635
2	15,000	×	.826	=	12,390
3	15,000	×	.751	=	11,265
4	15,000	×	.683	=	10,245
5	15,000	×	.621	=	9,315
6	15,000	×	.564	=	8,460
7	15,000	×	.513	=	7,695
8	15,000	×	.467	=	7,005
9	15,000	×	.424	=	6,360
10	15,000	×	.386	=	5,790
Present value of net cash flow					$ 92,160
Amount to be invested					100,000
Excess of amount to be invested over the present value of net cash flow					$ (7,840)

Capital Expenditure Analysis Illustrated. To illustrate the simultaneous use of all three methods of analyzing capital expenditure proposals, let us assume that an organization has the following proposals under consideration:

Proposal	*Estimated Cost*	*Estimated Useful Life*	*Estimated Annual Earnings*
A	$100,000	5 years	$20,000
B	120,000	5 years	26,000
C	160,000	8 years	16,000

Let us also assume that all capital expenditure proposals are initially evaluated against the following criteria:

1. Average rate of return must be equal to or greater than 10%.
2. Payback period is not to exceed 50% of the estimated useful life of the project or asset.
3. Discounted net cash flow must be equal to or greater than 30%.

We can see in Schedules C, D, and E (Tables 3–5) that all three

TABLE 3

SCHEDULE C

AVERAGE RATE OF RETURN

Proposal	*Estimated Annual Earnings*		*Average Investment* *		*Average Rate of Return*
A	$20,000	÷	$50,000	=	40%
B	26,000	÷	60,000	=	43.3%
C	16,000	÷	80,000	=	20%

* Estimated cost divided by 2.

TABLE 4

SCHEDULE D

PAYBACK PERIOD

Proposal	*Cost*		*Annual Net Cash Flow*		*Payback Period*
A	$100,000	÷	$40,000 *	=	2.5 years
B	120,000	÷	50,000 *	=	2.4 years
C	160,000	÷	36,000 *	=	4.4 years †

* Estimated annual earnings plus depreciation.
† Does not meet the requirement.

TABLE 5

SCHEDULE E

NET CASH FLOW DISCOUNTED AT 30%

		Proposal A		*Proposal B*	
Year	*Present Value of 1 at 30%*	*Net Cash Flow*	*Present Value of Net Cash Flow*	*Net Cash Flow*	*Present Value of Net Cash Flow*
1	0.769	$40,000	$ 30,760	$50,000	$ 38,450
2	0.592	40,000	23,680	50,000	29,600
3	0.455	40,000	18,200	50,000	22,750
4	0.350	40,000	14,000	50,000	17,500
5	0.269	40,000	10,760	50,000	13,450
Present value of net cash flow			$ 97,400		$121,750
Amount to be invested			100,000		120,000
Excess			$ (2,600) *		$ 1,750

* Does not meet the requirement.

proposals meet the average rate of return requirement, but that proposal C "falls out" of consideration when it cannot meet the payback period requirement, and proposal A falls out when it fails to meet the discounted cash flow requirement.

The following problem is illustrative of the CPA Examination requirements in the area of capital expenditure analysis.

Problem: The Capital Budget Committee of the Walton Corporation was established to appraise and screen departmental requests for plant expansions and improvements at a time when these requests totaled $10 million. The committee thereupon sought your professional advice and help in establishing minimum performance standards which it should demand of these projects in the way of anticipated rates of return before interest and taxes.

The Walton Corporation is a closely held family corporation in which the stockholders exert an active and unified influence on the management. At this date, the company has no long-term debt and has 1,000,000 shares of common capital stock outstanding. It is currently earning $5 million (net income before interest and taxes) per year. The applicable tax rate is 50%.

Should the projects under consideration be approved, management is confident the $10 million of required funds can be obtained either:

1. By borrowing—via the medium of an issue of $10 million, 4%, 20-year bonds.
2. By equity financing—via the medium of an issue of 500,000 shares of common stock to the general public. It is expected and anticipated that the ownership of these 500,000 shares would be widely dispersed and scattered.

The company has been earning a 12.5% return after taxes. The management and the dominant stockholders consider this rate of earnings to be a fair capitalization rate (eight times earnings) as long as the company remains free of long-term debt. An increase to 15% or six and two-thirds times earnings would constitute an adequate adjustment to compensate for the risk of carrying $10 million of long-term debt. They believe that this reflects, and is consistent with, current market appraisals.

Required:

a. Prepare columnar schedules comparing minimum returns, considering interests, taxes, and earnings ratio, which should be produced by each alternative to maintain the present capitalized value per share.

b. What minimum rate of return on new investment is necessary for each alternative to maintain the present capitalized value per share?

Solution:

a.

WALTON CORPORATION

COMPARISON OF MINIMUM RETURNS

	Before	*After*	
		Bonds	*Stock*
Earnings before interest and taxes	$5,000,000	$6,400,000	$7,500,000
Interest on bonds	–0–	400,000	–0–
Net income before taxes	$5,000,000	$6,000,000	$7,500,000
Taxes at 50%	2,500,000	3,000,000	3,750,000
Net income after taxes	$2,500,000	$3,000,000	$3,750,000
Number of shares of *common stock*	1,000,000	1,000,000	1,500,000
Earnings per share	$2.50	$3.00	$2.50
Price–earnings ratio	8	$6\frac{2}{3}$	8
Capitalized value per share	$20.00	$20.00	$20.00

b. The interests of the stockholders are paramount. To protect their investment from the danger of dilution, any new investment should earn *at least* 14% before interest and taxes in the case of bond financing and *at least* 25% before interest and taxes in the case of stock financing.

mathematics of inventory management

Mathematical techniques applicable to inventory management have been recognized for several years, but little use was made of them prior to the advent of automatic data processing. At present, considerable attention is being directed on the CPA examination toward two of the more important of these procedures, namely, the determination of the economic order quantity and the reorder point.

Economic Order Quantity (EOQ). The *economic order quantity* is the optimal amount of an inventoriable item to be ordered at a given time, the quantity to be ordered which will not only meet inventory requirements but will also result in the lowest total annual cost to an organization. Inasmuch as ordering creates procurement costs (order processing, etc.) and possession involves carrying or holding costs (insurance, storage, taxes, obsolescence, interest, etc.), the lowest total annual cost generally will correspond to the point where the *cost to order* is equal to the *cost to hold.* To illustrate the arithmetic computation of the EOQ, let us assume that the cost to place an order for item A is $2.50, the holding cost is 10% per year on the average inventory investment, and annual usage is $1,800. Table 6 arrays the estimated total cost of twelve alternative purchase order size/frequency policies:

TABLE 6

ECONOMIC ORDER QUANTITY

(DETERMINED ARITHMETICALLY)

Months' Supply	*Orders per Year*	*Value per Order*	*Average Inventory*	*Cost to Hold*	*Cost to Buy*	*Total Cost* *
12	1.0	$1800	$900	$90.00	$ 2.50	$92.50
11	1.1	1650	825	82.50	2.75	85.25
10	1.2	1500	750	75.00	3.00	78.00
9	1.3	1350	675	67.50	3.25	70.75
8	1.5	1200	600	60.00	3.75	63.75
7	1.7	1050	525	52.50	4.25	56.75
6	2.0	900	450	45.00	5.00	50.00
5	2.4	750	375	37.50	6.00	43.50
4	3.0	600	300	30.00	7.50	37.50
3	4.0	450	225	22.50	10.00	32.50
2	**6.0**	**300**	**150**	**15.00**	**15.00**	**30.00**
1	12.0	150	75	7.50	30.00	37.50

* Cost to hold plus cost to buy.

Of the listed alternatives, $300 per order every two months appears optimal. This corresponds to the point at which the cost to buy ($15.00) and the cost to hold ($15.00) are equal. This is also the point at which the total cost ($30.00) is the lowest. The candidate should also bear in mind that an EOQ stated in dollars may be readily stated in terms of units simply by the division of the dollar amount by the cost per unit. Thus, if we assume a unit cost of $0.50, an EOQ of $300 could also be stated as an EOQ of 600 units.

The relations of the cost to buy, cost to hold, and cost to both buy and hold to the EOQ expressed in units may be illustrated graphically as in Figure 4.

FIGURE 4

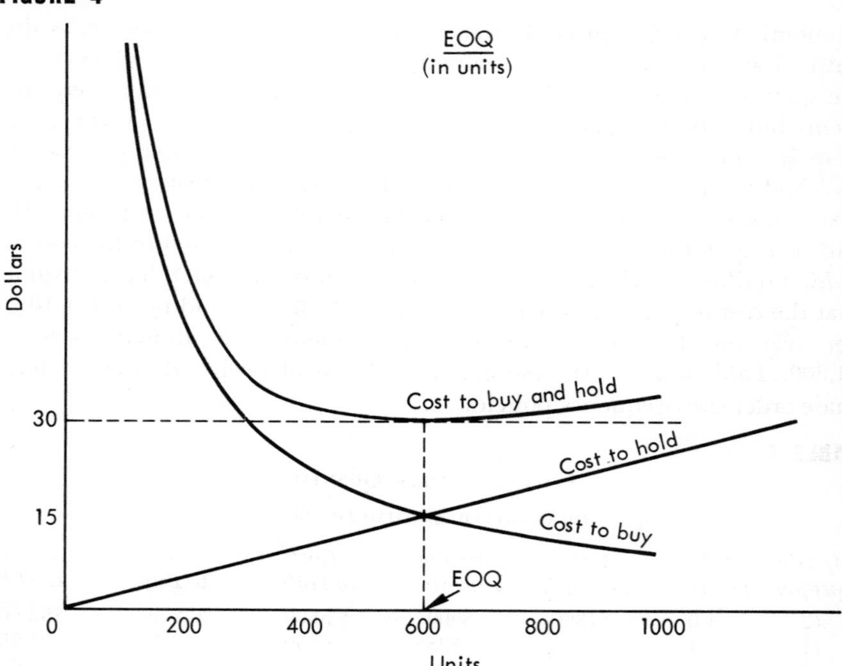

The low point on the total cost curve may be computed much more easily by using an algebraic formula than by listing several alternatives as previously. To illustrate, using the foregoing data, if we let:

Q = economic order quantity in dollars
A = the annual value of the usage of the item
C = the cost to order in dollars
H = the cost to hold, expressed as a percentage per year on the average inventory investment

the algebraic computation may be expressed as follows:

$$Q = \sqrt{2AC/H}$$

$$Q = \sqrt{\frac{2(\$1800)(\$2.50)}{10\%}}$$

$$Q = \sqrt{\$9000/0.10}$$

$$Q = \sqrt{\$90{,}000}$$

$$Q = \underline{\underline{\$300}}$$

Reorder Point (ROP). The *reorder point* is that quantitative point at which an inventoriable item should be reordered in order to ensure that sufficient stock will be continuously available to meet requirements, thus avoiding possible sales losses in merchandising organizations or production stoppages in manufacturing organizations. Whereas the EOQ is an indicator of *how much to buy,* the ROP is an indicator of *when to buy.*

Mathematically, the reorder point is the sum of the delivery lead time quantity and the safety level quantity. The *delivery lead time quantity* is the amount of an inventoriable item that is needed to fulfill inventory requirements from the time an order is initiated until delivery is accomplished. This quantity ordinarily is based on normal usage and normal delivery times. For example, if normal usage of item A is 12 units per day and 20 working days normally are required for delivery, the delivery lead time quantity will be 240 units (12 × 20).

The *safety level quantity* is the amount of an inventoriable item needed to ensure continued operations during the procurement period in the event that delivery time is longer than normal or usage is greater than anticipated. Although there are numerous variations, for purposes of simplicity the safety level quantity is often based on maximum usage and the delivery lead time is assumed to be relatively constant. For example, if the maximum daily usage in our illustration that reasonably can be anticipated is 18 units, the safety level quantity will be 120 units [20 working days × (18 units − 12 units)].

If we let *ROP* equal the reorder point, *DLTQ* equal the delivery lead time quantity, and *SLQ* equal the safety level quantity, we can compute a reorder point of 360 units as follows:

$$ROP = DLTQ + SLQ$$
$$ROP = 240 \text{ units} + 120 \text{ units}$$
$$ROP = \underline{\underline{360}} \text{ units}$$

Figure 5, based on the data that were employed in our ROP and EOQ illustrations, depicts graphically both the concept of the reorder point and its relation to the economic order quantity.

FIGURE 5

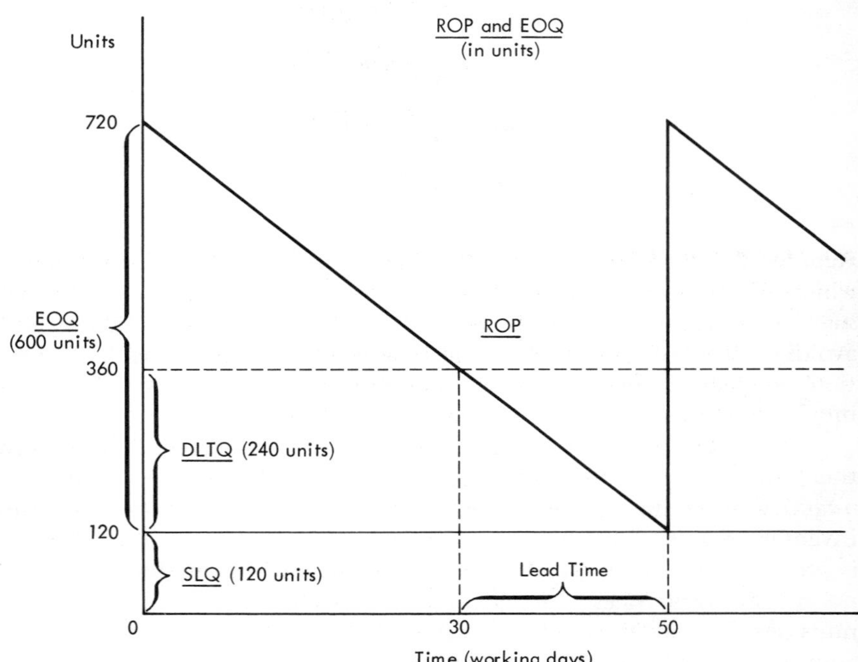

ROP and Probability Theory. If usage and delivery times during the procurement period could be forecast with certainty, the determination of the reorder point would be a simple matter; we would need to know the delivery lead time quantity only, and no safety level quantity would be required. However, although delivery times can be determined ordinarily with a certain degree of accuracy, the precise amount of usage is seldom known in advance. As a consequence, management may be faced with a problem that perhaps can be solved best by the employment of probability theory.

The "when-to-buy" (ROP) decision is essentially a safety-level decision, which in turn is an "acceptable-level-of-customer-service" decision. If the possibility of running out of stock is completely unacceptable to management, ROP computations would have to be based on rates of usage and delivery times that could not possibly be exceeded. Needless to say, an inventory policy of this nature could result in excessively high carrying costs. Therefore, instead of trying to guard against all possible stockouts, management customarily assumes some degree of stockout risk by establishing an acceptable level of customer service at something less than 100%. The level accepted in any given situation, of course, should be the result of sound decisions regarding the possible loss of profits due to stockouts as opposed to the cost of carrying additional safety stock in order to avoid or reduce the possibility of stockouts.

If we assume the term *normal* to be synonymous with the term *average,* a reorder point based solely upon normal usage (containing no safety stock provision) provides a 50% probability of no stockouts occurring during the procurement period. Therefore, if an inventoriable item is ordered six times a year, and the possibility of three stockouts a year constitutes an acceptable level of customer service, there is no need for a safety stock provision. However, if management wishes to maintain a higher level of customer service, a safety stock provision is necessary. For instance, if an item is ordered six times a year and management decides that only one stockout a year is acceptable, a sufficient quantity of safety stock should be included in the reorder point formula to provide for stockout protection in five of the six times yearly that actual usage during the procurement period is likely to exceed normal usage. In other words, management wants an 83.3% assurance that stockouts will not occur.

To illustrate the use of probability theory in ROP computations, let us assume the data employed in our ROP illustration; that is, normal usage of item A is 12 units per day and 20 working days are normally required for delivery. We based our safety level in the ROP illustration on the maximum usage that could reasonably be expected during the procurement period, while the delivery time was held constant. Let us now assume that there is one chance in ten that usage may be as high as 22 units per day, and one in twenty that it may be as high as 25. If management protects against the one-in-ten chance, it has a 90% assurance that no stockout will occur during the procurement period; if it protects against the one-in-twenty chance, it has a 95% assurance. If management accepts the one-in-ten odds, the reorder point will be 440 units, determined as follows:

$$
\begin{aligned}
ROP &= DLTQ + SLQ \\
ROP &= (12 \times 20) + [20 \times (22 - 12)] \\
ROP &= 240 + 200 \\
ROP &= \underline{\underline{440}} \text{ units}
\end{aligned}
$$

If management accepts the one-in-twenty odds, the reorder point will be 500 units, determined as follows:

$$
\begin{aligned}
ROP &= DLTQ + SLQ \\
ROP &= (12 \times 20) + [20 \times (25 - 12)] \\
ROP &= 240 + 260 \\
ROP &= \underline{\underline{500}} \text{ units}
\end{aligned}
$$

In the problem which follows, the CPA candidate was required not only to compute the EOQ and ROP, but also the cost of a stockout.

Problem: You have been engaged to install an accounting system for the Kaufman Corporation. Among the inventory control features Kaufman desires as a part of the system are indicators of "how much" to order "when." The following information is furnished for one item, called a komtronic, which is carried in inventory:

1. Komtronics are sold by the gross (twelve dozen) at a list price of $800 per gross F.O.B. shipper. Kaufman receives a 40% trade discount off list price on purchases in gross lots.
2. Freight cost is $20 per gross from the shipping point to Kaufman's plant.
3. Kaufman uses about 5000 komtronics during a 259-day production year and must purchase a total of 36 gross per year to allow for normal breakage. Minimum and maximum usages are 12 and 28 komtronics per day, respectively.
4. Normal delivery time to receive an order is 20 working days from the date a purchase request is initiated. A rush order in full gross lots can be received by air freight in five working days at an extra cost of $52 per gross. A stockout (complete exhaustion of the inventory) of komtronics would stop production, and Kaufman would purchase komtronics locally at list price rather than shut down.
5. The cost of placing an order is $10; the cost of receiving an order is $20.
6. Space storage cost is $12 per year per gross stored.
7. Insurance and taxes are approximately 12% of the net delivered cost of average inventory and Kaufman expects a return of at least 8% on its average investment (ignore return on order and carrying cost for simplicity).

Required:

a. Prepare a schedule computing the total annual cost of komtronics based on uniform order lot sizes of one, two, three, four, five, and six gross of komtronics. (The schedule should show the total annual cost according to each lot size.) Indicate the economic order quantity (economic lot size to order).
b. Prepare a schedule computing the minimum stock reorder point for komtronics. The komtronics inventory should not fall below this point without reordering if the company is to guard against a stockout. Factors to be considered include average lead-period usage and safety stock requirements.
c. Prepare a schedule computing the cost of a stockout of komtronics. Factors to be considered include the excess costs for local purchases and for rush orders.

a.

KAUFMAN CORPORATION

COMPUTATION OF ECONOMIC ORDER QUANTITY
FOR KOMTRONICS

Gross Ordered	*Orders Per Year*	*Net Cost Per Order (1)*	*Freight Per Order*	*Net Delivered Cost Per Order*	*Average Inventory (2)*	*Annual Carrying Cost (3)*	*Annual Storage Cost*	*Annual Order Placing and Receiving Cost (4)*	*Total Annual Cost (5)*
1	36	$ 480	$ 20	$ 500	$ 250	$ 50	$12	$1,080	$19,142
2	18	960	40	1,000	500	100	24	540	18,664
3	12	1,440	60	1,500	750	150	36	360	18,546
4	9	1,920	80	2,000	1,000	200	48	270	18,518 *
5	7.2	2,400	100	2,500	1,250	250	60	216	18,526
6	6	2,880	120	3,000	1,500	300	72	180	18,552

NOTES:

(1) List price per gross $800
Less 40% trade discount 320
Net cost per gross $480

(2) average inventory $= \frac{\text{beginning} + \text{ending inventory}}{2}$

(3) Insurance and taxes 12%
Imputed interest 8%
Total 20% × average inventory

(4) Order cost $10
Receiving cost 20
Total $ 30 × orders per year

(5) orders per year × net delivered cost per order = $18,000 + annual carrying cost + annual storage cost + annual order placing and receiving cost.

* Economic order quantity is at point of least total annual cost (this is also the point where annual carrying and storage costs are approximately equal to annual order placing and receiving costs).

b.

KAUFMAN CORPORATION

Computation of Minimum Stock Reorder Point
for Komtronics

Average daily usage $= \dfrac{5{,}184 \text{ annual usage}}{259 \text{ working days}} = 20$ per day.			
Normal lead time = 20 working days			
Average lead-period usage: 20 × 20 =	400	units	(A)
Maximum daily usage	28	per day	
Less average daily usage	20		
Excess above average	8	per day	
Normal lead time	20	days	
Safety stock	160	units	(B)
Average lead-period usage	400	units	(A)
Safety stock	160	units	(B)
Minimum stock order point (based on reasonable maximum usage prior to receipt of newly ordered stock)	560	units	

c.

KAUFMAN CORPORATION

Computation of Cost of a Stockout
of Komtronics

Excess cost for local purchase of one gross (1):		
List price locally per gross	$800	
Kaufman's net delivered cost per gross ($480 + $20)	500	
Excess cost for one gross	300	
Order and receiving cost	30	
Total cost first five days of stockout		$330
Extra cost for rush orders:		
Extra freight and order costs for each order	52	
Order and receiving cost	30	
Extra cost per order each additional five days	82	
Number of potential extra orders (2)	× 3	
Total extra cost for rush order		246
Total potential cost of stockout		$576

Notes:

(1) One gross purchased on a local basis will be sufficient because a rush order will be received in five working days and maximum usage in a five-day period is 140 units (5 × 28).

(2) 28 units × 20 days = 560 ÷ 144 = 3.9 gross maximum requirement during the 20-day period which must elapse before normal delivery of a regular order can be received. However, since 1 gross must be purchased locally, only 2.9 gross need be ordered by air freight, but the order must be rounded up to 3 gross because only full gross lots are obtainable.

Cost Accounting

In general, cost problems appearing on the CPA Examination may be classified according to the type of cost system to which they are related. The candidate can expect to encounter problems dealing with job order or job lot costs, process costs, and standard costs. Problems within the various systems ordinarily involve the determination of unit costs, the valuation of inventories, and the determination of cost of sales. Unit cost computations may be subdivided further into the appropriate material, labor, or overhead (burden) unit cost. Inventory valuation problems may deal with work in process, finished goods, or cost of sales. In connection with standard costs, there is the additional possibility of problems appearing on the examination which deal with the determination and analysis of variations from standards.

Although we shall examine each of the basic cost systems in some detail, we should perhaps first review the fundamental principles, concepts, and procedures that underlie the accumulation of cost data in general.

elements of manufacturing cost

Three major elements enter into the cost of a manufactured product: direct material, direct labor, and factory overhead (occasionally called manufacturing overhead, manufacturing expenses, factory burden, or simply, indirect costs). In cost terminology the sum of the first two—direct material and direct labor—is called *prime cost,* whereas the sum of the latter two—direct labor and factory overhead—is known as *conversion cost.*

Direct Material. Direct material is that portion of raw material utilized in the manufacturing process which is readily identifiable and measurable as an integral part of the finished product. In contrast, *indirect material* is defined as that portion of raw material which either cannot be readily identified as a basic component of the finished product or which is used in such small quantities that the cost of accounting for it would be prohibitive. Direct material is treated as a separate element of manufacturing cost, whereas indirect material is included as part of factory overhead.

Direct Labor. Direct labor is that portion of work performed by factory employees which is directly associated with the finished product. Conversely, *indirect labor* is employee labor that does not have immediate bearing on the production of the finished product. Like indirect material, indirect labor employed in the manufacturing process is considered as part of factory overhead.

Factory Overhead. Factory overhead is that portion of costs associated with the manufacturing process which cannot be readily identified as part of the cost of the finished product. In addition to indirect material and labor, it includes such items as factory rent, heat, light, power, insurance, and depreciation.

product costs versus period costs

Two kinds of costs are involved in accounting for manufacturing concerns. Costs associated with the units of output are generally known as *product costs.* Costs that are charged off as expenses in the period in which they are incurred are called *period costs.* Stated another way, product costs are inventoriable costs, but period costs are not.

As the candidate will recall from his previous study, the terms "cost" and "expense" in accounting are not mutually exclusive. The AICPA, however, has repeatedly emphasized in its terminology bulletins that items entering into the computation of the cost of manufacturing, such as material, labor, and overhead, should be described as costs rather than as expenses.

full costing versus variable costing

Accountants have long recognized the importance of the product as an appropriate vehicle for matching manufacturing costs and revenues when determining periodic income. They are not, however, in complete agreement about exactly what should be included in the cost of a product. Two schools of thought prevail: Full, or absorption, costing is favored by many "traditional" accountants, whereas others prefer what is known as variable, or direct, costing.

Full and Variable Costing Defined. Under the *full costing* concept, both fixed and variable costs are considered as integral parts of the total cost of manufacturing a product. In contrast, under the *variable costing* concept, the cost of manufacturing a product is considered to be composed only of those costs that vary with production. Thus, in the valuation of inventories and the determination of cost of goods sold, only direct material, direct labor, and variable factory overhead costs are taken into consideration under variable costing. Fixed factory overhead costs are charged against revenue as period costs in the period of their incurrence.

In sum, accounting for direct material and direct labor is the same under both concepts, but only variable factory overhead is charged to the product under variable costing, whereas both fixed and variable factory overhead are charged to the product under full costing.

Full and Variable Costing Illustrated. The basic differences between full and variable costing can perhaps be best illustrated by contrasting income statements prepared under the respective approaches.

In the problem that follows, the CPA candidate not only was required to prepare income statements under the two approaches, but he also had to perform several other operations. For review purposes, all parts of the problem are included here.

Problem: Flear Company has a maximum productive capacity of 210,000 units per year. Normal capacity is regarded as 180,000 units per year. Standard variable manufacturing costs are $11 per unit. Fixed factory overhead is $360,000 per year. Variable selling expenses are $3 per unit and fixed selling expenses are $252,000 per year. The unit sales price is $20.

The operating results for 19X2 are: sales, 150,000 units; production, 160,000 units; beginning inventory, 10,000 units; and net unfavorable variance for standard variable manufacturing costs, $40,000. All variances are written off as additions to (or deductions from) standard cost of sales.

Required: (For items a, b, and c, assume no variances from standards for manufacturing costs.)

a. What is the break-even point expressed in *dollar* sales?

b. How many *units* must be sold to earn a net income of $60,000 per year?

c. How many *units* must be sold to earn a net income of 10% on sales?

d. Prepare formal income statements for 19X2 under:
   1. "Conventional" or "full" costing
   2. "Direct" or "variable" costing

e. Briefly account for the difference in net income between the two income statements.

Solution:

a.

$$\begin{aligned} \text{Let } X &= \text{number of units at break-even point} \\ 20X &= 14X + 360{,}000 + 252{,}000 \\ X &= 102{,}000 \text{ units} \\ \text{Break-even point} &= \$20 \times 102{,}000 \\ &= \underline{\underline{\$2{,}040{,}000.}} \end{aligned}$$

b.

$$X = \frac{\text{fixed expenses} + \text{net profit}}{\text{contribution margin per unit}}$$

$$X = \frac{612{,}000 + 60{,}000}{6}$$

$$X = \underline{\underline{112{,}000 \text{ units}}}$$

c.

$$20X = 14X + 612{,}000 + 0.10\,(20X)$$

$$X = \underline{\underline{153{,}000 \text{ units}}}$$

d.

FLEAR COMPANY

CONVENTIONAL COSTING INCOME STATEMENT
FOR THE YEAR ENDED DECEMBER 31, 19X2

Sales (150,000 at $20)		$3,000,000
Cost of sales:		
Beginning inventory (10,000 at $13)	$ 130,000	
Production (160,000 at $13)	2,080,000	
Available for sale	2,210,000	
Ending inventory (20,000 at $13)	260,000	
Standard cost of sales	1,950,000	
Add unfavorable variances:		
Variable manufacturing costs	40,000	
Volume variance (20,000 at $2)	40,000	
Cost of sales		2,030,000
Gross margin		970,000
Selling expenses:		
Variable (150,000 at $3)	450,000	
Fixed	252,000	
Total selling expenses		702,000
Net income		$ 268,000

FLEAR COMPANY

DIRECT COSTING INCOME STATEMENT
FOR THE YEAR ENDED DECEMBER 31, 19X2

Sales (150,000 at $20)		$3,000,000
Direct costs and expenses:		
Beginning inventory (10,000 at $11)	$ 110,000	
Production (160,000 at $11)	1,760,000	
Available for sale	1,870,000	
Ending inventory (20,000 at $11)	220,000	
Standard variable cost of sales	1,650,000	
Add variance in variable production costs	40,000	
Variable manufacturing cost of sales	1,690,000	
Variable selling expense (150,000 at $3)	450,000	
Total direct costs and expenses		2,140,000
Marginal income		860,000
Less period costs:		
Fixed factory overhead	360,000	
Fixed selling expenses	252,000	
Total period costs		612,000
Net income		$ 248,000

e.

STATEMENT ACCOUNTING FOR DIFFERENCE IN NET INCOME

Net income per conventional costing		$ 268,000
Net income per direct costing		248,000
Net difference		$ 20,000
Difference accounted for:		
Ending inventory (conventional costing)	$ 260,000	
Ending inventory (direct costing)	220,000	
Difference between ending inventories		$ 40,000
Beginning inventory (conventional costing)	130,000	
Beginning inventory (direct costing)	110,000	
Difference between beginning inventories		20,000
Net difference		$ 20,000

The $20,000 difference in net income is traceable to the methods of valuing the beginning and ending inventories. The inventories under conventional costing include an application of fixed factory overhead, whereas under direct costing there is no application of fixed overhead. In other words, $20,000 of prior-year fixed overhead was charged to the current period, $40,000 of current-year fixed overhead was capitalized in inventory under conventional costing, and all fixed overhead was charged to the current period under direct costing.

manufacturing accounts

In addition to the usual accounts found in a merchandising concern, the typical manufacturing organization generally has some accounts that are peculiar to its particular type of activity. Many variations exist among manufacturing organizations, especially in relation to manufacturing costs, but their accounts differ from those of the typical merchandising concern chiefly in the inventory area. The Merchandise Inventory account of the merchandising concern is ordinarily replaced in the manufacturing organization by at least three inventory accounts, both in the ledger and on the financial statements. Since a manufacturing organization may have on hand at any one time a certain amount of raw material, partially completed products, and fully completed products, these items customarily appear in separate inventory accounts, typically entitled: Raw Materials Inventory, Work in Process Inventory, and Finished Goods Inventory.

When perpetual inventories are employed in a manufacturing concern, the Raw Materials Inventory account is debited for the cost of materials purchased and credited for the cost of materials put into production. Likewise, the Work in Process Inventory account is debited for all costs (material, labor, and overhead) put into production and credited for the cost associated with completed production, this cost being transferred to the Finished Goods Inventory account. The Finished Goods Inventory account in turn is debited for all costs transferred to it from the Work in Process Inventory account and credited for all costs associated with the goods sold. The flow of costs through the inventory accounts may be illustrated in abbreviated form as in Figure 6.

accounting for factory overhead

Since factory overhead, unlike direct labor and material, cannot be readily identified as part of the cost of a specific job or product, it must be allocated to production by some method of approximation. This could be done at the close of each accounting period by spreading all overhead costs incurred among the products manufactured. However, it is more often accomplished by using predetermined overhead rates.

FIGURE 6

FLOW OF COSTS THROUGH INVENTORY ACCOUNTS

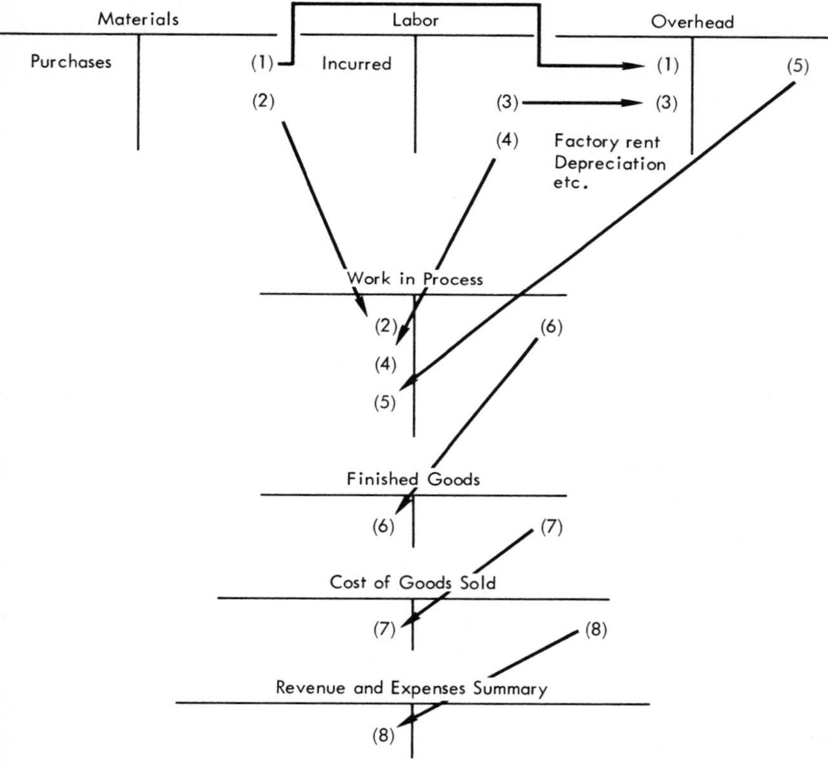

KEY:

(1) Indirect materials used in production.
(2) Direct materials used in production.
(3) Indirect labor used in production.
(4) Direct labor used in production.
(5) Overhead charged to production.
(6) Cost of completed production transferred to the Finished Goods Inventory account.
(7) Cost of goods sold transferred from the Finished Goods Inventory account to the Cost of Goods Sold account.
(8) Cost of Goods Sold account closed into the Revenue and Expense Summary account.

Predetermined Overhead Rates. Ideally, the method employed to allocate factory overhead to specific jobs or products should be based on a factor that is common to all jobs or products and that measures precisely the extent to which the overhead was utilized in their production. In practice, however, conditions are seldom such that the selection of an ideal base is possible. This is particularly true in organizations that make a variety of products, whose production utilizes overhead in varying degrees and causes it to be incurred in different ways. Such organizations must choose between (a) the use of several bases, each of which is appropriate for a single overhead item or group of items, and (b) the use of a single base that results in a reasonable although not precise allocation of the overhead. The bases most frequently used, regardless of approach, include:

1. Direct labor costs
2. Direct labor hours
3. Machine hours
4. Units of production

Computing Overhead Rates. The procedure for computing overhead rates is as follows:

1. Estimate the amount of overhead expected to be incurred at the planned level of activity.
2. Estimate production in terms of the basis selected (e.g., if overhead is to be allocated on a machine-hour basis, production should be estimated in terms of machine hours).
3. Divide the estimated overhead costs determined in step 1 by the estimated production determined in step 2.

To illustrate, let us assume that Company A estimates overhead expenses for the upcoming year to be $300,000. The company allocates overhead on a machine-hour basis and estimates that it will use 120,000 machine hours during the year. Overhead should be allocated at the rate of $2.50 per machine hour, determined as follows:

$$\text{overhead rate} = \frac{\text{estimated overhead}}{\text{estimated machine hours}}$$

$$\text{overhead rate} = \frac{\$300{,}000}{120{,}000 \text{ machine hours}}$$

$$\text{overhead rate} = \$2.50 \text{ per machine hour}$$

Advantages and Disadvantages of Overhead Bases. One of the major advantages of an overhead rate based on *direct labor costs* is its simplicity of operation. Because all requisite data are readily available from the payroll summary, no additional record keeping is necessary. The primary drawback to the method is that it tends to ignore contributions to a specific job or product by factors of production other than direct labor. For example, in some manufacturing operations machinery is the prime production factor and direct labor is only incidental. When machine operators are paid at different rates, the use of an overhead rate based on direct labor costs could result in a misleading allocation, because production of highly paid employees would be charged with proportionately more overhead than that of lower-paid workers.

An overhead rate based on *direct labor hours* overcomes the objection to the direct labor costs method arising from differences in labor rates; but its use necessitates the collection of additional data, namely, direct labor hours per job or product.

In organizations in which machinery is the chief factor in production, a rate based on *machine hours* usually constitutes the best method of allocating overhead. However, an important disadvantage of this method is that additional data not otherwise needed must be provided in detail. For example, records of the amount of machine time spent on various operations must be maintained. Because this increases accounting costs, some organizations do not find it practical to use a machine hour rate.

An overhead rate per *unit of production* is the simplest and most direct method of allocating overhead. Its usefulness, however, is limited to those situations in which one or a few closely related products possessing a common denominator (for example, weight or volume) are produced.

Overhead Application Illustrated. The terms "overhead allocation" and "overhead application" frequently appear interchangeably. As used here, *overhead allocation* pertains to the assignment of overhead costs tc a department or other subdivision of an organization, whereas the term *overhead application* pertains to the assignment of overhead to the product or job.

To illustrate overhead application using direct labor costs as a basis, let us assume that factory overhead in Company A is estimated to be $60,000 for a year and that direct labor costs will total $100,000. In a month in which $8,000 of direct labor costs is incurred, $4,800 ($60,000/ $100,000, or 60%, of $8,000) of overhead will be applied as follows:

Work in process	4,800	
Factory overhead		4,800

Rather than credit the Factory Overhead account when overhead is applied to production, some accountants prefer an additional account typically entitled Factory Overhead Applied. This account is credited when overhead is applied to production during the period, and at the end of the period it is closed to the Factory Overhead account. Since the

FIGURE 7

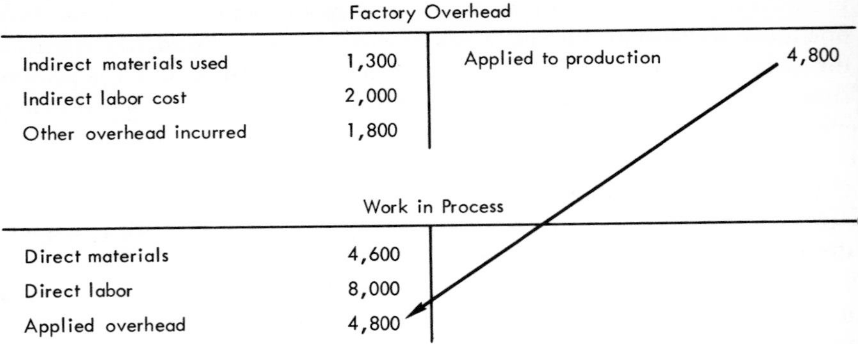

end result is the same, we shall use the simpler approach and merely credit the Factory Overhead account when applying overhead to production (see Figure 7).

Underapplied and Overapplied Overhead. As a general rule, debits to factory overhead accounts for a period seldom, if ever, equal the credits. If the account has a debit balance, as is the case in our illustration, the amount of overhead applied to production is less than the amount actually incurred. Conversely, a credit balance in the account means that more overhead has been charged to production than has actually been incurred. When the amount of overhead actually incurred (as reflected on the debit side of the account) is more than the amount applied (as reflected on the credit side), the difference is commonly called *underapplied,* or *underabsorbed, overhead.* When the amount of overhead applied exceeds the amount incurred, the difference is called *overapplied, or overabsorbed, overhead.*

When the amount of actual overhead incurred differs from that applied to production, there are implications for both control and financial statements. For control purposes, the deviation must be analyzed in terms of its causes. Since the overhead rate is computed by dividing estimated overhead by estimated production stated in terms of the basis selected, underapplied or overapplied overhead may result from (a) a difference between the estimated and actual overhead, (b) a difference between the estimated and actual production activity, or (c) a combination of (a) and (b). (We shall treat the topic of overhead variances more fully later in this section.)

With regard to the financial statements, the accountant has the problem of handling both monthly and year-end overhead balances. Monthly balances normally are carried forward on the balance sheet as deferred charges or deferred credits. An underapplied balance is classified as a deferred charge, and an overapplied balance as a deferred credit.

Year-end balances, on the other hand, should be closed out. Theoretically, they should be closed proportionately to the Cost of Goods Sold account, the Finished Goods Inventory account, and the Work in Progress Inventory account. Practically, however, they frequently are closed in their entirety to the Cost of Goods Sold account. This approach is particularly useful when the balances are not material.

To illustrate both the theoretical and practical treatment of a year-end overhead balance, let us assume that we have a Factory Overhead account with a year-end debit balance of $300. Let us also assume that of the $4,800 of overhead applied to production during the year, 50% was associated with the goods sold, 30% with the finished goods still on hand, and 20% with the production still in process. The first entry illustrates the theoretical treatment, and the second, the practical treatment.

(1)

Cost of goods sold (50% × $300)	150	
Finished goods inventory (30% × $300)	90	
Work in process inventory (20% × $300)	60	
Factory overhead		300

(2)

Cost of goods sold	300	
Factory overhead		300

Departmentalization of Factory Overhead. To enhance operational efficiency, most large business organizations, as well as many medium and smaller-sized ones, are divided into departments, which individually take responsibility for one or more of the organization's operations. For accounting purposes, factories are often further divided into *cost centers.* These are the smallest units of activity or areas of responsibility for which manufacturing costs are accumulated; a department may itself be a cost center or it may contain several cost centers.

In accounting, a major advantage of both departmentalization and the utilization of cost centers is that they are means of maintaining closer control over manufacturing costs and greater accuracy in the costing of jobs and products. For example, the responsibility for costs incurred in a department or cost center falls directly upon its manager or foreman, and he must answer to management if costs for his department are out of line. Greater accuracy in costing jobs and products is possible because departmentalization generally results in the use of different overhead rates for individual departments and cost centers. If a factory-wide overhead rate is used, the result may be an incorrect application of overhead to jobs or products that require processing only in specific departments or cost centers.

Production Departments and Service Departments. Departmentalized factories are generally divided into production departments and service departments. As the terms imply, *production departments* are directly involved in converting raw materials into finished products, whereas *service departments* render auxiliary services to the production departments. Examples of service departments are production planning, maintenance, and power.

A predetermined departmental overhead rate is based on two factors: the producing department's overhead and its portion of the cost of operating the service departments. Obviously the latter cost should be allocated to the producing departments on some equitable basis. The cost of operating the power department in a factory, for example, may be allocated to the producing departments on the basis of power consumed. Let us assume that the cost of operating the Power Department of the Ace Manufacturing Company was $9,000 during a month in which it produced 600,000 kilowatt hours. If Producing Departments A, B, and C used 100,000, 200,000, and 300,000 hours, respectively, the $9,000 cost would be allocated as follows:

Factory overhead—Department A (1/6 × $9,000)	1,500	
Factory overhead—Department B (2/6 × $9,000)	3,000	
Factory overhead—Department C (3/6 × $9,000)	4,500	
Power department		9,000

There are times, however, when the use of a single basis for the allocation of service department costs may not result in the most equitable distribution. This is particularly true when a significant part of the cost of operating such a department is a function of time (fixed costs) and a significant part a function of activity (variable costs). If a service department's costs can be segregated into fixed and variable elements, a dual-basis approach may be the most appropriate for the allocation of its costs. In a power department, for example, the fixed costs (depreciation, insurance, taxes, etc.) are primarily associated with the department's physical capacity to produce power, whereas the variable costs (wages, maintenance, fuel, etc.) are primarily associated with the actual power output. Thus, in the allocation of power department costs, the fixed elements may be allocated to the producing departments in the ratio of these departments' capacities to consume power, and the variable elements may be allocated to them in the ratio of their actual consumption of power. The former ratio is frequently referred to as the *capacity ratio* and the latter as the *consumption ratio.*

To illustrate the use of a dual basis, let us assume the same data used in our preceding illustration; in addition, let us assume that the power department's $9,000 cost was composed of fixed costs of $6,000 and variable costs of $3,000 and that the capacities of Producing Departments A, B, and C to consume power were 300,000, 300,000, and 400,000 kilowatt hours per month, respectively. Under the dual-basis approach, the $9,000 cost of operating the power department would be allocated as follows:

Factory overhead—Department A	2,300 *	
Factory overhead—Department B	2,800 *	
Factory overhead—Department C	3,900 *	
Power department		9,000

* Departments	*A*	*B*	*C*	*Total*
Fixed costs (3 3 4)	$1,800	$1,800	$2,400	$6,000
Variable costs (1 2 3)	500	1,000	1,500	3,000
	$2,300	$2,800	$3,900	$9,000

job order cost systems

A *job order cost system* is one in which manufacturing costs are accumulated for each separate job, or lot, of production. For such a system to be feasible, the different jobs must be readily identifiable. Job order cost systems are especially applicable in manufacturing organizations where customers' orders are manufactured to their specifications, for example: orders for 200 orange and blue band uniforms in a garment factory or for 100 specially designed planes in an aircraft factory. In the construction industry, orders for one or more houses, apartment buildings, or garages would be examples. Other users of job order cost systems include the motion picture, machine tool, and job printing industries.

Under a job order cost system, the costs of direct materials and direct labor employed on a specific job and the applicable factory overhead must be accumulated and accounted for as the job is being worked upon. Generally, this is accomplished on *job cost sheets,* or *job order sheets.* Figure 8 is typical of their format.

Job Cost Sheets as Subsidiary Records. In a job order cost system, the Work in Process account, which is primarily a controlling account, is supported by the job cost sheets of the unfinished jobs. When a job is finished, the completed cost sheet becomes the basis for the entry that transfers the cost of the job from the Work in Process account to the Finished Goods Inventory account.

To illustrate the role of the cost sheet as a subsidiary record, let us assume that during the first month of its operations Company A, which employs a job cost system, began Jobs No. 101, 102, and 103, and that

FIGURE 8

JOB COST SHEET

Job Order No. ______ Date order received ______

Item ______ Date delivery promised ______

For ______ Date job completed ______

Direct Material			Direct Labor			Factory Overhead	
Date	Reference	Amount	Date	Reference	Amount	Date	Amount
	(Materials requisition number)			(Time expenditure record)			(Based on predetermined rate)

SUMMARY

Direct material ______
Direct labor ______
Factory overhead ______
Total cost ______

Number of units ______
Unit cost ______

Jobs No. 101 and 102 were completed during the month, leaving only Job No. 103 in process as of the end of the month. In addition, let us assume that direct materials costing $4,600 and direct labor amounting to

$8,000 were charged to the month's production, and that $4,800 of factory overhead was applied to the month's production. The entries in the Work in Process account and the cost ledger would appear as in Figures 9a and 9b, respectively. (The costs accumulated for the jobs are assumed, and to simplify the illustration only summaries from the cost sheets are used.)

FIGURE 9a

GENERAL LEDGER

Work in Process

Direct materials	4,600	Job No. 101	8,200
Direct labor	8,000	Job No. 102	5,340
Factory overhead	4,800	Balance (Job No. 103)	3,860
	17,400		17,400
Balance (Job No. 103)	3,860		

FIGURE 9b

COST LEDGER

(Cost Sheet Summaries)

Job No. 101

Direct materials	1,800
Direct labor	4,000
Factory overhead	2,400
Total cost	8,200
(Finished)	

Job No. 102

Direct materials	1,500
Direct labor	2,400
Factory overhead	1,440
Total cost	5,340
(Finished)	

Job No. 103

Direct materials	1,300
Direct labor	1,600
Factory overhead	960
Cost to date	3,860
(Unfinished)	

The relation between the data appearing in the Work in Process account and the job cost sheets are summarized as in Table 7.

TABLE 7

Work in Process (Controlling Account in the General Ledger)		*Job Cost Sheets (Subsidiary Records in the Cost Ledger)*	
Beginning balance	$ -0-		$ -0-
		↗ Job No. 101	$ 1,800
Direct materials	4,600	→ Job No. 102	1,500
		↘ Job No. 103	1,300
		↗ Job No. 101	4,000
Direct labor	8,000	→ Job No. 102	2,400
		↘ Job No. 103	1,600
		↗ Job No. 101	2,400
Factory overhead	4,800	→ Job No. 102	1,440
		↘ Job No. 103	960
Total cost	$17,400		$17,400
Cost of jobs finished	(13,540)	↗ Job No. 101	(8,200)
		↘ Job No. 102	(5,340)
Balance (cost of jobs unfinished)	$ 3,860	→ Job No. 103	$ 3,860

Job Cost System Illustrated. In order to more fully set forth the job cost system, let us continue our illustration for the following month. Assume that Job No. 103 was completed and Jobs No. 104, 105, and 106 were begun during this month. At the end of the month Job No. 106 is still in process, but Jobs No. 104 and 105 have been completed. In summary form, the transactions related to the manufacturing operations for the month are as follows:

1. Raw materials purchased: material A, $5,000; material B, $6,000; material C, $9,000. All raw materials are purchased on open account.
2. Raw materials requisitioned and used:

	Material A	*Material B*	*Material C*	*Total*
Job No. 103	$ 100	$ -0-	$ 150	$ 250
Job No. 104	1,000	1,200	2,800	5,000
Job No. 105	1,500	1,300	4,000	6,800
Job No. 106	1,800	2,000	-0-	3,800
Factory overhead	-0-	1,000	1,600	2,600
Totals	$4,400	$5,500	$8,550	$18,450

3. Factory labor incurred:

Job No. 103	$ 800
Job No. 104	3,200
Job No. 105	4,400
Job No. 106	2,000
Factory overhead	2,100
Total	$12,500

4. Factory overhead, other than indirect labor and materials, incurred:

Accrued expenses	$ 500
Expiration of prepaid expenses	400
Depreciation of plant and equipment	1,000
Total	$1,900

5. Factory overhead applied to production at the rate of 60% of direct labor cost (see item 3):

Job No. 103	$ 480
Job No. 104	1,920
Job No. 105	2,640
Job No. 106	1,200
Total	$6,240

6. Jobs completed and transferred to the Finished Goods Inventory account:

Job No. 103	$ 5,390
Job No. 104	10,120
Job No. 105	13,840
Total	$29,350

7. Jobs No. 103 and 104 were sold on account at 25% above cost:

Job No. 103:	$ 5,390 × 1.25 =	$ 6,737.50
Job No. 104:	$10,120 × 1.25 =	12,650.00
Total		$19,387.50

The manufacturing operations for the month would be recorded as shown. (Journal entries are made in general journal form, and postings are shown only for the Work in Process account and the appropriate cost sheets; see Figures 10a and 10b, respectively.)

(1)

Raw materials inventory	20,000	
Accounts payable (Vouchers payable)		20,000
To record the purchase of raw materials.		

(2)

Work in process	15,850	
Factory overhead	2,600	
Raw materials inventory		18,450
To record raw materials used in production.		

(3)

Work in process	10,400	
Factory overhead	2,100	
Accrued payroll payable		12,500
To record labor used in production.		

(4)

Factory overhead	1,900	
Accrued expenses		500
Prepaid expenses		400
Accumulated depreciation—Plant and equipment		1,000
To record factory overhead, other than indirect labor and materials, incurred.		

(5)

Work in process	6,240	
Factory overhead		6,240
To record the application of overhead to production.		

(6)

Finished goods inventory	29,350	
Work in process		29,350
To transfer the cost of finished jobs from the Work in Process account to the Finished Goods Inventory account.		

(7)

Accounts receivable	19,387.50	
Sales		19,387.50
To record the sale of Jobs No. 103 and 104.		
Cost of goods sold	15,510	
Finished goods inventory		15,510
To transfer the costs of Jobs No. 103 and 104 from the Finished Goods Inventory account to the Cost of Goods Sold account.		

FIGURE 10a

GENERAL LEDGER
Work in Process

Beginning balance (Job No. 103)	3,860	Jobs No. 103, 104, & 105	29,350
Direct materials	15,850		
Direct labor	10,400		
Factory overhead	6,240	Balance (Job No. 106)	7,000
	36,350		36,350
Balance (Job No. 106)	7,000		

FIGURE 10b

COST LEDGER
(Cost Sheet Summaries)

Job No. 103

Beginning balance	3,860
Direct materials	250
Direct labor	800
Factory overhead	480
Total cost	5,390
(Finished)	

Job No. 104

Direct materials	5,000
Direct labor	3,200
Factory overhead	1,920
Total cost	10,120
(Finished)	

Job No. 105

Direct materials	6,800
Direct labor	4,400
Factory overhead	2,640
Total cost	13,840
(Finished)	

Job No. 106

Direct materials	3,800
Direct labor	2,000
Factory overhead	1,200
Total cost	7,000
(Unfinished)	

The next problem was taken from the Practice section of one CPA examination and the question from the Theory section of another. They are illustrative of the examination requirements in the job order cost system area.

Problem: The Gamma Manufacturing Company uses a job order cost system. The following data pertain to the month of June, the company's first operating month:

1. Raw materials used on:

Job No. 101	$ 2,200
Job No. 102	1,900
Job No. 103	1,700
Job No. 104	1,600
	$ 7,400

2. Direct labor incurred on:

Job No. 101	$ 4,500
Job No. 102	2,000
Job No. 103	2,100
Job No. 104	1,900
	$10,500

3. Factory overhead is applied to production at the rate of 125% of direct labor costs.

Required: Assuming that factory overhead amounted to $13,300 during the month and that Jobs No. 101 and 102 were completed during the month and billed to customers at a markup of 20% on cost:

1. Journalize the June operations.
2. Determine the balance in the Work in Process account as of June 30.
3. Determine the amount of overapplied or underapplied factory overhead for the month.

Solution:

(1)

Work in process	7,400	
Raw materials inventory		7,400
Work in process	10,500	
Accrued payroll payable		10,500
Work in process	13,125	
Factory overhead (1.25 × $10,500)		13,125
Finished goods inventory	18,725	
Work in process		18,725

	Job No. 101	Job No. 102
Material	$ 2,200	$1,900
Labor	4,500	2,000
Overhead (1.25 × D.L.)	5,625	2,500
	$12,325	$6,400

Accounts receivable	22,470	
Sales		22,470
(1.20 × $18,725)		
Cost of goods sold	18,725	
Finished goods inventory		18,725

(2)

$12,300.

	Job No. 103	Job No. 104
Material	$1,700	$1,600
Labor	2,100	1,900
Overhead (1.25 × D.L.)	2,625	2,375
	$6,425	$5,875

(3)

$175 (Underapplied). ($13,300 – $13,125)

Question: The H Manufacturing Company is engaged in manufacturing items to fill specific orders received from its customers. At any given time it may have substantial inventories of work in process and finished goods, but all such amounts are assignable to firm sales orders it has received.

The company's operations, including the administrative and sales functions, are completely departmentalized. Its cost system is on a job order basis. Direct materials and direct labor are identified with jobs by the use of material issue tickets and daily time cards. Overhead costs are accumulated for each factory service, administrative, and selling department. These overhead costs, including administrative and selling expenses, are then allocated to producing departments, and an overhead rate is computed for each producing department. This rate is used to apply overhead to jobs on the basis of direct labor hours. The result is that all costs and expenses incurred during any month are charged to Work in Process accounts for the jobs.

Required:

1. Compare the H Company's cost system, as it affects inventory valuation, with the usual job cost system.

2. Criticize the system as it affects inventory valuation and income determination.

3. State any justification you see for the use of H Company's system.

Answer:

1. The main difference between the system used by H Manufacturing Company and the conventional system is the inclusion of administrative and selling costs in the cost of the product. The usual system views these as period costs rather than product costs and charges them off to the period in which incurred. As a result of this difference, inventory valuations will be higher than under the usual system. Because the cost system is on a job order basis, the significant increase will be in work in process inventory. There would be little, if any, finished goods inventory since sales would be recorded on completion of the goods.

2. The system used by H Manufacturing Company can be criticized on the following points:

a. It is not generally accepted.

b. Administrative and selling expenses are clearly period costs and not product costs. They should be charged to the period in which incurred in order to produce generally accepted financial statements.

c. The direct labor hours basis (or any other single basis) is a poor measure of the administrative and selling efforts put forth.

3. Possible justifications for using the system:

a. Many of the arguments stated against the system would also apply to conventional systems (i.e., fixed factory overhead costs such as straight-line depreciation or plant superintendent's salary) are as much period costs as selling and administrative costs are.

b. The system aids in setting selling prices. Since all costs are included in the production costs, management can clearly see what the full cost to produce and sell a given product has been in the past.

c. It affords a better matching of cost and revenue than conventional systems since it defers at least some of the administrative and selling expenses.

d. The selling and administrative expenses may be so small that they are immaterial so far as total costs are concerned.

Unit Costs and Job Costing. Note on the job cost sheet illustrated on page 472 that a section is included for the computation of a cost per unit. To compute unit costs under a job order cost system, we simply divide the total cost of the lot by the number of units in the lot. For example, if we assume that Job No. 101 is composed of 1,000 units, the unit cost would be \$8.20 (\$8,200 ÷ 1,000). Likewise, if we assume that Job. No. 105 consists of two units, the unit cost would be \$6,920 (\$13,840 ÷ 2). Unit cost computations are relatively simple under a job order cost system; however, this is not always true under a process cost system, as we shall see in the next section.

process cost systems

A process cost system is one in which both manufacturing costs and quantities of production are accumulated and reduced to a cost per unit of production; from this cost the cost of any quantity of production can be determined. Unlike a job order cost system in which costs are accumulated by the specific job, a process cost system accumulates costs by *processes* or *departments*.

A process cost system is particularly useful for product costing in mass-production operations where the product is more or less standardized and production more or less continuous. Process costing is feasible in operations of this nature because each unit of finished product requires essentially the same amount of material, labor, and overhead, thus permitting costs incurred during a particular period to be spread over the production of the period through the use of broad averages. This system is used by organizations in such diverse industries as paper, petroleum, pharmaceuticals, and plastics.

Cost of Production Report. Under process costing, a report is prepared periodically for each processing department. It summarizes the disposition of both the units and the costs for which the department is accountable. This report, ordinarily referred to as the *cost of production report,* fulfills a dual purpose: It serves as a vehicle for control purposes and as a basis for product costing. In organizations in which considerable cost control must be exercised, the report may be prepared daily or weekly, whereas in others a monthly report may be adequate.

Although we are interested primarily in product costing at this time, it should be recognized that from a control standpoint any significant variation in product costs from one period to another should be analyzed in order to determine its causes and to permit corrective action. Tables 8 and 9 are typical of the form and arrangement of the cost of production report and the data usually included.

Note that the cost of production report encompasses five rather distinct phases of activity. The study of process costing can best be approached by examining these phases in their logical sequence. As evidenced in the report, process costing requires that we:

1. Determine the physical flow of production.
2. Express production in terms of equivalent units.
3. Determine total costs to be accounted for.
4. Determine unit costs of production.
5. Account for both total costs and units.

TABLE 8

DEPARTMENT B

COST OF PRODUCTION REPORT
FOR THE MONTH ENDED JUNE 30, 19X1

Units to be accounted for:		
Units in process at beginning of period		1,200
Units started (or transferred in) during period		2,800
Total units to be accounted for		4,000
Disposition of units:		
Units completed		3,000
Units in process at end of period		1,000
Total units accounted for		4,000
Costs to be accounted for:		
Costs in process at beginning of period		$ 5,200
Costs transferred in from previous process or department (2800 units at $2 per unit)		5,600
Costs added during period:		
Material (2800 units at $1 per unit)		2,800
Labor (3000 units at $2 per unit)		6,000
Overhead (3000 units at $3 per unit)		9,000
Total cost to be accounted for		$28,600
Disposition of costs:		
Transferred out (to finished goods or next process or department)		$24,100 *
Work in process at end of period:		
Cost from previous process or department: (1000 units at $2 per unit)	$2,000	
Material added this period: (1000 units at $1 per unit)	1,000	
Labor added this period: (1000 units × 30% × $2)	600	
Overhead added this period: (1000 units × 30% × $3)	900	4,500
Total cost accounted for		$28,600

* See notes and computations, Table 9.

TABLE 9

NOTES

Material is added at the beginning of processing in Department B.
Work in process at the beginning of the period: approximately 25% complete.
Work in process at the end of the period: approximately 30% complete.

Equivalent units of production:	
Work done on beginning inventory:	
(1200 units × 75%)	900
Work done on units started and finished:	
(2800 units − 1000 units)	1,800
Work done on ending inventory:	
(1000 units × 30%)	300
Equivalent units of production	3,000
Cost added per unit in department or process:	
Material ($2800 ÷ 2800 units)	$1.00
Labor ($6000 ÷ 3000 units)	2.00
Overhead ($9000 ÷ 3000 units)	3.00
Total cost added per unit	$6.00
Cost of units transferred out of department or process:	
Units in process at beginning of period:	
Costs in process at beginning of period	$ 5,200
Costs added this period:	
Material (none added)	–0–
Labor (1200 × 75% × $2)	1,800
Overhead (1200 × 75% × $3)	2,700
Units started and finished:	
Costs transferred in (1800 × $2)	3,600
Costs added this period:	
Material (1800 × $1)	1,800
Labor (1800 × $2)	3,600
Overhead (1800 × $3)	5,400
Cost of 3000 units transferred out	$24,100

Physical Flow of Production. To understand process costing fully, we must first be able to visualize the physical flow of production through a factory. Physical flow may be expressed in terms of both units and costs; hence we should be aware of where the units come from and where they go as they progress through the manufacturing operations and also where the costs come from and where they go as they flow through the accounts.

The physical flow of production is frequently depicted on flowcharts showing the various accounts through which the data flow. A flowchart, properly constructed, can often serve the CPA candidate as a basis and guide for an entire solution. The use of such charts whenever and wherever feasible is highly recommended. Figure 11 illustrates a situation in which units are processed through two departments, incurring costs for material, labor, and overhead in both.

FIGURE 11

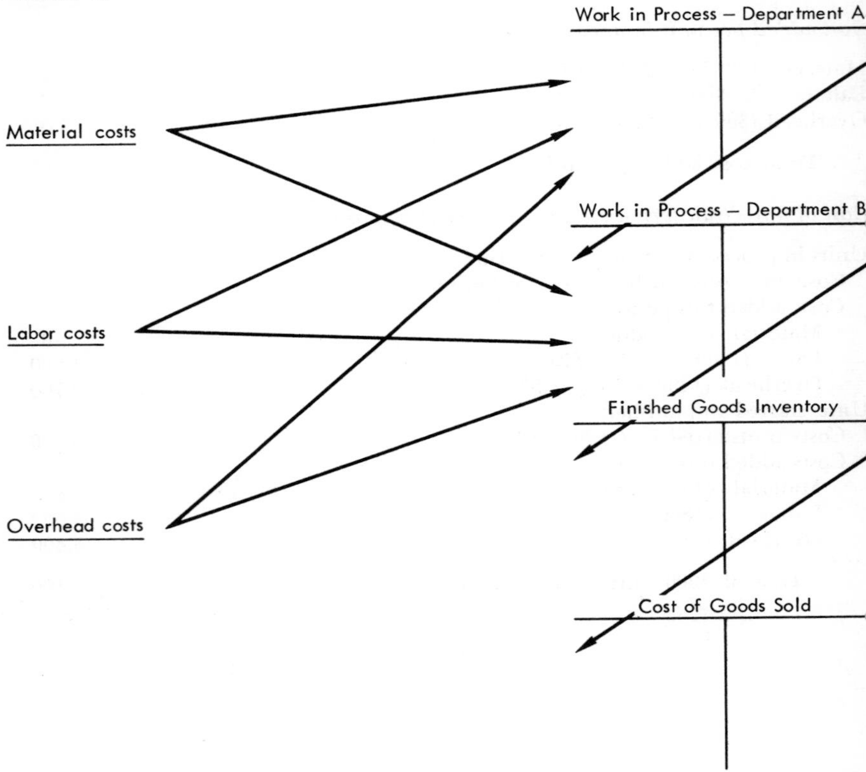

Work in Process Account. Whereas flowcharts present an overall view of the physical flow of production, the flow of costs can most readily be followed by examining the individual accounts, particularly the Work in

Process account. The Work in Process account for the month of June, 19X1, constructed from the data of Tables 8 and 9, would appear in T-account form as follows:

Work in Process – Department B

Beginning balance (1200 units)	5,200	Transferred out (3000 units)	24,100
Transferred in (2800 units)	5,600	Ending balance (1000 units)	4,500
Material added	2,800		
Labor added	6,000		
Overhead added	9,000		
	28,600		28,600
Beginning balance (1000 units)	4,500		

The relation between the cost data in the Work in Process account and the cost of production report in our illustration may be summarized by Table 10.

TABLE 10

Work in Process Department B		*Cost of Production Report*	
Beginning balance	$ 5,200 →	Transferred out	$ 5,200 *
Transferred in	5,600 →	Transferred out	3,600 *
	↘	Still in process	2,000
Material added	2,800 →	Transferred out	1,800 *
	↘	Still in process	1,000
Labor added	6,000 →	Transferred out	5,400 *
	↘	Still in process	600
Overhead added	9,000 →	Transferred out	8,100 *
	↘	Still in process	900
Total cost	$28,600		$28,600
Transferred out	(24,100) *		(24,100) *
Balance (still in process) ...	$ 4,500		$ 4,500

* $5,200 + $3,600 + $1,800 + $5,400 + $8,100 = $24,100.

Equivalent Units of Production (EUP). In order to allocate properly the costs incurred in a department or process during a period between the units completed in the course of the period and those still unfinished at the end of the period, we must express the production in terms of whole units. To do this, we must reduce the number of units in process as of the beginning and end of the period to the equivalent of completed units and add the result to the number of units that were completely processed (started and finished) during the period.

When there are no unfinished units in process at either the beginning or end of a period, the equivalent units of production are, of course, simply the number of units completed. However, when a department or process has either a beginning inventory of work in process, an ending inventory of work in process, or both beginning and ending inventories of work in process, the degree of completion must be estimated in order to reduce the number of partially completed units to the equivalent of completed units. For example, 200 units in an ending inventory estimated to be 50% complete would be the equivalent of 100 completed units; 400 units in an ending inventory estimated to be 25% complete would be the equivalent of 100 completed units. Thus, if 1000 units were put into production during the month, with 600 being completed and the remaining 400 estimated to be 25% complete, the equivalent units of production for the month would be 700 units [600 + $\frac{1}{4}$(400)]. The following data and the computations in Table 11 illustrate the procedure for computing equivalent units:

Case 1. No beginning or ending inventory of work in process; 4,000 units were started and finished.

Case 2. No beginning inventory of work in process, but 1,000 units were estimated to be 40% complete as of the end of the period; 4,000 units were started.

Case 3. No ending inventory of work in process, but 1,200 units were estimated to have been 30% complete as of the beginning of the period; 4,000 units were started.

Case 4. A beginning inventory of work in process of 1,000 units was estimated to have been 40% complete as of the beginning of the period, and an ending inventory of 1,200 units was estimated to be 20% complete as of the end of the period; 4,000 units were started.

TABLE II

EQUIVALENT UNITS OF PRODUCTION

Work done on:	*Case 1*	*Case 2*	*Case 3*	*Case 4*
Units in beginning inventory of work in process	–0–	–0–	840 [3]	600 [4]
Units started and finished	4,000	3,000 [1]	4,000	2,800 [5]
Units in ending inventory of work in process	–0–	400 [2]	–0–	240 [6]
Equivalent units of production	4,000	3,400	4,840	3,640

[1] 4,000 − 1,000 = 3,000
[2] 1,000 × 40% = 400
[3] 1,200 × 70% = 840
[4] 1,000 × 60% = 600
[5] 4,000 − 1,200 = 2,800
[6] 1,200 × 20% = 240

When we say that the units in process at the beginning or end of a period are estimated to be completed to a certain degree, it should be recognized that this is merely an estimated average stage of completion and does not necessarily mean that each unit in process is completed to precisely that degree. Typically, units in process at inventory time will be "strung out" throughout the department, with some nearing completion and others just beginning to be processed. In addition, as is the case in our cost of production report, units in process at inventory time may have received all their material, thereby incurring all their material costs. However, since the materials are only partially converted into finished products, only part of their conversion costs (labor and overhead) have been applied. When computing EUPs in such cases, we may have one EUP for material and another for conversion costs. For example, in our illustration the EUP for material is 2,800 units (the number of units started), whereas the EUP for labor and overhead is 3,000 units.

In addition to the possibility of having different EUPs for material and conversion costs in a given department or process, it is not unusual to have more than one EUP for material. For example, the production process may require the addition of one type of material at the beginning of the process, with another type added uniformly throughout the process, and yet another type added at the end of the process. To illustrate, let us assume the basic data used in our cost of production report (Tables 8 and 9); that is, 1,200 units approximately 25% complete in the beginning inventory of work in process, 2,800 units started during the period with 1,800 of them being completed during the period, and the remaining 1,000 approximately 30% complete at the end of the period. In addition, for illustrative purposes let us assume that three different materials are used: material A is added at the beginning of the process, material B is added uniformly throughout the process, and material C is added at the end of the process. The EUPs for material would be determined as in Table 12.

TABLE 12

EQUIVALENT UNITS OF PRODUCTION

	Material A	*Material B*	*Material C*
Beginning inventory of work in process	–0–	900	1,200
Units started and finished	1,800	1,800	1,800
Ending inventory of work in process	1,000	300	–0–
Equivalent units of production	2,800	3,000	3,000

Unit Costs of Production. Under process costing, the production costs of a period are spread over the production of the period through the use of broad averages, resulting in an average cost per unit. If all units worked on during a period are completely processed during that period, the determination of a unit cost is merely a matter of dividing total costs by the number of units processed. If, however, all units worked on are not completely processed during a given period, the various cost elements must be divided by their equivalent units of production; the resulting unit costs per element then must be summed in order to arrive at a total unit cost. (If production flows through more than one department or process, unit costs are ordinarily broken down, again by the use of averages, by department or process.)

In our cost of production report, the $1 unit cost for material was determined by dividing the total cost of material used ($2,800) by the EUP for material (2,800 units). Likewise, the $2 unit cost for labor was computed by dividing $6,000 (the total cost of labor) by 3,000 units (the EUP for labor), and the $3 unit cost for overhead was determined by dividing $9,000 (total overhead incurred) by 3,000 units (the EUP for overhead). In summarized form the computations are:

UNIT COSTS OF PRODUCTION—DEPARTMENT B

	Total Costs		*EUPs*		*Unit Costs*
Material	$2,800	÷	2,800	=	$1.00
Labor	6,000	÷	3,000	=	2.00
Overhead	9,000	÷	3,000	=	3.00

It should be noted parenthetically that in process costing, overhead may be applied to production as it is incurred or by the use of a predetermined rate, as is ordinarily done in job order costing. In organizations where the physical flow of production is not only continuous but also relatively stable from period to period, the application of the actual overhead incurred is usually satisfactory, since the regularity of production tends to normalize the amount of overhead applied to production from one period to another. However, in organizations where the physical flow of production is not constant from period to period, it is generally preferable that overhead be applied to production by the use of a predetermined rate.

When units are transferred out of a department or process, the average unit cost is determined simply by dividing the total costs associated with the units by the number of units involved. For example, in our cost of production report for June (Tables 8 and 9), a unit cost of $8.0333 would be determined by dividing $24,100 by 3,000 units.

Process Cost System Illustrated. To illustrate the process cost system more fully, let us continue our illustration for the month of July. In addition to studying the operations of Department B for the month, we shall also study Department A. For Department B we shall use the basic data from our previous illustration; you will recall that one unit of material—let us call it material Z—is added at the beginning of the process for each unit of production, and 1,000 units approximately 30% complete with an accumulated cost of $4,500 were in process as of the end of June.

In regard to Department A, let us assume that one unit of material X is added at the beginning of the process for each unit of production; one unit of material Y is added at the end of the process for each completed unit; and that as of the end of June, 800 units approximately 60% complete with an accumulated cost of $1,200 were still in process. Table 13 summarizes the transactions related to the manufacturing operations of Departments A and B for the month of July. With the journal entries in general journal form and postings shown in a skeletal fashion, the manufacturing operations for July would be recorded and posted as in Table 14 and Figure 12.

TABLE 13

1. Raw materials purchased:

	Number of Units	*Unit Cost*	*Total Cost*
Material X	5,000	$ .90	$ 4,500
Material Y	5,000	.10	500
Material Z	5,000	1.00	5,000
			$10,000

2. Direct materials requisitioned and used:

	Number of Units	*Unit Cost*	*Total Cost*
Material X	4,000	$ .90	$ 3,600
Material Y	3,000	.10	300
Material Z	3,000	1.00	3,000
			$ 6,900

3. Direct factory labor incurred:

Department A	$ 1,512
Department B	5,945
Total	$ 7,457

Table 13 (continued)

4. Factory overhead incurred:

Department A	$ 2,268
Department B	8,410
Total	$10,678

5. Units completed and transferred:

Department A	3,000
Department B	3,000

Units still in process as of July 31:

	Number of Units	*Percentage of Completion*
Department A	1,800	70%
Department B	1,000	20%

6. The 3,000 units produced in June and 2,000 units from the July production were sold on open account at $12 per unit. Sales are costed out of the Finished Goods Inventory account on the FIFO basis.

TABLE 14

(1)

Raw materials inventory	10,000	
Accounts payable (vouchers payable)		10,000
To record the purchase of raw materials.		

(2)

Work in process—Department A	3,900	
Work in process—Department B	3,000	
Raw materials inventory		6,900
To record direct materials used in production.		

(3)

Work in process—Department A	1,512	
Work in process—Department B	5,945	
Accrued payroll payable		7,457
To record direct labor used in production.		

(4)

Work in process—Department A	2,268	
Work in process—Department B	8,410	
Factory overhead		10,678
To record the application of overhead to production.		

Table 14 (continued)

(5)

Work in process—Department B	6,000	
Work in process—Department A		6,000
To transfer production costs from Department A to Department B.		
Finished goods inventory	23,865	
Work in process—Department B		23,865
To transfer production costs from Department B to the Finished Goods Inventory account.		

(6)

Accounts receivable	60,000	
Sales		60,000
To record the sale of 5,000 units at $12 per unit.		
Cost of goods sold	40,015	
Finished good inventory		40,015
To record the cost of sales.		

COMPOSITION OF COST OF SALES

June production:	3,000 units	$24,100
July production:	1,000 units	7,965 *
	1,000 units	7,950 †
		$40,015

* Units in process at beginning of period.
† From current production.

See also Figure 12 (page 492).

The following problem is representative of the CPA examination requirements in the area of process costing.

Problem: The Incredible Gadget Corporation manufactures a single product. Its operations are a continuing process carried on in two departments—the *Machining Department* and the *Assembly and Finishing Department. Materials are added to the product in each department without increasing the number of units produced.*

In the month of February the records showed that 75,000 units were put in production in the Machining Department. Of these units, 60,000 were completed and transferred to assembly and finishing, and 15,000 were left in process with all materials applied but with only one-third of the required labor and overhead.

FIGURE 12

GENERAL LEDGER

Work in Process – Department A

Beginning balance	1,200	Transferred to Dept. B	6,000
Material added	3,900	Ending balance	2,880
Labor added	1,512		
Overhead added	2,268		
	8,880		8,880
Beginning balance	2,880		

Work in Process – Department B

Beginning balance	4,500	Transferred to Fin. Goods	23,865
Transferred in	6,000	Ending balance	3,990
Material added	3,000		
Labor added	5,945		
Overhead added	8,410		
	27,855		27,855
Beginning balance	3,990		

Finished Goods Inventory

Beginning balance	24,100	Cost of sales	40,015
Transferred in	23,865		

Cost of Goods Sold

	40,015		

In the Assembly and Finishing Department 50,000 units were completed and transferred to the finished stock room during the month. Nine thousand units were in process on February 28, 1,000 units having been destroyed in production with no scrap value. All required materials had been applied to the 9,000 units and two-thirds of the labor and overhead, but only half the prescribed material and labor had been applied to the 1,000 units lost in process.

There was no work in process in either department at the first of the month.

The cost of units lost in production should be treated as additional overhead in the Assembly and Finishing Department.

Cost records showed the following charges during the month:

	Materials	*Labor*	*Overhead*
Machining department	$120,000	$ 87,100	$39,000
Assembly and finishing department	41,650	101,700	56,810 *

* Does not include the cost of spoiled units.

Required:

a. Prepare in good form a statement showing the unit cost for the month.

b. Prepare a schedule showing the details of the work in process inventory in each department.

Solution:

a.

INCREDIBLE GADGET CORPORATION

COST STATEMENT
MONTH OF FEBRUARY

	Units	*Amount*	*Cost per Unit*
Machining Department			
Materials	75,000	$120,000	$1.60
Labor	65,000	87,100	1.34
Overhead	65,000	39,000	.60
Total		$246,100	$3.54
Transferred to finishing	60,000	212,400	3.54
Work in process inventory		$ 33,700	
Assembly and Finishing Department			
Transferred from machining	60,000	$212,400	$3.54
Materials	59,500	41,650	.70
Labor	56,500	101,700	1.80
Total exclusive of overhead		$355,750	$6.04
Overhead:			
Expenses incurred		$ 56,810	

(continued)

Cost of spoiled units:			
Transferred cost	1,000	$ 3,540	
Materials	500	350	
Labor	500	900	
Overhead to be assigned	56,000	$ 61,600	$1.10
Total cost		$412,560	$7.14
Transferred to finished goods	50,000	357,000	7.14
Work in process inventory		$ 55,560	

b.

DETAILS OF WORK IN PROCESS INVENTORIES

	Units	*Cost per Unit*	*Amount*
Machining Department			
Materials	15,000	$1.60	$24,000
Labor	5,000	1.34	6,700
Overhead	5,000	.60	3,000
Total			$33,700
Assembly and Finishing Department			
Transferred cost	9,000	$3.54	$31,860
Materials	9,000	.70	6,300
Labor	6,000	1.80	10,800
Overhead	6,000	1.10	6,600
Total			$55,560

costing by-products and joint products

When more than one kind of product is obtained from a single manufacturing process, the problem arises of how to allocate the costs of manufacturing to the various products. For accounting purposes such products are classified either as by-products or joint products.

The distinction between the two is a relative matter, frequently more practical than theoretical. Generally, *by-products* are minor products of comparatively small value which are produced simultaneously with major products of greater value. Examples are buttermilk, a by-product in the production of butter, and coal tar, a by-product in the conversion of coal into coke. *Joint products,* on the other hand, are products of comparable value which are produced simultaneously from the same raw material. Gasoline, fuel oil, and lubricants in the petroleum industry, and ham, pork loins, and bacon in the meat-packing industry are examples of joint products.

The basic difference in accounting for the costs of by-products and joint products relates to the costs incurred prior to their separation from the main product or other joint products. This point is commonly called the *split-off point,* or the *point of separation.* In the case of joint products, all costs incurred prior to the point of separation must be allocated to the separate products. Such costs ordinarily are not allocated to by-products, but instead are treated in their entirety as costs of the main product.

Accounting for By-products. There are several methods of accounting for by-products. Theoretically, one of the better ways would be to determine the net realizable value (sales value less estimated cost of disposal) of the by-product and then deduct it from the cost of producing the main product. From a practical standpoint, however, based on expediency and materiality, the revenue received from the sale of a by-product is usually handled either as miscellaneous income or as a reduction of the cost of the main product. If we assume by-product sales of $100, the following entries are illustrative of the practical approach:

(1)

Cash	100	
Miscellaneous income		100
To record by-product sales (revenue from by-products considered as miscellaneous income).		

(2)

Cash	100	
Work in process		100
To record by-product sales (revenue from by-products considered as cost reduction).		

Accounting for Joint Products. When accounting for joint products, the accountant allocates common costs to the individual products. The two principal bases for allocating such costs are quantities produced and relative market (selling market) values.

The quantities produced method requires the use of a common unit of measurement such as pounds, gallons, or tons, for all products. The relative market value method is based on the premise that common costs should be allocated to joint products in proportion to the revenue earned by each product. When joint products incur additional costs of processing beyond the point of separation, such costs are deducted from the gross revenue of each product in order that net market values at the point of separation may be obtained.

The relative market value method is applicable for almost all types of joint products, whereas the quantities produced method is acceptable only when its results are substantially the same as those that would be obtained if the relative market value method were used. To illustrate both methods, let us assume that 10,000 units of product A and 20,000 units of product B were produced jointly at a total cost of $90,000. In addition, let us assume that product A had a sales value of $2 per unit and product B a sales value of $5 per unit. As Table 15 demonstrates, the $90,000 cost is assigned to products A and B in different amounts, depending on the method used.

TABLE 15

QUANTITIES PRODUCED METHOD

Product	*Units Produced*	*Computations*		*Cost Assigned*
A	10,000	10,000/30,000 × $90,000	=	$30,000
B	20,000	20,000/30,000 × $90,000	=	60,000
	30,000			$90,000

MARKET VALUE METHOD

Product	*Market Value*	*Computations*		*Cost Assigned*
A	$ 20,000 *	20,000/120,000 × $90,000	=	$15,000
B	100,000 †	100,000/120,000 × $90,000	=	75,000
	$120,000			$90,000

* 10,000 units at $2 per unit.
† 20,000 units at $5 per unit.

The problem which follows is illustrative of the CPA Examination requirements with respect to joint products.

Problem: The LaBreck Company's common, or joint, cost of producing 1,000 units of product A, 500 units of product B, and 500 units of product C is $100,000. The unit sales values of the three products at the split-off point are product A—$20; product B—$200; product C—$160. Ending inventories include 100 units of product A, 300 units of product B, and 200 units of product C.

Required: Determine the amount of common cost that would be included in the ending inventory valuation of the three products, assuming that common costs are assigned to joint products on the basis of their relative sales value and on the basis of physical units produced.

Solution:

a.

RELATIVE SALES VALUE BASIS

	Products			
	A	*B*	*C*	*Inventory*
1. Number of units produced	1,000	500	500	
2. Unit sales price	$20	$200	$160	
3. Sales value (item 1 × item 2)	$20,000	$100,000	$80,000	
4. Percentage of sales value	10%	50%	40%	
5. Allocation of common cost of $100,000	$10,000	$ 50,000	$40,000	
6. Allocated common cost per unit (item 5 ÷ item 1)	$10	$100	$80	
7. Units in ending inventory	100	300	200	
8. Common cost included in ending inventory valuation (item 6 × item 7)	$ 1,000	$ 30,000	$16,000	$47,000

b.

PHYSICAL UNIT BASIS

	Products			
	A	*B*	*C*	*Inventory*
1. Number of units produced	1,000	500	500	
2. Percent of total units	50%	25%	25%	
3. Allocation of common cost of $100,000	$50,000	$25,000	$25,000	
4. Allocated common cost per unit (item 3 ÷ item 1)	$50	$50	$50	
5. Units in ending inventory	100	300	200	
6. Common cost included in ending inventory valuation (item 4 × item 5)	$5,000	$15,000	$10,000	$30,000

standard costs

Simply stated, standard costs are forecasts of what costs for products or services should be under specified conditions. They generally are determined as a result of detailed engineering studies, time and motion studies, and other analyses of cost and production relationships.

Cost control through the use of standards is usually accomplished in manufacturing organizations in three basic steps:

1. Standards are established for each element of cost (material, labor, and overhead).
2. Actual costs are compared with the established standards.
3. When necessary, investigative and corrective action is taken.

When the actual cost incurred for material, labor, or overhead differs from the standard amount allowed, the difference is known as a *variance*. If the standard cost is greater than the actual cost, the variance is said to be favorable, whereas if the actual cost exceeds the standard amount, an unfavorable variance results.

The analysis of variances is an essential element of cost control. It is important that deviations between actual and standard costs be reported to the person or department responsible for the incurrence of the actual costs, in order that corrective action may be taken. Although variances may be stated in terms of physical units, it is customary to emphasize their economic significance by expressing them in dollar amounts.

Materials Standards. Cost standards for materials are composed of two basic factors: the quantity of material that should be used to produce the desired end product and the price that should be paid for the material used. Thus two major variances are possible, one related to the *quantity* of material used and the other related to the *price* paid for the material. To illustrate briefly, let us assume that the standards established for product X allow for ten units of material A at a standard price of $2 per unit. If production of product X requires eleven units of material A, the quantity standard will be exceeded by one unit. Likewise, if the actual price paid for the material used is only $1.90 per unit, it will be $0.10 per unit under the price standard.

The dollar value of the material's quantity variance is determined by multiplying the difference between the actual quantity of material used and the standard quantity allowed for the production by the standard price. It should be realized that the use of the standard price rather than the actual price screens out the effect of any price changes, which as a rule are not within the influence of the manager (e.g., a foreman) who is held responsible for the quantity variance. Stated as a formula, letting MQV equal materials quantity variance, AQ equal actual quantity, SQ equal standard quantity, and SP equal standard price, we have

$$MQV = (AQ - SQ) \times SP \qquad or$$
$$MQV = (SQ - AQ) \times SP$$

Example: A standard quantity of 2,000 units of material Z is allowed for the production of 1,000 units of product A. The standard price for material Z is \$2 per unit. Materials requisitions for the production of 1,000 units of product A show that 1,920 units of material Z were requisitioned and used. The materials quantity variation of \$160 would be computed as follows:

$$\begin{aligned} MQV &= (SQ - AQ) \times SP \\ MQV &= (2{,}000 - 1{,}920) \times \$2 \\ MQV &= 80 \times \$2 \\ MQV &= \$160 \end{aligned}$$

Since the actual quantity of material used was less than the standard quantity allowed for the production, the \$160 figure constitutes the dollar value of a favorable quantity variance. If the actual quantity of material used had exceeded the standard quantity allowed for the production, the variance would have been unfavorable.

The dollar value of a materials price variance is determined by multiplying the difference between the actual price incurred and the standard price by the actual quantity of material used. Stated as a formula, using our previous abbreviations and letting *MPV* equal materials price variance and *AP* equal actual price, we have:

$$\begin{aligned} MPV &= (AP - SP) \times AQ \quad \textit{or} \\ MPV &= (SP - AP) \times AQ \end{aligned}$$

Example: Assume the data used in our previous illustration; that is, that 2,000 units of material Z with a standard price of \$2 per unit were allowed for the production of 1,000 units of product A, and that 1,920 units of material Z were requisitioned and used. In addition, assume that the actual price of material Z was \$2.10 per unit. The materials price variation of \$192 would be computed as follows:

$$\begin{aligned} MPV &= (AP - SP) \times AQ \\ MPV &= (\$2.10 - \$2.00) \times 1{,}920 \\ MPV &= \$.10 \times 1{,}920 \\ MPV &= \$192 \end{aligned}$$

Since the actual price of material used exceeded the standard price, the \$192 figure constitutes the dollar value of an unfavorable materials price variance. If the actual price had been less than the standard price, the variance would have been favorable.

The following data provide a review of the computations involved in the determination of the two materials variances and at the same time show the combined effect of the variances.

Actual cost of material used:	
(1,920 units at \$2.10 per unit)	\$4,032
Standard cost of material that should have been used:	
(2,000 units at \$2.00 per unit)	4,000
Net unfavorable variance	\$ 32

The net unfavorable variance of \$32 was the result of:

Unfavorable price variance:	
(1,920 units at \$0.10 per unit)	\$192
Favorable quantity variance:	
(80 units at \$2.00 per unit)	160
Net unfavorable variance	\$ 32

Labor Standards. Cost standards for labor, like those for materials, are composed of two basic factors: the amount of labor that should be utilized to produce the desired end product and the price that should be paid for the labor. Thus again two variations are possible, one related to the *quantity* of labor used and the other related to the *price* paid for the labor.

To illustrate, let us assume that the standards established for product X allow for two hours of labor per unit at a standard price of \$5 per hour. If production of product X requires only one and one-half hours of labor per unit, it will be one-half hour per unit under the quantity standard. Likewise, if the actual price paid for labor is \$5.25 per hour, the price standard will be exceeded by \$0.25 per hour.

The dollar value of the labor quantity variance is determined by multiplying the difference between the actual amount of time required for production and the standard time allowed by the standard price. A formula, using our previous abbreviations and letting *LQV* equal labor quantity variance, is

$$LQV = (AQ - SQ) \times SP \quad or$$
$$LQV = (SQ - AQ) \times SP$$

Example: A standard quantity of 4,000 hours of direct labor at a standard price of \$3 per hour is allowed for the production of 1,000 units of product A. However, labor records for the production of 1,000 units of product A show that 4,200 hours of direct labor were actually incurred. We then have:

$$LQV = (AQ - SQ) \times SP$$
$$LQV = (4{,}200 - 4{,}000) \times \$3$$
$$LQV = 200 \times \$3$$
$$LQV = \$600$$

Since the actual amount of labor used exceeded the standard quantity allowed for the production, the $600 figure constitutes the dollar value of an unfavorable labor quantity variance. Had the amount of labor been less than the standard quantity allowed, the variance would have been favorable.

The dollar value of the labor price variance is determined by multiplying the difference between the actual price incurred and the standard price by the actual quantity of labor performed. The appropriate formula, using our previous abbreviations and letting *LPV* equal labor price variance, is

$$LPV = (AP - SP) \times AQ \quad \textit{or}$$
$$LPV = (SP - AP) \times AQ$$

Example: Assume the data used in our labor quantity illustration; that is, that 1,000 units of product A require 4,000 hours of direct labor at a standard price of $3 per hour, and that 4,200 hours of direct labor actually were performed to produce 1,000 units of product A. In addition, assume that the actual price of direct labor was $2.95 per hour. We then have

$$LPV = (SP - AP) \times AQ$$
$$LPV = (\$3.00 - \$2.95) \times 4{,}200$$
$$LPV = \$0.05 \times 4{,}200$$
$$LPV = \$210$$

Since the actual price of the labor was less than the standard price allowed, the $210 figure constitutes the dollar value of a favorable price variance. Had the price of the labor been more than the standard price allowed, the variance would have been unfavorable.

The following data provide a review of the computations involved in the determination of the two labor variances, and at the same time show the combined effect of the variances.

Actual cost of labor used:	
(4,200 hours at $2.95 per hour)	$12,390
Standard cost of labor that should have been used:	
(4,000 hours at $3 per hour)	12,000
Net unfavorable variance	$ 390

The net unfavorable variance of $390 was the result of:

Unfavorable quantity variance:	
(200 hours at $3 per hour)	$600
Favorable price variance:	
(4,200 hours at $0.05 per hour)	210
Net unfavorable variance	$390

Overhead Standards. Our earlier discussion of factory overhead applies equally well here, with one major exception which pertains to the determination of the overhead rate.

In developing predetermined overhead rates, which are commonly used to apply overhead to production by organizations not employing standard cost systems, we divided estimated overhead costs by estimated production. However, when standard costs are used, overhead is applied to production on the basis of a *standard overhead rate,* which is determined by dividing standard overhead costs by standard production. If SOR equals standard overhead rate, we have

$$SOR = \frac{\text{standard overhead costs}}{\text{standard production}}$$

Standard overhead costs are determined by establishing standards for each item of overhead expense. These standards are based on what costs should be under specified conditions rather than on what they were in the past or are expected to be in the future.

When establishing overhead standards, management must decide on the level of production at which the standards should be set. Although there are many variations in practice, standard production is often stated in terms of *normal capacity,* which in turn is ordinarily expressed in direct labor hours per month or year, machine hours per month or year, or units of production. Other terms used synonymously with normal capacity include normal activity, normal production, normal volume, average activity, average capacity, average volume, and simply, standard production.

In establishing normal capacity, management must make allowances for a normal amount of unavoidable work stoppage due to lack of sales orders, delays in delivery of materials or supplies, breakdown in machinery and equipment, labor shortages and absenteeism, and like factors.

Overhead Variances. Since the standard overhead rate per unit is determined by dividing standard overhead costs by standard production, a deviation between the actual overhead incurred and that applied to production during a specific period may result from differences between:

1. Standard overhead allowed and actual overhead incurred.
2. Standard production and actual production.
3. A combination of 1 and 2.

Up to this time, we have assumed that fixed expenses for a given period of time and a specified range of output do not change in response to changes in volume, and that variable expenses change more or less proportionately in response to changes in volume. Our assumption regarding fixed expenses is reasonably sound, but it does not always hold true in regard to variable expenses. They often tend to be somewhat "sticky," and therefore seldom vary in exact ratio to variations in volume. As a consequence, deviations between actual and standard overhead result primarily from:

1. Incurrence of variable expenses in an amount other than that called for by the standard.
2. Spreading of fixed expenses over more or fewer units than called for by the standard.
3. A combination of 1 and 2.

We can visualize the two basic deviations if we study Table 16. Assume that actual production for a given period is 40,000 units, normal capacity is 50,000 units, and that the actual variable expenses incurred amount to $32,000. As Table 16 reveals, the variable expenses at the 40,000 unit level should be only $30,000; thus there is an unfavorable deviation of $2,000. Similarly, when the standard overhead rate of $1.75 per unit, based on normal capacity of 50,000 units, is employed, only $1 of fixed expense per unit is applied to production; at the 40,000 unit level, however, $1.25 per unit should be applied if all the fixed expenses are to be charged to production. Since $10,000 of the fixed expenses [40,000 units × ($1.25 – $1.00)] would not be charged to production, we would have another unfavorable deviation.

TABLE 16

COST BEHAVIOR SCHEDULE

Production (Units)	*20,000*	*30,000*	*40,000*	*50,000 (Normal Capacity)*	*60,000*
Overhead costs:					
Fixed expenses	$50,000	$50,000	$50,000	$50,000	$50,000
Variable expenses	15,000	22,500	30,000	37,500	45,000
Total	$65,000	$72,500	$80,000	$87,500	$95,000
Overhead cost per unit:					
Fixed expenses	$2.50	$1.667	$1.25	$1.00	$ .833
Variable expenses	.75	.75	.75	.75	.75
Total	$3.25	$2.417	$2.00	$1.75	$1.583

The basic deviations associated with the variable expense elements of overhead are commonly known as *controllable variances,* and those associated with the fixed expense elements are referred to as *volume variances.*

The controllable variance is determined by comparing the actual amount of variable expense incurred with the standard amount that should have been incurred for the level of production attained. Letting *SVE* equal standard variable expenses and *AVE* equal actual variable expenses, we have

$$\text{controllable variance} = SVE - AVE \qquad \textit{or}$$
$$\text{controllable variance} = AVE - SVE$$

Example: Assume the basic data in our cost behavior schedule and also assume that $82,000 of overhead is incurred during a period in which 45,000 units are produced.

$$\text{controllable variance} = SVE - AVE$$
$$\text{controllable variance} = \$33{,}750 - \$32{,}000$$
$$\text{controllable variance} = \$1{,}750,$$

where the $33,750 is for 45,000 units at $0.75 per unit for variable expenses, and the $32,000 represents $82,000 minus fixed expenses of $50,000.

Since we assume that the fixed expenses are rigidly fixed, we can also determine the controllable variance in another way; that is, by comparing the total amount of overhead incurred with the total standard amount that should have been incurred for the level of production actually attained. Using this approach and letting *STO* equal standard total overhead and *ATO* equal actual total overhead, we would have

$$\text{controllable variance} = STO - ATO$$
$$\text{controllable variance} = \$83{,}750 - \$82{,}000$$
$$\text{controllable variance} = \$1{,}750,$$

where the $83,750 represents $50,000 fixed expense plus $33,750 variable expense (45,000 units at $0.75 per unit), and the $82,000 is as given in the basic data.

Since the actual variable expenses incurred were less than the standard amount allowed for the production, the $1,750 figure constitutes the dollar amount of a favorable controllable variance. If the actual variable expenses were to exceed the standard, the variance would be unfavorable.

The volume variance is determined by comparing the amount of fixed expense incurred with the amount applied to production. This is accomplished by multiplying the difference between actual and standard production by the fixed expense element of the overhead rate. Letting *ACP* equal actual production, *STP* equal standard production, and *FOR* equal the fixed expense element of the overhead rate, we have

volume variance = $(ACP - STP) \times FOR$ *or*
volume variance = $(STP - ACP) \times FOR$

Example: Using the basic data in our cost behavior schedule and the additional data in our preceding illustration, we would determine a volume variance of $5,000 as follows:

volume variance = $(STP - ACP) \times FOR$
volume variance = (50,000 − 45,000) × $1
volume variance = $5,000

where $1 is the fixed expense element of the standard overhead rate.

Since actual production was less than standard production, the $5,000 figure constitutes the dollar amount of an unfavorable volume variance. If the actual production were to exceed the standard, the volume variance would be favorable.

The following data provide a review of the computations involved in the determination of the overhead variances, and at the same time show their combined effect.

Actual overhead (given)	$82,000
Applied overhead:	
(45,000 units at $1.75 per unit)	78,750
Net unfavorable variance	$ 3,250

The net unfavorable variance of $3,250 was the result of:

Unfavorable volume variance:	
(5,000 units at $1 * per unit)	$5,000
Favorable controllable variance:	
(Standard variable expenses of $33,750 minus actual variable expenses of $32,000)	1,750
Net unfavorable variance	$3,250

* Fixed expense element of the standard overhead rate.

Standard Costs in the Accounts. Standard costs may be recorded in the accounts by one of three methods. All three ordinarily credit the Work in Process account for standard costs, but they differ regarding the amounts to be charged to the account. One method charges the Work in Process account with actual quantities at actual prices; a second method charges the account with actual quantities at standard prices; and a third charges the account with standard quantities at standard prices. The differences are illustrated in T-account form as follows:

First Method		Second Method		Third Method	
Work in Process		*Work in Process*		*Work in Process*	
$AQ \times AP$	$SQ \times SP$	$AQ \times SP$	$SQ \times SP$	$SQ \times SP$	$SQ \times SP$

Although the end results are the same (production is costed at standard cost), under the first method all variances are reflected in the Work in Process account; under the second method *price variances* are determined before the costs are transferred to the Work in Process account; and under the third method *all variances* are determined prior to the transfer of the costs to the Work in Process account.

When variances are determined before the costs are transferred to the Work in Process account, as in the second and third methods, they are ordinarily recognized in the accounts as they occur. For example, a material price variance would be recognized at the time of purchase rather than at the time of use. Each method has advantages and disadvantages, but because of the simplicity and economy of operation of the first method, we shall use it in the illustration that follows.

Standard Cost System Illustrated. To illustrate the standard cost system more fully, let us assume that the Arcat Company employs standard costs when accounting for its principal product, Arcat. Standard specifications per unit of Arcat are:

Material A	2 units at $10.00 per unit
Material B	3 units at $6.00 per unit
Direct labor	100 hours at $3.00 per hour
Overhead	100 hours at the standard overhead rate

The Arcat Company's standard overhead rate is based on normal capacity of 10,000 direct labor hours per month and standard costs of $4,000 and $5,000 for fixed and variable expenses, respectively.

The actual costs and production of Arcat during the month of June were:

Material A	188 units at $9.95 per unit
Material B	274 units at $6.04 per unit
Direct labor	8,980 hours at $3.06 per hour
Overhead	$10,920
Units of Arcat produced	90

The Arcat Company's manufacturing operations for June would be recorded as follows and posted as in Figure 13 and Table 17.

(1)

Work in process	1,870.60	
Raw materials inventory		1,870.60
To record the cost of material A charged to production (188 units at $9.95 per unit).		

(2)

Work in process	1,654.96	
Raw materials inventory		1,654.96
To record the cost of material B charged to production (274 units at $6.04 per unit).		

(3)

Work in process	27,478.80	
Accrued payroll payable		27,478.80
To record direct labor charged to production (8,980 hours at $3.06 per hour).		

(4)

Work in process	10,920.00	
Factory overhead		10,920.00
To record factory overhead charged to production.		

(5)

Finished goods inventory	38,520.00	
Work in process		38,520.00
To transfer standard production costs from the Work in Process account to the Finished Goods Inventory account (90 units at a standard cost of $428.00 * per unit).		

* The standard cost of a unit of Arcat is:

Material A: 2 units at $10.00 per unit	$ 20.00
Material B: 3 units at $6.00 per unit	18.00
Labor: 100 hours at $3.00 per hour	300.00
Overhead: 100 hours at $.90 † per hour	90.00
Standard cost per unit	$428.00

$$\dagger \text{ standard overhead rate} = \frac{\text{standard overhead costs}}{\text{standard production}}$$

$$\text{standard overhead rate} = \frac{\$4{,}000\ FE + \$5{,}000\ VE}{10{,}000 \text{ direct labor hours}}$$

$$\text{standard overhead rate} = \$0.90 \text{ per direct labor hour}$$

(6)

To illustrate the entries involved when a sale is made by an organization employing a standard cost system, let us assume that the Arcat Company sold 50 units of Arcat during the month of June at $600 per unit.

Accounts receivable	30,000.00	
Sales		30,000.00
To record the sale of 50 units of Arcat at $600 per unit.		
Cost of goods sold	21,400.00	
Finished goods inventory		21,400.00
To record the cost of sales (50 units at a standard cost of $428 per unit).		

FIGURE 13

GENERAL LEDGER

Work in Process

Material A (actual)	1,870.60	Material A (standard)	1,800.00[1]
Material B (actual)	1,654.96	Material B (standard)	1,620.00[2]
Labor (actual)	27,478.80	Labor (standard)	27,000.00[3]
Overhead (actual)	10,920.00	Overhead (standard)	8,100.00[4]
Actual costs incurred	41,924.36	Standard cost of work done	38,520.00
		Variances from standard	3,404.36
	41,924.36		41,924.36
Variances from standard	3,404.36*		

Finished Goods Inventory

	38,520.00		21,400.00

Cost of Goods Sold

	21,400.00		

* See Table 17

1 (90 × 2 × $10) = $1,800

2 (90 × 3 × $6) = $1,620

3 (90 × 100 × $3) = $27,000

4 (90 × 100 × $0.90) = $8,100

TABLE 17

SCHEDULE A

VARIANCES FROM STANDARD

Material A	
Quantity variance (8 units at $10 per unit)	$ 80.00 *
Price variance (188 units at $0.05 per unit)	9.40
Material B	
Quantity variance (4 units at $6 per unit)	24.00 *
Price variance (274 units at $0.04 per unit)	10.96 *
Labor	
Quantity variance (20 hours at $3 per hour)	60.00
Price variance (8,980 hours at $0.06 per hour)	538.80 *
Overhead †	
Controllable variance ($6,920 − $4,500)	2,420.00 *
Volume variance (1,000 hours at $0.40 per hour)	400.00 *
Total	$3,404.36 *

* Unfavorable variance.

† The $6,920 is $10,920 − $4,000, the $4,500 is 9,000 hours at $.50 per hour, and the 1,000 hour figure represents 10,000 "normal" hours − 9,000 actual hours.

Disposition of Variances. When monthly or other interim statements are prepared, variances from standard costs ordinarily are carried forward on the balance sheet, with net unfavorable variances being classified as deferred charges and net favorable variances as deferred credits. Year-end variances, however, are generally closed out. This may be accomplished in one of two ways. Theoretically, each variance should be closed proportionately to the Cost of Goods Sold account and the pertinent inventory accounts. Practically, however, based on expediency and materiality, a variance usually is closed in its entirety directly to the Revenue and Expense Summary account.

To illustrate the two methods, let us assume the same operating data as in our Arcat illustration, and also assume that the data are for the year ended June 30, 19X1, rather than only for the month of June. In addition, for purposes of simplicity, let us assume that the only other Arcat income activities of the year were the incurrence of $2,000 of selling expenses and $3,000 of administrative expenses. In studying Tables 18 and 19, note that when the variances are closed to the Revenue and Expense Summary account, they appear as deductions from gross margin before selling and administrative expenses are deducted. It should also be noted that the difference of $1,513.05 between the two reported net income figures ($1,708.69 − $195.64) is equal to the amount of the variances allocated to the finished goods inventory ($\frac{4}{9} \times$ $3,404.36). This, of course, is the amount of the variances prorated to the 40 units that were produced but not sold.

TABLE 18

ARCAT COMPANY

INCOME STATEMENT
FOR THE YEAR ENDED JUNE 30, 19X1
(VARIANCES CLOSED DIRECTLY TO R & E SUMMARY)

Sales		$30,000.00
Cost of goods sold (at standard cost)		21,400.00
Gross margin (based on standard costs)		$ 8,600.00
Adjustments for standard cost variances:		
Material quantity variance ($80.00 + $24.00)	$ 104.00	
Material price variance ($10.96 − $9.40)	1.56	
Labor quantity variance	(60.00)	
Labor price variance	538.80	
Overhead controllable variance	2,420.00	
Overhead volume variance	400.00	3,404.36
Gross margin—adjusted		$ 5,195.64
Less: Selling expenses	$2,000.00	
Administrative expenses	3,000.00	5,000.00
Net income		$ 195.64

TABLE 19

ARCAT COMPANY

INCOME STATEMENT
FOR THE YEAR ENDED JUNE 30, 19X1
(VARIANCES PRORATED)

Sales		$30,000.00
Cost of goods sold (at actual cost)		23,291.31 *
Gross margin		$ 6,708.69
Less: Selling expenses	$2,000.00	
Administrative expenses	3,000.00	5,000.00
Net income		$ 1,708.69

* Standard cost	$21,400.00
Plus $\frac{5}{9}$ of the variances from standard ($\frac{5}{9}$ × $3,404.36)	1,891.31
	$23,291.31

Three-way Analysis of Overhead Variance. Although the two-way analysis used in our previous illustrations is frequently called for on the CPA Examination, it is not unusual for the candidate to be required to further subdivide the two basic variances. When this is the case, the overall overhead variance is broken down into the following:

1. Expense variance.
2. Activity variance.
3. Efficiency variance.

The *expense variance,* often referred to as the spending or budget variance, is the difference between the actual variable expenses incurred and those budgeted for the actual activity. The expense variance in the Arcat illustration would be $2,430 (unfavorable), computed as follows:

Actual variable expenses incurred ($10,920 – $4,000)	$6,920
Variable expenses budgeted for the actual activity (8,980 hours at $0.50 per hour)	4,490
Unfavorable expense variance	$2,430

The *activity variance* is the difference between the actual fixed expenses incurred and those charged to production. The activity variance in the Arcat illustration would be $408 (unfavorable), computed as follows:

Actual fixed expenses incurred	$4,000
Fixed expenses charged to production (8,980 hours at $0.40 per hour)	3,592
Unfavorable activity variance	$ 408

The *efficiency variance* is the difference between the overhead budgeted for the actual activity and that budgeted for the standard activity. The efficiency variance in the Arcat illustration would be $18 (favorable), computed as follows:

Overhead budgeted for the actual activity (8,980 hours at $0.90 per hour)	$8,082
Overhead budgeted for the standard activity (9,000 hours at $0.90 per hour)	8,100
Favorable efficiency variance	$ 18

The following problems are indicative of the examination requirements in the area of standard costs. When studying them, note that problem 1 requires the two-way analysis of the overhead variance whereas problem 2 requires the three-way analysis.

Problem 1: The standard cost of a unit of product Q, based on "normal" production of 100,000 units per month, is as follows:

Materials (½ lb)	$0.50
Labor (¼ hr)	0.70
Variable overhead	0.20
Fixed overhead	0.10
Total	$1.50

The following costs apply to the month of March (a month in which 104,000 units were produced):

Materials (52,300 lb at $.98/lb)	$ 51,254
Labor (25,800 hr at $2.83/hr)	73,014
Variable overhead	20,600
Fixed overhead	10,000
Total	$154,868

Required: To the extent possible, determine the

a. Material quantity variance
b. Material price variance
c. Labor quantity variance
d. Labor price variance
e. Controllable overhead variance
f. Overhead volume variance

Solution:

a. $ 300 (unfavorable). [52,300 − (104,000 × ½) × $1.00]
b. $1,046 (favorable). [52,300 × ($1.00 − $.98)]
c. $ 560 (favorable). [(104,000 × ¼) − 25,800 × $2.80]
d. $ 774 (unfavorable). [25,800 × ($2.83 − $2.80)]
e. $ 200 (favorable). [($10,000 *FE* + $20,800 *VE*) − $30,600]
f. $ 400 (favorable). [(104,000 − 100,000) × $0.10]

Problem 2: The Smith Company uses a standard cost system. The standards are based on a budget for operations at the rate of production anticipated for the current period. The Company records in its general ledger variations in material prices and usage, wage rates, and labor efficiency. The accounts for manufacturing expenses reflect variations in activity from the projected rate of operations, variations of actual expenses from amounts budgeted, and variations in the efficiency of production.

Current standards are as follows:		
Materials:		
Material A	$1.20 per unit	
Material B	2.60 per unit	
Direct labor	$2.05 per hour	
	Special Widgets	*De Luxe Widgets*
Finished products (content of each unit):		
Material A	12 units	12 units
Material B	6 units	8 units
Direct labor	14 hours	20 hours

The general ledger does not include a finished goods inventory account; costs are transferred directly from work in process to cost of sales at the time finished products are sold.

The budget and operating data for the month of August are summarized as follows:

Budget:		
Projected direct labor hours	(hours)	9,000
Fixed manufacturing expenses		$ 4,500
Variable manufacturing expenses		13,500
Selling expenses		4,000
Administrative expenses		7,500
Operating data:		
Sales:		
500 special widgets		$52,700
100 de luxe widgets		16,400
Purchases:		
Material A	8,500 units	$ 9,725
Material B	1,800 units	5,635
Material requisitions:	*Material A*	*Material B*
Issued from stores:		
Standard quantity	8,400 units	3,200 units
Over standard	400 units	150 units
Returned to stores	75 units	
Direct labor hours:		
Standard		9,600 hours
Actual		10,000 hours

Wages paid:	
500 hours at	$2.10
8,000 hours at	2.00
1,500 hours at	1.90
Expenses:	
Manufacturing	$20,125
Selling	3,250
Administrative	6,460

Required:

a. Prepare journal entries to record operations for the month of August. Show computations of the amounts used in each journal entry. Raw material purchases are recorded at standard.

b. Prepare a statement of profit and loss for the month supported by an analysis of variations.

Solution:

a.

JOURNAL ENTRIES

(1)

Accounts receivable	69,100	
Cost of sales	54,970	
Work in process		54,970
Sales		69,100

To record sales and cost of sales:

	Cost of Sales		
	Unit	*Total*	*Sales*
500 special widgets	$ 86.70	$43,350	$52,700
100 deluxe widgets	116.20	11,620	16,400
		$54,970	$69,100

Computation of unit costs:

	Per	*Special Widgets*		*De Luxe Widgets*	
	Unit	*Units*	*Amount*	*Units*	*Amount*
Material A	$1.20	12	$14.40	12	$ 14.40
Material B	2.60	6	15.60	8	20.80
Labor	2.05	14	28.70	20	41.00
Burden	2.00	14	28.00	20	40.00
			$86.70		$116.20

Burden (manufacturing overhead) rate:

	Total	*Per Hour*
Fixed manufacturing expenses	$ 4,500	$ .50
Variable manufacturing expenses	13,500	1.50
	$18,000	$2.00

Based on budget for 9,000 direct labor hours.

(2)

Raw material inventory	14,880	
Material price variation	480	
Accounts payable		15,360

To record purchases:

	Standard Cost		*Actual*
	Unit	*Total*	*Cost*
8500 units Material A	$1.20	$10,200	$ 9,725
1800 units Material B	2.60	4,680	5,635
		$14,880	$15,360
Material price variation			$ 480

(3)

Work in process	18,400	
Material usage variation	780	
Raw material inventory		19,180

To record requisitions:

	Per	*Standard*		*Over Standard*	
	Unit	*Units*	*Amount*	*Units*	*Amount*
Issued:					
Material A	$1.20	8,400	$10,080	400	$480
Material B	2.60	3,200	8,320	150	390
Returned:					
Material A	1.20			(75)	(90)
			$18,400		$780

(4)

Work in process	19,680	
Labor efficiency variation	820	
Wage rate variation		600
Accrued payroll		19,900

To record direct labor at standard and variations:

Standard labor: 9,600 hours at $2.05	$19,680
Labor efficiency variation: 400 excess hours at $2.05	$ 820

Wage rate variation:		
Wages at standard:		
10,000 hours at $2.05		$20,500
Less wages paid:		
500 hours at $2.10	$ 1,050	
8,000 hours at 2.00	16,000	
1,500 hours at 1.90	2,850	19,900
		$ 600

(5)

Work in process	19,200	
Burden expense variation	625	
Burden efficiency variation	800	
Burden activity variation		500
Manufacturing expense absorbed		20,125
To record manufacturing expense at standard and variations:		

Manufacturing expense at standard:		
9,600 hours at $2.00		$19,200
Burden expense variation:		
Actual expenses		$20,125
Expenses at standard:		
Fixed expenses	$ 4,500	
Variable expenses		
10,000 hours at $1.50	15,000	19,500
Variation		$ 625
Burden efficiency variation:		
400 hours over standard at $2.00		$ 800
Burden activity variation:		
Actual direct labor		10,000 hr
Budgeted direct labor		9,000 hr
Excess hours		1,000 hr
1,000 hours at fixed manufacturing expense rate of $0.50		$ 500

(6)

Manufacturing expenses	20,125	
Selling expenses	3,250	
Administrative expenses	6,460	
Accounts payable, etc.		29,835
To record expenses.		

b.

SMITH COMPANY

STATEMENT OF PROFIT AND LOSS
MONTH OF AUGUST

Sales		$69,100
Cost of sales:		
Standard cost	$54,970	
Variations from standard—see schedule	2,405	57,375
Gross Profit		$11,725
Expenses:		
Selling	$ 3,250	
Administrative	6,460	$ 9,710
Net Profit		$ 2,015

SUMMARY OF VARIATIONS

Materials:		
Price	$ 480	
Usage	780	$ 1,260
Labor:		
Wage rate	$ 600 *	
Efficiency	820	220
Manufacturing expense:		
Activity	$ 500 *	
Expense	625	
Efficiency	800	925
		$ 2,405

* Indicates credit variation.

Budgeting

Whereas a standard cost is a predetermined cost intended to serve as a yardstick or standard of performance, a *budget* is an estimated plan of operations for the future expressed in financial terms. In golfing jargon, both provide management with "pars" to "shoot at." Although one may be utilized without the other, maximum benefits are ordinarily realized when the two are employed together. This is particularly true if they are interlocked; that is, if the budget is based upon standard costs and standard costs in turn are based upon the budget. Standard costs and budgets are particularly valuable to management because their use emphasizes variations between preset standards and actual performance. This, of course, is most compatible with the "management-by-exception" principle.

(The management-by-exception principle, which is more or less fundamental to the study of management, is based on the assumption that performances which meet a preset standard are satisfactory and that only those which vary from standard require management's attention.)

Budgeting generally embraces the entire field of management in a business organization, and as a consequence all supervisory and executive personnel are involved to varying degrees in the preparation and execution of the organizational budgets. With the aid of all available information, management must determine how the organization can best attain its desired goals, and in so doing it must prepare detailed plans for reaching these goals. The planning phase is known as *budgeting;* the written plans, expressed in financial terms, constitute the *budget.* In large and complex organizations it often becomes necessary to employ a master budget in which all plans are summarized; the details are then "spelled out" in various departmental and specialized budgets, which in turn may be supplemented by supporting schedules.

Although there is no set order in which the various budgets are prepared, in profit-oriented organizations budgeting ordinarily begins with a sales forecast (an estimate of sales for the budget period), and operating plans for all segments of the organization are then developed. Thus the usual procedure is to start with the sales budget and plan the other budgets around it.

Sales Budget. Since each of the other budgets is either directly or indirectly related to it, the sales budget, which is based on a sales forecast, is the foundation of the entire budgeting process. Although there are a number of methods of making sales forecasts, most of them are based on a projected *sales volume* and a projected *sales price,* and these in turn normally are based upon an analysis of:

1. Past sales performances.
2. Present and prospective general business conditions.
3. Relative status of competitors.

To illustrate the preparation of a sales budget, let us assume that Company B manufactures and sells products X, Y, and Z. During 19X1, Company B sold 10,000 units of product X at $25 each, 1,000 units of product Y at $600 each, and 100,000 units of product Z at $1 each. After a careful analysis of past sales performance, present and prospective general business conditions, and the relative status of its competition, Company B decides to raise the price of product X by 20%, and the price of product Y by 30% and at the same time to lower the price of product Z by 5%. Based on the new price list, the company expects to sell 10% fewer units of product X during 19X2 than during 19X1, 5% fewer units of product Y, but twice the number of units of product Z. Based on these actions and projections, the sales budget for 19X2 would appear as in Table 20.

TABLE 20

COMPANY B

SALES BUDGET
FOR THE YEAR ENDING DECEMBER 31, 19X2

Product	*Volume (units)*	*Sales Price*	*Total Sales*
X	9,000 [1]	$ 30.00 [4]	$ 270,000
Y	950 [2]	780.00 [5]	741,000
Z	200,000 [3]	0.95 [6]	190,000
			$1,201,000

[1] 10,000 − (10% × 10,000)
[2] 1,000 − (5% × 1,000)
[3] 2 × 100,000
[4] $25 + (20% × $25)
[5] $600 + (30% × $600)
[6] $1 − (5% × $1)

Production Budget. The major purpose of the production budget, which is predicated on the sales budget, is to assure the continuous availability of finished goods in an amount sufficient to meet the demands of the sales department and at the same time to maintain the inventory at its proper level. If the amount of finished goods on hand becomes too small, there is a danger of losing sales because the goods are not available; and if the amount becomes too large, a financial loss could result from such factors as deterioration, spoilage, obsolescence, and excess storage and handling costs.

To illustrate the preparation of a production budget, let us assume the basic data used in the preceding illustration. In addition, let us assume that the finished goods inventory as of December 31, 19X1, was composed of 2,000 units of product X, 100 units of product Y, and 40,000 units of product Z, and that Company B's plans call for having on hand 2,500 units of product X, 75 units of product Y, and 50,000 units of product Z as of December 31, 19X2. As indicated in Table 21, in order to meet both the sales and inventory requirements, Company B must produce 9,500 units of product X, 925 units of product Y, and 210,000 units of product Z during 19X2.

TABLE 21

SCHEDULE A

PRODUCTION IN UNITS
FOR THE YEAR ENDING DECEMBER 31, 19X2

	Units		
	Product X	*Product Y*	*Product Z*
Planned sales	9,000	950	200,000
Desired ending inventory	2,500	75	50,000
Total units needed	11,500	1,025	250,000
Less: Beginning inventory	2,000	100	40,000
Units to be produced	9,500	925	210,000

If we assume that Company B has a standard cost system in operation, and that the standard cost per unit of product is as shown in Table 22, Company B's production budget for the year ending December 31, 19X2, would appear as in Table 23.

TABLE 22

SCHEDULE B

STANDARD COST PER UNIT OF PRODUCT
FOR THE YEAR ENDING DECEMBER 31, 19X2

	Product X	*Product Y*	*Product Z*
Material	$ 4.00	$ 38.00	$0.25
Labor	12.00	300.00	0.15
Overhead	1.75	90.00	0.30
Total	$17.75	$428.00	$0.70

TABLE 23

COMPANY B

PRODUCTION BUDGET
FOR THE YEAR ENDING DECEMBER 31, 19X2

Product	*Quantity* *	*Standard Cost* †	*Total Costs*
X	9,500	$ 17.75	$168,625
Y	925	428.00	395,900
Z	210,000	0.70	147,000
			$711,525

* See Table 21.
† See Table 22.

Cash Budget. Although analyses of past cash flows are of considerable value to management, there is probably no more important aspect of planning for the future than that concerned with the management of future cash flows. Effective cash planning requires that management not only make provision for having adequate cash available to meet needs as they arise, but also that it formulate plans for effectively utilizing any excess cash as it becomes available. The questions then become: Where is the cash to come from? and How is it to be used? It is the purpose of the cash budget to provide answers to these questions. Although cash budgets may be prepared for any period of time, they usually are set up on a monthly, quarterly, or yearly basis.

To illustrate the preparation of a quarterly cash budget, let us assume that as of January 1, 19X2, Company B's Cash account has a $50,-000 debit balance and, for simplicity, that its Accounts Receivable account has a zero balance. In addition, assume the data given directly in the budget (Table 24) and in Schedule C (Table 25), pages 522–23.

flexible budgeting

Because they are based on estimates for specific volumes or levels of activity, the budgets that have been discussed and illustrated thus far are commonly known as *fixed* or *static budgets.* Our sales budget, for example, was based on a specific volume of sales and our production budget on a given level of production. When the volume of an organization's activities can be very closely estimated, the fixed budget as a rule is satisfactory for planning and control purposes. Modern business, however, is dynamic rather than static; as a consequence, management may find it very difficult to forecast precisely such activities as sales and production. In organizations where this is the case, it is common practice to employ what are known as flexible or variable budgets.

Flexible budgets are composed of a number of individual budgets that have been prepared for different levels of activity. For example, a flexible production budget may consist of separate budgets prepared for each 10% level of activity ranging from the 60% level to the 100% level. Thus budgets of this kind reflect what costs should be at different levels of activity, rather than at one specific level.

A knowledge of cost behavior is fundamental to a sound understanding of flexible budgeting. As the candidate will recall from our earlier study of break-even analysis, costs behave in different ways but as a general rule may be categorized as either fixed or variable. Fixed costs, synonymously called fixed expenses, do not change in response to changes in activity, whereas variable costs or expenses change proportionately with changes in activity. Since fixed costs are constant in total, the amount

TABLE 24

COMPANY B

CASH BUDGET
FOR THE YEAR ENDING DECEMBER 31, 19X2

	1st Quarter	*2nd Quarter*	*3rd Quarter*	*4th Quarter*
Beginning balance	$ 50,000	$ 77,000	$147,500	$190,000
Estimated receipts:				
Cash sales	160,000	170,400	185,000	205,200
Collections on receivables *	50,000	85,000	111,200	132,420
Sale of machinery		7,600		
Issuance of bonds			48,800	
Total cash available	$260,000	$340,000	$492,500	$527,620
Estimated disbursements:				
Payment of current payables	$180,500	$190,000	$220,000	$210,500
Retirement of mortgage				250,000
Purchase of equipment			80,000	
Payment of dividends	2,500	2,500	2,500	2,500
Total cash disbursements	$183,000	$192,500	$302,500	$463,000
Ending balance	$ 77,000	$147,500	$190,000	$ 64,620

* See Table 25.

TABLE 25

SCHEDULE C

COLLECTION OF ACCOUNTS RECEIVABLE
FOR THE YEAR ENDING DECEMBER 31, 19X2

		Collections *			
	Credit Sales	*1st Quarter*	*2nd Quarter*	*3rd Quarter*	*4th Quarter*
1st quarter	$100,000	$50,000	$30,000	$ 19,000	
2nd quarter	110,000		55,000	33,000	$ 20,900
3rd quarter	118,400			59,200	35,520
4th quarter	152,000				76,000
	$480,400	$50,000	$85,000	$111,200	$132,420

* Collections on credit sales are generally made as follows:

During quarter of sale	50%
During first subsequent quarter	30%
During second subsequent quarter	19%
Uncollectible	1%

of fixed cost associated with each unit of output will vary depending on the number of units produced, whereas the amount of variable cost associated with each unit will remain the same. Although somewhat condensed, Table 26 is illustrative of the general idea underlying flexible budgeting.

TABLE 26

COMPANY A

PRODUCTION BUDGET
FOR THE YEAR ENDING DECEMBER 31, 19X2

	Production in Units			
	7,000	*8,000*	*9,000*	*10,000*
Material costs	$ 35,000	$ 40,000	$ 45,000	$ 50,000
Labor costs	49,000	56,000	63,000	70,000
Fixed overhead costs:				
Depreciation on plant	30,000	30,000	30,000	30,000
Insurance	2,000	2,000	2,000	2,000
Supervision	5,000	5,000	5,000	5,000
Taxes	1,000	1,000	1,000	1,000
Variable overhead costs:				
Depreciation on machinery	7,000	8,000	9,000	10,000
Heat, light, and power	10,500	12,000	13,500	15,000
Indirect labor	3,500	4,000	4,500	5,000
Supplies	1,400	1,600	1,800	2,000
Total cost of production	$144,400	$159,600	$174,800	$190,000
Cost per unit	$20.63 *	$19.95	$19.42 *	$19.00

* Rounded off.

Flexible Budgeting and Overhead Application. Flexible budgeting is particularly useful in the analysis and control of factory overhead costs. As the candidate will recall when we discussed job order and process cost systems, we used a predetermined overhead rate based on an estimated level of activity. In situations where the actual amounts of overhead and production closely coincide with the estimated amounts, this approach ordinarily is satisfactory. However, at times management may find it difficult to estimate overhead and production with any degree of accuracy. If actual production turns out to be more or less than the estimated production, or if the actual and the estimated costs differ to any extent, comparisons of such data may not be too useful. For example, the results obtained by comparing costs estimated for an output of 10,000 units with those actually incurred for an output of 8,000 units would be of limited value. The significant comparison is one that relates budgeted and actual costs to the same level of activity. Flexible budgeting provides a means whereby this may be accomplished.

To illustrate the importance of flexible budgeting to the application of overhead costs, let us assume that a predetermined overhead rate of $2 per unit is determined by dividing $20,000 of estimated overhead by 10,000 units of estimated production. If actual production is 10,000 units and the actual amount of overhead incurred is $20,000 as was estimated, we have no problem. Let us assume, however, that actual production is only 8,000 units and the actual amount of overhead incurred is $17,000. If we use the $2 rate to apply the overhead, $16,000 of overhead will be applied to production (8,000 units × $2 per unit) resulting in a $1,000 underapplied overhead variation. Using flexible budgeting, however, and assuming a variable cost per unit of $1.50 (any amount under $2 per unit could be assumed), we find that in reality no variation is involved. Table 27 illustrates this.

TABLE 27

FLEXIBLE BUDGET

FACTORY OVERHEAD

	Production in Units			
	7,000	*8,000*	*9,000*	*10,000*
Fixed expenses *	$ 5,000	$ 5,000	$ 5,000	$ 5,000
Variable expenses *	10,500	12,000	13,500	15,000
Total cost	$15,500	$17,000	$18,500	$20,000
Fixed cost per unit	$0.714	$0.625	$0.556	$0.50
Variable cost per unit	1.50	1.50	1.50	1.50
Total cost per unit	$2.214	$2.125	$2.056	$2.00

* Since the variable cost per unit was given as $1.50 and the total cost incurred at the 10,000 unit level is $20,000, the amount of fixed overhead is $5,000 [$20,000 minus the variable overhead of $15,000 (10,000 units at $1.50 per unit)].

As can be deduced from Table 27, the $1,000 difference between the actual amount of overhead incurred ($17,000) and the amount applied to production ($16,000) was the result of fixed expenses being charged to production at the rate of $0.50 per unit (the amount chargeable at the 10,000 unit level) instead of $0.625 (the amount that should be charged at the 8,000 unit level). The $0.125 per unit difference ($0.625 – $0.50), when multiplied by 8,000 units (the actual production), is equal, of course, to the $1,000 difference between the actual and the applied overhead.

Glossary of Cost Terminology

Needless to say, the serious CPA candidate must be fully conversant with the appropriate terminology. The American Accounting Association's Committee on Cost Concepts and Standards (*Accounting Review*, Vol. XXVII) defines the following terms:

1. *Historical cost* is cost measured by actual cash payments or their equivalent at the time of outlay.
2. *Future costs* are costs expected to be incurred at a later date.
3. *Replacement cost* is cost in the present market.
4. *Standard costs* are scientifically predetermined costs.
5. *Estimated costs* are predetermined costs.
6. *Product cost* is cost associated with units of output.
7. *Period cost* is that cost associated with the income of a time period.
8. *Direct costs* are those costs obviously traceable to a unit of output or a segment of business operations.
9. *Prime costs* are the labor and materials costs directly traceable to a unit of output.
10. *Indirect costs* are those costs not obviously traceable to a unit of output or to a segment of business operations.
11. *Fixed costs* are those costs which do not change in total as the rate of output of a concern or process varies.
12. *Variable costs* are those costs which do change in total with changes in the rate of output.
13. *Opportunity cost* is the measurable advantage foregone as a result of the rejection of alternative uses of resources, whether of materials, labor, or facilities.
14. *Imputed costs* are costs that do not involve at any time actual cash outlay and which do not, as a consequence, appear in the financial records; nevertheless such costs involve a foregoing on the part of the person or persons whose costs are being calculated.
15. *Controllable costs* are those costs subject to direct control at some level of managerial supervision.
16. *Noncontrollable costs* are those costs not subject to control at some level of managerial authority.
17. *Joint costs* exist when from any single unit, source, materials, or process, there are produced more than one type of product or service.

18. *Sunk costs* are historical costs which are irrecoverable in a given situation.

19. *Discretionary costs,* often termed "escapable" or "avoidable" costs, are those costs which are not essential to the accomplishment of a managerial objective.

20. *Postponable costs* are those costs which may be shifted to the future with little or no effect on the efficiency of current operations.

21. *Out-of-pocket costs* are those costs which, with respect to a given decision of management, give rise to cash expenditure.

22. *Differential costs* are the increases or decreases in total cost, or the changes in specific elements of cost, that result from any variation in operations.

7 sundry topics[1]

Herbert E. Miller

No accounting topic is unimportant. A professional accountant should endeavor to be thoroughly familiar with all phases of accounting. For purposes of preparation and review for the CPA Examination, however, some subjects are relatively more important than others. The degree of importance is determined primarily by two criteria:

1. A topic that appears rather frequently (e.g., four times in ten years) on the examinations cannot safely be ignored.
2. The degree of difficulty that candidates experience in certain topics is a factor of obvious significance.

The following selection of assorted topics, although far from exhaustive, does appear to meet one or the other of the two criteria just mentioned. Generally material has been prepared under the assumption that the reader has had some previous exposure to each topic.

Consignments

Definitions. A *consignment* is a transfer of possession of merchandise from the owner, called the *consignor,* to another party, called the *consignee,* who becomes the agent of the owner for the purpose of selling the goods. From the standpoint of the consignor, a consignment is a consignment out; from the standpoint of the consignee, it is a consignment in.

[1] Adapted from Finney and Miller's *Principles of Accounting* (Englewood Cliffs, N.J.: Prentice-Hall, Inc., 1970).

Sale and Consignment Distinguished. The fundamental distinction between a sale and a consignment is that in a sale the title to the goods passes from the seller to the buyer, whereas in a consignment the title to unsold goods remains with the consignor. This distinction must be borne in mind for three reasons.

First, since a consignment is not a sale, no profit results from the transaction, and none should be taken up until the goods have been sold by the consignee.

Second, since the title to the goods remains with the consignor, any goods out on consignment must be included in the consignor's inventory when financial statements are prepared.

Finally, if the consignee becomes insolvent, the consignor may be able to recover his goods, whereas if a sale had been made instead of a consignment, the seller would have had to take his place with the other creditors and accept a pro-rata settlement.

Rights of the Consignee. The principal rights of the consignee are:

1. The right to be reimbursed for advances and expenses.
2. The right to compensation.
3. The right to warrant. The consignee, in making sales, has authority to make the usual, but not extraordinary, warranties, and the consignor will be bound by such warranties.
4. The right to extend credit. If the extending of credit is a custom of the business, and if the consignor has not expressly restrained the consignee from extending credit, the consignee has a right to sell goods on account. The account thus created is the property of the consignor, and any loss on the collection of the account must be borne by the consignor. The consignee may, by special agreement, guarantee the accounts; if he makes such a guarantee, he is known as a "*del credere* agent" and is entitled to an extra compensation for the guarantee.

Duties of the Consignee. The principal duties of the consignee are:

1. To care for the consignor's property. The consignee must give the consignor's property such care as an ordinarily prudent man would give it. Having done this, he is not liable for damages to the goods.
2. To exercise prudence in granting credit and diligence in making collections.
3. To keep the consignor's property separate from his own. This duty may be discussed under two headings. a) The consignee must keep the merchandise separate from his own in order that it may be identified as the property of the consignor. This does not mean that there must be actual physical separation, but there must at least be records sufficient to show what property in the consignee's possession

belongs to the consignor. b) If the consignee sells goods on account, the records he keeps must make a distinction between his own accounts receivable and accounts receivable originating from sales of consigned goods and thus belonging to the consignor.

4. To make reports of and settlements for sales in accordance with the terms of the consignments. These terms may require settlement after the sale of the entire consignment, settlement after certain portions of the consignment have been sold, or settlements at stated intervals.

The report of the consignee is called an *account sales,* and customarily it includes the data shown in the following example:

ACCOUNT SALES

OF SHIPMENT OF FIVE WASHING MACHINES
RECEIVED FROM C. D. JONES & COMPANY, CHICAGO,
TO BE SOLD FOR THEIR ACCOUNT AND RISK

Rendered by Weston Company, Elgin, Illinois

Sales for your account:		
5 washing machines at $200		$1,000
Charges:		
Freight	$ 30	
Local transportation	10	
Commission—25% of $1,000	250	290
Net proceeds—check enclosed		$ 710

Consignee's Entries. Following are the entries to be made by Weston Company to record the transactions relative to the consignment received from C. D. Jones & Company.

Entry for receipt of goods: Open a consignment in account and make a memorandum of the number and nature of the articles received, as follows:

Consignment In—C. D. Jones & Company

5 washing machines received	

Entry for expenses:

Consignment in—C. D. Jones & Company	40	
Cash (or expense accounts)		40
For freight, $30, and local transportation, $10.		

Entry for sales:

Cash	1,000	
Consignment in—C. D. Jones & Company		1,000

Entry for commission:

Consignment in—C. D. Jones & Company	250	
Commissions earned		250

Entry for settlement:

Consignment in—C. D. Jones & Company	710	
Cash		710

After final settlement, the consignment account will appear as follows:

Consignment In—C. D. Jones & Company

5 washing machines received		Sales—5 machines	1,000
Freight	30		
Cartage	10		
Commission	250		
Proceeds remitted	710		
	1,000		1,000

"Consignment-in" Accounts in the Balance Sheet. When the consignee closes his books and prepares a balance sheet, some consignment-in accounts may have debit balances, representing the excess of expenses, commissions, and advances over the proceeds of sales. These balances represent assets, and should so appear in the balance sheet. Other accounts may have credit balances, representing the excess of the proceeds of sales over the expenses, commissions, and advances. These balances represent liabilities of the consignee to consignors, and should be so shown.

If a controlling account is kept with all consignments in, the balance of the controlling account will be the difference between the debit and the credit balances of the individual accounts. But the balance sheet should show the total debit balances and total credit balances of the individual consignment accounts as assets and liabilities, respectively, and not merely the net balance of the controlling account.

Before the balances to appear as assets or liabilities are obtained, any commissions that have been earned but not recorded should be put on the books.

Consignor's Records. The consignor should keep a separate account for ach consignment. If any goods sent out on consignment are unsold when he consignor prepares his financial statements, they should be included n the consignor's inventory. The inventory value should list the cost of he goods consigned plus any inventoriable charges incurred by either he consignor or the consignee which are applicable to the unsold goods. This can be achieved most readily if all costs directly associated with each onsignment are accumulated in a consignment-out account.

To illustrate the entries associated with consignments out, assume he following additional facts regarding the consignment to Weston ompany of five washing machines:

> The machines cost the consignor, C. D. Jones & Company, $100 each.
>
> The cost of hauling the machines to the freight depot in Chicago, paid by the consignor, was $20.
>
> Packing costs were estimated to be $15; the consignor charges all such costs to a packing expense account; the $15 regarded as applicable to this consignment is merely a portion of the total of such expenses.
>
> The consignee remitted $710 as the proceeds of the consignment.

Entries:

Shipment:

onsignment out—Weston Company	500	
Inventory		500

(Note: If the consignor does not maintain perpetual inventory records, the credit ay be made to a suspense account, Consignment Shipments.)

Local transportation:

onsignment out—Weston Company	20	
Cash		20

Packing:

onsignment out—Weston Company	15	
Packing expense		15

Sales and proceeds (see account sales, p. 531):

ash	710	
ransportation on consignment sales	60	
acking expense—consignment sales	15	
lling commission—consignment sales	250	
ost of sales—consignments	500	
Consignment out—Weston Company		535
Sales—consignments		1,000

(NOTE: If the Consignment Shipments account mentioned previously had beer used, it would be debited in the foregoing entry in place of Cost of Sales—Consign ments.)

Partial Sales. If the consignee renders an account sales after selling a portion of the consignment, he has a right to deduct from the proceeds of the first sale all costs incurred on the entire consignment. But the con signor, when recording the settlement, may properly carry forward as an element of the consigned goods inventory the costs which are applicable to the unsold goods.

To illustrate, assume that Weston Company sold one washing machine and rendered an account sales as illustrated.

Sales for your account: 1 washing machine		$200
Charges:		
Freight	$30	
Local transportation	10	
Commission—25%	50	90
Net proceeds—check enclosed		$110

Prior to recording the account sales, the consignment-out account will be as follows: (see prior illustration)

Consignment Out—Weston Company

Cost of 5 washing machines	500	
Local transportation	20	
Packing	15	

The entries to record the account sales are:

Cash	110	
Consignment out—Weston Company:		
Freight	30	
Local transportation	10	
Selling commission	50	
Sales—consignments		20
Account sales from Weston Company		
Transportation on consignment sales	12	
Packing expense—consignment sales	3	
Selling commission—consignment sales	50	
Cost of sales—consignments	100	
Consignment out—Weston Company		16
Costs applicable to the machine sold assigned to expense.		

The balance in the consignment-out account will be $460, the in-
entoriable costs applicable to the four unsold washing machines out on
onsignment.

states and Trusts

administration and distribution of an estate

The laws governing the administration and distribution of estates ary to some extent among the states. The discussion of estates and estate ccounting in this text should be understood to be a generalization from country-wide standpoint, subject to exceptions arising from the differing tatutes and court decisions of the several states. For this reason, and ecause the treatment of the subject in a text devoted to accounting ust necessarily be limited, the section on estates and trusts presents only survey of the subject.

If a person dies intestate—that is to say, without leaving a will, or eaving an invalid will—his estate will be distributed among his dis-ributees in accordance with the laws of descent and distribution: the aws of descent determining the disposition of the real estate to the heirs, nd the laws of distribution determining the disposition of the personal roperty to the next of kin. The administration and disposition of the roperty is controlled by a court known variously in different states as he *probate, surrogate's,* or *orphans' court*. The work of dealing with the ntestate's assets, paying the debts and charges, and making distribution placed in the hands of an administrator, who is appointed by the court nd to whom the court issues letters of administration evidencing his uthority. If a will, although valid, directs the disposition of only a por-ion of the estate property, a condition of *partial intestacy* exists.

If the decedent leaves a valid will disposing of his entire estate, the aws of descent and distribution will not be operative, and the estate will e distributed in accordance with the wishes of the testator or testatrix, s expressed in this will. (This statement is subject to such exceptions as he widow's option to renounce her rights under the will and claim her lective or distributive share under the law.) Before the will can become perative, it must be admitted to probate; that is, it must be duly proved.

If an executor is named in the will, and if he is competent and willing serve, he will be granted letters testamentary by the court. If no ex-cutor is named in the will, or if one is named but is unwilling or incom-etent to serve, the court will appoint an administrator with the will nnexed *(administrator c. t. a.—cum testamento annexo)*.

uties of the Executor or the Administrator. The executor or the ad-inistrator (referred to hereafter by the general term *fiduciary*) is expected to seek out and take possession of the personal property of the deceased; to keep the estate funds separate from his own; to dispose of perishable property as quickly as possible and, unless authorized by testamentary direction to retain them, to dispose of any investments not legally permissible for fiduciaries; to preserve and administer the estate in a prudent manner; to keep excess funds invested to the fullest extent possible; to pay the funeral and administration expenses, the just debts, the estate and inheritance taxes, and all other proper charges; to distribute the estate to the persons entitled thereto; and to account to the court and all interested parties.

If there is a will, the real estate goes to the devisees, and the personal property, through the fiduciary, to the legatees. If there is no will, the administrator distributes the property in accordance with the applicable law of intestacy. The fiduciary does not ordinarily administer or distribute the realty; the heirs take title to it directly from the decedent. The personal representative (fiduciary) of a testate decedent must carry out all the directions in the will, including the erection of any trusts.

Title to personal property vests in the fiduciary and passes through him to the distributees, except that in many states certain household effects, a limited amount of cash, the decedent's clothes, and certain other personal effects may be exempt, title thereto passing directly to the widow or to minor children.

It is only rarely that the fiduciary exercises any control over the real estate, since, by the laws of most states, title vests in the heirs or devisees immediately upon the death of the legator. If, however, the personal property is not sufficient to pay the debts and charges, the fiduciary generally possesses, or may apply to the court for, authority to sell, mortgage or lease any parcels of realty in order to obtain funds with which to pay the debts. Or the will may specifically direct the fiduciary to administer the realty for various purposes. Where the testator has made a contract to sell real estate, the title to the real estate passes to the heir subject to the obligation of the heir to convey title to the vendee; and, since the claim against the vendee is personal property, it passes into the executor's control as part of the inventory.

The proceeds of life insurance policies payable to the estate pass into the hands of the fiduciary and must be accounted for by him; the proceeds of policies payable to specific beneficiaries are payable directly to them and are not part of the decedent's estate.

Inventory of Assets. As soon as the fiduciary is appointed, he should marshal and take possession of the decedent's personal estate. Although the laws differ in the various states, it is desirable, and in some states obligatory, to file an inventory of the assets with the court. This inven tory should show items and values; the valuations may be determined by the fiduciary unless the law or practice requires that the valuations be made by independent appraisers. The inventory should include all personal property of the decedent except exempt property.

If a testate decedent has made refundable advances to persons who are beneficiaries of his estate, such advances should be included in the inventory as estate assets, plus the interest thereon (unless a contrary intent appears) from the dates thereof to the dates of collection or distribution. The total represents the estate to be divided. In the case of intestacy, the treatment of advancements to the decedent's children is somewhat similar, except that interest is not generally charged. However, if the advancement to such child equals or exceeds his portion of the estate, he is entitled to no further participation, but he is not obligated to return any excess of the advance over his distributable share. If the advancement is less than the child's share, he is entitled to receive the balance of his share.

Income accrued to and including the day of death is a part of the principal of the estate and should be included in the inventory. If assets are thought to be valueless, they should, nevertheless, be included in the inventory, with a statement that they have no value. (A subsequent section, "Questions of accrual," covers the classes of income that are recognized as accruing in the field of estates and trusts.)

Although real estate titles pass directly to heirs or devisees without passing through the fiduciary, it may be desirable that real estate be inventoried in order to fulfill the requirements of state inheritance laws and the federal estate tax laws. Moreover, in some states the real estate must be included in the inventory because the inventory, filed with the proper county officer, serves as evidence of the passing of title.

Any assets discovered after the inventory is completed should be reported in a supplementary inventory.

Legacies and Devises. A *legacy* (or *bequest*) is a gift of personal property made by a decedent in his will; the recipient thereof is called a *legatee.* A *devise* is a gift of real estate made by a decedent in his will; the recipient of the gift is called a *devisee.*

A *specific legacy* is a gift of some particular property, such as a watch, a library, or a specifically described investment.

A *demonstrative legacy* is a legacy payable in cash out of a designated fund.

A *general legacy* is a gift of a sum of money.

A *residuary legacy* includes all personal property remaining after the payment of debts and charges and all other legacies. The residuary legatee receives "all the rest, residue, and remainder" of the personal estate.

Legacies may be paid at any time after the fiduciary takes charge; but unless the estate is clearly sufficient to pay all debts, charges, and legacies, the fiduciary should defer the payment of the legacies at least for the legal executorial period, to enable him to determine the amounts of the debts and charges. Otherwise he may incur a personal liability to creditors. Any liability owed to the estate by a legatee should be offset against his legacy.

Does accrued income on a specific legacy at the date of the decedent's death belong to corpus or does it go with the gift to the legatee? The law on this subject does not seem to be well settled, and a fiduciary faced with the question should apply to the court for a ruling.

Interest on all unpaid legacies begins to accrue at the end of the executorial period, which varies in different states.

Liabilities. The fiduciary should include a statement in his accounting to the court showing the nature and extent of the claims filed. The executor should reject any claims that he considers invalid; he is in duty bound to set up all legitimate defenses, including the statute of limitations and the statute of frauds. In some states, creditors whose claims have been rejected may appeal to the probate court; in other states, they must bring suit in the ordinary manner.

The debts and charges must be paid in full before legacies can be paid. If the residuary personal estate is not sufficient to pay the debts and charges, provision for their payment will generally be made by abatement (i.e., by scaling down) of legacies, in the following order:

1. General legacies (including such part of any demonstrative legacy as is not covered by the fund indicated for the payment thereof).
2. Specific legacies.

If the entire personal estate is insufficient to pay the debts and charges, the fiduciary may sell, mortgage, or lease the decedent's realty to obtain funds for the payment of all proper debts and charges.

Trusts. The testator may provide in his will that all or some portion of the principal of the estate shall be placed in the hands of a trustee or trustees, who shall keep the fund invested, distribute the income to one class of beneficiary during a stated period of time, and eventually turn over the principal of the trust to another class of beneficiary, both being designated in the will. For instance, the testator may direct that the income shall be paid to his widow during her life and that, at her death, the principal shall be paid to his children or to some institution. Or he may direct that the income shall be distributed in equal parts to his children until the youngest surviving child reaches the age of, for example, twenty-five, and that the principal shall then be divided equally among them or their surviving children.

A trust created by a will is called a *testamentary trust*. The person who is entitled to receive the income during a stated period and the person who is entitled eventually to receive the principal, or *corpus*, are both beneficiaries of the trust. The income beneficiary is called the *cestui que trust*. The *cestui que trust* is called a *life tenant* if he is entitled to the income during the entire period of his life; if he is entitled to the income for a shorter period, he may be referred to merely as the *income beneficiary*. The person who is entitled eventually to receive the principal of the trust is called the *remainderman*.

The trustee does not take over the duties of the trusteeship until the trust property is duly received by him. He takes title to the real estate as of the date of the testator's death, but he does not take title to personal property until it is duly turned over to him. However, the trust takes effect as of the date of death; hence, the income beneficiary is entitled to the income from the trust assets from the date of death.

Principal and Income. If a trust is created by the will, the records of the executor and the trustee must distinguish clearly between the principal and the income. The income beneficiary is entitled to the income (i.e., the earnings on principal) during his tenancy, and the remainderman is entitled to the principal (or corpus). Therefore, if cash or property is received, the fiduciary must know, and must indicate in his records, whether the cash or property belongs in the principal account or in the income account. Similarly a careful distinction must be made between disbursements that are payable out of principal and those payable out of income. A strict distinction must be made between principal and income in all accountings for trusts or for an estate in which a trust is involved.

The distinctions between principal and income must be made by the fiduciary in accordance with the law, unless a contrary treatment is prescribed in the will. However, the testator does not have *carte blanche* in his testamentary directions; for example, he must not violate such paramount legal restrictions as the prohibition against illegal accumulations of income. In cases of doubt about the proper classification of an item as principal or income, the fiduciary should apply to the court for a ruling.

The situations calling for a distinction between principal and income may be broadly classified as follows:

1. Questions of accrual, or apportionment on a time basis.
2. Questions of classification.
3. Questions of impairment.

Questions of Accrual. The distinction between the cash basis and the accrual basis of accounting is well understood as applied to ordinary commercial accounts. But some items of income and expense that are treated on an accrual basis in commercial accounting are not so treated in estate and trust accounting.

There are two important dates to be noted in connection with the apportionment of items of receipt or expenditure as between the income beneficiary and the remainderman:

1. The date of the death of the testator.
2. The date when the tenancy terminates and the remainderman receives the corpus.

Accruable income on trust assets arising prior to the death of the testator belongs to the corpus of the estate, even though it is not collected until a subsequent date; similarly, any such expenses accrued prior to that date are payable out of principal cash.

Such income as accrues after the testator's death up to the termination of the tenancy belongs to the income beneficiary or his estate, regardless of the date of collection; and expenses accrued between these two dates are payable from income cash. Income and expenses accrued after the termination of the tenancy affect the interest of the remainderman. If there are several successive income beneficiaries, accruals must be recognized at the close of each tenancy.

The laws relative to the distinction between principal and income differ somewhat in the several states; therefore, the rules stated in this chapter should be regarded as generalizations subject to state exceptions. Given this restriction, we can list the following points in answer to the question: What earnings and expenses accrue and must be apportioned between principal and income?

1. Interest, in general, accrues from day to day; the interest accrued on receivables and investments to and including the date of death of the testator is principal, and interest accruing during the tenancy is income. Interest expense is similarly accrued. Interest on savings bank deposits is generally not considered to accrue, but is treated as income of the period when it is declared to be available to depositors.
2. Ordinary cash dividends do not accrue, but are generally considered income of the period when declared. Thus a dividend declared prior to the testator's death is corpus, even though it is not collected until after his death; and an ordinary cash dividend declared during the tenancy is income, although paid from profits earned prior to the testator's death or paid after the termination of the tenancy. In some states the governing date is that on which the

corporation's stock records are closed to determine the stockholders of record to whom the dividends are payable.

A corporation may occasionally elect, instead of paying an ordinary cash dividend, to pay a stock dividend of approximately the same amount in order to preserve the corporation's current position; such dividends are generally treated in the same fashion as ordinary cash dividends.

The rule is not so simple in the case of extraordinary cash and stock dividends, since the relevant laws differ in the various states. In some states such dividends during the tenancy are classified as income, in others they are classified as corpus, and in some states extraordinary dividends are apportioned between income and corpus. In states where apportionment is required, the computation is made by determining the book value per share of stock owned at the date of death (as shown by the paying corporation's books) and the book value per share after the payment of the dividend; if the book value after the payment of the dividend is less than that at the date of death, enough of the dividend must be allocated to corpus so that the book value of the stock after the payment of the dividend plus the dividend so allocated will be equal to the original book value of the stock at the date of the creation of the trust.

3. Rents accrue in most states, although not in all. In the states in which they do accrue, rents earned prior to the death of the decedent are corpus, and the portion accruing during the tenancy is income. A similar rule applies to rents paid.

4. Taxes on trust property do not generally accrue. Taxes that became a lien on the property before the date of the decedent's death are payable out of principal cash; taxes that became a lien on the property during the tenancy are a charge against income. In many states a specific devisee of realty must pay any taxes accrued thereon before the death of the testator and remaining unpaid at that time. Special assessments for improvements may be chargeable to principal or may be apportioned according to the benefits conferred.

5. Partnership profits do not accrue. The death of a partner dissolves the partnership; if the books are closed as of the date of his death, the question of accrual does not arise, since the profits to that date will be determined and will be classified as principal.

6. Contract profits do not accrue. A contract for other than personal services entered into by the testator must be completed by the fiduciary, but the profits belong to the principal.

7. Livestock born during the life tenancy is income, except to the extent necessary to keep the herd intact where such an intention is expressed or implied.

8. If the trust principal includes land, crops harvested during the tenancy are income. If land is given as a devise, crops growing at the date of the testator's death go with the land.

Questions of Classification. Many items do not involve the question of accrual and apportionment on a time basis but involve the equally important question of determining whether the whole amount should be classified as principal or as income.

Increases or decreases in assets forming part of the corpus are classified as corpus; increases or decreases in assets representing undistributed income are classified as income.

Other matters related to the classification of items between principal and income are discussed under the following headings of items applicable to principal and items applicable to income.

1. Items Applicable to Principal. In general, it may be said that corpus should be charged with expenditures that represent the payment of obligations incurred prior or incident to the death of the decedent, expenses of administration prior to the setting up of a trust, and, thereafter, those expenditures which result in ultimate benefit to the remainderman.

The following are some of the expenditures ordinarily chargeable to principal:

1. Debts of the decedent, expenses of the last illness, and funeral and administration expenses.
2. Legal fees and court costs incurred in probating the will, in defending it against a contest, and in interpreting it.
3. Costs of defending the estate against claims rejected by the fiduciary.
4. Legal fees incurred in connection with a change in fiduciaries.
5. Federal estate tax and state inheritance tax (except where otherwise prescribed by law).
6. Legal fees and other costs of preserving the principal of the estate.
7. Carrying charges on property which produces no income are usually chargeable to principal; otherwise, the desires of the testator with respect to the income beneficiary might not be fulfilled because income from other trust assets would be applied to the carrying of unproductive assets for the benefit of the remainderman and to the detriment of the income beneficiary.

Premiums on fire insurance policies are usually considered to be payable out of income; but in case of loss, the proceeds of the policy are considered to be a replacement of principal.

2. Items Applicable to Income. All ordinary operating expenses of the estate or the trust are payable out of income. These include such items as:

1. The fiduciary's commissions for collection and disbursement of income.
2. Legal fees paid in matters pertaining to the earning of income, as distinguished from matters pertaining to the preservation of the estate.
3. Wages of clerks and of workmen employed to care for the property.
4. Costs of caring for and harvesting crops.
5. Ordinary repairs to trust property.
6. Interest accrued during the tenancy on mortgages and other liabilities.
7. Insurance premiums (generally).
8. Taxes on undistributed income accumulated for the benefit of the income beneficiary.

Repairs are classified in accordance with the usual accounting rule: ordinary repairs are chargeable to income, extraordinary repairs are chargeable to principal. Replacements and betterments may be apportioned—the portion that makes good wear and tear during the period of the trust being charged to income and the balance being charged to principal. (Although this rule is not difficult to state, it is often very difficult to apply.)

Special assessments for local benefits may be paid out of principal if the benefits are expected to add lasting value; otherwise, they should be paid out of income. In some cases a portion may be paid from principal and the remainder from income.

Mortgages and other investments may become delinquent, and for this and for other reasons the amount received in liquidation and settlement after foreclosure thereof may be less than the sum of the original value of the investment, the expenses incurred in attempting to preserve and collect the investment, and the uncollected income. Such receipts are generally apportioned between principal and income so that the loss occasioned by the salvage operation will be shared by the income beneficiary and the remainderman without entirely depriving the life tenant of his income during the barren period.

Questions of Impairment. If the trust property includes wasting assets (e.g., such natural resources as mines, quarries, oil wells, and timber, or such other types as leaseholds and copyrights), or assets subject to depreciation (such as a building), the fiduciary must consider whether a portion of any receipts therefrom should be regarded and retained as principal, in order to prevent the impairment of the trust corpus. The intention of the decedent is controlling in these cases and must be sought out carefully. If it appears that the testator intended to give the full, undiminished income to the income beneficiary even though the principal would thereby ultimately be completely exhausted, no deduction from income for the depletion or depreciation factor is permitted. If, however, the express or implied intention to preserve the principal intact appears, the fiduciary must retain out of the income an amount that will be sufficient to maintain the integrity of the original investment.

The same rules apply to income derived from similar investments held in corporate form—for instance, stock in a corporation engaged in exploiting a wasting asset.

Extraordinary repairs are payable from corpus. Permanent improvements to trust property generally are payable out of corpus; improvements made solely for the purpose of increasing the income-producing power of the property are chargeable to income unless there is strong justification for an apportionment.

Any losses or gains on the realization of assets forming a part of the principal are generally considered to be applicable to principal. The principal of the estate is composed of the assets left by the decedent, or whatever these assets ultimately realize.

In accordance with this general theory, if bonds left by the decedent are inventoried at a premium, turned over to a trustee, and held by him until maturity, there will be a book loss of the difference between the inventory value and par. But this loss is to be borne by principal, for the principal is not considered to be impaired if it contains the actual assets left by the decedent or the proceeds of these assets.

Similarly, if bonds left by the decedent are inventoried at a discount, the income beneficiary is not entitled to any income representing accumulation of discount; any discount realized at maturity, or upon disposition of the bonds, is regarded as an ordinary gain to be added to the corpus.

For bonds purchased by the fiduciary at a premium or a discount, any desire with respect to amortization expressed by the testator will govern. In the absence of any such expressed desire, it has been held generally that premiums should be amortized but that discounts should not be; there is, however, a strong minority opinion that discounts also should be amortized. In the determination of the amount of any premium or discount, brokerage fees should be regarded as part of the cost of the investment. Amortization, when required, may be made by either the straight-line method or an actuarial method. If bonds purchased at a premium are disposed of before maturity and the unamortized portion of the premium is not realized, the loss is generally chargeable to corpus; similarly, a gain would be credited to principal.

The right to subscribe for stock is inherent in the stock, which is corpus; if, instead of exercising the rights, the fiduciary sells them, the estate's interest in the corporation is diluted by reason of the reduction of its percentage of stock ownership. Therefore, all receipts from the sale of subscription rights, including any gain, should be regarded as principal.

fiduciary's accounts

Accounting for the Estate Principal. A fiduciary is placed in possession of certain assets, and his records should show how he has discharged his accountability for them. His accounts, therefore, are based on the following fundamental equation:

$$\text{assets} = \text{accountability}$$

The books of an executor or administrator are opened by debiting asset accounts with the valuations shown by the inventory and crediting a fiduciary accountability account called Estate Corpus or Estate Principal. Liabilities are not recorded until the fiduciary pays them, thus reducing the total assets for which he is accountable. Enough asset accounts should be kept to classify the property adequately. In general, it is desirable to keep separate accounts with assets included in the inventory and similar assets purchased by the fiduciary. One reason is that the nature of the fiduciary's responsibility for losses on assets purchased by him is somewhat different from his responsibility for the difference between the inventory valuation of assets left by the decedent and the amount ultimately realized therefrom; also, bonds included in the inventory and those acquired by the fiduciary may be subject to different amortization procedures.

The fiduciary's accountability is increased if additional assets are discovered after the original inventory is completed; any such subsequently discovered assets should be reported in a supplementary inventory and should be recorded by debiting asset accounts and crediting an account called Assets Subsequently Discovered. This is an accountability account and is a supplement to the Estate Corpus account.

The executor's accountability as to corpus is also increased by any gains on the disposal of assets, because gains increase the total assets of the estate; his accountability is decreased by losses. When an asset is disposed of, the asset account should be credited with the inventory value; gains should be credited to a Gain on Realization account, and losses should be charged to a Loss on Realization account.

The executor's accountability is also decreased by the payment of funeral and administration expenses. These may be charged to a single Funeral and Administration Expense account if there are only a few expenditures of this nature. If there are enough expenditures to warrant doing so, separate accounts may be kept with various classes of administration expenses.

The executor's accountability is also decreased (or, expressed more precisely, discharged) by the payment of liabilities incurred by the decedent. No entry should be made for liabilities until they are paid, thus effecting a decrease in the executor's accountability; when a liability is paid, an entry should be made debiting Debts of Decedent Paid (an accountability account) and crediting Cash.

The executor's accountability is also decreased by the payment of legacies. If there are only a few legacies, one account entitled "legacies paid" may suffice. If there are numerous legacies, it may be desirable to use several accounts, such as Specific Legacies Delivered, General Legacies Paid, and so on. If there are a great many legacies, if inheritance taxes are to be charged against the legacies, or if legacies are to be abated in order to pay debts, an account should be kept with each legatee, either in the general ledger or in a subsidiary ledger.

Entries in legacy accounts are illustrated below:

Legacy—John Doe
    Cash
  Payment of inheritance tax.
Cash
    Legacy—John Doe
  Refund from Doe for inheritance tax paid.
Legacy—John Doe
    Bonds of XY Company
  Delivery of legacy to Doe.

The will may direct that the total inheritance tax shall be paid by the estate, thus reducing the residuary legacy.

The accounts Assets Subsequently Discovered, Gain on Realization, Loss on Realization, Funeral and Administration Expense, Debts of Decedent Paid, and Legacies are temporary accountability accounts set up to provide information required for the executor's report to the court; after they have served their purpose, they are closed to Estate Corpus (generally when the fiduciary's report has been accepted).

Accounting for Estate Income. All the income of a small estate may be credited to a single income account; in a large estate, it is preferable to open separate accounts with the various classes of income, such as interest income and dividend income. All expenses deductible from income may be charged to one account called Expense—Income; or separate accounts may be kept with various kinds of expense.

In connection with the recording of declared dividends and accrued interest, it should be understood that the cash basis of accounting usually is satisfactory until the executor makes his final accounting; and even then it is acceptable unless the recording of accruals is necessary in order to effect an equitable distribution.

If cash collected as income is paid to beneficiaries, the charges should be made to an account called Distributions to Income Beneficiaries. If desired, a separate account may be kept with each beneficiary.

Principal and Income Cash. A fiduciary's records should distinguish between principal cash and income cash. Separate bank accounts may be kept with principal cash and income cash, or both may be deposited in one account; if the latter procedure is followed, the amounts applicable to principal and income can be determined from the balances of the Cash—Principal and Cash—Income accounts in the ledger.

Summary of Estate Accounts. As indicated previously, a fiduciary's accounts should show the assets and accountability as to corpus, and the assets and accountability as to income. The following trial balance data are assumed to have been prepared from the accounts of an executor of an estate involving a trust before the final statement to the court was prepared and the books were closed.

ESTATE OF GEORGE HENDERSON
W. C. TURNER, EXECUTOR

ACCOUNTS AS TO PRINCIPAL

	Debit	*Credit*
Accountability Accounts:		
Estate corpus		81,050
(The original amount for which the executor was accountable, as shown by the inventory.)		
Assets subsequently discovered		450
(Increase in accountability resulting from discovery of additional assets.)		
Gain on realization		500
(Increase in accountability representing excess of amount realized for assets over inventory value.)		
Loss on realization	300	
(Decrease in accountability resulting from losses on asset disposals.)		
Funeral and administration expense	535	
(Decrease in accountability resulting from disposal of assets in payment of expenses.)		
Debts of decedent paid	3,360	
(Decrease in accountability resulting from payment of debts.)		
Legacies—Mary Henderson	13,000	
Legacy—W. C. Turner	1,000	
(Decreases in accountability resulting from payments to legatees.)		
(The net credit balance of the foregoing accounts is $63,805, representing the executor's accountability for the remaining corpus assets.)		

Asset Accounts (Remaining assets, totaling $63,805, for which the executor is still acountable):		
PQ Company stock	10,000	
ST Company bonds	25,000	
LM Company bonds	5,000	
Cash—principal	23,805	
Total balances of accounts as to principal	82,000	82,000

Accounts as to Income

Accountability Accounts:		
Income		4,525
(The gross amount for which the executor has assumed accountability to the income beneficiaries.)		
Expense—income	250	
(Decrease in accountability as to income, resulting from payment of expenses applicable to income.)		
Distributions to income beneficiaries	500	
(Decrease, or discharge, of accountability, resulting from distributions to income beneficiaries.)		
(The net credit balance of $3,775 in these accounts reflects the executor's accountability for the following income assets.)		
Asset Accounts (Remaining income assets, totaling $3,775, for which the executor is still accountable):		
Accrued interest receivable	450	
Dividends receivable	500	
Cash—income	2,825	
Total balances of accounts as to income	4,525	4,525
Total balances of all accounts, combined	86,525	86,525

Fiduciary's Report to the Court. The exact form of the statements to be rendered by a fiduciary is generally prescribed by the forum to which they are presented. The requirements vary considerably among the several states. The charge and discharge statements illustrated in this chapter, together with a transcript or summary of the cash records, will serve the requirements of examination candidates and will indicate the nature of the *information* generally required to be submitted by a fiduciary; the presentation of the information in the *form* prescribed is largely a matter of mechanics.

Illustration Continued. The following statements and closing entries are based on the accounts of the estate of George Henderson, as given in the trial balance data just set forth.

ESTATE OF GEORGE HENDERSON

W. C. TURNER, EXECUTOR

Charge and Discharge Statement as to Principal
March 31, 1971 to October 31, 1971

I charge myself with:		
Assets per inventory (Schedule *A*)	$81,050	
Assets subsequently discovered (Schedule *B*)	450	
Gain on realization (Schedule *C*)	500	
Total charges		$82,000
I credit myself with:		
Loss on realization (Schedule *C*)	$ 300	
Funeral and administration expense (Schedule *D*)	535	
Debts of decedent paid (Schedule *E*)	3,360	
Legacies paid or delivered (Schedule *F*)	14,000	
Total credits		18,195
Balance as to Principal		$63,805
Consisting of:		
PQ Company stock	$10,000	
ST Company bonds	25,000	
LM Company bonds	5,000	
Cash	23,805	
Total	$63,805	

Inventory of Assets
March 31, 1971

Schedule A

Cash	$ 700
Life insurance policies	20,000
XY Company stock	1,000
ST Company bonds	25,000
Accrued interest on ST Company bonds	250
PQ Company stock	10,000
Dividend declared on PQ Company stock	600
Patents	19,000
Household furniture	3,000
Automobile	1,500
Total	$81,050

Assets Subsequently Discovered — *Schedule B*

Savings bank account	$ 450

Assets Realized — *Schedule C*

	Inventory Value	*Price Realized*	*Gain*	*Loss*
Insurance policies	$20,000	$20,000		
Dividends receivable on PQ Company stock	600	600		
Accrued interest in ST Company bonds	250	250		
Patents	19,000	19,500	$500	
Automobile	1,500	1,200		$300
Total	$41,350	$41,550	$500	$300

Funeral and Administration Expenses — *Schedule D*

Funeral expenses	$ 300
Administration expenses	235
Total	$ 535

Debts of Decedent Paid — *Schedule E*

John Smith	$ 1,000
Wm. Green	2,100
Personal property taxes, due by decedent	260
Total	$ 3,360

Legacies Paid or Delivered — *Schedule F*

Mary Henderson:		
Household furniture	$ 3,000	
Cash	10,000	$13,000
W. C. Turner:		
XY Company stock		1,000
Plus $30 dividend thereon		
Total		$14,000

ESTATE OF GEORGE HENDERSON
W. C. TURNER, EXECUTOR

CHARGE AND DISCHARGE STATEMENT AS TO INCOME
MARCH 31, 1971 TO OCTOBER 31, 1971

I charge myself with:			
Interest on ST Company bonds:			
Collected, August 1	$750		
Less: Accrued at date of death, March 31	250	$ 500	
Accrued, August 1 to October 31		375	$ 875
Interest on LM Company bonds:			
Collected, August 1	$150		
Less: Accrued at purchase, April 30	75	$ 75	
Accrued, August 1 to October 31		75	150
Dividend on PQ Company stock:			
Declared but not collected			500
Royalty on patents			3,000
Total charges			$4,525
I credit myself with:			
Expenses applicable to royalties		$ 250	
Distribution to income beneficiary—widow		500	
Total credits			750
Balance as to Income			$3,775
Consisting of:			
Dividends receivable:			
Declared on PQ Company stock		$ 500	
Accrued interest:			
On ST Company bonds		375	
On LM Company bonds		75	
Cash		2,825	
Total		$3,775	

If all the assets have been distributed, or if the residue of the estate has been transferred to a trustee, the charges and credits in the statements will be equal and the charge and discharge statements will show no balances.

If a testamentary trust is not created and the principal and income go to the same beneficiary, the separation of principal and income in the accounts and statements of an executor may not be of great significance and the report to the court may be made in one charge and discharge statement instead of two.

Closing the Executor's Books. After the executor has rendered his final report to the court, his books should be closed. If all the assets have been distributed to the beneficiaries, the asset accounts will have no balances and only the accountability accounts will remain open. These should be closed in the following manner:

Corpus accountability accounts:

> Close to Estate Corpus account the Assets Subsequently Discovered and Gain on Realization accounts showing increases in accountability and the Loss on Realization, Funeral and Administration Expense, Debts of Decedent Paid, and Legacy accounts showing decreases in accountability.

Income accountability accounts:

> Close to Undistributed Income the income account (or accounts), the expense account (or accounts) applicable to income, and the Distributions to Income Beneficiaries account.

If, as in the illustration of the estate of George Henderson, assets remain for transfer to a trustee, balances will remain in asset and accountability accounts after making the entries just indicated. These assets and accountability accounts should be closed to an account with the trustee, thus completing the closing of the books.

Illustration Continued Further. The following entries close the accounts of W. C. Turner as executor of the estate of George Henderson.

EXECUTOR'S JOURNAL

1971			
November 1	Assets subsequently discovered	450	
	Gain on realization	500	
	Estate corpus		950
	To close accountability accounts showing increases in corpus.		
1	Estate corpus	18,195	
	Loss on realization		300
	Funeral and administration expense		535
	Debts of decedent paid		3,360
	Legacies—Mary Henderson		13,000
	Legacy—W. C. Turner		1,000
	To close accountability accounts showing decreases in corpus.		
1	Income	4,525	
	Undistributed income		4,525
	To close the Income account.		

		Debit	Credit
1	Undistributed income	750	
	Expense—income		250
	Distributions to income beneficiary		500
	To close accountability accounts showing charges against income.		
1	Estate corpus	63,805	
	Undistributed income	3,775	
	W. C. Turner, trustee		67,580
	To close the two accountability accounts by transfer to the trustee.		
1	W. C. Turner, trustee	63,805	
	PQ Company stock		10,000
	ST Company bonds		25,000
	LM Company bonds		5,000
	Cash—principal		23,805
	To record the transfer to the trustee of corpus assets.		
1	W. C. Turner, trustee	3,775	
	Dividends receivable		500
	Accrued interest receivable		450
	Cash—income		2,825
	To record the transfer to the trustee of income assets.		

The Trustee's Accounts. Since the trustee is not responsible for paying the debts of the deceased and conducting operations incident to administration of the estate, his accounts will be somewhat less numerous than those of the executor. In studying his accounts, as typified here, it should be understood that the number of accounts and the desirability of using controlling accounts will depend on the size and nature of the trust.

Accountability Accounts—Principal:

Original accountability:

Trust principal.

This account is credited with the original amount of the trust, and to it are closed periodically the temporary accounts used to record the following increases and decreases.

Increases:

Gains on sales or other realizations.

Increases recognized at distribution.

This account is credited with any excess of the agreed value at which a beneficiary accepts a trust principal asset in distribution over the book value thereof.

Decreases:

Losses on sales or other realizations.

Decreases recognized at distribution.

Expense accounts applicable to principal.

Asset Accounts—Principal:
 The nature of the asset accounts will depend on what assets are owned by the trust.

Accountability Accounts—Income:
 Accounts with interest, dividends, etc., or a single income account.
 Expense accounts in such detail as required.
 Gains on disposal of income assets.
 Losses on disposal of income assets.
 Accounts with income beneficiaries.
  These accounts are credited with the beneficiaries' distributive shares of income and are charged with any distributions to them.

Asset Accounts—Income:
 Cash.
 Accrued interest receivable.
 Accounts with any other assets pertaining to income.

Liabilities will not normally exist, and therefore no accounts for them have been mentioned; if any must be recorded, accounts can be provided for them.

Illustration Continued—Opening Trustee's Books. The following entries will open the accounts of W. C. Turner as trustee:

TRUSTEE'S JOURNAL

1971			
November 1	Cash—Principal	23,805	
	PQ Company stock	10,000	
	ST Company bonds	25,000	
	LM Company bonds	5,000	
	Trust principal		63,805
	To record the principal assets at the inception of the trust.		
1	Cash—Income	2,825	
	Dividends receivable	500	
	Accrued interest receivable	450	
	Income		3,775
	To record the income assets at the inception of the trust.		

Trustee's Reports. The trustee's periodic reports may be prepared in the charge and discharge form. The charges and credits shown therein are the credit and debit balances of the accounts in the trustee's ledger, as indicated by the list above (pp. 553–54). Two statements should be prepared: one for principal and one for income.

Closing the Trustee's Books. The trustee's accounts should be closed periodically. The accounts showing increases and decreases in accountability as to principal should be closed to the trust principal account. The accounts showing increases and decreases in accountability as to income are closed to the accounts with the income beneficiaries.

Accounting for Fire Losses

Fire Loss Account. When a fire occurs, a Fire Loss account should be set up immediately. It should be charged with:

1. The carrying value of the fixed assets destroyed or the appropriate portion of the carrying value of those damaged.
   (Note: If the fire occurs between closing dates, depreciation for the fractional period should be recognized in the accounts. In other words, the carrying value of the fixed assets should be adjusted as of the date on which the loss occurred.)
2. The estimated value of the inventories destroyed or damaged.
3. Any expense arising directly from the fire.

It should be credited with:

1. The value of any salvage, if retained by the insured.
2. The settlement received from the insurance company.

The final balance of the account should not necessarily be regarded as a gain or loss from the fire; it is presumably a composite of several elements: adjustment of prior depreciation provisions, realization of changes in market values, and the difference between the sound value of the property lost and the insurance collected.

Inventory Losses. The procedure used by the insured to account for inventories, whether *lifo* (last-in, first-out), average cost, or cost or market, whichever is lower, will not determine the insurance settlement. Settlements for losses are usually based on the insurable value of the property at the date of the loss, which is often described as the actual cash value of the property, which may or may not equal cost or some other basis of valuation used and acceptable for accounting purposes. Replacement cost data can provide a good indication of insurable value, but no single basis can be relied on as being pertinent under all, or even most, circumstances.

For settlement purposes, some evidence of quantities and kinds of goods on hand at the date of loss is desirable. In most cases, the method of estimating the inventories on hand will depend on the accounting records kept. If perpetual inventories are maintained, they usually furnish the best possible evidence of quantities and kinds of goods on hand. If there are not perpetual inventory records, the gross profit method may be used.

To illustrate, assuming an inventory of $30,000 at the last closing, purchases with a net cost of $60,000, including freight charges, and net sales of $75,000, both for the current year to the date of the fire, and an estimated gross profit of 33.3%, the inventory at the date of the fire might be estimated as follows:

Inventory, at date of last closing		$30,000
Add: Purchases, at net cost		60,000
Total		$90,000
Less: Estimated cost of sales:		
Net sales	$75,000	
Less: Gross profit—33.3%	25,000	50,000
Estimated inventory at date of fire		$40,000

The dollar amount ascertained by the gross profit method or other means of estimate may be subject to scaling down by the adjuster for a reduction in the value of goods that were shopworn, damaged prior to the fire, obsolete, or out of style. It might be equally appropriate to adjust such dollar amounts upward in order to arrive at the insurable value of the inventory damaged or destroyed. Incidentally, the insurance company has the right to whatever salvage is obtainable from property on which a total loss has been paid. Or, if the insured wishes to keep the damaged property, the claim is reduced by the agreed-upon salvage value.

The Coinsurance Clause. Because losses are often only partial, there is a tendency to insure for only a portion of the value of the property. To combat this tendency, policies may contain a coinsurance clause, in which the insured consents, in consideration of a reduction in the rate, to carry insurance in an amount equal to a stipulated per cent of the value of the property.

If the insured does not carry insurance in an amount equal to the coinsurance requirements, he is regarded as being himself a coinsurer with the insurance company; that is, he carries a portion of the risk. For example, if, under an 80% coinsurance policy, the insured carries insurance equal to only 70% of the value of the property at the date of the loss, he is a coinsurer. Seven-eighths of any loss will be borne by the company and one-eighth by the insured; however, the company will not be liable for more than the face of the policy. If the amount of insurance carried is 80% or more of the insurable value of the property, the company will be liable for all losses up to the face of the policy.

The operation of an 80% coinsurance clause may be illustrated thus:

First illustration:

Insurable value of property at date of loss	\$10,000
Policy	8,000

Since the amount of insurance carried satisfies the coinsurance clause, the insurance company is liable for all losses up to \$8,000.

Second illustration:

Insurable value of property at date of loss	\$10,000
Policy	8,500

In this illustration, the insurance carried exceeds the coinsurance clause requirement. Hence, the insurance company is liable for all losses up to \$8,500.

Third illustration:

Insurable value of property at date of loss	\$10,000
Policy	7,000
Loss	4,000

Here the insurance carried is less than the coinsurance clause percentage, being equal to only 70% of the insurable value of the property. Therefore, the insured is a coinsurer for $\frac{1}{8}$ of any loss up to \$8,000. Hence, the insurance company's liability is $\frac{7}{8}$ of \$4,000, or \$3,500.

Fourth illustration:

Insurable value of property at date of loss	\$10,000
Policy	6,500
Loss	4,000

As in the preceding illustration, the insurance carried is less than the coinsurance clause percentage, in this case being equal to 65% of the insurable value of the property. Accordingly, the insured is a coinsurer for $\frac{15}{80}$ of any loss up to \$8,000. Hence, the insurance company's liability is $\frac{65}{80}$ of \$4,000, or \$3,250.

Fifth illustration:

Insurable value of property at date of loss	\$10,000
Policy (same as above)	6,500
Loss	Total

$\frac{65}{80}$ of \$10,000 is \$8,125, but the policy is for only \$6,500; hence, the insurance company's liability is \$6,500.

From these illustrations the following general rule may be derived. To determine the insurance company's liability under a policy with the 80% coinsurance clause: when the policy is less than 80% of the insurable value of the property, multiply the loss by a fraction whose numerator is the face of the policy and whose denominator is 80% of the insurable value of the property. The product is the liability of the insurance company, except that the liability cannot be more than the face of the policy.

If the insured amount is 80% or more of the insurable value of the property, the coinsurance clause does not affect the settlement.

The following illustration is based on a problem from the May, 1961, Examination, which required the use of the gross profit method to determine the amount of work in process which was lost when the processing building was completely destroyed by fire on May 31, 1960. The insurance policies carried an 80% coinsurance clause. Only that portion of the problem concerned with the inventories appears here.

After the fire a physical inventory was taken. The raw materials were valued at $30,000, the finished goods at $60,000, and supplies at $5,000.

The inventories on January 1, 1960, consisted of:

Raw materials	$ 15,000
Work in process	50,000
Finished goods	70,000
Supplies	2,000
Total	$137,000

A review of the accounts showed that the sales and gross profit for the last five years were:

	Sales	*Gross Profit*
1955	$300,000	$ 86,200
1956	320,000	102,400
1957	330,000	108,900
1958	250,000	62,500
1959	280,000	84,000

The sales for the first five months of 1960 were $150,000. Raw material purchases were $50,000. Freight on purchases was $5,000. Direct labor for the five months was $40,000; for the past five years manufacturing overhead was 50% of direct labor.

Insurance on the inventory was carried with three companies. Each policy included an 80% coinsurance clause. The amount of insurance carried with the various companies was:

	Inventories
Company A	$38,000
Company B	35,000
Company C	35,000

The in-process inventory destroyed by the fire can be estimated by making the following computations:

Gross profit percentage:

$$\frac{\text{gross profit (1955–1959)}}{\text{sales (1955–1959)}} = \frac{\$444{,}000}{\$1{,}480{,}000} = 30\%$$

In-process inventory destroyed by fire:

All inventories, except supplies—January 1, 1960		$135,000
Purchases—raw materials		50,000
Freight on purchases		5,000
Direct labor		40,000
Overhead (50% of direct labor)		20,000
Total		$250,000
Less: Cost of sales:		
Sales	$150,000	
Less: Gross profit—30%	45,000	105,000
All inventories, except supplies—May 31, 1960		$145,000
Deduct inventories—per physical count after fire:		
Raw materials	$ 30,000	
Finished goods	60,000	90,000
Work in process inventory destroyed by fire		$ 55,000

The following computations indicate that the 80% coinsurance clause was not satisfied:

Inventories—May 31, 1960:	
Raw materials	$ 30,000
Finished goods	60,000
Work in process—per estimate	55,000
Supplies	5,000
	$150,000

Coverage to satisfy coinsurance clause:

$$80\% \text{ of } \$150{,}000 = \$120{,}000$$

Insurance carried—$108,000.

The amount of the claim and its apportionment among the insurance companies follow.

	Share	*Claim*
Company A	38/108	$17,416
Company B	35/108	16,042
Company C	35/108	16,042
Total (108/120 of $55,000)		$49,500

The assignment of the loss among the insurance companies was simplified because all the policies carried identical coinsurance clauses. Given different coinsurance clauses, a company's portion of the loss may be determined by multiplying the total loss by a fraction whose numerator is the face amount of the policy and whose denominator is either:

1. The face amount of all policies.

   The face amount of all policies is used as a denominator if the insurer's policy has no coinsurance clause (see Company A in the following tabulation) or if the insurance carrier meets the coinsurance requirement of the policy (see Company B).

or

2. The insurance required under the coinsurance clause.

   The coinsurance requirement is used as a denominator if the insurer's policy contains such a clause and its requirement has not been met (see Company C).

Let us illustrate by assuming that property has an insurable value of $100,000, that it is insured under the policies described below, and that a loss of $75,000 is incurred. The amount collectible from each company is computed as follows:

		Insurance				
Company	*Coinsurance Clause*	*Required by Coins. Clause*	*Carried*	*Fraction*	*Loss*	*Amount Collectible*
A	None	—	$40,000	40/80	$75,000	$37,500
B	75%	$75,000	20,000	20/80	75,000	18,750
C	90%	90,000	20,000	20/90	75,000	16,667
Total			$80,000			$72,917

Funds Statements

Most candidates are familiar with funds statements before they begin to review for the CPA Examination. However, unless the candidate more or less regularly prepares these statements in the course of his accounting work, he does run some risk of losing points on problems covering this topic merely from lack of recent exposure to funds problems and their occasional peculiarities.

nature of funds statements

Various definitions of funds have been used in the preparation of funds statements, ranging from cash, a narrow definition, to all financial resources, a broad definition. As traditionally prepared, the term "funds" was equated with working capital. Following this definition, a funds statement accounts for the change in working capital that has occurred during a period of time. Thus it shows the sources and applications of working capital, working capital being defined as the excess of current assets over current liabilities. An alternative, and more appropriate, title for such statement is statement of sources and uses of working capital.

The traditional funds statement is customarily supported by a schedule of working capital setting forth in comparative form the balances of the current asset and current liability accounts at the beginning and end of the period covered by the funds statement.

Definition of Working Capital. Defining *working capital* as the excess of current assets over current liabilities is somewhat inadequate unless accompanied by definitions of current assets and current liabilities. The Committee on Accounting Procedure in ARB No. 43 has defined these terms as follows:

> The term *current assets* is used to designate cash and other assets or resources commonly identified as those which are reasonably expected to be realized in cash or sold or consumed during the normal operating cycle of the business.
>
> * * *
>
> The term *current liabilities* is used principally to designate obligations whose liquidation is reasonably expected to require the use of existing resources properly classifiable as current assets, or the creation of other current liabilities.

An important feature of the definition of current assets is that prepaid expenses are included in the working capital group. However, the *Bulletin* states that "long-term prepayments which are fairly chargeable to the operations of several years, or deferred charges such as unamortized debt discount and expense, bonus payments under a long-term lease . . ." are not included.

Illustrative Statement. Many variations in funds statement arrangement can be found in accounting texts and among published financial statements. A traditional form is used for the following illustration.

STATE COMPANY

STATEMENT OF SOURCES AND USES OF WORKING CAPITAL
FOR THE YEAR ENDED DECEMBER 31, 19X1

Working capital sources:			
Operations:			
Net income for the year		$14,885	
Add charges to operations not affecting working capital:			
Depreciation:			
Building	$1,250		
Office equipment	650		
Delivery equipment	1,500		
Loss on sale of delivery equipment	200	3,600	$18,485
Issuance of capital stock at par			10,000
Sale of delivery equipment			100
Total			$28,585
Working capital uses:			
Payment of cash dividend		$15,000	
Purchase of fixed assets:			
Office equipment	$3,000		
Delivery equipment	1,500	4,500	19,500
Increase in working capital—per schedule			$ 9,085

STATE COMPANY

SCHEDULE OF WORKING CAPITAL
DECEMBER 31, 19X1 AND 19X0

	December 31,		*Working Capital Increase-Decrease* *
	19X1	*19X0*	
Current assets:			
Cash	$ 8,500	$ 6,250	$2,250
Accounts receivable—net of allowance for doubtful accounts	33,675	31,160	2,515
Notes receivable	20,000	22,500	2,500 *
Inventory	48,000	44,625	3,375
Prepaid expenses	640	545	95
Total	$110,815	$105,080	$5,735
Current liabilities:			
Accounts payable	$ 7,900	$ 9,250	$1,350
Notes payable	10,000	12,000	2,000
Total	$ 17,900	$ 21,250	$3,350
Working capital	$ 92,915	$ 83,830	$9,085

source of data for funds statement

The data needed to prepare a statement of sources and uses of working capital can be found in the noncurrent accounts, as is illustrated by the following analysis of some of the noncurrent accounts of State Company. Noncurrent accounts are those other than the current asset or current liability accounts.

Office Equipment

Beginning-of-year balance	10,000		
Purchase for cash	3,000		

For funds statement purposes, any entry that causes a change in working capital is relevant. Because the acquisition of office equipment reduced the company's cash, and hence its working capital, it was necessary to show it as a use of working capital in the illustrative funds statement.

Accumulated Depreciation—Office Equipment

		Beginning-of-year balance	4,000
		Depreciation for 19X1	650

Depreciation reduces the net income without reducing the working capital. Therefore, the $650 depreciation taken in 19X1 was added to the net income to determine the increase in working capital attributable to operations.

Delivery Equipment

Beginning-of-year balance	7,500	Sale of partially depreciated equipment	1,000
Purchase on account; terms, 60 days	1,500		

Accumulated Depreciation—Delivery Equipment

Accumulated depreciation on equipment sold	700	Beginning-of-year balance	2,800
		Depreciation for 19X1	1,500

Because the acquisition of delivery equipment increased current liabilities, which thus reduced the working capital, it appeared as a use of working capital.

The $1,500 of depreciation for 19X1 was added to net income, for the reasons mentioned when depreciation of office equipment was being considered.

The sale of the partially depreciated delivery equipment was recorded as follows:

Cash	100	
Accumulated depreciation—delivery equipment	700	
Loss on sale of delivery equipment	200	
Delivery equipment		1,000

The $100 was shown as a source of working capital and the $200 loss, which reduced the net income without reducing the working capital, was added to net income to determine the increase in working capital attributable to operations.

Capital Stock

		Beginning-of-year balance	75,000
		Issuance for cash	10,000
		Stock dividend	15,000

Retained Earnings

Stock dividend	15,000	Beginning-of-year balance	61,53[illegible]
Cash dividend	15,000	Net income	14,88[illegible]

The stock dividend was ignored because it had no effect on working capital. The changes in working capital due to the issuance of capital stock and the payment of the cash dividend were included in the statement.

Working Papers. The working papers on page 565 show a convenient device for assembling the information required for the preparation of a statement of sources and uses of working capital. Because the working capital schedule can be prepared before the statement of sources and uses of working capital, details of current assets and current liabilities may be omitted from the working papers and only the net change in working capital need be shown.

The statement of sources and uses of working capital does not give the noncurrent account balances at the beginning and end of the year, but only the changes therein. Therefore, only the changes in the balances need be accounted for in the working papers.

Solutions Without Working Papers. Some of the CPA Examination problems are designed to permit the preparation of funds statements without the necessity of preparing underlying working papers. When a problem does not require working papers as a part of the solution, the candidate should not take the time to prepare them unless he is convinced that only by their use will he be able to solve the problem.

The relevance of the preceding paragraphs is indicated by the following problem taken from the May, 1960, Examination. The solution

STATE COMPANY

Working Papers for Statement of Sources and Uses of Working Capital
For the Year Ended December 31, 19X1

	Analysis of Year's Changes		Adjustments		Working Capital Uses	Working Capital Sources: Operations	Working Capital Sources: Other
Increase in working capital	9,085						
Noncurrent accounts:							
Land—no change							
Building—no change							
Office equipment:							
Purchase	3,000				3,000		
Delivery equipment:							
Purchase	1,500				1,500		
Sale		1,000	(a) 900				100
Accumulated depreciation—building:							
Depreciation for year		1,250				1,250	
Accumulated depreciation—office equipment:							
Depreciation for year		650				650	
Accumulated depreciation—delivery equipment:							
Depreciation for year		1,500				1,500	
Accumulated depreciation on equipment sold	700			(a) 700			
Capital stock:							
Issuance at par		10,000					10,000
Issuance as a stock dividend		15,000	(b) 15,000				
Retained earnings:							
Stock dividend	15,000			(b) 15,000			
Cash dividend	15,000				15,000		
Net income		14,885		(a) 200		15,085	
	44,285	44,285	15,900	15,900			
Working capital provided by operations						18,485	18,485
Working capital from all sources							28,585
Working capital uses					19,500		19,500
Increase in working capital							9,085

(a) Nonworking-capital elements of sale transaction.
(b) Stock dividend.

which follows the statement of the problem, omits the use of working papers and illustrates the need to develop some of the required data.

Statement of Problem The net changes in the balance sheet accounts of *X* Company for the year 19X0 are shown below:

	Debit	*Credit*
Investments		$25,000
Land	$ 3,200	
Buildings	35,000	
Machinery	6,000	
Office equipment		1,500
Allowance for depreciation:		
Buildings		2,000
Machinery		900
Office equipment	600	
Discount on bonds	2,000	
Bonds payable		40,000
Capital stock—preferred	10,000	
Capital stock—common		12,400
Premium on common stock		5,600
Retained earnings		6,800
Working capital	37,400	
	$94,200	$94,200

Additional information:

1. Cash dividends of $18,000 were declared December 15, 19X0, payable January 15, 19X1. A 2% stock dividend was issued March 31, 19X0, when the market value was $12.50 per share.

2. The investments were sold for $27,500.

3. A building which cost $45,000 and had a depreciated basis of $40,500 was sold for $50,000.

4. The following entry was made to record an exchange of an old machine for a new one:

Machinery	13,000	
Allowance for depreciation—machinery	5,000	
Machinery		7,000
Cash		11,000

5. A fully depreciated office machine costing $1,500 was written off.

6. Preferred stock of $10,000 par value was redeemed for $10,200.

7. The company sold 1,000 shares of its common stock (par value $10) on June 15, 19X0 for $15 a share. There were 13,240 shares outstanding on December 31, 19X0.

Required: A statement of source and application of funds for the year 19X0.

Solution:

X COMPANY

STATEMENT OF SOURCE AND APPLICATION OF FUNDS
FOR THE YEAR ENDED DECEMBER 31, 19X0

Sources of funds:		
Operations:		
Operating income—see supporting computation	$16,000	
Depreciation charges—see supporting computation	13,300	
Total		$ 29,300
Sale of investments		27,500
Sale of building		50,000
Sale of bonds		38,000
Sale of stock		15,000
Total		$159,800
Funds applied:		
Purchases of land, building, and machinery—see supporting computation		$ 94,200
Redemption of preferred stock		10,200
Dividends declared		18,000
Total		$122,400
Net increase in working capital		$ 37,400

The candidate should not expect that all the data needed for a funds statement will be set forth in the problem directly; he will undoubtedly have to develop some of the data by analysis and computation.

Supporting Computations

Net increase in retained earnings		$ 6,800
Cash dividends declared		18,000
Stock dividend (240 shares at $12.50 per share)		3,000
Premium paid on redemption of preferred stock		200
Net income		$ 28,000
Deduct:		
Gain on sale of investments	$ 2,500	
Gain on sale of building	9,500	12,000
Operating income		$ 16,000

(continued)

Building:		
Net increase in allowance	$ 2,000	
Allowance applicable to building sold	4,500	
Depreciation—building		$ 6,500
Machinery:		
Net increase in allowance	$ 900	
Allowance applicable to machine exchanged	5,000	
Depreciation—machinery		5,900
Office equipment:		
Net decrease in allowance	$ (600)	
Allowance applicable to equipment written off	1,500	
Depreciation—office equipment		900
Total depreciation		$ 13,300
Land purchased		$ 3,200
Net increase in building account	$35,000	
Cost of building sold	45,000	
Cost of building purchased		80,000
Machinery purchased		11,000
Total purchases of fixed assets		$ 94,200

The foregoing solution illustrates the desirability of grouping some of the data in order to show the correct amount of working capital change resulting from a particular transaction. For example, the $2,500 gain on sale of investments is associated with the $25,000 change in the Investments account to report the correct amount ($27,500) of funds provided by the sale of investments. Similarly, the $15,000 of funds received from the issuance of common stock is shown as a single source of funds although two accounts, Capital Stock—Common and Premium on Common Stock, were affected by the transaction.

opinion of accounting principles board

In March, 1971, the Accounting Principles Board of the American Institute of Certified Public Accountants published an Opinion dealing with "reporting changes in financial position." The following is quoted from that Opinion:

> The Board concludes that . . . when financial statements . . . are issued, a statement summarizing changes in financial position should also be presented as a basic financial statement for each period for

which an income statement is presented. . . . The Board also concludes that the statement summarizing changes in financial position should be based on a broad concept embracing all changes in financial position and that the title of the statement should reflect this broad concept. The Board therefore recommends that the title be Statement of Changes in Financial Position. . . . The Statement should prominently disclose working capital or cash provided from or used in operations for the period, and the Board believes that the disclosure is most informative if the effects of extraordinary items are reported separately from the effects of normal items.

The Opinion concluded by the Board strongly recommending:

. . . that isolated statistics of working capital or cash provided from operations, especially per-share amounts, not be presented in annual reports to shareholders.

In addition to accounting for the change in working capital, the statement, prepared under this concept, should give a comprehensive picture of other changes in financial condition by including the following items:

1. Under the Funds Sources caption:

   All credits to noncurrent accounts resulting from transactions (but not mere book entries) regardless of whether the offsetting debit was to a working capital account or to some other noncurrent account.

2. Under the Funds Uses caption:

   All debits to noncurrent accounts resulting from transactions (but not mere book entries) regardless of whether the offsetting credit was to a working capital account or to some other noncurrent account.

Illustrations. An illustrative statement prepared in accordance with this concept is presented on page 571. It is based on the following condensed comparative balance sheet.

THE FM COMPANY

CONDENSED COMPARATIVE BALANCE SHEET
DECEMBER 31, 19X1 AND 19X0

	December 31,		*Net Change*	
Assets	*19X1*	*19X0*	*Debit*	*Credit*
Working capital	$24,000	$20,000	$ 4,000	
Investment securities		5,000		$ 5,000
Land	8,000	5,000	3,000	

(continued)

Buildings	50,000	30,000	20,000	
Accumulated depreciation—buildings	4,000 *	3,000 *		1,000
Equipment	22,000	15,000	7,000	
Accumulated depreciation—equipment	3,000 *	2,250 *		750
Goodwill		5,000		5,000
	$97,000	$74,750		

Liabilities and Stockholders' Equity

Long-term unsecured notes payable		$10,000	10,000	
Mortgage payable	$15,000			15,000
Capital stock	65,000	50,000		15,000
Retained earnings	17,000	14,750		2,250
	$97,000	$74,750	$44,000	$44,000

* Deduction.

The causes of the changes in the noncurrent accounts are:

Depreciation of buildings during the year was $1,000; depreciation of equipment was $750.

The $5,000 Goodwill account was written off. This was a mere book entry and will not be reflected in the statement.

Capital stock of $10,000 par value was issued to retire the long-term notes payable.

Capital stock of $5,000 par value was issued for cash.

A dividend of $3,500 was paid.

The net income for the year was $10,750.

A purchase of fixed assets was made as follows:

Acquired from seller:	
Land	$ 3,000
Buildings	20,000
Equipment	7,000
Total	$30,000
Given to seller:	
Investment securities	$ 5,000
Mortgage payable	15,000
Cash	10,000
Total	$30,000

THE FM COMPANY

STATEMENT OF CHANGES IN FINANCIAL POSITION
FOR THE YEAR ENDED DECEMBER 31, 19X1

Funds sources:			
Operations:			
Net income for the year		$10,750	
Depreciation of buildings		1,000	
Depreciation of equipment		750	$12,500
Issuance of capital stock			15,000
Issuance of mortgage			15,000
Disposal of investment securities			5,000
Total funds from all sources			$47,500
Funds uses:			
Acquisitions of fixed assets:			
Land	$ 3,000		
Buildings	20,000		
Equipment	7,000	$30,000	
Retirement of long-term unsecured notes payable		10,000	
Payment of dividend		3,500	
Total funds uses			43,500
Increase in working capital			$ 4,000

The following question from the Theory of Accounts section of the May, 1969, Examination, and its unofficial answer, provide a second illustration and a helpful indication of the kind of general knowledge expected of the candidate in relation to funds statements.

The following statement of Source and Application of Funds was prepared by the controller of the Clovis Company. The controller indicated that this statement was prepared under the "all financial resources" concept of funds, which is the broadest concept of funds and includes all transactions providing or requiring funds.

Problem:

CLOVIS COMPANY

STATEMENT OF SOURCE AND APPLICATION OF FUNDS
DECEMBER 31, 1968

Funds were provided by:	
Contribution of plant site by the City of Camden (1)	$115,000
Net income after extraordinary items per income statement (2)	75,000
Issuance of note payable—due 1972	60,000

(continued)

Depreciation and amortization	50,000
Deferred income taxes relating to accelerated depreciation	10,000
Sale of equipment—book value (3)	5,000
Total funds provided	$315,000
Funds were applied to:	
Acquisition of future plant site (1)	$250,000
Increase in working capital	30,000
Cash dividends declared but not paid	20,000
Acquisition of equipment	15,000
Total funds applied	$315,000

NOTES:

(1) The City of Camden donated a plant site to Clovis Company valued by the board of directors at $115,000. The company purchased adjoining property for $135,000.

(2) Research and development expenditures of $25,000 incurred in 1968 were expensed. These expenses were considered abnormal.

(3) Equipment with a book value of $5,000 was sold for $8,000. The gain was included as an extraordinary item on the income statement.

Required:

a. Why is it considered desirable to present a statement of source and application of funds in financial reports?

b. Define and discuss the relative merits of the following three concepts used in funds flow analysis in terms of their measurement accuracy and freedom from manipulation (window dressing) in one accounting period:

1. Cash concept of funds.
2. Net monetary assets (quick assets) concept of funds.
3. Working capital concept of funds.

c. Identify and discuss the weaknesses in presentation and disclosure in the Statement of Source and Application of Funds for Clovis Company. Your discussion should explain why you consider them to be weaknesses and what you consider the proper treatment of the items to be. Do not prepare a revised statement.

Answer:

a. It is considered desirable to present a statement of source and application of funds as supplementary information in financial reports because such information is useful for a variety of purposes affecting both operating and investment decisions. A statement of source and application of funds is helpful because it presents information that cannot easily be obtained from the financial statements and because it presents articulated information about the movement of funds. A statement of source and application of funds cannot supplant the income statement, but it can provide a useful and significant summary of certain transactions. The statement of source and application of funds is particularly helpful in appraising financial policies of the past and in planning financial activities of the future.

b. 1. When the funds concept denotes cash, all noncash balance sheet changes are analyzed in terms of their effect upon the movement of cash. Under the cash concept of funds flow analysis, the statement of source and application of funds is designed to explain the sources and uses of cash.

Cash flow can be more precisely measured than can other concepts of funds because the valuation problems of cash are not as great as for other financial resources. However, movement of cash may be easily influenced. For example payments of liabilities may be temporarily delayed or marketable securities may be sold, increasing cash flow for a given period.

2. Net monetary assets are defined as the quick current assets (i.e., cash, accounts receivable, and marketable securities) less current liabilities. Thus a statement of source and application of funds prepared under the net monetary assets concept of funds flow analysis reports the changes in all nonquick current assets and noncurrent liabilities in terms of their effect upon the movement of net monetary assets.

Under the net monetary assets concept of funds, the problem of valuation for marketable securities and accounts receivable arises. As a result, precision in the measurement of funds flow is decreased. Although selected alternatives are available which may influence the movement of net monetary assets, such as the temporary postponement of inventory purchases, the range of possibilities is not as great as for cash movements. For example, selling marketable securities or postponing the payment of current liabilities will not influence the flow of net monetary assets.

3. Working capital is defined as current assets less current liabilities. A statement of source and application of funds prepared under the working capital concept of funds flow analysis reports the changes in the noncurrent accounts that affect the movement of current items.

The working capital concept of funds enlarges the problem of valuation because it includes inventory and prepaid items. Thus the measurement of working capital flows is less precise than for cash or net monetary assets. However, this concept further reduces the areas for window dressing. For example, the postponement of the purchase of merchandise on open account will not influence working capital flows.

c. Weaknesses in presentation and disclosure of Clovis Company's Statement of Source and Application of Funds include the following:

Date. The date of the statement should indicate the time period covered by the statement.

Arrangement. As the major recurring activity of the firm is operations, it is recommended practice to report, as the first item in a statement of source and application of funds, resources provided by operations with the related adjustments for nonfund items such as depreciation and amortization, deferred income taxes, and gains and losses on the disposition of noncurrent assets.

As an alternative arrangement, gross inflows of funds from operations could be reported with a deduction for operating expenses requiring the use of funds. Under this alternative, nonfund items such as depreciation and amortization and deferred income taxes would not appear on the statement. Abnormal operating revenues or expenses should be separately stated. Extraordinary gains and losses should not be reported, but rather should be included in the funds provided (if any) by the extraordinary event.

Research and development expenditures. In order to reflect accurately the funds provided by normal operations, the deduction for abnormal research and development expenditures should be excluded from the computation of funds provided by operations and reported separately as an application.

Depreciation and amortization. Depreciation and amortization should be reported as an adjustment to net income which did not require the use of funds. As presented, it erroneously implies that depreciation and amortization were sources of funds.

Deferred income taxes. Like depreciation and amortization, deferred income taxes relating to accelerated depreciation should be reported also as an adjustment to net income which did not require the use of financial resources during the period.

Gain on sale of equipment. The $3,000 gain on the equipment sale should be deducted as an adjustment to net income. The actual funds provided by the sale should be reported as $8,000.

Acquisition of future plant site. To achieve improved clarity in reporting, the acquisition of future plant site should be separated into its two components—the portion donated by the City of Camden and the portion acquired through the use of corporate funds.

An acceptable but less desirable alternative is to report the donation of plant site by the City of Camden as follows:

Funds were applied to:		
Acquisition of future plant site (1)	$250,000	
Less portion donated by the City of Camden	115,000	$135,000

Disclosure. The footnotes do not disclose commitments to use funds in the future or contractual rights to funds available but not executed in 1968.

Retail and Dollar-Value Methods of Inventory Valuation

Retail Method. The intent of the retail inventory method, as conventionally applied, is to value the inventory so that its sale at prevailing prices will yield at least the normal or prevailing rate of gross profit. The dollar amounts thus determined are intended to conform generally to the cost-or-market rule.

To apply the retail method of inventory valuation, it is necessary to maintain records of purchases at both cost and selling price and of sales at selling price.

With this information it is possible to determine a ratio of cost to retail, which has the following uses:

1. To estimate the inventory at any time without taking a physical inventory; the procedure is as follows:

	Cost	*Retail*
Inventory at beginning of period	$ 10,000	$ 15,000
Purchases during the period	110,000	185,000
Totals	$120,000	$200,000
(Ratio of cost to retail—60%)		
Sales		180,000
Estimated inventory at retail		$ 20,000

Inventory computation—60% of $20,000 = $12,000.

The retail method makes it possible to prepare monthly, weekly, or even daily estimates of the inventory. Such estimates may be useful for purposes of inventory control and formulating purchasing policy.

2. To permit pricing a physical inventory at marked selling prices and reducing the selling price valuation by applying to it the ratio of cost to retail.

Using retail prices eliminates the necessity of marking costs on the merchandise, referring to invoices, and dealing with the problem of identical merchandise acquired at different costs.

Physical inventories, priced by the retail method, should be taken from time to time as a check on the accuracy of the estimated inventories determined by the procedure described under 1. If the inventory determined by procedure 2 is less than the amount estimated by procedure 1, the difference may be attributable to "shrinkages" resulting from theft, breakage, or other causes. However, the difference may be attributable in part to errors in the retail inventory records or in the physical inventory priced at retail.

Special Terms. The foregoing illustration ignores the problem created whenever changes are made in selling prices after the original pricing of goods. The fact that businessmen do revise or modify prices of goods on hand necessitates an understanding of the following terms:

Original retail is the price at which goods are first offered for sale.

Markups are additions that raise the selling price above the original retail.

Markdowns are deductions that lower the price below the original retail.

Markdown cancellations are additions that do not increase the selling price above the original retail.

Markup cancellations are deductions that do not decrease the selling price below the original retail.

To illustrate, assume the following facts:

The goods cost $100	
The original retail was	$140
There was a markup of	20
which advanced the selling price to	$160
There was a markup cancellation of	5
which reduced the selling price to	$155
The selling price was reduced $30:	
This included a markup cancellation of	15
which reduced the selling price to original retail	$140
It also included a markdown of	15
New selling price	$125
There was a markdown cancellation of	5
which increased the selling price to	$130

Markups minus markup cancellations may be referred to as *net markup;* markdowns minus markdown cancellations may be referred to as *net markdown.*

An understanding of markups, markup cancellations, markdowns, and markdown cancellations, and a careful differentiation thereof in the records, are necessary because, in determining the ratio of cost to retail, it is customary to include markups and markup cancellations, but to ignore markdowns and markdown cancellations. To illustrate, let us assume the following facts:

	Cost	*Retail*
Inventory at beginning of period	$ 20,000	$ 30,000
Purchases	80,000	120,000
Markups		10,000
Markup cancellations		2,000 *
Markdowns		7,000 *
Markdown cancellations		1,000

The percentage to be used in determining the inventory value by the retail method (including net markups and excluding net markdowns) is computed as follows:

	Cost	*Retail*
Inventory at beginning of period	$ 20,000	$ 30,000
Purchases	80,000	120,000
Markups		10,000
Markup cancellations		2,000 *
Totals (Ratio of cost to retail—63.29%)	$100,000	$158,000

Markon is the difference between the cost and the original retail plus net markups. In the foregoing example, the markon is $58,000; the percentage of markon is 36.71% ($58,000 ÷ $158,000); and the ratio of cost to retail is the complement of this percentage or 63.29%. This rate is used in the following computation of inventory value.

	Cost	*Retail*
Inventory at beginning of period	$ 20,000	$ 30,000
Purchases	80,000	120,000
Markups		10,000
Markup cancellations		2,000 *
Totals (cost ratio—63.29%)	$100,000	$158,000
Markdowns		7,000 *
Markdown cancellations		1,000
Remainder		$152,000
Sales		120,000
Inventory at retail		$ 32,000

Inventory valuation: 63.29% of $32,000, or $20,253.

Freight, Discounts, Returns. Transportation and other charges which, in accordance with good accounting theory, are proper additions to merchandise costs, should be added to purchase costs in the retail record. If cash discounts are regarded as deductions from purchases, the purchases should appear net in the retail inventory records. If such discounts are regarded as financial income, they should not be included in the retail inventory computations.

Purchases should be entered at cost and at retail in the inventory computation; returned purchases should be similarly indicated. Returned sales should be deducted from sales to obtain a net sales figure for use in the computation.

Special Note. The retail inventory method is based on the assumption that high-cost-ratio and low-cost-ratio goods will be found in the same proportions in the final inventory as in the total goods offered for sale. Conditions which may negate this assumption will require special consideration. For example:

1. If the cost ratios vary by departments and the ratios of ending inventory to goods available for sale are not the same in all departments, the basic assumption stated previously is not warranted. This condition can be dealt with by developing departmental cost ratios, thereby permitting departmental inventory computations.
2. For similar reasons, separate inventory computations for special sale merchandise may be desirable.
3. A year is too long a period to embrace in the inventory computation unless approximately the same cost ratio prevails throughout the year.

In spite of such complications associated with the retail inventory method, it does have commendable features:

1. It simplifies the task of inventory pricing.
2. It permits frequent, even daily, computations of inventory with relative ease.
3. By comparing a computed inventory with a physical inventory, an element of inventory control is provided.

lifo and the retail method

When an accountant applies the *lifo* concept to the retail method, he must use procedures somewhat different from those used under the conventional retail method.

First Difference:

Include markdowns as well as markups in the determination of the cost ratio.

As previously stated, the conventional retail method produces an inventory valuation closely approximating the amount that would be obtained by taking a physical inventory and pricing the goods at the lower of cost or market. *Lifo,* on the other hand, is a cost method. It is possible to modify the retail method to produce results reasonably conforming to a cost basis by including markdowns as well as markups in the determination of the cost ratio.

Second Difference:

Ignore the beginning inventory in the determination of the cost ratio.

After the *lifo* method has been in use for a period of time, the difference between current costs and the "old" costs that are considered by the *lifo* method to be applicable to the inventory becomes quite significant. Because the cost ratio is intended to indicate the current relationship between costs and selling prices, the beginning inventory data are not used in the computation of the cost ratio because their inclusion could have a distorting effect on the cost ratio.

The contrasting procedures under the conventional retail method (intended to produce an inventory valuation on the basis of the lower of cost or market) and under the *lifo* method (intended to produce an inventory valuation on a cost basis) are illustrated next.

	Conventional Retail		*Lifo Retail*	
	Cost	*Retail*	*Cost*	*Retail*
→ Inventory—beginning of year	$ 3,200	$ 5,500	Omitted from cost ratio	
Purchases	15,600	24,500	$15,600	$24,500
Transportation in	400		400	
Markups		2,000		2,000
Total	$19,200	$32,000		$26,500
Conventional cost ratio: $19,2000 ÷ $32,000	(60%)			
Markdowns		2,500		2,500
Remainder			$16,000	$24,000
Lifo cost ratio: $16,000 ÷ $24,000			(66⅔%)	
→ Inventory—beginning of year				5,500
Total goods, at retail		$29,500		$29,500
Sales		23,500		23,500
Inventory at retail—end of year		$ 6,000		$ 6,000
Applicable cost ratio		60%		66⅔%
Inventory valuation		$ 3,600		$ 4,000

It will be noted that, in the foregoing computation of the *lifo* cost ratio, the markups and markdowns were applied to the selling price of the goods purchased, although they presumably applied in part to the opening inventory. Obviously, this is not strictly correct; however, the slight theoretical impropriety usually is ignored.

The practice of disregarding the beginning inventory when computing the cost ratio is a feature of the *lifo* retail method and, therefore, is followed in all subsequent years and not confined merely to the computation of the base or beginning *lifo* inventory.

Dollar-Value *Lifo*. As indicated by the word *lifo,* the dollar-value *lifo* method is a form of last-in, first-out inventory valuation. Under the dollar-value method, dollars, rather than physical quantities, are used to determine whether there has been an increment (a new *lifo* layer) or a reduction to the *lifo* inventory. For example, assuming no change in the price level during the current year, if last year's inventory was $1,000 (at cost) and this year's inventory was $1,100 (at cost), it can be inferred that the inventory has increased 10%. Under *lifo* this would mean that we have an additional layer to deal with. In a sense, this approach views an inventory as a pool or aggregate, in contrast to an item-by-item approach. In practice, the inventory would probably be divided by broad product categories or by departments, with separate *lifo* bases and layers for each grouping.

Of course, the price level changes. So before the dollar amount of a current inventory can be compared with the dollar amount of a previous inventory to determine whether there has been an increase or decrease, the two inventories being compared must be stated in dollars "of the same size." This could be done by the use of index numbers which measure the extent of changes in the price level. For instance, if it were known that the prices of goods purchased for resale had increased 10% during the current year, an inventory of $11,550, priced by using the current year's costs, could be converted to last year's price level by dividing by 1.10; thus $11,550 ÷ 1.10 = $10,500.

If last year's inventory amounted to $10,000, the comparison between the $10,500 amount and the $10,000 amount would indicate that the inventory has increased 5%, or by $500 in terms of last year's prices. For purposes of determining the *lifo* inventory, this layer should be stated in terms of the current year's price level, or $550, which is computed by multiplying $500 by 1.10.

Because price index numbers are not available for many industries or lines of business, some alternative device for measuring price changes as it affects the inventory of a particular business must be applied. The approach used is to compute the inventory first in terms of current costs and second in terms of the costs prevailing when *lifo* was adopted.

For example, if the current inventory amounts to $110,000 at current costs and to $100,000 in terms of costs prevailing when the *lifo* method was adopted (see below), it can be concluded that as far as this company is concerned, prices of inventory items have gone up 10%.

INVENTORY

		Unit Costs		*Total*	
Description	*Current Quantity*	*Current Period*	*Prevailing When Lifo Was Adopted*	*At Current Costs*	*At Costs Prevailing When Lifo Was Adopted*
A	80	$3.00	$2.75	$ 240	$ 220
B	100	2.45	2.25	245	225
C	200	5.50	5.00	1,100	1,000
				$110,000	$100,000

In the previous paragraph it was stated that each inventory is computed twice—once using current year's costs and again using costs prevailing when the *lifo* method was adopted. It should be pointed out that only a representative sample of the inventory need be thus double-priced, because the purpose of the extra computation is to obtain an index or measure of price change. It should also be mentioned that, as a practical matter, some provision must be made for the effects of discontinued and new products in developing a measure of price change.

The basic techniques of dollar-value *lifo* are illustrated below. Zero is used to designate the year when *lifo* was adopted.

	Inventory of Year			
	0	*1*	*2*	*3*
Priced by using costs of year 0	$10,000			
Priced by using costs of year 1		$10,710		
Priced by using costs of year 2			$11,340	
Priced by using costs of year 3				$11,880
Priced by using costs of year 0	$10,000	$10,500	$10,800	$10,800
Index of price change since year 0, when *lifo* was adopted:				
$10,710 ÷ $10,500		102		
$11,340 ÷ $10,800			105	
$11,880 ÷ $10,800				110

Inventory—*lifo* cost:

Year 0: $10,000

Year 1:

By comparing the year 1 inventory with the year 0 inventory, both stated in dollars of the same price level (year 0), it is seen that there has been an increment to the inventory. This layer amounts to $500 ($10,500 – $10,000) in terms of the price level at year 0. But a new layer must be computed in terms of the current price level, or $500 × 1.02.

Year 1 layer	$ 510
Base	10,000
Inventory—*lifo* cost	$10,510

Year 2:

By comparing year 2 and year 1 inventories, both stated in dollars of the same price level (year 0), it is seen that there has been a further increment to the *lifo* inventory. The year 2 layer amounts to $300 ($10,800 – $10,500) in terms of the price level when *lifo* was adopted. To convert to the year 2 price level, the $300 is multiplied by 1.05.

Year 2 layer ($300 × 1.05)	$ 315
Year 1 layer	510
Base	10,000
Inventory—*lifo* cost	$10,825

Year 3:

By comparing year 3 and year 2 inventories, both stated in dollars of the same price level (year 0), it is seen that there has been no change in the aggregate inventory ($10,800 – $10,800). Therefore, the *lifo* inventory for year 3 is the same as for year 2.

Inventory—*lifo* cost	$10,825

Inventory Reductions. Reductions in *lifo* inventories are subtracted first from the most recent layer (or layers, depending on the extent of the reduction), and, after all layers have been utilized, they are then deducted from the base inventory. To show how a reduction is handled under dollar-value *lifo,* continue the illustration for an additional year and assume that the inventory for year 4 is as follows:

Priced using costs of year 4	$11,770
Priced using cost of year 0	$10,700

By comparing year 4 and year 3 inventories, both stated in dollars of the same price level (year 0), it is seen that there has been a reduction of $100 ($10,800 – $10,700). This reduction is taken from the year 2 layer, as follows:

Year 2 layer stated in terms of year 0 prices	$300	
Reduction occurring during year 4	100	
Remaining layer	$200	
Price index for year 2	1.05	
Remainder of year 2 layer in terms of *lifo* cost	$210	

Inventory—*lifo* cost:	
Year 4:	
Year 2 layer	$ 210
Year 1 layer	510
Base	10,000
Inventory—*lifo* cost	$10,720

Reorganizations

The CPA candidate should be prepared for the type of problem that requires him to submit accounting entries to give effect to a plan of reorganization. Frequently *pro forma* (after giving effect to) financial statements or parts of financial statements are required. Usually the company described in the Examination question is in financial difficulty and the proposed plan will necessitate adjustment or revision of several of the account balances. Such proposals are customarily referred to as *financial reorganizations* if the only accounts affected are those representing securities issued by the company. If a restatement of certain asset balances is also involved, the procedure is more aptly labeled an *accounting* or *quasi-reorganization*. As a general rule, an acceptable solution requires the application of a general knowledge of financial and accounting principles rather than of special statement forms.

In the typical case, rather detailed financial and accounting data describing the condition of the given business are given in the problem. Some combination of the following circumstances is usually present:

1. Dividends in arrears on cumulative shares.
2. Two or more classes of share capital, one class clearly senior or preferred in relation to the common stock.
3. One or more issues of notes or bonds outstanding, perhaps with an interest default existing or imminent.
4. Operating losses, past and perhaps prospective.
5. Overvalued properties.
6. A deficit (debit balance in Retained Earnings).

Typical Entries. The adjusting entries required to give effect to the proposed plan of reorganization usually involve some combination of the following types of entries:

1. Asset values are written down. The amount of the write-down will be specified by the problem data. The candidate should charge the write-down to retained earnings—irrespective of whether the Retained Earnings account has or will have a debit balance.

2. After all losses or write-downs have been recognized, if the Retained Earnings account has a debit balance, it may be transferred by journal entry to any paid-in surplus previously existing or created by the reorganization. It is improper to increase a credit balance in Retained Earnings by a financial or accounting reorganization, but it is acceptable to wipe out a deficit and start the post-reorganization period with a zero balance in Retained Earnings. If a deficit has been transferred to paid-in surplus at the time of the reorganization, it is important for the candidate to remember that any subsequent Retained Earnings balance presented on the balance sheet must be dated to disclose that it has arisen since the date of the reorganization. For example,

Retained earnings, since January 1, 19X1 $845,000

3. Additional shares of stock may be issued, either of a new class or from previously authorized unissued shares. The shares may be issued in exchange for other shares, or perhaps exchanged for existing indebtedness. For instance, bondholders may agree to accept stock in lieu of back interest. In some cases a stockholder group may agree to subscribe to additional shares in order to provide new money for the corporation. In preparing the accounting entries to reflect any of the foregoing situations, the candidate's principal concern will be to follow carefully the rather detailed plan as described in the Examination question. As a general rule, the problem instructions leave little to the candidate's judgment. However, there are a few basic points relating to the issuance of capital shares on which the problem may remain silent. In these instances, the candidate is expected to apply generally accepted accounting principles. These principles include:

a. A careful distinction must be maintained in the accounts between Paid-In Surplus and Retained Earnings. For example, if the shareholders of $25 par value stock agree to exchange their shares on a basis of three shares of a new class of stock having a $5 stated value for each share of old, the amount of stated or legal capital released by the exchange must be credited to Paid-In Surplus, not Retained Earnings. A sample entry follows:

$25 par value stock	25	
$5 stated value stock		15
Paid-in surplus		10
Exchange of $25 par value stock for $5 stated value on a basis of 3 new shares for 1 old.		

Similarly, if an accrued interest liability is settled by an issuance of capital shares, if the aggregate par or stated value of shares issued is less than the amount of the interest accrual eliminated, the credit should be assigned to Paid-In Surplus. On the other hand, if the interest accrual is less than the aggregate par or stated value of the shares issued, the debit may be assigned to Retained Earnings on the theory that the difference represents additional consideration for surrendering a creditor position for a less preferred status.

Retained earnings	1,000	
Accrued interest payable	9,000	
Common stock, $5 stated value		10,000
Issuance of shares in settlement of interest accrual.		

In some instances, surrounding circumstances might suggest that a stock discount account should receive the debit.

b. If a creditor group has agreed to relinquish its preferred position by exchanging bonds or notes for stock, it is important that the accounting entries reflecting the exchange eliminate all contra and adjunct accounts associated with the main liability account. In other words, any bond premium or bond discount must be eliminated proportionately to the par value of the bonds exchanged. A sample entry follows:

Bonds payable	100,000	
Bond discount		800
Preferred stock, $5 stated value		90,000
Paid-in surplus		9,200
To reflect presentation of company's bonds in exchange for preferred stock pursuant to reorganization plan.		

Disclosure. Many candidates weaken an otherwise acceptable solution by failing to recognize the importance of disclosure in reorganization situations. This matter is particularly significant if the problem calls for the presentation of financial statements or some portion of the financial statements; for example, the Stockholders' Equity section. In many instances, one or more footnotes may be required in order to disclose pertinent information about the changes produced by the reorganization.

Without these disclosures, a statement user would not understand or appreciate the significance of the reorganization. An excellent example of the type of information that should be disclosed in a thoroughly acceptable solution is provided by reference to a problem from an old CPA Examination. In that problem, the candidate was asked to submit a statement of the stockholders' equity of the Fayetteville Company showing the condition as it would exist on January 1 if the reorganization plan were made effective as of that date. The plan included a provision for the settlement of dividends in arrears by the payment of $360,750 cash and the issuance of 216,450 shares of "B" stock having a par value of $10 per share. A solution would be incomplete if it failed to disclose that "The 'B' shares are nonvoting and are not entitled to dividends. They are redeemable at $20 per share and entitled to $20 per share after preferred but prior to common in liquidation." Similarly, a solution would be incomplete if the following footnote disclosure were omitted:

> The liquidating preference of the preferred stock when added to the liquidating value of the class "B" stock creates a deficiency with respect to the common stock amounting to $1,556,457.

The Fayetteville Company problem may be used as a basis for the reminder that a corporate Stockholders' Equity section is incomplete if the account titles are not supplemented by information regarding the par or stated value of capital stock, the number of shares authorized and outstanding, the dividend rate, and the preference with respect to dividends and liquidation. It is quite evident that a solution to the Fayetteville Company problem would lose points if the preferred stock were listed in the Stockholders' Equity section as follows:

Preferred stock	$3,848,000

A more acceptable listing would be:

$3 Cumulative preferred stock—par value, $40. Entitled to $50 per share on liquidation, redeemable at $55 per share. 96,200 shares outstanding	$3,848,000

Concluding Note. In the area of reorganization problems, the writer is inclined to venture the opinion that unsatisfactory solutions to problems of this type are probably the result of a failure on the part of the candidate to follow the problem data with sufficient care, rather than a lack of accounting background. Inadequate attention to details of form and disclosure is the second most important source of penalty.

Last, and to repeat, do not forget to date any subsequent retained earnings.

Price-Level Changes and Supplementary Statements

A Basic Assumption of Accounting. Accounting uses the dollar as its unit of measurement and assumes that fluctuations in the dollar's purchasing power will be too insignificant to undermine its usefulness as a unit of measurement. During certain periods this assumption has squared substantially with reality. But it is also true that during other periods the purchasing power of the dollar has changed significantly. Nevertheless, during these periods of change, accounting regarded all dollars as though they were the same size, and it continues to regard as identical all dollars appearing in the financial statements.

Although financial statements show dollars of "mixed and varying dimensions," it is doubtful whether statement users make any allowances therefor. The consequences and repercussions flowing from the use of an unstable dollar in the accounting process are not fully known or understood. This situation is potentially dangerous because financial statements may prove to be misleading or of little value, and it may have contributed to the concern of the Accounting Principles Board when it went on record in 1961 stating "that the assumption in accounting that fluctuations in the value of the dollar may be ignored is unrealistic" and directed that research be undertaken to study the problem. This resulted in the 1963 publication of *Reporting the Effects of Price-level Changes*,[2] which in turn probably resulted in the issuance of APB Statement No. 3. That statement reaffirmed an earlier position of the Committee on Accounting Procedure which supported the use of supplementary financial schedules (ARB No. 43, Chapter 9A) and expanded that support to encompass price-level-adjusted financial statements, but only as supplementary information. The APB made its belief clear that general price-level information is not required at this time (June, 1969) to achieve a fair presentation of financial position and results of operations.

Supplementary Financial Statements. From the foregoing discussion it seems evident that, if an accountant desires to give recognition to the effects of changes in the size of the dollar on financial statements, he may use supplementary statements for the purpose. That is, such price-level-adjusted statements (in which historical dollars are converted to current dollars) cannot replace or be a substitute for conventional financial statements. The supplementary statements would serve as companions to the conventional financial statements, which would continue to be prepared in the usual fashion.

[2] Accounting Research Study No. 6 authored by the Staff of the Accounting Research Division of the AICPA.

Supplementary statements are technically feasible. Enough research studies have been made to support this conclusion. It is generally agreed that the index used for conversion purposes should be a general price index designed to measure the overall purchasing power of the dollar. According to the accounting research study, which investigated this matter in considerable depth, at least one such index is now available (the GNP implicit price deflator).

The use of supplementary statements would:

1. Leave the conventional financial statements and accounting principles undisturbed.
2. Disclose the effects of changes in the price level on the financial position and results of operations of business enterprises.

The use of supplementary statements would *not:*

1. Provide information on replacement costs or current values.
2. Resolve any questions, at least for some time, about the need for a revision of some basic accounting concepts because of the instability of the dollar.
3. Represent a departure from the cost basis of accounting (costs would continue to be used but would be stated in dollars of uniform size).

Preparation of Supplementary Statements Demonstrated. Pertinent data about Vision Company and the period since its incorporation are presented below.

Year	*Events*	*Price Index*
19X0	Company organized and facilities rented	100
19X1	$21,000 of equipment purchased and $6,000 bank loan negotiated	105
19X2		108
19X3	Ending inventory was $5,500	110
19X4	$3,000 of additional equipment purchased	120
19X5	Bank loan partially retired on December 31, by special permission of the bank	126

These index numbers are an annual series in contrast to a monthly or quarterly series. If available, index numbers relating to shorter periods offer the advantage of introducing greater refinement in the adjusted data. However, such refinement would not usually be necessary under conditions of generally "creeping" inflation, which typified the decade preceding the time of this writing.

Some conventional financial statements for the company are given next.

VISION COMPANY

Comparative Income Statement
For 19X4 and 19X5

	19X4		19X5	
Sales		$48,000		$50,000
Cost of sales	$30,000		$32,000	
Depreciation (10% per year)	2,400		2,400	
Other expenses (including interest and taxes)	12,000	44,400	12,600	47,000
Net income		$ 3,600		$ 3,000

VISION COMPANY

Comparative Balance Sheet
For 19X4 and 19X5

Assets	19X4		19X5	
Current assets:				
Cash	$ 5,000		$ 4,000	
Current receivables	12,600		15,000	
Inventory (at cost on *fifo* basis)	6,000	$23,600	8,000	$27,000
Fixed assets:				
Equipment	$24,000		$24,000	
Less: Accumulated depreciation	8,700	15,300	11,100	12,900
		$38,900		$39,900
Liabilities and Stockholders' Equity				
Current liabilities:				
Current payables		$ 4,000		$ 5,000
Long-term liabilities:				
Bank loan		6,000		4,000
Stockholders' equity:				
Capital stock	$20,000		$20,000	
Retained earnings	8,900	28,900	10,900	30,900
		$38,900		$39,900

VISION COMPANY

Statement of Retained Earnings
For the Year Ended December 31, 19X5

Retained earnings, December 31, 19X4	$ 8,900
Net income	3,000
Total	$11,900
Dividends	1,000
Retained earnings, December 31, 19X5	$10,900

The following schedules show the conversions required for supplementary statements in order that all balances shown thereon will be stated in uniform, December 31, 19X5, dollars. In order to convert old dollars into current dollars, a conversion ratio is used; the index number for the current year-end is the numerator and the index number for the year with which the dollars being converted are identified is the denominator. Assume that the price level advanced 5% early in 19X5, carrying the index to 126, and remained steady thereafter.

19X5 Account Balances Converted to Current Dollars

		Conversion Ratio	*December 31, 19X5 Dollars*
Balances stated in 19X0 dollars:			
Capital stock	$20,000	126/100	$25,200
Balances stated in 19X1 dollars:			
Equipment—original acquisition	$21,000	126/105	$25,200
Accumulated depreciation—5 years	10,500	126/105	12,600
Depreciation for 19X5 (10%)	2,100	126/105	2,520
Although the bank loan originated in 19X1, no conversion is required for the balance outstanding at the end of the current period. Because the loan is a fixed dollar obligation, its account balance automatically shows the number of current dollars required to satisfy the debt.			
Balances stated in 19X4 dollars:			
Equipment—additional acquisition	$ 3,000	126/120	$3,150
Accumulated depreciation thereon—2 years	600	126/120	630
Depreciation on addition for 19X5 (10%)	300	126/120	315
Beginning inventory portion of cost of sales	6,000	126/120	6,300

Balances stated in 19X5 (current) dollars (no conversion required):

Cash		$ 4,000
Current receivables		15,000
Inventory		8,000
Current payables		5,000
Bank loan		4,000
Sales		50,000
Cost of Sales	$32,000	
Less: Beginning inventory element converted above	6,000	
Balance, from 19X5 purchases		26,000
Other expenses		12,600
Dividends		1,000

19X4 ACCOUNT BALANCES
CONVERTED TO CURRENT DOLLARS

		Conversion Ratio	*December 31, 19X5 Dollars*
Balances stated in 19X0 dollars:			
Capital stock	$20,000	126/100	$25,200
Balances stated in 19X1 dollars:			
Equipment—original acquisition	$21,000	126/105	$25,200
Accumulated depreciation—4 years	8,400	126/105	10,080
Depreciation for 19X4	2,100	126/105	2,520
Balances stated in 19X3 dollars:			
Beginning inventory portion of cost of sales	$ 5,500	126/110	$ 6,300
Balances stated in 19X4 dollars:			
Cash	$ 5,000	126/120	$ 5,250
Current receivables	12,600	126/120	13,230
Inventory	6,000	126/120	6,300
Equipment—additional acquisition	3,000	126/120	3,150
Accumulated depreciation thereon—1 year	300	126/120	315
Depreciation on addition for 19X4 (10%)	300	126/120	315
Current payables	4,000	126/120	4,200
Bank loan	6,000	126/120	6,300
Sales	48,000	126/120	50,400
Cost of sales $30,000			
Less: Beginning inventory element converted above 5,500			
Balance, from 19X4 purchases	24,500	126/120	25,725
Other expenses	12,000	126/120	12,600

The dollars in several of the accounts originated in more than one year, and must be combined as indicated by the following groupings.

	Dollars		
	19X1	*19X4*	*19X5*
Equipment:			
Original acquisition	$21,000		$25,200
Addition		$ 3,000	3,150
Total			$28,350
Accumulated depreciation—19X4:			
On original acquisition	$ 8,400		$10,080
On addition		$ 300	315
Total			$10,395
Accumulated depreciation—19X5:			
On original acquisition	$10,500		$12,600
On addition		$ 600	630
Total			$13,230
Depreciation expense:			
On original acquisition	$ 2,100		$ 2,520
On addition		$ 300	315
Total			$ 2,835
Cost of sales—19X4:			
From beginning inventory	$ 5,500		$ 6,300
From purchases		$24,500	25,725
Total			$32,025
Cost of sales—19X5:			
From beginning inventory		$ 6,000	$ 6,300
From purchases			26,000
Total			$32,300

The data in the 19X5 Dollars column of the above conversion schedules have been used to prepare the following supplementary financial statements. The Retained Earnings, renamed "Balance of Stockholders' Equity" in the supplementary statements, is the balancing figure for the supplementary balance sheet. Note also that the phrase "Capital Invested by Stockholders" has been substituted for "Capital Stock" in the supplementary balance sheet.

VISION COMPANY

Supplementary Comparative Income Statement
In Current Dollars
For 19X4 and 19X5

	19X4		*19X5*	
Sales		$50,400		$50,000
Cost of sales	$32,025		$32,300	
Depreciation	2,835		2,835	
Other expenses	12,600	47,460	12,600	47,735
Net income		$ 2,940		$ 2,265

VISION COMPANY

Supplementary Comparative Balance Sheet
In Current Dollars
December 31, 19X4 and 19X5

Assets	*19X4*		*19X5*	
Current assets:				
Cash	$ 5,250		$ 4,000	
Current receivables	13,230		15,000	
Inventory	6,300	$24,780	8,000	$27,000
Fixed assets:				
Equipment	$28,350		$28,350	
Less: Accumulated depreciation	10,395	17,955	13,230	15,120
		$42,735		$42,120
Liabilities and Stockholders' Equity				
Current liabilities:				
Current payables		$ 4,200		$ 5,000
Long-term liabilities:				
Bank loan		6,300		4,000
Stockholders' equity:				
Capital investment by stockholders	$25,200		$25,200	
Balance of stockholders' equity	7,035	32,235	7,920	33,120
		$42,735		$42,120

VISION COMPANY

STATEMENT OF CHANGES IN BALANCE OF STOCKHOLDERS' EQUITY
IN CURRENT DOLLARS
FOR THE YEAR ENDED DECEMBER 31, 19X5

Balance of stockholders' equity, December 31, 19X4, per above		$7,035
Net income for 19X5—per supplementary statement	$2,265	
Less: Price-level adjustment for monetary items	380	1,885
Total		$8,920
Deduct:		
Dividends		1,000
Balance of stockholders' equity, December 31, 19X5, per above		$7,920

Price-Level Adjustment of Monetary Items. Monetary items consist of cash, receivables, and liabilities. When monetary assets are held during a period of rising prices, the holder suffers a loss in purchasing power. A gain in purchasing power is experienced when monetary assets are held during a period of declining prices. Last year Vision Company had a cash balance of $5,000 when the general price index was 120. Early in the current year (19X5), the price level increased 5%, which carried the index to 126. A cash balance of $5,000 × 1.05, or $5,250, is required in 19X5 to equal the purchasing power of last year's cash balance of $5,000. By holding cash, the company incurred a loss in purchasing power in the amount of 250 current dollars. Similarly, a purchasing power loss of $630 has resulted from the $12,600 of current receivables held by the company.

Purchasing power gains and losses can also arise from liabilities. Less purchasing power is required to settle a liability incurred when the price level was lower. In the case of Vision Company, less purchasing power is required in 19X5 to settle the liabilities carried over from 19X4.

In the Vision Company illustration, a net purchasing power loss of $380 has resulted from the 5% increase in the price level at the beginning of the current year (19X5). This appeared in the supplementary statement reporting the changes that have occurred in the stockholders' equity during the current year. The $380 amount is the difference between the prior-year book balances of the monetary items and their converted balances, as follows:

	19X4 Book Balances		*Conversion*	*Dec. 31, 19X5*	
	Debit	*Credit*	*Ratio*	*Dollars*	*Difference*
Monetary items:					
Cash	$ 5,000		126/120	$ 5,250	$250 loss
Current receivables	12,600			13,230	630 loss
Current payables		$4,000		4,200	200 gain
Bank loan		6,000		6,300	300 gain
Net loss					$380

To complete the determination of the purchasing power gain or loss, both the beginning of year amount of net monetary items and all the year's transactions (which involved inflows and outflows of monetary assets and liabilities) must be converted into year-end dollar terms. The difference between the year-end balance thus computed and the actual year-end amount of net monetary items measures the gain or loss. This is illustrated below, using Vision Company data:

		Conversion Ratio	*December 31, 19X5 Dollars*
Net monetary items, December 31, 19X4	$ 7,600	126/120	$ 7,980
Add: Sales	50,000	126/126	50,000
Total	$57,600		$57,980
Deduct:			
Purchases	$34,000	126/126	$47,600
Other expenses	12,600		
Dividends	1,000		
Total	$47,600		$47,600
Net monetary items, December 31, 19X5	$10,000		$10,380
Deduct unadjusted balance, per above			10,000
Purchasing power loss			$ 380

Sales, purchases, other expenses, and dividends are assumed to have been cash (or other monetary item) transactions. Their conversion ratio is 126:126 in this illustration because the price level is assumed to have increased early in the year and then held steady. The Skadden Company problem, included below, illustrates this approach when the price level increases steadily during the year.

Accountants agree that gains and losses on monetary items should be disclosed if supplementary statements are prepared, but differences of opinion exist concerning the proper method of disclosure. Those accountants who view the primary purpose of supplementary statements as being to set forth all amounts in the conventional statements in dollars of uniform size in order to offset the unreality of the assumption regarding the stability of the dollar, see no reason to include gains or losses in purchasing power as elements in arriving at net income. Such inclusion would bring a new factor into the income-measurement process, one not now included among those accounting concepts concerned with a cost-basis approach to income measurement.

The alternative view has the support of the APB. In its Statement No. 3 it "concluded that these gains and losses should be recognized as part of the net income of the period in which the general price level changes."

liabilities and changes in the purchasing power of the dollar

The following paragraphs are included for those candidates who might welcome some additional exposure to the reasoning underlying the handling of liabilities in price-level-adjusted statements.

Although the dollar amount for a given liability is fixed, it does not follow that a comparison such as that presented next is the most meaningful comparison that can be made.

	19XX	*19X5*
Long-term loan	$50,000	$50,000

The comparison implies that nothing affecting the loan has happened between 19XX and 19X5 (19X5 being the current year). But if the general price level has increased during this period (causing the purchasing power of the dollar to decrease), something *has* happened; the purchasing power of the dollars borrowed was greater than the purchasing power of the dollars that would be required to repay the loan. Normally the borrower spends the money borrowed and hence uses the amount of purchasing power provided by the loan. When the loan matures, the borrower is committed to repay the same number of dollars borrowed, not the same amount of purchasing power. Thus during a period of rising prices it generally works out that creditors will have lost purchasing power and debtors will have gained purchasing power. Inflation tends to be less harmful financially to those in debt because they can pay back money borrowed with "cheaper" dollars; that is, with dollars of smaller size in terms of purchasing power. It can be said that an increase in the price level reduces outstanding liabilities, not in terms of dollars, but in terms of purchasing power.

Consider the preceding long-term loan under the assumption that the price level had increased 60% between 19XX and 19X5. Although $50,000 must be repaid, the effective reduction in the liability that has occurred is not disclosed by a comparison using unadjusted data. If the 19XX liability amount and the 19X5 liability amount are stated in dollars of the same size, the comparison becomes more meaningful. The 19X5 amount for the liability is already stated in current dollars. The 19XX amount is out of date and is the amount that should be converted to improve comparability.

	19XX	*19X5*	*Percentage Decrease*
Unadjusted Data:			
Long-term loan	$50,000	$50,000	–0–
Adjusted Data:			
Long-term loan stated in 19X5 dollars *	$80,000	$50,000	37.5%

* 50,000 19XX dollars $\times \frac{160}{100}$ = 80,000 19X5 dollars.

Using the adjusted data, the comparison indicates that in 19XX the size of the loan was equivalent to 80,000 19X5 dollars. Actually the burden associated with the long-term debt has declined by about 37.5% between 19XX and 19X5. This reduction is revealed by the comparison using the adjusted data.

Illustrative CPA Problem. A problem from the May, 1970, Examination and an unofficial solution are offered as an indication of the relevance of this topic for CPA candidates.

Problem: Skadden, Inc., a retailer, was organized during 1966. Skadden's management has decided to supplement its December 31, 1969, historical dollar financial statements with general price-level financial statements. The following general ledger trial balance (historical dollar) and additional information have been furnished:

SKADDEN, INC.

TRIAL BALANCE
DECEMBER 31, 1969

	Debit	*Credit*
Cash and receivables (net)	$ 540,000	
Marketable securities (common stock)	400,000	
Inventory	440,000	
Equipment	650,000	
Equipment—Accumulated depreciation		$ 164,000
Accounts payable		300,000
6% first mortgage bonds, due 1987		500,000
Common stock, $10 par		1,000,000
Retained earnings, December 31, 1968	46,000	
Sales		1,900,000
Cost of sales	1,508,000	
Depreciation	65,000	
Other operating expenses and interest	215,000	
	$3,864,000	$3,864,000

1. Monetary assets (cash and receivables) exceeded monetary liabilities (accounts payable and bonds payable) by $445,000 at December 31, 1968. The amounts of monetary items are fixed in terms of numbers of dollars regardless of changes in specific prices or in the general price level.

2. Purchases ($1,840,000 in 1969) and sales are made uniformly throughout the year.

3. Depreciation is computed on a straight-line basis, with a full year's depreciation being taken in the year of acquisition and none in the year of retirement. The depreciation rate is 10% and no salvage value is anticipated. Acquisitions and retirements have been made fairly evenly over each year and the retirements in 1969 consisted of assets purchased during 1967 which were scrapped. An analysis of the equipment account reveals the following:

Year	*Beginning Balance*	*Additions*	*Retirements*	*Ending Balance*
1967	—	$550,000	—	$550,000
1968	$550,000	10,000	—	560,000
1969	560,000	150,000	$60,000	650,000

4. The bonds were issued in 1967 and the marketable securities were purchased fairly evenly over 1969. Other operating expenses and interest are assumed to be incurred evenly throughout the year.

5. Assume that Gross National Product Implicit Price Deflators (1958 = 100) were as follows:

Annual Averages		*Index*	*Conversion Factors (1969 4th Qtr. = 1.000)*
1966		113.9	1.128
1967		116.8	1.100
1968		121.8	1.055
1969		126.7	1.014
Quarterly Averages			
1968	4th	123.5	1.040
1969	1st	124.9	1.029
	2nd	126.1	1.019
	3rd	127.3	1.009
	4th	128.5	1.000

Required:

a. Prepare a schedule to convert the Equipment account balance at December 31, 1969, from historical cost to general price-level-adjusted dollars.

b. Prepare a schedule to analyze in historical dollars the Equipment—Accumulated Depreciation account for the year 1969.

c. Prepare a schedule to analyze in general price-level dollars the Equipment—Accumulated Depreciation account for the year 1969.

d. Prepare a schedule to compute Skadden, Inc.'s general price-level gain or loss on its net holdings of monetary assets for 1969 (ignore income tax implications). The schedule should give consideration to appropriate items on or related to the balance sheet and income statement.

Solution:

a.

SKADDEN, INC.

SCHEDULE TO ANALYZE EQUIPMENT FOR GENERAL PRICE–LEVEL RESTATEMENT
DECEMBER 31, 1969

Year Acquired	*Amount (Historical)*	*Conversion Factor*	*Amount (General Price-Level)*
1967	$490,000	1.100	$539,000
1968	10,000	1.055	10,550
1969	150,000	1.014	152,100
	$650,000		$701,650

b.

SKADDEN, INC.

SCHEDULE TO ANALYZE EQUIPMENT—
ACCUMULATED DEPRECIATION
(HISTORICAL DOLLARS)
FOR THE YEAR 1969

Year Assets Acquired	*Balance 12/31/68*	*Depreciation for 1969*	*Retirements in 1969*	*Balance 12/31/69*
1967	$110,000	$49,000	$12,000	$147,000
1968	1,000	1,000		2,000
1969		15,000		15,000
	$111,000	$65,000	$12,000	$164,000

c.

SKADDEN, INC.

SCHEDULE TO ANALYZE EQUIPMENT—
ACCUMULATED DEPRECIATION
(GENERAL PRICE-LEVEL DOLLARS)
FOR THE YEAR 1969

Year Assets Acquired	*Conversion Factor*	*Balance 12/31/68*	*Depreciation*	*Retirement*	*Balance 12/31/69*
1967	1.100	$121,000	$53,900	$13,200	$161,700
1968	1.055	1,055	1,055		2,110
1969	1.014		15,210		15,210
		$122,055	$70,165	$13,200	$179,020

d.

SKADDEN, INC.

Schedule to Compute General Price–Level Gain or Loss For 1969

	12/31/68			*12/31/69*
	Historical	*Conversion Factor*	*Restated to 12/31/69 Dollars*	*Historical (stated in 12/31/69 Dollars)*
Net monetary items:				
Cash and receivables				$ 540,000
Accounts payable				(300,000)
Bonds payable				(500,000)
Net	$ 445,000	1.040	$462,800	$ (260,000)

			Restated to 12/31/69 Dollars
General price-level gain or loss			
Net monetary items—12/31/68	$ 445,000	1.040	$ 462,800
Add: Sales	1,900,000	1.014	1,926,600
	2,345,000		2,389,400
Deduct:			
Purchases	1,840,000		
Operating expenses and interest	215,000		
Purchase of marketable securities	400,000		
Acquisitions of equipment	150,000		
	2,605,000	1.014	2,641,470
Net monetary items—historical	$ (260,000)		
Net monetary items—historical —restated—12/31/69			(252,070)
Net monetary items—12/31/69 (as above)			(260,000)
General price-level loss			$ (7,930)

8
law

Robert L. Black

Introduction

A study of recent Examinations in Business Law (Commercial Law) of the Uniform Certified Public Accountant Examinations reveals certain patterns of structure and content. Assuming that these patterns will continue to be followed, helpful predictions can be made. First, candidates can expect that this test will be administered for three and one-half hours on the morning of the last day (Friday) and that it will contain eight major questions. Of these, three should be objective in nature, and consist of thirty to sixty true–false questions each. The grade for the objective questions is determined by deducting a penalty for incorrect answers from the candidate's total of correct ones. Omitted answers are not considered to be incorrect. Thus outright guessing is discouraged. The remaining five questions should require an essay answer that: defines a legal term (such as listing the requirements of a holder in due course), states a rule of law, or provides the solution to issues raised by a hypothetical fact situation. These five essay questions are usually divided into several parts. It is recommended that all the parts be read and understood before the candidate begins to write his answers to them. Often some parts give useful clues to the answers to others. In addition, one may find that in answering part "a", he has included information required in part "b". A complete reading might save valuable time by preventing unnecessary repetition. The answer to a hypothetical essay question should contain a conclusion, statements of the appropriate rules of law *and* their exceptions, as well as an explanation of how these rules were applied to the facts to reach the conclusion. The knowledge required to answer the objective questions correctly is the same as that needed for the essay ones.

At least six, probably seven, and possibly all eight of the major questions are likely to be selected from the areas of law listed below. Therefore, a thorough familiarity with these is essential to obtaining a passing score for the law section.

Contracts	Accountants' Legal Obligations
Agency	Sales and Bailments
Partnerships	Commercial Paper
Corporations	Security Devices and Suretyship
Insurance	Bankruptcy

Questions involving other business law topics, such as Wills, Estates, Trusts, Personal Property, Real Property, Mortgages, Patents, and Copyrights and Trademarks, also have appeared on the Examination, but with much less frequency.

In his review, the candidate should concentrate on learning and understanding the rules that are applicable in the majority of jurisdictions. These are governed by the common law in some areas of law and by statutes which have been enacted by most states in others. Particularly important are the state Uniform Acts, mainly the Uniform Commercial Code and the Uniform Partnership Act. Of course, the federal Bankruptcy Act has nationwide application. In general, minority rules can be disregarded, except those which have been adopted by a substantial number of states.

Besides general provisions, the Uniform Commercial Code (referred to here as the "Code" or "UCC") contains articles on Sales, Commercial Paper, Bank Deposits and Collections, Letters of Credit, Bulk Transfers, Documents of Title (Warehouse Receipts, Bills of Lading, and others), Investment Securities, and Secured Transactions. However, if the common law has not been changed by the Code in these areas, it remains applicable. In addition to dealing with specialized matters relating to the foregoing subjects, the Code modifies some of the principles of *general* contract law. It must be emphasized that these particular changes apply *only* to contracts involving the sale of goods, wares, or merchandise, or in other words, tangible personal property. The candidate, therefore, must acquire a knowledge of two different rules of general contract law in some instances—that which applies when the contract is for a sale of goods and that which is applicable to all other contracts, such as those dealing with construction, personal services, and sales of real estate. These situations are discussed in the sections on contracts immediately following. In a few cases, we shall see that the Code changes apply only if one or both of the parties to the sale are merchants in goods of the kind being sold.

This chapter of the *Manual* attempts to set forth those principles of law with which candidates should be familiar. However, it must be understood that, in the space allotted, it is impossible to cover all matters that might be raised on a given examination.

Contracts

1. Definition. A contract is an agreement that is enforceable in law. The requirements for a valid contract are: agreement (offer and acceptance), consideration, two or more competent parties, and a legal purpose or object. The first step in the formation of a contract consists of the making of an offer or proposition by one of the parties, who is then called the *offeror.* The party to whom the offer is made is called the *offeree.* The agreement takes place when the offeree accepts the offer.

agreement

2. Nature of Offer. An offer is a proposal that is communicated to the offeree by the offeror. It is not effective until the offeree has obtained knowledge of it from the offeror or through the agent he has selected. A communication started by the offeror through certain channels but stopped prior to its receipt is not effective as an offer merely because the offeree learns of its terms indirectly by some unauthorized means.

An offer must be definite; that is, it must state clearly enough what the offeror is willing to do and what he is asking the offeree to do in exchange. It must also definitely show a present contractual intent, or willingness to do business with the offeree on the terms stated. An advertisement, circular letter, or catalog usually is written in a way that suggests no present willingness to deal with those receiving it or learning of it. These communications are also deficient as offers in most cases because they do not specify the quantity available to each person, thus making the terms indefinite. Much of this preliminary material is circulated merely for the purpose of inducing offers. However, if the terms of an advertisement are clearly worded, and the notice shows a willingness on the part of the person inserting it to deal with any member of the public who learns of it, it may constitute an offer.

A mere quotation of price is not an offer, since it indicates no willingness to deal on the terms quoted. Suppose that B writes to S inquiring the price of 5000 bushels of grade A Grimes Golden apples. In reply he receives a telegram which reads as follows: "Price $1.80 a bushel." No offer has been made, since S merely quoted the current price of apples. He did not say he had any for sale or that he was willing to sell them to B. If B had asked S for a price on 5000 bushels that he was willing to deliver to B within ten days, and the above telegram had been received, an offer would have been made by S. Under such circumstances, the telegram of S would have been more than a mere quotation of price because it was in response to B's invitation for an offer.

Bids made at an auction or on construction work are offers rather than acts of acceptance. The person submitting the goods for sale or asking for the construction work makes no offer and, as a consequence, is free to accept one of the bids or to reject them all.

3. Duration of Offer. Unless the terms of an offer set a limit on its duration, the offer remains open for a reasonable time, after which it is said to *lapse*. The reasonableness of the time is determined by such matters as the nature of the subject matter, the means of communication used in transmitting the offer, and the past dealings between the parties. The death or adjudged insanity of either the offeror or the offeree causes an offer to lapse immediately. In cases of lapse, the offer terminates automatically, and no notice is required.

An offer can be withdrawn or revoked by the offeror at any time prior to its acceptance. Although in general revocation is possible even though the offeror promised to hold the offer open for a given period, a revocation is not effective until it has been received by the offeree. No knowledge of the contents of a letter of revocation is required. But until the revocation has arrived at a place where the offeree normally receives mail, the offeree is free to accept—unless, of course, he has had information that the offeror no longer intends to keep his offer open. Indirect knowledge of revocation also terminates an offer.

The rejection of an offer by the offeree causes the offer to terminate. The offeree may not thereafter change his mind and accept. Any attempt at acceptance after a rejection amounts to a new offer on the part of the original offeree. The rejection does not become operative until it is received by the offeror. Thus it is possible for a person who has mailed a letter of rejection to change his mind and send an acceptance. If the acceptance becomes effective before the rejection reaches the offeror, a contract has been formed. However, if the offeror detrimentally relies on the rejection before he learns of the acceptance, equity would prevent or estop the offeree from asserting his acceptance and enforcing the agreement.

4. Irrevocable Offers. Although in most cases an offer can be withdrawn in spite of the fact that the offeror has promised to keep it open, there are two important situations in which such an offer is irrevocable. In the first case, the offeror has entered into an *option contract* with the offeree. An option contract is an enforceable agreement whereby the offeror surrenders his right to withdraw for an agreed period of time in exchange for some consideration furnished by the offeree. Often this consideration is a promise to pay or the payment of money. An option expires at the close of the period unless it has been accepted or extended by a new agreement. The death or adjudged insanity of the offeror in an option contract does not cause the offer to lapse. It remains open for the agreed period, with the burden of carrying out the agreement resting on the offeror's estate in case the offer is accepted after death, or on his conservator in the event of acceptance following insanity.

Offers normally are not assignable, for the named offeree is the only person who can accept. An option contract can be assigned, however, subject to the same conditions that apply to assignments generally.

The second case in which an offer is irrevocable is governed by the UCC, and therefore can arise only when it involves a sale of tangible personal property or goods. The Code provides that a firm offer to buy or sell goods (i.e., an offer that gives the assurance that it will be held open) is irrevocable without consideration or payment under certain circumstances. The firm offer must be made by a merchant in writing and signed by the maker. If it is on a form supplied by the offeree, it must be signed separately. The period of irrevocability will not be enforceable beyond three months. If a firm offer does not state a time period, it must be held open for a reasonable time.

5. *Acceptance.* What constitutes an acceptance depends on whether the offer in question is unilateral or bilateral. A *unilateral* offer is worded so that it requires the *performance* of certain acts as its acceptance, in exchange for a promise by the offeror. No contract exists until completion by the offeree of all the acts requested, and the offer can be withdrawn at any time before substantial performance of them. If there is a revocation by the offeror after partial completion, the offeree is entitled to no compensation unless the offeror has received some benefit. In such a case, the offeror is not bound to a contract but is required as a matter of law to pay the offeree the reasonable value of the benefit. If the offer is ambiguous, the courts tend to construe it as bilateral.

A *bilateral* offer is worded so that it requires a *promise* to perform certain acts as its acceptance, in exchange for a promise by the offeror. Any language or other conduct of the offeree which clearly indicates to the offeror the former's willingness to be bound by the terms of a bilateral offer constitutes an acceptance. It may consist of the delivery of a signed writing, a nod of the head, or a handclasp. However, the words or conduct used must be unambiguous. Generally, mere silence does not qualify as an acceptance. Even though the offer suggests that silence shall be considered an acceptance, the offeror cannot impose on the offeree the burden of taking some action in order to avoid a contractual relationship. There are two exceptions to this rule. First, if two parties through a long course of dealing have treated silence as an acceptance, the courts, in a later case, will reach the same result. Second, if a seller has sent out a solicitor to obtain orders for merchandise and a buyer submits an order which is subject to approval at the office of the seller, continued silence by the seller for a long period of time may be taken by the purchaser as approval. The seller who fails to reject the buyer's solicited order within a reasonable time is deemed to have accepted it.

Under the Code, when a person orders goods for current shipment, he invites the acceptance of the seller either by the seller's prompt promise to ship the goods or by their current shipment. Thus such an order may be treated as either a unilateral or bilateral offer at the option of the seller.

An acceptance must conform to the terms of the offer. An offeree who adds new terms or changes the original ones in his acceptance makes, in effect, a counteroffer, which the original offeror is free to accept or reject. This counteroffer, unless worded to indicate otherwise, acts as a rejection of the original offer, which cannot thereafter be accepted. A mere request by the offeree for additional information is not considered a counteroffer and has no effect on the original offer.

Under the Code, an expression of acceptance of an offer to buy or sell goods creates a contract and is not a rejection even though it states different or additional terms. (However, this is not the result if the acceptance is expressly conditioned on the inclusion of the changed provisions.) Generally, the parties are bound according to the original offer, unless the offeror agrees to incorporate the changes. If the agreement is between merchants, though, *minor* changes in the acceptance become part of the contract of sale unless: the offer expressly limited acceptance to its terms or the offeror gives notice of his objection to the changes within a reasonable time after learning of them. In these two cases the parties still have a contract, but on the terms originally proposed by the offeror. *Major* changes in the acceptance are ignored.

Printed material on identification tickets received by persons who have left items for repair or storage does not form part of the contract of bailment unless it is called to the attention of the bailor at the time possession of the goods is surrendered by him. Similarly, printed material on the back of a contract is not a part of it unless incorporated by some language in the body of the instrument.

6. *Time Acceptance Effective.* The acceptance of a *unilateral* offer is effective when performance of the acts requested by the offeror have taken place. No notice to the offeror is required.

The acceptance of a *bilateral* offer is effective when the offeree's promise to perform is properly communicated to the offeror. If the parties are not dealing directly, an acceptance becomes effective when sent if the offeree uses the communicating agency which was used or suggested by the offeror. If a different means of communication is used, the acceptance dates from the time it is received by the offeror. Consequently, if an offer is received and accepted by mail, the acceptance is effective from the moment the letter, properly addressed and stamped, is deposited with postal authorities. Similarly, an offer made by telegram is accepted as soon as the reply is placed with the telegraph company. Thus a contract may exist even though the acceptance is never received by the offeror. However, if an offer arrives by telegram, an acceptance by letter is effective only when it reaches the offeror. Likewise, if an an offer by letter suggests that the offeree reply by wire, the acceptance will be effective when sent only if it is telegraphed.

If the offeror holds out no means of communication, it is assumed that he has authorized the mails. Therefore, whereas an oral offer usually lapses when the parties separate, if they understand that the offer is to remain open, an acceptance by mail creates a contract as soon as it is posted.

Under the Code, the acceptance of an offer to buy or sell tangible personal property is effective when sent by *any* reasonable medium, unless the offer clearly specifies otherwise. If A offers by letter to sell his car to B, a contract would be created at the time B either wires or mails his acceptance.

consideration

7. *Defined.* An agreement is not enforceable as a contract unless, under its terms, each of its parties is furnishing consideration. A person provides consideration if he gives up or promises to give up a legal right. That is, he must do or promise to do something he is not already legally bound to do. In addition, each must have the purpose of bargaining or exchanging with the other. In essence, consideration is the price paid or to be paid for another's promise.

For example, assume that A promises to give B a particular painting and B agrees to accept it. B has given up no legal right in exchange, so consideration is not present. The agreement is unenforceable. Thus a promise to make a gift is not legally binding. If, at A's request, B had promised to pay $100 for A's promise to deliver the painting, a binding contract would have existed. Both A and B would have incurred a detriment, or promised to give up some legal right in an exchange.

Generally, the value of consideration is not a factor in determining the validity of a contract. Although the values exchanged may appear to be unequal, the law permits the parties to make their own bargain as long as each incurs some legal detriment.

8. Performing a Legal Duty. Doing no more than one is already legally obligated to do does not, as a rule, constitute consideration. No legal right is given up in such a case. Suppose that a contractor refuses to complete a building, as he has previously bound himself to do, unless the owner promises to pay an additional sum. Even if the owner grants the promise, he is not obligated to pay the extra amount on completion of the work because the contractor incurred no detriment in exchange. Under the Code, however, the parties to an existing contract for the sale of goods are bound to a modification of their agreement without consideration. Assume that a seller has contracted to sell certain merchandise for $100 but later encounters certain difficulties and persuades the buyer to accept a new price of $120. Although the buyer receives no new consideration, he is now bound to pay the $120 for the goods.

Similarly, a promise to accept less than the full amount of a debt in full satisfaction of it is unenforceable unless the debtor pays it before it falls due or does some other act at the request of the creditor which he was not obligated to do. Giving a note for less than the amount due will not eliminate a larger indebtedness unless the note is secured by collateral. A promise to pay to a different person or at a different place has been held consideration for a promised discount. If the creditor accepts the lesser sum in full satisfaction of the debt and indicates that he is making a gift of the balance, no recovery of the balance can be had later. The foregoing rule applies to debts that are certain in amount. If the debt is uncertain in amount (e.g., a tort claim or a contract claim that is disputed in good faith), the debt can be discharged for any amount agreed to by the parties. Even though evidence is later produced to confirm a contention by one of them that the obligation actually is smaller or larger than the settlement, the debt is discharged in full by the compromise. The right to go into court and have the issue settled there is good consideration for the release of the full amount of the claim.

9. Gratuitous and Illusory Promises. Although a promise to make a gift is usually unenforceable, it is binding if made to a religious, charitable, or educational organization for a definite purpose, provided the promisee incurs liability in reliance upon the promise before it is withdrawn. An executed gift—one that is completed by delivery of the subject matter and its acceptance—cannot be revoked by the donor on grounds of lack of consideration. Also, under the UCC, the rights for breach of contract involving the sale of goods are discharged in whole or in part by a waiver, in writing, delivered by the injured party to the other.

An illusory promise is one that at first inspection appears to bind the promisor, but, analyzed, requires him to do nothing. Such a promise makes an agreement unenforceable because of lack of mutuality. Suppose that A promises to deliver to B all of A's production that B desires to have during the next six months at a given price, and B agrees to buy all he desires of A's product. B has promised nothing, since he did not agree to desire any, so A's promise continues as an offer until it is withdrawn, lapses, or is accepted. However, if B promises to buy all his *needs* or *requirements* at that price and is in a business which had required such products, his promise to buy supports A's promise to sell, provided the quantity ordered bears a reasonable relation to estimates given or to past requirements.

10. Past Consideration. Past consideration will not support a present promise. That is, something that has already taken place may not serve as consideration for something presently promised, since the requirement of a bargain or exchange is lacking. Assume that A loaned B money on an unsecured note but that, before the note fell due, A doubted B's ability to pay. Some time later C was persuaded to sign the note directly under the signature of B. When the note fell due, B was unable to pay it and A sought to recover from C, whose defense was lack of consideration. A would be unable to recover because the loan previously made could not act as consideration for C's later promise. If C had signed at the time the loan was made, the mere making of the loan to B (which in any event A was not obligated to do) would have been good consideration for both B's and C's promise to pay. Claims that have been outlawed or barred by bankruptcy may be revived by a new promise without the necessity for any new consideration. In such cases, some states require the new promise to be in writing.

capacity to contract

11. Minors' Contracts Voidable. Contracts entered into by a minor (usually a person under twenty-one years of age) are voidable by him, although they are binding on the adult if the minor cares to enforce them. The contract is voidable whether it is fully or partially executed or is wholly executory. To avoid an executory contract, the minor needs only to indicate his unwillingness to carry out its terms. A contract that has been executed by the adult can be avoided only by the minor's offering to return what remains of the consideration he received and denying any liability on his part. If he has squandered, depreciated, or lost the consideration received, he is nevertheless free in most states to avoid the agreement. Should he have the consideration received in a different form because of some trade or improvement, it is his duty to return the new or improved article. The fact that the minor has executed his part of the contract by performing as agreed does not bar him from later avoiding the contract. He is entitled to the return of the consideration he gave in full, although he is unable to restore the consideration he has received.

A minor who has sold real estate cannot avoid the contract until he reaches his majority, although his other contracts can be avoided while he is still a minor. He is permitted to control the income from real estate he has sold during his minority, but the complete rescission must await his majority.

The fact that a minor misrepresents his age or appears to be older than twenty-one does not impair his right to avoid. As is suggested later, however, he may be liable for fraud if he is guilty of intentional misrepresentation.

A partnership agreement entered into by a minor may be avoided at any time; but if his investment is required to meet firm obligations, he cannot obtain its return. A minor's appointment of an agent is held in some states to be void from the beginning. Other states treat such appointments as merely voidable, thus making it necessary for the minor to take affirmative action to rescind contracts made by his agent in order to escape liability.

12. Ratification. Ratification or approval of a contract made by a minor has the legal effect of making it binding on him, as if it had never been voidable. Ratification can take place, however, only after the individual has reached his majority. A minor has a reasonable time after becoming of age in which to avoid or ratify his contracts. Retention of the benefits received for an unreasonable period following his majority will constitute a ratification. Any other act on his part which clearly indicates his approval of a contract made during his minority is a ratification. Selling or offering for sale the article received as a minor is a ratification when it takes place following adulthood.

13. Necessaries. Contracts of a minor for necessaries, like other contracts he makes, are voidable. However, if necessaries contracted for have been furnished to him, he is liable for their reasonable value (*not* their contract price). He has no liability on executory contracts for necessaries. The list of necessaries include food, clothing, shelter, medical care, tools of a trade, and a reasonable amount of education. The economic station in life of the minor does not expand the list of necessaries, although the quality and quantity of necessaries may vary as a consequence of one's economic status. If he has higher status, his need and thus his possibility of liability are greater.

Necessaries become such only when they are actually needed, the minor's station in life being properly considered. If the minor has an ample supply at the time of purchase, any items given him then can not be considered necessities. If his parent or guardian is adequately caring for his needs, items that he purchases are not deemed necessities.

Parents have no liability on contracts made by their minor children, except where the minor has been appointed an agent with authority to make contracts for his parent. The parent, like any principal, must carry out agreements made for him. A parent who has abandoned or failed to support a minor child is liable to one who has supplied the minor with his necessaries for their reasonable value.

14. Minor's Torts. A minor is liable for his torts. Having due regard for the age and experience of the minor, he is held responsible for any injury to the person or property of another growing out of the minor's willful or negligent misconduct. Fraud is a tort. Consequently, if a minor intentionally misrepresents his age and the other contracting party is injured as a result, the minor may be liable for the injury sustained. In some states the minor is free to avoid the contract but must pay the adult for the injury resulting from the use or destruction of the property which the minor has had in his possession as a result of his fraud. Other states, however, refuse to hold the minor liable for fraud in this situation, since they feel that doing so would have the effect of enforcing the contract indirectly.

15. Insane Persons and Drunkards. Contracts made by insane persons and people who are so intoxicated that they fail to appreciate the consequences of their acts are voidable. These contracts differ from those of a minor in that they cannot be avoided without the return of the consideration received unless the other party knowingly took advantage of their status. The contracts of a person adjudicated insane are absolutely void and of no effect. Only his court-appointed conservator can enter into contracts affecting his property.

fraud

16. Nature. Fraud consists of an intentional misrepresentation of a material fact which induces another to enter into a contract. This definition embraces at least four elements: intent, misrepresentation, material fact, and reliance causing damage. Fraud is present only when the party responsible for the misrepresentation was aware of its untruth at the time the statement was made or was grossly careless in making the statement. The misrepresentation may consist of a direct misstatement or may be the result of a series of statements, each of which is true but the net effect of which is to create a misimpression or to mislead.

Mere silence or failure to volunteer information normally does not constitute a misstatement, although in at least two instances there is a duty when entering into a contract to volunteer information of importance to the other party. When an article sold has a hidden defect known to the seller but not to the buyer, it is the duty of the seller to disclose this fact. Silence in such a case is the same as a misrepresentation. Likewise, if there is a fiduciary relationship between the parties—one of trust and confidence such as exists between parent and child, priest and parishioner, principal and agent—there is a duty to disclose any pertinent information that is not known to the other party. It is understood under such circumstances that the parties do not deal at arm's length, although normally each party to a contract is expected to look after his own interests.

Silence plus physical action taken to conceal the facts is in effect a misrepresentation. Turning back the odometer on a used car or hiding a defect with paint are illustrative of this type of fraud.

17. Material Fact. Intentional misrepresentation constitutes fraud only when it relates to some fact and that fact is material in inducing the contract which has been made. A mere expression of opinion or a promise that the thing sold will perform in a certain fashion in the future is not a statement of present or past fact. At best, statements regarding the value of property or relating to its expected performance can be only opinions of the person expressing them. However, when one misrepresents his own opinion, he misstates a fact and he may be held accountable. This is particularly true of experts. An opinion rendered by a real estate broker about the value of property being sold gives no relief if it is later shown to have been unsound; but if the broker did not give his true opinion, he may well be guilty of fraud. The same is true of one who promises to do something in the future. Provided he intends to carry out his promise, no fraud takes place just because he later breaches the contract. But if he had no intention of performing when the promise was made, he has misstated his intention. Thus a failure to disclose his insolvency by a purchaser on credit is not fraud; although, if he never intends to pay for the goods, his promise to do so under the circumstances constitutes a misrepresentation.

18. Reliance. An intentional misrepresentation of fact does not result in fraud unless the person to whom the statement is made acts in reliance on it. If he makes his own investigation and lends no credence or weight to what has been said, he has not been injured by the statement and should have no relief. Fraud is present only when the party takes action because of the misstatement. Several states go beyond this and hold that a buyer has no right to rely on misinformation if correct information is readily available. In such cases, the buyer should check the accuracy of the seller's statements.

19. Effect of Fraud. Fraud gives the injured party a choice of one of two remedies against the guilty party. He may rescind the agreement and recover what he parted with upon returning what he has received. Or, he may affirm the contract and recover damages for the injury sustained in a tort action of deceit. To rescind, the injured party must act promptly after the fraud is discovered.

At common law these remedies are mutually exclusive. However, the UCC has established that this restriction does not apply to contracts involving a sale of goods. Under it, a buyer of tangible personal property who is injured by fraud can rescind or reject the goods and also recover any money damages he suffers.

20. Unintentional Misrepresentation. Unintentional misrepresentation requires the same elements as fraud except the intent to deceive. One who enters into a contract in reliance on an unintentional misrepresentation made by the other party is entitled to rescind. This is his only remedy, however. Since no tort exists because of the lack of intent, an action for damages is not available. However, a misstatement made recklessly or with gross negligence has been held by many courts to be tantamount to an intentional misstatement and thus fraudulent. An accountant who recklessly prepares financial statements that are relied upon by third parties in extending credit to the accountant's client may be held liable for damage incurred because of such reliance.

mistake and duress

21. Unilateral Mistake. A unilateral mistake occurs when one of the parties is induced to enter into a contract because of a misunderstanding by him alone regarding some material fact. Such a mistake, usually the result of his own carelessness or lack of investigation, affords him no grounds for relief. Thus one who submits a construction bid because of an error in his computations or makes an offer to sell merchandise in ignorance of its true value has no basis for rescission, if his offer is accepted in good faith. However, if the seriousness of a computational mistake is so great that the other party must have known of it when he accepted the offer, the courts permit rescission or cancellation of the contract. One is not permitted to take advantage of another's mistake knowingly. Relief is granted when the error is known by the other party or is so glaring that he should notice it.

22. Bilateral Mistake. A bilateral mistake is made when both parties to the contract have based their agreement on an incorrect assumption of material fact. Such a mistake exists, for example, when the acreage of a farm being sold is thought by both the buyer and the seller to be different from what it actually is. Any contract based on a mutual mistake regarding some material fact may be avoided by the one suffering damage due to the error.

A contract that is incorrectly reduced to writing by the scrivener and is signed by the parties may be reformed in court action so that it conforms to the original intention of the parties. Reformation is not available, however, unless it can be shown that neither party originally intended the instrument to be drawn as it was.

23. Duress. Contracts are enforceable only when the parties enter into them of their own free will. Consequently, a contract entered into because of force or threat is voidable if the mind of one of the parties was truly overcome by fear. Threat of bodily injury or of criminal prosecution of a near relative is usually considered sufficient to constitute duress.

Business duress arises when one of the parties is induced to enter into a contract because of the other's threat to detain wrongfully the former's property or to destroy it. Contracts so induced also may be avoided because they are not entered into by the parties of their own volition.

illegal agreements

24. Nature. Agreements are illegal because some statute makes them so or because the courts rule that they are opposed to sound public policy. When an agreement is found to be illegal, it is unenforceable by either party. And, in most cases, the courts will not permit rescission of a fully or partially executed agreement. The parties are usually left as they are found. Since both are equally guilty, neither should be given aid by the law. For example, gambling contracts are deemed to be illegal and unenforceable under the laws of most states. Furthermore, under the Code, if the court rules that a contract for the sale of goods, or any term thereof, is *unconscionable,* it may decline to enforce the contract or unconscionable provision. What is unconscionable is not clearly defined. However, the official Comment to the UCC indicates that terms so one-sided that they serve to oppress or unfairly surprise one of the parties should be held as such.

25. Exculpatory Clauses. An exculpatory clause attempts to relieve one of the parties to a contract of liability for his own wrongful or negligent act. For example, the lessee of a car may persuade the owner to agree that the lessee will not be responsible for damage to the car while it is in his possession, even if the damage results from the lessee's own carelessness. If their bargaining positions are equal, such a provision is binding on the owner, who must bear the risk of any loss.

A quasi-public concern—one which the public is more or less bound to make use of in the ordinary routine of life—may not use an exculpatory clause to immunize itself from liability due to its own fault. Public utilities, carriers, warehouses, parking lots, eating houses, and banks are illustrative of quasi-public enterprises. Because of their superior bargaining position, they can force, to an exculpatory term, an agreement that has not been arrived at freely. Assume that a parking-lot owner posts signs on the premises and informs his customers that if cars are stolen or destroyed by fire, the owner of the car is to assume responsibility for the loss even though the loss is caused by the carelessness of the bailee or his agents. Such a provision is unenforceable, however, and even though it becomes part of the bailment contract, the parking-lot owner will be liable for a fire loss resulting from his carelessness or that of his employees.

26. Usury. Most of the states limit the amount of interest that may be charged on money loaned. A contract that provides for excessive interest is usually enforceable only as to the principal indebtedness. If usury exists, any payment of interest made by the debtor is applied by the courts to the debt itself. A few of the states allow the lender to recover the legal rate of interest as well as the principal indebtedness. Any attempt to circumvent the law by charging a commission in addition to the maximum interest, or by having the borrower sell an article and agree to buy it again at a substantial increase in price is futile, since the court treats these contracts the same as any usurious agreement.

The lender may charge the borrower the maximum rate of interest and a service charge for handling the loan. The charge must have a reasonable relation to the actual cost of legal, investigative, bookkeeping, or other expenses related to carrying the loan. Corporations, not being natural persons, generally can be charged any rate of interest they are willing to pay. Sellers of merchandise are entitled to add a carrying or finance charge to the price of goods when they are sold on credit. In the absence of statute, such a charge is not treated as interest and may be set at any figure agreeable to the parties. Furthermore, most states license small-loan companies, which are permitted to charge a high rate of interest on their loans because of the risk involved.

27. Agreements in Restraint of Trade. Today, many federal and state statutes deal with agreements in restraint of trade. In addition, the common law has long held them to be illegal and unenforceable. Any agreement to control prices, limit competition, or restrain the freedom of trade is illegal. However, in many states fair trade legislation permits the producer of merchandise with a brand or trade name to protect his goodwill by contracts controlling the retail price at which his products may be sold.

Three exceptions have been recognized to the general rule just stated. One who sells his business may legally agree not to compete with the buyer for a reasonable period of time; an employee may agree with his employer not to compete with the employer when the employment relationship is severed; and the seller of real property may so limit its use that it does not compete with his business. These limitations are enforceable, however, only if they are a part of the original contract of sale or employment and are reasonably necessary to protect the goodwill involved. If the restriction is unreasonably severe, covering a longer period of time or a larger area than necessary, it is unenforceable to any degree. In such a case, the seller or employee may compete without any limitation.

statute of frauds

28. Requirement of a Writing. Although in general oral contracts are just as binding as written ones, the Statute of Frauds requires that certain kinds of contracts be evidenced by a writing to be enforceable. The original Statute of Frauds was enacted in England in 1677 and was called "An Act for Prevention of Frauds and Perjuries." Its purpose was to prevent a fraud on the court by requiring written evidence of some types of contracts; thus false testimony by "witnesses" could not be used to establish nonexistent agreements. Today similar provisions are found in state statutes and in the UCC. The writing required must contain the major provisions, it must identify the parties, and it must be signed by the party to be held. Note that the original contract itself need not be written. The evidence necessary is adequate if obtained at any time prior to the date when suit is brought, and it may consist of a series of writings. A single contract may fall within the provisions of more than one part of the Statute. If so, it must satisfy the exceptions of all, or a writing is essential.

Of course, a written contract is advantageous even if it is not required, since a written instrument is easier to prove in the event of a dispute. The terms of a written contract cannot be altered by parol evidence that there were additional oral provisions agreed to at the time of the writing. However, they can be modified by a *later* oral agreement, provided the Statute of Frauds is satisfied. Once a written agreement is signed and delivered by the parties, they are bound even if they have not read the terms.

29. Real Estate. Contracts for the sale of real estate must be evidenced by a writing. Real estate involves land or any interest therein; it includes a life interest, easement, estate for years (lease of over one year's duration), as well as the fee simple title to land. All property that is not real estate is personal property. Sales of personalty are subject to the Statute of Frauds provisions of the UCC. If a particular item of tangible property is attached to land, it may or may not be real property. The UCC states that contracts for the sale of timber, minerals, or a structure constitute sales of goods and not land if they are to be severed by the seller (e.g., when the seller has a duty under the contract to deliver). Such agreements, therefore, are governed by the Code. If the buyer is to sever in a sale of the foregoing, land is involved. Contracts for the sale of growing crops separate from the land, or for other things that also are attached and capable of being severed without material harm to it (like trade fixtures), involve goods under the UCC regardless of whether the buyer or seller is to sever.

Under the real property section of the Statute, an oral contract is not enforceable merely because the purchaser has paid all or a part of the purchase price. In such a case, if the seller refuses to perform and no writing is available, the buyer is entitled to the return of his payment. However, if the buyer refuses to proceed with the contract, the seller may retain all payments made. Even if the buyer has entered and taken possession of the property, the requirement for written evidence is not dispensed with. An exception does exist in favor of the buyer, who, in reliance upon an oral agreement, changes his position so greatly that it would be exceedingly inequitable to require a writing. Thus a buyer who has surrendered possession of other property, moved in, and improved the newly acquired property to a considerable degree is usually allowed to enforce the oral agreement. Improvements added in reliance upon an oral agreement must be paid for by the seller in the event that he fails to carry out the oral agreement.

30. Contracts of Guaranty. An agreement whereby one assumes a secondary liability for the debt, default, or miscarriage of another must be evidenced by a writing. Guaranty arises only when the primary responsibility for performance rests on the principal debtor, the guarantor to be liable only if the primary party fails to perform. No guaranty exists when one person assumes another's debt, because the person who assumes then becomes the primary debtor. Thus if D owes C $500 and G makes a contract with C to pay it in case D fails, the agreement is enforceable only when written evidence signed by G is available. However, if G makes a contract with D to pay the debt, an oral agreement is enforceable. Several states hold that an oral guaranty is enforceable if the guarantor makes his promise because of an interest he has in the transaction himself.

31. Long-Term Contracts. Contracts which by their terms are incapable of completion within one year of the time of their making are unenforceable unless evidenced by a writing. The fact that a contract takes longer than one year to perform is unimportant if, at the time the contract was made, it could have been completed within a year in accordance with its provisions. An oral contract to build a house for another at a cost of $20,000 is enforceable. It is no less enforceable because the contractor spreads his work out over fifteen months. However, an oral agreement to build a house with the express stipulation that work is not to start for fifteen months is unenforceable. By its terms performance must necessarily extend beyond one year.

An oral agreement to support a person for life at an annual rate is enforceable, regardless of how long the person lives. When the agreement was made, it was possible that it could have been completed within one year by the death of the one being cared for.

Under this section of the Statute of Frauds, complete performance by one of the parties makes the agreement binding on the other.

32. Sales of Personal Property. Contracts for the sale of personal property are subject to one of three different Statute of Frauds provisions of the UCC.

First, if a contract for the sale of goods, wares, or merchandise (tangible personal property) is for $500 or more, it must be evidenced by a writing unless one of the following exceptions is met:

1. If the goods are to be specially manufactured for the buyer, are not ordinarily suitable for sale by the seller, and if the seller has relied on the agreement before receiving notice of repudiation.

2. If either party admits the existence of the contract in his pleadings or evidence. (Under the sections of the Statute not governed by the Code, one may admit the existence of the oral contract, but plea the Statute as a defense.)

3. Where both parties to the agreement are merchants, and one sends to the other a written confirmation that is sufficient against the sender, the agreement is enforceable against the receiver, unless he gives written notice of his objection to the confirmation within 10 days of its receipt.

4. If there is part performance by either the buyer or the seller, either may enforce the agreement to the extent of his part performance.

Second, if a contract is for the sale of investment securities (stocks or bonds) of *any* value, written evidence is necessary. The exceptions to this provision are essentially the same as those controlling the sale of goods. Of course, exception (1) does not apply to securities. And, for exception (3) to dispense with the requirement of a writing, it is not necessary for either of the parties to be a "merchant."

Third, a contract to sell any other kind of personal property for $5000 or more must be evidenced by a writing. This covers all intangibles (other than investment securities) such as good will, trademarks, accounts receivable, patents, and copyrights. No exception to this provision is stated.

third parties

33. What Rights Are Assignable. An assignment is a transfer of a contractual right. Any party to a contract may assign his rights to a third party without the necessity of obtaining the consent of the other party to the agreement, unless the rights are personal in character. The right to the services of an employee may not be assigned, and the right to protection under a policy of fire insurance is likewise unassignable without the consent of the other party to the agreement—the insurer, in the latter case.

Wages earned or to be earned may be assigned, so long as they grow out of a current contract of employment. Many states limit the percentage of future wages that can be assigned at any one time, and some permit assignment of future wages without a present contract of employment. All other money claims are assignable without limit, the assignee taking over the right of the assignor to the money when it falls due. A contract to sell or to buy may be assigned by either the seller or the buyer; however, an agreement to buy on unsecured credit may not be transferred by the purchaser without the seller's assent, since the credit standing of the assignee may be inferior to that of the original purchaser.

An assignment is effective without any consideration to support it, such being in the nature of a promise to make a gift. An assignment without consideration can be canceled by the assignor at any time before performance for the assignee. A gift is not completed until delivery to the donee.

34. Rights of Assignee. The rights acquired by an assignee are no better than those possessed by the assignor. The assignee of a money claim takes it subject to the same defenses the debtor held against his original creditor. To illustrate, a money claim may grow out of a sale of a used car, the seller immediately assigning the right to the purchase price. If the seller is guilty of fraud, the buyer of the car could assert fraud as effectively against an innocent assignee as he could have against the assignor. However, under the Code, if a buyer of goods waives any defense he has against the seller, should the seller assign the contract, an innocent assignee generally takes the rights free of such defense.

As between debtor and creditor, mutual claims, when both are due, may be set off against each other, only the difference being payable. Setoff may be used against the assignee when it would have been available against the assignor.

Generally a person who buys a contract right, regardless of whether it is a money claim, has no claim against the assignor in case the third party obligor is unable or refuses to perform, unless the assignment is expressly "with recourse." The assignor makes only one warranty; namely, that the right assigned is a genuine enforceable claim without defenses against it. If the third party fails to perform because of a defense he has against the assignor, then the latter becomes liable to the assignee. Otherwise, failure of the obligor to perform gives the assignee no action against the assignor.

The assignee of the contract should give immediate notice of his assignment to the person expected to perform. This is necessary for two reasons. If no notice is received, the third party is quite likely to perform for the original contracting party. Thus if a money claim is assigned and the debtor not notified of the assignment, payment may be made by him to the original creditor. In such a case, the assignee has a claim only against the assignor to recover what has been collected. Occasionally, persons have been known to make two or more assignments of the same right. Although the states are in conflict, a slight majority hold that the first of two innocent assignees to give notice to the third-party obligor obtains the better right. The other states hold that the first person to receive the assignment has the better claim, regardless of which party gives notice first.

35. Delegation of Duties. It is sometimes said that contracts are assigned, although it is more accurate to indicate that the rights are assigned and the duties delegated. A true assignee acquires only the rights and has no responsibility for the duties unless he has expressly or impliedly assumed them. Accepting the benefits where duties remain to be performed implies the assumption of them. Of course, if the duties are to be performed before the right can be enforced, the assignee either forfeits the right or must perform the duty. For example, let us assume that A has contracted to sell B a residence for $15,000. B assigns the contract to C, receiving $1,000 for the rights it gave him. If the prices of realty drop substantially, C is not obligated to take the property, for he has promised no one to buy it; he acquired only the right to purchase the property.

The UCC provides that the assignee of all the rights under a contract for the sale of goods assumes all the duties of the assignor, unless the agreement states otherwise or the assignment is given as security.

Even when the assignee assumes the duties of the assignor, the assignor remains liable. If the assignee fails to perform, the third party may enforce the agreement against either. The transferor of a contract may be released only by a novation in which the third party joins, agreeing to discharge him and to look solely to the transferee for performance.

36. Contract for Benefit of Third Party. A contract for the benefit of a third party arises whenever a person not a party to the contract is to benefit from it. In a life insurance policy, for example, the named beneficiary is the third party. Contracts for the benefit of third parties are of two types, one being for the benefit of a donee and the other for the benefit of a creditor. The insurance contract illustrates the donee type, since the terms are enforceable by the one for whose benefit the contract was made. Although some conflict exists, most states enforce donee beneficiary contracts if the benefit is intended to be direct, and the majority hold that the contract may not be rescinded or altered without the consent of third party unless the right to do so is reserved in the agreement. An incidental donee beneficiary of a contract has no remedy for its breach.

A contract for the benefit of a creditor develops whenever one person contracts to pay another's debt. For example, assume that O borrows $50,000 of M and gives the latter his note secured by a mortgage on a business building. O sells the building to A, who as part of the purchase price assumes and agrees to pay the indebtedness. Although M has no contract with A, most states permit M to sue either O or A when the debt falls due. If O is compelled to pay, he then has a cause of action against A.

remedies for breach

37. Damages. For *every* breach of contract, the injured party has a right to money damages. The amount is assessed by the jury as a finding of fact; it is that figure which is required to leave the injured party in as good a position as he would have enjoyed if performance had taken place. Compensatory damages must be proved by evidence. If such proof is lacking, the plaintiff is still entitled to nominal damages or to some small amount to indicate that a cause of action existed. To be recoverable, damages must be a direct, foreseeable result of the breach. A seller of goods who fails to make delivery should be required to pay the difference between the contract price and the amount the buyer expended (market) to replace the articles contracted for. Loss of profits, where demonstrable, may also be recovered. So far as possible, after a breach occurs, the injured party must keep his losses as small as possible—it is his duty to mitigate damages.

Some agreements include a clause by which the parties agree in advance on the amount of damages to be paid in the event of a particular breach by one of them. This is called a *liquidated damages clause*. In such a case the actual amount of damages suffered is unimportant, the amount recoverable being the figure established in the contract, no more, no less. A liquidated damages clause should be distinguished from a penalty clause, which is unenforceable. A penalty clause is one which the court feels was inserted as a whip to discourage nonperformance and not for the purpose of compensating for the injury sustained. A liquidated damages clause must have a reasonable relation to damages that could be suffered in event of a breach.

38. Rescission. Not every breach of contract will permit the injured party to rescind. If the terms violated are trivial or minor in nature, substantial performance has taken place and the injured party must perform his part of the bargain, less the damages he has suffered. However, if the breach is major, or is the breach of a *condition,* the injured party may, at his option, choose to rescind in lieu of recovering damages.

Many contracts are drawn in a way that makes it clear that one of the parties must perform before any duty to do so is imposed on the other. In such cases, performance by the first party is said to be a *condition precedent* to the duty of the second to perform. If a contract is silent regarding the time for its performance, the agreed-on act must be performed within a reasonable time. Where the date for performance is stipulated, performance on that very date may or may not be a condition precedent, depending on contract terms and also on how important to the parties the time provision is. A clause in a contract to the effect that time "is of the essence" signifies that the parties are agreed that performance on time is important. In contracts, between merchants for the sale and purchase of goods, the courts imply that time is of the essence. Unless the goods are received on time, or nearly so, the buyer is not obligated to accept them. In the case of nonmarketable goods, however, the buyer must accept them somewhat later than agreed, although he may deduct damages. Thus a buyer for calendars bearing his business name which were to be delivered by November 1 for early free distribution to his customers could not properly decline to accept them if they arrived as late as the fifteenth day of December, unless by the terms of the contract time was made of the essence. A delivery as late as February or March, however, would probably be a breach substantial enough to justify rescission. Extended delay in the performance of any contract eventually becomes important.

In a contract that requires simultaneous performance by the parties, the conditions are said to be *concurrent*. Neither party is in default until the other has *tendered* performance. A proper tender is an offer to perform in the proper manner, at the proper time and place, with the capacity to do so. If the person to whom such a tender is made fails to perform, he is guilty of a breach. The injured party has a cause of action even though he did not actually perform himself.

After a money obligation falls due, a proper tender of payment does not satisfy the indebtedness. If refused by the creditor, the tender merely stops interest from accumulating thereafter, shifts court costs to the creditor if suit is later brought, and releases any liens that secure the debt.

A statement made prior to the time performance is to begin that the party will not perform is an *anticipatory breach*. The other party may accept the statement at its face value, enter into a similar contract with another, and immediately bring a suit to recover money damages. The guilty party can retract such a breach at any time before it is relied upon and perform without penalty. Under the UCC, an anticipatory breach of a contract to sell goods cannot be retracted after notice of cancellation is given by the injured party. There can never be an anticipatory breach of a money obligation. The creditor must wait until the obligation falls due to recover, even though the debtor states in advance that he does not intend to pay it.

39. Specific Performance. Specific performance is a remedy whereby a court of equity orders the defendant to actually perform his part of the contract as agreed. This gives the one injured by a breach what he bargained for instead of just the money damages which a court of law is empowered to award. Specific performance is only available at the discretion of the court and will be granted only when money damages would not provide adequate relief. Contracts to purchase items that are unique are usually specifically enforced. Examples are purchases of works of art, real estate, and stock in a closely held corporation where control is involved.

40. Partial Performance. The right of a person who has only partially completed his contract to recover for the benefits conferred depends entirely on the circumstances. If impossibility arises after part performance, the injured party is entitled to recover the reasonable value of all work done. In other cases, recovery, if permitted, is limited to the reasonable value of the net benefit, also.

In the case of a willful breach, the one who receives part performance is not required to pay for it if he returns the performance or is unable to do so. Thus a contractor who willfully leaves a construction job after partially completing it is generally denied any recovery. However, a buyer of goods who receives and retains part of them must pay for the goods delivered, less his damages for not receiving the balance.

41. Quasi-Contract. A true contract may be either express (arising from the words exchanged by the parties) or implied in fact (arising totally or in part from their conduct other than language). An implied-in-fact contract exists if a person accepts a benefit from another, knowing that no gift is intended. In such a case, his conduct implies a promise to pay for the reasonable value of the benefit.

A *quasi-contract* (or contract implied in law), however, is not a true contract at all. This term is used to identify the situation in which a court imposes a contract-like duty upon a person to pay for a benefit he has received, even though he did not expressly or impliedly agree to do so. Generally, a court will imply a duty to pay for the reasonable value of a benefit conferred if it feels that the recipient has been unjustly enriched. The benefit conferred cannot be intended as a gift, and the one conferring it cannot be at fault or officious. For example, if a buyer of a tractor is unable to finance the purchase and he and the seller agree to rescind the contract of sale, the buyer is liable for the reasonable rental value of the tractor while it was in his possession before the rescission.

excuses for nonperformance

42. Waiver and Prevention. Waiver consists of any conduct on the part of one of the parties which indicates an intention to disregard a past or future violation of contract terms.

Prevention, as the word indicates, is conduct by one of the parties which makes performance by the other impossible or more burdensome. Every contract contains an implied provision that neither party will interfere with performance by the other. If interference occurs, the injured party is excused from performing and, in addition, may recover damages for the breach.

43. Impossibility. Unanticipated burden or hardship does not excuse one from his contractual duties. An unexpected increase in the price of materials, a strike, a fire, shortage of supplies, or a transportation difficulty neither releases one from his obligation nor offers legal justification for requesting additional compensation. Provision for such contingencies should be made in the original contract between the parties.

True impossibility does relieve a contracting party from further performance unless he has assumed the risk of becoming unable to perform by the terms of the agreement. If not excused, he must pay damages for breach. The courts have recognized at least three cases of true impossibility: (a) legislation that makes performance illegal, (b) death or incapacitating illness of a party to a contract clearly involving the personal services, and (c) destruction or lack of essential subject matter. Illustrative of the first situation are those contracts necessarily abandoned during a war period because of government controls on the distribution of certain products.

An ordinary agreement is not affected by the death of one of the parties. A contract to sell or buy merchandise is not disturbed by the death of the seller or buyer. The estate must perform the duty of the deceased. A contract to build a house according to specifications for the owner of property falls in the same category, although an agreement to work for the owner as an employee is terminated by the death or incapacitating illness of either. Similarly, an agreement by an eminent artist to paint a portrait would be terminated by the death of the artist, since his personal services are essential to performance of such an agreement.

The destruction of the specific thing agreed to be delivered, stored, or worked on terminates the duty of performance: it is no longer possible to perform. Likewise, the destruction of a source of supply that is absolutely essential to performance excuses a failure to perform. In such a case it must be clear that performance cannot be had elsewhere in compliance with the terms of the contract. Thus an agreement to deliver 5000 cases of a certain kind of orange would not be terminated by *impossibility* because the seller's orchard was destroyed or his crop damaged by an early freeze. If all oranges of the kind under consideration are destroyed or if the oranges to be delivered were, by the terms of the contract, to come from the seller's orchard, destruction would result in impossibility.

44. Impracticability. Under the UCC, if the seller of goods finds that performance has become *impracticable,* he may be wholly or partially excused for nondelivery or a delay in delivery. Impracticability may result from compliance with government regulation or from the happening or nonhappening of an event that was a basic assumption on which the agreement was made. It is not brought about by general price level changes, but severe shortage due to crop failure or shutdown of a source of supply constitute valid excuses. In the event of impracticability, the seller must fairly allocate his production or inventory to his regular customers and give them notice. However, the customers are not required to accept just part performance if there will be a substantial impairment of the contract, and they may rescind to look elsewhere for their needs.

discharge

45. Novation; Accord and Satisfaction. A *novation* is the substitution of a new party for one of the original parties to a contract. It can be accomplished only when all three of the parties consent and the new party assumes the liability of the one to be released. The original party accepting the substitution must clearly agree to release the withdrawing one. Merely to agree that an assignee of a contract may perform does not discharge the assignor unless performance takes place. In the meantime, the original obligor is a surety for the one who has promised to perform. Assume that S contracted to sell supplies to B for $300. With S's consent, B assigned the contract as a whole to Y, who assumed its duties. No novation has taken place.

An *accord and satisfaction* is like a novation in that there is a substitution, but it is of consideration, not of parties. The person entitled to performance agrees to take something different from that for which he contracted. Unless clearly agreed otherwise, the promise to supply something different does not discharge the old duty. It is only when the new promise is performed or satisfied that the old obligation is eliminated.

46. Statute of Limitations. The statute of limitations of each state sets forth the time in which a suit must be brought after the cause of action accrues or a breach occurs. Matured debts are said to be outlawed unless suit is brought against the debtor within the period permitted by law, often six years after the maturity date. Under the Code, the statutory limit for suit is four years after the breach of a contract for the sale of goods by either the buyer or seller. Even if suit has been outlawed, the statute usually starts running anew from the beginning if the wrongful party promises to perform, partially performs, or acknowledges his obligation. Such conduct furnishes fresh evidence of its existence. The running of the statute is suspended for any period the debtor is outside the state, extending the time within which the action can be brought.

When a debtor makes a payment, he has the right to stipulate how it is to be applied in case he owes several obligations to the creditor. If the debtor fails to so indicate, the creditor is at liberty to apply payments where his interest is best served, provided the obligations credited are past due.

Agency

1. Defined. An agency relationship exists when one person, (the principal) grants to another (the agent) the authority to make, alter, or terminate a contract for him. If an agent acts within the actual or apparent authority conferred upon him, his principal is bound the same as if the principal had acted for himself. Many states hold that the appointment of an agent must be accompanied by the same formality required by the execution of the contract he makes. In these states contracts made by the agent that require written evidence or contracts that must be made under seal are unenforceable unless the appointment is in writing or under seal.

An agent has no implied power to appoint other agents for the principal unless his position is one that includes that responsibility. However, an agent may appoint a subagent to perform his duties, provided they are purely ministerial in character, not involving any discretion.

An agency may be created by estoppel or by ratification as well as by express appointment. Such cases are discussed in the next two sections.

An agent is to be distinguished from an independent contractor in that the latter is engaged to accomplish a certain result and is relatively free in his choice of the means used in obtaining the result. An agent need not be an employee in the technical sense. Local fire insurance agents possess authority to bind their companies, but they are not considered employees of the company for tax purposes. Commission merchants act as agents of the consignor in the sale of merchandise but are in no sense employees.

2. Extent of Authority. The authority of an agent stems from that which is expressly conferred upon him and includes that which usage and custom have added as incidental to the actual authority that has been conferred. Likewise, it includes such apparent authority as may be implied from the conduct of the principal. It is the duty of the person dealing with the agent to ascertain the limits of his authority. But if the principal by his conduct has reasonably led a third person into believing that an agency exists even if there is no actual authority, the principal may not deny responsibility for the ostensible agent's acts. This is known as *agency by estoppel.* No estoppel exists unless the third party knew of the principal's conduct and relied upon it in his dealings with the assumed agent. Nothing an agent does can create estoppel; it is only the conduct of the principal which justifies a third party in assuming that an agency exists.

For example, assume that A was the bookkeeper of P with authority to stamp all incoming checks for deposit and carry them to the bank for deposit. On two or three occasions A, without authority, indorsed a few small checks and received the money for use as change in the business. P reprimanded A but said nothing about the matter to the bank, and some time later A cashed a larger check, took the money, and disappeared. Although A had no authority to indorse checks generally, the loss must fall upon P, since he neglected to caution the bank after the first ones were cashed. This led it reasonably to believe that the agent was possessed of such authority and to rely on that belief.

An agent's power may be enlarged by the existence of an emergency, but only to the extent necessary to care for the immediate situation. Also, his power is enlarged only if he is unable to contact the principal for instructions.

Any limitation on the authority of an agent below that customarily held by similar agents is said to be a *secret* limitation. Such a limitation does not affect the rights of third parties unless they have knowledge of it.

3. Ratification. A principal is not bound by acts of an agent which exceed his actual or apparent authority unless the principal later ratifies or approves them in some manner. For a valid ratification to take place, it is only necessary that the agent profess to represent the principal at the time he acts, that the principal have full knowledge of the facts when he ratifies, and that he show in some manner approval of the agent's act. No notice to the third party is necessary. Also, since the effect of ratification is the same as though the agent had authority at the time the act was committed, the ratification must be in writing if the appointment was required to be written. Because the principal is not bound prior to ratification, the third party is at liberty to withdraw any time before then.

4. Implied Power to Collect. An agent has no implied power to collect money for his principal except in two instances. Unless otherwise indicated to the customer, a salesman who delivers goods sold under a cash sale has the implied power to collect for them. Similarly, where it is customary to accept a partial payment at the time the contract is made, the salesman may collect and bind his principal. The buyer has no right to assume that a sales agent or solicitor has the power to collect under other circumstances.

5. Undisclosed Principal. For one reason or another, the principal may not care to have his identity known, and therefore may request the agent to conduct the business at hand in his own name. Under these circumstances, the contracts are made in the name of the agent; and people dealing with the agent, being unaware of the existence of a principal, may hold the agent liable on them. The principal is also liable if the agent acted within the scope of his authority. When later discovered, the principal may be sued, unless he has, prior to his disclosure, made a good-faith settlement with the agent (supplied the agent with the money to make a purchase or other means of performance).

After the principal and agent are both known to the third party, if there has been no settlement between principal and agent, the third party may elect to recover from either. Having made an election of one, he may not thereafter look to the other. His election must be very clear and conclusive in order to release one of the parties. Merely sending a bill to one of them or requesting payment does not signify an election. However, a suit prosecuted to judgment will constitute an election even if the third party finds it impossible to collect because of the debtor's insolvency. It should be emphasized that election never arises unless the third party knows of the existence of the principal.

6. *Employees' Torts.* An employer (or principal) is liable for the torts of his employee (or agent) committed while the latter is acting in the course of his employment. In other words, the employee must be acting in furtherance of his employer's business at the time of the tort for this vicarious liability to be imposed. For example, if a truck driver is negligent and injures a third party while making deliveries for his company, the company is liable, for at the time of the accident the employee was about the employer's business. However, if the employee had been totally about his own business but in possession of his employer's truck when the accident occurred, the company would not have been liable. If the employee is combining the business of both, the employer can be held.

An employer is liable for the *intentional* torts committed by his employee in only three situations: (a) where the injury occurs on his business premises at a time when the guest is there to transact business, (b) when the employee has been entrusted with force and uses excessive force—as he may do when he is authorized to repossess goods sold on credit, and (c) where the employee, by his conduct, is definitely attempting to further the interests of his employer. It must be emphasized that an employee is *always* liable for his own torts. The third party has the choice of looking either to him or the employer. No election is required. This rule holds true even though the employee is acting in good faith while following instructions. In such a case it is the duty of the employer to indemnify him against loss. On the other hand, if the tort results from the negligent or willful misconduct of the employee and his company is held by the third party, the company may recover from the employee, since the latter owes a duty to exercise reasonable care.

In general, a proprietor has no liability for the torts committed by an independent contractor who is accomplishing some end result for him, unless the activities involved are inherently dangerous to others.

7. *Duties of an Agent.* The duties of an agent to his principal may essentially be embraced within one statement; namely, the obligation to be *loyal.* Duties growing out of this central one may be listed as follows:

1. A duty not to compete with the principal.

2. A salesman's duty not to carry a sideline profitable to the agent while on the principal's time or expense account without the approval of the principal. Profits made in violation of this duty may be recovered by the principal.

3. A duty not to sell to himself or buy from himself without the approval of the principal while acting for him.

4. The duties to follow carefully all instructions given by the principal which fall within the scope of employment, and not to be negligent. Loss from any deviation falls upon the agent.

5. The duty to account accurately for all funds of the principal entrusted to the agent and not to commingle them with his own.

6. The duty not to use confidential information acquired while working for the principal in a manner that is adverse to the principal's interests. Even following the termination of employment, the use of such information is forbidden by the agent's prior duty of loyalty. Only skills learned and acquaintances made may be utilized when employment ceases.

8. *Principal's Duties to Agent.* The basic duties of a principal to his agent grow out of the contract of employment. There is a duty to compensate and one to reimburse for any money reasonably expended by the agent in the principal's behalf. The principal has a duty to employ the agent for the agreed period. Any premature and unjustified dismissal makes him liable in damages. Also, the principal must indemnify his agent against any loss suffered as a result of following instructions in good faith.

9. *Liability of Agent to Third Party.* An agent who conducts business in his principal's name incurs no liability on the contracts he makes, provided they are properly signed. He should sign his principal's

name and, for purposes of identification, add his own name, preceded by the word "by" or "per." If the signature is ambiguous, as it often is when an agent adds his office after his name—A, Cashier of X Co.—he is risking the possibility of being personally bound.

An agent warrants that he possesses the authority he undertakes to exercise. Should it develop later that he possesses no such authority, he has breached his warranty and is liable for damages suffered by the third party. Likewise, when an agent makes a contract for his principal, he warrants to the third party that he represents a competent principal, one with power to contract. Thus he warrants that his principal is not a minor or an unincorporated association. Should he represent a principal of this character, the agent assumes full responsibility for the obligations growing out of the contract. These warranties are not made if, at the time of the contract, he makes full disclosure with respect to his authority or character of the principal.

An agent who has collected money to which his principal is not entitled—such as an overpayment—is obligated to return it if the error is discovered before the money is surrendered to the principal. However, if an agent's own carelessness is the cause of an erroneous collection, he remains liable to the third party even if he has paid it to the principal.

10. Termination. An agency is terminated by operation of law by the death or insanity of either principal or agent or by the destruction of the subject matter of the agency. Such termination is automatic and requires no notice to third parties.

The authority of an agent can also be terminated by the act of his principal or himself; even if such act is in breach of their contract of employment, the agent possesses no more authority to bind his principal. However, upon termination of the agency by act of one of the parties, the principal has a duty to give notice thereof to third parties. Failure to do so makes him liable for acts of the agent which occur after dismissal. Those who have previously dealt with the principal through the agent are entitled to direct notice. Receipt of written or verbal notice is required to warn them that the agent no longer is authorized to bind the principal. To those who knew of the agency but had not dealt with the agent, public notice through advertisements in newspapers, trade journals, or other media generally available to interested third parties is sufficient. No knowledge of the notice by such third parties is necessary.

An agency coupled with an interest of the agent in the subject matter with which the agency is concerned cannot be terminated within the lifetime of the principal and is not terminated by his death. As an illustration, consider a mortgage that gives the mortgagee the right to sell the mortgaged property as the debtor's agent, on the default by the debtor. Here, because of the agent's interest in the property, the mortgagor cannot terminate the agent's power of sale.

Partnerships

1. Nature of a Partnership. In addition to individual proprietorships, there are several other forms of business organizations; the most important of these are partnerships and corporations. In most states the law relating to partnerships is found in the Uniform Partnership Act (UPA). A *partnership* is the result of an agreement, whereas a *corporation* is a creation of the state. Whenever two or more persons agree to carry on, as co-owners, a business for profit, a partnership results. There can be no partnership unless the members have by voluntary conduct indicating common consent, or by formal agreement, entered into such a relationship. Each partner has unlimited personal liability for all obligations and liabilities of the firm.

Mere co-ownership of property or authority to represent another in business transactions does not establish a partnership. However, an agreement to share the net profits of a business is *prima facie* evidence of a partnership, except where the share of profits is received in lieu of interest, as wages or salary, as rent, for goodwill, or as an annuity to the widow of a deceased partner.

It is possible for a person to incur partnership liability by estoppel without actually being a member of a firm. Partnership by estoppel arises when one person holds himself out or permits another to hold him out as though he were a partner and a third person relies on this conduct to his damage. Assume that A permits B to publish a statement to the effect that they are partners. C, who knows of the statement, sells B merchandise on credit because of A's assumed connection with B. A is liable to C as though he were a partner if B defaults.

2. Partnership Property. Property invested by the partners or acquired with partnership funds becomes partnership property. However, property owned by one or more of the partners but used by the firm in the business is not thereby owned by the firm. Unless the owners invest it in the business, the property continues as an individual asset, even though the firm pays no rent and maintains the property at firm expense.

An individual partner has no interest in any specific piece of firm property which he can sell or mortgage as his own but has the right and power to use it in the ordinary conduct of the firm business. The property is owned by the firm, and the creditors of an individual partner cannot reach it. The partner has an interest in the firm as such, and this interest may be voluntarily sold or his creditors may force a sale of it through proper court action. Such a sale does not of itself work a dissolution of the partnership, and the buyer of the interest does not thereby become a partner. Unless the other partners accept him as a partner, the buyer's only rights are to receive the share of profits to which the partner would have been entitled and to effect a dissolution, liquidation, and return of capital at such time as the debtor partner could properly have done so. Otherwise, the creditor has no voice in the management of the business.

Title to personal property is held in the firm name and is sold or mortgaged under that name. At common law, title to real property was necessarily held in the individual name of one or more of the partners but the Uniform Partnership Act permits it to be held in the firm name.

3. Powers and Duties of Partners. In addition to being an owner and manager of the firm, each partner is a general agent of it. Thus the law of agency has significant application to the law of partnerships. Each partner has the apparent authority to bind the firm to contracts if he acts within the scope of the firm business. He also may bind the firm to contracts outside the ordinary course of its business if he has been given actual authority. The articles of copartnership may limit the authority possessed by a particular partner, but a limitation of this kind does not affect the rights of third parties unless it is known to them. In addition, the firm is liable for the torts of a partner which are committed while he is acting in the course of the partnership business.

The power of a partner to borrow money and execute firm notes exists only when such act has been expressly or impliedly authorized. Partners in a trading concern—one that buys and sells—have implied power to borrow because the nature of the business is such that borrowing at certain seasons is customarily necessary. Those in a nontrading firm have no such implied power.

Any one of the partners presumably has the right and power to sell inventory in the ordinary course of the partnership business. If he has the right to borrow money, he may also execute a chattel mortgage on the personal property which will bind the firm, except if so much property of the firm is included that a foreclosure of the mortgage would put the partnership out of business. The sale of fixtures or equipment is outside the ordinary scope of the firm business. To bind the partnership to such a contract, a partner must have actual authority.

Title to real property held in the firm name may be effectively conveyed by one member of the firm if the firm is engaged in the business of buying and selling such property. Otherwise a partner has no implied authority to dispose of firm realty, and a purchaser from him would not get good title, since the other partners could avoid the conveyance. If the person who acquired title because of a partner's wrongful sale resells it to an innocent third party, the firm may not regain the property. The contract of sale can be avoided only against the immediate purchaser from the firm. When real property is held in the name of one of the partners, any purchaser who is innocent of the fact that it is firm property will take good title.

Unless provided otherwise in the agreement, each partner has an equal voice in the management of the business, regardless of his investment. In case of a dispute, the firm's internal business affairs are controlled by a majority of the partners, so long as they deal with matters within the scope of the partnership business. However, the partnership agreement can be amended only by unanimous approval. Thus a provision for increasing capital investment, adding a new partner, or changing the nature of the business becomes operative only when assented to by each partner, unless amendment of the partnership agreement is otherwise provided for. In addition, the UPA provides that the approval of all partners must be obtained in order to submit a claim to arbitration, confess judgment against the firm, make an assignment for the benefit of firm creditors, or do any other act that might make the continuance of the business impossible.

A partner has a fiduciary relationship with the firm and his copartners. He owes them a duty of loyalty which is similar to that an agent owes his principal.

4. Rights of Partners. Partners have the right to share in the profits of the enterprise in conformity with the partnership agreement; but if no agreement has been made, profits are shared equally. Losses, including losses of capital, are shared in the same ratio as profits unless the partnership agreement reads otherwise. If one partner is unable to contribute his full share of the loss, the others divide his loss in the same ratio in which they share profits, one to the other.

A partner receives no compensation for his services and no interest on his investment in the absence of an agreement, since it is assumed that these matters are taken into consideration in arriving at his share of the profits. A partner who spends time liquidating the partnership business is entitled to compensation for such services, since no profits are anticipated from this work. Likewise, a partner who has made advances to the firm is entitled to interest on the advance. Profits left in the business are not considered to be an advance unless the partners agree to treat them as such.

A partner has a right to inspect the books and to have an accounting as provided for in the articles of copartnership. If profits are withheld, if a partner is barred from inspecting the records, or if he has wrongfully refused to account for profits, a formal court accounting may be had. Normally, a partner has no right to sue a copartner on any matter concerning the partnership until there has been a formal accounting to determine their respective rights, and the courts refuse to order an accounting to settle minor disagreements between the parties.

5. *Dissolution.* Dissolution results from a change in the relationship among the partners. It is not the same as termination. After a dissolution, a new firm may continue in business; or, if operations are to be ended, the old firm remains in existence for the time necessary to wind up its affairs. The dissolution of a partnership terminates the authority of any partner to bind the firm on any matter other than liquidation. Any contracts made thereafter for any purpose other than liquidation become his own individual responsibility. However, if a contract were made following the death or bankruptcy of a partner, of which the contracting partner had no notice, all partners must share in the responsibility for the agreement. Under the UPA a partner is entitled to notice of termination in such cases.

Unless proper notice has been given to third parties following dissolution, contracts improperly made in the firm name by one of the partners will bind the firm. Notice is required when dissolution is caused by the death of a partner or by any act of a partner or partners. If dissolution is caused by court decree or bankruptcy, power to bind the firm is terminated without notice, for it is assumed that the general public will have knowledge of such events. Under the UPA, direct notice need be given only to those who have had credit dealings with the firm. Public notice through newspapers, trade journals, and the like is sufficient in other cases. A dormant partner, one who is both silent and secret, is not required to give notice of his withdrawal, since credit to the firm could not have been extended on the basis of his connection with it.

6. *Causes of Dissolution.* Partnerships may be dissolved by acts of the partners, by operation of law, or by court decree. A partnership is dissolved by the acts of the partners when the period provided for the life of the partnership has expired, when all the partners—or the requisite number under the agreement—agree to dissolution, or when any

one partner notifies the others of his intention to withdraw. Under a partnership at will, any partner is free to dissolve the firm at any time he desires.

Although the partnership agreement specifies the time for its existence and the period has not expired, one partner has the power, but not the right, to terminate it earlier. Such conduct on his part constitutes a breach of contract and makes him liable for the damages his partners suffer as a consequence. He also forfeits all interest in firm goodwill and loses his right to participate in the liquidation of the firm.

The partnership may be dissolved in conformity with the terms of the partnership agreement. The expulsion of a member from the firm causes a dissolution; under such circumstances, the right to expel and the method of liquidation or compensation for loss of interest depend entirely on the terms expressed in the articles of copartnership.

The death of a partner, the bankruptcy of the firm or a partner, or the illegality of the business of the firm dissolves the firm by the operation of law. Such acts dissolve the partnership automatically, and no additional act is required.

Upon petition by one of the partners, the court will decree a dissolution for proper cause. A showing that the business cannot be continued at a profit, that one of the partners has become incapacitated by illness, or that one of the partners has been guilty of grave abuse of his powers should result in a court order of dissolution. Similarly, a partner who has been induced to become such because of fraud may have the agreement rescinded, provided he acts promptly after the fraud is discovered. For the period during which he has been a partner, however, he has a partner's liability for firm obligations.

7. *Withdrawal or Addition of Partner.* The withdrawal of a partner or the addition of a new partner causes a dissolution of the old firm and the creation of a new one. Because this often happens without complete liquidation, the UPA provides that, if the business is continued by one or more of the survivors, the old firm creditors become new firm creditors and all share alike in firm assets if the new firm becomes insolvent. The same holds true if the new firm contains no old member, provided the old firm debts have been assumed. Thus if A, B, and C are partners and C, with the approval of A and B, sells his interest to D, the business may be continued without liquidation. In that event, the creditors of the firm A, B, and C become the creditors of the firm A, B, and D.

Unless a novation occurs, a withdrawing party continues liable for all firm obligations incurred prior to his withdrawal and possibly, if proper notice of dissolution has not been given, for debts of the new firm.

An incoming partner incurs no personal liability for old firm debts unless he assumes them. To the extent that he invests in the firm, his capital may be used to pay either set of creditors, but his personal liability extends only to the creditors who became such after he joined the firm. Consequently, D, on becoming a member of the firm in which C formerly held the interest, has no *personal* liability to the creditors of the firm A, B, and C in event of the failure of the new firm unless, when he acquired C's interest, he expressly assumed responsibility for outstanding liabilities.

8. Liquidation. A partnership that has been dissolved should be promptly liquidated by the survivors. The particular method of liquidation may be determined by the majority, acting in good faith, but it is their duty to turn all assets into cash, including goodwill. This applies to land as well as personal property, unless all the interested parties are willing to distribute the assets in kind.

The partnership agreement or the will of a deceased partner can effectively provide for the retention by the survivors of the interest of the deceased in the business for a reasonable period of time. If so, the estate of the deceased does not become a member of the firm and is in no way liable for the new obligations incurred, except that the interest of the deceased may be increased or decreased as profits or losses develop. A will that provides for retention of the partner's capital after his death gives the firm no right to retain accumulated profits. Profits currently unwithdrawn do not become capital.

9. Distribution. So long as a partnership continues to operate by mutual agreement of the partners, it may dispose of its assets as it sees fit. The assets may be used to pay the debts of individual partners, unless the transfer becomes a fraud on the firm creditors. Following liquidation, however, the UPA does provide an order of payment. Creditors are to be paid first, followed by advances that have been made by the partners. Partners should not be repaid their advances until charged with their share of losses. If the capital is unable to bear the loss, only the net advance over and above the share of losses is repaid. Capital is next in line for payment, and any additional sum realized is divided in the profit-and-loss ratio.

Problems concerning the liquidation and distribution of partnership assets frequently appear on CPA Examinations. For example, assume that the ABC partnership has the following trial balance and is in the process of winding up:

ABC PARTNERSHIP

TRIAL BALANCE
(DATE)

Cash	$31,000	Creditors	$20,000
Other assets	59,000	B, advance	5,000
		A, capital	30,000
		B, capital	10,000
		C, capital	25,000
	$90,000		$90,000

Creditors should be paid first:

Debit: Creditors	20,000	
Credit: Cash		20,000

Assume that $1,000 will be sufficient to meet liquidation expenses, that the profit-and-loss ratio is one-third each, and that the partners wish to pay out the remaining $10,000 in cash as an installment distribution without waiting for further realization on the other assets.

Although B has a preferred claim of $5,000, he is not entitled to share in the $10,000 installment distribution unless his capital account is adequate to absorb his share of all *possible* losses which the firm might encounter during dissolution.

In the present illustration, the $10,000 should be distributed to A and C according to the following computation:

	A	*B*	*C*
Balances:			
Advance	$ –0–	$ 5,000	$ –0–
Capital	30,000	10,000	25,000
Total	$30,000	$15,000	$25,000
Possible losses and liquidating expenses	20,000	20,000	20,000
	$10,000	($ 5,000)	$ 5,000
Possible further loss assignable to A and C	(2,500)	5,000	(2,500)
Installment distribution	$ 7,500	–0–	$ 2,500

10. Insolvent Partnerships. If the partnership assets are in the hands of a court for distribution, firm assets are used first to pay firm creditors. The claim of an individual partner against the firm is deferred until other firm creditors are satisfied. Similarly, a claim of a former partner for money owing to him because of a sale of his interest is paid only after other firm creditors have been satisfied.

Individual creditors have first claim to individual assets in case a partner's assets are under court control or supervision. A partner's claim against his insolvent copartner which grew out of the partnership relation is not paid until other individual creditors have been paid in full. His claim, like the claim of the firm for contribution to losses, is deferred until individual creditors are satisfied. In those few instances in which there are no firm assets and no solvent partners, the firm creditors may share with the individual creditors in the assets of a partner. Normally, however, individual creditors must be paid in full before firm creditors may reach the individual assets of an insolvent partner.

If one of the partners has been conducting the firm business in his own name (and the other partners are dormant or silent), his individual creditors have the right to share proportionately with firm creditors in the firm assets, and the firm creditors share in like manner with the individual creditors in the individual assets of that partner.

If a firm has complied with the requirements of the Uniform Limited Partnership Act, its limited partners have no personal liability for firm debts and stand to lose only their investment. However, there is a requirement that such partnerships have at least one partner with unlimited liability.

Corporations

1. Nature. A *corporation* is a legal entity competent to contract and to hold title to property in its corporate name. It is created by the state and is subject to such regulatory statutes as exist in the state in which it is chartered. These regulatory statutes differ from state to state. Such an entity generally has unlimited life, its shares are readily transferable, profits are divided according to the number of shares owned, and the owners of the shares have no personal liability for corporate debts. Occasionally the courts will disregard the corporate entity in order to mete out justice, usually in cases of a corporation that has been organized to perpetrate a fraud or is dominated in rather detailed fashion by a parent corporation.

To illustrate, let us assume that A and B have sold a business and have agreed not to compete with the buyer for a given period of time. Later, to avoid the effect of this restriction, A and B form a corporation which they completely control to operate a business in competition with the buyer. Under these circumstances, the courts have consistently disregarded the corporate entity and have enjoined it from conducting business, although it, as such, had never agreed not to compete.

Parent corporations have so closely controlled and regulated the activities of a subsidiary that the latter becomes in effect their agent. Under such circumstances, the courts have made the parent stockholder responsible for obligations of the subsidiary incurred in activities that have been strictly controlled by the parent.

A corporation may be either *de jure* or *de facto.* A *de jure corporation* is one that has complied in full with the provisions of the law concerned with its creation. A *de facto corporation* has obtained a charter under a valid state law and has operated under the charter in good faith, but has failed in some minor way to comply with the law. No one except the state can object to the continued operation of a *de facto corporation.* A corporation organized so defectively that it falls short of a *de facto* corporation is usually held to be a partnership composed of those actively engaged in its business.

A foreign corporation—one chartered in one state and "doing business" in another—must obtain a license in order to do business in the second state. If it fails to obtain such a license, it is usually denied the use of the courts of the second state in enforcing its rights against third parties, although it may be sued there itself. A foreign corporation is not considered as doing business in a state unless it has more than an occasional transaction there. Doing business in a state requires substantial activity. Business is not being done in a state when all transactions are conducted by mail from without the state or by a solicitor within the state whose orders must all be approved by the home office and the goods shipped from outside the state.

2. Incorporation. The procedure for forming a corporation is governed by the business corporation act of the state in which it is organized. Usually the promoters submit to the state a fee and an application containing all required information, including: the name of the proposed corporation; the amount and kind of stock to be authorized and the portion to be presently issued, the object and powers of the corporation, and the time for which it is to continue (usually perpetual). As soon as the application for charter is approved by the Secretary of State, it becomes the corporate charter and is recorded in the county in which the corporation establishes its registered office.

Promoters are not entitled to compensation for their services unless an independent board of directors approves payment after the corporation is organized. Contracts made by promoters before incorporation do not bind the corporation unless it adopts them. The promoters are personally liable on all contracts made by them, unless the contracting party agreed to look exclusively to the corporation to be organized. Promoters hold a fiduciary relation to the prospective corporation and are held accountable in much the same way as an agent.

3. Corporate Powers. A corporation possesses those powers expressly conferred upon it by its charter and those which are incidental and useful in carrying out the express powers. For illustration, take a corporation organized to operate a retail clothing store. It has incidental power to buy, sell, employ salesmen, borrow money, rent a place in which to do business, and do many other things that grow out of the operation of such a business. Assume, however, that the corporation guarantees the payment of an obligation of one of its customers. The courts would normally hold that such an act was outside the scope of its business—*ultra vires*—unless, in entering into the contract of guaranty, the corporation was in some manner trying to protect its own interests.

Unless provided for by statute or charter provision, a corporation is denied the right to be a partner in a firm or to invest generally in the stock of other corporations whose business is foreign to its own, since to permit such conduct would be to risk the investment of the stockholders of the first corporation in an enterprise not anticipated at the time they purchased their stock. Corporations may properly invest idle funds in other corporations, and in most states they are authorized to acquire stock in related enterprises in order to expand their own business. Several states permit corporations to enter a partnership to accomplish a similar purpose. However, it is improper to buy stock in another corporation for the purpose of eliminating competition, through controlling the activities of the second firm. A corporation has the right to acquire its own stock by purchase from its stockholders, provided the purchase can be financed out of retained earnings and will not render the company insolvent in the sense that it is unable to meet current obligations as they fall due. This limitation is imposed to protect the creditors against the injurious effect of the reduction in capital indirectly accomplished by such a purchase. Stock purchased by the corporation is called *treasury stock* and lies dormant until it has been reissued. It may not be voted and does not draw dividends.

4. Ultra Vires *Contracts.* Contracts made by a corporation which exceed the powers conferred upon it by the charter are said to be *ultra vires.* Even though a contract is *ultra vires,* it is binding on both parties, whether it be executed or executory. No one may take action against a corporation because it is engaged in an *ultra vires* business except the state and one or more of the stockholders of the corporation. Either can obtain an injunction to block future *ultra vires* conduct, and the state may have the charter forfeited for continued *ultra vires* action. Directors who authorize *ultra vires* business are personally liable for any loss suffered by the corporation as a consequence.

5. Subscriptions. A person becomes a member of a stock corporation by acquiring a share of stock. He may purchase it from an existing stockholder, subscribe to a new issue of stock, or subscribe for stock in a corporation that is in the process of being organized. A subscription to stock in a new enterprise is considered an offer on the part of the subscriber which can be withdrawn at any time prior to incorporation by giving notice to the promoters. If this offer is not withdrawn, the subscriber becomes a stockholder as soon as the charter is issued. Several states make a subscription irrevocable for a limited period in order to give the organizers time to bring the corporation into being. Contracts between subscribers not to withdraw their subscriptions are enforced by most courts.

A subscription for stock is impliedly conditioned on the creation of a corporation exactly like the one held out at the time the subscription was made. If the nature of the business is altered or the capital structure changed, or if the corporation is not a *de jure* one, the subscription is not enforceable by the corporation.

The rights and liabilities of a subscriber to a new issue of stock are largely determined by the contract he signs with the corporation. It may be drawn so that he becomes a stockholder as soon as he subscribes, or it may be so worded that he engages to buy stock at some date in the future.

A share of stock, once acquired, makes the holder a member of the corporation and gives him a "bundle of rights." These rights, to be discussed later, are largely determined by the corporate charter, its bylaws, the language of the certificate of stock, and the general corporation law in force in the state of incorporation. The stock certificate is merely evidence of stock ownership and should not be confused with the stock itself, which is intangible personal property. Stock warrants, on the other hand, are certificates that give to the holder an option to purchase a number of shares of stock upon the terms and conditions outlined therein. They may or may not be transferable, depending on the agreement, and they are valuable only when the price set forth in the warrant is less than the market price of the stock.

6. Preferred Stock. Stock issued by a corporation may be either common or preferred if provision therefor is made in the charter. Unless otherwise stated, shares of stock are common, no one share of stock having preference or priority over any other share; common stock may be broken up into classes, however, so that some shares carry rights different from the rights of other shares. *Preferred stock* is so named because the holder of it is given a preference of some kind over holders of the common stock, usually a preference with respect to dividends or to assets at time of liquidation. If it is preferred with respect to dividends, dividends on it at the stipulated rate must be paid before any dividends on common stock are paid.

Stock preferred with respect to dividends may be noncumulative, cumulative, or partially cumulative, depending on the wording of the contract. Dividends on cumulative stock that are not paid in any particular year accumulate and must be paid in the future with the current dividend before any dividend may be paid on common stock. Many companies have preferred stock outstanding which is cumulative for only a few years or for the years in which the dividends are earned. If the contract says nothing about cumulation, stock preferred with respect to dividends is generally held to be cumulative.

Preferred stock may be either participating or nonparticipating, again depending on the contract. Participating stock, after having been paid its stipulated dividend, shares with common stock in any dividend in excess of that rate, whereas nonparticipating stock receives only its stated rate. In the absence of any stipulation, preferred stock is probably nonparticipating, although there is authority to the contrary.

At dissolution, preferred stock has no preference in the assets over common stock unless the right is expressly conferred by contract.

7. Watered Stock. Stock that has been issued for less than its par value is called *watered stock.* Stock issued as a bonus to induce the purchase of bonds or other stock, stock issued at a discount, or stock issued in exchange for property that has been intentionally overvalued falls into this category. Since the issuance of stock for less than its face value tends to mislead creditors or to reduce the equity that should be available to protect them during the lean years, the persons originally acquiring such stock may be compelled to make good the discount in case the corporation becomes insolvent. It is generally held that they are not liable to the corporation; in fact, they are required to pay only for the benefit of creditors when the corporation becomes insolvent.

Some courts hold that the creditors may recover on a *trust fund theory,* which suggests that the full par value should be paid in full and held intact for them. Other states by court decision use the *fraud theory,* under which the creditors are considered to have relied upon the stock's being paid in full. Under the latter view, which appears to be the doctrine currently in favor, the stockholders are liable only to creditors who became such after the stock was issued and who had no knowledge of the discount. In any event, only the original stockholders are obligated to make good the "water." Later purchasers of stock in good faith cannot be forced to contribute to aid the creditors.

There are times when stock cannot be sold at a given par, and, to avoid the consequences resulting from a sale at a discount, most of the states now authorize the issuance of no-par stock. No-par stock can be sold at any figure established by the board of directors, unless the state has set a minimum. The directors are also authorized to determine the amount of the sale price to be credited to capital stock and the amount to be credited to capital surplus, if any. The right of no-par stock to share in dividends and in assets at time of liquidation should be clearly set forth in the by-laws and in the stock certificate. Otherwise, the right of no-par stock in these areas is not clear.

8. Transfers of Stock. The transfer of stock is governed by Article 8 of the UCC. Under it, investment securities—bonds, certificates of stock, and stock warrants—are negotiable. This is true even if the instruments do not meet the formal requirements for the negotiability of commercial paper found in Article 3 of the Code; however, securities are not subject to Article 3 even if they do comply with it. Negotiability gives to the bona fide purchaser of a security greater rights than he would have if he had bought ordinary personal property. That is, he is free of any adverse claims such as one that the transfer was wrongful or that another owns an interest in the security. In addition, one who takes from a good-faith purchaser has the same rights as his transferor, even if the transferee is not a good-faith purchaser in his own right.

The Code Statute of Frauds provision requires written evidence of any contract for the sale of an investment security, regardless of price, unless one of several exceptions is met. (See section 32 of the material on Contracts, page 621.) Unless restricted by a by-law which was approved by all the stockholders, shares of stock are readily transferable. Any limitation found in the by-laws must be reasonable and must have been known to the buyer of the shares or printed in the stock certificate. A provision in the by-laws that stock must first be offered to the corporation or to other stockholders before it is sold to the public is enforceable.

The transfer of stock takes place when the certificate is delivered with any required indorsement. The purchaser may not be able to enforce in full his rights against the corporation until his name has been entered on corporate records after surrender to it of the old certificate and issuance by it of a new one. But, as between seller and buyer, the exchange of ownership is usually evidenced by the transfer of the certificate alone. A forged indorsement of a certificate is ineffective to pass title, and the named stockholder continues to be the stockholder although he no longer possesses the certificate. However, if the certificate bearing the forged indorsement is surrendered to the corporation for cancellation and a new certificate is issued, and if the new certificate is later sold itself to an innocent purchaser, the corporation finds itself liable to two parties. The original holder must have notified the corporation promptly after he discovered the loss or theft of his certificates. The original stockholder continues as such and the innocent purchaser either becomes a stockholder or has an action against the corporation for damages. The corporation, in turn, has an action against the person surrendering the old certificate for a new one. That person had no title and should, in the end, assume liability for the loss.

A security may be indorsed in blank (the signature of the indorser alone) or specially (where the indorser signs and specifies the name of the transferee). An indorsement of a security may be on a separate document. A security issued to bearer can be transferred by delivery alone, and a special indorsement of it does not change this characteristic. However, a registered security indorsed by the owner in blank may thereafter be transferred by delivery without further indorsement until the name of a transferee is filled in. If a security that is transferable by delivery alone is stolen or improperly transferred, an innocent purchaser of it obtains good title.

A person by transferring a security to a purchaser for value warrants that: his transfer is effective and rightful, the security is genuine and has not been materially altered, and he knows no fact that might impair the validity of the security. However, in the absence of a special agreement, the transferor or indorser does not guarantee that the issuer will honor the security.

9. Rights of Stockholders. Unless denied by corporate charter or contract, all stock carries with it the right to vote; each share has one vote, regardless of its par value.

A stockholder has the right to inspect any and all corporate records for any proper purpose. He has the right to obtain a list of stockholders in order to fight for proxy control in the election of new directors, and he has a right to check the operating records to determine whether management is functioning properly. The stockholder is not free, however, to use the information obtained adversely to the best interest of the corporation or to serve his outside interests.

Each share of stock carries with it a *preemptive right* to share proportionately in any new issue of old or newly authorized stock. Before a new issue of stock can be sold to the public, it must first have been offered to existing shareholders so that they may have an opportunity to preserve their equity in the surplus and their comparative voting strength. The preemptive right may be, and often is, limited in the charter; and some states by legislation make possible the sale to employees of stock free of any preemptive right. Preferred stock that carries either the right to vote or the right to participate in dividends is considered as possessing the preemptive right. This right may be sold by the stockholder if he does not care to purchase added stock. The preemptive right is generally held not to apply to treasury stock. The directors are free to sell treasury stock to any person at any time.

Under unusual circumstances, shareholders are permitted to sue third parties who have injured the corporation in a stockholder's derivative action. In the event that a recovery is obtained, the proceeds belong to the corporation as a whole and not to the particular stockholder who instituted the suit. Before bringing suit, such stockholders must first request the directors to take action or must show that it would have been useless to do so, as where the suit is against the directors themselves.

10. Right to Dividends. A corporation may declare dividends in cash, property, or its own shares out of accumulated earnings (i.e., "retained income" or "earned surplus") if such exists. For other cases, the statutes vary from state to state, but there appear to be two distinct approaches. One group approves of a dividend whenever the capital stock (par or stated value) is not and will not be impaired because of it. Apparently in states adopting this view, capital or paid-in surplus as well as retained income may be used for dividends. This is probably the majority rule and is that adopted by the Model Business Corporation Act. Under it, revaluation surplus may be used only for stock dividends. And, if a stock dividend is declared, the Act requires a transfer from surplus to stated capital of an amount equal to: the total par value of the shares issued; or, if no-par stock is given, the total stated value of it as fixed by the board of directors. Also, the Act prohibits any distribution of dividends if the corporation is insolvent (unable to pay current liabilities as they fall due) or if the payment of them would render it insolvent. Another group of states seems to make the existence of net profits the controlling test. In these states, dividends may be declared out of profits earned from current operations even if a deficit exists because of the operations of previous years. It appears that this view follows the common law and does not permit either capital surplus or revaluation surplus to be used for dividends of any kind.

Dividends on preferred stock must be payable in cash unless the stockholders are willing to take something else. Stock dividends may be declared only where unissued stock is available for the purpose. Property dividends are most commonly paid in the stock of some other company, but occasionally other corporate property serves this purpose.

The wisdom of declaring a dividend rests exclusively with the board of directors, but they may not wantonly abuse their discretion.

By court action, stockholders may compel the declaration of a dividend by showing that cash and profits are available and that the directors are capricious, having no plan for the use of the assets. Also, directors may not accumulate profits over extremely long periods of time without distributing some of them to the stockholders.

11. Ownership of Dividends. Property and cash dividends become a debt of the corporation as of the date on which they are declared. Once notice of the declaration has been made public, the dividend may not be rescinded by the board of directors. Stock dividends, however, create no immediate debt and can be rescinded by later action of the board of directors.

As between a seller and buyer of stock, the dividend usually belongs to the owner of the stock at the date of the declaration unless their agreement reads otherwise. When the dividend is declared at one date, is payable to all stockholders of record at a later date, with the date of payment being still later, the dividend belongs to the owner of the stock at the record date. The actual recording of the certificate has no bearing on the issue as between seller and buyer. If the buyer fails to receive the dividend because he has failed to record his ownership, the person receiving it will hold the funds for the owner's benefit.

12. Stockholders' Meetings. Stockholders' meetings can properly be held only when the requisite notice has been given to all stockholders, unless all are present at the meeting. Lack of notice to a few of the stockholders may be used to invalidate the action taken at a meeting. Business at a meeting can be conducted only in the presence of a quorum, which consists of holders of a majority of the stock, except when a different figure is established by the charter or the by-laws. Each shareholder is entitled to one vote for each share of stock held by him, and he may vote in person or by proxy. The proxy acts as an agent of the stockholder and may vote as he sees fit unless limited by the proxy agreement that authorizes him to act. When several directors are to be elected, most of the states permit cumulative voting, the number of shares owned being multiplied by the number of directors to be elected and then divided among the candidates as the owner elects. This gives minority interests an opportunity to be represented.

Voting trusts and pools, whereby a stockholder surrenders his stock to a trustee for voting purposes or agrees to vote it as a unit with certain other stockholders for a given period of time, are enforceable if reasonable in their duration and not created for an improper purpose.

13. Directors. Directors are elected by the shareholders and need not be stockholders unless required to be by statute or corporate by-law.

They are the active managers of the corporate business and cannot be interfered with by the shareholders. Generally, directors are not liable for losses due to errors in judgment as long as they have acted honestly and have exercised reasonable care. They receive no compensation for their services as directors unless the by-laws so provide, but they may receive compensation for other services rendered.

Directors have a fiduciary relationship with the corporation. Thus they should not vote on any matter in which they have a personal interest. If they do, their vote may not be counted and the action taken may later be rescinded in a court action. This appears to be true even though the vote was not needed for passage of the motion. Some courts have gone so far as to hold that any action taken on a matter of this kind when the director is present is voidable. A director who is also an officer should not be present at a meeting during which the salary of the officer is being established; or, if he has been present, such director should have the action of the directors approved at the annual meeting of the stockholders.

Meetings of the board of directors may be held at regularly scheduled times or at irregular intervals. For any action taken at a special meeting to be valid, all directors must have received proper notice of the meeting or must have attended it. Directors may not vote by proxy, and action taken by the board must be in a formal meeting with a quorum present. A majority constitutes a quorum.

14. Dissolution or Charter Amendment. The laws relating to dissolution, consolidation, merger, and other charter changes are highly technical and are set forth in detail in statutory form. Since they vary materially from state to state, no attempt is made to deal with them here.

Bankruptcy

1. Nature. Bankruptcy is a procedure in federal courts whereby an insolvent's assets are taken for the benefit of his creditors and the debtor is released of further liability for his existing obligations. A voluntary petition in bankruptcy may be filed in Federal District Court by any person, partnership, association, or corporation, except banking, building and loan, insurance, municipal, and railway corporations. An involuntary petition may be filed against any person, partnership, association, or corporation, with the exception of: the five types of corporations just named, farmers, nonbusiness corporations, and wage earners who are compensated at the rate of $1500 or less a year. The status of a bankrupt, in case he changes his vocation, is determined as of the date he commits his act of bankruptcy.

A petition in involuntary bankruptcy will fail unless: the debtor has liabilities of at least $1000, the petitioning creditors have total unsecured claims of at least $500, the signing creditors are at least three in number if there are twelve or more creditors (if less than twelve, only one signer is required), and unless the creditors show that the debtor has committed one of the acts of bankruptcy.

2. *Acts of Bankruptcy.* The purpose of involuntary bankruptcy is to work out a fair distribution of a debtor's assets among his creditors. A debtor cannot be forced into bankruptcy merely because he is insolvent. He must have committed some act that may impair the position of some of his creditors, and the Bankruptcy Act lists the acts of bankruptcy as follows:

1. Conveyed, transferred, concealed, or removed, or permitted to be concealed or removed, any part of his property with intent to hinder, delay, or defraud his creditors, or any of them.
2. Transferred, while insolvent, any portion of his property to one or more of his creditors with intent to prefer such creditors over his other creditors.
3. Suffered or permitted, while insolvent, any creditor to obtain a lien on his property through legal proceedings and not having vacated or discharged such lien within thirty days from the date thereof or at least five days before the date set for the sale or other disposition of such property.
4. Made a general assignment for the benefit of creditors.
5. While insolvent or unable to pay his debts as they mature, procured, permitted, or suffered voluntarily or involuntarily the appointment of a receiver or trustee to take charge of his property.
6. Admitted in writing his inability to pay his debts and his willingness to be adjudged a bankrupt.

Solvency at the time the petition is filed is a good defense to the action under only the first act of bankruptcy. Under some of the others, insolvency at the time of the act is required but solvency at the date the petition is filed is of no importance.

The petition in bankruptcy must be filed not later than four months following the alleged act of bankruptcy. If the act of bankruptcy is one which is usually accompanied by filing or recording some document, the four-month period dates from the time of recording, which is usually some time after the preferential or fraudulent transfer takes place.

3. Officers of the Court. After a petition in bankruptcy is filed, the court appoints a referee to hear the evidence and report his findings. In a general way, the referee supervises the bankruptcy proceeding and must approve all dividend payments made by the trustee.

The trustee in bankruptcy, elected by the creditors, takes title to the bankrupt's property as of the date the petition is filed, since the adjudication dates back to that time. Property acquired by the bankrupt following the filing of the petition becomes part of his new estate, except that bequests, devises, and inheritances received within the first six months following the filing of the petition become part of the bankrupt estate to be handled by the trustee. Executory contracts of the bankrupt may be either accepted or rejected by the trustee. If he rejects them, the injured party files a claim against the estate.

A receiver in an ordinary bankruptcy proceeding is appointed by the court to preserve wasting assets until such time as a trustee can be elected. In a reorganization proceeding, he is usually charged with operating the business until a plan of reorganization is approved.

4. Recoverable Preferences. Any transfer of property as payment, or security, for an existing unsecured debt by one who is insolvent is a preference. If at the time he makes the transfer or payment he intends to prefer the creditor and the creditor knows, or has reason to believe, the debtor to be insolvent, the trustee may have the preference set aside. Preferences can be avoided only if they have been received within the four months immediately preceding the institution of the bankruptcy proceeding. If the creditor is compelled to surrender his payment or security, he then becomes an ordinary creditor of the bankrupt estate. However, a creditor who receives his preference more than four months prior to bankruptcy or who receives it without knowledge of the debtor's insolvency may retain the property or security received. A judgment lien obtained within four months of bankruptcy is voidable without proof of knowledge of insolvency on the part of the creditor. It becomes an unsecured claim against the bankrupt estate.

Payment of an adequately secured claim or a transfer for present consideration creates no preference, being rather an exchange of assets. Thus a mortgage given to secure a current loan is valid, although the debtor is known by the lender to be insolvent.

Mutual debts between the debtor and his creditors are set off against one another and a claim for the difference only is filed. Claims cannot be purchased for the express purpose of being set off but must arise in good faith out of the normal transactions between the parties. A creditor who extends additional credit to the insolvent debtor, because of payments made on account, has been preferred only to the extent of the net difference. Thus if a creditor, with full knowledge of the debtor's insolvency, accepts a $10,000 payment on account and thereafter permits the debtor to obtain $8,000 worth of merchandise on credit, he may be compelled to return only $2,000 of the $10,000 received.

5. *Provable Claims.* It may be said that all claims against a bankrupt estate, with the exception of certain tort claims, are provable; thus the right to share in the assets exists. All judgments, all contract claims and negotiable instruments, workmen's compensation awards, costs involved in a suit by or against the bankrupt, and claims for taxes are provable. If the amount of the claim is uncertain, time is given to adjust it or determine the issue in court. A creditor who has knowingly received a preference may not file other claims until he returns the preference.

Tort claims that have been reduced to judgments or contracts prior to bankruptcy are provable. Also provable are tort claims based on the carelessness of the bankrupt on whom suit has been started at the time the petition in bankruptcy is filed. Otherwise, tort claims are not provable. Since they are not provable, they are not discharged and remain as claims against the bankrupt's new estate. Other claims not discharged by bankruptcy are those for breach of trust, fraud, taxes due within three years of bankruptcy, and wages earned within three months of it.

The bankrupt is obligated to compile a list of his creditors with their addresses, so far as he knows them. They are then given notice of the proceeding and must file their claims within six months after the first meeting of creditors is held.

6. *Discharge of Bankrupt.* A bankrupt becomes entitled to an automatic discharge six months after the first meeting of creditors unless cause is shown why the discharge should be denied. It is his duty to be present at the first meeting of creditors for questioning; if he refuses to be present, he has no right to the discharge. In addition, the Bankruptcy Act has the following to say about the discharge:

> The court shall grant the discharge unless satisfied that the bankrupt has (1) committed an offense punishable by imprisonment as provided under this Act; or (2) destroyed, mutilated, falsified, concealed, or failed to keep or preserve books of account or records, from which his financial condition and business transactions might be ascertained, unless the court deems such failure to have been justified under all the circumstances of the case; or (3) obtained, as an individual proprietor, partner, or executive of a corporation, for such business money or property on credit, by making or publishing or causing to be made or published, in any manner whatsoever, a materially false statement in writing respecting his financial condition or the financial condition of such

> partnership or corporation; or (4) at any time subsequent to the first day of the twelve months immediately preceding the filing of the petition in bankruptcy, transferred, removed, destroyed, or concealed, or permitted to be removed, destroyed, or concealed, any of his property, with intent to hinder, delay, or defraud his creditors; or (5) has within six years prior to bankruptcy been granted a discharge . . . ; or (6) in the course of a proceeding under this Act refused to obey any lawful order of, or answer any material question approved by, the court; or (7) has failed to explain satisfactorily any losses of assets or deficiency of assets to meet liabilities.

Any one of the foregoing facts, if presented to the court by the creditors, should bar the issuance of the discharge to the bankrupt. Even though a discharge is obtained, however, certain provable claims are not discharged. To the extent that they are not paid out of the bankrupt estate, they carry over and may be enforced against any new assets acquired by the bankrupt. The most important of these claims are taxes, wages earned within the three months immediately prior to bankruptcy, claims arising from willful or malicious torts, claims not listed by the bankrupt where the creditor does not learn of the proceeding in time to file, and claims based upon fraud or upon breach of trust by one acting in a fiduciary capacity. Thus an agent who absconds with funds belonging to his principal cannot rid himself of the debt by obtaining his discharge in bankruptcy.

7. *Priority of Payment.* The trustee's title to a bankrupt's property is precisely that previously held by the bankrupt, being subject to the same liens or mortgages. Thus, if the trustee disposes of such property clear of the liens, he must use the proceeds first to settle the claims secured by the liens. Therefore, real estate taxes, mortgages, and liens are the very first claims to be paid, provided the property that secures them has a value equal to the claims. If the property is worth less than the indebtedness, the difference may be filed as an ordinary claim.

A debtor is allowed by the state of his residence certain exempt property which is not subject to the claims of his creditors. The Bankruptcy Act allows him the same exemption that his state authorizes. If exempt or partially exempt property is taken by the trustee, the bankrupt must be compensated in line with the particular state statute involved.

After the above cited rules have been complied with, the order of payment is as follows, each group being paid in full before the next group shares:

1. The costs of preserving and administering the estate.
2. Claims of wage earners not exceeding $600 to each claimant, provided the wages have accrued within the three months immediately preceding bankruptcy.

3. Claims for money expended in defending against or setting aside an arrangement of the bankrupt debtor.
4. Claims for taxes that have become due within three years preceding bankruptcy. No particular tax has priority over others.
5. Claims for rent if granted priority by state statute and any claims of the United States which by the statutes of the federal government are granted priority.
6. General claims.

Real Property and Mortgages

real property

1. Nature. Real property consists of land and things permanently attached thereto. It includes timber and minerals until such time as they are severed. Personalty (personal property) that is attached to real property becomes a part of it unless the affixation is only temporary. Much conflict in the courts has developed around the right to remove fixtures, particularly as between landlord and tenant, seller and buyer, and as between the seller of the personal property and a later purchaser or mortgagee of the realty. In general, the answer depends on the intention of the person who attaches the personalty to the realty, the intention being shown by his connection with the realty (owner, tenant, or conditional vendor of the personalty), his method of affixation, and the extent to which the personalty affixed contributes to the normal use of the property (called adaptation).

Quite often the seller of the fixtures as personal property retains a security interest in them to protect collection of the purchase price. His right to repossess the fixture after it has been attached to the realty and the realty has been later sold or mortgaged to a third party is often at issue. The UCC protects the security of the original seller, provided he can restore the real property to its condition prior to the time the fixture was added.

2. Interests in Real Property. An *estate in fee simple* is the complete ownership of real property; it is all the right, title, and interest, including the right to dispose of the property. A *life estate* in real property gives the life tenant the right to use and control the property and the income therefrom so long as he lives. A *life tenant* may sell or mortgage his life estate unless restricted by the instrument that created it. The buyer of the life estate would hold the interest until the death of the original life tenant. A mortgagee of the interest would doubtless carry life insurance on the life of the mortgagor to protect his interest.

After the life estate expires, the estate in fee reverts to the former owner who is known prior to the death of the life tenant as a *reversioner,* or to someone to whom it has been conveyed, called a *remainderman.* A reversionary interest or a remainder may be sold or mortgaged, but the deed or mortgage must be subject to the interest of the life tenant.

During the period of the life estate, it is the duty of the life tenant to pay taxes, maintain the property, and pay the interest on any outstanding mortgage; and the tenant is limited in this respect only when the income from the property is inadequate to meet these items. At the maturity of a mortgage placed on the property before the life estate was created, it is not the burden of the life tenant to remove it unless he has contracted to do so. However, if the remainderman pays the mortgage to protect his remainder, the life tenant must continue to pay interest, since neither party may demand that the other improve his position. The life tenant has no right to commit waste, thus destroying or reducing the remainderman's interest. He has no right to cut timber, drill for and remove oil, or mine coal unless this right was conferred when the estate was created or implied because such operations were under way or anticipated at that time.

An *easement* in real property, which gives the holder a limited right to use the land, normally consists of a right of way over, under, or across the land. Unless limited in the grant, the right is continuous, lasting until abandoned or released by the holder.

Many of the states still retain *common-law dower,* which gives the widow a life estate in one-third of the real property owned by her husband at his death. She also has an *inchoate right of dower,* which makes it impossible for the husband to convey good title during the marriage relationship unless the wife joins with him. The husband's interest in his deceased wife's property, formerly known as *curtesy,* has been abolished in this country. Many states give the husband a *dower interest* in his wife's property.

3. Title to Real Property. Title to real property is usually acquired by deed, will, descent, or adverse possession. The Statute of Limitations establishes a limit within which the owner of real property must eject a trespasser who is claiming it. The period is generally twenty years. Therefore, one who is in open and notorious possession of real property for a period of twenty years, claiming it as his own, adversely to the true owner, gains title to it. The Statute of Limitations does not run against the state nor fully against minors; the latter are always given a limited time after arriving at maturity in which to enforce their rights.

The formalities that must accompany the creation of a *valid will* are established by state statutes. In general, a will must be in writing and signed by the testator in the presence of two or more disinterested witnesses and can be made only by one who is of sound mind and disposing memory. A will never becomes operative until the death of the testator, being at all times prior thereto subject to change or revocation unless the testator has relinquished these rights via some binding contract. A person may dispose of his property in any manner he sees fit, with one exception. The right of dower or other statutory provision made for the surviving spouse cannot be defeated by a will. In general, there is no necessity to make provision for children, who can be cut off in favor of a stranger or an organization in which the testator has interested himself.

Whether taken by will or under the law of descent, real property descends directly to the parties entitled to it, and the executor or administrator takes title only to the personal property. He may, however, have real property sold in order to pay debts of the estate when the personal property is not sufficient for that purpose. The dower interest is usually not subject to the claims of creditors, however. In the absence of a will, a person is said to die *intestate,* and the property descends in the manner provided by the statute of the state where the real property lies.

4. Conveyance by Deed. Deeds to real property may be either *warranty* or *quitclaim* in character. The grantor of property by a *warranty deed* impliedly warrants that: the grantor has good title, the land is free of all liens and encumbrances except those noted, the grantor has the right to convey the property, no one having a better interest will interfere with the grantee's quiet enjoyment of the property, and if they do, the grantor will defend in any suit brought against the grantee.

A *quitclaim deed* carries no warranty and acts to convey merely such interest as may be possessed by the grantor. Such title as is held by the grantor is conveyed with equal effectiveness by a quitclaim and by a warranty deed.

A deed of any character is not effective unless it describes the property to be conveyed, names the grantee, is signed, sworn to or witnessed, as the case may be, sealed, and delivered. A deed may be *conditionally delivered* or it may be *delivered in escrow,* the escrow agent to complete delivery when the established condition has been met. In no case, however, does a deed become effective unless the grantor has surrendered possession and control over it at least temporarily. In those states having dower, the deed should be signed by both husband and wife in order to eliminate the inchoate right of dower. The deed should be recorded in the county in which the property is located in order to protect against a second sale or a later mortgage of the land by the grantor, although if the grantee is in possession, his very possession is constructive notice to the world of such interest as he claims in the property.

Deeds may contain either covenants or conditions. A *covenant* in a deed is a restriction on the use that can be made of the land and, in effect, it becomes a promise of the grantee not to violate the restriction. Once on record, a covenant runs against any later taker and can be enforced by other property owners who are subject to the same restriction, since it is presumed that the grantor included it for their benefit. A *condition* is a provision that, if violated, causes the property to revert to the grantor or his heirs. In case of doubt, the courts tend to construe provisions to be covenants rather than conditions.

5. Co-ownership. Property owned by two or more persons may be held by them as tenants in common, joint tenants, co-owners of community property, or tenants by entirety. In the absence of statute or express provision in the deed or will, when two or more persons jointly take title to real property, they become tenants in common. Each has the right to make use of the property but may not bar the other from such use. Any income from the property is divided in accordance with the tenants' interest in the land, which in the case of a tenancy in common may be unequal. That is, one owner may have a two-fifths interest in the property whereas two other co-owners have a three-tenths interest each. The property as a whole may not be leased, mortgaged, or sold without the consent of all the tenants in common, although each co-owner may lease, mortgage, or sell his interest without the consent of the others. Co-ownership does not of itself create a partnership; only an agreement of the co-owners can make the property a partnership asset.

Many states permit co-owners to hold property as *joint tenants,* which carries with it the right of survivorship. At the death of one of the tenants, his interest passes to the survivor. A joint tenancy can be created only by very clear and explicit language, suggesting that the parties take as joint tenants with the right of survivorship and not as tenants in common and, in this case, the interests in the property must be equal. If there are two joint tenants, each has a one-half interest and if there are three joint tenants, each has a one-third interest. While the parties are living, joint tenancy is much like tenancy in common. Either party may sell or mortgage his interest successfully, and creditors of one of the parties may force a sale of his interest. Any voluntary or involuntary sale or mortgage by one of the parties destroys the joint tenancy, and thereafter the parties become tenants in common. After the death of a joint tenant, the tenancy has not been destroyed, and the survivor takes all, the creditors or heirs of the deceased having no enforceable claim against the property.

Several of the states operate under *community property laws,* which provide that property acquired out of earnings during the marriage relationship becomes the joint property of husband and wife. The husband is generally allowed to control the property during lifetime, but at death either party is free to dispose of half of the then-existing property by will.

A few of the states retain *tenancy by entirety,* a relationship which can exist only between husband and wife. It is similar to joint tenancy but cannot be destroyed by either party acting alone.

mortgages

6. Nature. A mortgage on real estate results from the execution of a formal document quite similar to a deed. In many states, however, it must be signed by both husband and wife to void possible prior claims of right of dower. In effect it creates a lien on the property as security for some obligation, usually an indebtedness of the mortgagor. A mortgage has no inherent value and, unless some debt or obligation exists for which it is security, is worthless. Unless the mortgagee takes possession of the property, the mortgage should be recorded. The mortgagor in most states is permitted to remain in possession unless the contract provides otherwise, although some states hold and most contracts provide that after default the mortgagee may enter and take possession. Any mortgagee in possession is obligated to exercise care in making the property productive and must account for the income derived from his control.

The courts will construe an ordinary deed to be a mortgage, provided it is given to secure an indebtedness. A *trust deed* is in effect a mortgage except that the lien is, or may be, held by someone other than the holder of the indebtedness. It is most often used when two or more obligations are secured by the same lien, the trustee holding the security for the benefit of all the noteholders. Unless the trust indenture reads otherwise, at time of the default, the judgment of the trustee as to the advisability of immediate foreclosure is controlling.

If the trustee is also the fiscal agent of the debtor to pay interest and to redeem bonds, payments to him by the debtor are not payments on the debt. Unless the trust deed and bonds provide otherwise, the trustee is deemed to be a paying agent of the debtor rather than a collecting agent of the creditors. Any loss growing out of the trustee's insolvency or misconduct as a paying agent must be borne by the debtor.

A *purchase money mortgage* is one given to the lender of part of the purchase price of real property. It is usually given to the grantor at the same time he gives his deed, as security for the unpaid portion of the purchase price and, if given to somebody else, it must be given at the time the deed is received. The purchaser of the property is considered as though he had purchased property previously mortgaged. He acquires only the equity over and above the mortgage with a personal liability for the secured indebtedness. As a consequence, the wife need not sign such a mortgage, since any dower interest acquired exists only in the equity over and above the mortgage.

7. Transfer of Mortgaged Property. One who purchases property with full knowledge of an outstanding mortgage against it may, when the seller is willing, buy it either "subject to" the mortgage or "assuming" the mortgage. In either case he pays the seller only the difference between the face of the mortgage and the value of the property; but if he acquires the property "subject to" the mortgage, he has no personal liability for the mortgage indebtedness. When the mortgage falls due, he pays it only if at that time he considers the land to be worth as much or more than the mortgage indebtedness. Otherwise he permits foreclosure, whereby he has no liability for any deficit but loses his original investment. On the other hand, if the purchaser assumes the mortgage, he takes on a personal liability for the indebtedness and is liable for the full amount regardless of the value of the land when the mortgage falls due.

The original mortgagor is not released when the buyer assumes the mortgage, since his release can be accomplished only by a *novation.* However, most states treat the original mortgagor in such a case as if he were a surety, thus releasing him entirely if the original mortgagee extends time to the new owner without the assent of the mortgagor. Many states hold that an extension of time given to the "subject to" purchaser releases the original mortgagor to the extent that he is damaged by the extension, this usually being measured by the drop in the value of the land during the period of extension.

8. Transfer of the Mortgage. The holder of a mortgage is free to sell the mortgage indebtedness and assign the mortgage to the purchaser. If the note is negotiable, this frees both the note and the mortgage of personal defenses, provided the purchaser is a holder in due course. The debtor, as usual with negotiable paper, is obligated to locate the note and pay it to the holder. However, if the new holder of the note and mortgage fails to notify the mortgagor and does not record his assignment, a release obtained upon payment to the original mortgagee may destroy the mortgage, but the negotiable note is still enforceable. Of course, if the note is nonnegotiable, the debtor is entitled to notice of the assignment, and, if he receives none, is free to pay his original creditor. If the indebtedness is nonnegotiable, the mortgagee can transfer no better right under either note or mortgage than he possesses.

9. Foreclosure. The owner of mortgaged property can redeem it by payment of the indebtedness and interest at any time prior to foreclosure, provided the indebtedness is due. Many states permit redemption for a limited time after foreclosure and sale, although strict foreclosure, where permitted, eliminates the right to redeem after foreclosure. Strict foreclosure is permitted only where the debtor is insolvent, the creditor is willing to accept the land in full satisfaction of the indebtedness, and the land is worth materially less than the mortgage debt.

Foreclosure cuts off all inferior liens outstanding against the property but leaves all superior liens undisturbed. Thus the buyer of property at a second-mortgage foreclosure would take the property free from an outstanding third mortgage but subject to the first mortgage. The money realized from the foreclosure is used first to meet the expenses of the foreclosure; second, to pay the mortgage indebtedness for which the property is being foreclosed; and third, if any surplus remains, to pay the inferior-lien claimants in the order of their priority. No money is used to satisfy a superior lien. If a deficit results from the foreclosure, the mortgagor and anyone who has assumed the mortgage are liable for it.

The doctrine of *marshalling assets* is called into play when one person has available two sources from which he may effect payment if the debtor fails while a second party has only an inferior right to look to one of these sources. As applied to mortgages, A has a first mortgage on two pieces of property as security for a loan, whereas B has a second mortgage on one of these pieces. At foreclosure B may insist that A foreclose first on the piece having no second mortgage, thus saving for B an equity in the second piece, provided it is not all required to settle the first-mortgage indebtedness.

10. Mechanic's Lien. A *mechanic's lien* is much like a mortgage in effect and is given by statute to contractors, materialmen, and laborers who combine to improve the owner's property. Such liens, to be effective against innocent purchasers or mortgagees of the property, must be filed within a limited time after the work or improvement is completed. Claims of laborers are usually given preference. The lien applies both to the improvement and to the property which is improved, except that a prior mortgage on the property is first on the unimproved realty but the mechanic's lien is first on the improvement or on the amount the improvement has added to the value of the property. Appraisals are often required in these cases to determine how much the improvement added to the value of the property.

11. Leases. A lease given on property previously mortgaged is inferior to the mortgage, with the result that a foreclosure of the mortgage often terminates the lease. No one should pay a lump-sum rental for a long-term lease on heavily mortgaged property. However, a mortgage given on leased property is inferior to the lease and its foreclosure can in no manner impair the position of the tenant. Only bankruptcy of the tenant can terminate this long-term lease; the lease, having been given at a time when no mortgage lien existed against the leased premises, is not affected by foreclosure.

Rental payments are payable to the owner of the property at the time the rent falls due in accord with contract terms. If nothing is said, rent is payable at the end of the period. As between seller and buyer, if the contract is silent, there is no apportionment of the rental money, which is payable to the one having title at the time the rent is payable. The rental income growing out of a lease is assignable; and if the assignee has notified the tenant, the rent is thereafter payable to the assignee. A sale of the property thereafter creates some difficulty in that the majority of the courts hold the rights of the assignee to be superior to those of the new owner of the property.

A lease may be created to run for a definite period of time—being known as a lease for years—or it may be a lease from period to period—month to month or year to year—depending in large measure on how it arose. A lease for years expires automatically at the close of the period, with no notice required, and the tenant who has a right to remove fixtures must remove them before the expiration date. A lease from period to period can be terminated only at the end of a period, but advance written notice of from thirty to sixty days is usually required to terminate it at that time.

The owner of leased property has no duty to keep the buildings in repair unless required to do so by the terms of the lease. The tenant should make a careful inspection of the property, ask questions concerning its condition, or insist on the insertion in the lease of a provision which requires the landlord to maintain the property in a good state of repair. The parts of a building used in common by several tenants remain under the control of the landlord, and it is his duty to see that they are continued in a fair state of repair.

Unless forbidden by its terms, a lease may be assigned without obtaining the assent of the owner. The assignee takes over the rights of the tenant against the owner and impliedly assumes the duties of the tenant so long as the assignee remains in possession. A subtenant—one to whom a portion of the premises is transferred or one to whom the entire premises are transferred for a lesser period than that held by the tenant—derives his rights from the original tenant and owes any duties to him. The subtenant is not liable to the owner for rent but can be ejected along with the tenant if the latter fails to pay the rent.

Suretyship

1. Nature. A suretyship relation exists whenever one person, the surety, contracts to be liable to a creditor for the obligation of another person, the principal debtor. In the broad sense of the term, a surety can have either primary or secondary liability for the debt. However, in the narrow sense, a surety is one who has primary liability; that is, recovery can be sought from him in the first instance by the creditor, without any attempt to collect from the principal debtor. In contrast, a guarantor is one who assumes just secondary liability. He promises to pay only if the debtor does not, thus requiring the creditor to look first to the principal for payment, seeking recovery from the guarantor only if the debtor refuses or otherwise fails to meet his obligation.

A conditional guaranty is one in which the debt is guaranteed to be collectible. Here the guarantor's liability is conditioned on the insolvency of the primary party when the obligation falls due. The creditor must actually sue the debtor (or show that suit would be useless), attempt to collect, and fail. He must also give the guarantor prompt notice of any default. Failure to receive such notice releases the guarantor of liability to the extent of any damage he suffers as a consequence. A few states require notice for all types of guaranty, although it is not required in technical suretyship unless the contract is so worded. Unless otherwise indicated, the text that follows is applicable to both sureties and guarantors.

2. Duration of Relationship. In the ordinary case, the surety continues liable until the obligation for which he is surety has been satisfied or has been outlawed by the Statute of Limitations. In this connection, it should be observed that the principal debtor and the surety each has his own Statute of Limitations. Nothing the principal does, such as making a part payment, can extend the duration of the surety's liability. Similarly, nothing the surety does can extend the period in which the principal is liable to the creditor.

A contract of guaranty that is not explicit with respect to its life and places no limit on the amount of credit that may be extended to the principal debtor is usually construed as applying only to one transaction. Thus, A writes to R, "Let B have what leather he needs, and if he fails to pay for it, I will." This language would not create a continuous guaranty, A being secondarily liable only for the initial purchase of leather. However, if A had placed a limit on the amount, guaranteeing B's credit up to $10,000, the offer of guaranty would have continued until it was withdrawn by the guarantor or otherwise terminated. Such a continuous guaranty of credit has no reference to any particular purchase or any number of purchases. So long as the guarantor has not withdrawn and the debtor has an obligation to the creditor, the guarantor remains secondarily liable, being limited only by the maximum set in the letter of guaranty. After the guarantor gives notice of his withdrawal, he continues secondarily liable on obligations created prior to the date on which his notice reached the creditor.

3. Extension of Time. A contractual extension of time given by the creditor to the principal debtor releases the surety from liability thereafter unless he assents to it; the theory is that the change in the contract terms may prove injurious to the surety. The release is automatic. It is not incumbent upon the surety to show that damages resulted from the extension. The consent of the surety to the extension is effective if obtained either before or after the extension is granted. The surety is released only when the extension is contractual in character, involving consideration and a definite period. Mere indulgence or lack of diligence in collection is not an extension of time and has no effect upon the liability of the surety.

There are four recognized exceptions to the extension of time rule. The surety is not released by an extension of time if he (a) is amply protected by collateral or other security, (b) is a paid surety and undamaged by the extension, (c) is a continuous guarantor, or (d) has rights reserved against him at the time the extension is granted. A simple statement made by the creditor to the debtor at the time the extension is granted that he reserves his rights against the surety is sufficient to continue the liability of the surety. This is the case even if the surety is uninformed about either the extension or the reservation of rights. Regarding the surety, an extension of time with reservation of rights is construed by the courts as mere indulgence. His rights remain unaffected by such an extension, and he is free to pay the debt at any time and to look immediately to the principal for reimbursement. The extension of time, where rights are reserved, does not bind the surety, for the extension is enforceable only between the principal and the creditor. From the viewpoint of the principal debtor, such an extension of time is not entirely satisfactory, since the surety may force payment prior to the close of the period of extension.

Any other material change in the contract terms made by the principal and creditor without the approval of the surety effectively discharges the latter. He has a right to stand on the contract as made. Thus if there are two or more principal debtors and the creditor releases one of them upon payment of a small sum because of insolvency, the surety is released unless he (the surety) assents, rights are reserved, or he has ample security to protect him. A release of one of several cosureties, however, is generally held to release the remaining sureties in part only, the cosureties are released of that portion of the debt which the released surety would otherwise have been compelled to pay.

4. Defenses Available to the Surety. A surety called upon to pay his principal's debt may assert his own defenses against the creditor. His minority, fraud on the part of the creditor, or setoff are a few of the defenses that he may assert. It is also generally conceded that he may use such defenses as are available to the principal debtor, with the exception of the minor's defense and the defense of bankruptcy. The surety's bankruptcy is always a defense, even though it occurred prior to the time the principal indebtedness fell due, but the bankruptcy or minority of his principal will not excuse the surety.

The surety is bound to the creditor although he has been induced by the principal's fraud to become secondarily liable, unless the creditor knows of the fraud at the time he accepts the surety. It is the responsibility of the surety to make certain of his position at the time he assumes his suretyship.

5. Subrogation. In effect, *subrogation* means the right of one person to be substituted to the position of another in his relation to a third party. In suretyship it works in either of two directions. First, if the principal debtor has deposited collateral or other security with the surety for the latter's protection against loss, the creditor may be subrogated to that collateral when the debt falls due and is unpaid. If the surety proposes to return the collateral to the principal, the creditor may have it impounded for his protection in a court action. The protection given the surety is deemed to be for the protection of the creditor as well. If the collateral is given the surety to protect him against loss on many obligations of the debtor, the creditors share in it proportionately. This right of subrogation applies only to security given the surety by the principal debtor. Security given the surety by third parties may not be appropriated by the creditor.

Second, full payment by the surety of the indebtedness secured by collateral in the hands of the creditor entitles the surety to the collateral.

This right of subrogation applies only when all the obligations secured by the collateral have been paid in full. No partial subrogation develops upon the payment of a particular obligation or a part of an obligation. Any voluntary surrender of collateral by the creditor or any negligent loss of it releases the surety to the extent that he is damaged. His right of subrogation has been lost by reason of the creditor's act, and any injury should fall upon the latter.

6. *Rights against the Principal.* A surety who has partially or fully paid his principal's debt is entitled to immediate reimbursement. The Statute of Limitations begins to run from the moment payment takes place. Since the duty to reimburse the surety is implied from the relationship, the contract is considered an oral one for Statute purposes unless the promise to reimburse has been reduced to writing.

A surety who obtains his principal's collateral through subrogation is entitled to utilize it the same as if he had been the original creditor.

The surety is also entitled to exoneration by the principal; that is, to have the principal perform in a way that relieves the surety of the duty to do so. By proper court action, the surety may compel the principal to perform where he has the ability to do so.

7. *Cosuretyship.* Whenever two or more parties are secondarily liable for the same obligation of the principal debtor, they are considered to be *cosureties.* Each surety who pays more than his share of the loss has a right to expect contribution from his cosureties. Unless they agree otherwise, it is assumed that they will share any loss equally except where they are liable in different amounts. In the latter case, they agree by implication to share any loss in proportion to their maximum liability. Thus, let us assumed that P owes C $15,000, and that X, Y, and Z are cosureties. If X is compelled to pay the entire $15,000, he has a claim of $5000 against each of the others. However, if X had guaranteed the credit of P up to $10,000 and Y and Z had guaranteed up to $5000 each, X would have had to absorb $7500 of the loss and Y and Z $3750 each. As soon as the loss has been distributed, each surety has an independent action against the debtor for the amount which the surety has paid.

The loss is first spread among the solvent sureties residing within the state. Each one who contributes on this basis then has an action against the insolvent surety or the one who is a nonresident. Thus in our illustration, if Z had been insolvent or a nonresident, the loss would have been divided between X and Y. Then X and Y would each have had an action against Z for the overpayment they were compelled to make.

Since it is assumed that all losses will be borne by the sureties either equally or proportionately, any collateral that one of the sureties receives from the principal must be shared with the other sureties. It can be held for the protection of the one surety alone only when the others have agreed to such an arrangement.

Secured Transactions

1. Introduction. Secured transactions are governed by Article 9 of the UCC. A secured transaction is one in which a debtor (or obligor) gives a security interest in personal property (the collateral) to his creditor (the secured party). For example, assume that a bank lends X money and takes X's note payable in one year, as well as an interest in X's equipment, to secure payment of the note at maturity. X is the debtor, the bank is the secured party, and the equipment is the collateral. The holder of a validly perfected security interest in personal property is a preferred creditor in that asset. In other words, generally the collateral must be used to satisfy the claim the holder has against the debtor before it may be applied to any other of the debtor's obligations. To illustrate, assume that a proper sale of the collateral nets cash which exceeds the amount of the debt. The secured party's claim will be paid in full, and only the balance of the proceeds will be available for general creditors. If the secured party's claim exceeds the value of the collateral, he will be paid the total amount realized from its sale and will become a general creditor as to the balance. Since the claims of general creditors of a bankrupt may be discharged by payment of only a few cents on the dollar, the advantage of taking a security interest in a debtor's personal property is evident.

The operation of the rules of law pertaining to secured transactions may vary, depending on the nature of the collateral involved. The Code identifies the three general categories of collateral as goods, paper, and intangibles. Each is defined in separate paragraphs.

Goods are tangible personal property. The term embraces all things that are movable at the time the security interest attaches, including fixtures, the unborn young of animals, and growing crops. The four types of goods are consumer goods, equipment, farm products, and inventory. Consumer goods are those which are to be used mainly for personal or household purposes. Equipment consists of goods to be used primarily in business, farming, a profession, a nonprofit organization, or a governmental agency (if not included in the definitions of the three other kinds of goods). Farm products are crops, livestock, or supplies used or produced in a farming operation. In addition, products of crops or of livestock in their unmanufactured state such as milk, eggs, and ginned cotton fall into this classification if they are in the possession of a debtor engaged in farming operations. Goods that are farm products are neither equipment nor inventory. Inventory includes goods held for sale or lease, as well as raw materials, work in process, and materials used or consumed in a business. Inventory may not be classified as equipment. The status of the debtor and his intended use for the goods, as well as their nature, must be considered to properly classify goods that are collateral. For example, eggs are farm products when in the possession of the farmer, inventory when held by a retail grocer who is selling them, and consumer goods when purchased by a housewife for her family's breakfast.

Paper, the second type of collateral, includes documents, instruments, and chattel paper. Documents are documents of title such as bills of lading, warehouse receipts, dock receipts, and dock warrants. An instrument is a negotiable instrument, investment security, or any other writing evidencing a right to the payment of money that is transferred in the ordinary course of business. Chattel paper is a writing (or writings) that evidences both an obligation to pay money and a security interest in or lease of specific goods. If a transaction involves both such a security agreement and an instrument, the writings taken together constitute chattel paper. Such would be the classification of the conditional sales contract and note signed by a customer buying goods from a seller on installment payments.

Intangibles, the third type of collateral, are either accounts, contract rights, or general intangibles. An account is an account receivable, or any right to payment for goods sold or leased or services rendered, provided it is not evidenced by an instrument or chattel paper. A contract right is a right to payment under a contract which has not been earned by performance, provided it is not evidenced by an instrument or chattel paper. General intangibles are any kinds of personal property other than those already defined. In other words, they are any personal property other than goods, paper, accounts, and contract rights. Goodwill, patents, and copyrights all fall into this category.

In order to acquire a security interest that affords him the maximum protection, the secured party must make a security agreement with the debtor, the security interest must attach to the collateral, and the secured party must perfect the interest.

2. *The Security Agreement.* The security agreement between the secured party and the debtor must be in writing and signed by the debtor, unless the secured party has possession of the collateral, in which case it can be oral. It must contain a reasonable description of the collateral. Generally it may contain other provisions as desired by the parties, such

as the amount of the debt to be secured and the terms of repayment agreed upon. If the collateral consists of crops, or oil, gas or minerals to be extracted, or timber to be cut, a description of the land concerned must also be included.

3. *Attachment of the Security Interest.* A security interest cannot attach to the collateral until: (a) there is a security agreement, (b) value is given the debtor by the secured party, and (c) the debtor has rights in the collateral. When all three have occurred, in any order, the security interest attaches unless the time of attaching has been postponed by the explicit agreement of the parties. Generally, value includes any consideration that would be sufficient to support a simple contrast. Also, the secured party has given value when he has a preexisting claim against the debtor. A debtor has no rights in a contract until it is made, in an account until it comes into existence, in crops until they are planted or become growing crops, in fish until caught, in timber until cut, or in oil, gas, or minerals until they are extracted.

The UCC permits a security agreement to provide that collateral acquired after the agreement shall secure all the obligations covered by it. In addition, a security interest is not invalid or fraudulent against third parties because the debtor is permitted to use, commingle, or dispose of the collateral or otherwise deal with it in the course of business. Furthermore, the security agreement may cover future advances made to the debtor. Thus the Code provides for a "floating lien" if it is desired by the parties. Assume that a merchant needs funds to purchase inventory for resale and obtains a loan from a bank for that purpose, executing a security agreement describing his inventory as the collateral. He may be permitted to use the collateral in the normal course of operating his business, by selling it to customers, without invalidating the security interest. When he buys new inventory, it becomes part of the collateral if the security agreement contained an after-acquired clause. If the debtor pays the first loan but later obtains another from the bank, it will be unnecessary for the parties to execute a new security agreement if the original one stated that it covered future advances. The floating lien is provided in the main for commercial transactions. The use of it is strictly limited when the collateral is consumer goods or crops. The Code provides that no security interest can attach under an after-acquired property clause to crops that become property more than one year after the security agreement is executed or to consumer goods that are to be additional security, unless the debtor acquires rights in them within ten days after the secured party gives value.

When a security interest has attached to the collateral, the rights and duties of the secured party and the debtor with respect to the collateral are established. However, the secured party must *perfect* the security interest in order to protect his rights in the collateral against possible claims of third parties. These could be other creditors of the debtor or a purchaser of the collateral from the debtor. Even if a security interest is perfected, some third parties will have superior rights in the collateral. For example, a purchaser of inventory in the ordinary course of business takes good title free of any interest of the secured party. Priorities are discussed in more detail in Section 6.

4. Perfection of the Security Interest. A security interest may be perfected by: (a) the secured party's taking possession of the collateral, (b) filing a financing statement, or (c) attachment alone, in some cases.

If the secured party takes possession of the collateral, the security interest is perfected without the necessity of filing a financing statement. This method would not be practical where the collateral is needed by the debtor, as when it is inventory. However, the method affords a simple way of giving notice to third parties of the secured party's interest if possession of the collateral is not needed by the debtor (e.g., the collateral is investment securities). The *only* method of perfection where the collateral is negotiable instruments or securities is by possession. It is optional if the collateral consists of goods, negotiable documents of title, or chattel paper. However, if the secured party does not take possession of goods, documents, or chattel paper, he may lose his interest to a third party. For example, if the debtor negotiates a document of title, the holder has better rights in it than the secured party, even if the security interest was filed. And, if the debtor sells chattel paper to a purchaser who gives *new* value and takes possession in the ordinary course of business without actual knowledge of the security interest, such a purchaser also has better rights than the secured party.

The filing of a financing statement at the proper public office is a second method of perfecting a security interest. A financing statement is a writing signed by both the secured party and the debtor, describing the collateral. It also states that the two parties have entered into a security agreement regarding it. The security agreement itself may be filed as a financing statement, if it meets these requirements. But often it contains details which the parties do not wish to make public, such as the amount of the debt. The bare financing statement simply gives public notice of the possibility that the secured party *might* have some interest in the collateral. It may be filed before the security interest attaches and still be valid. Unless stated otherwise, it is effective for five years, after which it may be renewed for another five years if the secured party signs and files a continuation statement. If the secured party no longer has a right to a security interest, however, he must file a termination statement to indicate that fact, and he must do so within ten days after receiving a written demand by the debtor. If he does not comply, the secured party is liable to the debtor for $100 plus any loss caused to him. The proper place for filing varies from state to state. The system adopted may be exclusively central filing (in the office of the Secretary of State), local filing, or a combination of the two. If the secured party does not perfect his security interest in *goods* by possession, he must do so by filing (with the exceptions noted in the next paragraph concerning sales to consumers and sales of farm equipment). The secured party also may perfect by filing instead of obtaining possession if the collateral is chattel paper or negotiable documents. (Filing is ineffective regarding the third type of paper, instruments.) Of course, if the collateral consists of intangibles (accounts, contract rights, or general intangibles), physical possession is impossible and the only way to perfect is by filing.

A purchase money security interest is one that is taken by the seller of the collateral to secure payment of the price by the buyer. Such an interest also exists when it is taken by a person who gives value to the debtor so that he can obtain the collateral, if such value actually is used for that purpose. Attachment alone of a *purchase money security interest* will perfect it if the collateral consists of farm equipment with a price of $2500 or less or of consumer goods. (Nevertheless, filing is *required* for a fixture or for a motor vehicle that is required to be licensed.) Such a perfected interest is subject to limitations. It is ineffective against a buyer of the goods for personal use who, without knowing of the security interest, gives value before a financing statement has been filed. However, in such cases, the secured party's rights in the collateral are superior to those of creditors of the debtor and persons to whom he may later give another security interest in it. In addition, a purchase money security interest is perfected by attachment for ten days after the secured party gives value, regardless of the nature of the personal property purchased by the debtor. In order to take advantage of its protection and to have priority over the rights of bulk purchasers from the debtor and his lien creditors, the secured party must file within this ten-day period. (A lien creditor is one who has obtained a lien on property by attachment; the category includes an assignee for the benefit of creditors, a trustee in bankruptcy, and a receiver.) Even if the secured party does file a financing statement within the ten-day grace period, he is not protected from a sale by the debtor of the collateral, or a transaction in which the collateral is given as security for a loan to the debtor, if either occurs prior to the time of the filing.

If the debtor disposes of the collateral, the secured party has a security interest in the resulting identifiable proceeds, such as cash, negotiable instruments, or accounts receivable. In addition, if the disposition of the collateral by the debtor was unauthorized, the security interest in it generally continues. If the financing statement pertaining to the collateral provided that a security interest would exist in proceeds, no additional filing is necessary to perfect it. If the financing statement did not so provide, or if the original interest was perfected by possession or attachment, the perfected interest in proceeds is good for ten days. To take advantage of this provision, the secured party must file a financing statement concerning such proceeds or take possession of them within the ten days.

5. *Rights of the Secured Party.* When the collateral is in the possession of the secured party, reasonable expenses concerning it are chargeable to the debtor and secured by the collateral. Although the secured party is required to exercise reasonable care over the collateral, the risk of any accidental loss is on the debtor to the extent that it is not covered by insurance. Any increase in it or profits (except money) may be held as additional security. Money received must be applied to the debt or given to the debtor.

If the debtor does not pay his debt or perform any other obligation as agreed, the secured party may look to the collateral to satisfy his claim. The secured party has the right to take possession of the collateral upon default and may do so without judicial process, if this can be accomplished without breaching the peace. If the collateral is an account or an instrument, the secured party may, upon notice, require the account debtor or obligor on the instrument to make payment to him. In this event, the secured party must account to the debtor for any amounts collected over the amount of the indebtedness secured, but the debtor remains liable for any deficiency.

Upon default, the secured party may dispose of any collateral he has in his possession, provided he does so in a commercially reasonable manner. He may sell it at a public or private sale, and the purchaser for value who acts in good faith will obtain all rights free and clear of any claim of the debtor or any lien or security interest, including those subordinate to those of the secured party. The secured party may buy at a public sale. He also may buy at a private sale if the collateral has an easily determined market value. In general, reasonable written notice of a sale must be given to the debtor and (except for consumer goods) any other secured party who has filed or who is known by the secured party to have a security interest in the collateral. The proceeds of the sale are applied in the following order: (a) to reasonable expenses of the sale, including attorney's fees; (b) to the satisfaction of the indebtedness to the secured party; and (c) to the satisfaction of any indebtedness secured by a subordinate security interest, if written demand is received before distribution of the proceeds. If any surplus remains, the secured party must account for it to the debtor, but the debtor remains liable for any deficiency.

Instead of selling the collateral upon default, a secured party in possession may propose to retain it in full satisfaction of the debtor's obligation. In this case, he must notify the debtor and (except for consumer goods) any other secured party who has filed or who is known by him to have a security interest in the collateral. If none of these parties objects in writing, within thirty days of receipt of notice, the secured party may keep the collateral. However, any other party who has a security interest in the collateral, but is not entitled to notice, may object within thirty days after the secured party obtained possession of it, and defeat his right to retain it. If any of the above mentioned parties objects to the proposal, the secured party *must* dispose of the collateral by sale, as previously discussed. In addition, if the collateral is consumer goods and the debtor has paid 60% of the cash price or loan, the secured party *must* sell the collateral within ninety days after he takes possession. (However, the debtor may waive this requirement in writing, after his default.) When a secured party takes possession of collateral other than consumer goods for which the debtor has paid 60% of the cash price or loan, there is no time limit in which he must act to dispose of it.

The debtor, or any other party with a security interest, may redeem the collateral by tendering to the secured party the full obligation secured by it, along with the amount of the expenses reasonably incurred. However, such a redemption must take place before the secured party has sold or contracted to sell the collateral and before he has discharged the obligation by retaining the collateral in full satisfaction.

When the secured party does not proceed in accordance with the Code, a court may order disposition of the collateral, or restrain such, in an appropriate manner. If the disposition of the collateral has taken place, the debtor, and any secured party entitled to notice or whose interest was previously made known to the secured party, may recover damages for any loss suffered by a failure to comply with the Code. Where the collateral is consumer goods, the debtor has the right to damages for conversion in tort or to recovery of at least the amount of the credit service charge plus 10% of the principal amount of the debt, or the time–price differential plus 10% of the cash price.

6. Priorities. Generally, if a secured party has not perfected his interest, he only has priority in the collateral over third parties who acquire it or become lien creditors of it with knowledge of his security interest. Otherwise, although he has rights against the debtor, his interest is subordinate to third persons who may claim an interest in the property.

If a secured party *has* perfected his interest in the collateral, his rights as against third parties who also claim an interest in it are governed by Code rules which set up certain priorities. Any buyer of goods from the debtor in the ordinary course of business takes the collateral free and clear of a security interest, even if it is perfected and the buyer is aware of it. In addition, a buyer of consumer goods or farm equipment having an original price not over $2500 (even if outside the ordinary course of business) is free of any security interest if he buys without knowledge of it and for his own or household use. A holder in due course of a negotiable instrument (defined in the material on commercial paper), a holder of a negotiable document of title to goods, and a good-faith purchaser of an investment security all have priority over an earlier perfected security interest. The public notice given by filing does not constitute notice to these parties of the security interest in the collateral. A purchase money security interest in inventory has priority over another security interest if (a) the purchase money security interest was perfected when the debtor took possession of the collateral and (b) the holder of the purchase money security interest has given notice of it (before the debtor receives possession of the collateral) to any other secured party whose interest is known to him or who has filed a financing statement covering the inventory. If the collateral is not inventory, a purchase money security interest has priority if it is perfected within ten days of the time the debtor receives possession. Common-law liens for the repair, storage, or transportation of goods, as well as statutory liens, have priority over a prior perfected security interest as long as possession of the goods is kept by the claimant. If two or more kinds of raw materials are collateral and are combined to make a finished product, the secured parties may share in the finished goods proportionately to the cost of the materials. In other cases (a) the first security interest filed prevails over others filed, regardless of when each attached; (b) if both were not perfected by filing, the first to be perfected prevails, regardless of when each attached; and (c) the first security interest to attach has priority if neither is perfected.

Sales and Bailments

1. Introduction. A sale is a contract by which the seller agrees to transfer his ownership (title) in goods to the buyer for a price. By definition, it involves tangible personal property or goods, wares, or merchandise, only. Unique problems inherent in such an agreement require special rules. Many of these are furnished by Article 2 of the UCC and are summarized in the sections that follow. In any case with which the Code does not deal, it may be assumed that the common law rules relating to ordinary contracts are controlling.

2. *The Sales Contract.* Many of the rules of law that have been changed by the Code were pointed out in the sections on contracts. Additional Code rules relating to the formation and performance of sales contracts are dealt with here.

A contract for the sale of goods may result from conduct of the parties which recognizes its existence, or it may be made in any other manner indicating agreement. It is not necessary that the exact moment of the making of the contract be determinable. Also, the UCC is much more liberal than the common law regarding the requirement that the terms of an agreement be definite. If the parties intended to contract and there is a reasonably certain basis for giving an appropriate remedy, a contract will be formed even if one or more of the terms are left open, are to be agreed upon later, or are missing. Thus commercial standards of what is "definite" are adopted, and the UCC itself has sections that make provision for open price, remedies, and the like. For example, if the price is not settled, it is considered to be a reasonable price at the time of delivery if: nothing is said about price; the price is to be agreed to by the parties later and they do not agree; or, the price is to be fixed by some standard such as market as set by some agency, but it is not so set. However, if the parties do not intend to be bound unless the price is fixed in a manner agreed upon, then there is no contract if it is not so fixed. If either the buyer or seller is to fix the price alone, he must do so in good faith. When the price is not fixed owing to the fault of one of the parties (and it was not to be set by mutual agreement), the other may either fix a reasonable price or treat the contract as being canceled.

In general, the seller's obligation is to transfer and deliver the goods and the buyer's duty is to accept and pay for them. Each party is entitled to performance by the other strictly according to their agreement.

Unless otherwise agreed, the seller has no duty to move the goods. His duty to tender delivery requires him to hold conforming goods for the buyer's disposition at the seller's place of business (or residence, if he has no place of business) and to give the buyer any notice necessary to effect delivery. Tender must be at a reasonable hour and the goods must be kept available to the buyer for a reasonable period of time. If the goods are in the hands of a bailee and are to be delivered without being moved, the seller is required either to tender a negotiable document of title covering them or obtain acknowledgment by the bailee of the buyer's right to them. (Tender of a nonnegotiable document of title or a written direction by the seller to the bailee to deliver is sufficient, however, unless the buyer seasonably objects. Refusal by the bailee to honor the document or instruction invalidates such a tender.)

If the contract requires the seller to deliver at a particular destination, he must tender conforming goods to the buyer there. If the contract requires or authorizes the seller to ship but not to deliver at a particular destination, he must put conforming goods in the possession of a carrier and make a contract for their transportation which is reasonable. The seller must also obtain and tender any document to the buyer which is needed to obtain the goods and must give the buyer prompt notice of the shipment.

If the buyer rejects tender or delivery of the goods because they are nonconforming, the seller has a right to "cure" or make a conforming tender. The right to cure exists only if the time for performance has not yet expired, except when the seller had a reasonable basis to believe that the nonconforming tender would be acceptable to the buyer. In the latter case, the seller has a further reasonable time to cure. In any event, the seller must seasonably notify the buyer of his intention to cure his defective tender. Tender of delivery is a condition to the buyer's duty to accept and pay for the goods and entitles the seller to acceptance and payment when properly made.

Tender of payment by the buyer is a condition to the seller's duty to tender and complete delivery of the goods. Thus the conditions of performance in a sales contract are usually concurrent. The buyer's tender may be made in any way that is currently acceptable in the ordinary course of business, unless the seller demands payment in legal tender. Therefore, tender by a check is proper, except when the seller demands cash and gives the buyer a reasonable time to obtain it. If accepted, payment by check is conditional on the check's being honored by the bank upon which it was drawn. Even if the place of shipment is the place of technical delivery, the buyer's payment is due at the time and place he actually is to receive the goods or, if delivery is authorized by documents of title, at the time and place he is to receive the documents. Under the Code, there is a presumption against the extension of credit. In general, the buyer has the right to inspect the goods at a reasonable time and place before accepting them or making payment, and the inspection may be made after their arrival when the seller is authorized to send them. There is no such right to inspection before payment if the contract provides for delivery C.O.D. (collect on delivery) or for payment against documents of title. Although the buyer must bear all expenses related to inspection, he may recover them from the seller if the goods are nonconforming and he rejects them. If the contract requires the buyer to pay for the goods before inspection, he is not excused from making the payment by the fact that the goods are nonconforming, unless such is apparent without making an inspection. If the buyer does make the required payment, he is not impaired in any of his rights.

The Code defines certain technical terms which are frequently used in sales contracts: F.O.B. means free on board. If F.O.B. the place of shipment is the delivery term of the contract, the seller must put the goods in the hands of the carrier there at his own expense and the buyer bears the freight costs. The term F.O.B. the place of destination requires the seller to transport the goods to the destination and tender them there, bearing the freight costs himself. If the delivery term is F.A.S. (free alongside) vessel, the seller must deliver the goods, at his own expense, alongside the vessel specified or to a dock designated and provided by the buyer. The expression C.I.F. means that the cost of the goods and the insurance and freight to the named destination is included in a lump sum in the price; C. & F. means the same, except the cost of insurance is not included in the price. The term C.I.F. requires the seller, at his own expense, to load the goods on the carrier and obtain a negotiable bill of lading for their transportation and a receipt for payment of the freight, obtain a reasonable policy of insurance covering the goods, and, with commercial promptness, tender all documents, including necessary invoices, to the buyer.

If the contract contains a "no-arrival, no-sale" term, the seller must properly ship conforming goods and tender them on arrival, but he has no obligation that they will in fact arrive. Of course, he cannot cause the nonarrival himself. Such a term is employed when the hazards of transportation are great, as in an overseas shipment, and it protects the seller from a suit for damages for breach in the event the goods are not delivered. In a no-arrival, no-sale contract, where the goods are lost, late, or damaged to the extent that they are no longer conforming, the buyer may treat the contract as voided. Or he may accept the goods, deducting his damages from the purchase price.

It should be kept in mind that, as a general rule, the parties are free to make their own contract and can alter the effect of the UCC by their agreement. However, an attempted disclaimer of an obligation of good faith, diligence, or reasonableness and care imposed by the Code on one of the parties is void.

3. *Title.* The Code deemphasizes the importance of the role of title in a sale of goods. Under the UCC, the rights of buyer, seller, or third parties are determined mainly by specific rules and are not affected by whether title to the goods has passed. However, title may be important in applying a public regulation or taxing statute. In addition, of course, only those goods to which a business has title may be properly included in its inventory. Thus the accountant uses the rules concerned with

passage of title in preparing purchases and sales cut-off statements and in arriving at a correct inventory valuation for the end or beginning of any given period.

The express agreement of the buyer and seller of goods will control the time at which title to them passes. However, title cannot pass to existing goods until they are *identified* to the contract, or to future goods (those not yet both in existence and identified).

Identification occurs at the time of the contract if the specific goods that are being sold are agreed upon by the parties then. It occurs with respect to future goods when the seller ships, marks, or in some way designates them as those to which the contract refers. If the future goods are crops or unborn young they are identified when the crops are planted or the young are conceived. Identification of the goods is required before the buyer can obtain title, but it does not necessarily give him ownership in itself. When goods have been identified to the contract, however, the buyer does obtain what the Code calls a "special property" which carries with it certain special rights. First he has an insurable interest in them (even if they are nonconforming and can later be rejected). Second, his right to obtain the goods themselves is superior to the rights of unsecured creditors of the seller in two situations:

1. The buyer is unable to cover (find a suitable replacement for the goods elsewhere).
2. The buyer has paid part of the price (and has kept open a tender of the balance), if the seller becomes insolvent in ten days after receiving the first installment.

If the parties have not expressly agreed on title, its passage depends on whether the seller has a duty to physically deliver the goods by moving them. Here are the rules that come into play.

1. Seller Has Duty to Move Goods

Where the seller has a duty to deliver the goods by moving them, title passes only when he performs this obligation. The seller has no such duty unless he has agreed to it. He may use his own means of transportation to accomplish the delivery. If so, title passes when he properly tenders the goods to the buyer. A common carrier may be employed, however, in which case the following F.O.B. rules control:

> If the term concerning delivery specifies F.O.B. place of destination, title passes when the seller properly tenders goods *at the destination* by putting and holding conforming goods at the buyer's disposition there.
>
> If the term concerning delivery specifies F.O.B. place of shipment, title passes when the seller places the goods in the possession of the carrier.

If the delivery term is F.A.S. vessel, title passes when the seller has delivered the goods alongside the vessel specified or on a dock designated and provided by the buyer.

2. Seller Has No Duty to Move Goods

If the contract does not require the seller to deliver the goods by moving them, the following rules control:

When documents of title covering the goods (such as bills of lading or warehouse receipts) are required to be delivered to the buyer, title passes at the time of such delivery.

If no documents of title are to be delivered and the goods are specifically identified, title passes at the time of the contract.

If the specific goods are not identified at the time of the contract and no documents are involved, title passes when the seller tenders conforming goods to the buyer at the seller's place of business.

Some sales contracts permit the buyer to return the goods to the seller after delivery, even if they conform to the terms. In the absence of an intent expressed by the parties, title passage in such cases depends on the purpose for which the goods were bought. If the goods were bought primarily for *use* or *consumption,* a "sale on approval" exists. Title here passes only when the buyer indicates his approval even though the goods are identified. Until approval, the goods are not subject to the claims of the buyer's creditors. The buyer's approval may be indicated by use of the goods in a manner inconsistent with the purpose of the trial or failure to notify the seller seasonably of the buyer's decision to return the goods. After proper notification by the buyer of his election to return, the act is at the seller's expense. If the goods are delivered primarily as inventory to be *resold* by the buyer, a "sale or return" exists. In this case, title passes to the buyer according to the general rules already discussed. However, the buyer, if he acts seasonably, may elect to revest title to any commercial unit of the goods in the seller. In this case, the return is at the buyer's expense, and the goods are subject to claims of his creditors while in his possession. Of course, the effect of these rules may be altered by the agreement of the parties. However, if goods are delivered for resale on consignment and title is reserved by the seller until payment or resale, they are still subject to the claims of the creditors of the buyer while in his possession, with the following exceptions: the seller's interest is evidenced by a sign, the seller perfects a security interest, or the seller shows that the buyer's creditors generally know he deals in the goods belonging to others.

The reservation of title by the seller of goods does not affect the operation of the preceding rules but amounts to a security interest for payment. When title has passed, if the buyer rejects or refuses the goods (wrongfully or rightfully), such conduct causes title to revest in the seller.

A buyer acquires the title his seller had, or had the power to transfer. Thus a purchaser from a thief obtains no title, and the true owner is entitled to the goods. However, one who has voidable title can transfer good title to a good-faith purchaser for value. Therefore, a seller who acquired goods by fraud or one who acquired them from a minor can pass good title to a buyer in good faith for value. In addition, if the possession of goods is *entrusted* to a *merchant* who deals in goods of that kind, he can transfer all the rights of the entruster to a buyer in the ordinary course of business. This is so in spite of any condition imposed on the entrusting party by the owner and regardless of whether the delivery was procured by conduct of the merchant that is larcenous under criminal law.

4. Risk of Loss. As in the case of title, the express agreement of the buyer and seller of goods will control who bears the risk of loss if the goods are damaged or destroyed. If there is no such agreement, the placement of this risk depends on whether there has been a breach of the sales contract.

No Breach of Contract

Generally, when neither the buyer nor the seller has breached the sales contract, risk of loss of the goods is on the party *in possession* (or constructive possession through a third party). The official comment to the Code states that "the underlying theory of this rule is that a merchant who is to make physical delivery at his own place continues meanwhile to control the goods and can be expected to insure his interest in them. The buyer, on the other hand, has no control of the goods and it is extremely unlikely that he will carry insurance on goods not yet in his possession." [1] The following rules govern risk of loss where there has not been breach of contract by either party:

If the goods are in the possession of a third party bailee (such as a carrier or warehouseman) and the seller has no duty to move them, risk of loss passes to the buyer when (a) he receives a negotiable document of title to the goods or (b) when the bailee acknowledges the buyer's right to the goods if there is no document or (c) after the buyer receives a nonnegotiable document of title or written direction to the bailee to deliver to him. In this last case, risk of loss passes only when the buyer has had a reasonable time to present the document or direction to the bailee.

If the seller *is not to deliver by carrier,* the passage of risk of loss depends on whether the seller is a merchant. With a merchant seller, risk of loss passes when the buyer actually *receives* the goods. (This includes both the case of the merchant seller required to

[1] Uniform Commercial Code, § 2-509, Comment 3 (Official Text, 1962).

deliver personally and the merchant seller who is to hold the goods for the buyer to pick up.) *If the seller is a nonmerchant,* the risk of loss passes to the buyer as soon as the seller *tenders or offers* to give up possession of the goods. Thus the Code places a higher duty on merchant sellers to carry insurance on sold goods that are in their possession than it does on nonmerchants.

If the seller *is required or authorized to deliver by carrier,* rules similar to the F.O.B. rules discussed previously are applicable. In an F.O.B. shipping point contract, risk of loss passes when the goods are delivered to the carrier. If the contract is F.O.B. destination, risk of loss passes when the goods are duly tendered at the destination.

Breach of Contract Has Occurred

In general, if either the seller or buyer has breached the sales contract, he bears the risk of loss of the goods. However, this shift from the general rules applies only to the extent that the insurance of the innocent party fails to cover the loss. Thus if the insurance of the party injured by a breach of the sales contract is insufficient to cover a loss, the loss shifts to the guilty party to the extent of the deficiency.

A special rule applies to sales on approval. In such sales, the risk of loss does not pass to the buyer until he has approved the goods. However, in a sale or return, the risk of loss will pass to the buyer under the general principles governing such risk, until a return of the goods is seasonably made by him.

5. *Warranties.* A warranty is an affirmation of fact or a promise relating to goods that are sold. It can be expressly stated or can arise by implication from the fact of the sale or from surrounding circumstances. Upon breach of a warranty, the buyer may recover money damages for any loss he has suffered and generally has the right to cancel the contract if he chooses. The Uniform Commercial Code provides for several types of warranties which may be part of the contractual obligation of a seller.

A promise or statement of fact by the seller relating to goods creates an express warranty by him. It is not necessary for the seller to use formal words such as "warranty" or "guaranty" or even to have the specific intent to make a warranty. However, mere statements of the value or of commendation of the goods (known as puffing) or of the seller's opinion concerning them are not considered statements of fact; consequently, they do not give rise to an express warranty. The seller also expressly warrants that where the goods are sold by description, sample, or model, they shall conform to such description, sample, or model. Any attempt to limit an express warranty is ineffective to the extent that it would be unreasonable to construe the limitation as consistent with the warranty.

Where the seller is a *merchant* with respect to the type of goods involved, there is an implied warranty that the goods are "merchantable." This means, generally, that the goods are fit for their ordinary use and must be of a quality that would pass without objection in the trade. They must be of even kind and quality within and among all their units. They must also be adequately packaged and labeled if the agreement requires, and they must conform to any statement made on the label. If the goods are fungible, they must be of fair average quality for the kind being sold. The warranty of merchantability also arises when food or drink is served for consumption. Other implied warranties can arise from a course of dealing or usage of trade.

The warranty of merchantability can be eliminated or modified by agreement of the parties, but the language must specifically mention merchantability. If in writing, the disclaimer must be conspicuous. Also, if the goods are expressly sold "as is" or "with all faults," *all* implied warranties are eliminated, including those of merchantability and fitness. A former course of dealing of the parties or a usage of the trade may also result in eliminating or modifying any implied warranty. If the buyer has examined or had the right to examine the goods (or a sample), no warranty of merchantability arises concerning those defects which his inspection should have revealed.

If the buyer has a particular use for the goods and the seller has reason to know of this purpose and that the buyer is relying on his judgment to select the goods, then there is an implied warranty by the seller that the goods will be fit for that purpose. This warranty extends to purchases made under a patent or trade name and can coexist with the warranty of merchantability. It is not necessary for the buyer to *expressly* make his purpose known, as long as the seller has reason to know of it from some source. The warranty of fitness for a particular purpose applies only to a special use of the buyer which is different from the ordinary use of the goods. It can be excluded by general language such as: "There are no warranties which extend beyond the face hereof." The disclaimer must be in writing in the sales agreement and must be conspicuous.

The seller warrants that he is rightfully conveying good title to the goods, free from any lien that is not known to the buyer. The warranty of title can be excluded only by specific language or by circumstances under which the buyer should know that the seller does not claim to be passing completely good title (such as a sheriff at a foreclosure sale). In addition, a *merchant* seller warrants that no third party will have a claim of infringement of a patent or trademark. Conversely, a buyer who furnishes the seller specifications is liable to the seller for such claims by third parties which arise from following the specifications. Under the

UCC the warranty of title is designated neither as an express warranty nor as an implied warranty.

Express and implied warranties are to be interpreted as consistent with each other and as cumulative, unless that interpretation would be unreasonable. Then, the intention of the parties determines which warranty governs. Exact specifications prevail over an inconsistent sample or model or general description of the goods. Also, a sample prevails over an inconsistent general description. In general, express warranties will displace any inconsistent implied ones except that of fitness for a particular purpose.

The express and implied warranties made by a seller extend to all members of the family and household of the buyer as well as to guests in his home. The seller cannot exclude or modify the operation of this provision by the sales agreement. Whether a manufacturer, grower, or producer of goods is liable for breach of warranty to consumers who are not in privity of contract with him is not uniform from state to state. The UCC is silent on this issue. However, the trend is to make such persons liable to the remote purchaser for damages due to defects that are a serious threat to health or life, such as those in food, cosmetics, and mechanical equipment. Of course, in the states adhering to this trend, the foregoing Code provision applies to expand the manufacturer's liability beyond that to the buyer alone.

6. Breach, Repudiation, and Excuse. If the seller breaches because the goods or tender of delivery does not conform to the terms of the contract in any way, the buyer has the option of rejecting the whole, accepting the whole, or accepting any commercial unit and rejecting the rest. To be effective, rejection must take place a reasonable time after the goods are delivered or tendered and the buyer must seasonably notify the seller of the rejection. Afterward, of course, the buyer must exercise reasonable care in holding the goods in his possession for the seller to remove them, and any attempt to exercise any rights of ownership over them is wrongful except where the Code requires the buyer to sell them. In addition, a *merchant* buyer must follow any reasonable instructions of the seller regarding the goods, if the seller has no agent or place of business at the market where the rejection was made. The seller must furnish the buyer indemnity for his reasonable expenses in following instructions, upon demand by the buyer. In the absence of instructions, the merchant buyer must make a reasonable effort to sell the goods for the seller if the goods are perishable or for another reason may decline in value rapidly. The merchant buyer who sells goods may recover his reasonable expenses out of the proceeds of sale. In addition, he is entitled to the selling commission customary in the trade, or if there is none, to a reasonable amount not in excess of 10% of the sales price. If the goods are not of such a character as to require the merchant buyer to sell them on account of the seller, he has three options, provided the seller gives no instructions within a reasonable time after he has received notice of rejection. He may store the goods for the seller's account, reship them to him, or resell them for the seller, with reimbursement as in the case of a sale of perishable goods.

If the buyer can ascertain a particular defect by a reasonable inspection and fails to state it to the seller, he loses his right to reject nonconforming goods or to establish a breach in two cases: (a) where the seller could have cured if the defect had been stated seasonably and (b) between merchants, when the seller has made a written request to the buyer after a rejection by him for a complete written statement of all the defects on which the buyer intends to rely. Also, if payments are made for documents without a reservation of rights, the payments may not be recovered for defects that are apparent on the face of the documents.

Acceptance of goods by the buyer takes place when, after having a reasonable opportunity to inspect them, he fails to make an effective rejection or states to the seller that they are conforming or that he will accept them even though they are nonconforming. If the buyer accepts any part of a commercial unit, that amounts to acceptance of the whole unit. Acceptance of goods obligates the buyer to pay at the contract rate for them and precludes his rejection of them, unless he has the right to revoke his acceptance as indicated below. Acceptance in itself does not impair any other remedy given the buyer. However he loses all remedies if he fails to notify the seller of any breach within a reasonable time after he discovers it or should have discovered it. In two cases, a buyer may revoke his acceptance and obtain with respect to the goods the same rights and duties he would have had if he had rejected them. Such revocation may take place if the buyer accepted the goods on the reasonable assumption that their nonconformity would be cured by the seller, but such has not been seasonably cured. He may also revoke if he accepted the goods without discovering their nonconformity because of the difficulty of doing so or because the acceptance was induced by the seller's assurances that the goods were conforming. Such a revocation must take place within a reasonable time after the buyer discovers or should have discovered the basis for it and before the condition of the goods has substantially changed for any cause other than their own defects.

Under certain circumstances, one of the parties may have reasonable grounds for feeling insecure about the performance of the other. For example, a seller may learn that his buyer has unjustifiably failed to pay for goods purchased elsewhere. Or, the buyer may learn that his seller has repeatedly cut corners in producing the goods that he sells. In such a case, the party with grounds for insecurity may (in writing) demand adequate assurance of due performance from the other. What is adequate will vary from one case to another. The promise of a reputable seller that a defective delivery will not be repeated would probably be sufficient. However, a guaranty of payment might be required of a buyer who is in a particularly poor financial condition. The party entitled to the assurance may suspend his own performance until he receives it, except with respect to performance for which he has already been paid or received the goods. The failure to provide adequate assurance of performance within a reasonable time (not to exceed thirty days) after the receipt of a justified demand for it constitutes a repudiation of the contract.

The excuses for nonperformance are discussed in the sections on contracts.

7. *Remedies of the Seller and Buyer.* Certain remedies are available to the seller in the event of breach by the buyer. The buyer breaches if he wrongfully rejects or revokes acceptance of the goods, fails to make a payment due on or before delivery, or repudiates the contract in part or whole. After such a breach, with respect to goods affected or the undelivered balance, the injured seller may, in general (a) withhold delivery, (b) stop delivery by a bailee, (c) resell the goods and recover damages, (d) recover damages for nonacceptance (or in a proper case recover the price), or (e) cancel. These remedies are cumulative and include the right to recover incidental damages. If necessary for proper relief, pursuit of one or more of them does not bar pursuit of another in addition.

The seller's right to stop delivery by a carrier or other bailee because of breach is limited to carload, planeload, truckload, or larger shipments. If the seller's notice is such that the bailee can by reasonable diligence prevent delivery, the bailee must hold and deliver the goods according to the directions of the seller. Of course, the seller must pay any resulting damages. If a negotiable document of title has been issued for the goods, the bailee is not required to stop delivery until surrender of the document. In addition, the seller cannot stop delivery after an acknowledgment to the buyer by a bailee that the bailee holds the goods for the buyer. This restriction does not apply to goods in the hands of a carrier while in transit during their original shipment.

If the seller elects to resell, he may do so at a public or private sale and is not liable to the buyer for profits he makes on resale. However, if the sale is made reasonably and in good faith and a loss results, the seller may recover the difference between the resale price and the contract price from the buyer (less any expense he has saved because of the breach). Reasonable notice of the intended resale must be given the buyer, and every aspect of the sale must be commercially reasonable. Any public sale must be made at a usual market, if one is available and the seller is permitted to buy.

In general, the measure of the seller's damages is the difference between market price (at the time for tender) and the contract price, less expenses saved because of the buyer's breach. However, the seller may recover the agreed contract price of goods that have been accepted by the buyer or have been lost or damaged after the risk of loss has passed to the buyer. The seller may also recover the price of goods that have been identified to the contract if he is unable to resell them at a reasonable price after breach by the buyer.

Even if there has been no breach, when the seller discovers that the buyer is insolvent, he may refuse delivery (except upon payment of all cash due). If the goods are in the hands of a bailee, the seller may also stop delivery of them to an insolvent buyer (as in the case of a breach) regardless of the size of the shipment. In addition, if the seller discovers that an insolvent buyer has received goods that were sold on credit, the seller may reclaim the goods by demanding them within ten days after their receipt. The ten-day limit on the seller's demand does not apply if the buyer misrepresented his solvency, in writing, within three months before delivery of the goods.

In addition to his other remedies, the aggrieved seller has the right to recover his incidental damages, including reasonable expenses incurred in stopping delivery, the return or resale of the goods, and the transportation and care of goods after the buyer's breach.

The Code also provides the buyer several remedies where the seller breaches by repudiating the contract or failing to make delivery of the goods. In summary, the buyer may choose among the following alternatives:

1. Obtain specific performance (if the case is appropriate), or replevy the goods (obtain possession of them) in certain instances.
2. Cancel, recover any part of the price paid, and recover damages for nondelivery.
3. Cancel, recover any part of the price paid, "cover" (obtain substitute goods elsewhere), and obtain damages.

The Code also gives the remedies outlined in items 2 and 3 to a buyer who rightfully rejects goods or justifiably revokes an acceptance of them. In addition, such a buyer has a security interest in rejected goods in his possession for any payments he has made on their price and any expenses incurred with regard to them. He may resell such goods in the same manner that an injured seller can resell after breach by a buyer.

The remedy of specific performance was discussed in the sections on contracts. It is only available in cases of goods that are unique, or in similar unusual circumstances. Replevin is the name of the common-law remedy to recover possession of personal property where one has been deprived of it wrongfully. The Code makes replevin available to an injured buyer if the goods have been identified to the contract and he is unable to recover after a reasonable effort, or it would be useless to try; or the seller shipped the goods reserving a security interest for the price and satisfaction of the security interest has been made or tendered by the buyer.

If the buyer chooses to cancel and recover the amount of the price he has already paid, he may also recover his damages for nondelivery. In such a case, the measure of damages is the difference between the market price (at the time the buyer learned of the breach) and the contract price, less expenses saved by the buyer because of the seller's breach. Note here that cancellation (or rescission) of the contract by *either* the buyer or the seller does not discharge a claim for damages for a breach by the other which occurred before the cancellation.

If the buyer chooses to cancel and recover the amount of the price he has already paid, he may elect to recover instead of seeking damages for nondelivery. If so, his purchase of substitute goods must be reasonable, in good faith, and without undue delay. The UCC recognizes that the buyer may still suffer some damages, so the buyer may also recover the difference between the cost of cover and the contract price, less expenses saved because of the seller's breach.

None of the foregoing remedies, of course, is given to the buyer who has accepted goods. However, the buyer who accepts nonconforming goods may recover any loss he suffers in the ordinary course of events by reason of the nonconformity, provided he has given the seller proper notice. Such damages may be determined in any way that is reasonable. Generally, where a breach of warranty has occurred and the goods are accepted, the amount of damages is the difference in value of the goods accepted and the value they would have had if they had been as warranted. The values used are those at the time and place of acceptance.

In addition to any of his other remedies, the injured buyer may recover his incidental and consequential damages. Incidental damages include expenses incurred in inspection, receipt, and care of goods rightfully rejected, as well as those reasonable expenses incurred in effecting cover. Consequential damages include losses of the buyer due to the lack of goods to fill his needs (if the seller had reason to know of the needs and the losses could not have been prevented by cover) and injury to person or property which is a proximate result of any breach of warranty by the seller.

Even if the buyer is guilty of a breach, he may have an action against the seller. In some situations, the buyer is given a right to partial restitution of a downpayment or deposit which was given the seller. Of course, such a payment is first subject to the seller's right to damages (other than liquidated damages provided for in the sales contract), as well as his right to obtain the value of any benefits conferred on the buyer. Then, if the seller justifiably withholds delivery of goods, the buyer is entitled to restitution of that amount of his payment which is in excess of the amount of liquidated damages provided for in the contract. In the absence of a liquidated damages term, the buyer may recover the smaller of 20% of the contract price or $500.

8. Bailments. A *bailment* consists of a transfer of possession and temporary control over personal property without a transfer of ownership. Ultimately, possession of the identical property bailed is to be returned to the bailor or to some third party selected by him. Since, as a general principle, one can transfer no better title to property than he possesses, a bailee, even though he has possession, cannot sell and pass title to bailed property unless he has been authorized to do so by the bailor.

The ordinary bailee of property is not an insurer of its safekeeping unless the contract of bailment is so drawn. He has a duty to exercise reasonable care if the bailment is one for the mutual benefit of the parties, such as a contract for the repair or storage of goods. A bailment for the benefit of the bailor imposes a duty upon the bailee to exercise only slight care, although slight care varies with the value of the property and may, in the case of very valuable property, be a grave responsibility. A bailment for the benefit of the bailee gives rise to a duty to use extraordinary care. If the property is lost or damaged through the failure to exercise this high degree of care, the loss is visited upon the bailee.

The bailor is obligated to notify the bailee of any defects in the property that may prove injurious to the bailee, provided the bailor was aware of them at the time the property was delivered to the bailee. In a bailment for the mutual benefit of the parties, the bailor rests under a duty to disclose all defects he could reasonably have been conversant with. A bailor who leases a car with defective brakes is liable to the bailee who is injured as a consequence, assuming that the bailor could reasonably have discovered the defect prior to the bailment.

A bailment to a public carrier gives somewhat greater rights to the bailor than is true of an ordinary bailment. During the contract of carriage, the carrier is an insurer of safe delivery unless the loss in transit is caused by: (a) the nature of the property; (b) faulty packing, loading, or other misconduct of the shipper; (c) act of God; (d) action of an alien enemy; or (e) action of public authority. The carrier thus assumes responsibility for the acts of all third parties other than those enumerated.

A public carrier is obligated to accept goods for shipment but is given a lien on them as security for transportation charges.

A bailee must stay within the bailment contract, becoming liable for loss from any cause if at the time of loss he is acting beyond the authority conferred. Thus a bailor who stores goods with a bailee at a particular location assumes the risk at that location and no other. If the goods are moved by the bailee without the bailor's knowledge and are destroyed by windstorm or fire, the loss falls upon the bailee.

Commercial Paper

1. Introduction. The law of commercial paper deals with negotiable instruments, those specialized types of contracts which are designed to serve as substitutes for money. Article 3 of the UCC, which governs commercial paper, states that a negotiable instrument is one of the following:

a. a "draft" ("bill of exchange") if it is an order;
b. a "check" if it is a draft drawn on a bank and payable on demand;
c. a "certificate of deposit" if it is an acknowledgment by a bank of receipt of money with an engagement to repay it;
d. a "note" if it is a promise (to pay) other than a certificate of deposit.

The person to whom a negotiable instrument is made payable is called the *payee*. One who issues a draft is known as the *drawer*. The person to whom a drawer issues the order to pay is the *drawee*. One who issues a note is called the *maker*.

Money passes freely from hand to hand as a medium of exchange. A *simple* contract right to the payment of money cannot so move for a number of reasons. For example, if the contract creating the right is oral, its proof could be difficult, making it unacceptable to the creditor as cash. Also, the general contract rule concerning assignees of contract debts is that they obtain only the rights of their assignors, regardless of their good faith in purchasing a claim. Thus, if C has a claim for $50 against D for goods delivered, and sells the claim to X for $45 cash, X may obtain rights against D *or* he may not. Any defense D has against C may be asserted against X. Therefore, if C breached a warranty regarding the goods and D can cancel against C, he can cancel against X. Likewise, if D has a counterclaim against C which can be set off against the purchase price it can be set off against X's claim.

In order to make a contract more acceptable as a medium of exchange to transferees of it, the law gives special attributes to negotiable instruments, with the result that they are more like money. The central rule that accomplishes this result is: a holder in due course of a negotiable instrument is not subject to the personal defenses of any prior party who has undertaken liability on the instrument. Applying this rule to the previous situation, X could recover the $50 from C if C had given a note or check to D instead of a simple contract promise to pay money. Generally X would be a holder in due course as a good-faith purchaser, assuming that C properly negotiated the instrument to him. And, the defenses of breach of warranty or of a counterclaim are personal defenses; that is, they are available only between the immediate parties to the transaction in connection with which the defense arose.

The holder in due course rule just stated involves many complex issues and ties together most of the law of commercial paper. In order to understand how the rule operates and predict the outcome of a given case, the following questions must be answered:

1. What are the formal requirements to create a *negotiable instrument?*
2. How is an instrument negotiated in a manner that will make the transferee a *holder* of it?
3. What requirements must a *holder* meet in order to be a *holder in due course?*
4. What are the *defenses* a party to a negotiable instrument might have, and which of these are *personal?* (Although a holder in due course is not subject to personal defenses, he is subject to *real* ones, such as forgery of the signature of the party from whom he is seeking recovery.)
5. What is the nature of the *liability* that the different types of parties to negotiable instruments assume (e.g., makers of notes, drawers of drafts, acceptors of drafts, and indorsers), and *what steps* must a holder take (if any) in order to perfect his rights against them?

Each of these questions is discussed in the sections that follow.

2. *Requirements of Negotiability.* The UCC states that, in order for a *writing* to be negotiable, it must:

a. be signed by the maker or drawer; and
b. contain an unconditional promise or order to pay a sum certain in money . . . ; and
c. be payable on demand or at a definite time, and
d. be payable to order or to bearer.

Each of these requirements is now outlined, in order.

Note that the preface to the other requirements indicates that a negotiable instrument must be in writing. Any kind of writing materials may be used. The signature of the maker or drawer may be printed, written, typed, or stamped and may consist of any symbol adopted with the intent to authenticate the writing.

A promise or order to pay may be present even though these exact words are not used, as long as it is clear that a promise is being made or an order given. (The promise is required in a two-party instrument, such as a note, where the maker promises to pay money to the bearer of it. An order is necessary in a three-party instrument, such as a check, where the drawer orders his drawee bank to pay money to the bearer of the check.) An acknowledgment of debt or an I.O.U. is not a promise; a mere request or authorization to pay is not an order.

The promise or order must be unconditional so that a transferee will not have to look outside the terms of the instrument to determine that it will be payable in any case. This enhances it as a substitute for money. An order or promise is unconditional if its payment does not depend on the happening of some event that may not happen. Thus a clause making the instrument "subject to" the terms or performance of an underlying contract renders the instrument nonnegotiable. However, it may state the transaction that gave rise to it, such as "payment of July rent" or that it is given "as per" a certain contract. It may also otherwise simply refer to a separate agreement or state that it is secured by collateral. In general, an instrument is conditional and nonnegotiable if it states that it is to be paid only out of a particular fund or source, such as "the proceeds of the sale of my home," since no obligation is undertaken unless the source is in existence. The UCC provides two exceptions to this rule. First, such a limitation is not a condition if it is imposed by a governmental unit, since fund accounting is required by law and employed by such units. Second, an instrument may be limited to payment out of the entire assets of a partnership, unincorporated association, trust, or estate, if issued by it. Also, negotiability is not destroyed if an instrument indicates a particular fund out of which reimbursement is to be made, such as "debit payroll account." This is simply an accounting instruction and not a condition of payment.

The sum payable is a sum certain if the exact amount payable at any time of payment can be calculated by the holder from the instrument itself, without reference to any outside source. Therefore, an instrument may be payable with stated interest (even if the stated rates are different before and after a given date), with a specified discount or addition in the event it is paid before or after maturity, or by stated installments. A note payable with interest "at the current rate" does not have the interest stated and is not negotiable. However, the UCC provides that the sum is certain even if the instrument calls for its payment with or deducting exchange, whether the rate of exchange is fixed or is to be the current rate.

Also, a clause requiring the payment of costs of collection or an attorney's fee on default by the party liable is permitted. Such a clause may make the sum uncertain from the standpoint of the obligor who defaults, but it makes the instrument more acceptable to those who may accept or reject it as a substitute for money. The amount of such expenses collectible need not be stated; but if it is, it may not exceed a reasonable amount or it is illegal as a penalty.

An instrument is payable in money if it is payable, at the time it is made, in a medium of exchange authorized or adopted by a domestic or foreign government as a part of its currency. If payable in "currency" or "current funds," an instrument is payable in money. Unless it specifies a foreign currency *as the medium* of payment, an instrument that states the sum in a foreign currency may be paid in the number of dollars which the amount in foreign currency will purchase on the date payment is due. Generally, if an instrument contains a promise or order to do an act in addition to paying money, it is not negotiable unless such is authorized by the Code. An instrument may give the holder (not the maker or drawee) an option to require something to be done in lieu of the payment of money, however. In addition, it may authorize the sale of collateral securities in case it is not paid at maturity and may waive the benefit of any law intended for the protection of the obligor.

Included as instruments payable on demand are those which are payable at sight or on presentation, as well as those in which no time for payment is stated. Typical of the last type is a check. An instrument is payable at a definite time when it states the date of maturity, such as "payable June 1, 1975." It also meets this requirement if it is payable on *or before* a stated date, or at a fixed period after a stated date or sight, such as "payable 30 days after June 1, 1975." However, if it is undated and states it is "payable 30 days after date," the time is indefinite until its date is filled in. An instrument is nonnegotiable if it is payable only on the happening of an act or an event that is uncertain with respect to the time of its occurrence; for example, one payable on the death of an ancestor of the maker or drawer. As long as an instrument is payable at a definite time, its negotiability is not affected by any acceleration clause (one permitting the date of maturity to be sped up at the option of one of the parties or on the happening of some event). In addition, an instrument's maturity date may be subject to extension on the happening of some event or at the option of the maker, acceptor, or holder. Such an extension, except when made by the holder, must be to another definite time, however.

The requirement that an instrument be payable to "order" or to "bearer" generally can be satisfied only if it contains one of those words (the words of negotiability) or one having the same meaning. Thus, the language "Pay John Smith $50" is deficient. Such an instrument would be governed by Article 3 of the UCC if it is otherwise negotiable and if its terms do not prevent transfer. No one could become a holder in due course of the paper, however. An instrument is payable to order on its face when it states that it is payable to the order of a person specified, such as "Pay $50 to the order of John Smith." It could also be made payable to the assigns of John Smith, to John Smith, or to order. Also, an instrument is payable to order when it names a payee and is clearly designated as "exchange" on its face. The payee may be the maker, drawer, drawee, or some other person and two or more payees may be named. When the payee named is an estate or trust, it is payable to the order of the representative (or his successor). If the payee is an office or officer by title (such as "the Secretary of State of Illinois") the instrument is payable to the principal, but the incumbent in office (or his successor) is permitted to act as the holder. Also, a partnership or unincorporated association may be named as the payee. Words like "payable upon return of this instrument properly indorsed" do not make an instrument payable to order and negotiable. An instrument is payable to bearer on its face if it states that it is payable to bearer (or holder), to the order of bearer, or to a certain person or bearer. Also, instruments payable to "cash," or to the order of "cash," or to similar words that do not purport to represent a person, are payable to bearer. If an instrument is made payable to the order of a person *and* to bearer, it is payable to the order of the person named. However, if the bearer words are *handwritten* or *typewritten,* it is payable to bearer.

The last two provisions of the UCC (cited previously) resolve an ambiguity that may arise from the use of certain printed forms. Other rules related to ambiguous terms are also given. If it is not clear whether an instrument is a draft or note, it may be treated as either. If there are both handwritten and typed or printed words, the handwritten ones are controlling; typed words control printed ones. If the amount varies as stated in words and figures, the words determine it. But, if the words are ambiguous themselves, the figures control.

An instrument may be undated, postdated, or antedated if it otherwise meets the requirements of negotiability. It may also contain a clause authorizing a confession of judgment by someone else on behalf of the party who is liable on the instrument. Such a term would allow the holder of a note which is not paid when due to obtain a judgment against the maker without his knowledge and in summary fashion. By it, the maker would agree in advance that any attorney could represent him in court for the purpose of admitting liability on the note upon default. If a clause authorizes a confession of judgment *before* an instrument is due, however, it destroys negotiability.

3. *Transfer and Negotiation.* When an instrument is transferred by a proper negotiation, the transferee becomes a holder of it. If it is payable to bearer, it is negotiated even if the transfer is by delivery to the transferee only. If it is payable to the order of a named person, it must be negotiated by the indorsement of that person, completed by delivery, Mere delivery of order paper is not sufficient to constitute the transferee as the holder of it. But a transferee of an order instrument who gave value for it does obtain the specifically enforceable right to obtain the unqualified indorsement of the transferor. *Negotiation* of such an instrument takes place only when the necessary indorsement is made. Until that time there is no presumption that the transferee is the owner and, of course, he cannot be a holder in due course, since he is not even a holder. However, a mere transfer does vest in the transferee whatever rights the transferor had in the instrument. The indorsement must be written by the holder or on his behalf on the instrument itself, or it may be written on an allonge—a paper attached so firmly that it becomes a part of the instrument. The signature of the indorser without additional words is sufficient, and the addition of words of assignment, guaranty, condition, or disclaimer do not change its character as an indorsement. The indorsement must be of the entire instrument (or unpaid residue) or it operates only as a partial assignment. In the event an instrument is payable to the order of two payees such as A *and* B, both must indorse to negotiate. However, if the payees are stated to be A *or* B, either may indorse and constitute the transferee as a holder.

An indorsement is either blank or special. A blank indorsement may be the signature of the indorser alone and does not specify any particular indorsee. A special indorsement, in addition to containing the signature of the indorser, specifies the person to whom or to whose order the instrument is to be payable, such as: "Pay John Smith (signed) Peter Payee." A blank indorsement may be converted into a special one by the holder's writing over it any contract consistent with its character. The *last* indorsement on any instrument determines how it may be further negotiated. If the last indorsement is blank, the instrument is bearer paper and may be negotiated then by delivery alone. If the last indorsement is special, it is payable to the order of the indorsee and may be negotiated only by his indorsement and delivery.

In addition to being blank or special, an indorsement may contain words that qualify it or render it restrictive. A qualified indorsement adds to the indorser's signature the words "without recourse," or any similar language. It does not impair the negotiability of the instrument. Its effect is to eliminate the conditional (secondary) liability of a general indorser to pay the instrument if it is presented properly, dishonored, and the indorser is given proper notice. However, qualified indorsers retain their unconditional liability to all subsequent parties if they breach one of the warranties the UCC provides that they make on transfer. These matters are discussed in more detail in Section 6.

A restrictive indorsement is one that either (a) purports to prohibit the further transfer of the instrument, such as "Pay John Doe *only*"; (b) adds the words "for collection," "for deposit," "pay any bank," or others that indicate the intent of deposit or collection; (c) states that it is for the use of the indorser or some other person, such as "Pay John Smith to hold in trust for my daughter Ann"; or (d) is conditional. A conditional indorsement states that the instrument is to be paid to the indorsee on the happening of some event; for example, "Pay John Doe when he has finished building my house." None of these restrictive indorsements impairs the negotiable character of an instrument, nor will any of them prevent further transfer or negotiation of it. The effect of restrictive indorsements is severely limited as they apply to banks in the collection process. Such indorsements can be ignored by an intermediary bank or a payor bank which is not the depositary bank (the first bank to which an item is transferred for collection) unless made by the bank's immediate transferor. But, any transferee (except an intermediary bank) after a conditional indorsement or one that states "for deposit," "pay any bank," or the like, must pay any value given by him consistently with the indorsement. Only the first taker under an indorsement for the benefit of the indorser or another person must pay any value given by him consistently with the indorsement. A later holder is not affected by this kind of restrictive indorsement, unless he has knowledge that a person has negotiated the instrument in breach of fiduciary duty, such as for his own benefit. Any transferee under a restrictive indorsement who properly pays value becomes a holder for value to the extent that he does so.

A negotiation is effective to transfer an instrument even if it may be rescinded later by the transferor. This includes negotiations made by persons without capacity and those obtained by fraud, mistake, or duress, as well as those which are part of an illegal transaction or made in breach of duty. The transferee in such cases may further negotiate the instrument. Even so, the right of the transferor to rescind and recover the instrument is available against all subsequent parties, except a holder in due course.

4. Rights of Holders and Holders in Due Course. Regardless of whether he is the owner of an instrument, the holder may transfer or negotiate it and generally may discharge it or enforce it in his own name. However, a holder who is not a holder in due course (or does not have the rights of one) is subject to all valid claims of any person and any defenses of any party, whether they are personal or real. For example, assume that M makes a $50 note payable to the order of P, delivers it to P as a gift, and P negotiates it to H by indorsement and delivery. H is a holder, but if H does not meet all the other requirements of a holder in due course, he will be unable to collect from M. H will be subject to M's defense that P gave no consideration and M's promise was only gratuitous. (If M had had no defense, H could have recovered from him.) But, a person who has the rights of a holder in due course is free from all claims to the instrument on the part of any person as well as all personal defenses of any party to it (with whom he has not dealt himself). Since lack of consideration is a personal defense, a holder in due course would be able to enforce payment of the note by M in the foregoing situation.

There are two ways in which a person can obtain the *rights* of a holder in due course. One is by meeting the UCC requirements to become a holder in due course, himself. The other is for him to take an instrument that has passed through the hands of some prior party who met these requirements. Obviously, a holder in due course must first be a holder. In addition, he must meet three other requirements. He must take the instrument for value, in good faith, and without notice that it is overdue, that it has been dishonored, or that any person has any defense against or claim to it. The Code provides that one does *not* become a holder in due course of an instrument, if he purchases it at a judicial sale, takes it under legal process, acquires it in taking over an estate, purchases it as part of a bulk transaction not in the regular course of the business of the seller. However, a payee can be a holder in due course, as can a purchaser of a limited interest, to the extent of the interest purchased.

A holder takes an instrument for value to the extent that he has *performed* the consideration he agreed to give for it. Thus if H, a holder, agrees to pay P $25 for a $50 note and H actually pays the $25 to P, H is a holder for value of the note to the full extent of its face amount, $50. But, if H pays P $24 of the $25, he is a holder for value only for $24, and is free of personal defenses just up to that sum. If a transferee learns of any infirmity in the instrument or defect in the title of the person negotiating it before he has paid the *full* amount agreed upon, he is a holder for value only to the extent of the amount actually paid by him before he learned of the defect. Thus a simple promise to pay money or give other consideration is not value. When a bank credits an account for an instrument being deposited, it has merely promised to pay. It has not given value until it has paid the amount out, following the first-in, first-out rule. However, a negotiable instrument is value. The holder who gives a check for another instrument gives value because he cannot refuse to pay a holder in due course. Likewise, the making of an irrevocable commitment to a third person (someone other than the transferor), such as issuing a letter of credit when an instrument is taken, constitutes giving value for it. To the extent that a holder acquires a security interest in an instrument he takes it for value. For example, suppose D owes C $100 and negotiates a $150 note, made by M, to C as security for payment of the debt. C is a holder for value of the note to the extent of $100. Giving value includes discharging a preexisting claim for an instrument. If C had *discharged* D's $100 debt in exchange for M's $150 note, C would have been a holder for value to the extent of $150. Here, C would have given the total consideration agreed upon.

A holder takes an instrument in good faith if he has no actual knowledge of any defects in it and is honest in fact. His mere suspicion of some defect, or even negligence in not discovering one, will not prevent him from being a holder in due course.

In addition to taking an instrument for value and in good faith, a holder in due course must take it without notice that it is overdue or has been dishonored. Clearly, if an instrument is payable at a definite time and a holder takes it after the stated maturity date, he has notice that it is overdue. He also has such notice if he has reason to know that an acceleration of an instrument has been made, even if he takes it before its stated maturity. In addition, if the purchaser has reason to know that any part of the principal amount of the instrument is overdue (as in the case of an installment note) he cannot be a holder in due course. However, mere knowledge of a default in payment of *interest* on the instrument, or in the payment of another instrument does not prevent him from attaining this status. If the instrument is payable on demand, the purchaser has notice that it is ovedue if he has reason to know that he is taking it after a demand has been made or more than a reasonable time after its issue. What is reasonable depends on all the facts and circumstances. However, the UCC states that a reasonable time for a check is presumed to be thirty days after issue.

Finally, a holder in due course must take an instrument without notice that any person has a defense against or claim to it. If it is so incomplete or irregular, or has such visible evidence of forgery or alteration that he is made to question its validity or terms, the purchaser has notice of a claim or defense. An instrument may contain blanks relating to unnecessary matters, or it may have minor erasures; still it will not put the purchaser on notice of any irregularity. Also, some alterations, such as a change in date from January 3, 1973, to January 3, 1974, should cause no suspicion in January of 1974. In other words, the irregularity must be of a nature that would put a reasonable person on notice that something is wrong. Also, a purchaser has notice of a defense if he knows that any party's obligation is voidable or that all parties have been discharged. Finally, a purchaser has notice of a claim when he knows that a fiduciary has negotiated the instrument in breach of duty, such as for the payment of the fiduciary's own debt or otherwise for his own benefit. However, mere notice that a person negotiating an instrument is a fiduciary does not of itself give notice of a claim. Knowledge that an incomplete instrument was completed, even if done in the purchaser's presence, will not give him notice of a defense unless he knows that the completion was improper. In addition, a purchaser may be a holder in due course even if he knows that the instrument is antedated or postdated or that it was given for an executory promise or separate agreement.

Since a transferor can transfer whatever rights he has in an instrument, a holder in due course generally transfers his rights to all subsequent transferees, provided they are not a party to any wrongdoing affecting the instrument. Thus personal defenses that arose before the instrument was negotiated to a holder in due course are cut off once the instrument has been in his hands, to the benefit of all subsequent transferees. This is so even if such a transferee were to take an overdue instrument, or have knowledge of a defect, or part with no value. For example, suppose that M makes a note for $100 payable to the order of P and delivers it to P in payment for goods which P never delivers to M. P negotiates the note to H, a holder in due course. After the note is overdue, H negotiates it as a gift to A. Because A is a transferee from a holder in due course, he can collect the note from M. M's defense of failure of consideration is only personal. H would not be subject to the defense, so A is not. If A had transferred the note to B, B would have been able to enforce the note against M under the same principle. (Note that a holder in due course has no effect on defenses that arise *after* he has become a party to the instrument.) The foregoing rule does not operate in favor of a *reacquirer,* who is placed by the law in the original position he occupied. Thus, continuing our example, if B had negotiated the note back to P (the original payee), P would be subject to M's defense and unable to collect. Although a reacquirer may either reissue or further negotiate the instrument, all intervening parties are discharged as against him and as against all subsequent holders who are not holders in due course. Therefore, in this example, P would have no rights against H, A, or B as prior indorsers.

If an instrument is lost by destruction, theft, or otherwise, the owner may recover from any party liable on it upon proving his ownership, the terms of the instrument, and his reason for not being able to produce it. However, the court may require the owner to indemnify the defendant against loss due to other claims.

5. *Defenses.* All defenses are personal or real. As was indicated, a person with the rights of a holder in due course is not subject to the

personal defenses of any prior party to a negotiable instrument, but he is subject to those which are real.

The unauthorized signature of a person is completely inoperative as his. Thus he has a real defense, unless he ratifies it or is estopped from denying it by his own conduct, such as negligence. The term "unauthorized signature" includes both a forgery and a signature by an agent who exceeds his authority. It does operate as the signature of the unauthorized signer himself with respect to anyone who in good faith pays the instrument or takes it for value.

Infancy is a real defense to the extent that it is a defense to a simple contract obligation under local state law. This is so even though the effect is to render the instrument merely voidable and not void. However, in order for any other incapacity, as well as duress and illegality, to be a real defense, it must be of a nature that renders the obligation of the party a nullity under local law. This means that the obligation must be void by reason of incapacity, duress, or illegality in order to be effective against a holder in due course. If the contract of the obligor is made merely voidable, then these defenses are personal. In most states, for example, whether duress makes a contract void or voidable depends on its degree. If the maker of a note is required to sign it at gunpoint, the note is void and he has a real defense. If he signs because of a threat to prosecute his son, the note is only voidable and the defense personal.

Fraud in the inception or execution of an instrument is a real defense, whereas fraud in the inducement of it is only personal. The Code states that a holder in due course is subject to the defense of a party that he signed an instrument because of another's misrepresentation that the paper was something other than a negotiable instrument or that its essential terms were different from those actually contained in the instrument. The party signing it must have had neither knowledge of nor a reasonable opportunity to obtain knowledge of its nature or its terms. For example, a person might be able to assert this defense as a real one if he is tricked into signing a note by someone who represents that it is merely a receipt. However, negligence of the signer in failing to discover the nature or terms of the instrument makes fraud in the execution a personal defense. All facts are taken into account in deciding whether a reasonable opportunity for such discovery existed or not. Such matters as age, sex, intelligence, business experience, the ability to read or understand English, the representation made, the reason to rely on or have confidence in the one making it, and the presence or absence of a third person to read or explain the instrument are among those which would be relevant. Fraud in the inducement exists when a person is persuaded to sign an instrument by fraudulent misrepresentations concerning the *consideration* for which it is being given. However, the signer does know that he is signing a negotiable instrument and he is aware of its essential terms. For example, suppose one who signs a note, which he knows to be one, delivers it in payment for a car. If the seller knowingly misrepresented that the car had been driven only 10,000 miles when in fact it had been driven 50,000, the maker of the note would have only a personal defense.

Discharge of a party in bankruptcy or other insolvency proceedings, or any other discharge of which the holder has notice when he takes the instrument, is a real defense. However, a purchaser can still become a holder in due course with notice of a discharge which leaves other parties liable on the instrument. For example, a person would still be a holder in due course if he knows that one of the indorsers of an instrument has been discharged, such as by cancellation of his indorsement. Of course, the holder would acquire no rights against the discharged indorser. If a person has been discharged other than in insolvency proceedings, he only has a personal defense (except with respect to purchasers who took with knowledge of the discharge).

A material alteration of an instrument (other than its unauthorized completion) gives prior parties a real defense to the extent of the alteration. However, they can have at best only a personal defense regarding its original terms. Any alteration is material which changes the contract of the one who has signed by changing the number of relations of the parties or the writing by adding to or removing part of it. Scissoring instruments that are part of another contract is a material alteration where no separation is authorized by dotted lines or the like. A note has been materially altered if its amount is changed from $5 to $500. In such a case, a holder in due course would not be able to collect from the maker to the extent of the alteration, $495, but would be able to collect to the extent of the original terms, $5. Negligence of the party asserting material alteration changes it to a personal defense, as does any other conduct creating an estoppel. Therefore, if the maker of the $5 note had carelessly left spaces that facilitated its alteration upward to $500, a holder in due course could collect the full $500 from him. An instrument that is signed but is incomplete in some necessary way cannot be enforced until it is completed. When this has been done properly, the instrument is effective. If an incomplete instrument is completed outside the authority given, it has been materially altered; but at most this can be no more than a personal defense. Suppose a payee is authorized to complete a check for any amount up to $10 but completes it for $100 instead. A holder in due course could enforce it as actually completed and collect $100.

Generally a person without the rights of a holder in due course has no rights against any prior party whose contract is changed by a material alteration. (This is assuming that the prior party has not agreed to the change and is not estopped from asserting the defense.) However, for such a discharge of the prior party to occur, the alteration must not only be material but also must be fraudulent and must have been made by a former holder (and not just some third party). Otherwise, even one who is not a holder in due course may enforce the instrument according to its original terms; or he may enforce an improperly completed instrument according to the authority given to complete it. For example, assume that an incomplete check is issued with authority to fill it in for $10. If a holder fills it in for $25, honestly believing that this is the amount authorized, a material alteration by a holder would exist but would not be fraudulent. Thus even a person who does not have the rights of a holder in due course could recover $10 on this particular check from those parties whose contract was changed by the alteration.

The lack or failure of consideration to support the instrument is a personal defense, as is the nonperformance of a condition precedent. If a note is given by its maker as a gift to the payee, a later holder may not enforce it, but a holder in due course may. However, no consideration is required for an instrument given as payment of or security for a preexisting claim.

Nondelivery of an instrument or delivery of it for only a special purpose is a personal defense. A check payable to "Cash" (i.e., bearer paper) which is stolen can be enforced by a later holder in due course but cannot be enforced by one not having that status. The same is true of a check payable to order if the last valid indorsement is in blank, since it is also bearer paper. However, if *order* paper is lost or stolen, the thief or finder must forge the indorsement of the payee or last special indorsee to make a further transfer appear to be legitimate. A forged indorsement passes no title, and no person who afterward takes the instrument can become a holder. Therefore, a subsequent taker may not enforce the instrument (except with respect to intervening parties after the nondelivery) and possesses it subject to the right of the true owner to recover it. As was noted in Section 3, if order paper *is delivered* by a holder without his indorsement, the transferee obtains the rights of the transferor plus the specifically enforceable right to have his indorsement.

If payment or satisfaction to a holder would violate the terms of a restrictive indorsement, a personal defense exists. In addition, all defenses that would be available in an action on a simple contract are personal. Thus if the maker of a note has a counterclaim or right of set-off against the payee, he will have the same defense against any other person who does not have the rights of a holder in due course. Similarly, payment of a note by the maker is a personal defense. Of course, if payment is made after a person has notice that it is overdue, that individual cannot be a holder in due course.

6. Liability of Parties. The rights of the owner of a negotiable instrument are determined, in part, by the nature of the obligation undertaken by the party from whom he is trying to recover. Of course, any party can escape his liability if he has a defense that is available against the person trying to recover. If the defense is only personal, it cannot be used to avoid obligations owed one with the rights of a holder in due course, but it can be used against all others. If the defense is real, it can be used against all persons seeking recovery. A person cannot be liable on a negotiable instrument unless his signature appears thereon. Anyone who signs with a trade or assumed name or any word or mark is liable to the same extent as if he had signed his own name. Any signature may be made by a duly authorized agent. However, unless an agent who signs his own name indicates on the instrument *both* that he signed in a representative capacity and the name of the person represented, the agent is personally obligated. In such a case, the principal is not liable, even if the agent was duly authorized. The UCC states that naming an organization and adding the name and office of an authorized person is a signature of the organization in a representative capacity. The three types of liability are primary liability to pay the instrument, secondary liability to pay the instrument (conditional liability), and liability for breach of some warranty (unconditional liability).

Primary liability arises out of a promise to pay the instrument in the first instance (without attaching the condition of the holder's seeking payment from some other party first). It is undertaken by the maker of a note or the acceptor of a draft. The maker of a note or the acceptor of a draft engages that he will pay it according to its tenor or terms at the time he makes his promise or as it is later completed, if it is incomplete at that time. In addition, these parties admit the existence of the payee and his capacity to indorse at the time of their engagement. The acceptor of a draft also admits the existence of the drawer, the genuineness of his signature, and his capacity and authority to draw the instrument.

A draft is not an assignment by the drawer of his funds in the hands of the drawee. Therefore, the drawee is not liable to the holder, and there is no primary party on an unaccepted draft which, however, may still be negotiated. The drawee becomes primarily liable on a draft drawn on him only after he accepts, at which time he is called the acceptor. The acceptance of a draft is the signification by the drawee of his agreement to follow the order of the drawer. It must be in writing, on the draft itself, and signed by the drawee-acceptor. It may use such language as "accepted (date)" followed by the signature of the drawee, or it may consist of his signature alone. It is not operative until completed by delivery or notice of acceptance. Even though a draft has not been signed by the drawer, is incomplete or overdue, or has been dishonored, it may still be accepted. A holder may, in good faith, supply the date of an undated acceptance of a draft that is payable a fixed period after sight.

A qualified acceptance is one in which the drawee accepts the draft, but not exactly in accordance with the order of the drawer. For example, he may agree to pay at a later date than its maturity or to pay a smaller sum than stated. The holder may treat such an acceptance as a dishonor and proceed against parties with secondary liability even though the draft is not yet due by its terms. Or, the holder may elect to take the acceptance, in which case each drawer and indorser who does not affirmatively assent to it is discharged.

If the drawee accepts a bill on which the drawer's signature is forged or unauthorized, the drawee-acceptor will nevertheless be liable to a holder in due course, since by accepting he admits the genuineness of the drawer's signature. Likewise, if the drawee, without accepting, pays a draft on which the drawer's signature is forged or unauthorized, he will be unable to recover the payment from a holder in due course or a person who has changed his position in good-faith reliance on the payment. The policy here is that a drawee should be able to recognize the signature of his customer. The drawee in these situations may not debit the account of the drawer but may recover from the forger, or the person paid if he does not have the rights of a holder in due course. Similar rules apply to the case of a person who pays a note on which his name was forged as the maker.

If the drawee accepts a draft on which a necessary indorsement was forged, he is not liable even to a purchaser in good faith after the forgery. Since a forged indorsement is inoperative, it cannot effect a negotiation and no one after it can take title to order paper. If the drawee has paid such a draft, he may recover the amount from the person paid or any prior transferor who has breached his warranty that he had a good title to the instrument. Similar rules apply when the maker of a note pays it to a person who does not have title due to a forged indorsement. A party who accepts or pays does *not* admit the genuineness of indorsements and is not required by the Code to recognize the signatures of indorsers. The true owner of the order paper—the one whose indorsement was forged—is entitled to recover the instrument and enforce it against any person who is liable thereon. Of course, if an instrument is bearer paper at the time an indorsement is forged on it, the preceding rules do not apply. Bearer paper can be negotiated by delivery alone; thus such a forgery does not prevent the passage of title and subsequent purchasers can be holders in due course. As such, they are not subject to the personal defense of nondelivery of the instrument. If bearer paper is lost or stolen, the true owner has only rights against the finder or thief or any holder without the rights of a holder in due course, who is in the same position as the finder or thief.

In certain special cases, the effect of the rules relating to forged indorsements of order paper are changed by the Code. These situations would usually arise in connection with the issuance of a check, but the principles are equally applicable to other drafts and to notes as well. First, where an impostor induces the drawer of a check to issue it to him in the name of the payee, an indorsement by any person in the name of the designated payee *is* effective. This is so whether the impersonation is by use of the mails or otherwise (e.g., face to face or over the telephone). Of course, it is highly likely that the indorsement will be forged by the impostor or a confederate of his. Second, in the course of certain schemes to embezzle funds of an employer, the named payee may not be intended to receive the proceeds of a check by (a) the authorized agent who creates the instrument by signing it on behalf of his employer or (b) an agent or employee who supplies the name of the payee. In either case an indorsement by any person in the name of the designated payee is effective. Here it is highly likely that the indorsement will be forged by an embezzling agent or employee. In both the impostor and the fictitious payee situations, the forged indorsements are made effective only to the extent that they will negotiate the check. The forger remains criminally liable for his wrongful act, and the named payee has no liability as an indorser. The purpose of these provisions is to shift the loss resulting from a forged indorsement from the drawee of a check or the innocent purchasers of it to the drawer, when he could and should have prevented it. Although all but the forger are innocent, the drawer is relatively more at fault. Because the forged indorsement is effective in these cases, any subsequent holder can become a holder in due course and can obtain title to the instrument and the right to payment. By the same token, the drawee who accepts or pays the check does have the right to charge the drawer's account for it and is following his order. The drawer in these cases could have taken more precaution in identifying the impostor, or he could have instituted a better system of internal control. At the very least, he should not permit employees who are authorized to sign checks or to furnish the names of their payees to obtain possession of the checks before they are mailed to the payees designated.

Secondary (conditional) liability to pay an instrument is the obligation to pay it in the second instance. That is, the obligation to pay only *after* the holder seeks payment from the maker of a note, or the drawee or acceptor of a draft, but is refused, and gives notice to the secondary party of the refusal. The obligation also arises when a time draft is presented to the drawee for acceptance prior to maturity, and he refuses to accept. This kind of liability is imposed by the UCC on all general (or unqualified) indorsers and drawers of drafts. In addition, a drawer admits the existence of the payee and his capacity at the time to indorse. Just as qualified indorsers eliminate secondary liability, the drawer may limit or negate his, as by drawing "without recourse." The secondary liability extends to the holder and all subsequent indorsers who take up and pay the instrument. It is often referred to as the conditional liability because the obligation is to pay *only* if the following conditions occur: *presentment* (for payment or acceptance) to the maker, drawee, or acceptor; *dishonor* by nonpayment or nonacceptance; and *notice* of dishonor to the drawer or indorser. (These conditions are discussed in Section 7.) Secondary parties only undertake to pay the instrument according to its tenor at the time they became liable on it. With respect to one another, indorsers are presumed to be liable in the order in which they indorse, unless they have agreed otherwise. For example, if A, B, and C have indorsed in that order, A is liable to B and C; B is liable to C.

Liability for breach of warranty (unconditional liability) does not arise out of an obligation to pay the instrument but out of its presentment or transfer. By presenting an instrument for payment or acceptance, or by transferring it, a party affirms (or warrants) certain facts. If the alleged circumstances are not true, he is liable for damages caused by his breach. Warranty liability is called unconditional because it exists regardless of whether the conditions of presentment, dishonor, and notice have been performed.

A person who presents a note or draft for payment or who presents a draft for acceptance warrants three things to the party who pays or accepts in good faith. These warranties are (a) that he has good title to the instrument, (b) that he has *no knowledge* that the signature of the maker or drawer is unauthorized, and (c) that the instrument has not been materially altered. Any prior transferor also makes these same warranties. The Code qualifies and reduces the liability of a holder in due course with respect to the second and third warranties.

Any person who transfers an instrument by indorsement and receives consideration warrants to any subsequent holder in good faith that (a) he has good title and the transfer is otherwise lawful, (b) all signatures are genuine or authorized, (c) the instrument has not been materially altered, (d) no defense of any party is good against him, and (e) he has no knowledge of any insolvency proceeding that has been instituted against the maker, the acceptor, or the drawer of an unaccepted draft. A qualified indorser (one who transfers "without recourse") makes all these warranties, except that represented by item (d). There his warranty is simply that he has no *knowledge* of a defense of any party that is good against him. A transferor of bearer paper who does not indorse makes the same warranties as an unqualified indorser, except that they extend only to his immediate transferee.

An accommodation party is one who has signed an instrument as maker, drawer, acceptor, or indorser for the purpose of lending his name and credit to some other person. Such a party is liable on the instrument in the capacity in which he signs to a holder for value before it is due, even if the holder knew that he was only an accommodation party. An accommodation indorser has only conditional liability to pay the instrument. He makes no warranties, since he is not a transferor.

The UCC expressly states the contract of a guarantor. "Payment guaranteed" added to a signature means that if the instrument is not paid when due, the signer will pay it *without* resort by the holder to any other party. Words of guaranty, which do not specify otherwise, guarantee payment. "Collection guaranteed" added to a signature means that the signer will pay the instrument if it is not paid when due, but only after the holder has reduced his claims against the maker or acceptor to a judgment and execution has been returned unsatisfied. However, the signer must also pay after it is apparent that it would be useless to proceed against the primary party, as, for example, when he has become insolvent. Presentment, dishonor, and notice are not necessary to charge a person using words of guaranty.

The conversion of the property of a person is a tort that consists of its unauthorized appropriation and use by another and gives the injured party a cause of action for damages. The UCC provides that a negotiable instrument is converted when it is delivered for acceptance to a drawee and he refuses to return it on demand, when it is delivered for payment to any person who refuses either to pay or return it on demand, or when it is paid on a forged indorsement.

The holder of a negotiable instrument may discharge any party in any apparent way, such as by intentionally canceling the party's signature. Such a discharge is effective without consideration and cannot affect the title to the instrument unless the instrument is surrendered.

If an instrument does not clearly indicate that a signature is made in some other capacity, the signing party is liable as an indorser.

7. *Presentment and Notice of Dishonor.* If the conditions of presentment, dishonor, and notice of dishonor are not performed properly in every respect (unless excused), unqualified indorsers are discharged from their conditional liability to pay. Performance of these conditions is also necessary to charge a drawer, but failure to do so properly will only discharge him from this secondary liability in a narrowly defined situation; that is, if the drawee (or payor bank) becomes insolvent during an unexcused delay in presentment or notice of dishonor and, because of the insolvency, the drawer is deprived of funds maintained with the drawee to cover payment of the instrument. To effect his discharge in such a case, the drawer must assign in writing his rights against the drawee to the holder of the instrument. (The rules applicable to drawers also operate to discharge an acceptor of a draft *payable at a bank* or the maker of a note *payable at a bank* from liability on an instrument. Otherwise, the conditions need not be performed to hold makers or acceptors on their primary liability to pay.) The conditions need not be performed for any drawer or indorser if a waiver of them is on the face of the instrument, nor need they be performed for any indorser whose signature directly follows a waiver on the back. In effect, parties waiving the conditions are primarily liable. Of course, the conditions need not be performed to hold transferors or qualified or unqualified indorsers for breach of warranty (unconditional liability), or any person who indorsed after maturity of the instrument.

Presentment is a demand for payment made by the holder upon the maker, acceptor, or drawee. It may be made to any one of two or more makers, acceptors, or drawees. Technically, a demand is all that is needed and dishonor occurs if payment is refused (other than for lack of proper presentment). Thus the instrument need not necessarily be present or exhibited. However, the one to whom presentment is made *may* require (a) exhibition of the instrument; (b) reasonable identification; (c) the instrument, produced for payment at a place specified in it, or if there is none, at any reasonable place; or (d) a signed receipt for any partial or full payment and surrender of the instrument upon full payment. Failure to comply with any of these requirements, if imposed by the party to whom presentment is made, invalidates the presentment and refusal to pay is not a dishonor.

Presentment may be made at the stated address where the instrument is to be paid. If none is given, it may be made at the place of business of the party to pay or at his residence. If the person to pay cannot be found at these places, presentment is excused. Presentment may also be made by mail or through a clearing house. If it is mailed, it is effective as of the time of its receipt.

Presentment must be made at a reasonable hour or, if made at a bank, at any time during its banking day. All time instruments (those bearing a definite maturity date) must be presented for payment on the day they fall due, or on the next business day if the due date is not a full business day either for the party presenting or for the one to whom presentment is made. However, if a consent to extension of the due date is expressed in the instrument, it is binding on secondary parties and accommodation makers. Such a consent authorizes the holder to only a single extension for not longer than the original period, unless otherwise specified. If the maker, acceptor, or drawee tenders full payment when the instrument is mature and objects to an extension of the due date, the holder may not exercise his option. The proper time for presentment of all demand instruments is within a reasonable time after the party with conditional liability became a party to the instrument. Thus a presentment might be proper with respect to a recent indorser, but improper for another indorser. It is presumed that a reasonable time in which to present an uncertified check drawn and payable in the United States is

> with respect to the drawer, thirty days after date or issue, whichever is later;
>
> with respect to any indorser, seven days after his indorsement.

Delay in making presentment for payment or in giving notice of dishonor is excused when the delay is caused by circumstances beyond the control of the holder or when he is without notice that the instrument is due. When the cause of the delay ceases to operate, presentment must be made with reasonable diligence. Presentment for payment or notice of dishonor is dispensed with when the drawee is a fictitious person, when presentment is waived, or when by reasonable diligence it cannot be made or given. It is also entirely excused with respect to anyone who has dishonored the instrument, countermanded payment, or has no reason to expect or require that the instrument be paid.

Presentment for acceptance is applicable only to drafts and must be made in order to obtain the primary liability of a drawee. It may be made at any time after the issue and before the maturity of a time draft. Generally the drawee of a demand draft has no duty to accept it, since he could pay the instrument and discharge his duty to the drawer. Refusal to *accept* in such a case is not a dishonor. Refusal by the drawee to accept a time draft is a dishonor; and unless the holder acts promptly to give proper notice, secondary parties will be discharged from their conditional liability to pay, even though the instrument is not yet due. No dishonor occurs if acceptance is deferred by the drawee up to the close of the next business day following presentment for acceptance. The holder may allow postponement of acceptance for an additional business day, without dishonor or discharge of secondary parties, in a good-faith attempt to obtain acceptance. In a few cases, the holder *must* present a draft for acceptance: when an instrument is payable a certain number of days after sight, it must be presented to fix its maturity date; when the instrument itself provides that it must be presented; and when it is payable at a place other than the place of business or residence of the drawee. An accepted draft must be presented for payment properly.

An instrument is dishonored by nonpayment when it is properly presented for payment and this is refused or cannot be obtained. It is also dishonored if presentment is excused and the instrument is overdue and unpaid. Payment of an instrument may be deferred without dishonor of it for a reasonable examination (to determine if the instrument is properly payable) up to the close of business on the day of presentment.

When an instrument has been dishonored by nonpayment or nonacceptance, the holder must give notice of that fact to the drawer and to each indorser. Such notice may be either oral or written, and it also serves as notice for the benefit of all subsequent holders and all prior parties who have recourse against the party to whom it is given. That is, once properly given by any holder, notice establishes the conditional liability of the one receiving it to any party who might have a right against him. Notice may be given by an agent, by the holder, or by anyone who has received notice or may be compelled to pay. If given by an agent to a principal, the principal has an additional proper period of time so that he himself may give notice to others. A bank must give notice before its midnight deadline (midnight of the next banking day following dishonor or receipt of notice of dishonor). Any person other than a bank must give notice before midnight of the third business day after dishonor or receipt of notice of dishonor. It should be emphasized that when a party has received notice of dishonor, he has the same time (after receipt) for giving notice to his prior parties that the holder has after dishonor itself.

A fourth condition, protest, must be performed in the case of the dishonor of a bill of exchange that is drawn or payable outside of the United States. The purpose is to preserve evidence of the fact of the performance of the other conditions precedent in a situation in which this might otherwise be very difficult to prove. Protest is a certificate of dishonor under the hand and seal of a United States consul or vice consul or a notary public or other person authorized to certify dishonor by the law of the place in which it occurs. It may be made when any information satisfactory to such a person is given. Protest is due at the time notice of dishonor is—unless, before notice is due, the instrument has been noted for protest by the officer to make it. In the latter case, protest can be made at any time after it is noted, as of the date of noting. The term "protest waived" includes a waiver of presentment and notice of dishonor, even if protest of the instrument in question would not have been required.

8. Checks. A check is a demand draft drawn on a bank. The rules applicable to other drafts generally are applicable to checks. In addition, the UCC contains provisions that pertain only to checks, because of the special nature of these instruments.

A bank has the duty to pay out money deposited in a checking account only if and when ordered to do so by its depositor, and then only in strict accordance with his order. The depositor gives his orders by issuing checks. If the drawee bank pays a check without a proper order from its depositor, the bank must return any amount charged to his account. A customer has the right to issue an order countermanding payment of checks previously issued. An oral stop order is effective for fourteen days and a written stop order is effective for six months. Either may be renewed in writing. The customer bears the burden of proving the amount of loss resulting from payment in spite of the stop order. Of course, the stop order must be received in time to afford the bank a reasonable opportunity to act on it. The drawer cannot stop payment on a check that has been certified. A bank has no right to pay a check until the date of issue stated on it. If it does so, the customer may countermand payment before that date and the bank will be liable for any loss suffered by him. If the drawee bank knows of the adjudication of incompetence of the depositor in time to have reasonable opportunity to act on such knowledge, it has no authority to pay checks drawn by the depositor. Similar knowledge of the death of a depositor also terminates authority to pay, except that the bank may for ten days after the date of death continue to pay checks previously drawn by the depositor, unless it is ordered to stop by a person who claims an interest in the account. A bank not having such knowledge of the adjudicated incompetence or death of a depositor continues to have authority to pay checks that are or were drawn by him.

A drawee bank is liable to its customers for damages proximately caused by its wrongful dishonor of a check drawn by him. The customer can collect only the actual damages he proves he has suffered if the dishonor was caused by mistake. Damages caused by arrest or prosecution of the customer or other consequential damages can be included. It should be noted that a deposit of money in a bank is available for withdrawal as a matter of right only at the opening of the bank's next banking day following receipt of deposit. The holder of a check has no rights against the drawee bank unless it has certified the check, even if the drawer has sufficient funds on deposit. Under the UCC, a bank has no obligation to its customer to pay an uncertified check presented more than six months after its date, but the bank *may* pay such a check in good faith and charge the drawer's account. In addition, the bank may charge any properly payable check even if it causes an overdraft.

If a check is certified by the bank on which it is drawn, the certification is equivalent to an acceptance, and the bank is primarily liable on it. Where the holder of a check procures its acceptance or certification, the drawer and all prior indorsers are discharged from liability thereon. If the drawer has it certified, he is not released. Refusal to certify a check is not a dishonor, since the check is payable on demand.

A depositor has the duty to examine with reasonable care and promptness a bank statement and relevant checks that are paid in good faith and sent to him by his bank, to discover any unauthorized signatures or any alterations. He must notify the bank promptly after discovering instances of either irregularity. If the bank has exercised ordinary care in paying such a check and suffers a loss because the depositor has failed to perform these duties, the depositor cannot assert the unauthorized signature or the alteration against the bank. (If a holder has deposited a check without signing his indorsement, the depositary bank may supply his signature if it is necessary to title.) Even if the bank was negligent, a depositor cannot object to an unauthorized signature or alteration unless he acts within one year from the time the statement and checks were made available to him. For unauthorized indorsements, the maximum period in which to act is three years. In the case of a single irregularity that has been overlooked, even for some time, the bank could have difficulty in proving that the depositor's negligence caused the loss. In most cases, timely notification would not have enabled the bank to recover anyway. But the situation is different when there are a series of unauthorized signatures or alterations by the same wrongdoer. Here, if the depositor does not notify the bank of the *first* irregularity within fourteen days after he receives his bank statement, he bears all losses due to payments by the bank on *additional* unauthorized or altered checks after this fourteen-day period, until he notifies the bank. Regardless of the care or lack of care of either the depositor or the bank, the customer is precluded from asserting (a) his unauthorized signature or any alteration on a check if he does not report it within one year from the time the statement is made available to him or (b) any unauthorized indorsement, if he does not report it within three years from the time the bank statement is made available to him.

Legal Obligations of Certified Public Accountants

1. Common Law Obligations of CPA to Client. The legal relation between a CPA and his client arises out of their contract. Therefore, the principles of general contract law previously discussed are applicable in spelling out their rights and duties. For example, since the accountant's duties are personal, his death excuses his estate from liability for nonperformance of an audit on the grounds of impossibility. Also, a CPA may not delegate his contractual duties to another over the objection of the client, by the law of assignment. As another example, the contract between an accountant and his client is enforceable even if oral, unless it falls within the provision of the statute of frauds which requires contracts of over one year's duration to be evidenced by a writing. Failure to comply with state licensing statutes relating to the practice of public accounting renders the contract between the auditor and his client void, since it is against public policy and illegal.

An accountant must perform his contractual duties to his client in a reasonable manner. If his negligence or carelessness causes the client a loss, the CPA is guilty of a breach of contract and is liable to the client for all damages resulting from the breach. What is reasonable care is a question of fact that must be resolved by considering all the facts and circumstances of the case at hand. It cannot be defined precisely. However, it seems that a failure by an accountant to follow generally accepted auditing standards should be indicative of negligence. The client's loss must proximately result from the CPA's negligence. If the accountant fails to uncover an embezzlement but has performed his audit in a nonnegligent manner, he is not liable to the client. Even if an audit is performed negligently and an embezzlement by an employee is not discovered as a result, the accountant may not be liable. For example, the client might have been unable to recover his losses from the employee even if the latter's defalcation had been uncovered because the employee was insolvent. However, if a negligent audit permits an employee to *continue* a scheme of embezzlement, the accountant is clearly liable for the losses suffered by his client thereafter. Contributory negligence on the part of the one seeking damages for the negligence of another is a complete bar to recovery, whatever its degree. However, it should be noted that the accountant must exercise that degree of care which a reasonably prudent and competent CPA would use under similar circumstances. The standard of care required of a lay client probably would be lower. If the CPA is guilty of gross negligence (recklessness), contributory negligence on the part of his client is not a defense.

An accountant has a duty of loyalty to his client which is similar to the duty of loyalty an agent owes his principal. Because of this he cannot without permission legally disclose confidential or secret information that he obtains in the process of performing professional services for the client unless ordered to do so by subpoena. This duty does not prevent a firm from having clients who are competitors, as long as the confidential affairs of one of them are not disclosed to the other. Thus the working papers related to an engagement are the property of the CPA, but his ownership is limited with respect to their use. He is allowed to retain them to provide evidence of the nature and extent of the services he rendered and may not be required to turn them over to his client. However, he must produce his working papers and give testimony concerning them when required to do so by legal process. That is, there is no common law accountant–client privilege similar to the attorney–client privilege concerning confidential communications. Such evidence is inadmissible, due to privilege asserted on the client's behalf, only in a small minority of states which have specifically created the necessary exemption by statute.

Just as the general law of contracts is applicable to CPAs, so is the law of agency. Thus an accountant who has an agent or employee may be held liable for certain acts of the agent or employee, in either contract or tort, regardless of the CPA's personal fault or intent. Likewise, the law of partnerships governs the legal relationships of a CPA who is the member of a firm with both his partners and others.

2. *Common Law Obligations of CPA to Third Parties.* Generally a CPA has no common law liability to third parties because of his negligence. His duty to perform his services in a reasonable manner arises out of contract, and he is not in privity of contract with anyone other than his client. An exception to this rule exists in favor of a specific third-party beneficiary who is intended to benefit from, and rely upon, the performance of an audit and opinions rendered by a CPA. For example, suppose that ABC Company engages a CPA to perform an audit, making it known to him that the purpose is to enable it to obtain a loan from B Bank. The CPA performs the audit in a negligent manner and renders an unqualified opinion concerning the state-

ment of financial position of ABC. The statement indicates that ABC has a substantial amount of retained earnings, when in fact the company has a deficit. If B bank lends money to ABC in reliance on CPA's opinion and suffers a loss, the amount thereof is recoverable from CPA. On the other hand, if ABC uses the statement to obtain a loan from XYZ Company, CPA has no liability for any loss suffered by XYZ, which was not a direct third-party beneficiary of the audit because it was not indicated as such when the audit was performed.

Usually an accountant's common law liability to third parties must be based on his commission of the tort of actual or constructive fraud. Actual fraud by a CPA exists when he intentionally misstates material facts and a third party relies on the misstatements to his damage, such as by extending credit to an insolvent corporation which was represented to be solvent. Of course, this is a rare case. *Constructive* fraud, however, is present when a material fact is misstated recklessly (i.e., due to gross negligence) and is relied upon by a third person to his damage. If a CPA misstates a fact with utter disregard for its truth or falsity, knowing that others are likely to rely upon what he says, the law makes the misstatement tantamount to an intentional one. In one case, a CPA prepared financial statements on stationery bearing his letterhead without revealing that he had performed no audit and was merely using the balances in the general ledger accounts as they were represented by the client. Although these statements indicated that the client was in sound condition, he was in fact insolvent. A third party who made large advances to the client was able to recover these from the CPA on the grounds of constructive fraud.

3. Statutory Liability of Accountants. A CPA may incur liability to purchasers or sellers of securities under the provisions of the Securities Act of 1933 or the Securities Exchange Act of 1934 without being in privity of contract with the one seeking damages. When a security that is subject to the Securities Act is issued, the issuer must file a registration statement with the Securities and Exchange Commission. The law requires that the registration statement include financial statements and an auditor's opinion concerning them. If there is a false statement or misleading omission of material fact in these statements, the CPA who rendered his opinion is liable to *any* person who purchases the securities described and suffers a loss on them. In addition, the court may assess court costs and reasonable attorney's fees against the CPA. There is no need for the purchaser to prove fraud or negligence on the part of the auditor, or even the purchaser's reliance on the misstatement or omission. (This is in distinct contrast to the third-party plaintiff's position at common law.) The purchaser must show only that he suffered a loss and that there was a material false statement or misleading omission in the financial statements. However, the CPA may successfully defend and escape liability by affirmatively proving (a) that the plaintiff knew of the untruth or omission at the time of his purchase, (b) the absence of fraud or negligence on his part, (c) that the buyer's loss resulted from causes other than the false statement or misleading omission, or (d) that the CPA, having made a reasonable investigation, had reasonable grounds to believe and did believe that the financial statements were true and that there were no material omissions. In order to avail himself of these defenses, the CPA must show that he was free of fault as of the time the *registration statement* became effective, and not merely as of the date of his opinion concerning the financial statements in question. Thus he must be alert during this interim period to discover events or facts that would necessitate amendment of the original financial statements. The statute of limitations for such an action by a buyer is one year from the time he discovers or should have discovered the auditor's error. Other provisions impose similar liability on CPAs for false statements or misleading omissions of material fact in *any* document or report required to be filed with the SEC. Anyone who *buys or sells* a security in reliance on such a statement or omission has an action for damages caused by his reliance. Here the CPA cannot escape liability unless he proves that he acted in good faith, had no knowledge of the omission, and did not know that the statement was false or misleading.

The Securities Act also contains criminal sanctions. Anyone who intentionally violates this law or the rules and regulations of the SEC, or willfully makes an untrue statement or misleading omission of material fact in a registration statement, is subject to a fine of up to $5000 or imprisonment of up to five years or both.

Insurance

1. Introduction. Insurance is a form of risk sharing. Each insured contributes to the losses of others by the payment of his premium, the insurance company acting as the clearinghouse and being paid for its services. Life insurance also partakes in some respects of the nature of an investment. There are numerous kinds of insurance, including life, fire, fidelity, theft, marine, and workmen's compensation, to name only a few. Since fire and life represent two distinct types of insurance, discussion is limited primarily to these two. Most of the statements made with reference to fire insurance are applicable to other kinds of insurance in which the objective is to protect the insured against loss from events over which he has little or no control.

2. *Contract of Insurance.* The terms of an insurance contract are usually found in the provisions of the policy. The application of the insured constitutes the offer, and, unless some act shows an earlier acceptance, the contract is perfected by the issuance of the policy. If the terms of the policy differ from those requested in the application, the policy acts as a counteroffer, and when retained by the insured, is deemed to be accepted by him. Consequently, the terms of the policy generally are controlling.

Local agents of fire insurance companies are usually authorized by their companies to accept risks, and in such cases the contract of insurance becomes effective from the moment the agent, by some act or statement, accepts for an insurance company the oral or written application. It is not essential that the policy be delivered or that the premium be paid in order for the insurance to become operative. Occasionally, the agent issues a binder that gives temporary protection pending a decision on whether to accept or reject the risk on the terms requested.

The exact date upon which life insurance protection begins is dependent on the type of insurance involved. If a physical examination is required, the receipt given for the initial premium often provides that the insurance is to be effective from the date of the physical examination, provided the applicant is at that time an acceptable risk according to company standards. Thus, even before the policy is issued, if the insured is a standard risk and has paid the first premium, his beneficiary is protected in event of death. If the receipt makes no such provision, the protection becomes effective only when the company indicates its acceptance, normally by mailing the policy. For the industrial-type policy and others that require no physical examination, the application form usually provides for the insurance to take effect upon delivery of the policy to the insured in good health, provided the first premium has been paid. Courts consider the policy to have been delivered as soon as it leaves the home office, whether sent to the insured or to the agent of the insurer. The applicant is considered to be in good health when he is free of any serious disorder.

It is the duty of an agent to act promptly after he receives an application. His company becomes liable for any loss resulting from an unreasonable delay in acting upon the application.

3. *Representations and Warranties.* In the absence of state statute, any intentional or unintentional misrepresentation of facts by the insured which has a material bearing on the risk assumed by the in-

surer gives the latter the right to avoid the policy and thus avoid liability for a loss incurred by the insured. The facts misrepresented must be material to the risk, although not necessarily material to the loss, in order to justify rescission. Misrepresentation of immaterial factors has no bearing on the liability of the insurer. Companies early incorporated clauses in the application or policy which made warranties out of all statements of the applicant. Although in most contracts a breach of warranty always justifies rescission, the states by court decision or legislation now permit rescission of an insurance policy only if the warranty relates to something material. Many states give the insured additional protection in the field of life insurance by legislation which provides that no misrepresentation shall be used as a defense unless a photostatic copy of the statement is made a part of the policy. Since such statements are usually a part of the application, a photostatic copy of it is customarily incorporated in the policy.

As a result of state statute or policy provision, a life insurance policy cannot be contested by the company after it has been in effect for a given period of time, usually two years. Regardless of fraud or misrepresentation, unless the company has contested the policy in court within the limited period of time, the policy is enforceable.

4. Insurable Interest. An insurance contract in which the insured has no interest to protect in the person or thing insured is illegal because it is in the nature of a gambling contract and, perhaps, contrary to public policy since it may induce the insured to destroy the person or property insured. For fire insurance, an insurable interest consists of a legal or equitable interest in the property insured. An owner, mortgagee, tenant, bailee, conditional vendor, and conditional vendee are considered as being interested in the continued existence of property. An ordinary unsecured creditor has no insurable interest in the property of his debtor, and insurance carried by him gives no protection if the property is destroyed unless the company is willing to volunteer payment.

An insurable interest in the life of another rests on the probability of financial loss by reason of the death of the insured. Thus a creditor may insure the life of a debtor to the extent of the indebtedness, a wife the life of a husband, a partner the life of a copartner, and an employer the life of a valuable employee. Other similar relationships may be protected by life insurance, the test being the financial relationship. If an insured procures insurance upon his own life, he is free to name anyone as his beneficiary. In such a case, most states hold that it is not necessary for the beneficiary to have an insurable interest in the life insured.

The life insurance contract is enforceable if the insurable interest exists only at the time the policy is issued. A later loss of interest does not destroy the policy. A fire insurance policy is enforceable, however, only if the insurable interest exists at the time the loss develops.

5. Life Insurance Risks. Life insurance contracts may be either term, whole life, endowment, or a combination of these. Under any type, the proceeds are payable at time of death of the insured if the policy is then in force. *Term insurance* carries the lowest annual rate, but the protection extends only over the term specified—five or ten years—unless within that time it is converted into one of the other forms of life insurance.

The premium on *whole life* is payable during the lifetime of the insured unless it is modified by a paid-up provision. This paid-up clause calls for a slightly higher premium, but after a given number of years premiums need no longer be paid. *Endowment insurance* is both protective and a form of investment. It calls for a still higher premium rate, but after a given number of years the proceeds are payable even though the insured has not died.

A life insurance contract is much like a continuing offer which the insurer is not free to withdraw—a kind of option contract. The insured is not obligated to continue the payment of premiums, but each time one is paid, the policy protection is extended for an additional period. If the insured receives proper notice that a premium is due and fails to pay it within the grace period allowed, usually thirty days, the policy is said to *lapse.* A payment is considered as having been made as soon as it is mailed, provided it is stamped and properly addressed. When the payment is made by check, the payment is effective when mailed only if the check is supported by an adequate bank balance.

The holder of a lapsed policy is accorded the choice of three, and usually four, rights. He is entitled to the cash surrender value of the policy, assuming that he has not exhausted it by borrowing; he may demand a paid-up policy for such amount as the reserve will buy; or he may elect to receive extended insurance for the full face of the policy for the period that the reserve will pay the premiums. If he fails to make an election within the time provided, the policy provides which of the latter two will become operative. In addition, the insured is usually given the right to reinstate the policy within a given number of years by showing that he is in good health and by paying back premiums with interest.

6. Fire Insurance Risks. A fire insurance policy protects the insured against the natural and proximate results of an unfriendly fire. A fire is deemed unfriendly whenever it is burning outside its proper container. Thus smoke or heat damage caused by an overheated furnace is not covered unless the fire leaves the furnace and burns elsewhere. The standard fire insurance policy covers any loss that is the natural result of the fire, although the fire never reaches the insured property. Damage caused by smoke, water, falling walls, explosion, or theft is covered if it is the result of an unfriendly fire. Recovery for lightning loss, theft, and explosion is generally controlled by policy terms.

The carelessness of the insured in handling his property will not defeat his recovery, since this is one of the risks insured against. The owner is obligated to remove his goods from the path of an oncoming fire of which he has notice.

Location of property is quite often an important element of risk, and property insured at a particular location is generally unprotected if moved without obtaining the consent of the insurer. A rider to cover the property at the new location should be obtained from the insurer and attached to the policy.

A fire insurance policy on business property quite often includes a *coinsurance clause,* which has the effect of making the owner a coinsurer of the property to the extent that he fails to carry the requisite amount of insurance. Thus if A owns property worth $100,000 and carries insurance of $60,000 which has an 80% coinsurance clause, he bears one-fourth of any loss which develops. The premium rate for a policy with a coinsurance clause is much lower than for straight insurance, but such a policy requires vigilance on the part of the owner in a period when values are advancing.

7. Termination of Fire Insurance. Fire insurance contracts usually run for a definite period—one, three, or five years—and are drawn in a manner that gives either party the right to terminate. The company is usually required to give the owner five days' written notice before the policy can be terminated. The unearned premium is returnable on a proportionate basis if the company terminates the policy. When the insured terminates the insurance, he is charged the short rate for the time the policy is in effect, receiving the balance of the premium.

A fire loss that is settled by the insurer reduces the face of the policy by the amount of the loss that is paid, unless special provision has been made for such a contingency. More recently, it is customary for the policy to carry a clause automatically reinstating the policy for the full amount following a loss. Therefore, if the property is restored to its former condition by the owner, by reason of such a clause he need not take out additional coverage.

Insurance companies divide the loss proportionately when two or more insure the same property. If for any reason one of the policies is unenforceable or uncollectible, the other company pays only its share of the loss. By the language of the policy, it assumes no responsibility for the failure of its coinsurer to perform.

8. Subrogation. Subrogation—the right of the insurer to take over the claim of the insured against a third party—has no application to life insurance but is important in fire and auto collision insurance. A fire caused by the negligence of a third party gives the owner an action against the third party or against the insurer, as he elects. If he collects of the insurer, the latter takes over the claim against the third party. Similarly with collision insurance, the company which pays a collision loss may recover of a third person who occasioned the loss. The insured should never release his claim against the third party without the approval of the insurer. Since such a release robs the insurer of his right of subrogation, it also releases the insurer.

9. Company Protective Clauses. Policies of fire insurance include several clauses to protect the insurer against increased risk growing out of the conduct of the insured. Quite generally, policies are suspended while the property is vacant or unoccupied beyond a given period of time or when the risk is increased by anything within the control or knowledge of the insured. The policy protection is automatically resumed when the property is again occupied or the risk is reduced to normal, but the contractual period of insurance is not extended by the period when the insured was unprotected. The number of such clauses depends on the statutes of a particular state and the whim of the insurer.

Policies require the insured to give prompt notice of loss and, unless a settlement is obtained, to make a sworn written statement of loss in which the nature of the fire, its cause, and the estimated loss are set forth. Failure to meet these conditions deprives the insured of the right to recover, although insurance companies have been fairly liberal in refusing to be technical when these terms are violated.

10. Mortgage Clause. A mortgagee has no equity in the proceeds of insurance carried by the owner of the mortgaged property unless the mortgage requires the owner to carry the insurance for the benefit of the mortgagee or unless the policy of insurance contains a provision whereby the loss is payable to the mortgagee. Two types of mortgage clauses are to be found in fire insurance policies. One is a *simple loss-payable clause* which states that, in event of a fire, the proceeds shall be payable to the mortgagee until his claim has been satisfied, any excess being paid to the owner. This clause gives the mortgagee no better right on the policy than is possessed by the owner.

A second type, called the *standard mortgage clause,* has the same loss-payable feature but gives added protection in that the insurance is payable to the mortgagee even though the owner is in default of the policy terms at time of loss. The policy may not be terminated with respect to the mortgagee without first giving him ten days' written notice. Thus if a loss arises when the property has been vacant over the allotted time, the insurer is liable to the mortgagee up to the face of the mortgage, if the loss is that much. In such a case, since the insurer owes no duty to the owner, it takes, by subrogation, the mortgage from the mortgagee with the right to enforce it against the owner. However, if both mortgagor and mortgagee are in good standing with the insurer, any payment made to the mortgagee effectively reduces the amount of the mortgage indebtedness.

11. Rights of Beneficiary. A life insurance policy which reserves for the insured no right to alter or change it gives to the beneficiary a vested claim from the date of issuance. In such a case the insured has no right to borrow on the policy, surrender it for the cash-surrender value, or change the beneficiary. It is customary for the insured to have these rights reserved in the policy, and as a consequence the insured may change the beneficiary by giving notice to the insurer and having the change indorsed on the policy. If the insured dies after the policy has been forwarded for a change but before the company has had time to indorse the change, the courts construe the policy as though the change had taken place.

12. Rights of Creditors in Life Insurance. A bankrupt who has reserved the right to change the beneficiary in his life insurance possesses an asset that becomes a part of the bankrupt estate. He may be compelled to borrow the cash-surrender value or to surrender the insurance to the trustee in bankruptcy. A policy made payable to the estate of the insured is like any other asset and can be reached by creditors if it has any value. Some states by legislation have exempted a certain amount of insurance from the claims of creditors.

An insurance policy may be pledged as security for a loan if the right to change beneficiaries has been reserved or if the policy is payable to the estate of the insured. Otherwise, the beneficiary must join in the pledging to make it effective. Most lenders have their interest indorsed on the policy as a partial change of beneficiary, although mere delivery of the policy is adequate to effect a valid pledge. Notice should be given to the insurer to make certain that the pledgee will obtain payment of the loan in the event the insured dies before discharging his debt.

Upon the death of the insured, creditors have no right to the proceeds of the policy of life insurance that names a beneficiary and has not been pledged. Policies payable to the estate of the insured increase the assets of the estate, and the proceeds of such policies may be used to pay claims against the estate unless they are exempt under some state statute.

Occasionally the beneficiary named in the policy is also a creditor of the insured. If the insurance was taken out to secure the creditor, the latter is entitled to retain only enough to pay the indebtedness. He must return the excess to the estate of the insured. This rule also appears to hold if the creditor takes out the insurance on the life of the debtor and pays the premiums. If the debt is reduced below the face of the policy at time of death, the full face of the policy is payable, but the creditor is permitted to retain only enough to pay the indebtedness. The creditor is not permitted to profit by the death of the insured.

13. Transfer of Insurance. Unless restricted by the nature of the policy, the insured may sell his life insurance policy as freely as any other asset. Likewise, he may give it away if he desires. If he is the beneficiary, it is not necessary to change beneficiaries, but this should be done to make the transaction clear. The new owner continues to pay the premiums and at death collects the full face of the policy.

A fire insurance policy is not assignable without the consent of the insurer. Consequently, an owner who sells his property and desires to transfer his insurance protection to the purchaser must obtain a rider from the company in which the new owner is named as the insured. There is some authority, however, to the effect that the mortgagee who sells his mortgage may transfer his rights under a loss payable clause.

Like any other money claim, the right to proceeds of insurance growing out of death or a fire loss is assignable. It is the risk in fire insurance which is personal in character and, therefore, unassignable without company approval.

index

index

A

C

G

M

N

O

P

Q

R

S

T

U

V

W

Z